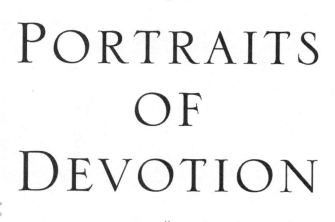

# PORTRAITS
# OF
# DEVOTION

BETH MOORE

# PORTRAITS
# OF
# DEVOTION

PUBLISHING GROUP

NASHVILLE, TENNESSEE

978-1-4627-9674-8


Printed by B&H Publishing Group
Nashville, Tennessee


Dewey Decimal Classification: 242.2
Subject Heading: DEVOTIONAL LITERATURE \ WOMEN \
BIBLE—STUDY

Unless otherwise stated, all Scripture passages are taken from the New International
Version (NIV), copyright © 1973, 1978, 1984 by International Bible Society, used by
permission of Zondervan Bible Publishers. Other versions include the New King
James Version (NKJV), copyright © 1979, 1980, 1982, Thomas Nelson Publishers; The
Amplified Bible, Old Testament copyright © 1962, 1964 by Zondervan Publishing
House, used by permission, the Holman Christian Standard Bible (HCSB), copyright ©
1999, 2000, 2002, 2003 by Holman Bible Publishers, and the King James Version (KJV).

All Scripture passages used in the opening of each devotion are taken from the
Holman Christian Standard Bible (HCSB), copyright © 1999, 2000, 2002, 2003 by
Holman Bible Publishers.

Unless otherwise stated, all Greek word definitions used throughout this book are
taken from *The Complete Word Study Dictionary: New Testament* by Spiros Zodhiates,
et. al., eds. (Chattanooga, TN: AMG Publishers, 1992). Definitions marked
"Strong's" are taken from *A Concise Dictionary of the Words in the Greek Testament* by
James Strong (New York: The Methodist Book Concern, 1890).


1 2 3 4 5 6 7 8 • 22 21 20 19 18

# DAY 1
### Genesis 1:26–2:3

—⁂—

God saw all that He had made, and it was very good (v. 31a).

—⁂—

Can you imagine the fellowship of the Trinity on the seventh day? As they rested and looked upon the very good work they had accomplished, one planet had been tended like no other to our knowledge. Perfectly placed in the universe with adequate distance from sun, moon, and stars to sustain human life, it was chosen for divine infiltration.

"For God loved the world." Scripture doesn't tell us He loved the sun, the most impressive of the heavenly bodies we can see. Nor are we told that He loved the stars, even though He knows every one of them by name. John goes out of his way, however, to tell us that God loved the world.

In a universe so vast, so incomprehensible, why does God single out one little planet to love? Beloved, absorb this into the marrow of your bones: because we are on it. As despicable as humanity can be, God loves us. Inconceivably, we are His treasures, His prize creation. He can't help it. He just loves us. So much, in fact, that He did something I, with my comparatively pitiful love for my children, would not do for anyone. He "gave His One and Only Son, so that everyone who believes in Him will not perish but have eternal life" (John 3:16 HCSB).

Dear one, let it fall afresh. I myself am overcome with emotion. Elohim is so huge; we are so small. Yet the vastness of His love—so high, so wide, so deep, so long—envelops us like the endless universe envelops a crude little planet God first called Earth.

My Amanda was one of the dreamiest, most tenderhearted toddlers you can imagine. I often stooped down to talk to her so I could look her right in those big blue-green eyes. Every time I squatted down to talk to her, she squatted down, too . . . and there we'd be. The gesture was so precious I always had to fight the urge to laugh. I dared not, because she was often very serious about those contemplative moments between the two of us.

Of his God, the psalmist wrote, "Your right hand sustains me; you stoop down to make me great" (Ps. 18:35). The Amplified Version says it this way: "Your gentleness and condescension have made me great." I don't think the Scripture applies to us in the modern world's terms of greatness. I think it says of us, "You stoop down and make me significant." Yes, indeed. And when the God of all the universe stoops down and a single child recognizes the tender condescension and bends her knee to stoop as well, the heart of God surges with unbridled emotion. And there they are. Just the two of them.

# DAY 2
## Genesis 17:1–11

———∞∞∞———

"This is My covenant, which you are to keep, between Me and you and your offspring after you: Every one of your males must be circumcised" (v. 10).

———∞∞∞———

Paul grew up in an orthodox Jewish home in a Gentile city. The Bible gives us only a few pieces of information about his upbringing, but based on these tidbits, we may draw a number of conclusions. The following narrative describes the events that most likely took place soon after his birth. The story line is fictional to help you picture the events, but the circumstances and practices are drawn from Scripture and the Jewish code of law.

"I thank Thee, O living and eternal King, Who hast mercifully restored my soul within me; Thy faithfulness is great."[1]

The words fell from his tongue while his eyes were still heavy from the night's rest. His morning prayers invited unexpected emotion this particular dawn as he soberly considered the honor that lay before him. Eight days had passed since the birth of his friend's son. Today would be the child's *Berit Milah,* an infant boy's first initiation into Judaism. He would stand beside the father at the infant's circumcision in the role of *sandek,* the Jewish godfather, assuming solemn responsibility—second only to the parents—over the child's devout religious upbringing.

He had intended to arrive first so he could assist the father with preparations, but a few members of the Minyan, a quorum of ten Jewish men, had already gathered at the door. The small house was filled with people. The father, a Pharisee and Roman citizen, was an impressive man. He was one of a few men in the community who seemed to command a certain amount of respect from both Jew and Gentile. When all had finally gathered, the ceremony began. The sandek took his place in a chair next to the father, who remained standing. The infant was placed on the sandek's knees, and the father leaned over him with greatest care to oversee the circumcision of his beloved son. He then handed the knife to the *mohel,* the most upright and expert circumcisor available in Tarsus. The father watched anxiously for the interval between the cutting of the foreskin and its actual removal. He could not help but smile as he competed with his wailing son for the attention of the quorum as he spoke the benediction, "Who hath sanctified us by His commandments and hath commanded us to bring him into the covenant of our father Abraham."[2] With the exception of the sandek, all who gathered stood for the ceremony and responded to this benediction with the words, "Just as he has been initiated into the covenant, so may he be initiated into the study of the Torah, to his nuptial [marriage] canopy, and to the performance of good deeds."[3]

No one could deny the blessings of good health God had already bestowed on the infant boy. The sandek had to hold him securely between his calloused palms to keep the child from squirming completely off his lap. His tiny face was blood red, his volume at full scale. This may have been his first bout with anger, but it would not be his last. Had the ceremony not held such sober significance, the sandek might have snickered at the infant's zeal. He dared not grin, but he did wonder if God was. The child lying on his lap was yet another piece of tangible evidence that God was faithful to do as He promised. Yes, God had been faithful to a thousand generations.

The circumcision was completed but not soon enough for the master of ceremonies. The sandek cradled the child with a moment's comfort and then handed him to his father, whose voice resonated throughout the candlelit home, "His name is Saul!" A perfectly noble name for a Hebrew boy from the tribe of Benjamin, named for the first king of the chosen nation of Israel. A fine choice met with great approval. While a great feast ensued, the mother slipped the agitated infant from his father's arms and excused herself to nurse the child.

Custom demanded that the father host a feast to the limits of his wealth. A man who offered less than he could afford at his son's circumcision was entirely improper. If baby Saul's father was anything at all, he was painfully proper. Yes, this would indeed be a child well reared. "I have much to learn from the father of Saul," the sandek surmised.

Darkness was quickly falling when the sandek and his wife finally reached their home. The day had been long but the fellowship sweet. Gathered with those who feared God and worshiped Him only, he had almost forgotten this city was not their own. Tarsus, the city of the Greeks, had given birth to another Hebrew. "Dear wife," the sandek thought out loud, "our Saul seems special, does he not?"

"Dear man," she teased, "he looked like every other eight-day-old infant boy I've ever seen: mad as a wronged ruler!" They both laughed heartily. She prepared for bed as he reached for the Torah, trying to fight off the sleep quickly overtaking him. He repeated the words of the *Shema*, and then he walked over to the *mezuzah* fastened to the doorpost of the house and placed his fingers on it. He responded to the touch with the familiar words of his own father every night of his life, "The Lord is my keeper."[4] He crawled into bed and smiled once again. Then he whispered as his thoughts drifted into the night, "I still say he's special. Full of zeal, he is. Just something about him . . ."

# DAY 3
## Deuteronomy 6:4–9

---

"Bind them as a sign on your hand and let them be a symbol on your forehead.
Write them on the doorposts of your house and on your gates" (vv. 8–9).

---

By the time Saul was thirteen years of age, he was considered a son of the law.
He assumed all the religious responsibilities of the adult Jew. He started wearing
phylacteries, called tefillin, during weekday morning prayers. Phylacteries were
made up of two black leather cubes with long leather straps. Each cube held
certain passages from the Torah written on strips of parchment. Saul wore one
of the cubes on his left arm facing his heart. The other cube was placed in the
center of his forehead. The leather straps on the left arm were wound precisely
seven times around his arm.

The *Code of Jewish Law* prescribed that a Jewish man thirteen years or older
was to put on the tefillin at the first moment in the morning when enough daylight was present to recognize a neighbor at a distance of four cubits.[5] These
practices seem very strange to us perhaps, but we should appreciate their attempt
to interpret Scripture as literally as they knew how.

Exodus 13:9 says the annual observance of the Feast of Unleavened Bread
was to "serve as a sign for you on your hand and as a reminder on your forehead,
so that the law of the Lord may be in your mouth" (hcsb). You can see that for
the strict Jew, the phylacteries were a literal act of obedience.

The left arm was chosen because it was ordinarily the weaker. They were to
wear God's Word as a banner and shield over their weakness. We don't practice
the outward expression of the Jew, but we are wise to share the inward principle.

Saul would have placed the phylacteries around his forehead and arm in
total silence. If interrupted while putting on the phylacteries on any given morning, he would have started the procedure all over again, repeating the appropriate
benedictions. You see, a thirteen-year-old Hebrew boy could not even get out of
bed in the morning without remembering to whom he belonged. As he wound
the straps of the phylacteries around his head and arm, he was reminded of his
binding relationship to his Creator. Soberly he assumed the responsibility of one
associated with God. The law of the Lord was his life.

# DAY 4
## 1 Samuel 1:1–8

—◦◦◦◦◦—

"Hannah, why are you crying?" her husband Elkanah asked. "Why won't you eat?
Why are you troubled? Am I not better to you than 10 sons?" (v. 8).

—◦◦◦◦◦—

One of the blessed gifts God has given our ministry over the years is Lee Sizemore, who long produced our videos with LifeWay Christian Resources. When we were talking about David and the forces that shaped his life, the time in which he lived, and the people who preceded him, Lee said, "In video production terms, that is David's 'back story.'"

What a wonderful term. We all come with a "back story." Some of us come with a heritage of faith and faithfulness. Some of us come with the testimony of God's ability to rescue us from terrible circumstances.

So to understand and appreciate David, we need to venture into his back story, where we get to meet both some heroic characters and some despicable ones.

We will look in the coming days at one of the high points in David's back story, looking at the time when Samuel anointed him to be the king. But we would have no Samuel without a brave and obedient mother named Hannah.

As 1 Samuel begins, we meet Elkanah and his two wives, Hannah and Peninnah. Peninnah had children, but Hannah was childless. They had gone up to the tabernacle at Shiloh to offer sacrifices.

> *Because the LORD had closed her [Hannah's] womb, her rival
> kept provoking her in order to irritate her. This went on year
> after year. Whenever Hannah went up to the house of the LORD,
> her rival provoked her till she wept and would not eat. Elkanah
> her husband would say to her, "Hannah, why are you weeping?
> Why don't you eat? Why are you downhearted? Don't I mean
> more to you than ten sons?" (1 Sam. 1:6–8).*

I'm sorry to report that Elkanah reminds me of one of the thinly developed characters in a TV sitcom. To his credit we read of his making the appropriate sacrifices with his family, but we also find he is married to two wives. Ultimately the word "clueless" comes to mind to describe Elkanah. There he is, married to two wives, one of them childless in a society where childbearing is everything. And the wife with children is torturing the wife without. In that situation he said, "Hannah, why are you weeping? Why don't you eat? Why are you downhearted? Don't I mean more to you than ten sons?"

Does this guy deserve the "I just don't get it" award, or what? I'm jumping ahead, but when Hannah gave birth to Samuel and later prepared to give him up to be reared by the priests, instead of making an attempt at leadership or at least just an opinion, Elkanah said to his wife: "Do what seems best to you" (1 Sam. 1:23).

Guys, don't follow Elkanah's example. Get involved at home. If God has given you a wife, put the effort into understanding her. Is it an impossible task? Most assuredly. But sometimes the challenging jobs are the most rewarding. Wives need men who engage and participate, not abdicate as parent and spouse. For too many husbands the lights are on, but nobody is home.

This is certainly true with Elkanah, which is not surprising when you consider the serious problems that naturally arise from polygamy. This situation certainly adds to Elkanah's inability to understand or meet his wife's needs. Simply stated, he had too many wives!

Let's take a look at where polygamy first crawled into history. Genesis 4:19 tells us: "Lamech married two women, one named Adah and the other Zillah." Lamech disobeyed God's very specific directive in Genesis 2:24: "A man will leave his father and mother and be united to his wife, and they will become one flesh." Tough assignment becoming one flesh when three or more get involved.

We need to nail solidly into our lives two important precepts that come from these Scriptures. First, prevalence does not equal acceptance. Just because polygamy became a common practice, God did not change the rules. Polygamy did not become acceptable with God because it became common with man, any more than research polls cause Him to change His mind about any other sin. Our God is incredibly "public opinion resistant."

Second, *a man cannot be one flesh with two women.* Nor can a woman be one flesh with two men. According to God's math, only two can become one. Both of Elkanah's wives suffered because of his disobedience to God.

As we have all discovered in our individual lives, one problem unchecked invariably leads to plenty of others. "Year after year" the mother of Elkanah's children baited Hannah, and "year after year" the woman of Elkanah's heart bit the bait. Small wonder Hannah felt "bitterness of soul" (1 Sam. 1:10).

# DAY 5
## 1 Samuel 1:9–18

Deeply hurt, Hannah prayed to the LORD and wept with many tears. . . . Then Hannah
went on her way; she ate and no longer appeared downcast (vv. 10, 18).

What constitutes the most bitter pill you've ever had to swallow? All of us
have them. Compared to each other they may seem major or minor, but just as
the only minor surgery is one that happens to someone else, the bitterness we feel
is never minor.

Hannah's situation certainly involved no small pain. Childless. Tormented.
Alone. A plight many have faced, but company proves small solace for misery.

Yet Hannah made the right choices about what to do with her bitterness.
She "wept much and prayed to the LORD" (v. 10). In her prayer, she made two
almost unimaginable commitments. One was by far the easiest of the pair. She
promised no razor would be used on his head. This meant the child would be a
Nazirite, especially consecrated to the Lord. The other promise was to give him
to the Lord for all the days of his life.

We could accuse her of bargaining with God, who does not bargain, but our
God does search the earth for those with a heart toward Him so He can bless
them (2 Chron. 16:9). Chronicles had not yet been written when Hannah was
praying for a son, but somehow she sought in God what David later learned to
be true: "The LORD searches every heart and understands every motive behind
the thoughts. If you seek him, he will be found by you" (1 Chron. 28:9). In her
bitterness she sought her Lord.

I believe God responded to Hannah's prayer for two reasons. First, *He is
gracious*. He longs to pour His love on us. Second, *He knew her heart*. He knew
that what she said, she would do.

Hannah demonstrated that she took her vow to God seriously. For three
years she would hold and love this child. Then she would fulfill her vow, loving
her son even as she gave him to the One who gave him to her.

I never fail to be moved by this account in Scripture. How deeply this
woman wanted a child. How easy to promise anything to get what we want,
but Hannah did not voice empty words. Even in her bitterness of soul and great
weeping, she made her vow to God with the steadfast determination to fulfill it.

## DAY 6
### 1 Samuel 1:19–28

———⸜⸝———

"I prayed for this boy, and since the LORD gave me what I asked Him for, I now give the boy to the LORD. For as long as he lives, he is given to the LORD" (vv. 27–28a).

———⸜⸝———

Hannah named him Samuel. So precious. So prayed for. So deeply loved. And so very important to the Hebrew nation. "She named him Samuel, saying, 'Because I asked the LORD for him'" (1 Sam. 1:20).

Hannah vowed to the Lord that she would give the son she asked for to the Lord and that the child would be a Nazirite. Can you imagine how much easier it would be to say those words about a hypothetical baby, before you held the child in your arms—before your heart became so wrapped up in his that you could hardly keep them separate? Imagine the emotion that filled Hannah's heart. Elkanah went up to make the annual sacrifice. Hannah did not go along, but she told him, "After the boy is weaned, I will take him and present him before the LORD, and he will live there always" (v. 22).

And that's just what she did.

> *After he was weaned, she took the boy with her, young as he was, along with a three-year-old bull, an ephah of flour and a skin of wine, and brought him to the house of the LORD at Shiloh (1 Sam. 1:24).*

Hebrew mothers, according to the accounts recorded in the Apocrypha (2 Mac. 7:27), customarily nursed their children until they were about three years old. I cannot imagine a more difficult age to tear myself away from a child. Still young enough to be such a baby! Old enough to question why. I cried the first time I let mine go to Mother's Day Out for half a day!

If Hannah mustered up the strength to take him there, you would never expect that she could walk away and leave him. In fact, these days we would question such a mother's love for her child.

Oh, but God had a plan. A marvelous plan. He allowed Hannah to be childless so that she would petition God for a child instead of assuming it would be the normal result of marital relations. He also allowed Hannah to be deeply desirous of a child so she would dedicate him entirely to the Lord. He sovereignly planned for His word to come through Eli at the temple so that she would return him to the exact place where she made the vow. Why? Because God had a plan for Samuel that was far more significant than even the most loving set of parents could devise.

Surely while nursing him, Hannah looked into the face of her precious son, and with love overflowing, rehearsed the faithfulness of God in his tiny ears. No doubt he was weaned to know he was appointed to grow up in the house of the Lord. What did the child do when she took him there? "He worshiped the LORD" (v. 28). The Hebrew word is *shachah*. The *Complete Word Study Old Testament* tells us that "*shachah* was not used in the general sense of worship, but specifically to bow down, to prostrate oneself as an act of respect before a superior being."[6]

I recall a scene, engraved in many of our memories, of a tiny boy stepping forward from his grieving mother, saluting the flag-draped coffin of a man who was not only his daddy but the President of the United States. Imagine another scene: A tiny three-year-old boy, still with creases of satiny baby skin around his plump little thighs, bending his knee and bowing before El Elyon, the sovereign God of all creation. How precious this child must have been to God. How in the world could a child that age have such respect for the God of the universe? We get a clue from Hannah's prayer of praise, found in 1 Samuel 2:1–10 . . .

> "There is no one holy like the LORD; there is no one besides
> you; there is no Rock like our God" (v. 2).

Samuel learned faith from his mother—a woman whose faithfulness evidenced her faith, a woman with compulsory praise on her lips. She met painful sacrifice with a song.

God does not ask of us that we take our children to the temple and leave them there to be reared by priests, but we must give them to God in other, equally important ways.

Remember the faith of Hannah. She sought God in her deep need. She made a vow that, by its very nature, was either a deep commitment or a hollow mockery. Then she fulfilled her vow with a mother's sacrifice.

## DAY 7
### 1 Samuel 2:12–26

⎯⎯⎯⎯

Eli's sons were wicked men; they had no regard for the LORD. . . .
By contrast, the boy Samuel continued to grow in stature and in favor
with the LORD and with men (vv. 12, 26).

⎯⎯⎯⎯

Eli was the priest in charge of the tabernacle at Shiloh. At the time of our story, he was an old man. His two sons, Hophni and Phinehas, had followed him as priests in charge. Worshipers came to Shiloh from all the tribes of Israel, bringing with them offerings. We read that "Eli's sons were wicked men; they had no regard for the LORD" (v. 12). They abused worshipers, flaunted the sacrificial laws and customs, and even committed adultery with the women who served at the tabernacle.

At first look, the situation with Eli, his sons, and Samuel seems unfathomable. As credentials for effective parenting, Eli's sons would get him expelled from any waiting list for adoptive parents. Why would God entrust Samuel to a man who had two such sons? One friend of mine observed that Eli demonstrated God's willingness to recommission us. No matter how badly we've messed up in the past, God can still use us. What an expression of His grace to Eli, to give him another chance at fathering!

As we see the unbending character of the man that Samuel became, remember the influences that shaped his life. Possibly he chose to learn from the negative example of Hophni and Phinehas. Most certainly he learned from his mother's respect for God and her commitment to obedience. From Samuel's example we can conclude at least the following truths:

• *We cannot use even the worst of our leaders' failures as excuses before God for lives of negligence and compromise.* Knowing what we do about Eli's sons, we are not surprised to learn that "the word of the LORD was rare" in their days (1 Sam. 3:1). They did not hear from God because they did not honor God. God did not speak because they did not listen. Yet despite the example of Eli's sons, Samuel chose a life of unparalleled faithfulness to God.

• *Parents, like Hannah, do a tremendous service to their children when they rear them to worship and adore God and God alone.* Hannah could not train Samuel to depend on her because she knew she wouldn't be there. But as we witness his life, we never see Samuel confuse God and man. His mother's influence still came through.

# DAY 8
## 1 Samuel 4:1–11

When the ark of the covenant of the LORD entered the camp,
all the Israelites raised such a loud shout that the ground shook (v. 5).

I have noticed something specific to religious people who do not walk with God. They cannot tell the difference between legitimate faith and superstition. This was certainly true of Israel throughout much of the period of the judges. Finding themselves under the heel of the Philistines—a neighboring, but not neighborly, country—they had gone out to fight against them. But the Israelites met bitter defeat. About four thousand soldiers lost their lives in the battle.

Yet as a people who had rejected and ignored God for a generation, their first question upon being slaughtered by their enemy was, "Why did the LORD bring defeat upon us today?" (v. 3). That's when the leaders sent for the ark of the covenant. No doubt their thinking ran that their ancestors had carried the ark when God won great victories, so if they had the ark, they would be victorious.

We can take a great lesson from their presumption. The sovereign God loves deeply, but He will not be disrespected. He will not permit us to take Him for granted. He will not honor our neglect.

Genuinely spiritual people recognize that the trappings of God's presence—such as church buildings, human organizations, even the sacred ark—have no meaning apart from Him. Those who honor Him will *respect* the symbols of His presence, but they will not *worship* those symbols. They certainly will not allow them to take His place.

According to the 1 Samuel account, the very ones who despised and disrespected the sacred things of God, Hophni and Phinehas, came with the ark. No way under heaven was God going to give them this victory. They were treating the ark of the covenant as a good-luck charm. The ark had no power to save. Only the God who graced the ark with His presence had that power.

Likewise, the cross has no power to save—only the Christ who graced it with His presence. We must be very cautious to avoid ever approaching the Divine as a talisman.

# DAY 9
## 1 Samuel 6:1–12

—⊗∞⊗—

"Take the ark of the LORD, place it on the cart, and put
the gold objects in a box beside it, which you're sending
Him as a guilt offering. Send it off and let it go its way" (v. 8).

—⊗∞⊗—

David's back story continues through 1 Samuel 5 and 6, where the Philistines capture the ark of the covenant but are frightened when, in a classic show of "my god's bigger than your god," the presence of the Lord caused the Philistine god Dagon to fall facedown before the ark in a position of worship.

But God wasn't through showin' He's God. So He sent a plague on the Philistines in Ashdod.

They moved the ark to Gath. God moved the plague to Gath.

To Ekron. To Ekron.

You get the picture?

Finally the Philistines cried "uncle." They included an offering to the God of the Hebrews and sent the ark back to Israel . . . sort of.

Any farmer would recognize that the Philistines tried to rig the return of the ark. They put the ark on a cart pulled by two cows that had never pulled a cart, cows with nursing calves penned up at home, and sent the cows on their way with the ark. The Philistine leaders obviously did everything they could to keep the cows from taking the ark away.

Have you ever wanted a certain answer from God so desperately that you consciously or subconsciously tried to "rig" the results? Reading things into the answer that just weren't there? Grabbing the first thing out of someone's mouth as your answer? I think we all have. It's easy to do, but it invariably leads to pain because we end up claiming a promise or a position God never gave us.

Obviously, the cows wouldn't pull the cart together, and certainly they wouldn't leave their calves. Certainly, that is, except for God. The cows obeyed the Creator of cows.

I guess this story proves another basic truth about life: *sin makes you stupid*. The cows had better sense than the Philistines. God can appoint even the beasts of the field to do His bidding.

# DAY 10
## 1 Samuel 8:1–22

———✖———

Listen to them, but you must solemnly warn them and tell them
about the rights of the king who will rule over them (v. 9).

———✖———

Samuel judged Israel all the days of his life. Then, when he grew old, he appointed his two sons to serve in his place. But like Eli before him, his sons dishonored the Lord. We don't know what went wrong. What we do know is that the people demanded a king.

I believe this request from the people devastated Samuel. *Hadn't he loved and sacrificially served these people?*

Then, in a move that seemed to justify and reward their misplaced values and shortsightedness, the Lord told him to grant their request because they had not rejected Samuel as judge; they had rejected God as king.

As always, Samuel obeyed.

Still, he told the people of the taxes they would pay, the freedoms they would lose, and ultimately how their sons and daughters would be reduced to virtual slavery by the fulfillment of their request. No matter how Samuel reasoned, however, the people wanted a king. They wanted a king for all the wrong reasons. Ultimately, they wanted a king because the other nations had them.

We can see so many truths in the situation. One lesson speaks of *patience.* God had already planned a king for the people. Their lack of patience was to cost them dearly. If they had waited for the Lord's choice instead of demanding their way, how different might the story have been?

Another lesson from the story deals with *rejection.* None of us enjoys rejection, but when we are serving Christ, any rejection falls to His broad shoulders rather than our narrow ones. The next time you feel rejection's sting, remember God's words to Samuel: "It is not you they have rejected, but they have rejected me" (v. 7).

Samuel warned the Israelites about what they were getting into. Often when God does not readily give us what we want, it is because He knows what our desire would cost us. Faith sometimes means forgoing our desires because we trust Christ to have a better plan for our lives.

# DAY 11
## 1 Samuel 9:14b–25

---

Then Samuel said, "Notice that the reserved piece is set before you.
Eat it because it was saved for you for this solemn event at the time I said,
'I've invited the people.'" So Saul ate with Samuel that day (v. 24).

---

The people rejected the sons of Samuel and demanded a king. Because they did, we meet one of the great and tragic figures of the Bible. He stood a head taller than anyone else in Israel yet showed all the characteristics of a poor self-concept. His name was Saul, and he would be king. We learn volumes about the shepherd king, David, from his peculiar relationship with his predecessor, Saul.

God arranged for Saul to encounter Samuel while Saul and a servant were out searching for lost donkeys. God had already told Samuel that Saul was coming. But Saul got a puzzled understanding of Samuel's statement:

> *"As for the donkeys you lost three days ago, do not worry about them; they have been found. And to whom is all the desire of Israel turned, if not to you and all your father's family?" (1 Sam. 9:20).*

Saul's response gives us a glimpse of a root problem in his life. The future king replied, "But am I not a Benjamite, from the smallest tribe of Israel, and is not my clan the least of all the clans of the tribe of Benjamin?" (v. 21).

How do we distinguish between godly humility and low self-esteem? Which did Saul display? One key lies in our focus. A person with godly humility looks to the Master. He or she neither exalts nor denigrates self, because to do either is to make self the center of our universe. When we're really serving Christ, our reputations and abilities simply cease to be so important. We must decrease that He may increase.

Saul exhibited the core sin of all self-centered people: he focused on himself. We need to recognize that a lack of confidence does not equal humility. In fact, genuinely humble people have enormous confidence because it rests in a great God. Saul's self-centeredness eventually cost him dearly, as a self-focus always does.

# DAY 12
## 1 Samuel 10:17–27

———∞∞∞———

Some wicked men said, "How can this guy save us?"
They despised him and did not bring a gift, but Saul said nothing (v. 27).

———∞∞∞———

Samuel summoned all of Israel and led them through a dramatic selection process to reveal their king. Only two people knew the eventual outcome: Samuel and Saul. From all the tribes, Samuel selected Benjamin. From all the clans of Benjamin, he chose Matri. From all the families of Matri, the family of Kish. When the big moment arrived—no Saul.

Again we get a glimpse of Saul's root problem: Saul was hiding among the baggage. Self-consciousness constitutes the opposite of God-consciousness. Rather than gratefully rejoicing in the privilege God was freely extending to him, Saul's concern ran to himself and what others would think of him.

Once messengers had retrieved Saul from hiding, Samuel presented the new king and explained to the people the regulations of their new form of government. That's when we immediately get another hint of Saul's deficiency. Most of the people shouted for joy at the stature of the new king, but a few troublemakers reacted differently. They despised Saul and publicly insulted him. Another characteristic of Saul's self-consciousness appeared: he kept silent. Possibly he wanted everybody to like him. Another Saul wrote a prescription this one could have used:

> Am I now trying to win the approval of men, or of God? Or am I
> trying to please men? If I were still trying to please men, I would
> not be a servant of Christ (Gal. 1:10).

Saul, like all people pleasers, had difficulty standing up for right or righteousness because he desired the approval of men. Instead of confrontation, he looked for the easy way out. Saul didn't deal with the problem before him; maybe he hoped it would go away. However, the greater problem lay in himself: he prioritized self over the God who had chosen him.

We are about to see Saul at his best, but like a mighty oak with a fatal infestation of insects, his blight would continue to eat away at his soul. We soon see quite a different portrait of the man who might have been a great king had he consistently placed himself under the authority of God.

Saul returned to his father's farm. Events didn't leave him there long. Nahash the Ammonite attacked Jabesh Gilead, a city of Israel about twenty-five miles south of the Sea of Galilee. The leaders knew they could not hold out against his superior force, so they began to bargain. Nahash agreed to let them live, but at an awful price. He said, "I will make a treaty with you only on the condition that I gouge out the right eye of every one of you and so bring disgrace on all Israel" (1 Sam. 11:2). The people agreed on the condition that they have one week for their fellow Israelites to come to their rescue.

What happened next revealed some important things about the new king. The messenger from Jabesh Gilead found Saul returning with his oxen after plowing a field. I am encouraged that Saul was touched by the tears of "his" people. Scripture tells us that "the Spirit of God came upon him in power, and he burned with anger" (1 Sam. 11:6). The Israelites were about to receive a "special delivery" from their new king.

Saul took a pair of oxen, cut them to pieces, and sent the pieces throughout Israel, proclaiming, "This is what will be done to the oxen of anyone who does not follow Saul and Samuel" (1 Sam. 11:7). Samuel had warned the people that a king would mean forced servitude. Hello selective service!

His approach worked. Verse 7 ends, "Then the terror of the LORD fell on the people, and they turned out as one man." Saul marched his army to Jabesh Gilead and relieved the siege. In the process he won two mighty victories: one over the Ammonites and one over his detractors. The victorious Israelites gathered those who had slighted Saul and . . .

> *The people then said to Samuel, "Who was it that asked, 'Shall Saul reign over us?' Bring these men to us and we will put them to death." But Saul said, "No one shall be put to death today, for this day the LORD has rescued Israel" (1 Sam. 11:12–13).*

For Saul's sake I wish I could report that Saul was simply a compassionate king, but something else may have been going on. If indeed he felt compassion, in the days ahead we will see him lose it. Rather, his actions seem to be the cry of a people pleaser, desiring to be liked rather than demanding to be respected.

# DAY 13
## 1 Samuel 13:6–14

⊸⊶⊷

"You have not kept the command which the LORD your God gave you. It was at this time that the LORD would have permanently established your reign over Israel" (v. 13).

⊸⊶⊷

Any serious student of Israel, or of David, must face why God rejected Saul as king of Israel. We begin to comprehend the reason by examining the time when Saul mustered an army for war against the Philistines, but the Israelite army was so badly outnumbered that they hid in caves.

God gave Saul a chance to shine. He could have taken his place among the great men and women of faith. According to verse 8, he "waited seven days, the time set by Samuel." God was teaching his new king to wait on the Lord.

Imagine the strain on the fledgling king as he watched his army melt away before his eyes. The prophet told Saul to wait until he came to offer the sacrifice before battle. By the seventh day, Saul's patience snapped. He could no longer stand to see his army disintegrate. No doubt he chafed under the criticism of his men. He dared not go into battle without making an offering to God, so he offered the sacrifice himself.

Have you noticed the truth in the old statement that God is seldom in a hurry but He's never late? How often do we give up on God and on obedience just five minutes before deliverance? As Saul made the offering, Samuel arrived. At first glance Saul's infraction may seem minor and Samuel's reaction harsh, but we must remember, Saul was king of God's people. If you aspire to greater authority, you must accept the greater accountability that goes with it.

Samuel demanded to know what Saul had done. The king's response reflected his fear of public opinion, his lack of trust in God, and his cavalier attitude toward obedience. Saul said when he saw the men scattering and Samuel didn't come, he "felt compelled to offer the burnt offering" (v. 12).

We dare not minimize disobedience to God. The prophet responded to Saul's excuses and blaming with harsh words. Saul had a clear command from God. He disobeyed, and it cost him the kingdom.

# DAY 14
## 1 Samuel 14:1–14

———∞∞∞———

Saul's son Jonathan said to the attendant who carried his weapons,
"Come on, let's cross over to the Philistine garrison on the other side."
However, he did not tell his father (v. 1).

———∞∞∞———

Saul, a man with such potential, squandered the kingdom through his disobedience. Now we meet a character who was as noble as Saul was disappointing—Jonathan, son of King Saul, a man vastly different from his father. The one who became so dear to David is sure to become dear to us.

Once again Saul, Jonathan, and the Israelite army faced a far superior force of Philistines. The Israelites were literally hiding in fear. Jonathan obviously decided the army of the mighty God need not hide.

In one of the great statements of faith backed by action, Jonathan said to his armor-bearer:

> *"Come, let's go over to the outpost of those uncircumcised fellows.*
> *Perhaps the LORD will act in our behalf. Nothing can hinder the*
> *Lord from saving, whether by many or by few" (1 Sam. 14:6).*

They challenged the Philistine detachment holding the pass at Micmash. God showed them they should attack. So the two climbed up to the soldiers, killed twenty men, and began the battle. Before the day ended, the Israelites won a great victory over the Philistines.

Jonathan and his armor-bearer were impressive and worthy men. I am amazed by them in two ways. First, Jonathan's perception of the Lord's ways impresses me. His keen perception of the Lord certainly did not come from his father, because Jonathan's understanding exceeded that of Saul. Second, Jonathan had his own relationship with the Lord, completely separate from his father's. He made two profound statements in verse 6:

1. "Perhaps the LORD will act in our behalf."

2. "Nothing can hinder the LORD from saving, whether by many or by few."

Consider how these statements reveal Jonathan's distinct perception of God's ways: Jonathan knew the Lord could save, no matter who or how many were fighting the battle. In fact, he knew that if God chose to save, nothing could hinder Him! His faith in God's strength and determination stood solidly; God could do anything. Jonathan's only question was whether God would choose to do it through them that day. Whether or not He did, Jonathan understood God's response to be based on sovereignty, not weakness.

Jonathan began the battle that quickly turned into a rout. God sent panic on the Philistines until they killed one another. The Israelites merely chased the Philistines in a mopping-up operation.

Then Jonathan's father, the king, entered the picture. Saul saw the Philistine army in disarray and ordered the Israelites into battle. In the process he did an impulsive and stupid thing. Saul "bound the people under an oath, saying, 'Cursed be any man who eats food before evening comes, before I have avenged myself on my enemies!'" (1 Sam. 14:24). He forced the army into an ill-advised and non-God-directed fast.

I believe we need to take a lesson in two ways from Saul's impulsive action. First, *we simply need to beware of decisions made on impulse.* Saul displayed an excessive capacity for action without consulting either God or good sense. The second lesson from Saul's action relates specifically to our eating habits. Many people indulge in fasting that does not come from God. Some carry dieting to fatal extremes. I have known friends who have died as a result of depriving their bodies of food. Remember from Saul's impulsive command: *only God has the right to call a fast.*

Hasty self-centered vows can cost us. Since Jonathan was not in the camp, he did not hear his father's command. As the army chased the Philistines, they became exhausted. They came to a place where a beehive had been broken open. Jonathan ate some of the honey.

In this story we encounter an amazing and humbling truth: God expected the people to obey the king even when his edicts made no sense. So the next day when they inquired of God, He remained silent. Through a process of elimination, they discovered that Jonathan had disobeyed the command of Saul. The king would have put his own son to death, but the men would not allow it.

God tried to teach Saul a very serious lesson that day. Saul's pride could have caused him to keep a foolish vow. Better to repent than to add foolishness to foolishness.

In the account of the battle and its aftermath, we see evidence that God is for us, not against us. He wants us fortified before our enemy with faith like Jonathan's, obedience like the armor-bearer's, and proper fuel like Saul's army should have received.

## DAY 15
### 1 Samuel 15:12–29

—oⱋo—

"Does the LORD take pleasure in burnt offerings and sacrifices as much as
in obeying the LORD? Look: to obey is better than sacrifice" (v. 22).

—oⱋo—

God commanded Saul to utterly destroy the Amalekites, including all the
people and all the livestock. God is sovereign. He owes us no explanation as
to why He desired for this entire population to be exterminated. However, we
can assume they were a vile and godless people, because God is merciful and
compassionate.

We do know from Deuteronomy 25:17–19 that the Amalekites had once
attacked Israel when they were traveling from Egypt to the Promised Land.
They had followed the Israelites and attacked the stragglers. But whatever the
reasons God had for ordering the destruction of the Amalekites, Saul led the
Israelite army to victory but then disobeyed. They kept the king and the best of
the livestock.

Have you noticed how a small disobedience left unchecked always grows?
Saul's actions back in chapter 13 grew from fear and concern for public opinion.
In chapter 15, however, he had *nothing* to fear; his disobedience had become open
and self-serving.

When God told Samuel what Saul had done, the prophet cried out all night
in grief. Then he proceeded to confront Saul directly. The confrontation speaks
to us as we consider our approach to God's instructions. When God speaks, we
must learn to follow Him with complete obedience.

Saul made some very serious presumptions. He kept King Agag alive to
present him as a trophy—a public exhibit. He did not slaughter the sheep and
cattle for the very same reason: he saved the best to make himself look better.
Verse 9 ends with a sad commentary on Saul's actions:

> *These they were unwilling to destroy completely, but everything
> that was despised and weak they totally destroyed.*

Saul had the audacity to improve on God's command. Several breaches in
Saul's character become evident in this dramatic chapter.

First, Saul was *arrogant*. Remember that we said he was self-centered? If we
needed any further proof of Saul's pride and audacity, verse 12 certainly provides
it. Saul went directly to Carmel and built a monument to himself.

Next, note how Saul refused to take *responsibility for his actions*. He first
excused himself for disobeying God by claiming he spared the best of the sheep
and cattle for a sacrifice to the Lord. Amazing, isn't it? Believe it or not, we can

sometimes use God as our excuse for disobedience too. One woman told me she was certain God's will was for her to leave her husband because she simply wasn't happy. Another woman explained to me that she had found the man God intended her to marry, though she was already married.

Saul not only tried to use God as his excuse for disobedience; he also claimed he was afraid of, and gave in to, the people (v. 24). When we've done something wrong or foolish, we find shouldering the responsibility difficult, don't we? At times we are all tempted to blame someone else when we've blown it. I wonder if the outcome might have been different if Saul simply had admitted that he made a wrong choice.

Saul minimized the seriousness of disobedience. In verse 23, Samuel made a striking statement. He said, "Rebellion is like the sin of divination, and arrogance like the evil of idolatry."

The comparison seems puzzling until we consider that rebellion is a means by which we attempt to set the course of our futures. We try to choose our own futures by our independent actions. Divination attempts to foretell or sway the future. In the same verse, God likens arrogance to the evil of idolatry. When we are arrogant, who becomes God in our lives?

We see the final stage of Saul's disobedience and disintegration later on in chapter 28. Once again he had to go into battle. By this time Samuel was dead. Saul sought without success to contact God. Since the Lord chose to remain silent, Saul, in an attempt to contact Samuel, consulted a medium known as the witch of Endor. We see the fleshing out of Samuel's earlier statement. Saul's rebellion became literal witchcraft.

How does a man who is the people's choice lose a kingdom? Saul provides a sad object lesson. All his life he focused on himself instead of his God. Therefore, he feared public opinion; he would not trust God but rather had to feel he was in control. He disobeyed, because obedience requires the trust and humility he did not possess.

Saul. The first king of Israel. The people's choice. Not an accident waiting for a place to happen but a train wreck mangling the lives of others. Sad but true. A head taller but a heart shorter.

# DAY 16
## 1 Samuel 16:1–7

——— 

But the LORD said to Samuel, "Do not look at his appearance or his stature,
because I have rejected him. Man does not see what the LORD sees,
for man sees what is visible, but the LORD sees the heart" (v. 7).

——— 

I love to discover new truths through Scripture, but I also love wrapping
the familiar passages around me like a security blanket and feeling their warmth.
Perhaps we'll have the joy of experiencing the best of both worlds as we go
through these next days together, examining the life of David.

From the first glimpses we get of him in Scripture, you begin to wonder how
one person could be so utterly typical in some ways and so completely atypical in
others. That one question will both bless and haunt us intermittently throughout
our look at David's life—first in his youth and then in the relationships that
shaped his future.

He appears first to us in 1 Samuel 16, amid turbulent circumstances. The
opening words of the chapter ring with change:

> *The LORD said to Samuel, "How long will you mourn for Saul,*
> *since I have rejected him as king over Israel? Fill your horn with*
> *oil and be on your way; I am sending you to Jesse of Bethlehem. I*
> *have chosen one of his sons to be king" (1 Sam. 16:1).*

This verse supplies some interesting facts to file away. Saul had been rejected
as king of Israel, and Samuel the prophet had been grieving over him. So when
told to play a part in appointing Saul's successor, Samuel uncharacteristically
argued with God. He said, "How can I go? Saul will hear about it and kill me"
(v. 2).

The plot thickens.

Samuel the prophet took a heifer for a sacrifice *(when engaging in matters of
espionage, it always pays to have a good cover story)* and set out for the Bethlehem
home of a man named Jesse. Jesse had six of the finest sons in all Israel, and—did
I mention?—those six had a kid brother.

When Samuel arrived in Bethlehem, the town council trembled with fear.
Nobody to trifle with, that Samuel. But he announced his peaceful intentions
and invited the village to attend the sacrifice. When Jesse arrived, Samuel's heart
leaped at the sight. The eldest son, Eliab, was certainly king material, but God
gave a clear no. Each of the sons of Jesse followed—each with the same result.

A slightly puzzled Samuel inquired, "Are these all the sons you have?" (v. 11).

Have you ever felt like the youngest son, the consummate "little brother?" You don't have to be male and you don't have to have siblings to feel that way. In fact, I don't think anyone escapes the feeling completely. Sometime, somewhere, you've probably been treated as if you didn't exist, weren't wanted, didn't matter.

For example, when a friend of mine was about four years old, his two older brothers had company, and he wanted to tag along. Probably he annoyed his older siblings into a brilliant idea. They took him to an anthill, and with a couple of serving spoons and a coffee can, soon had his pants filled with very angry insects.

The few glimpses we see of David and his brothers suggest that he too knew the "sting" of being left out. I believe his wisdom and meditative nature got their start in the loneliness of a little brother accustomed to being put down and ostracized. Did he inherit the duties of keeping sheep, or were the woolly creatures preferable to the company of taunting brothers?

When Samuel asked Jesse if he had any other sons, Jesse answered, "There is still the youngest . . . but he is tending the sheep" (v. 11).

Samuel's stubbornness amuses me. Notice his response to Jesse once he learned that Jesse had one more son: "Send for him; we will not sit down until he arrives" (v. 11). He certainly knew how to get them moving! Don't forget how everyone trembled when he arrived in Bethlehem.

David, a young teenager, arrived on the scene with no idea what awaited him. He was handsome, with a reddish complexion, and no doubt smelled like sheep. He obviously was not his own father's first choice, nor Samuel's.

But God taught Samuel a very important lesson: "Man looks at the outward appearance, but the LORD looks at the heart" (v. 7). God reminded Samuel that the human mind has an overwhelming tendency to make assumptions based on appearances. God's choices don't always make sense to us, but they are never haphazard or random.

# DAY 17
## 1 Samuel 16:8–13

⁕

So Samuel took the horn of oil, anointed him in the presence of his brothers, and the Spirit of the LORD took control of David from that day forward (v. 13).

⁕

I think you'll enjoy knowing that the name Jesse is a personal name meaning "man."[7] Christ, you remember, referred to Himself as the "Son of Man" more than any other title. Isn't it interesting that the King of Israel who often prefigured Jesus was technically also the "son of man"?

David's occupation made him a candidate for kingship. Do you find God's activity as fascinating as I do? We might be tempted to go overboard and believe only His grace matters—that we are the hole in the proverbial doughnut. Of David we might think, "God called him in spite of the fact that he was a common shepherd." The facts prove otherwise. God was working in David's life from the beginning.

David received invaluable experience in the process of keeping sheep. Psalm 78:70–72 states, "He chose David his servant and took him from the sheep pens; from tending the sheep he brought him to be the shepherd of his people Jacob, of Israel his inheritance. And David shepherded them with integrity of heart; with skillful hands he led them."

I believe God takes the building blocks of our lives and uses them to His glory. Never assume that to follow Him means to throw away who He has made you to be. Few things seem less spiritual than keeping a bunch of smelly sheep, yet God used David's skills for eternal purposes.

When David arrived at home, Samuel saw that he was "ruddy, with a fine appearance and handsome features" (v. 12). Still, Samuel did not move. He had already made a mistake based on appearances. Then God said, "Rise and anoint him; he is the one" (v. 12). The next few words send chills up my spine.

> *So Samuel took the horn of oil and anointed him in the presence of his brothers, and from that day on the Spirit of the LORD came upon David in power (1 Sam. 16:13).*

The Holy Spirit just can't seem to arrive without power, can He? As we study the life of a shepherd boy, we will no doubt see testimony of that power again and again. Samuel stood before a young lad and with awe and reverence poured the oil on his head. Although the oil surely blurred the vision of the one whose eyes it bathed, God's vision was crystal clear. He had said, "I will send thee to Jesse the Bethlehemite: for I have provided me a king among his sons" (1 Sam. 16:1b KJV).

The Hebrew word for "provided" is *ra'ah*. It means "to see, to look at, view, inspect, regard, to perceive; . . . to feel; to experience."[8] Second Chronicles 16:9 says, "For the eyes of the LORD run to and fro throughout the whole earth, to show Himself strong on behalf of those whose heart is loyal to Him" (NKJV).

That day so many years ago, the eyes of the Lord looked throughout the whole earth and fell upon an obscure little village called Bethlehem. There He found a heart—one like unto His own. He found a heart tender to little lost sheep, and He showed Himself strong on behalf of that heart, just as He promised.

# DAY 18
## 1 Samuel 16:14–23

---

I have seen a son of Jesse of Bethlehem who knows how to play the harp. He is also a valiant man, a warrior, eloquent, handsome, and the LORD is with him (v. 18).

---

The Scripture combines two descriptions of David we would not expect to find together: he played the harp; he was a warrior. In two simple descriptions, God tells us volumes about "the man after His own heart."

We find that David had the tenderness and the sensitivity of an artist. He was a musician and a songwriter. David did not simply have talent. Talent alone could not have soothed the torment of Saul. David plucked the strings of his harp with tenderness and sensitivity. He chose melodies that ministered to the aching soul. You may rightly imagine that many of your favorite psalms were first sung by the young voice of David, wavering and cracking somewhere between boyhood and manhood to the accompaniment of a well-worn and deeply loved harp. Yet we are also told he was a warrior, brave and strong. The fingers that gently plucked the strings of a harp could also wind fiercely around a sling or a sword.

These complementary parts of David's character will appear throughout this book. David was a complex man. He could be both passionate and withdrawn; dependable and shocking; righteous and wicked—just like us.

Two qualities I've come to admire most in both men and women are tenderness and strength. I no longer see them as exclusive terms. Quite the contrary, I've come to realize that one without the other leaves an individual lacking wholeness. I deeply desire to be a woman of tenderness and strength because my dearest role model possessed both.

Christ Jesus is the artist. He created the world with colors and textures human artists have tried for thousands of years to imitate. Christ Jesus is the musician. He gave the angels their voices. Christ Jesus is the tenderhearted, ministering to our every need.

Christ Jesus is also the warrior, forever leading us in triumphant procession, if only we will follow (2 Cor. 2:14). In our greatest weakness, He is strong. Christ Jesus is the blessed embodiment of both characteristics. He has set an example before us of true manhood and true womanhood. No greater man or woman exists than one in whom tenderness and strength can be found. David was such a man.

# DAY 19
## 1 Samuel 17:1–30

---

David was the youngest. The three oldest had followed Saul, but David kept going
back and forth from Saul to tend his father's flock in Bethlehem (vv. 14–15).

---

We arrive today at an account in Scripture that has captured the imaginations of every little boy and girl who ever sat in a circle of small, wooden chairs in
a Sunday school room. This is the story of David and Goliath.

But today, I want you to notice just this one thing: David knew the sting of
disapproval by his brothers. When his oldest brother, Eliab, heard him talking
about Goliath, he became angry. Eliab accused David of wrong motives: "Why
have you come down here? And with whom did you leave those few sheep in the
desert? I know how conceited you are and how wicked your heart is; you came
down only to watch the battle" (v. 28).

Eliab said everything he could to discourage David. He said he didn't
belong; he made fun of David's trade; he accused him of conceit and deceit.

David's response, "Now what have I done?" (v. 29)—perhaps more clearly
understood when you turn it around a little to read, "What have I done now?"—
evidenced the fact that Eliab and David were not at odds for the first time. I
have to wonder if Eliab's response resulted from almost being anointed king. The first
drop of oil had almost fallen on his head when God stopped Samuel and chided
him for looking on the outward appearance.

I'm not sure anyone can encourage or discourage us like family. The views
of our family members toward us are very convincing, aren't they? If people
who know us the best encourage us the least, we have few chances to develop
confidence.

David remained undaunted by Eliab's criticisms for one reason: David
took God's Word over the opinions of others. As a Hebrew lad, David heard
the promises of victory God made to the nation that would call upon His name.
David believed those promises.

Whenever you feel alone, rejected, or misunderstood, stand your situation
up next to David's. The boy had as pure a heart as humanly possible, and his own
family blasted him. Ouch. I don't want to minimize your hurts, but in David you
can certainly find someone who has been there, done that.

# DAY 20
### 1 Samuel 17:31–58

---

Instead, he took his staff in his hand and chose five smooth stones
from the wadi and put them in the pouch, in his shepherd's bag.
Then, with his sling in his hand, he approached the Philistine (v. 40).

---

When David volunteered to fight the giant, Saul promptly dressed David in the king's armor. Imagine this picture: a young shepherd boy, dressed in the armor of the middle-aged king who was twice his size. Is it any wonder David could hardly walk, let alone fight?

David made a wise choice that is a lesson for us: "'I cannot go in these,' he said to Saul, 'because I am not used to them'" (v. 39). What wisdom from such a youth. David was comfortable enough with himself to say, "This just isn't me."

So David shed the armor of Saul, picked up five smooth stones, took his shepherd's sling, and went out to meet Goliath—in the power of God. You know the rest. No giant will ever be a match for a big God with a little rock.

David's example teaches us some wonderful, practical truths we can use to deal with the giants in our lives. First, he illustrates what God's Word tells us—that we are *loved, gifted, and blessed*. We can do anything God calls us to do through Christ who strengthens us (Phil. 4:13). We must develop more confidence in God's Word than in the opinions of others.

Second, David reminds us to *measure the size of our obstacles against the size of our God*. Goliath was nine feet tall, with 140 pounds of armor shielding him. We tend to measure our obstacles against our own strength. We often feel overwhelmed and defeated before the battle begins. I am not suggesting that if we measure our obstacles against God our battles will be effortless. David still had to face his giant obstacle and use the strength he possessed, but his confidence in God caused a simple pebble to hit like a boulder.

Third, David shows us our need to *acknowledge an active and living God in our lives*. Look how David referred to God in 1 Samuel 17:26: "Who is this uncircumcised Philistine that he should defy the armies of the living God?"

We're often intimidated in battle because we are uncertain of our faith. But we must remember we don't stand in victory because of our faith. We stand in victory because of our God. Faith in faith is pointless, but faith in a living, active God moves mountains.

# DAY 21
## 1 Samuel 18:1–4

———∞∞∞———

Jonathan made a covenant with David because he loved him as much as himself (v. 3).

———∞∞∞———

Who but God can explain the ways of the heart? Sometimes friendships bloom over months or years. At other times someone touches your heart almost instantly, and you seem to have known him or her forever. Have you ever felt an almost instant bond to a new friend? Such was the deep and abiding friendship between Jonathan and David.

Jonathan's expressions of love and friendship toward David paint one of the most beautiful portraits of a covenant in the Word of God. The word "covenant" in verse 3 derives from the Hebrew term *berith*, which means "determination, stipulation, covenant. It was a treaty, alliance of friendship, a pledge, an obligation between a monarch and his subjects, a constitution. It was a contract which was accompanied by signs, sacrifices and a solemn oath which sealed the relationship with promises of blessing for obedience and curses for disobedience."[9]

According to the definition, three elements accompanied the making of a covenant: signs, sacrifice, and a spoken commitment. Although in the covenant of Jonathan and David these three elements are less obvious than in other covenants in Scripture, their covenant includes each of the parts.

*The sign:* Jonathan demonstrated his covenant with David by giving him his robe, tunic, and weapons. We will see the greater significance of Jonathan's sign as we consider the sacrifice and the spoken commitment.

*The sacrifice:* In Jonathan's covenant with David, the sacrifice is less obvious than other examples in Scripture, but it is profound. Clearly Saul intended for Jonathan to become the second king of Israel (1 Sam. 20:30–31), but this son had other plans. In David, Jonathan saw character fit for a king. He was so determined that the throne be occupied by God's chosen instrument that he offered everything he had. In this unique covenant, Jonathan sacrificed himself. He removed his royal regalia—his robe and tunic—and placed it on David, symbolizing that David would be king instead of him. Can you picture the face of the recipient, whose clothing probably still carried the faint scent of sheep?

Jonathan acknowledged David as prince of the Hebrew nation, a position which he could have jealously and vehemently claimed as his own. Men like Jonathan are a rarity. Few people we meet in life have "in mind the things of God" at risk of their own favor and position (Matt. 16:23).

*The spoken commitment:* The oath of Jonathan's covenant with David does not take place in words in chapter 18. Jonathan symbolized the solemn oath by giving David his weapons of protection: his sword, bow, and belt. He symbolically gave all he had to protect David from harm and ensure his position as future king.

Jonathan verbalized his solemn oath by pledging in 1 Samuel 20:13 to protect David from harm at great personal risk.

We have examined three elements of covenant, but we have not yet noted the most critical issue: the basis of the covenant.

Deuteronomy makes a bold assertion about why God chose the nation of Israel. It simply and majestically declares that God redeemed Israel "because the Lord loved you and kept the oath he swore to your forefathers" (Deut. 7:8). Reconsider Jonathan's covenant with David. You will see that they had the same basis to their covenant. In fact, 1 Samuel 18:1–4 shows something else about the covenant. If you go back and read the passage, you will find no mention of David returning Jonathan's love.

God's covenant with the nation of Israel was based on His love for them—not their love for Him. Amazing! In this same way, Jonathan's covenant with David was based on Jonathan's love, not David's response. We who have accepted Christ as Savior are part of the most wonderful covenant God ever made with man. God loves us for a singular reason—because He chooses to.

Look at a final Scripture as we consider the covenant God has made with us. Examine these two verses from 1 John 4, and reflect on how our covenant compares to Jonathan's covenant with David:

> *This is love: not that we loved God, but that he loved us*
> *and sent his Son as an atoning sacrifice for our sins. . . .*
> *If anyone acknowledges that Jesus is the Son of God, God*
> *lives in him and he in God (1 John 4:10, 15).*

*The sign:* God sent His only Son.

*The sacrifice:* He "sent his Son as an atoning sacrifice for our sins" (v. 10).

*The spoken commitment:* "If anyone acknowledges that Jesus is the Son of God, God lives in him and he in God" (v. 15).

The basis of this covenant is the same as the basis of Jonathan's covenant with David: "not that we loved God, but that he loved us" (v. 10). What greater covenant could possibly exist?

# DAY 22
## 1 Samuel 18:5–16

—⁂—

Saul was furious and resented this song. "They credited tens of thousands
to David," he complained, "but they only credited me with thousands.
What more can he have but the kingdom?" (v. 8).

—⁂—

In stark contrast to Jonathan's self-sacrifice and solemn allegiance, Saul
regarded David as the ultimate threat. The praise of the people that was directed
at David planted a seed of jealousy in Saul that would express itself with a vengeance over many chapters and years.

Motivated by jealousy, Saul sent David to fight with the army. The king
hoped young David would come to harm, yet David effectively performed the
duties Saul assigned to him. As he came in from battle, the women of Israel sang,
"Saul has slain his thousands, and David his tens of thousands" (v. 7).

A man as big in character as Saul stood in stature could have rejoiced with
David, but Saul was no such man. The words galled him. He decided it would be
only a matter of time until David took his kingdom.

So the next day Saul tried to kill David. As the loyal harpist played for his
master, Saul threw a spear in an attempt to pin David to the wall, but David
avoided Saul's attacks twice.

The Hebrew word for the kind of anger Saul experienced is informative:
*charah*—"to burn, be kindled, glow with anger, be incensed, grow indignant; to
be zealous, act zealously." Unlike some of its synonyms, *charah* points to the fire
or heat of the anger just after it has been ignited.[10] *Charah* captures the moment
a person explodes with anger—the moment anger is ignited before any sense of
control takes over, before a rational thought can be processed.

Rarely do we accomplish anything profitable at the moment we become
angry. Actions or words immediately following the ignition of anger are almost
always regrettable. Moments like the one *charah* describes are exactly the reason
I never want to approach a day without praying to be filled with the Holy Spirit.
Through the life of Saul, we see a portrait of what our lives might be like if the
Holy Spirit either departed or was quenched in us. No thanks!

# DAY 23
## 1 Samuel 18:17–30

———

Saul realized that the LORD was with David and that his daughter Michal
loved him, and he became even more afraid of David. As a result,
Saul was David's enemy from then on (vv. 28–29).

———

Saul felt many things toward David, but the most consistent emotion was
jealousy. Few experiences are more miserable than being the subject of someone's
unleashed jealousy. Perhaps the only thing worse is being the one in whom the
jealousy rages. As we travel along, we will see some of the suffering that jealousy
showered on the lives of both Saul and David.

We know, interestingly, that God reveals Himself to be a "jealous God"
(Exod. 20:5). But His is a selfless jealousy motivated by love. He is jealous on
our behalf—jealous for us to know Him, to be kept from evil, to be ready for our
Bridegroom. Saul's jealousy of David, however, was anything but holy.

In 1 Samuel 18, we see an amazing and disgusting picture of what jealousy
can do in our hearts. Saul had promised his daughter to the man who would fight
Goliath, so he offered his oldest daughter, Merab, to David. If David had been
interested in social climbing, he certainly would have jumped at the chance, but
he deferred. So Saul married Merab to another man. Michal, however—Saul's
second daughter—was in love with David.

The king hatched a plan. Possibly he thought that the Philistines would go
to extra lengths to kill David if he was the king's son-in-law. Saul offered Michal
to David in marriage, but David had no dowry. So Saul took his plotting a step
further:

> *Saul replied, "Say to David, 'The king wants no other price for
> the bride than a hundred Philistine foreskins, to take revenge on
> his enemies.'" Saul's plan was to have David fall by the hands of
> the Philistines (1 Sam. 18:25).*

So our David is married, having accomplished this daunting task. We know
little about his bride Michal, but Saul considered the marriage a way to destroy
David (v. 21). Can you imagine the evil in the heart of a man who would use his
own daughter as a pawn in a personal vendetta? Saul obviously had high hopes
that Michal would be the death of David, but David had something much greater
than high hopes. He had a Most High God.

# DAY 24
## 1 Samuel 19:9–18

———⟨∞⟩———

Saul sent agents to David's house to watch for him and kill him
in the morning. But his wife Michal warned David:
"If you don't escape tonight, you will be dead tomorrow!" (v. 11).

———⟨∞⟩———

Once the seed of jealousy was sown in the heart of Saul, fear, anger, and bitterness fueled a jealousy that quickly grew out of control and continued to grow. Read 1 Samuel 19, and you can almost see the scene unfold on stage. Picture the scene with me.

Saul's madness led him through a series of pendulum swings. He would become paranoid and homicidal toward David, then he would temporarily become rational, only to let his madness consume him again.

We've probably all been in Saul's place at one time or another. Something makes us furious; then someone tries to talk some sense into us. We feel a little better, pledging to put our anger away forever. Then here it comes again with the power of gale-force winds.

Jealousy is a powerful emotion, isn't it?

But so is love. When Saul married his daughter Michal to David, he thought she would be a snare to him. When the king discovered his daughter loved David, he became even more afraid (1 Sam. 18:28–29). He was right about love threatening his plans for Michal to bring harm to David. The power of love often exceeds the power of loyalty. Before long, Saul once again sought to kill David. Saul threw a spear at the young warrior, but once again he escaped. Saul sent soldiers to kill him—again—but Michal warned her husband. She helped him escape out a window and put an idol in the bed to look like David (vv. 11–13).

Saul thought he could trust Michal to make David miserable. He thought she would be a puppet in his hands against the young warrior—until he realized she loved him. Her masterful deception could easily have led to her death. She was spared only because she convinced her father that David would have killed her if she hadn't let him get away.

Truly, love is more powerful than jealousy, just as godliness is more powerful than wickedness, and the Spirit of God is more powerful than anything! That's what it takes to burst the walls of rage and jealousy within us. First John 3:20 says, "God is greater than our hearts." As children of God, we do not have to be derailed by the way we feel. Our God is greater. Give Him your heart!

# DAY 25
## 1 Samuel 20:1–17

———— ∞∞ ————

"If I continue to live, treat me with the Lord's faithful love, but if I die, don't ever withdraw your faithful love from my household—not even when the Lord cuts off every one of David's enemies from the face of the earth" (vv. 14–15).

———— ∞∞ ————

The Spirit of God sometimes cements two people together as part of His plan. God would never have chosen David to be His future king if He had not planned to sustain him and ultimately deliver him safely to his throne. Jonathan was an important part of God's plan. They were uncommon friends joined by a common bond: the Spirit of God.

Consider these evidences of an uncommon friendship.

1. *Uncommon friends can speak their minds without fear.* Imagine the tone David probably used with Jonathan when he came to him, demanding to know why Saul was seeking his life. David asked, "What have I done? What is my crime? How have I wronged your father, that he is trying to take my life?" (v. 1).

Jonathan replied, "Look, my father doesn't do anything, great or small, without confiding in me. Why would he hide this from me? It's not so!" (v. 2).

David's words suggest nothing less than panic. Jonathan could easily have received David's words as an insult. After all, David practically took his frustration out on Jonathan and asked him to explain his father's actions. As you carefully consider the words they traded, you can almost hear them shouting at each other.

Jonathan responded to David's panic with the words, "Why would he hide this from me? It's not so!" David came very close to holding Jonathan responsible for Saul's actions, and Jonathan came very close to getting defensive.

Their initial words to one another were natural under these circumstances. What is *not* natural, however, was their freedom to speak their minds and move on to resolution without great incident. At this point Jonathan didn't believe that Saul was really trying to take David's life, yet he acknowledged that David's feelings were authentic by saying, "Whatever you want me to do, I'll do for you" (v. 4). He didn't necessarily agree with David, but he agreed that David was upset and needed his help instead of his doubt.

Allowing others to speak their fears even when we can't understand is characteristic of uncommon friendship. Willingness to listen, then to let the potential insults pass, is not a sign of weakness. It is a sign of strength. The bonds of uncommon friends are deeper than the width of their differences.

2. *Uncommon friends can share their hearts without shame.* The scene between Jonathan and David in 1 Samuel 20:41 touches my heart every time I read it.

Jonathan signaled David that he must run for his life. Then Jonathan sent the boy that was with him away and went to David.

> *After the boy had gone, David got up from the south side of the stone and bowed down before Jonathan three times, with his face to the ground. Then they kissed each other and wept together—but David wept the most.*

Something about two men unafraid to share their hearts with one another never fails to move me. Uncommon friends can be vulnerable with one another and still retain their dignity. The friendship between them was far more than emotion. It was a safe place to trust and show feelings. They shared a common goal: the will of God. Each life complemented the other. They had separate lives but inseparable bonds.

3. *Uncommon friends can stay close even at a distance.* Most friendships require time and attention. We saw that Jonathan and David's friendship did not grow out of a lengthy period of time as most friendships do. They were brought together by spiritual ties, not sequences of time. They had "sworn friendship with each other in the name of the LORD" (v. 42). God brought them together. Their friendship was a bond of three.

I am struck by how Ecclesiastes 4:9–12 pictures the friendship of David and Jonathan. We are not sure that Solomon wrote the Book of Ecclesiastes, but if he did, I wonder if the inspiration from this passage came from the stories he heard at his father David's knee.

> *Two are better than one, because they have a good return for their work: If one falls down, his friend can help him up. But pity the man who falls and has no one to help him up! . . . A cord of three strands is not quickly broken. (Eccles. 4:9–10, 12b)*

This Scripture applies perfectly to Jonathan and David, but especially the last line. Doesn't this statement picture God's part in Jonathan and David's friendship? If God is not an active part in your friendships, you are missing one of life's most important treasures.

# DAY 26
## 1 Samuel 21:1–9

—∞∞—

The priest told him, "There is no ordinary bread on hand.
However, there is consecrated bread" (v. 4).

—∞∞—

David was scarcely twenty years old when he was forced to leave his home, his livelihood, and his beloved friend Jonathan as he fled from the madman who happened to be king of Israel.

When David resigned to live as a fugitive, he first went to Nob, to Ahimelech the priest. David did not haphazardly end up there. He sought relief in the "city of priests." Nob, a village between Jerusalem and Gibeah, was the venue where the tabernacle was relocated after the destruction of Shiloh. Like many of us in times of crisis, David may have desired to draw closest to those who seem closest to God—not a bad idea.

When Ahimelech asked David's reason for coming, David responded to the priest with a lie. Throughout our look at his life, we will be witness to more than a few compromises in David's character. In this case the compromise was David's willingness to lie. He was probably attempting to spare the priest's life, hoping that Saul would not hold Ahimelech responsible for helping David.

Famished from his flight, David asked the priest for bread. He asked for five loaves. The request strikes a familiar chord to those schooled in the Scriptures. Christ fed the multitudes with five loaves of bread in Matthew 14:19. In 1 Samuel 21:3, David requested of Ahimelech, "Give me five loaves of bread, or whatever you can find." In all four of the Gospels, as Christ sent the disciples to search for food, five loaves were all they could find. For David, no bread could be found except the bread of the Presence.

Perhaps God had a point to make with the five loaves. The bread of the Presence has always been connected to God's covenant. The regulation concerning the bread of the Presence appears in Leviticus 24:5–9. Verse 8 says, "This bread is to be set out before the LORD regularly, Sabbath after Sabbath, on behalf of the Israelites, as a lasting covenant."

Consider two possible reasons why God might have purposely used the bread of the Presence to feed David. First, the bread of the Presence might have symbolized *God's everlasting covenant with David*. Somewhat like the stars of the sky symbolized the offspring of Abram (Gen. 15:5), the bread of the Presence was placed before God as a reminder, or symbol, of the everlasting covenant. God may have used the bread of the Presence to remind David of the everlasting covenant He had made with David's kingdom.

Second, the bread of the Presence might have symbolized *the provision of God's presence in the life of David*. Just as the first possible reason was a corporate symbol for a kingdom covenant, the second reason might have been a private symbol for a personal covenant. The Hebrew term for presence is *paneh*, which means "countenance, presence, or face."[11] The everlasting covenant symbolized by the bread of the Presence was a reminder of the pledge of God's presence to His people. As He offered bread to David through Ahimelech the priest, I believe God pledged His presence to David throughout his exile and promised to be his complete sustainer. God was doing more in this moment in Nob than feeding David's hungry stomach.

God also extends His presence to you as your sustaining provision. Note the name Christ calls Himself in the Gospel of John:

> *"I tell you the truth, he who believes has everlasting life. I am the bread of life" (John 6:47–48).*

Did you notice how Jesus combined the bread of life with everlasting life? Christ is the bread of God's presence to us. His scars are placed before God as a perpetual memorial that the wages of our sins have been paid. Christ said, "This bread is my flesh, which I will give for the life of the world" (John 6:51b). Those who have eaten the bread of His presence enjoy the same everlasting covenant He made with David thousands of years ago. He renews His promise to us in Hebrews 13:5:

> *"Never will I leave you; never will I forsake you."*

God reminded David of His presence and provision not just through the priest of Nob; God also reminded David in another way. Does it seem coincidental that when David asked for a weapon, the only one in the city of Nob was Goliath's sword? Is it possible God was trying to remind David that he had overcome a greater enemy than Saul with God's help?

# DAY 27
## 1 Samuel 21:10–15

—∞∞—

"Look! You can see the man is crazy," Achish said to his servants.
"Why did you bring him to me?" (v. 14).

—∞∞—

David's relentless search for refuge led to a rather humorous scene, as we see in today's reading. He fled to Achish, the king of Gath, but the Philistine king quickly recognized David. This situation frightened David in his depleted state, but the Israelite was a quick thinker. He pretended to be insane, acting like a madman, "scribbling on the doors of the gate and letting saliva run down his beard" (v. 13). Had David been auditioning for a theatrical production, he would no doubt have gotten the part!

We see a new, creative, and shrewd side of our protagonist in this situation. Not only was he a harpist and a warrior, he could have won an Oscar for best actor! Some people act for pleasure. Others act for money. David was acting for his life. He pulled it off too.

You may be wondering why the men of Gath didn't kill him on the spot. David knew the pagan people of his day. They were terrified of a madman and far too superstitious to harm one. They feared he was a dangerous demon who had the power to cause them havoc from the next life. Apparently, David wasn't just sheep-smart, he was street-smart.

The Philistine king delivered one of those wonderful lines that show Scripture is not only the Word of God but the greatest literature you can find. Achish said: "Am I so short of madmen that you have to bring this fellow here to carry on like this in front of me?" (v. 15). (I confess that though good manners have precluded my using this line, the action of some people have made me think of it.)

David may have been short on patience and on perceiving God's constant reminders, but he certainly wasn't short on personality, was he? It does make for good story material, even though patience and perception might have helped him a little more than personality. In the days ahead, we are going to see David as he negotiates some pretty tough times. We'll begin to peek a little deeper into the heart God saw and loved. Keep praying for a hunger and thirst for God's Word. Ask God to make you aware of His constant presence so that you can have His assurance no matter your circumstances, no matter how crazy your life may sometimes get.

# DAY 28
## 1 Samuel 22:1–10

—⧞—

Every man who was desperate, in debt, or discontented
rallied around him, and he became their leader (v. 2).

—⧞—

We now begin to consider a vital season that provided painful preparation for the throne God had promised. David responded to life on the run as he fled a wildly jealous king. Can you imagine the devastation David must have experienced having all his hopes dashed to pieces? He probably had never been away from home before he was summoned to Saul's service. Filled with dreams and wonderful expectations, young David was met by a nightmare. He had not only left his home, now he'd run from his "home away from home." He was separated from his new wife and his best friend, and forced to beg bread from the priest of Nob.

Verse 1 tells us that "David left Gath and escaped to the cave of Adullam." The cave of Adullam, a word meaning "sealed off place," was about twenty miles southwest of Jerusalem.[12] David had traveled approximately ten miles by foot from Gath to this place of strange refuge he found in the crevice of a mountain.

Cave-pierced mountains are prevalent in the area of Palestine where David's exile took place. Evidence exists that many continued to find refuge in these caves up until the time of Roman rule, when they were common hideaways for Jews fleeing Roman persecution. I wonder how many of those Jews found solace in knowing their beloved King David had also escaped persecution in a similar refuge centuries earlier.

Obviously, David's brothers were at least beginning to change their tunes about their younger sibling, because his brothers and his father's household joined him in the cave. David asked the king of Moab if his parents could stay with him awhile. No doubt David feared for the lives of his parents when Saul found that his brothers had joined him.

Don't forget that this was David's first taste of independent leadership! What could be less appealing than leading a group made up of the three D's: the distressed, the debtors, and the discontented? Ultimately, David would rise to the throne as the forerunner of the King of kings. His kingdom would be known throughout the world. He would be favored by the living Lord as His chosen, His anointed. God had to bring David down to a lowly position before He could raise him up to stand on solid ground.

## DAY 29
### 1 Samuel 22:11–23

———∞∞∞———

Then the king ordered the guards standing by him, "Turn and kill
the priests of the LORD because they sided with David" (v. 17).

———∞∞∞———

We are about to see the depth of Saul's irreverence toward God and the
breadth of his madness toward David. This account shows how far the once
potentially noble Saul had fallen.

Remember the hinted reference to Doeg the Edomite in 1 Samuel 21:7?
He had been in Nob the day David had met with Ahimelech the priest and had
overheard their exchange. We sort of suspected that we hadn't seen the last of
this sinister figure.

Sure enough, he tattled to Saul about Ahimelech's helping David. So on the
word of Doeg, Saul sent for Ahimelech and all his family. The priest nobly and
bravely testified to the king that David was loyal to Saul. Enraged nonetheless,
Saul ordered the murder of all the priests, but his guards refused to carry out
the order. Doeg the Edomite then volunteered and murdered eighty-five priests
plus all the family members—including women, infants, and children. Only one
priest—Abiathar, the son of Ahimelech—escaped and fled to join David.

I'll never forget seeing this scene in the movie *King David*. I ran to God's
Word to see if the events portrayed were accurate, and to my horror, they were.
At that moment, I ceased to feel pity for Saul. In my opinion, David gave him far
too much credit. David gambled on the hope that Saul would never put to death
an innocent priest. He was wrong.

Once again, we have the great privilege of seeing the words God inspired
from David's pen after he learned of the tragic slaughter. The NIV note with
Psalm 52 reads: "When Doeg the Edomite had gone to Saul and told him: 'David
has gone to the house of Ahimelech.'" Take a moment to read this brief psalm
yourself.

Assuming David is addressing Saul, verse 1 of this psalm strongly suggests
that Saul not only had a multitude of innocent people put to death, many of them
priests, but he also bragged about it.

Verse 7 tells us something vile about the ego of King Saul. It says he "grew
strong" by destroying others. Have you ever known anyone who made him or
herself feel bigger or better by putting others down? Putting others down to
build ourselves up is perhaps the ultimate sign of gross insecurity. Thankfully,
most people with such insecurity don't have the kind of power Saul had to destroy
people physically. However, if we allow our insecurities to govern our lives, we
become destroyers just as certainly.

Don't miss a wonderful lesson in verse 8, as well. Remember, David was still on the run in the forest of Hereth (1 Sam. 22:5), but even on the run, not knowing where his next meal would come from, David knew that in comparison to Saul, he was "like an olive tree flourishing in the house of God." Do you see what David did in the face of unimaginable horror? Psalm 52 tells us. When he received the news of the slaughter of innocent people, David responded in four ways to the tragedy.

1. He placed blame where it should have been: on Saul, on evil (vv. 1–4).
2. He reminded himself that God will repay evil (v. 5).
3. He placed his hope solely in God (v. 9).
4. He reminded himself that God is good (v. 9).

I will never forget seeing the first film clips on television from the 1995 bombing of the federal building in Oklahoma City. I could not fathom how anyone could be so heartless and depraved. I cried for the children who had been lost or injured; then I tossed and turned most of the night. The day following the bombing I was scheduled to speak at a conference of 4,500 women from the Oklahoma City area—a commitment I had made two years prior to the time. I kept thinking that perhaps we would cancel the event; or perhaps many would not attend. The event was not canceled. Only one person who registered did not come; she was unaccounted for in the rubble of the federal building. Never have I been more frightened that I might give the wrong message. I begged God to be clear with me and not let me say a word on my own. My text was different from Psalm 52, yet the points He sent me to make were almost identical to the ones we've noted above:

1. God is not the author of destruction.
2. God will repay evil.
3. Our hope must be in God.
4. No matter how bad things look, God is good.

In the face of unimaginable horror, we must cast our imaginations on Christ, our only hope. His Word will be our anchor when our faith is tossed like the waves. David could not have survived the guilt or the pain of Saul's horrendous actions had he not cast himself on God and His Word. We must do the same. Keep having faith even in the face of unexplainable evil or disaster. You will be richly rewarded for your faith even when others have scorned you for still believing. God is the only hope in this depraved world. He is faithful who promised.

# DAY 30
## 1 Samuel 23:1–6

Once again, David inquired of the LORD, and the LORD answered him (v. 4).

First Samuel 23 shows God's faithfulness shining brightly against the bleak backdrop of David's life. David continued to evade the crazed King Saul, but he did more than hide. He took every possible opportunity to defend his people, even when he was repaid with betrayal.

David faced a dilemma. The Philistines were attacking the Israelite town of Keilah. What was David to do? Should he defend fellow Israelites and thereby put himself and his men at greater risk? In that difficult situation David did something characteristic of a man after God's heart. He inquired of the Lord.

"The LORD answered him, 'Go, attack the Philistines and save Keilah'" (v. 2). Not surprisingly, David's men greeted the news with less than enthusiasm. They said, "Here in Judah we are afraid. How much more, then, if we go to Keilah against the Philistine forces!" (v. 3).

David responded to them in an interesting way. He returned to ask God once again. Once again God told him to go attack the Philistines and save Keilah. So David and his men fought the Philistines and saved the people of Keilah (vv. 4–6).

Have you ever moved too quickly in a direction you believed God was sending you and later realized you were hasty and might have misunderstood? David's example reminds us that doubting God and doubting we understood God are two different things.

I find it interesting that rather than shame his men for questioning the word he had received from God, David went back to God and reconfirmed His direction. God rebuked neither David nor his men. God knew David felt great responsibility to them. If he misunderstood God, many lives could be lost.

David did not ask God a second time because he doubted God, but because he needed to be certain. In the same way, you or I might ask God to reconfirm His direction—not because we doubt God's Word, but because we question our understanding. To doubt God in the face of clear direction is disobedience, but to double-check our understanding and interpretation of God's will is prudent.

# DAY 31
## 1 Samuel 23:7–18

—∘∞∘—

Saul searched for him every day, but God did not hand David over to him (v. 14).

—∘∞∘—

When Saul heard that David had rescued the inhabitants of Keilah, the king thought he had trapped his prey in a walled city. When David learned that Saul was gathering his forces, David consulted God and asked two questions. He wanted to know if Saul would pursue him and if the people of Keilah would defend him.

David received both answers from God: Yes, Saul would pursue him, and yes, the citizens of Keilah would give him over to Saul. So David again fled, this time to the Desert of Ziph.

We have the blessing of studying several psalms that coincide with David's experiences. I wish I could invite you to expect a coinciding psalm at every venture, but God's Word only tells us the occasions surrounding a few of the psalms. God inspired David to write Psalm 54 after the Ziphites told Saul his whereabouts. David began the psalm with the words, "Save me, O God, by your name." Before David had finished, he called on God with a multitude of names. David seemed to have as many names for God as he had needs! Why? Because God was everything to him! One of my favorite ways David referred to God is the little word "my." In Psalm 62:6–7, he said, "He alone is my rock and my salvation; he is my fortress . . . my mighty rock, my refuge." Aren't you glad his God can be yours and mine as well? No wonder, in spite of his human frailties, David was a man after God's own heart!

Psalm 54 concludes with David's vowing to sacrifice a freewill offering to the Lord. According to Deuteronomy 16:10, the freewill offering was to be "in proportion to the blessings the LORD your God has given you." Do you remember that well-known hymn, "Count Your Many Blessings"? Counting our blessings when we are betrayed, wrongly accused, and hunted by ruthless men is a different kind of worship than counting our blessings in the safety of Sunday worship. David responded to his helpless estate by giving a freewill offering to God in proportion to His blessings.

He left us a wonderful example.

# DAY 32
## 1 Samuel 24:1–22

---

"Look at the corner of your robe in my hand, for I cut it off, but I didn't kill you.
Look and recognize that there is no evil or rebellion in me. I haven't sinned
against you even though you are hunting me down to take my life" (v. 11).

---

We have already considered God's unwavering devotion to prepare His
children for His service. Now we will see some of the fruit of God's preparation
in David. In those caves, God chiseled character into the heart of His king.

Once again the mad Saul came after David, this time with three thousand
men. David and his men were hiding in a cave when the king came in to relieve
himself. David could easily have killed Saul, but instead he crept up and cut off
a piece of Saul's robe.

Amazing! David resisted revenge after all Saul had done to him! After all
the lives he had taken! David wasn't even sure Saul had the sense to spare the
life of his own son Jonathan or daughter Michal. In this strange circumstance
David had an odd reaction to his own action. He became conscience-stricken for
cutting the king's robe. He said to his men,

> "*The* LORD *forbid that I should do such a thing to my master,
> the* LORD's *anointed, or lift my hand against him; for he is the
> anointed of the* LORD" *(1 Sam. 24:6).*

In spite of all that Saul had done, David continued to have a tenacious belief
that he must respect God's anointed king. After Saul left the cave, David called
to him from a safe distance. He offered the fact that he had just spared Saul's life
as proof of his loyalty.

David's men must have thought he was crazy! David apparently chose to risk
man's disapproval over God's, regardless of the consequences. David's change of
heart offers four evidences that he was greatly influenced by the Holy Spirit:

1. *David's conscience was immediately stricken.* The Holy Spirit convicts of sin
(John 16:8). When the Holy Spirit dwells in a person, He uses the individual's
conscience as the striking ground for conviction. David evidenced the work of
God by saying, "The LORD forbid that I should do such a thing" (v. 6). He was
suddenly aware that his actions were displeasing to God. You and I may want to
minimize David's sin against Saul because Saul's offense against David seems so
much worse. We tend to view sin in relative terms. David's standard for measuring sin was not the wickedness of Saul, but the holiness of God.

2. *David met conviction with a change in behavior.* The Holy Spirit always
does His job, but we don't always do ours! If we do not fully yield to the Spirit's

influence, we will often fight conviction. One sure measurement of our proximity to God, whether near or far, is the length of time between conviction and repentance. David responded to his Spirit-stricken conscience with an immediate change of behavior. His immediate response to conviction proves David was intimate with God at this point in his life. Remember, the same Holy Spirit who anointed David with His presence also dwells in New Testament believers. As we draw nearer to God, our sensitivity to conviction and our discernment of wrongdoing will increase. If we are filled by His Spirit, conviction will be met with a change in behavior.

3. *David exercised great restraint.* He must have been influenced by the Spirit. He had the perfect chance to get revenge and he didn't take it! No one would have blamed him. He easily could have argued that his actions were in self-defense. Such a level of restraint could only have been supernatural! Second Thessalonians 2:6–7 refers to the restraining work of the Holy Spirit. The Holy Spirit works restraint in us when we are tempted toward revenge; if we are fully yielded to the Spirit, we will obey. A moment's revenge is not worth the cost of alienation from God, not even the revenge we've been waiting for and feel so justified to seize!

4. *David respected God more than he desired revenge.* Consider again David's words in verse 6: "The LORD forbid that I should do such a thing to my master, the LORD's anointed." David withdrew from taking the life of Saul out of respect for God, not Saul. David's incomparable respect for God kept him from making a tragic and costly mistake.

If you are willing to honor a person out of respect for God, you can be assured that God will honor you. Several times I've been required to honor a person out of honor to God. A very strange thing has happened almost every time I've been obedient to God in this area: He has restored my respect for the person I had come to resent. God is always faithful. The results of your obedience may differ, but the blessing of your obedience is guaranteed. No doubt the time will come when you will face a window of opportunity to get back at a person who has wronged you. The only way to get through a window God doesn't open is to break it yourself. This is one window sure to leave you injured. Don't do it. Let the Holy Spirit perform His restraining work. Someday you'll be glad you did.

# DAY 33
## 1 Samuel 25:2–35

—∞∞—

"My lord should pay no attention to this worthless man Nabal, for he lives up
to his name: His name is Nabal, and stupidity is all he knows" (v. 25).

—∞∞—

David and his men always made it a practice to protect their fellow Israelites.
They had protected the animals and herdsmen of a wealthy landowner named
Nabal, a man who was surly and mean in his dealings. So in keeping with the
customs of the day, David sent his men at harvesttime to request provisions from
Nabal. To David's surprise the surly rancher insulted David, treated his men
discourteously, and sent them away empty-handed (vv. 10–11).

David obviously did not have the same patience with Nabal that he had with
Saul. David had many good character traits, but a high tolerance for insult was
not among them. He said, "Put on your swords" (v. 13), and four hundred of his
men prepared to "visit" Nabal. All he really needed, of course, was a sling and a
few smooth stones!

Enter Abigail, the intelligent and beautiful wife of Nabal. If Abigail had
been like her husband, the result would have been a tragedy. Fortunately, the servants knew their mistress had more sense than Nabal. A servant warned Abigail
about what Nabal had done. He said David's men had protected them in the
fields. He said, "Night and day they were a wall around us" (v. 16). The servant
asked Abigail, "See what you can do, because disaster is hanging over our master
and his whole household. He is such a wicked man that no one can talk to him"
(vv. 16–17).

Abigail prepared gifts for David and his men. Then she hurried to intercept
them before they brought retribution to her husband and household. When she
reached David, she bowed before him and asked him to forgive her wicked husband. Abigail continued by praising David and making her case for him to spare
her household. She asked him to accept her gift of thanks.

I think we see another glimpse of David's heart in his reply. He quickly
agreed to spare Nabal, praising God both for Abigail's good judgment and for
keeping him from bloodshed. While David was certainly capable of great violence, he did not harbor grudges or hang on to resentments.

# DAY 34
## 1 Samuel 25:36–44

———∞∞∞———

When David's servants came to Abigail at Carmel, they said to her,
"David sent us to bring you to him as a wife" (v. 40).

———∞∞∞———

David went a bit overboard in the marriage department. We could be understanding about his broken vows to Michal; after all, Saul had given her away to "Paltiel son of Laish" (v. 44). But then, who is Ahinoam? I thought we had been with David every minute! When did he come up with her?

Sometimes we can thank God not only for what He wrote in His Word but also for what He did not. We'll just try to celebrate Abigail's good fortune, although I'm not sure how happy you can be sharing your man with another wife!

Some things we may never understand, but one principle is definitely clear: polygamy has never been God's will (Gen. 2:24). I found myself wondering, "Did God tolerate David's actions? Did God make exceptions to His first commands regarding marriage in the lives of his kings?" Our dilemma calls for a brief consideration of other Scriptures.

Deuteronomy 17 contains regulations for the time when the Israelites would have kings. Kings were told not to multiply wives or else their heart "will be led astray" (v. 17). David knew that God intended him to be the next king of Israel, yet already he had disobeyed one of God's specific commands for kings: he had taken more than one wife.

As always, God's commands are for our sake, not for His. As we saw, kings had been commanded by God not to take "many wives." The word "many" was the Hebrew word *rabah*. It means to "increase, multiply, have more."[13] The Word of God is clear from the second chapter of Genesis that two wives is "more" than God planned. God's reason was clear: those who took many wives would have hearts led astray.

We can take a moment to inhale deeply and smell trouble brewing. God's Word will once again prove authentic. Eventually David's heart *will* be led astray. God presented the consequence as a promise, not a possibility. We will unfortunately be witnesses when David's straying heart ruptures like a volcano.

Until then, we'll praise the God of David who still has a fresh supply of mercy every morning, prompting hearts to ache when they are prone to stray. May we take God at His Word and not have to learn everything the hard way!

# DAY 35
## 1 Samuel 27:1–12

———∞∞———

*So Achish trusted David, thinking, "Since he has made himself detestable to his people Israel, he will be my servant forever" (v. 12).*

———∞∞———

We must now take a difficult look at the life of David; a situation we probably can't relate to as well. Chapter 26 of 1 Samuel tells one of the classic David stories. Again Saul came after David. While Saul and his men were asleep, David and Abishai crept into the camp and took Saul's spear and water jug.

The next morning David called to Saul and his general, Abner. David taunted Abner for failing to protect Saul and offered the purloined articles as evidence that David meant Saul no harm. Once again, the homicidal king recognized his error, apologized, and returned home. The event seems another clear victory for David, but his next action recorded in chapter 27 seems out of character. David thought to himself, "One of these days I will be destroyed by the hand of Saul" (v. 1). So he fled with his men to the land of the Philistines. They went to king Achish of Gath as political refugees.

In retrospect, Achish does not seem to have been the sharpest knife in the drawer, but we could see how he chose to receive David. Achish saw Saul as his greatest threat. In politics "the enemy of my enemy is my friend." So Achish gave David the town of Ziklag on the frontier with Judah. Finally David had a reasonably safe place. They lived in Ziklag a year and four months.

I am frankly somewhat at a loss to understand what happened next. David and his men became raiders attacking neighboring cities, and "he did not leave a man or woman alive" (v. 9).

My mind filled with questions when I first saw 1 Samuel 27. What has happened to David? Why was he taking up an alliance with the Philistines? Why was he on a rampage with every surrounding village? I believe two verses hold the keys for understanding David's uncharacteristic actions. In verse 1, he thought, "One of these days I will be destroyed by the hand of Saul." Then in verse 11 we read that David "did not leave a man or woman alive to be brought to Gath, for he thought, 'They might inform on us and say, "This is what David did."'"

Life on the run obviously had taken its toll. Fear, frustration, and exhaustion apparently caused David to feel hopeless. Possibly he was driven to the point of paranoia. The result was a literal case of overkill. You can hear the downward spiral of his mood in his thought: "One of these days I will be destroyed by the hand of Saul." David became convinced he would be destroyed.

David believed his only option was to escape to the land of the Philistines. He knew Saul was afraid of them. David surmised he would at least be safe for a while. He felt like giving up, but he couldn't because everyone had become an enemy in his eyes! Therefore, he fought everyone with a vengeance—everyone except his two clear enemies: Saul and the Philistines. We have no way of knowing how God responded to his alliance with the Philistines. To be sure, God had an opinion, but He kept the matter between Himself and David. Note, however, that God did not command David to kill all the inhabitants of the villages.

Scholars believe David penned Psalm 10 at this time in his life. Perhaps we gain some insight from it into the feelings he was experiencing. Obviously David felt that God was far away and hidden. In the first verse, he asked God: "Why do you hide yourself in times of trouble?" In verse 2, David characterized his enemy as arrogant and himself as weak: "In his arrogance the wicked man hunts down the weak." At this point David serves as an example of what happens when we focus more on our battles than on God. Our enemy appears bigger, we appear weaker, and our God appears smaller. Beware! Long-term battle can cause vision impairment if eyes focus anywhere but up!

Notice what David apparently believed Saul was saying to himself in verses 6 and 11 of Psalm 10: "Nothing will shake me; I'll always be happy and never have trouble" and "God has forgotten; he covers his face and never sees." In verse 13, David says the wicked man reviles God because he tells himself that he will not have to answer for his actions. But even in his despair, David never lost sight of God. In verse 14, he wrote his conviction that God remained the "helper of the fatherless." In verse 17, David cited three actions God takes in behalf of His children: "You hear, O Lord, the desire of the afflicted; you encourage them, and you listen to their cry."

We may have a difficult time relating to David's exact dilemma and his outrageous responses recorded in 1 Samuel 27, but we can certainly relate to his feelings. So the next time you battle an enemy so hard and so long that you feel like giving up or doing something rash, remember David. When you feel powerless over your real enemy and lash out at someone who is innocent, remember Psalm 10.

God has not forgotten. He has seen your battles. He has gathered your tears and blotted your brow. He knows those who have treated you unfairly. He knows when you're almost ready to give up or give in. Keep telling Him. Stay in His Word. Keep claiming His promises.

# DAY 36
## 1 Samuel 28:1–7

———∽∞∽———

*He inquired of the LORD, but the LORD did not answer him (v. 6).*

———∽∞∽———

In verse 3, we learn one of those tidbits of information that we suspect will come back to haunt somebody. Saul had expelled the mediums and spiritists from the land. When Saul learned that the Philistines were preparing for war, he was terrified. He sought God to learn the outcome of the battle. When the Lord did not answer Saul, he sent his attendants to find a medium.

God's occasional refusal to respond to the pleas of someone in His Word often strikes a humanitarian chord in us. At first we may wonder why God would not answer Saul since Saul first inquired of Him before he sought a spiritist? Does God seem a little unfair to you at first in His lack of response to Saul?

God never responds haphazardly, nor does He withhold an answer without regard. Why is God silent at times? Isaiah 59:1–3 gives us one very valid explanation for God's occasional silence, and one which certainly applied to Saul at this time. Isaiah wrote:

> *Your sins have hidden his face from you, so that he will not hear*
> *(Isa. 59:2).*

Remember, Saul continued in disobedience to God. He relentlessly sought the life of an innocent man and even attempted to spear his own son! He had the priests of the Lord slaughtered and gave approval to an entire town being wiped out. We've seen some regrets, but we've never seen him truly turn from wickedness to righteousness. Notice that Isaiah 59:2 does not say God can't hear but that He won't.

I can vividly remember times in my life when God seemed silent, and I realized He was waiting on me to confront and confess certain sins in my life. His silence suggested, "I will not go on to another matter in your life, my child, until we deal with this one."

One prayer God will surely hear even when we've been rebellious and sought our own way is the prayer of sincere repentance. The prayer for deliverance from sin must precede the prayer for deliverance from our enemies.

# DAY 37
## 1 Samuel 28:8–19

—∞∞∞—

Saul disguised himself by putting on different clothes and set out
with two of his men. They came to the woman at night, and Saul said,
"Consult a spirit for me. Bring up for me the one I tell you" (v. 8).

—∞∞∞—

When God refused to answer Saul, he asked where to find a spiritist. Isn't it interesting that Saul set out on a journey to seek that which he himself had expelled from Israel? Deuteronomy 18:10–12 specifically forbids spiritists and mediums. Saul knew God's Word. Early in his reign as king he did what God's Word commanded. But after his regard for God shrank and his flesh abounded, he sought the very thing he once had considered wrong.

We've done the same from time to time. We've felt convicted to get rid of something or to cease a certain practice; then, when our regard for God began to shrink and our regard for our own flesh began to grow, we were out the door hunting it down. Taking a few steps backward in our Christian walk is not very difficult. We used to call it "backsliding." I wish the only direction for a Christian was onward to maturity, but unfortunately some of our footprints in the sand look a lot like figure eights!

Can you think of any personal examples?

Have you ever given up R-rated movies yet found yourself at a later date with a ticket and popcorn in your hand, heading into a movie you formerly wouldn't have watched? Have you ever given up gossip magazines because God convicted you toward purity of mind, but you found yourself throwing one into your grocery basket again? At one time were you very sensitive about saying hurtful things to or about others, but now it doesn't bother you much anymore?

I find myself hoping even Saul's life had an ultimately happy ending. When Samuel said, "Tomorrow you and your sons will be with me" (v. 19), we don't know what he meant. He may simply have meant, "You are about to die." Or he may have meant Saul and his sons would join Samuel among the redeemed. I'd like to think that Saul and his sons took the opportunity to settle business with God, knowing of their imminent demise. Sometimes the most merciful thing God can do in a rebellious person's life is let him know he is going to die so he can beg for mercy.

# DAY 38
## 1 Samuel 30:1–31

———∞∞∞———

David was in a difficult position because the troops talked about stoning him,
for they were all very bitter over the loss of their sons and daughters.
But David found strength in the LORD his God (v. 6).

———∞∞∞———

David and his men returned to Ziklag after a three-day journey. When they arrived, they found that Ziklag had been raided, burned, and their wives and children had been taken captive. When the men saw what had happened to their families, "David and his men wept aloud until they had no strength left to weep" (v. 4). In their grief David's men even began to discuss stoning him.

David was greatly distressed over the blame his men cast on him, but the circumstance yielded one of the great glimpses of a man after God's own heart. David was distressed . . . but he found strength in the Lord his God. I'd like to draw a few points from this passage that paints some perfect portraits of human nature.

1. *Hurting people often find someone to blame.* When we've suffered a loss, just like David's men we often look for stones to throw—and for someone at whom to throw them. Notice that David also suffered the loss of his family. He did not know if he would ever see them again. He had taken many lives. I'm sure he assumed his enemy would not blink an eye at taking the lives of his wives and children. David cried the same tears the other men cried, but because they needed someone to blame, they focused their anger on him.

2. *Nothing hurts more than our children being in jeopardy.* Many things hurt and cause us to search for stones to throw, but, as in verse 6, nothing has the potential to cause bitterness in spirit like matters involving our children. They are our Achilles' heel, aren't they? Someone can treat our child unfairly, and we're ready to pounce. We almost can't help living by the philosophy, "If you want to make an enemy out of me, just mess with my kid." Can you imagine how many poor decisions have been made when parents have hastily thrown the stones of retaliation on behalf of their children? David's men ultimately arrived at a place of reason. They chose not to act at the peak of their emotions—a wise response for all of us.

3. *Nothing helps more than finding strength in our God.* Sometimes no one offers us encouragement or helps us find strength. We'd better be prepared to strengthen ourselves in the Lord. Others can help and be encouraging, but this kind of strength comes only from the Lord. After David and his men had poured out their initial cup of grief, they turned to find a solution. David inquired of the Lord if he should pursue the raiding party. God answered: "Pursue them. . . . You will certainly overtake them and succeed in the rescue" (v. 8).

David set out with his six hundred men. At Besor Ravine, two hundred of David's men were too exhausted to continue, so David left them and went on with the remaining four hundred. They overtook the Amalekites, who were celebrating prematurely. The ensuing battle lasted from dusk until the following evening, but David and his men recaptured all they had lost and much more plunder. Only four hundred young Amalekites escaped from David.

When the battle-weary group returned to the two hundred who had stayed behind, some of the men did not want to share the plunder, but David issued a decree that the "share of the man who stayed with the supplies is to be the same as that of him who went down to the battle. All will share alike" (v. 24).

We can make important life applications from the experiences of David and his men:

1. *Assured victory does not mean easy wins.* God told David in advance that he would "certainly overtake them and succeed in the rescue," yet we see references to exhaustion (v. 10), hard work (v. 17), a nonstop, twenty-four-hour battle (v. 17), and four hundred escapees (v. 17). God was absolutely true to His Word. The end was exactly as God had promised, but what we often don't count on is the means. Many times God gives us a victory that requires blood, sweat, and tears. Why? Because He is practical. When He can bring about a victory and strengthen and mature us all at the same time, He's likely to do it!

God revels in overcoming and undergirding all at once. You see, God's idea of victory has virtually nothing to do with plunder; it has to do with people. *What* comes out of a battle isn't nearly as important as *who* comes out of a battle. That day God not only worked a victory *through* David, He worked one *in* David. The man after God's own heart came out of battle with grace and mercy and a little better grasp of God's sovereignty.

2. *We don't have to "win big" to win.* No wholesale slaughter resulted. Quite the contrary. Four hundred men got away, yet God called it a victory! David could have been furious with himself because he let some guys get away. Instead, he chose to focus on the ones he brought home: their families, his family. If your family has come out of a serious battle intact, fall on your face and praise your faithful God. The victory is yours.

# DAY 39
## 1 Samuel 31:1–13

---

When the residents of Jabesh-gilead heard what the Philistines
had done to Saul, all their brave men set out, journeyed all night, and retrieved the
body of Saul and the bodies of his sons from the wall of Beth-shan (vv. 11–12).

---

Saul, critically wounded in battle, fell on his own sword rather than be taken alive by the enemy. He knew the Philistines made sport of their prize captives. But the Philistines did not need Saul alive to mock him. They cut off his head, surely in memory of their slain giant, and impaled his body on the wall of Beth Shan.

Sometimes the worst of events bring out the best in people. When the men of Jabesh Gilead heard of the death of Saul and his sons, they traveled all night and risked their lives to retrieve the bodies. They burned the bodies and buried the bones under a tamarisk tree at Jabesh (vv. 11–13).

The men of Jabesh Gilead performed a brave and loving act. Certainly the bodies were well-guarded. The men could have ended up impaled right beside the bodies they came to rescue. Why would they take such a chance?

Remember Saul's first act as king, recorded in 1 Samuel 11:1–11, when he marshaled the Israelite troops against the Ammonites who had laid siege to Jabesh Gilead?

> *During the morning watch, they invaded the Ammonite camp*
> *and slaughtered them until the heat of day. There were survivors,*
> *but they were so scattered that no two of them were left together*
> *(1 Sam. 11:11).*

I am encouraged to think that across forty-two years, the people of the village never forgot their debt of gratitude to a young king. The men of Jabesh Gilead paid a tribute to a king who started well. May we accept and imitate their example. May our memories of kindness be long and of offenses be short. It's not too late to say thanks.

Owe somebody a favor? How much better to repay it before you stand with them under the shade of a tamarisk tree. In the midst of a tragic scene, a group of heroes emerged, all because they had good memories. No doubt God's heroes are those who never forget His faithfulness. May we be counted among them.

# DAY 40
## 2 Samuel 1:1–27

∞∞

"The splendor of Israel lies slain on your heights.
How the mighty have fallen!" (v. 19).

∞∞

Second Samuel begins with David and his men's return from rescuing their families from the Amalekites. A young man who happened to be an Amalekite living in Israel arrived from the battle scene on Mount Gilboa. In his hands he carried the crown and armband of Saul. In his heart he carried dreams of reward. If he had known the heart and character of the man to whom he spoke, he would have behaved differently.

The young man told David that Saul and his sons were dead. He went on to claim that he had seen the wounded Saul and finished him off personally. He offered the articles from Saul as proof. Have you ever heard the saying, "He lies when the truth would fit better"? If a literal example of this expression ever existed, this is it. The messenger didn't get the result he had imagined.

> Then David and all the men with him took hold of their clothes and tore them. They mourned and wept and fasted till evening for Saul and his son Jonathan, and for the army of the LORD and the house of Israel, because they had fallen by the sword (2 Sam. 1:11–12).

The passage does not tell us how quickly David dealt with the messenger, but I wonder: If David grieved until evening before he responded, did the man begin to have misgivings? Few people living in the Middle East would have failed to hear rumors of Saul's pursuit of David. Many must have followed them as closely as a faithful watcher of a modern soap opera. People love conflict. We love reading about it and hearing about it. When the men were returning home after David had killed the Philistine giant, the women met King Saul singing: "Saul has slain his thousands, and David his tens of thousands" (1 Sam. 18:7). Those women started a jealousy that cost both men dearly.

Many days later, as the deceitful Amalekite lay slain at David's feet, that little song had caused another casualty. The opportunist was hoping he'd find favor with David by claiming he had taken the life of Saul. He was dead wrong. David poured out his love for Jonathan—and for Saul, in spite of all the years the mad king's jealousy had cost him. He wrote the lament that appears in 2 Samuel 1:19–27. Look at some of David's words of grief:

*O mountains of Gilboa, may you have neither dew nor rain, nor fields that yield offerings of grain. For there the shield of the mighty was defiled (v. 21).*

*Saul and Jonathan—in life they were loved and gracious, and in death they were not parted. They were swifter than eagles, they were stronger than lions (v. 23).*

*I grieve for you, Jonathan my brother; you were very dear to me. Your love for me was wonderful, more wonderful than that of women (v. 26).*

In David's song of lament, his words suddenly turned from the refrain of the assembly to the grief of a single heart: "I grieve for you, Jonathan my brother." The Hebrew word for brother in this verse was *ach*. It meant "a brother, near relative. *Ach* is any person or thing which is similar to another. It is generally a term of affection."[14] One was a shepherd; the other a prince. Yet they were "one in spirit" (1 Sam. 18:1). They were brothers.

David called his friend's love "wonderful" (v. 26). David distinguished the sacrificial nature of this friendship from anything else anyone had ever demonstrated to him. So determined was Jonathan that David be king, a position Jonathan stood to inherit, that he committed his entire life to that end. David found it astonishing.

I know what it's like to lose a best friend. My buddy and I were absolutely inseparable. We dressed alike, cut our hair alike, shared a locker, and had endless sleepovers. I had lots of boyfriends as a teenager, but I only had one best friend. Her name was Dodie. One day she dropped by the house to pick me up for a bite to eat. My parents would not let me go because we were preparing to leave town. Dodie never came back. Within half an hour, I heard the blood-curdling siren of an ambulance. I can hardly talk about it even today. I still visit her grave. I still ache for our friendship.

David grieved the tragic loss of life that took place on Mount Gilboa. His thoughts must have been consumed with how differently he wished it had all happened. Not coincidentally, the next chapter begins with the words, "In the course of time, David . . ." We share a moment of his grief when we see these words. Yes, some things just take "the course of time."

# DAY 41
## 2 Samuel 2:1–2

Some time later, David inquired of the LORD:
"Should I go to one of the towns of Judah?" (v. 1).

Did you notice that David kept asking until he had a specific answer from God? He did not want general directions. He wanted God's exact will for his life. David wasn't interested in simply getting to the throne. He wanted to get to the throne God's way.

At times I have asked God's direction, then assumed my first hunch was His will for my life. I'm learning to be more patient, allowing God to be more specific if He wishes.

No matter how long we may wait for direction, we are wise to ask before we advance. God is not going to speak to us from the clouds, nor can we toss the Urim and Thummim, but we have something David didn't have: God's written and completed Word. God will speak specifically to us through Scripture if we learn how to listen. God has taught me a method that never fails. It may take time but it always works. The method I use consists of four general steps:

1. *I acknowledge my specific need for direction.* Example: "Lord, I have been asked to serve on the pastor's council. I need to know whether this is Your will for my life at this time." I almost always write my question in a journal so that I can keep a record of God's activity in the matter.

2. *I continue to pray daily and study His Word.*

3. *I ask Him to help me recognize His answer.* He usually helps me recognize His answer by bringing His Word and the Holy Spirit He has placed within me into agreement over the matter. In other words, I resist reading into my situation everything God's Word says. I specifically ask Him to confirm with His Word and His Spirit what He desires to apply to my life. One or two weeks later I might be studying a particular passage of Scripture and His Holy Spirit will draw my attention to it and remind me of my question. The Holy Spirit almost seems to say, "Look, Beth, that's it!"

4. *I ask for a confirmation if I have any doubt.*

What if the Holy Spirit still hasn't given me an answer when the deadline comes? Then I usually assume the answer is no.

# DAY 42
## 2 Samuel 2:3–7

—∞∞∞—

*David brought the men who were with him, each one with his household,*
*and they settled in the towns near Hebron (v. 3).*

—∞∞∞—

At least fifteen years had passed since Samuel went to the home of Jesse and anointed the young shepherd. As chapter 2 begins to unfold, David is thirty years old.

Let's see what has transpired "in the course of time" (v. 1).

God instructed David to go to Hebron, a region rich in biblical history. It has been occupied almost continually since around 3300 BC. Hebron is located in the hill country of Judah about nineteen miles to the south of the city of Jerusalem. Some very important people and events are connected with Hebron.

Abraham settled in Hebron and built an altar to God (Gen. 13:18). There God spoke to Abram through three visitors and told him Sarah would bear a child (Gen. 18:1–15). Joshua gave Hebron to Caleb as his inheritance (Josh. 14:13). God chose to write some rich history on the map of Hebron, not the least of it in the life of David. Second Samuel 2:3 says, "David . . . with his family . . . settled in Hebron."

Settled. Nice word, isn't it? One that extends the invitation to rest awhile and put down a few roots.

David had been on the move constantly for years. God had probably been his only comfort. After settling in Hebron, "the men of Judah came . . . and there they anointed David king over the house of Judah" (v. 4).

What a significant moment in the life of our subject! At last, his private anointing from years earlier became public! He was anointed king over "the house of Judah," his first step to reigning as king over the entire nation of Israel.

From the moment David became king over the house of Judah, he began his official works of diplomacy. He sent word to the men of Jabesh Gilead expressing his appreciation for their "kindness to Saul" (v. 5) and pledged his favor to them.

But not all could be accomplished by words of diplomacy and pledges of protection. The entire nation of Israel would ultimately have to be under his authority. Much like Joshua in an earlier day, the land was to be David's, but he would have to take some of it by force.

# DAY 43
## 2 Samuel 3:1–39

---

The war between the house of Saul and the house of David was long and drawn out, with David growing stronger and the house of Saul becoming weaker (v. 1).

---

The "house of Judah" anointed David as their king, but the other tribes continued to recognize the family line of Saul as king. Abner, Saul's general, installed Saul's son Ish-Bosheth as king. We are told that he reigned for only two years. Although this kingdom was given to David by God, David would have to take it from the old aristocracy.

The pacifist in me would like to skip the bloody details of the civil war in Israel; the Bible teacher in me knows we shouldn't. Old regimes rarely crumble without bloodshed. Just like America's history, Israel's history was often written in blood.

The first of many battles in the civil war occurred at Gibeon. The results of the battle were to affect David for years to come. Abner commanded the army of Israel. Joab, along with his brothers Abishai and Asahel, commanded the men of Judah. Joab's troops routed those of Abner. Asahel, Joab's baby brother, was fleet of foot. He chased the battle-hardened Abner. Abner tried to talk Asahel out of the pursuit, but without success. Finally, Abner struck Asahel with the butt of his spear, merely trying to stop the youth, but the blow killed Asahel and launched a bitter blood-feud. The civil war in Israel lasted a long time.

We now see a fact sadly reflective of human life. Through their behavior, parents teach children to repeat the family sins. Jealousy proved the undoing of Saul. Now his son became jealous and suspicious of someone who had been on his side. Ish-Bosheth accused his general, Abner, of sleeping with one of Saul's concubines. The Bible offers no evidence to support Ish-Bosheth's accusation of Abner, but we do know the end result. The soldier completely transferred his loyalties to David. Abner sent a message to David saying, "Make an agreement with me, and I will help you bring all Israel over to you" (v. 12).

David greeted the offer with a demand: the return of his first wife Michal. The demand resulted in a heart-wrenching side story. Michal had been married for many years to Paltiel. When the soldiers took her away, Paltiel followed behind her weeping until Abner finally forced him to turn back (vv. 15–16).

God does not tell us David's motive for wanting Michal to return to him. He certainly did not lack for female companionship. Maybe he was indignant because he won her fair and square. Maybe he wanted everything back that was rightfully his. Maybe he used her to demonstrate his political and military power. Maybe he loved her. Clearly Paltiel loved her. Whatever David's motives might have been, these events mark a crucial change in Israel—and in David's career.

Since Ish-Bosheth gave the order to return Michal to David, he must have been a party to the agreement. I wonder how different the future might have been for the remaining son of Saul if bitterness had not intervened, but remember Joab and his little brother Asahel?

Abner conferred with the leaders of Israel and arranged for a peaceful transfer of power to King David. Abner even met with the leaders of Benjamin, Saul's tribe. Then he traveled to Hebron to meet with David. Shortly after Abner left David's presence, Joab returned from a raid. When he learned Abner had been there, he secretly sent for Abner and murdered the commander of the armies of Saul.

Though we may not feel a deep bond with Abner as we did with the noble Jonathan, his murder still saddens me. In all that we read about him, Abner acted with honor. He deserved better. Joab, on the other hand, was a vengeful and murderous man.

We would wonder why David put up with Joab's evil but for two facts. First, we learn in 1 Chronicles 2:13–17 that Joab was David's nephew. Second, David doubtless felt that he owed Joab loyalty because they had weathered the fugitive years together. Sometimes justice is more important than loyalty or lineage. In my opinion, David should have opted for justice.

David ordered and led in public mourning for Abner. His grief demonstrated that he had not participated in the murder, so the leaders of Israel proceeded to accept him as king. But the repercussions of the murder continued.

Since Abner was dead, two of Ish-Bosheth's junior officers took it upon themselves to kill Saul's heir. They would have done well to consider what David did to a certain Amalekite. They brought the severed head of Ish-Bosheth to David.

This time we don't have to wonder about the time frame of David's reply. He responded that since he killed the Amalekite, "Should I not now demand his blood from your hand and rid the earth of you!" (2 Sam. 4:11).

So at last the stage was set. The anointing from the now long-dead Samuel was about to reach fruition. David was about to become the king of all Israel.

# DAY 44
## 2 Samuel 5:1–5

—⊸∞⊶—

"Even while Saul was king over us, you were the one who led us
out to battle and brought us back. The LORD also said to you,
'You will shepherd My people Israel and be ruler over Israel'" (v. 2).

—⊸∞⊶—

What an exciting day! We are about to see David experience the fulfillment
of God's promise! As we witness a tremendous pivot in his life, we can assume
his introspective mind was swirling with many things, filling him with all sorts
of emotions.

In 2 Samuel 5, all the tribes of Israel came to David and acclaimed him as
king. The chapter gives some key numbers for the life of David: He was thirty
years old when he became king. He ruled for forty years. He reigned seven and
one-half years over Judah from Hebron. He ruled all Israel from Jerusalem for
thirty-three years. He waited a long time for the fulfillment of 1 Samuel 16.

God didn't choose the person Samuel expected. He chose a shepherd boy.
God called David not in spite of the fact that he was a common shepherd but
because he was a shepherd!

Strangely, David had come so far, yet he was back where he started. The
hand that wrapped around his weapon now as he waited for God's signal to overcome the Philistines looked far different from the hand that had searched for a
smooth stone many years before. The first time he ever used his hands in battle
was against the Philistines. Now he stood against them once more as king of
Israel. Perhaps God inspired David to write the words of Psalm 144:1–2 on this
very day:

> *Praise be to the Lord my Rock who trains my hands for war,*
> *my fingers for battle. He is my loving God and my fortress, my*
> *stronghold and my deliverer, my shield, in whom I take refuge,*
> *who subdues peoples under me.*

We began our study with a shepherd boy. Now we see a shepherd king. He
was still guarding the sheep with "integrity of heart" and "skillful hands" (Ps.
78:72)—hands prepared for war yet still for the same purpose: the protection of
sheep. Same shepherd, different sheep. God's sheep.

# DAY 45
## 2 Samuel 5:6–12

Then David knew that the LORD had established him as king over Israel
and had exalted his kingdom for the sake of His people Israel (v. 12).

Many things must have confused David in his previous fifteen years. So
many things he did not know:

- Why had God chosen him?
- Why did Saul turn on him?
- Why did Jonathan have to die?
- When would God's promise of the kingdom ever be fulfilled?

David did not know how he would ever live to be king. But when God
handed over the most fortified city in all Israel to David and placed favor in the
heart of the king of Tyre toward him, David knew the Lord had established him!

You may be going through a confusing time. You may not know how God is
going to use a situation in your life or why certain things have happened to you.
But you can be encouraged and strengthened by recalling what you know about
God in the midst of uncertainties. In confusing times, recounting what we do
know refreshes us.

David still had many unanswered questions. He would never know for sure
why God allowed certain things to happen, but he knew God had done exactly
what He promised. You may never know why or how, but you can always know
who is faithful. David knew without a doubt that God had given him the victory and subdued the people under his leadership. He still didn't know why. He
simply knew Who.

When David captured the fortress of Zion, the City of David, he must have
thought, "You have been to me what these walls have been to this city. No other
excuse exists for my safety or my success." He knew God was all those things
we looked at yesterday in Psalm 144: "my rock, my loving God, my fortress, my
stronghold, my deliverer, my shield, my refuge." The names David called his God
fell from the lips of experience, from things he knew. Sometimes we stand to
learn the most about God from the situations we understand the least.

# DAY 46
## 2 Samuel 6:1–11

———◦◦◦◦———

David feared the LORD that day and said,
"How can the ark of the LORD ever come to me?" (v. 9).

———◦◦◦◦———

David set out with thirty thousand men to bring the ark of God to Jerusalem. Unfortunately, we learn something in verse 3 that can only spell disaster: "They set the ark of God on a new cart" (v. 3).

According to the regulations for kings of Israel, they were to personally hand-copy the Law of God so that they would know every line. How then could David have set out to transport the ark in a wagon? God was extremely specific about every detail of the construction and treatment of the ark. According to Exodus 25:10–16 plus Numbers 4:5 and 4:15, the ark was to be transported only by the priests using poles through the rings on the ark. The poles were to be carried on their shoulders. God masterfully designed the transportation of His glory to literally rest on the shoulders of His revering priests, not on the backs of beasts.

David's actions not only disregarded the Lord's instructions, they included a greater insult. Do you remember when the Philistines captured the ark? After they had suffered seven months of devastation, the Philistines loaded the ark on a cart pulled by two cows. Now David imitated the actions of the Philistines rather than obey the commands of God.

Sure enough, while "David and the whole house of Israel were celebrating with all their might before the LORD" (v. 5), at the threshing floor of Nacon, Uzzah reached out to stabilize the ark, and God struck him dead (vv. 6–7).

Imagine becoming emotionally geared for a great celebration only to greet disaster instead. Uzzah's death would have been shocking under the most somber of circumstances, but can you imagine the shock in the midst of such celebration? David must have felt as if he jumped off an emotional cliff.

Surely all of us have experienced an unexpected, uninvited emotional dive. I have a friend who was left standing at the altar on her wedding day. I have another friend who was told he was being considered for a promotion, but when his boss called him into his office, he was laid off instead. Still others have joyfully expected a baby and miscarried. Devastation is always heartbreaking. Devastation that should have been celebration is almost more than we can take.

In times like these, we find out whether we have based our faith on who God is or on what He does. Because His ways are higher than our ways, we cannot always comprehend what God is doing or why He makes certain decisions. But when we sift His apparent activity through the standard of who He is, the fog begins to clear.

God is not telling us He is harsh in 2 Samuel 6. He's telling us He is holy. The words represent a big difference, although sometimes our limited understanding leads us to confuse them.

We have difficulty understanding how sacred the ark of the covenant was because we have the advantage of living after the incarnation of Christ. Think with me about the meaning of the ark. The awesomeness, the holiness, the majesty of God dwelled right there, between the cherubim on that sacred ark! Until God was incarnate among men many centuries later in the person of Jesus Christ, the ark was the sacred center of God's glory and presence. To treat the ark inappropriately was to treat God inappropriately, not just because of what it was but because of who God is. Based on who God is, I believe we can draw some conclusions about what He was doing when He killed Uzzah.

1. *God was setting ground rules for a new regime.* He was ushering in a new kingdom with a new king He had chosen to represent His heart. God had dealt with the disrespect of man through many judges as well as the reign of a selfish king. With a new day dawning, God was demanding a new reverence.

2. *God wanted His children to be different from the world.* The Philistines might transport the ark on an oxcart, but God's people would not. How careful we must be not to think that God is less holy because others seem to get away with irreverence! We are sometimes tempted to measure our respect for God by the lack of respect surrounding us. The godless, however, are not our standard. God is. Through the pen of King David, God told us to "praise him according to his excellent greatness," not according to public opinion (Ps. 150:2 KJV).

3. *God wanted His kingdom to be established on His Word.* The Israelites failed to consult God's designated commands for the ark's transportation. At the time David's kingdom was established, David certainly had access to the "Books of Moses," the first five books of the Bible.

4. *God was teaching the relationship between blessing and reverence.* After the death of Uzzah, David left the ark at the home of Obed-Edom. God greatly blessed that household. In the process, God demonstrated the relationship between reverence and blessing. God desires His presence and His glory to be a blessing, but reverence for Him is the necessary channel.

# DAY 47
## 2 Samuel 6:12–23

———◆◆◆———

David was dancing with all his might before the LORD wearing a linen ephod.
He and the whole house of Israel were bringing up the ark of the LORD
with shouts and the sound of the ram's horn (vv. 14–15).

———◆◆◆———

Hard lessons learned well undoubtedly usher in a fresh respect and new freedom. As strange as this statement may seem, the more we learn about and fear God, the more freedom we have to worship Him! We'll see this principle at work in David's life as we continue the next portion of 2 Samuel 6.

David reacted to the death of Uzzah with anger and fear, yet Scripture calls him "a man after God's own heart." I think one reason why this is true was his unwillingness to turn from God, even when he felt negative emotions. David allowed his anger and fear to motivate him to seek more insight into the heart of God.

We need to follow David's example by allowing our questions and confusion to motivate us to seek God. At first consideration, the account of Uzzah and the ark is hard to swallow. God almost seems mean-spirited. But David's attitude changed once he discovered that God had blessed the household of Obed-Edom. He again went down to get the ark, but this time his methods showed a change of attitude. This time the priests carried the ark. With every six steps they offered sacrifices, and David "danced before the LORD with all his might" (v. 14).

The success of the second attempt to transport the ark demonstrates the following points:

1. *All worship is based on sacrifice.* Just as our bold approach to the throne of grace could only have followed Christ's shed blood on Calvary, David's bold approach that day in Jerusalem could only have acceptably followed the shed blood of sacrifice. David was not free to worship acceptably until sacrifice had paved the way.

2. *Worship with abandon is an intimate experience.* We see David almost oblivious to everyone around him, totally liberated in the spirit, dancing through the streets of Jerusalem "with all his might" (v. 14). Oh, I love this scene! Centuries later, a group of disciples were stunned when Mary of Bethany poured the fragrance of abandoned worship on Christ's feet (John 12:1–8). Completely abandoned worship is often misunderstood.

Sadly we see the legacy of Saul bear more bitter fruit in this chapter of rejoicing. His daughter, David's wife Michal, looked out the window and saw David dancing through the streets of Jerusalem. We can imagine that she could have been filled with either of at least two emotions: she could have been filled with pride, honored by her husband and God; instead she burned with jealousy.

"When she saw King David leaping and dancing before the LORD, she despised him in her heart" (v. 16).

David went home to "bless his household," but he was met with ridicule and condemnation (v. 20). He did not allow Michal to quench his spirit. He responded to her with the words, "It was before the LORD" (v. 21). You can almost hear him say, "How dare you! My worship was not for you; it was for the Lord!"

Her scolding must have stung his heart. You can sense his reaction from the text, yet he resolved, "I will celebrate before the LORD." He seemed to be saying, "Whether or not my family does, whether or not my friends do, whether or not this nation does, I will celebrate!"

What a slice of life we see in this episode. We've gone from anger to rejoicing, devastation to celebration. We would miss a certain blessing if we did not conclude with David's words in Psalm 30:11–12:

> *You turned my wailing into dancing;*
> *    you removed my sackcloth and clothed me with joy,*
> *that my heart may sing to you and not be silent.*
> *    O LORD my God, I will give you thanks forever.*

I'm not sure we will ever be fully released to "dance" before the Lord until we've learned to wail. You'll never know the experience of being clothed with joy until you've allowed Him to remove your sackcloth. Like David, you may be angry at God for taking someone's life you cared for deeply. Perhaps you are still hurt and confused. We have no idea whether David ever fully understood Uzzah's death. We just know he was willing to wait, to study, to hear God's Word, and to approach Him again. Then came indescribable celebration. He may not have understood more about Uzzah's death, but he understood more about God, which made his loss more tolerable.

God is not harsh; He is holy. He is not selfish; He is sovereign. He is not unfeeling; He is all-knowing. Like David, we need to come to know Him, and respect Him; and like David, we will love Him more.

# DAY 48
## 2 Samuel 7:1–16

———◦◦◦◦———

"When your time comes and you rest with your fathers, I will raise up after you your descendant, who will come from your body, and I will establish his kingdom" (v. 12).

———◦◦◦◦———

With the confetti swept from the streets, the merchants back to work, and the children back in class, after what seemed like an endless struggle, "the king was settled in his palace and the LORD had given him rest from all his enemies around him" (v. 1). In the resulting peace, we get another glimpse of David's character.

Have you ever noticed how the body rests more readily than the mind? We may seize the opportunity to put our feet up for awhile, but the mind stays in overdrive. I think David had a little difficulty getting his mind to rest. Certain thoughts occurred to David after "the LORD had given him rest."

We've all experienced a sudden bout of sober realization, times when we are horror-struck by our own audacity. This was one of those times in the life of David. Life was calm. Enemies were subdued. Perhaps he was taking a load off, perched on his throne, when suddenly his eyes were unveiled to the splendor around him. The one who found refuge in a cave was now throned in a magnificent palace. He must have looked around and thought, *What's wrong with this picture?* He responded with shock: "Here I am, living in a palace of cedar, while the ark of God remains in a tent" (v. 2).

Perhaps several virtues could be noted in David's sudden reaction to his surroundings, but let's not miss the virtue of humility so present in his life at this point. He summoned the prophet Nathan as if lightning would strike if he didn't.

God's message through Nathan to His new king was so rich. He began with a gentle rebuke: "Are you the one to build me a house to dwell in?" (v. 5). In other words, "David, did I tell you to do that?" God reminded David that He is fully capable of appointing a servant for specific tasks. If we're seeking Him through prayer and Bible study, we will not likely miss His appointments. We need to wait on Him even when we have a great plan.

When we wait on God, He gives supernatural strength and accomplishes the inconceivable! Did you notice that God gave David the initial vision for the project (the temple), but his offspring was to build it? God can entrust a vision or an idea to us that may be ours to pray about and prepare for but never to participate in directly.

As I read God's gentle rebuke to Nathan and David, I saw another wonderful principle at work. God said, "I have not dwelt in a house from the day I brought the Israelites up out of Egypt to this day. I have been moving from place to place with a tent as my dwelling" (v. 6). God seemed to be saying, "As long as my people are on the move, I'm on the move! You can't tie me down as long as my people are mobile!"

Isn't He wonderful? The "tent" to which God was referring was the Old Testament tabernacle designed by God to move with the people! That's God's way. You can't leave home without Him. The New Testament says it this way: "The Word became flesh and made his dwelling among us" (John 1:14).

The climactic point in God's message to David comes in verse 11. Allow me to paraphrase: "David, you won't build a house for Me. I'm going to build a house for you!" What overwhelming words! We want to do so many things for God, then they suddenly pale in comparison to the realization of all He wants to do for us! Romans 8:32 says,

> *"He who did not spare his own Son, but gave him up for us all—how will he not also, along with him, graciously give us all things?"*

David discovered what we all eventually discover: you can't outgive God.

God drew His message to a close by issuing what is often called the Davidic Covenant. He issued His promise in the form of a declaration (vv. 11–16). Notice that the blessings and cursings of God on David's son might be conditional (v. 14), but God's kingdom covenant was completely unconditional. The covenant rested on God's faithfulness, not man's.

Interestingly, many years later David reflected on an additional reason why God did not choose him to build the temple. In 1 Chronicles 28:3, David remembered: "God said to me, 'You are not to build a house for my Name, because you are a warrior and have shed blood.'" God chose to have His temple built during a reign characterized by peace. I am touched by the mercy of God toward his beloved David. He did not snatch the privilege from him in judgment. Rather, He allowed David's son to receive the honor.

What could be better than being appointed to do a marvelous task for God? For me, it would be for *my child* to do a marvelous task for God! I would happily forfeit participation in the great things of God for my children to inherit the opportunity instead!

# DAY 49
## 2 Samuel 7:17

———⎯∞⎯———

Nathan spoke all these words and this entire vision to David (v. 17).

———⎯∞⎯———

The prophet Nathan emerged as a new figure in Israel's history. God sovereignly raised prophets to serve as His voice to Israel. God apparently never intended for civil leaders to have absolute and unquestioned authority. They were to listen to the voice of God through His Word and through His prophets.

Samuel was God's prophet through whom He spoke to King Saul. Elijah and Elisha were God's prophets through many years during the Jewish monarchy. Nathan served as the prophet in the royal court of David. These prophets were called to issue the word and will of God, not necessarily the message leaders wanted to hear.

David did not consider himself to be above reproach or the need for advice. The statement David made to Nathan in the verses we looked at yesterday (2 Sam. 7:1–2) assumed the question, "What am I to do about the ark of God?" His sudden sense of audacity drew him to accountability.

But sometimes even a fellow believer can offer wrong advice. We are wise to make sure a fellow believer's advice agrees with God's Word.

Nathan's initial response to David was mistaken. "Whatever you have in mind, go ahead and do it, for the LORD is with you" (v. 3). God taught both the king and his prophet a gentle lesson on making assumptions.

To David, God said, "Don't assume that every bright and noble idea in a godly man's mind is of Me." Good ideas and God's ideas are often completely different. To Nathan, God said, "Don't assume that a leader I have chosen is always right." The Lord can be "with" a man while that same man can make a decision "without" God.

We will discover a primary reason why God wanted to dissuade Nathan from thinking David's actions were always right. God was preparing Nathan in advance for a time when he would have to confront and rebuke David. Thankfully, at this point, the hearts of both men were right toward God. Their motive was right even if their move was wrong.

# DAY 50
## 2 Samuel 7:18–29

---

Then King David went in, sat in the LORD's presence, and said, "Who am I, Lord GOD, and what is my house that You have brought me this far?" (v. 18).

---

We have looked at the personality of David from many different angles, with many more to go. Few Scriptures allow us to dive into the depth of his passionate soul more deeply than this prayer. While others were prone to wander, he was prone to worship.

> *"What more can David say to you? For you know your servant, O Sovereign LORD. For the sake of your word and according to your will, you have done this great thing and made it known to your servant" (2 Sam. 7:20–21).*

When I am overwhelmed by something God has done for me or said to me, I often find that I have to sit a moment and wait for my heart to write words on my lips. Sometimes I weep for awhile before I can begin to speak. David might have done the same thing. So intimate were the words God spoke to him through Nathan that he left the messenger's presence and went straight to the One who sent the message.

For reasons I will never understand, God has given me opportunities for ministry in this season of my life, and I praise Him for that. Yet the moments that most often move me are extremely intimate and private. Because they are so personal, I will probably never share in a testimony some of the most wonderful things God has done for me. What David was feeling was not about grand positions; it was about personal petitions. We each have countless opportunities to be overwhelmed at the goodness of God on our behalf.

David said, "And as if this were not enough in your sight, O Sovereign LORD, you have also . . ." (v. 19). How like God to keep giving and giving! Suddenly overcome, David broke out in compulsory praises! "How great you are, O Sovereign LORD!" (v. 22).

Every now and then we enjoy a moment void of doubt and full of mystery, when we're overwhelmed with humility yet stunned with possibility. Moments when we realize with every one of our senses that God stands alone. "No one— no mate, no child, no preacher, no teacher, no ruler, no principality—no one is like You." Nothing is quite like suddenly realizing that nothing is like Him.

# DAY 51
## 2 Samuel 8:1–18

⸺∞⸺

So David reigned over all Israel, administering justice
and righteousness for all his people (v. 15).

⸺∞⸺

This chapter undoubtedly represents the zenith of David's career. God had given him success. David had it all: fame, fortune, power, and position. For just a little while, David handled the unabashed blessings of God with brilliant integrity. Up until now we've seen David's virtues presented as subtle themes in the shadow of God's own. In 2 Samuel 8, God directly pinpointed David's character, allowing him to take a moment in the spotlight. We can glean the following virtues from this chapter:

1. *David showed a spirit of cooperation.* In 2 Samuel 7:10–11, God promised David that He would give the nation of Israel rest from her enemies. Second Samuel 8:1 tells us that "in the course of time, David defeated the Philistines and subdued them." David did not sit on the throne and simply wait for God to fulfill His promise. He obeyed God's beckoning to the battlefield to participate in victory!

When God assures us of a promise, He desires for us to respond by cooperating in the fulfillment of that promise. Sometimes that means battle; at other times God directs us to sit still and wait. Wisdom involves learning to know the difference. Whether God tells us to sit, stand, or move, He calls us to respond with a spirit of cooperation.

2. *David kept a spirit of hope even through a violent event.* When David defeated his enemies, he did not annihilate them and simply leave the nations destroyed. When he defeated the Moabites, he allowed one-third of them to live (v. 2).

King David lived in a harsh and cruel time. That he would kill two-thirds of the people naturally offends our modern sensibilities—until we compare his actions with the standard of his day. "Normal" behavior would have called for complete destruction of the Moabites. What we remarkably do see is that David had a concern for the spiritual welfare of non-Jews. David's concern was a giant step forward for a man of his day. He left a remnant and exhibited hope for the nations to bend their knees to the King of all kings. I believe David's God-given motive was to bring the other nations to a place of obedience to God rather than to obliterate them.

3. *David had a literal dedication to God.* At this point David had never confused the source of his strength. He immediately dedicated any spoils of his feats to the Lord. Verse 11 tells us that King David dedicated all the articles of silver and gold from all the nations he conquered. If he was praised for his successes, he

quickly gave the praise to God. If he was exalted for his successes, he lifted the name of God even higher. When he was surrounded by splendor, he wanted God to have something more splendid. When he returned with gold, silver, and bronze, he dedicated them immediately to the Lord.

4. *David displayed a concern for justice and righteousness.* The definitive verse of 2 Samuel 8 says, "David reigned over all Israel, doing what was just and right for all his people" (v. 15). This verse describes the moment when David most clearly and completely fulfilled his calling! When God called David a man after His own heart, He meant it literally. For a season, the kingdom of David reflected the kingdom of the supreme King of all kings. These were the glory days of David's kingdom. God had given him the keys to the kingdom: justice and righteousness—keys to a kingdom that will never end.

5. *David employed a wisdom for administration.* He knew that growth meant a greater need for administration. As the eighth chapter concludes, we see one of the first orders of business: the delegation of authority and responsibility. You may not find verses 16–18 exciting, but they record an essential step in David's kingdom. Joab son of Zeruiah was over the army; Jehoshaphat son of Ahilud was recorder; Zadok son of Ahitub and Ahimelech son of Abiathar were priests; Seraiah was secretary; Benaiah son of Jehoiada was over the Kerethites and Pelethites; and David's sons were royal advisers.

David had obviously learned an important lesson in his initial leadership of the distressed, indebted, and discontented (1 Sam. 22:2). A leader needs help! A good administrator knows when and how to delegate.

In this chapter, we see David as a man after God's own heart more than ever before in our study. We see Christ's own heart illustrated over and over. No one was more humble. No one held himself more accountable to God. No one revealed a greater heart for worship. No one had such a depth of cooperation with God. In all these ways David provides a picture of Jesus. Christ dedicated His every treasure to God, His Father, and will return for us when the Father nods. He will rule in justice and righteousness. As Chief Administrator, He will delegate the responsibilities of the kingdom to the faithful on earth.

The characteristics God saw and loved so much in David are those most like His Son. God has one specific bent toward partiality: He loves anything that reminds Him of His only begotten Son. To be more like Christ is to be a man or woman after God's own heart.

# DAY 52
## 2 Samuel 9:1–8

—∞∞—

David asked, "Is there anyone remaining from Saul's family
I can show kindness to because of Jonathan?" (v. 1).

—∞∞—

David had conquered kingdoms and subdued enemies. He had servants at his beck and call. All was momentarily quiet and peaceful—but he missed his best friend. God had fulfilled Jonathan's wish and given David everything, but Jonathan wasn't there to share it with him.

So David sought the next best thing. Ziba, a servant of the house of Saul, told him about Jonathan's one remaining son named Mephibosheth.

The Bible first mentions Mephibosheth in 2 Samuel 4. The boy was still a small child when news came of Saul and Jonathan's death. The nurse dropped Mephibosheth, resulting in his being crippled in both feet. Physical deformity was a great source of shame in the ancient world. Ziba might have suspected the son's handicap to disqualify him from anything the king sought.

If so, David surprised the servant.

David immediately commanded that Mephibosheth be brought to the court. Picturing the scene brings me to tears. Imagine the king sitting on the throne, surrounded by splendor. His brightly adorned servants open the door, and before him stands a crippled man. The Word says, "When Mephibosheth son of Jonathan, the son of Saul, came to David, he bowed down to pay him honor" (v. 6). With crippled legs he crept before the king, then he bowed before him! Can you imagine the difficulty for a handicapped man to get down on his knees, press his forehead to the floor, as was the custom, then rise up? Mephibosheth was obviously humbled. "What is your servant, that you should notice a dead dog like me?" (v. 8).

How amazed Mephibosheth must have been. Possibly he feared that David had summoned him for punishment. Remember that his uncle Ish-Bosheth had been at war with David. Whatever he hoped or feared, he probably had no idea what he was about to receive.

David was just seeking someone to bless and love.

# DAY 53
## 2 Samuel 9:9–13

—∞∞∞—

Ziba said to the king, "Your servant will do all my lord the king commands." So
Mephibosheth ate at David's table just like one of the king's sons (v. 11).

—∞∞∞—

I see two wonderful pictures in the story of Mephibosheth. First, I see an
image of myself. Like Jonathan's son, apart from Christ I am broken, outcast, and
crippled in both feet. I could never even crawl into God's presence, but in Christ
I put my feet under His table as His child.

Have you ever felt like a Mephibosheth? Surely everyone who ever accepted
Christ as Savior has crept before Him, crippled from the fall of sin, overcome by
our unworthiness against the backdrop of His Majesty's brilliance.

The second picture in the story is God Himself. In the encounter of
Mephibosheth and the king, we see several characteristics of the Father. Consider
the following virtues of God:

1. *David displayed God's loving-kindness.* David searched for someone of the
house of Saul to whom he could show God's kindness, not his own (v. 3). The
Lord is, first of all, kind. Compassionate. He desires to deal with us first in
mercy. If we refuse to accept His mercy, He often deals with us in the way He
must; but He is above all kind. As a man after God's own heart, David was
tender. His heart was full of loving-kindness, and he was eager to pour it out on
a willing vessel.

2. *David initiated the relationship.* "Where is he?" David inquired. Then he
summoned Mephibosheth immediately. Note that Mephibosheth did not seek
David. David sought Mephibosheth. David was the king! What could he possibly
have needed? But he wanted someone to whom he could show God's kindness.
God is always the initiator of the relationship, always looking for someone who
will receive His loving-kindness!

3. *David completely accepted Mephibosheth.* He did not hesitate when Ziba
informed him of Mephibosheth's handicap. In the Old Testament, people considered physical imperfection to be shameful, but David summoned Mephibosheth
exactly as he was. How reflective of the heart of God! Many people wait until
they can get their act together before they approach God. If only they could
understand that God calls them just the way they are; then He empowers them
to get their act together!

4. *David displayed God's calming spirit.* As Mephibosheth practically came
crawling before the king, David exclaimed, "Mephibosheth!" He knew him by
name . . . just as Christ knows us (John 10:3). David's next words were, "Don't be
afraid" (v. 7). How many times have we seen those words come from the precious
lips of our Lord: "It is I. Don't be afraid."

- To the twelve as He sent them forth (Matt. 10:31).
- To a bunch of scaredy-cats in a storm (Matt. 14:27).
- To Peter, James, and John, overcome by His glory (Matt. 17:7).
- To the father of a dying child (Mark 5:36).

"Don't be afraid." How very Christlike David was in this moment.

5. *David delighted in restoration.* "I will restore to you all the land that belonged to your grandfather" (v. 7). David's first desire was to restore Mephibosheth. This son of Jonathan had been so hurt by the fall. He had lived with such shame. The king could hardly wait to see Mephibosheth's shame removed and his life restored. David knew about restoration. He penned the words, "He restores my soul" (Ps. 23:3). Perhaps the most grateful response we could ever offer God for our restoration is to help another be restored. I was nearly overcome when I looked up the name Mephibosheth and found that it means, "shame destroyer" or "image breaker."[15] What a precious portrait of our Savior! He has been my shame destroyer and my image breaker!

6. *David had a desire for another son.* Mephibosheth came stooped as a servant before the king. The king came before Mephibosheth to make him a son. He was family—invited to sit at the king's table to partake of his fellowship as one of his own! Imagine the sight when he first limped to the table set with sumptuous delights, surrounded by festive activity, and sat down, resting his crippled legs at the king's table. Hallelujah! We are like Mephibosheth! No matter how many sons the Father has, He still wants more to conform into the image of His first and only begotten. "How great is the love the Father has lavished on us, that we should be called children of God! And that is what we are!" (1 John 3:1).

That's us, all right. One day, when we sit down to the ultimate wedding feast, the lame will be healed, the blind will see, the restored will leap and skip with ecstatic joy! We will be surrounded by the ministering servants of heaven! He is a God of loving-kindness. He's just searching for someone with whom to share it. Not just the moment when we first bow before Him and acknowledge that He is king, but every single time we sit at His table. Joint heirs. Sons. Daughters. He is the shame destroyer. The lover of the lame.

I would never have learned to walk with God on healthy feet had I never experienced sitting at His table as a cripple. My emotional and spiritual healing has come from approaching God in my handicapped state and believing I was His child and worthy of His love.

## DAY 54
### 2 Samuel 10:1–19

—∞∞—

*Then David said, "I'll show kindness to Hanun son of Nahash,
just as his father showed kindness to me." So David sent his emissaries
to console Hanun concerning his father (v. 2).*

—∞∞—

With 2 Samuel 10, we mark the end of the golden period of David's reign. In the next chapter we will see him commit the sin that will dog the rest of his life, so let's enjoy these final unblemished examples of his character.

When Nahash the king of the Ammonites died, David demonstrated a remarkable degree of sympathy for the suffering. David knew better than anyone that a crown did not make a person void of feelings and oblivious to losses. Even though Saul was not his father and had often treated him with malice, David had grieved his death. Likewise, Hanun was assuming the throne of the Ammonites but at the cost of his father's life.

David was exhibiting the character of God as he extended sympathy to someone who had experienced loss. David knew the disappointment of reaching out to others for sympathy and not receiving it, but he learned from his experience that God is always compassionate and sympathetic. *You can depend on God in your need.* See how he described the sympathetic heart of God:

> *As a father has compassion on his children,
> so the LORD has compassion on those who fear him (Ps. 103:13).*

But His sympathy is not always accepted.

David experienced something similar when Hanun rejected his extension of sympathy. The Ammonite nobles led Hanun to believe that David had sinister motives for sending his men. They attempted to make the new king feel foolish for trusting David's motives. "Do you think David is honoring your father by sending men to you to express sympathy?" (v. 3).

A possible paraphrase might be, "Are you some kind of gullible idiot?" They said David was spying out Hanun's kingdom for conquest. Following his advisers' counsel, Hanun humiliated David's men by cutting off half their garments and beards. He was symbolically making them half the men they were.

I see an important similarity between David's rejected sympathies expressed by the humiliation of his delegates, and God's rejected sympathies expressed by humanity's rejection of Christ. God's most glorious extension of sympathy to a dying world was Christ, His Son. God sent Christ as the delegate of His sympathy to the misery of men.

Christ was also met by those who stirred up misunderstanding among the people, just like the Ammonite nobles. These people in Christ's day were called Pharisees. Ultimately, His message of sympathy was rejected by the very ones to whom it was extended, and Christ hung on a cross in complete humiliation. For those who have received Him, Christ remains our sympathizer, ever ready to lead us to a door of escape from temptation or a door of mercy when temptation has turned to participation.

We saw David's character reflect God's sympathy. We now turn to another aspect of God's character: *the king's fierce protectiveness toward his own*. David sent messengers to meet the men so they would not have to be publicly humiliated. He made provision for them to stay in Jericho until their beards had grown because he knew a shaved beard was considered an insult. In effect, he threw a cloak around their exposed bodies and formed a plan to spare their dignity.

I'm not sure we can understand what this kind of humiliation meant to a Hebrew. The thought of being exposed in such a heartless manner would be humiliating to anyone, but to a Hebrew such humiliation was virtually a fate worse than death. They were a very modest people. Their enemy had preyed on one of their worst nightmares. David fiercely protected the dignity of his men.

God is even more protective of us.

Finally in this incident, we see David reflecting another clear example of God's nature: *his vengeance toward the enemies of his people and the mockers of his mercy*. David did not just formulate a plan to spare the dignity of his men. He took on their enemy himself. God also takes on our enemies when we've been shamed.

Let me assure you, God can take on your enemy with far more power and might than you could ever muster. When someone persecutes you, your Father takes the persecution very personally, especially when you are persecuted for obeying Him, as David's men were. The battle is the Lord's!

God has extended His mercy to every single member of the human race. He sent His Delegate of sympathy for our sin problem to hang on a cross as the Divine Remedy. Those who reject His mercy and mock His motives will be punished sooner or later if they do not repent. Pray today for your enemies! Pray they will accept God's Delegate of mercy toward them!

# DAY 55
## 2 Samuel 11:1–5

---

*One evening David got up from his bed and strolled around on the roof of the palace.*
*From the roof he saw a woman bathing—a very beautiful woman (v. 2).*

---

The study of David intrigues me for many reasons. He, of all the characters in the Old Testament, may best prefigure Christ and the gospel message. In chapters 7–10, we scaled the heights of David's reign and the breadth of his character, but the qualities of God's character only comprise one side of the gospel.

We are about to encounter the dark side—human sin.

David painfully proved the depths to which one can fall after reaching such heights. The contrast between these consecutive seasons of David's life is staggering. Against God's warning, David multiplied wives and grew dangerously accustomed to having all he wanted. We will soon discover the outcome of his eroding self-control.

Through many chapters of Scripture we've seen the qualities of David extolled. Now in two short verses we see him tumble headlong into the pit of sin. Join me as we step out on the roof of an ancient Hebrew home to catch a fresh breath of spring air.

After Hanun shamed the men David sent to bear his sympathies, the Ammonite king knew he was in trouble, so he formed an alliance with the Arameans (Syrians). In chapter 10, Joab only began the job of punishing Hanun. David's general thoroughly defeated the Arameans, but then the season for warfare was past. Joab returned the army to Israel, pending the coming spring when he would resume the campaign against the Ammonites. In that context, hear the first words of chapter 11: "In the spring, at the time when kings go off to war, David sent Joab out with the king's men and the whole Israelite army" (v. 1). The first sign of trouble appears when David began to shirk his duty.

You probably know the story that follows. One night David couldn't sleep. He went for a walk on the roof of the palace, and from there he saw a beautiful woman bathing. He sent a messenger to find out about her. The messenger told him two facts, either of which should have stopped him cold. He said her name was Bathsheba, the wife of Uriah the Hittite, one of David's soldiers. David disregarded common decency. He sent for her. They committed adultery.

She went home. Time passed.

Soon she realized that she was pregnant.

Few things frighten me more than this testimony of David's life. We too could be persons of character and integrity and, without apparent warning, destroy our ministries and ourselves through the choice to gratify our sudden lusts. Like David, a few short verses could record the story of our downfall.

As you consider this familiar story, don't be drawn into their sin by romantic—and false—notions. We cannot afford to justify their behavior through sympathy. In our culture we justify immoral behavior with the excuse that two people were "in love." Even if two people are emotionally entangled, don't call self-gratification and breaking promises to God and others love. David and Bathsheba didn't even have that flimsy excuse. They were not in love. They simply chose to act in a dishonorable and destructive way. We could speculate that he was intoxicated by her beauty mixed with an opportunity to display his power. She may have been enamored with his wealth and prestige.

But we cannot lend this scene the sympathies we are tempted to offer "victims" of passion in romance novels. This trashy romance we're reading about today is down in the bottom of the barrel, down there with all the sticky stuff, where the stench is—the place we find ourselves when the line between wanting and getting erodes.

We may wish we could get everything we want—until we look at David and Bathsheba. The gap between wanting and getting is where we must flex the muscle of self-control to protect ourselves. David had risen to a position where his every wish was someone else's command. He had ceased to hear a very important word—one without which integrity cannot be maintained. The word *no*.

David was probably like most of us. He could say no rather easily to some things, but he had great difficulty with others. The difficulty was obviously regulated by how badly he wanted what he shouldn't have. In the midst of all his integrity in the other areas of his life, "David took more concubines and wives in Jerusalem" (2 Sam. 5:13). Obviously he lacked self-control in the area of sexual lust.

In Deuteronomy 17:17, God clearly stated the consequences of multiplying wives: the king "must not take many wives, or his heart will be led astray." Just as God warned, David's heart had gone astray. Suddenly the heart that had been so much like God's had wandered to an abyss of no resemblance. David didn't guard his heart, and it began to lie to him.

David, the man of God, the Lord's anointed, the one who enjoyed God's complete provision, took what did not belong to him and cast himself headlong into scandal. He believed his own cheating heart.

# DAY 56
## 2 Samuel 11:6–17

The next morning David wrote a letter to Joab and sent it with Uriah.
In the letter he wrote: "Put Uriah at the front of the fiercest fighting,
then withdraw from him so that he is struck down and dies" (vv. 14–15).

We saw David's sin begin in his thought life and end up in the conception of an innocent child with another man's wife. We may see the greatest evidence of his faraway heart in the way he reacted to the news of Bathsheba's pregnancy.

When David heard the news that Bathsheba was pregnant, he immediately tried to cover up his sin. He sent for her husband, Uriah, so he would have intercourse with her and thus think the baby was his. David's initial conversation with Uriah was at best disingenuous but, more accurately, was despicable.

Have you ever felt someone was faking an interest in you for an ulterior motive? Most of us know the sting of such behavior. The Scripture gives no hint that Uriah recognized the dishonesty of his king. To the contrary, Uriah's honor spoiled David's plan. Uriah refused to go home to his wife when his comrades were in the field. If only his commander in chief had acted with such honor.

Uriah's honor put David on the spot. The king had an opportunity to confess his sin or to cover it with still more evil. He chose the latter.

We have seen that Joab was a man of flawed character. He trusted God in matters of battle, but he apparently had no compunctions about murder. Note that when Joab murdered Abner, David clearly and publicly disavowed his actions, but now David found Joab's talents useful. In one of the great betrayals of history, David wrote orders for Joab to have Uriah killed in battle. David even gave the orders to Uriah to deliver to Joab. Thus Bathsheba's husband trustingly carried his own death warrant to his executioner.

I grieve to think how loyal Uriah must have felt when the troops around him in battle deserted him to die. I wonder if, in the last moments, he guessed that "good" King David and the wife to whom he had pledged his love were complicit in his death. One thing I know and David certainly should have known: the God of righteousness will not allow such behavior to stand.

# DAY 57
## 2 Samuel 11:18–27

—∞∞∞—

David told the messenger, "Say this to Joab: 'Don't let this matter upset you because the sword devours all alike. Intensify your fight against the city and demolish it.' Encourage him" (v. 25).

—∞∞∞—

Did you find yourself secretly hoping the story had changed this time? Imagine how the Father's heart is wounded when we behave so unlike one of His children. He was no doubt grief-stricken by David's sin, even though He saw it coming. Considering the events we've read, David's heart was obviously further away from God than we imagined. If David were accused of a faraway heart and tried in a court of law, how much evidence would there be to convict him? As members of the jury—not the judge—consider four evidences of David's faraway heart.

1. *David resisted many opportunities to repent of his sin and lessen the charges against himself.* Most of us have been carried away by an overwhelming and sudden craving of the flesh, but we've often cried out for help before sin was heaped on sin. Other times, we've thrown ourselves into a revolving door of sin, just like David, and continued in a destructive cycle.

Why do you think David didn't stop and repent? You might consider the answer from a personal standpoint by asking yourself, "Why have I not at times stopped and repented in the earlier stages of sin?"

After David committed the act of adultery, even though the consequences of the pregnancy were already at work, he could have fallen on his face before God, repented, asked for mercy, and begged God to help clean up the mess he had made. Throughout his encounters with Uriah, he had many opportunities to consider his actions and recant. He didn't.

David was a man with God's Spirit in him! You can be assured the Spirit was doing His job of conviction! Sadly, David had quenched the Spirit to such a degree that he was able to resist conviction repeatedly. Little should frighten us more than realizing the Holy Spirit's conviction has grown so faint we hardly sense it. We are dangerously far away when we can sin with little conviction. We should run home to the Father as quickly as we can!

2. *David was unmoved by Uriah's integrity.* David's faraway heart was unaffected by an encounter with authentic integrity. Psalm 78:72 says David once shepherded his people "with integrity of heart." Uriah's integrity should have spurred such a sense of loss in David that he could not bear to remain so far from the Father.

Unfortunately, when people have moved this far away from God, someone else's righteous behavior often only serves to make them angry and send them further into denial. While they recognize their faults, at that point the pull of sin is often stronger than the desire to set things right.

David surely recognized integrity. For most of his life, his character had been replete with it! When I confront godly character, I never fail to say to myself, "I want to reflect character like him, Lord!" or, "Please, God, make me an example like her!"

3. *David tried to cover his own sin.* Have you ever gotten tangled in a web of sin while you tried to cover the first one? Most of us have tried to cover our sin at one time or another!

In Psalm 32:1, David reminded us that the blessed person is the one "whose transgressions are forgiven, whose sins are covered." How sad that he learned the lesson through such bitter experience.

The word "covered" in the Hebrew is *kasah*, meaning "to cover, conceal, hide; to clothe; . . . to forgive; to keep secret; to hide oneself, wrap oneself up."[16] When we try desperately to cover up our sinful ways, we are bound for disaster as sin perpetuates. Only through repentance will God "cover" us and "clothe" us with His loving forgiveness. Only when we run to Him in the nakedness of our sin will He wrap us up with "garments of salvation" and a "robe of righteousness" (Isa. 61:10). David was trying to cover his tracks; God wanted to cover his sins. The latter means life; the former means death—to something or someone.

4. *David involved many others in his sin.* Apparently, David never stopped to consider the position in which he was placing others. We, too, can become so self-absorbed that we do not care what we are asking from others. We can be unmoved by the compromises of others on our behalf. Intense selfishness accompanies a faraway heart.

In David's selfishness, he involved a servant in his plans; he invited Bathsheba to a season of guilt and grief; he attempted to entice Uriah to compromise his values; he involved Joab in his sin; and he had Uriah killed. Most importantly "the thing David had done displeased the LORD" (v. 27). Still he did not repent. We may rightly conclude that David had ample evidence to convict him of a faraway heart.

The results were tragic.

# DAY 58
## 2 Samuel 12:1-12

—◦◦◦—

"Why then have you despised the command of the Lord
by doing what I consider evil?" (v. 9).

—◦◦◦—

This chapter is difficult and painful. The scene unfolds with Nathan sent to confront David's sin. We can take a lesson from this already. We need to be careful not to confront for any other reason than sin. Galatians 6:1 records one of the reasons: "Watch yourself, or you also may be tempted."

Nathan was God's man for this job, but he still needed the Lord's protection and leadership as he confronted the powerful, persuasive king. He probably dreaded his appointment like the plague, but he was obedient to the will of God.

When the prophet Nathan confronted David, he used a method any good preacher might have used. He used an illustration familiar to his hearer, and then drove the illustration home with the Word of God. Nathan's rebuke was God's way of saying to David, in effect, "I anointed you, delivered you, gave you Saul's kingdom and all that belonged to him. If you had needed more, I would have given it. But you didn't ask me for things I longed to give to you. Instead you took something that wasn't yours."

Nathan's method struck an immediate chord with David. David was ready to fine the man in Nathan's story "four times over" and kill him—until he found out *he* was the man!

What was God trying to accomplish? I believe He wanted David to recognize the grace of God in the midst of the grave consequences of his sin. God wanted David to recognize that he deserved to die. Bathsheba also deserved death, according to Hebrew law. So did Joab for setting up another person's death. God allowed David to sit as judge over his own life and pronounce a death sentence on himself so his heavenly Father could grant him the undeserved gift of life. No doubt, David never forgot that moment.

God was teaching the way to the Messiah through His chosen king. Through David's victories, God taught something of Himself. Now, through David's failures, God would teach the very foundation of all salvation—God will forgive the sinner, but He will still judge the sin. Because of David's sin, God said "the sword will never depart from your house" (v. 10). Ominous and predictive words indeed.

# DAY 59
## 2 Samuel 12:13-23

He answered, "While the baby was alive, I fasted and wept because I thought,
'Who knows? The LORD may be gracious to me and let him live'" (v. 22).

Nathan delivered a harsh word concerning the child born to David and
Bathsheba: "Because by doing this you have made the enemies of the LORD show
utter contempt, the son born to you will die" (v. 14).

And sure enough, the prophet had hardly turned the doorknob to leave
before David's child fell ill.

David had been warned that his son would die, and still he "pleaded with
God for the child" (v. 16) for seven days. David refused to eat. He spent the nights
lying on the ground. When the child died, the servants were terrified. They
thought David might kill himself. So they were afraid to tell him the child had
died. They were stunned when David received the news. He got up, washed his
face, changed clothes, and went into the house of the Lord and worshiped. Then
he went home and ate.

David's servants were mystified by his behavior. They asked him why he
wept when the child was ill but worshiped when the child died. David's reply in
verses 22–23 has brought comfort to bereaved parents across the centuries.

Did David waste his time pleading with God over the life of the child?
After all, God's message through Nathan was painfully clear. Before we attempt
(tomorrow) to determine whether or not David's efforts were wasted, today let's
peek quickly at just a little of the intense intimacy David shared with God.

When he fell on his face before God, the prodigal returned home to the
place he belonged. He was bankrupt in soul, demoralized, and terrified, but he
was back. Too many months had passed since he had last entered the indescribable place of God's presence, but he still recognized the Father.

Through David's crisis, he was reminded of all he knew of God's ways.
David did not plead with God out of ignorance or naïveté but out of his intimate
knowledge of Him. God does indeed hear our prayers and reserves the right to
relent if the change does not compromise an eternal necessity.

## DAY 60
### 2 Samuel 12:24–25

———∞∞———

Then David comforted his wife Bathsheba; he went and slept with her.
She gave birth to a son and named him Solomon. The LORD loved him (v. 24).

———∞∞———

We continue to see David during the most difficult season of his life. We find some of the events hard to study, but they overflow with vital life lessons. The nuggets of gold we will dig from the painful caverns of the coming chapters will captivate us until the winds of victory blow in our faces once again. Pause right now and ask God to tender your heart to His Word.

David knew something about his God that we need to realize as well. God did not create humanity in His own image to be unaffected by Him. More than any other creature, we are products not of His head but of His heart. Numerous times in Scripture God responds to the needs of His people with the words, "I have heard your cry." I would despair of life if I believed God is unaffected by our cries. The God of Scripture is One who feels.

Unlike us, God is never compromised by His feelings, but He is touched by the things of the heart. When David heard that he would live but his child would die, he probably begged God to allow him to die instead. Can you imagine God's being unaffected by a parent's painful pleas? You may be thinking, "But, Beth, God didn't do what David asked. David's prayers didn't change a thing. Where is grace? Where is mercy? What changed?"

Let's consider a few of the things that changed.

1. *David's painful pleas forced him back to a crucial place of depending on God.* Somewhere along the line, David had mistaken the power of God as his own. He had so often been told he could do anything, he started to believe it. God demands that we depend on Him because only He can keep us safe. When we depend on Him, He takes care of us. When we seek security in other places, He is obligated to turn us back toward home. When we refuse the less painful nudgings of the Holy Spirit, we risk more drastic measures. Tragedy caused David to depend on God. God's judgment seems harsh until we reconsider David's many transgressions. He multiplied wives and concubines, took another man's wife, took the man's life—all with no willingness to repent. Don't conclude that the loss of a child must be chastisement on sinful parents. God is not mean-spirited. Remember, David was the king of God's holy nation and had continued to rebel against God in spite of the Holy Spirit's urgings.

2. *David's pleas would satisfy his spirit in the many months of mourning to come.* As he grieved the loss, he needed to know he had done everything he could to prevent the child's death. David did not want his child to die because he did not ask God (see James 4:2).

3. *David's pleas ultimately ensured his survival through the tragedy he and his wife would suffer.* David's pleas returned him to intimacy with God. The return positioned him to make it through such loss with victory. David's restored relationship to God enabled him to comfort his grieving wife. When tragedy hits, if we cast ourselves on the Savior and rely on Him for the very breath we draw, we will one day get up again. We will even have the strength to comfort another mourner. Perhaps most difficult to fathom, we will have the strength to return to worship.

I'm glad Scripture does not record the scene when David first returned to public worship. The moment belonged to God and David alone. I cannot hold back the tears as I imagine how quickly David's words turned to sobs. I can picture him standing there acknowledging through wails of grief his God's sovereignty and loving-kindness.

Have you ever returned to the Lord in worship after a painful loss that you believe He could have stopped? If so, you may view your return to worship as one of the most difficult and painful experiences of life. I suspect David would concur, but his return restored his sanity. His rediscovered relationship with God became the pillar to hold him up through the painful repercussions of his sins.

4. *David's pleas touched the heart of God to respond.* God loved this man—just as He loves us. The one He loves He must discipline (Heb. 12:6). But does God's heart ache as He disciplines? I believe the answer is yes. Beautiful evidence of the Father's tender heart toward David emerges in this tragic account. God could not give David what he asked because He had to perform an eternal work and teach an eternal lesson.

But He did something else. Out of grace God removed the curse on the sinful union of David and Bathsheba. Their union had been wrong. Their motive was wrong. Even when David found out Bathsheba was pregnant, he tried to manipulate a way for her to stay out of his life. But now we see them drawn together by terrible tragedy. God removed the curse of their marriage and brought a child from their union. Jedidiah means "beloved of the Lord."

"The Lord loved him." God loves you. His chastisements can be painful, but God never turns His back on us. He will discipline us, but He will not forsake us. He will always seek to draw us back to a place where He can bless us once more.

# DAY 61
## 2 Samuel 13:1–20

---

"Don't, my brother!" she cried. "Don't humiliate me, for such a thing should never be done in Israel. Don't do this horrible thing!" (v. 12).

---

Sin never fails to bring painful repercussions. We will now see Nathan's prophecy regarding David's sin begin to find fulfillment. Turmoil will escalate within the private quarters of the palace, and David's responses will reveal that he was a far more effective king than father.

If you already know what's coming, you know Amnon's actions were inexcusable, but can you imagine the confusing messages David's children received as they grew up? They had siblings, half siblings, and siblings born to David's concubines. They grew up in a household saturated by sexual excess and lacking any example of parental restraint. We can't and must not excuse Amnon, but we can certainly understand.

These verses are replete with tragedy. The focus of this corruption was a beautiful young virgin daughter of the king, Tamar, no doubt awaiting the man she trusted God would one day bring her. Tamar's brother was Absalom, and their half brother was named Amnon. Amnon was infatuated with Tamar. I believe he was used to getting whatever he wanted, with the result that he became obsessed with the one thing he could not have—his half sister.

The events in chapter 13 are scandalous even by today's standards and as painful as the horrid descriptions of rapes we read in a big city newspaper. Amnon wanted Tamar. On the advice of his shrewd cousin Jonadab, Amnon pretended to be sick. He asked his father David to send Tamar to care for him. Then he raped her.

Those who have experienced the trauma of rape know the injury doesn't end with the event. The actions and reactions of others multiply the pain. In this case, Amnon quickly added to the hurt: "Then Amnon hated her with intense hatred. In fact, he hated her more than he had loved her" (v. 15).

The tragic irony of Tamar's dress also touches my heart (v. 19). The richly ornamented robe was her cloak of dignity and honor. She ripped the fabric of her robe as surely as Amnon had ripped the fabric of her honor. His crime against her was heinous. And her loss, incalculable.

# DAY 62
## 2 Samuel 13:21–39

———∞∞∞———

"Amnon is dead. In fact, Absalom has planned this
ever since the day Amnon disgraced his sister Tamar" (v. 32).

———∞∞∞———

I am acutely aware that many who read these words have been victims of
rape. I deeply desire to handle this subject with tenderness and reverence. I have
asked God to pour His Spirit through me so that I will be untrue to neither Him
nor you. First, we need to assign appropriate responsibility.

*Amnon.* He was David's firstborn. Ironically, his name meant "trustworthy"
and "faithful."[17] Obviously, he was neither. We see the immediate evidence of a
father's influence on his son. Amnon had watched his father take one wife after
another in a nation where polygamy was forbidden. As far as Amnon could see,
his father never wanted anything he didn't ultimately get.

Like his father, Amnon saw something beautiful and determined to have
it. He gave no consideration to the other party involved. Only his lust mattered.
He literally became sin-sick to the point of stopping at nothing to satisfy his
appetite. Tamar pled with him to spare her disgrace and his reputation, but "he
refused to listen."

I found one of the most sickening moments in the tragic events to be
Amnon's immediate reaction. After the rape, Amnon hated her with intense
hatred. We humans often practice a kind of blame shifting. When we have done
something sinful and shameful, we blame our actions on someone else—often
the victim of our behavior.

We can be assured that God will deal appropriately with Amnon. We see no
sign of repentance. When he sees the face of the Righteous Judge, he may utter
words like those in Revelation 6:16: "They called to the mountains and rocks,
'Fall on us and hide us from the face of him who sits on the throne and from the
wrath of the Lamb!'"

*Absalom.* Both Absalom and David reacted inappropriately toward Tamar
and the crime she suffered. Absalom obviously discovered his sister in extreme
distress. He guessed the nature of the crime against her from the tearing of the
virgin's robe. No one can doubt Absalom's love for his sister, but his reaction to
her could only have added further injury. Countless victims of rape and moles-
tation have been hurt by similar advice. Absalom told her to "be quiet" and not
"take this thing to heart" (v. 20).

Perhaps you have been the victim of shame in some way. If so, I offer
you company today. I've been there too. When I was a small child, someone
my parents should have been able to trust caused great pain and suffering by
crimes against me. Friends and family members of victims often ask me what

they can possibly say to their hurting loved one. I know from my own experience that the most important thing anyone can say to a victim of a shame-breeding crime is, "I am so sorry. I love you, and I support you." We often think we need to come up with answers when another has been hurt. Sometimes the words of comforters are well-meaning but hurtful.

Simple words like "I love you" and "I support you" work best for those of us who are not counselors. In case you've been a victim of shame and no one has ever said these words before: I am so sorry.

Absalom was wrong to tell Tamar to be quiet and not take it to heart. The shame was crushing her to pieces. He minimized the significance of the terrible crime against her. She was invited to live with him, but she was not invited to be honest with him. She was left desolate—like the living dead.

*David.* How did David react? We see just one description: "He was furious" (v. 21). But what did he do about the crime? Absolutely nothing. Why didn't David take control of his family tragedy? I believe the enemy may have been working on David just as he works on us when we really blow it. His own complicity and sin blinded him to the need of Tamar to find release for the fire of hurt and shame that burned in her. Satan uses sin and failure so effectively against us that even after sincere repentance we often remain completely disabled. He whispers all sorts of questions in our ears like, "How dare you expect obedience from your children after what you've done? How dare you walk into church again? You hypocrite!"

Two wrongs don't make a right! If we blow it as a parent, spouse, servant, employee, or leader, we should fall before God in complete repentance and ask Him what we must do to cooperate with restoration. Then we should follow Him in utmost obedience to His precepts. Restoration does not mean you can no longer stand for the truth because you fell. Restoration means you must stand!

David allowed his own failure to disable him to lead his household in justice and righteousness. He had been forgiven by God, but he had not chosen to live like a forgiven person. He allowed his own sense of guilt to handicap him as a parent.

"Be ye angry, and sin not" (Eph. 4:26 KJV) does not mean "be angry and do nothing." God created anger. It energizes us to respond when something is wrong. David needed to channel his anger and respond to the crime committed in his household. No weaker house exists than one that lacks appropriate authority. Lack of authority is a breeding ground for untold recklessness and sin. Just ask Tamar.

# DAY 63
2 Samuel 14:1–33

⸻

"For we will certainly die and be like water poured out on the ground,
which can't be recovered. But God would not take away a life; He would
devise plans so that the one banished from Him does not remain banished" (v. 14).

⸻

Two years had passed since Amnon's crime against Tamar. Two years with bitterness multiplying in Absalom's heart. He must have watched and waited to see if his father would call Amnon to account for his crime. His father didn't. Absalom did.

After ordering Amnon's death, Absalom fled to the king of Geshur. The tragedy ends with one son dead, one son missing, and one father grief-stricken. After a time Joab grew weary of seeing David mope and do nothing. Anyone who studies the life of Joab will see that the general was no fan of doing nothing. He had obviously witnessed David's irresponsibility toward Absalom for as long as he could. He devised a plan to capture David's attention. Through a concocted story of a woman and her prodigal son, Joab convinced David to summon Absalom.

David granted Joab's request and allowed him to summon Absalom. Joab was so thrilled, he "fell with his face to the ground . . . and he blessed the king" (v. 22). He joyfully hastened to bring the young man home, no doubt picturing the emotional but wonderful reunion of father and son. He brought Absalom back to Jerusalem, bracing himself and his charge for the glorious reunion. But he was met with these words from the king: "He must go to his own house; he must not see my face" (v. 24).

Often David's heart and actions show us a picture of Christ. In this case he shows the opposite. I am very grateful God will not call us to the heavenly Jerusalem and say, "She must not see my face." I've waited all my life to see His beautiful face! David did not respond like the father of the prodigal son in Christ's parable—the father who searched the horizon daily for his wandering son to come home. That father, who represents our heavenly Father, caught a glimpse of his son in the distance and "ran to his son, threw his arms around him and kissed him" (Luke 15:20).

God sometimes gives us a second chance to do something right. Some chances never come back around. The chance for David and Absalom to be genuinely reunited in their hearts would not come again. By the time David finally received Absalom, his son's heart was cold.

# DAY 64
## 2 Samuel 15:1–12

—∞∞—

Then Absalom sent messengers throughout the tribes of Israel
with this message: "When you hear the sound of the ram's horn,
you are to say, 'Absalom has become king in Hebron!'" (v. 10).

—∞∞—

We now see evidence of Absalom's deep dissatisfaction about his encounter with his father. Their meeting did nothing but fuel his bitterness. The relationship between David and Absalom teaches us an important object lesson: reuniting and reconciliation can be two very different things.

Many previously separated couples have returned to one another to live under the same roof for the sake of the children, finances, religious convictions, or the family business. They may live together the rest of their lives without healing or dealing with the problems. Reuniting is one thing; reconciliation is another.

Absalom was dissatisfied by his meeting with his father. Possibly he suffered from the same thing many adults suffer from today. When Absalom was a child, his daddy was his hero. He was strong and smart. He was his son's idol. David had plenty of shortcomings, but the boy could not see them until one day an emotional bombshell hit home—exploding in the bedroom of Amnon.

Although people got mad, no one cleaned up the mess. Lives continued to be torn by the shrapnel no one ever swept away. David did not—perhaps could not—live up to Absalom's expectations. The results were devastating. The revenge Absalom had taken on Amnon's life was not enough. The fact that his father still called him a son was not enough. He still cried out for vengeance and was determined his father would pay.

Obviously, Absalom tried everything he knew—good and bad—to get his father's attention. He could not get to David through his home, so he determined to get to him through the throne.

Absalom began a very deliberate campaign to win the hearts of the people. Each morning he arrived with a chariot and an entourage of men and horses. He looked impressive as he stood at the gate of the city. When anyone entered the city with a complaint, Absalom proclaimed that if he were appointed judge, anyone with a complaint would get justice. He was quite an effective politician. I wouldn't be surprised if he even kissed a few babies. Absalom proved a patient and diligent schemer. He continued to work through every step of his plan for four years, waiting for the right moment to attempt to overthrow the father he now hated.

Absalom spent two years waiting for David to punish Amnon, three years in hiding after killing his brother, two years in Jerusalem waiting for David to receive him, and four years working his devious plan of vengeance against his father. Unforgiveness and retaliation stole eleven years of his life! Eleven years is a long time for anyone to seethe, for anyone to harbor bitterness.

Has anger or bitterness stolen years of your life? God tells us to forgive those who hurt us, but He never qualifies the command by saying forgive only when someone asks for your forgiveness. He simply says, "Forgive" (Luke 6:37). Christ set the perfect example in Luke 23:34. From the cross He cried, "Father forgive them, for they do not know what they are doing." Those crucifying Jesus had not realized what they were doing. They had not asked forgiveness. Rather, they were gambling over His clothes.

I believe Christ asked God to forgive them, not to let His persecutors off the hook, but for Christ to disavow bitterness. He chose to continue His painful destiny with the love of the Father, not unforgiveness.

David never asked for forgiveness. He never took his rightful place of authority over family events. David made plenty of mistakes, but Absalom did not have to follow suit. He could have called on the mercy of God and forgiven David for failing him, even if his father never admitted how wrongly he had handled his family. God would have held David responsible, and Absalom would have been free. Instead, he locked himself in the prison of bitterness where character eroded in the darkness of his soul. We often resist forgiveness by saying, "It's too difficult to forgive." Forgiveness may be excruciating for a moment, but anger and bitterness are excruciating for a lifetime.

Often, the people who hurt us don't realize the magnitude of their actions. The people who mocked and crucified Christ had no idea they were dealing with the fullness of the Godhead bodily! The man who hurt me when I was a small child had no idea how much I would suffer for decades to come. Can we muster the courage to say regarding those who hurt us, "God, forgive them and help me to forgive them"?

Those who hurt us often have no idea how deeply we will suffer. If we follow Christ's example, we will be free. We can save ourselves a lot of heartache! Learning to forgive even if no one takes responsibility for his or her actions will save us from the kind of misery that ultimately destroyed Absalom.

# DAY 65
## 2 Samuel 15:13–31

David said to all the servants with him in Jerusalem, "Get up. We have to flee,
or we will not escape from Absalom! Leave quickly, or he will overtake us,
heap disaster on us, and strike the city with the edge of the sword" (v. 14).

When David heard of Absalom's rebellion, the warrior king did a remarkable thing. He packed up, abandoned Jerusalem, and ran (v. 14).

Is this the same David whom God had anointed as His chosen king? The one who conquered the giant? The one God prospered like no other? Did he not know that God gave him the kingdom, and only He could take it away? How could he run from his throne?

David found himself right in the middle of a cycle of self-appointed failure. Stricken with grief and dressed for mourning, he and his loyal followers trudged the Mount of Olives where people once worshiped God.

There on the Mount of Olives, continuing up to the summit, an amazing thing happened: "David prayed" (v. 31). Little by little, things began to happen. David had run from his throne practically hopeless. But somewhere on top of that mountain, David got down on his knees and prayed. See his prayer for yourself. God had him write it down. It's Psalm 3. It begins:

> *O LORD, how many are my foes! How many rise up against me!*
> > *Many are saying of me, "God will not deliver him."* . . .
> *Arise, O LORD! Deliver me, O my God!*
> > *Strike all my enemies on the jaw; break the teeth of the*
> > *wicked* . . .
> *From the LORD comes deliverance.*
> > *May your blessing be on your people (Ps. 3:1–2, 7–8).*

God did not answer every one of David's requests from this prayer immediately, but He returned enough strength to David for him to begin walking in faith instead of fear. On the Mount of Olives, David confronted the Spirit of God who had grown accustomed to being honored there. Many years later Jesus trudged that same path and found strength to walk on to a cross. I wonder if Christ thought of David when He prayed on that same mountain.

# DAY 66
### 2 Samuel 16:1–4

---

"Why, he's staying in Jerusalem," Ziba replied to the king, "for he said, 'Today, the house of Israel will restore my father's kingdom to me'" (v. 3).

---

The conflict between David and Absalom rekindled old supporters of Saul who were still nursing grudges against David. Have you ever noticed that mean-spirited people will kick a person when he's down? David had seemed invincible; yet the moment he appeared vulnerable, opportunists began to descend on him like vultures.

As David fled, he met Ziba, the steward of Mephibosheth, with donkeys loaded with provisions for the fleeing troops. David certainly needed the help, but Ziba's motives were less than pure.

David had no reason to disbelieve Ziba's claims in verse 3 that Mephibosheth was back at the palace, smugly and ungratefully aspiring to fill David's vacant throne. If Absalom, his own flesh and blood, could betray him, why not the adult son he adopted? David had suffered so much betrayal, he assumed no one was beyond turning on him. So the king said to Ziba, "All that belonged to Mephibosheth is now yours" (v. 3).

In fact, however, Ziba lied to David. The steward had abandoned his crippled master in Jerusalem in order to swindle him out of his property.

Can you remember ever feeling like someone had taken advantage of you at a time when you were vulnerable? Nothing makes us as vulnerable as family problems. Personal difficulties may cause us to lack discernment. David told Ziba he would give him everything Mephibosheth owned without confirming Ziba's claims. David's vulnerability caused him to believe the worst and respond with haste rather than prudence.

We are wise to be careful about the decisions and assumptions we make when we are stressed. We will tend to react rather than respond. When pain is acute, we often can't discriminate properly between good and bad decisions. I can't think of a situation when godly advice is more valuable than in times of great vulnerability.

David could have used a little advice before he gave Mephibosheth's belongings to Ziba. Perhaps the wisdom and insight of another would have prevented him from having such a knee-jerk reaction. Unfortunately, Ahithophel, his head counselor, was unavailable. He was busy advising Absalom! No wonder David was vulnerable!

# DAY 67
## 2 Samuel 16:5–14

---

The king replied, "Sons of Zeruiah, do we agree on anything?
He curses me this way because the LORD told him, 'Curse David!'
Therefore, who can say, 'Why did you do that?'" (v. 10).

---

On the heels of Ziba's claims about Mephibosheth, David encountered a profane, violent man by the name of Shimei, who began to curse David and throw stones at the deposed king. The stones hit him, yet I have a feeling the words hurt more than the stones. The man's actions were wrong, but David feared his words might be right. When Abishai wanted to kill Shimei, David forbade it, saying the Lord may have *told* him to curse. He said, "It may be that the LORD will see my distress and repay me with good for the cursing I am receiving today" (v. 12).

Through all his ups and downs, victories and failures, we've never seen David walk through this kind of humiliation.

Jesus also walked the road of humiliation as He went to the cross. People spat on Him and slapped Him in the face. Unlike David, He was completely innocent. He could have summoned the armies of heaven or ordered the earth to quake, yet He "for the joy set before him endured the cross, scorning its shame, and sat down at the right hand of the throne of God" (Heb. 12:2).

Like Christ, we could be in the middle of God's will and find ourselves on a path of humiliation. Or like David, we could suffer the further humiliation of knowing we chose our own path. God is still merciful to meet us on the humiliating paths of our lives whether or not we chose them through rebellion.

Consider the timing of Shimei's attack—just as David was regaining a shred of strength! Just when Satan suspects we are regaining a spark of hope, he hastens to greet us with discouragement and rejection. Notice David's response to Abishai's request to avenge David's persecution: "My son, who is of my own flesh, is trying to take my life. How much more, then, this Benjamite! Leave him alone" (v. 11). David might have been saying: "My own beloved son has rejected me. There is nothing anyone can do to injure me any more deeply. Let him go ahead. Maybe I deserve it."

I want to express something to you that I hope you'll receive with your whole heart: We can still cry out to God for help even when we think we're getting what we deserve! God comes to us even when our pain is self-inflicted. Times of humiliation and persecution do not have to be permanent injuries.

Few experiences are more exhausting than keeping your head up through the unjust attacks, but all journeys have an end. Finally, "The king and all the people with him arrived at their destination exhausted. And there he refreshed himself" (v. 14).

How can you refresh yourself when you've been down a rocky path? One way is to appreciate the support you do receive.

Read on in 2 Samuel 16–17, and you'll see how David's friend Hushai the Arkite risked his life by defecting to Absalom, and then gave him bad advice to offset the wise counsel of Ahithophel. Ahithophel encouraged Absalom to pursue David and kill him. Hushai convinced him to wait and consolidate his hold on the nation first. Thus Hushai saved David's life in the early days of the rebellion.

But Hushai wasn't the only person working in David's interests. The priests Zadok and Abiathar risked their lives and those of their sons to send messages to David. They warned him not to stop before crossing the Jordan and not to stay with the troops lest Absalom follow Ahithophel's advice.

Sometimes when we're down, it's hard to see how many people have come to our aid. We're often so focused on our circumstances that we don't realize how many people God has sent to encourage us. At times I've cried out, "God, please help me get through this difficult time!" or "Please help me meet this deadline!" I am often humbled as He opens my eyes to all He's done and says to my heart, "I was the One who sent Mary Helen to your house with home-baked cookies. I was the One who told Nancy to send you a note of encouragement. I was the One who gave you that good laugh. I've been there all along."

God was there all along for David too.

I'd like to consider one last question from these chapters in 2 Samuel. Why did Ahithophel betray David while Hushai remained faithful? Hushai risked exposure and death by entering the household of the enemy. He helped buy time for his king by "counseling" and deceiving Absalom so that David could strengthen his forces. Why did he respond so differently to a leader who appeared to be on his way out? First Chronicles 27:33 offers a beautiful explanation: "Ahithophel was the king's counselor. Hushai the Arkite was the king's friend."

You and I have a "friend who sticks closer than a brother" (Prov. 18:24), for "greater love has no one than this, that he lay down his life for his friends" (John 15:13). No matter what happens, no matter who rejects you or humiliates you, God will never betray you. Stay faithful, believer. You are on the winning team. The King of all kings will return and take His rightful throne.

# DAY 68
## 2 Samuel 18:1–18

———∞∞———

So he gave the pillar his name. It is still called Absalom's Monument today (v. 18).

———∞∞———

In David and Absalom we watched an emotional match involving two opponents torn between love and hate. Now we will see one go down tragically. We can't change the story. We can only agree to be changed through it.

We saw that David won the battle of the counselors. Now came the battle of blood and bone. Absalom drew up his army to fight his father. David sent forth his army to fight the men of Absalom, but he gave each of his commanders, in the hearing of their troops, the same command. "Be gentle with the young man Absalom for my sake" (v. 5).

Imagine how demoralizing David's behavior must have been for the men who were risking their lives for him. Small wonder how Joab responded. He'd had enough of David's behavior.

The battle took place in the forest of Ephraim with twenty thousand casualties. Absalom rode his mule under a tree and caught his head in the branches. A soldier brought word to Joab that Absalom was "hanging around" in the area. The soldier feared harming Absalom because of David's words, but Joab hurried to kill the king's son.

At one time Absalom was a handsome and compassionate man. He loved his sister deeply, grieving the shame Amnon had heaped on her. He made a place for his desolate sister in his own home. He named his daughter Tamar in her honor. He tried to do the right things for Tamar, but he ended up doing all the wrong things for himself.

My oldest daughter Amanda has always been relatively easy to discipline. When she was a little girl and misbehaved, all I had to do was walk toward the drawer that held a flimsy plastic spatula and she would sweetly say, "I feel better!" Though she could not state the situation clearly, she chose to respond to discipline in the least painful way: "I feel better."

One day a good friend of mine grabbed that same spatula and swatted her little boy for repeatedly disobeying her. The son wasn't hurt, but he was as mad as a hornet. Amanda stood right next to him while his mother paddled him and continued to ask, "Do you feel better?" If looks could kill, my precious angel would have been dead! He finally screamed, "No, I not feel better!"

Those words could apply to Absalom. He didn't feel better after Amnon was in the grave. He didn't feel better when David let him return to Jerusalem without punishment. He didn't feel better after he was summoned to the king's quarters and reunited with his father. And after stealing the hearts of his father's people, he still didn't feel any better. Absalom ultimately possessed as little self-control as the brother he despised. His lack of self-control finally killed him.

Can you imagine the thoughts going through the head of that beautiful but troubled young man as he struggled to set himself free from the tree branches? The picture of his death was the picture of his life: the noose of bitterness choking the captive's cry. In the end, those close enough to hear him choking no longer cared.

Like departing words on a tombstone, we read Absalom's eulogy in verse 18: "Absalom had taken a pillar and erected it in the King's Valley as a monument to himself." At first glance, the verse seems to fit the chapter like a square peg in a round hole. At second glance, the passage relates perfectly to the verse before it.

I see great irony in the fact that the record of Absalom's grave—the "huge mound of stones" piled over him by Joab's men—and the account of the monument he erected to himself appear together in Scripture. The verses demonstrate that Absalom's death as a traitor remains far more memorable than his self-absorbed life. Through bitterness, Absalom's heart became as hard and cold as the pillar he raised. Even though David committed many sins and was unfair to others, his heart did not grow cold.

After Absalom's death, word reached the waiting David. He cried out, "O Absalom, my son, my son!" (2 Sam. 18:33). The words send chills up a parent's spine, don't they? Suddenly, a heart of tragically suppressed love exploded. Tears he should have cried long ago poured from his eyes. Words he should have said the moment he first saw his prodigal finally burst from his lips: "My son, O, my son!" He did not speak about him. He spoke right to him, as if his voice would carry to the depths of the pit where the body lay.

"If only I had died instead of you!" (v. 33).

Death would have been far easier than life without him. What grieving parent hasn't cried those same words? Felt those same emotions? And where was God when David lost his son? Where was He when a king's own countrymen pierced his son? Where was He when the blood poured forth? The same place He was when He lost His own Son.

# DAY 69
## 2 Samuel 19:1–8

⊶⊷

So the king got up and sat in the gate, and all the people were told: "Look, the king is sitting in the gate." Then they all came into the king's presence (v. 8).

⊶⊷

Divided loyalties had left God's chosen nation in an upheaval, and grief over Absalom was crippling and consuming David. Once again Joab stepped in. He went to David and said:

> *"Today you have humiliated all your men, who have just saved your life. . . . You have made it clear today that the commanders and their men mean nothing to you. I see that you would be pleased if Absalom were alive today and all of us were dead" (2 Sam. 19:5–6).*

Joab was warning him that unless David started acting like a king again, everyone would desert him.

The next time I suffer a painful loss, remind me not to call someone like Joab for a sympathetic ear. Nothing is more natural than grieving a devastating loss, but David was met by immediate condemnation from Joab.

I think a pretty good rule for comforting a grieving friend is to offer hugs and say little. Joab did not confront King David as a friend, however. He approached him as commander over the king's armies. He had the best interests of his soldiers in mind and not the emotional well-being of a mourning father. He had seen many lives stolen in battle. If we give Joab the benefit of the doubt, we could see a shred of humanity in his desire to see David cease mourning. If we don't, we can assume his resistance to David's grief showed his guilt for having disobeyed David's order to spare Absalom's life.

Even though Joab's heart was wrong, David concluded his advice was right. He returned to the business of the kingdom. David also realized that his army had fought for him, and he could not have them return in shame. So he got up and took his seat in the gateway. The words represented a pivotal moment—the king became accessible once more. David was back—in his heart—if not yet on his throne.

# DAY 70
## 2 Samuel 19:14–30

—∞∞∞—

"Ziba slandered your servant to my lord the king. But my lord the king
is like the Angel of God, so do whatever you think best" (v. 27).

—∞∞∞—

Apparently David's victory combined with his fair treatment of the defeated alliance won over the hearts of the men of Judah. So they escorted him back across the Jordan to Jerusalem. On the trip, David had encounters that showed his intention to bring peace to the land.

Mephibosheth was one who came to meet the returning David. He had obviously been mourning the king's situation: he "had not taken care of his feet or trimmed his mustache or washed his clothes from the day the king left until the day he returned safely" (v. 24). When David asked about Ziba's story that Mephibosheth had allied himself with Absalom, he told him it was absolutely untrue.

David responded in a puzzling fashion. He ordered the land be split between Ziba and Mephibosheth.

One of two reasons may have been at the heart of David's order. Either David was attempting to end the rivalry as simply as possible, or he was testing Mephibosheth's heart. He may have been employing some of the same wisdom his son Solomon later applied between two women fighting over a child (1 Kings 3:24–26). When Solomon suggested the child be cut in half and divided between them, the true mother emerged, ready to sacrifice her own position to spare the life of her son. Likewise, Mephibosheth's integrity emerged as he responded, in effect, "Let Ziba have everything as long as I have you back safely."

No doubt, the encounter between David and Mephibosheth was a priceless moment—an example of authentic restoration. Ironically, the son of his own blood was never reconciled to David, but his adopted son escorted him back to his throne, inspired by love and loyalty.

I cannot help but notice an astonishing parallel. God's own beloved nation, His chosen ones, His natural descendants, refused to be reconciled to Him through Christ; yet the adopted sons—the church—accepted Him, loved Him, remained loyal to Him, and will escort Him to His rightful throne!

# DAY 71
## 2 Samuel 20:14–22

---

"I am a peaceful person, one of the faithful in Israel, but you are trying to destroy a city that is like a mother in Israel. Why would you devour the Lord's inheritance?" (v. 19).

---

When people begin to bicker, they provide an opportunity for slick trouble-makers. In this case his name was Sheba. He sounded a trumpet and called the Israelites to a rebellion against David. All the men of Israel followed him.

Once again David was faced with a civil war.

He sent Amasa, the new commanding general, to gather the army of Judah. But when Amasa returned, he found Joab waiting with the army ready to march. Joab took his cousin Amasa by the beard as if to give him the customary kiss of greeting and stabbed his rival, leaving him to bleed to death in the road. (We can't seem to get rid of Joab, can we? We may as well accept him as a permanent figure in this story, whether we like it or not!) So under new leadership, the army pursued Sheba to the city called Abel Beth Maacah. Joab laid siege to the city and prepared to break down the wall.

As the plot thickened, one woman was willing to become more than a spectator to imminent disaster. She negotiated a solution to the problem. At her urging and persuasion, the inhabitants tossed the head of Sheba over the wall, and Joab lifted the siege. As a result, an entire city was spared.

Let's allow her a moment's glory. We don't even know her name. She wasn't looking for recognition. She was looking for her city's salvation. An entire village could have perished because one person, Sheba, was such a troublemaker.

I know a woman whose son was openly pursued by a homosexual college professor. Her son could have been easy prey for the shrewd predator. The professor had confused many other young men, but no one was willing to confront him. The woman tried to enlist her husband's support. He did not want to get involved. She tried to enlist her pastor's support. He did not want to get involved. She finally approached the dean of students and an investigation ensued. Many people came forward, and mountains of evidence emerged. The professor never again pursued another young man on that campus. The woman's son is now a devoted husband and father. He credits his mother for having snatched him and others from the jaws of a ferocious lion.

# DAY 72
## 2 Samuel 21:1–9

———oee———

He asked the Gibeonites, "What should I do for you? How can I wipe out
this guilt so that you will bring a blessing on the LORD's inheritance?" (v. 3).

———oee———

A sobering realization falls on us from our next passage. Many years later,
the people of Israel were still suffering the ill effects of a king who was rebellious
to God. I once heard a preacher say, "Never forget, God can outwait you. Time
is always on His side." That preacher could have been thinking of what happened
next in Israel.

> *During the reign of David, there was a famine for three succes-*
> *sive years; so David sought the face of the LORD. The LORD said,*
> *"It is on account of Saul and his blood-stained house; it is because*
> *he put the Gibeonites to death" (2 Sam. 21:1).*

God was making an important point. He was holding the nation of Israel to
an old vow made with the Gibeonites generations prior to David's reign. I think
you will find the circumstances of the vow very interesting.

The story appears in Joshua 9. When the Israelites entered Canaan, the Lord
sent a great fear of them upon the peoples. Most of the people groups in Palestine
joined forces to fight the Israelites, but the people of Gibeon chose a wiser and
sneakier course of action. They dressed as if they had come from a distant country
to make a treaty with Israel. The elders of Israel did not inquire of the Lord and so
were fooled. They made a promise never to destroy the Gibeonites.

Fast forward three hundred years. During his forty-two years as king, Saul
sought to destroy the Gibeonites, but God has a long memory—much longer
than a few hundred years.

God meant for His people to be good for their word. He still does. Surely
one reason He expects His people to be good for their word is so that observers
will come to believe He is good for His. Israel had to keep her agreement with
the Gibeonites even though they should never have entered the agreement. Saul
broke the agreement with the probable aid of his sons and tried to annihilate
a people innocent of their father's sins. Ironically, Saul's sons were brought to
account for their father's sins.

God considers vows extremely important. Ecclesiastes 5:5–6 says, "It is better
not to vow than to make a vow and not fulfill it. Do not let your mouth lead you
into sin. And do not protest to the temple messenger, 'My vow was a mistake.'"
Countless men and women have broken marriage vows by claiming their marriage

was a mistake. Maybe they were like the Israelites who did not inquire of the Lord and were sorry later, but a vow is still a very serious thing. Others have vowed to honor their mates, but although they still live under the same roof, honor moved out long ago. Still others have decided they prefer richer over poorer. We don't live in a society that supports the seriousness of long-term vows, but we live under the heavenly authority who does.

Many young people have taken vows of purity to God through a wonderful program called True Love Waits. I spoke at a youth camp one summer in which several high schoolers came to me individually grieving their broken vows. They asked my advice, and I didn't have to think very long to answer based on what I understand about God and His Word.

I explained to them that I have also made promises to God along the way that I have not kept. Rather than continue in disobedience, God desires two responses to broken vows: repent and recommit! Several vows I made to God as a teenager I broke within the first couple of years; but after recommitment, most of those have been kept for decades through the grace of God.

Oh yes, I wish I had kept every vow just as I had promised from the very beginning; but I am so thankful to have had the opportunity by God's grace to recommit my life and try again successfully.

The Gibeonites made what seemed a horrible request. The very horror of it should remind us how very seriously God takes vows. They wanted pure blood revenge—seven of Saul's male descendants to kill and to expose their bodies to the elements.

I'm sure your stomach turns over as mine does, but again, a vow is a serious matter. The Israelites recommitted themselves to the vow they made with the Gibeonites by satisfying their demands.

Christ has led us to a new form of warfare far more effective than guns and tanks. We have weapons of grace, mercy, love, and the Sword of the Spirit which is the Word of God. Anybody out there need your forgiveness? Your acceptance? Your release? It's time for some old battles to end. Just like the Israelites, we will suffer in ways that seem totally unrelated when we allow matters to continue unsettled and outside the will of God. Rebellion inevitably leads to famine in our relationship to God. A new beginning is as close as the fresh smell of rain.

# DAY 73
## 2 Samuel 21:15–22

The Philistines again waged war against Israel. David went down with his soldiers,
and they fought the Philistines, but David became exhausted (v. 15).

King David returned to Jerusalem and realized he had to take back his
throne rather than receive it from cheerful givers. The business of politics and
inevitable battles must have seemed insurmountable. But one last enemy arose
before he could take a breath and proclaim a victory.

One very familiar enemy. One very persistent enemy.

The Philistines were at it again.

Again David went to fight them, but this time he became exhausted in
battle.

I am so thankful God chose to tell us David knew about exhaustion in
battle! I need to know that others have experienced the weariness of fighting the
same old enemy over and over. The word for exhausted in Hebrew is *uwph*. The
word even sounds like something you might say at a glimpse of an old enemy!
*Uwph* means "to cover, to fly, faint, flee away."[18] It is the overwhelming desire to
run and hide.

When was the last time you wanted to run and hide? Few things make us
want to flee more than the prospect of fighting an old battle. The moment an
old enemy reappears, we want to run into the nearest forest and never come out.
Have you ever noticed that Satan always chooses just the right time to haunt you
through an old enemy? When you haven't had enough rest, when things have
been emotional and turbulent, when you've been swinging from one extreme to
the other, when you're completely vulnerable—that's when the enemy strikes.

Satan is the counterfeit god of perfect timing. He's watching for just the
right moment to pull the rug out from under us, but even that rug is under God's
feet. And God always has victory in mind! He will never allow Satan to discourage you without a plan to lead you to victory! We may not always follow Christ
to victory, but He is always leading! "Thanks be to God, who always leads us in
triumphal procession in Christ and through us spreads everywhere the fragrance
of the knowledge of him" (2 Cor. 2:14).

One of the most important truths we can apply from David's ongoing battles with the Philistines is that God will always lead us to victory—but He will
lead us His way.

# DAY 74
## 2 Samuel 22:1–51

---

I called to the LORD in my distress; I called to my God.
From His temple He heard my voice, and my cry for help reached His ears (v. 7).

---

Nothing is more appropriate than celebrating a victory God has sovereignly and majestically won for us! After all the ups and downs of David's journey, in chapter 22 we get to experience the sheer pleasure of attending a celebration. Anyone who has ever experienced victory in Jesus is invited to attend. Someone else just wouldn't understand.

> David sang to the LORD the words of this song when the Lord
> delivered him from the hand of all his enemies and from the hand
> of Saul (2 Sam. 22:1).

Think about what motivated David to sing these words. Sometimes God puts a new song in our mouths—a hymn of praise to our God! Other times He brings us back to an old song, one which fell from our lips many years ago and has gathered a film of dust only a fresh breath could blow away. No doubt about it, sometimes God wants to hear an old song from a new heart. This was the case for David.

David remembered the words he had sung many years before, after God delivered him from the hand of Saul. I believe his recent victory over the Philistines rekindled the remembrance of his victory over Saul because of several similarities. Both conflicts seemed they would never end. Both conflicts sapped his strength. Both conflicts caused him to rely on another's strength.

Decades wedged their way between the solos of this one song. How different the sound of the same singer's voice—so young and daring when first he sang. Now the voice was old, but suddenly, unexpectedly filled with the passion of a young warrior. I believe the words comprise the testimony of an old man with a fresh passion. Praise God, we need never get too old to experience a young passion!

Chapter 22 is a lengthy song of praise, as David catalogued the ways God had worked in his life: "He reached down from on high and took hold of me; he drew me out of deep waters. He rescued me from my powerful enemy, from my foes, who were too strong for me" (vv. 17–18).

You will notice in chapter 22 that David is serving us a slice of his personal history with God. Are you actively building a history with God? Can you readily say that the two of you have done lots of living together since your salvation? Have you allowed Him to reveal Himself to you in the many experiences of life?

If you are a Christian but you've attempted a life of self-sufficiency, you may not be able to relate to having a close personal relationship with God. But claiming Him personally is the most precious right of any believer! Look at the revolutionary news the risen Lord told Mary Magdalene: "Go . . . to my brothers and tell them, 'I am returning to my Father and your Father, to my God and your God'" (John 20:17). Blessed Calvary, cheated grave that made Christ's God my very own! Glory in the cross!

The Book of 2 Samuel is not the only place David's words of victory are found. Psalm 18 contains an almost identical set of verses to those God placed in 2 Samuel 22. One of the exceptions is too precious to miss. Verse 1 of Psalm 18 simply declares, "I love you, O LORD, my strength."

"I love you, Lord." No demands. No despair. Just "I love you." The words might seem more fitting as the grand finale rather than the opening line. Their sudden appearance suggests they were words that could not wait. The psalmist considered his delivered state and his Father's stubborn love, and he burst forth with the words: "I love you, Lord."

The One who delivered David from his enemies was no distant deity. He was the object of the psalmist's deepest emotions, the One with whom he shared authentic relationship. David deeply loved God. David was a man after God's own heart because his desire was also the sheer pleasure of the Father. The Father's deepest desire is to be loved—genuinely loved—by His child.

If 2 Samuel 22 and Psalm 18 compel us to see one thing, it is that God is a personal God we each can call our own.

- He is my strength when I am weak.
- He is my rock when I am slipping.
- He is my deliverer when I am trapped.
- He is my fortress when I am crumbling.
- He is my refuge when I am pursued.
- He is my shield when I am exposed.
- He is my Lord when life spins out of control.

A heart that makes Him its own—one that can state, "He is mine"—is a heart that cannot help but love.

I love you, Lord.

# DAY 75
## 2 Samuel 23:8–17

—∞∞∞—

David was extremely thirsty and said, "If only someone would bring me water to drink from the well at the city gate of Bethlehem!" So three of the warriors broke through the Philistine camp and drew water from the well (vv. 15–16).

—∞∞∞—

God led David to victory through all four of the battles mentioned in 2 Samuel 21:15–22, but He brought the victory to David through someone else. Just like us, I'm sure David's preference would have been for God to make him the hero and leave others in awe over his great strength. But God had other plans. He saved David, all right, but He purposely made him dependent on someone else.

Several wonderful reasons might exist for the method God used, which we can pick up by reading through the list of David's mighty men in 2 Samuel 23. Consider a few of these rationales:

1. *For the sake of the people.* Israel did not need David to be like a god to them. He could not deal with being put on that kind of pedestal or subjected to that kind of pressure. He was bound to disappoint them. When it comes to hero worship, the line between love and hate is very fine! How many close followers have turned against their leaders? God will never allow any of us to be the only one through whom He appears to be working mightily.

2. *For the sake of King David.* Do you remember what happened when David was so highly exalted on his throne that he became disconnected from his people? Remember how lonely he was for his friend? Remember how isolated he became? Remember what happened when he thought he had risen above the normal duties of a king and stayed behind in the spring when other kings went off to war? That's when the nightmare began! David believed his own press. He came to believe he could not be overtaken. He was wrong. God protected David by not always letting him be the hero. He gave David a few heroes instead—men who commanded his respect. He humbled David and made him depend on them for his life. None of us will escape this important life lesson. God will force us to need help.

3. *For the sake of the men he empowered.* People can easily be discouraged if they perceive that God works mightily through others but never works through them. God does not play favorites. Anyone who cries out to Him, He answers. Anyone who surrenders to His call, He uses.

# DAY 76
## 2 Samuel 24:1–10

—◆◆◆—

The LORD's anger burned against Israel again, and it stirred up David
against them to say: "Go, count the people of Israel and Judah" (v. 1).

—◆◆◆—

Second Samuel 24 gives us an opportunity to do some research into an
easily misunderstood event in David's history. Satan always seeks to make us
believe that God is unfair or unkind. In this task, the adversary particularly likes
to use a few difficult-to-understand events recorded in Scripture.

Chapter 24 may be confusing and unsettling to us if we don't keep one
thought in mind: we do not know every fact about every event in Scripture. We
don't always have the explanations for certain events and acts of God. He is sovereign. He owes us no explanation. He purposes to teach us to walk by faith and
not by sight. When Scripture records an event or judgment of God that seems
cruel or unfair, we need to do two things:

1. *Acknowledge that His ways are higher than ours.* We do not have all the
information or understanding. We have no idea the depth of evil God may have
seen in human hearts that necessitated such serious judgment.

2. *Acknowledge what we do know about God.* Anytime you are overwhelmed by
what you do not know or understand about God, consider what you do know about
Him. Your heart and mind will be quieted, and you will be able to walk in faith.

In 2 Samuel 24, we get a chance to practice using this method:

> *Again the anger of the LORD burned against Israel, and he incited
> David against them, saying, "Go and take a census of Israel and
> Judah." So the king said to Joab and the army commanders with
> him, "Go throughout the tribes of Israel from Dan to Beersheba
> and enroll the fighting men, so that I may know how many there
> are" (2 Sam. 24:1–2).*

But the counting of the fighting men was barely completed when David realized he had made a serious mistake. He was conscience-stricken about his actions
and he said to the Lord, "I have sinned greatly in what I have done. Now, O LORD, I
beg you, take away the guilt of your servant. I have done a very foolish thing" (v. 10).

Before David got up the next morning, the word of the Lord had come to Gad
the prophet, David's seer: "Go and tell David, 'This is what the LORD says: I am
giving you three options. Choose one of them for me to carry out against you'" (v. 12).

God's three options were all dreadful: three years of famine, three months
of defeat in war, or three days of plague. David chose to fall into God's hand
rather than those of men. In the ensuing three days of plague, seventy thousand
Israelites died.

As you can see, this gives us the perfect opportunity to employ the method of Bible study I suggested—to measure what you don't know or understand by what you do! I see at least two occurrences that Satan could twist to cause doubt or dismay in the reader: (1) God's role in David's sin, and (2) punishment that appears to exceed the crime.

Let's consider the first point. The first verse of chapter 24 says, "[God] incited David against them, saying, 'Go and take a census of Israel and Judah.'" A brief look at this one verse may cause us to wonder why God would ask David to do something and then kill seventy thousand people as a result.

Just as God included four Gospels to tell the story of the incarnate Christ, He recorded many of the occurrences of David's reign in the books of 2 Samuel and 1 Chronicles. We can better understand passages or events by comparing these "parallel" accounts.

First Chronicles 21:1 sheds a little light on what happened to David. "Satan rose up against Israel and incited David to take a census of Israel" (1 Chron. 21:1).

So who did it? Who enticed David to sin—God or Satan? As we confront something we do not know, consider what we do know. How could the following Scriptures shed light on our understanding of 2 Samuel 24:1 and 1 Chronicles 21:1?

> "When tempted, no one should say, 'God is tempting me.' For God cannot be tempted by evil, nor does he tempt anyone; but each one is tempted when, by his own evil desire, he is dragged away and enticed" (James 1:13–14).

> "No temptation has seized you except what is common to man. And God is faithful; he will not let you be tempted beyond what you can bear. But when you are tempted, he will also provide a way out so that you can stand up under it" (1 Cor. 10:13).

From these two passages we know that God does not tempt us. He may allow us to be tempted to test, prove, or help us to grow; but He is definitely not the tempter. In our temptation He always makes a way of escape.

So how do we explain the activity of God in David's sin? His role must have been somewhat like His part in the suffering of Job. God did not tempt Job; God gave Satan permission to test Job. In the same way we can be assured that God did not tempt David to sin and then judge him harshly for it. God has no sin; therefore He is incapable of enticing one to sin. He did, however, allow David to be tempted because He saw something in David's heart that needed to be exposed.

# DAY 77
## 2 Samuel 24:11–17

⸺◦◦◦◦⸺

When David saw the angel striking the people, he said to the LORD,
"Look, I am the one who has sinned; I am the one who has done wrong" (v. 17).

⸺◦◦◦◦⸺

If we are not careful to study this text, it seems that seventy thousand men died solely as a result of David's sin. So let's apply our method from yesterday once again. What is the first thing we do *not know?* We do not know why God's anger burned against Israel. But what *can we know* in order to shed light on Israel's action that angered God?

Based on Deuteronomy, we can conclude that Israel's sin against God angered Him. Deuteronomy 28:1–24 contains the promises of blessing and cursing. In general, God promised blessing for obedience and cursing for disobedience.

We don't know what Israel had done to make God so angry, but we do know that His judgment was consistent with that which He had promised for rebellion against His commands. Somehow Israel had severely disobeyed God. Several scholars suggest God may have been judging Israel for their quickness to desert David, God's sovereign choice, and follow Absalom.

Why, then, was David also wrong? I'd like to suggest three possible reasons David was involved in the anger of God toward Israel.

1. *He deserted the throne God had given him and did not trust God to fight his battles for him.* Earlier, David had trusted God to direct his battles and to fight them for him. This time David ignored God and depended on human resources and wisdom.

2. *He did not stand in the gap and intercede for the sins of his nation.* In Exodus 32–33, God revoked a portion of His judgment on Israel as a direct result of the humility and intercession of Moses. David saw the evil ways of his nation and did not intercede or take any responsibility. David finally arrived at a place to cry out on behalf of the people, but not until the angel threatened his own area.

3. *He possessed wrong motives for taking the census.* David fell to the temptation of counting his fighting men either out of the sin of pride, distrust, or both. Anyway, as king of Israel, David's heart was wrong toward God. God had proved Himself many times in the life of this king. David had no grounds for pride or distrust.

# DAY 78
## 2 Samuel 24:18–25

———⊷⊶———

Araunah said, "Why has my lord the king come to his servant?" David replied,
"To buy the threshing floor from you in order to build an altar to the LORD,
so the plague on the people may be halted" (v. 21).

———⊷⊶———

The exact location of the threshing floor of Araunah the Jebusite was the most vital place in Israel's history. Scripture says God grieved when the angel reached the threshing floor of Araunah the Jebusite and stretched out his hand to destroy Jerusalem. The Hebrew word for "grieve" in this passage is *nacham*. It carries the idea of breathing deeply as "a physical display of one's feeling, usually sorrow, compassion, or comfort."[19] The word was used once before in 2 Samuel 12:24, where it meant "being consoled over the death of an infant child."[20]

When the angel of the Lord stretched out his hand at the threshing floor of Araunah the Jebusite, God seemed to cry. He "panted" in grief somewhat like one "being consoled over the death of an infant child."

I want to suggest that the primary reason God grieved as if over the death of a child at that exact location was related to an event that took place on that very soil many years before. In Genesis 22, Abraham obeyed God and almost sacrificed his son Isaac—in this very spot.

God did not coincidentally grieve at this exact spot generations later during David's reign, then coincidentally direct an altar, and ultimately the temple of God, to be built there as well. Each occurrence was based on the vivid lesson God taught about substitutionary death at the same location. Look at the similarities!

*The altar.* God commanded that an altar for sacrifice be built by both Abraham and David—and ultimately by Solomon—on the same spot. Something at that location obviously represented sacrifice and substitution.

*The timing.* Genesis 22:10–12 tells us that when Abraham reached out his hand and took the knife to slay his son, God intervened and stopped him. God then presented a sacrifice in his place. Consider the timing during David's reign: 1 Chronicles 21:16 tells us "David looked up and saw the angel of the LORD standing between heaven and earth, with a drawn sword in his hand extended over Jerusalem."

Of the same event, 2 Samuel 24:16 says,

> *When the angel stretched out his hand to destroy Jerusalem, the LORD was grieved because of the calamity and said to the angel who was afflicting the people, "Enough! Withdraw your hand."' The angel of the Lord was then at the threshing floor of Araunah the Jebusite.*

In both cases, the moment God saw a sword raised to destroy life at this location, He intervened and accepted substitutionary sacrifices. That both of these events happened at the same place and at the moment a sword was being drawn is no accident.

When the angel of the Lord drew his sword at the threshing floor of Araunah the Jebusite, I believe God remembered a father who was willing in obedience to take the life of his dearly loved son. I believe God not only cried over the memory of Abraham and Isaac but over the gospel they foretold—"For God so loved the world, that he gave his only begotten Son, that whosoever believeth in him should not perish, but have everlasting life" (John 3:16 KJV).

The day that Abraham offered Isaac portrayed the cross as the ultimate altar of sacrifice and the substitutionary death of the unblemished Lamb as the perfect sacrifice. Many years later, during David's reign, God saw the angel raise his sword over the lives of His people at that same location, and He grieved and said "Enough!" Why? Because when God saw the threshing floor at Mount Moriah, He saw mercy—mercy that would finally be complete on Calvary when God would look on the suffering of His Son and be satisfied (Isa. 53:11). The legacy of sacrifice on Mount Moriah would continue from Abraham to David to Solomon because access to God is forever based on sacrifice and mercy.

As we conclude, we must meditate for a moment on David's words as Araunah offered him the threshing floor free of charge. He said, "I will not sacrifice to the LORD my God burnt offerings that cost me nothing" (v. 24).

Mount Moriah did not represent a cheap offering. The sacrifice depicted on that mountain throughout the ages was costly. Abraham's sacrifice cost him dearly. God's sacrifice cost Him severely. The chastened king's sacrifice was costly as well. At the threshing floor of Araunah, the cost of sacrifice was counted—and God wept.

When faced in Scripture with something you don't understand and when God seems cruel, never forget how God identifies Himself: "Then the LORD came down in the cloud and stood there with him and proclaimed his name, the LORD. And he passed in front of Moses, proclaiming, 'The LORD, the LORD, the compassionate and gracious God, slow to anger, abounding in love and faithfulness'" (Exod. 34:5–6).

When you don't know why, a personal history with God will tell you Who.

# DAY 79
## 1 Kings 1:1–4

———∞∞∞———

Now King David was old and getting on in years. Although they
covered him with bedclothes, he could not get warm (v. 1).

———∞∞∞———

I am saddened by the initial words of 1 Kings. The words suggest the inevitable to us. One of the most well-documented lives in history was hastening to an end. Our David? The one who had killed a lion and a bear? The one who had thundered the ground with the frame of an overgrown Philistine? The one who had made caves his bed and had stolen the spear of a savage king? The one who had conquered nations and called on the might of heaven? I am almost shocked by his sudden mortality. As he lay chilled beneath the weight of heavy blankets, we realize his humanity and his frailty.

By the standards of his day, David was not an extremely old man. He was approaching his death at a far younger age than the patriarchs who preceded him. Perhaps his seventy years of active living could easily compare to one hundred years of simply being alive. He had known virtually every extremity of the human experience—unparalleled success, unabashed rebellion, unashamed mourning, and uninhibited celebration. Life rarely free of extremity can be life rarely free of anxiety. It takes its toll.

Much of my life has been lived in the extremes. I seem to find myself in the valley or on the mountain as often as in between. Some years ago God led me to express on paper my responses to the extremities of life. I'd like to share these words with you.

> *Satisfy me not with the lesser of You*
> *Find me no solace in shadows of the True*
> *No ordinary measure of extraordinary means*
> *The depth, the length, the breadth of You*
> *And nothing in between.*
> *Etch these words upon my heart, knowing all the while*
> *No ordinary roadblocks plague extraordinary miles*
> *Your power as my portion, Your glory as my fare*
> *Take me to extremities,*
> *But meet me fully there.*

# DAY 80
## 1 Kings 1:11–31

———⁕———

Bathsheba bowed with her face to the ground, paying homage to the king,
and said, "May my lord King David live forever!" (v. 31).

———⁕———

After a long absence from Scripture, the prophet Nathan reentered the
scene. He joined Bathsheba in the plan to (1) inform David that the king's oldest
surviving son, Adonijah, was following in the footsteps of his deceased half-
brother Absalom, declaring himself king, and (2) to put Solomon on the throne.

I am touched by his support of David and the union with Bathsheba after
acknowledgment of their grave sin. Nathan was the prophet God used to confront the sin between David and Bathsheba. He was also the one who warned
Bathsheba about Adonijah's plans, which probably would have resulted in death
for her and Solomon. Nathan showed himself to be a true prophet of God. He
could both confront sin and lovingly care for sinners.

Nathan knew Bathsheba was the key to restoring decision-making strength
to the king, so he sent her to inform David. Then he confirmed her words to the
king. Bathsheba captured David's full attention with the threat to Solomon's
succession. Then Nathan confirmed Bathsheba's claims. Apparently, Bathsheba
stepped out of the room so Nathan could have full access to the king. Then David
confirmed his promise to Bathsheba that Solomon was to be his successor.

David could easily have issued the orders without Bathsheba being present,
but he summoned his queen so that he could make an oath to her. The words were
addressed directly to Bathsheba, intimating to us that this was a matter not only
between king and queen but also between husband and wife—father and mother.

I wonder if Bathsheba was a sight for David's tired eyes. To the exclusion
of all good judgment, she had captivated his attention on a moonlit roof many
years before. Now after the passage of decades, I imagine he found her beautiful
once more.

Need has a way of breathing fresh life into a soul, if just for a moment. We
will see David, who seemed chilled with the onset of death, assume swift control,
perform the will of God, and meet the desires of his queen's heart. Whether on
his sickbed or on his throne, David was indeed still king.

# DAY 81
## 1 Kings 1:32–48

———∞∞∞———

All the people followed him, playing flutes and rejoicing with such
a great joy that the earth split open from the sound (v. 40).

———∞∞∞———

David purposely called three specific men to escort the new king Solomon
to his rightful place of authority. Nathan was the primary prophet of the day.
Zadok was the priest, and Benaiah was a mighty warrior. For the nation to be
strong, all four areas of authority needed to be present: prophet, priest, warrior,
and king. Interestingly, our Lord and Savior Jesus Christ will ultimately fill every
one of those positions. All authority has been given to Christ! (Matt. 28:18).
Under one Head, all nations will finally be unified.

David sent his most trustworthy warrior and his army to protect Solomon.
They were to put Solomon on King David's mule and escort him. Customarily, a
king rode on a mule to signify his intent to be a servant to the people. The mule
was often dressed with a wreath of flowers around its neck or a royal drape over
its back.

Solomon surely knew he would one day be king. He knew the time would
come, but I wonder if he knew what it would be like. Did a servant girl tell him
three VIPs were at the door to speak to him? Or did he hear the bray of the mule?
We simply read that Zadok, Nathan, Benaiah, the Kerethites, and the Pelethites
went down and put Solomon on King David's mule.

Picture the scene as Solomon took the ride of his life!

David specifically commanded the men to escort Solomon to Gihon. Two
springs provided Jerusalem's water supply: the En Rogel spring and the Gihon
spring. According to 1 Kings 1:9, Adonijah was staging his own coronation at
En Rogel.

The Gihon spring was directly east of the city wall. The ancient Hebrew
people believed God's glory and authority would come from the east. The Gihon
spring did not provide a steady flow, but gushed "out at irregular intervals, twice
a day in the dry season to four or five times in the rainy season. Water issues
from a crack sixteen feet long in the rock."[21] Even the name was significant. The
name Gihon comes from a Hebrew word that means "a bursting forth."[22] A new
king was bursting on the scene to supply the nation of Israel with security and
authority.

Zadok the priest took the horn of oil from the sacred tent and anointed
Solomon. Could this have been the same horn tipped by the hand of Samuel over
the head of a young shepherd boy? What other horn would have had a place in
the sacred tent?

Solomon is not described like Absalom and Adonijah, handsome and obvious choices for a would-be king. He may not have been the natural choice in the eyes of men. He was not the oldest of the sons of David. But he represented God's divine mercy. He was the embodiment of second chances. He was the innocence that came from guilt. He was God's choice, as history would prove.

I find enormous security in the consistency of God. He is always merciful. Christ Jesus would never have become flesh to dwell among us had it not been for man's scandalous sin. Jesus certainly did not display the image of the king that Israel was expecting, yet He was the embodiment of second chances. He took our guilt on His innocent shoulders and became sin for us so we could become the righteousness of God in Him (2 Cor. 5:21). Why? Because we were God's choice.

When David received the news from his royal officials, "the king bowed in worship on his bed and said, 'Praise be to the LORD'" (vv. 47–48). This verse records the last time God used the word "king" in the Book of 1 Kings in reference to His beloved David. God chose to pen this last reference to King David in a sentence eternally linked to two responses:

1. *Worship.* Too weak to move to the floor, David fell on his face right where he was.

2. *Praise.* "Praise be to the LORD, the God of Israel, who has allowed my eyes to see a successor on my throne today" (v. 48).

David's rule ended just as it officially began. His stiffened body bowed before God on his final day as king with the same abandon he demonstrated when he danced through the streets of Jerusalem.

Was it not he who said, "Bless the LORD, O my soul: and all that is within me, bless his holy name" (Ps. 103:1 KJV). With all that was within him, he once danced. On that last day as king, he bowed to worship.

David's actions were often contradictory, but one consistency he wove throughout his life and reign—he was a man of worship, a man after God's own heart.

I'm thankful David enjoyed a brief reprieve from his sickbed. I was not ready to part with him yet. Were you? Deep within the aging king we can still see glimpses of a heart after God's own. May God deal tenderly with us as we approach his journey's end.

# DAY 82
### 1 Chronicles 22:11–19

—

"The Lord your God is with you, isn't He? And hasn't He given you rest
on every side? . . . Get started building the Lord God's sanctuary" (vv. 18–19).

—

Historians generally agree that David lived somewhere between one to two
years after Solomon assumed his reign. God allowed David the strength to prepare the new king for public coronation and for an effective beginning.

The first order of business for the new king was the building of a house for
the "Name of the Lord" (1 Chron. 22:7). Before he died, the old king gathered
the materials and drafted the plans for the work.

The Book of 1 Chronicles records the vivid account of the extensive preparations David made before his death (1 Chron. 22:5). Then David shared with
Solomon all that had been gathered for the building of the sanctuary and all who
had been commissioned to help. I find his words so pertinent and applicable to us
today: "Now begin the work, and the Lord be with you" (v. 16). In other words,
"I've set aside everything you will need. You have all the materials and all the
support your task will require. Now get started."

When I was a little girl, I often remember my mother giving her children
various instructions that were often received with moans, complaints, and questions. She'd finally say, "I've already told you. Now, get busy." Her words, like
David's, were wise and practical. God provides what we need. Now we, like
Solomon, need to get busy.

God promised His plans are to prosper us, to give us hope and a future
(Jer. 29:11). The Word of God and Christ's indwelling Spirit equip us to fulfill
the works preordained for us in God's perfect plan. As my mom would say, "Get
busy!"

Some of the most important words ever formed on David's tongue appear in
1 Chronicles 22:19: "Now devote your heart and soul to seeking the Lord your
God." The Hebrew word for devote is *nathan*. It means "to give, place, add, send
forth. *Nathan* indicates fastening something in place."[23] I especially love the idea
this wonderful definition expresses in the word "fastening." David told Solomon
and the leaders of Israel to fasten their hearts to seeking the Lord.

David's choice of words challenges us too—to fasten our hearts to Him and
get busy!

# DAY 83
## 1 Chronicles 28:1–10

———◆———

"As for you, Solomon my son, know the God of your father,
and serve Him with a whole heart and a willing mind, for the LORD
searches every heart and understands the intention of every thought" (v. 9).

———◆———

Chapter 28 of 1 Chronicles rings with strong statements from David. He reminded Solomon that God had chosen both him and his task. God had said to David: "Solomon your son is the one who will build my house and my courts, for I have chosen him" (v. 6). Then David summed up his godly, fatherly advice in verse 9. Let's read it again:

> *You, my son Solomon, acknowledge the God of your father, and*
> *serve him with wholehearted devotion and with a willing mind,*
> *for the LORD searches every heart and understands every motive*
> *behind the thoughts.*

David's words to Solomon apply to us in every area of potential success. David gave his son three vital directives we would be wise to obey:

1. *Acknowledge God.* Acknowledging God first thing every morning transforms my day. I often begin my day by reconfirming His authority over me and submitting to Him as Lord in advance of my daily circumstances. I try to accept the words of Joshua 24:15 as a personal daily challenge: "Choose for yourselves this day whom you will serve." When I fail to begin my day by settling the matter of authority, I am often in a mess by noon! Remember, any day not surrendered to the Spirit of God will likely be lived in the flesh (Gal. 5:16–17). Spiritual living does not come naturally—sin does. The first step to victory is acknowledging the authority of God in our lives.

2. *Serve Him with wholehearted devotion.* The Hebrew word for "wholehearted" is *shalem* and means "unhewn, untouched stones." In the Old Testament, *shalem* often referred to rocks that were uncut.[24] Notice something quite interesting about the temple God commanded Solomon to build. First Kings 6:7 tells us, "In building the temple, only blocks dressed at the quarry were used, and no hammer, chisel or any other iron tool was heard at the temple site while it was being built." Do you see the significance? No stone could be cut in the temple. The uncut stones represented the kind of devotion God was demanding from His nation—Shalem, wholehearted devotion, uncut hearts. David was used of God to describe *shalem* perfectly in Psalm 86:11: "Teach me your way, O LORD, and I will walk in your truth; give me an undivided heart, that I may fear your name."

Do you have a divided heart? Does God have only a piece of your heart, but the rest belongs to you or someone else? If you've given your heart wholly to God, perhaps you remember a time when your heart *was* divided.

A divided heart places our entire lives in jeopardy. Only God can be totally trusted with our hearts. He doesn't demand our complete devotion to feed His ego but to provide for our safety. God uses an undivided heart to keep us out of trouble. David learned the price of a divided heart the hard way. He lived with the repercussions for the rest of his life. Let's just take his word for it and surrender now! Never forget, God's commands are for our good.

3. *Serve Him with a willing spirit.* The Hebrew word for "willing" in this reference is *chaphets*, which means "to find pleasure in, take delight in, be pleased with, have an affection for; to desire; to choose; to bend, bow. The main meaning is to feel a strong, positive attraction for something, to like someone or something very much."[25] Do you see what God is saying? He wants us to serve Him and honor Him because we want to! Because it pleases us! Because we choose to! You see, the Lord searches every heart and understands every motive behind the thoughts! Hear the beat of His tender heart as He says, "Choose me because you delight in me!"

Many motives exist for serving God other than pleasure and delight. God wants us to serve Him with a willing spirit, one that would choose no other way. Right now you may be frustrated because serving and knowing God is not your greatest pleasure. You may be able to instantly acknowledge a divided heart. Your question may be, *How can I change the way I feel?* You can't. But God can. Give Him your heart—your whole heart. Give Him permission to change it.

The words of Deuteronomy 30:6 have changed my life and my heart:

> The LORD your God will circumcise your hearts and the hearts of your descendants, so that you may love him with all your heart and with all your soul, and live.

I pray daily that God will circumcise my heart to love Him. I know we will never be men and women after God's own heart with halfhearted devotion. A heart wholly devoted to God is a heart like His.

We started this journey with a pair of underlying questions: Why was David a man after God's own heart? And how can I be a man or woman after God's own heart?

Any old heart will do. Any whole heart will do.

# DAY 84
## 1 Chronicles 29:1–9

---

"The task is great, for the temple will not be for man, but for the LORD God. So to the best of my ability I've made provision for the house of my God" (vv. 1–2).

---

One of my most heartfelt pleas before the throne of grace is this: Please surround my children with positive influences. Raise up godly friends for my children! David knew that little would influence Solomon's success more than being surrounded by leaders whose hearts were devoted to seeking the Lord.

Solomon lacked nothing but age and experience—a lack that probably scared his father half to death. Looking at a son full of dreams, David dared not say, "This will be the most difficult thing you have ever done." He could not explain how lonely Solomon would be at the top, the exhaustion of too much responsibility, the temptation of too much power, the loneliness of too few friends. Chances were good that Solomon would not have understood David anyway. He had too many stars in his eyes and accolades in his ears. So David looked at the whole assembly and basically said, "Give him a hand. He's going to need it."

Never underestimate the power of a positive example!

David himself proved this in giving sacrificially of his wealth to finance and outfit the temple. David could not have motivated the leaders of Israel to give freely and wholeheartedly to the Lord unless he too had given. He could have forced them, but the willing spirit God so deeply desired would have been forfeited. David knew their cheerful giving would be motivated by his own; therefore, he had to give more than what belonged to the kingdom. The third verse clearly tells us, "I now give my personal treasures of gold and silver for the temple of my God, over and above everything I have provided for this holy temple."

David gave what was his. What belonged to him. That which was personal. And the people overwhelmingly responded. I love the way the ninth verse captures the electricity of the moment: "The people rejoiced at the willing response of their leaders, for they had given freely and wholeheartedly to the LORD. David the king also rejoiced greatly."

What a glorious moment! I can't think of much that spurs the hearts of the people of God like the wholehearted devotion of their leaders. When leadership is sold out to God, the followers become willing to sell out too.

# DAY 85
## 1 Chronicles 29:10–20

---

"LORD God of Abraham, Isaac, and Israel, our ancestors, keep this desire forever in the thoughts of the hearts of Your people, and confirm their hearts toward You" (v. 18).

---

Surely time stood still in David's mind as the people fell prostrate before the Lord and before the king. Close your eyes for a moment and picture the scene. Keep the picture like a snapshot in your memory.

We've waited through more than fifty years of David's life to witness an entire kingdom in unity before God! As we compare verses 9 and 20, we know that David was the one to whom Scripture referred as "king." All the people fell before the Lord and His beloved David, God's first choice, a man after His own heart.

So there David stood, a man of many years and experiences. His legs trembled with illness and age. His heart blazed with emotion. The streets of the city of God were paved with praises, blanketed with the prostrate bodies of all who called Jehovah their God.

May we never forget the awesome benefits of authentic praise. God desires our praises for many reasons, but I believe among the most vital are these two.

1. *Praise reminds us who He is.* When I am overwhelmed and wonder if God can see me through, He often calls on me to rehearse out loud—before His ears and mine—some of His many virtues:

   • His wonders in the lives of those recorded in the Word.
   • His wonders in my own life.
   • His wonders in the lives of those I know.

I proclaim out loud His greatness and His power and His glory. Then when I consider my need compared to His strength and bounty, I can proclaim with confidence the words of the prophet Jeremiah: "Ah, Sovereign LORD, you have made the heavens and the earth by your great power and outstretched arm. Nothing is too hard for you" (Jer. 32:17).

2. *Praise reminds us who we are.* Praise is an exercise in perspective. Notice David's words in verse 14: "But who am I?" Authentic praise works every time! Things seem to fall right into perspective. I don't believe you can truly praise and worship without ending up with a humbled heart.

# DAY 86
## 1 Chronicles 29:23–30

—∞∞—

He died at a good old age, full of days, riches, and honor,
and his son Solomon became king in his place (v. 28).

—∞∞—

Indeed, our God gave no insignificant space to the chronicles of David's life. He was the object of much love and continues to be the object of much learning. As we near the end of our look at David, may it be no exception.

In Psalm 69:16, David wrote: "Answer me, O LORD, out of the goodness of your love." As his life came to its end, we see how God graciously answered. In Psalm 51, David begged forgiveness. Solomon was the tangible evidence of David's pardon, for of him Scripture says, "The LORD loved him" (2 Sam. 12:24). Just as the contrite father had asked, the Word says of Solomon, "He prospered and all Israel obeyed him. All the officers and mighty men, as well as all of King David's sons, pledged their submission to King Solomon" (vv. 23–24).

The unrelenting sword was finally at rest. David's house was in order. God had given a weary man strength and helped him prepare a family and a nation for life in his absence. Surely as he bowed on his sickbed, David had prayed the words of Psalm 71:9: "Do not cast me away when I am old; do not forsake me when my strength is gone."

God did not cast David away. God did not forsake him when he was old. The God whose faithfulness endures to all generations completed the good work He started in a shepherd. Now the work was finally finished. The empty grave pleaded to be filled, the warrior to cease fighting. His thoughts must have been like those of the writer of Psalm 102: "For my days vanish like smoke; my bones burn like glowing embers. My heart is blighted and withered like grass; I forget to eat my food. Because of my loud groaning I am reduced to skin and bones" (vv. 3–5).

David had no reason to resist death's call. He had lived the length of his days. His throne was filled. It was fitting that his grave be filled as well. He had turned over his crown and joyfully dedicated his personal riches to the building of the temple. He was too old to conquer kingdoms, too sick to fill a sling, too frail to feast on the fatted calf. But that which he treasured most was never so dear to him and never so real.

Scholars generally agree that the words of Psalm 71 were written in David's old age as he confronted his hastening death. In verse 14 he wrote, "But as for me, I will always have hope; I will praise you more and more." David proclaimed a specific hope as the cords of death encompassed him:

> *Though you have made me see troubles, many and bitter,*
>     *you will restore my life again;*
> *from the depths of the earth you will again bring me up*
>     *(Ps. 71:20).*

He had hope of the blessed resurrection, just as we do! Not just an empty wish, but an anxious and certain expectation! From his proclamation of hope came Psalm 71:22: "I will praise you with the harp for your faithfulness, O my God."

I picture the aged king praising God. Once more his fingers wrapped around the strings of his harp, his hands no longer the calloused young hands of a hardy shepherd boy. Bent with age, slowed with time, David's fingers brushed across the strings. His voice, once wavering with adolescence, now wavered with age. No sweeter voice could be heard than the one that flowed, however unevenly, from the sincere heart of the aged. No longer did David's voice resound with the richness that had once awed a tormented Saul. Resigned to the will of the Father, in perfect harmony with God's plan for his life, he sang a final song of hope. The One who would take him to the depths of the earth would bring him up.

So he departed this life with two magnificent treasures: peace with his family and hope in his resurrection.

"Then David rested with his fathers and was buried in the City of David" (1 Kings 2:10). The eyes that had peeked into the heart of God now closed in death. The earthly life of one of the most passionate and controversial figures ever to grace this planet ended. The deadly silence must have lasted only long enough for Bathsheba to place her ear close to his mouth and her hand on his heart. The faint rise and fall of his chest had ceased.

No doubt the silence gave way to wails of grief. Trumpets carried the news. A kind of mourning peculiar to the Hebrew nation filled the days that followed. The very instruments commissioned by David for the dedication of the temple ironically may have first played his funeral dirge. Multitudes heaped ashes on their heads and draped sackcloth on their bodies. Then after an intense period of national mourning with visits from foreign dignitaries, life continued—just as it has the audacity to do after we've lost a loved one.

Life went on, but forever marked by the life of God's chosen king. God sovereignly chose to chisel David's reign into a kingdom that would last forever.

# DAY 87
### Psalm 32:1–11

---

*When I kept silent, my bones became brittle from my groaning
all day long. For day and night Your hand was heavy on me; my strength
was drained as in the summer's heat (vv. 3–4).*

---

Over the next several days we will revisit a few major events from David's life as we gain new perspective from Psalms and Proverbs. Chapter 11 of 2 Samuel ended with some very solemn, hair-raising words: "But the thing David had done displeased the LORD" (2 Sam. 11:27). We now begin to assess the cost of a few moments of carnal pleasure.

When David penned the words of this Psalm, virtually a year had passed since his initial sin with Bathsheba. We know the baby had already been born, but we do not know exactly how old he was. Why was the time so important? Because David had shown no sign of repentance!

David appeared to be moving on with his life as if nothing had happened, but how do you suppose his sin affected his relationship with God? Had he simply picked up with God where he had been? Hardly! Most of us have had seasons of unrepentance when we outwardly attempt to go on with life as if we had not sinned against God. However, our unwillingness to repent has internal effects.

David wrote exactly how he felt during his season of unrepentance. I believe Psalm 32:3–5 describes a malady we might call *sin sickness*.

I know what it's like to be sin sick. Do you? During periods when I refused to repent, I felt sapped of strength and sick all over. I groaned in my sin. Thankfully, the seasons of my sin and rebellion were the most miserable periods of my life, worse than any uninvited suffering I've ever experienced.

God graciously forgave me once I repented, and He forgot my sin, but I am thankful He did not allow *me* to forget. Have you ever noticed God helps us to forgive ourselves, but He does not make us forget our sins?

Psalm 32:3–5 teaches us an important truth. Spiritual illness (unrepentance) can lead to emotional illness (groaning all day, heaviness all night) and physical illness (bones wasted away, strength sapped). Please do not misunderstand. Certainly not all emotional or physical illness is caused by an unrepentant heart, but a continued refusal to repent can take a serious emotional and physical toll.

I know. I've been there.

# DAY 88
## Psalm 51:1–5

⸻

*Against You—You alone— I have sinned and done this evil in Your sight. So You are right when You pass sentence; You are blameless when You judge (v. 4).*

⸻

Somewhere between confronting sin and restoring fellowship must come the bridge between those two vital works—contrite confession. We have the blueprint for the bridge of confession fresh from the heart of a grieving king. Psalm 51 will be a fitting addition to our study of the infamous transgressions of David. This psalm invites the vilest of sinners to drink from the fountains of forgiveness.

So great was David's need for cleansing, so urgent his plea, that he began his prayer with no introduction and no high praises. David understood experientially the teaching of Isaiah 59:2:

> *Your iniquities have separated you from your God; your sins have hidden his face from you, so that he will not hear.*

David knew his God was complex and multifaceted. In his history with God, David had called on His sovereignty, His might, His deliverance, His intervention. But at this moment, David called on the God of love and compassion. Only on the basis of covenant love could David dare ask for mercy. For those of us who have known God and experienced the presence of God, the biggest heartbreak over sin comes with the realization that we have offended Him. God takes our sin personally. When we leave sin unconfessed, we scoff at the cross.

A man who lived many centuries before David also had an opportunity to sleep with another man's wife. In Joseph's case the other woman was Potiphar's wife. He responded to her with the words we should always ask ourselves in time of temptation: "How then could I do such a wicked thing and sin against God?" (Gen. 39:9).

# DAY 89
## Psalm 51:6–13

❧

Let me hear joy and gladness; let the bones You have crushed rejoice (v. 8).

❧

This line from verse 8 is perhaps my favorite in Psalm 51—"Let the bones you have crushed rejoice." I know exactly what the psalmist was talking about. Do you? David mixes the pain of confessing and turning from sin with the pleasure of restored fellowship. God sometimes uses circumstances and discipline to figuratively break our legs from continuing on the path of sin. Only the repentant know what it's like to dance with joy and gladness on broken legs!

Then verse 10: "Create in me a pure heart." The Hebrew word for "create" is *bara*. Also used in Genesis 1:1, the word "refers only to an activity which can be performed by God" and describes "entirely new productions."[26] David was admitting his need for something only God could do. Pure hearts never come naturally. In fact, a pure human heart is perhaps God's most creative work.

Most of us have borrowed the precious words of verse 12 from time to time. Sometimes our prayers seem to go unanswered because, in our misery, we beg for our joy to be restored without the obedience of fully turning from our sin. Nothing equals the moment you begin to sense the return of the joy of His salvation, but we must have the willing spirit to cooperate in His marvelous work!

Finally, let's look at verse 13: "Then I will teach transgressors your ways, and sinners will turn back to you." What happens after God has created a pure heart in a repentant sinner, renewed his spirit, and restored the joy of His salvation? No more willing and effective evangelist and teacher exists than one who has been humbled, cleansed, renewed, and restored! God will never have to goad this person to witness. His or her life will have eternal impact.

David's entire purpose in writing Psalm 51 was to ask for mercy. Did God grant his request? Speaking for myself as a repentant sinner who has experienced the misery of broken fellowship with God and reveled in the freshness of forgiveness, I have a hunch that He was delighted to.

# DAY 90
## Psalm 139:1–24

---

If I say, "Surely the darkness will hide me, and the light around me
will become night"—even the darkness is not dark to You. The night shines
like the day; darkness and light are alike to You (vv. 11–12).

---

Be aware of the progressive nature of sin. We've all experienced this. Reread 2 Samuel 11:1–5 and note three progressive areas of sin.

Step 1: *David sinned in thought.* First of all, David saw the woman bathing and concluded she was very beautiful. Sight turned into desire. The seed of sin was first sown in his mind as he tarried on the rooftop, just as the seed of sin is first sown in our minds.

Step 2: *David sinned in word.* If we do not confess and repent the sin of the mind, it virtually always gives birth to the next stage. The meditation of David's mind turned into the conversation of his mouth. God knows that our meditations (the focus of our thoughts, what we think and rethink) will ultimately turn into conversations. That's why He tells us to meditate on Him and His Word!

Temptations rarely go from the mind to the deed. The second stop is usually the mouth. David saw Bathsheba and allowed himself to dwell on wrong desires (the participation of his mind), then he summoned someone and expressed his interest (the participation of his mouth). These two steps enticed a third.

Step 3: *David sinned in deed.* David flirted with adultery in thought and word, stopping at neither venue to repent and ask God for help. Action followed. David committed adultery and set in motion a hurricane of repercussions.

For years I've approached my time of confession and repentance by categorizing my sins according to the three areas we've addressed. In my prayer time, I ask God to bring to my mind any sins of thought, word, or deed. Virtually everything will fall into one of those three categories. Through David's example I realized how often the three areas can unite as participants in grievous sin.

If wrong thoughts give way to wrong words, often giving way to wrong actions, we must learn to allow God to halt sin in the place where it begins—the thought life! We are wise to aggressively confess the sins of our thoughts! The sins of our thought lives are so numerous that their familiarity tends to make them less noticeable. Jealous thoughts, sudden lusts, quick criticisms, and harsh judgments may be fueled in our minds without any regard toward them as sin.

A heightened awareness of wrong thoughts will work greatly to our advantage. Getting in the habit of confessing sin in the thought life is not to remind us constantly what wretches we are, but to remind us what victors we are! Confessing wrong thoughts stops sin in the first stages, before it comes out of our mouths and then directs our actions.

If I allow God to halt sin before it takes one step out of the mind into word or deed, the only person hurt will be me. Once sin progresses from the mind to the mouth and deeds, we've involved others, and the repercussions and chastisements escalate.

Unchecked thoughts will usually progress. Our minds can't be "fairly pure." Purity comes with a radical attitude toward the thought life. God was looking out for our best interest when He commanded us to love Him with our whole minds!

I encourage you to let the following Scriptures become staples in your prayer time to guide you through purity of thought, word, and deed before God.

Regarding thoughts:

> *Search me, O God, and know my heart;*
> > *test me and know my anxious thoughts.*
> *See if there is any offensive way in me,*
> > *and lead me in the way everlasting (Ps. 139:23–24).*

Regarding words:

> *May the words of my mouth and the meditation of my heart*
> > *be pleasing in your sight,*
> *O LORD, my Rock and my Redeemer (Ps. 19:14).*

Regarding deeds:

> *LORD, who may dwell in your sanctuary?*
> > *Who may live on your holy hill?*
> *He whose walk is blameless*
> > *and who does what is righteous,*
> *who speaks the truth from his heart (Ps. 15:1–2).*

Copy these words of Scripture. Memorize them. Let them guide your confession daily. None of us is beyond the sin of adultery. Two kinds of people are in greatest danger: those who think they could never be tempted and those who are presently being tempted. May we cast ourselves on the mercy of God and find help in our time of trouble. Big trouble.

# DAY 91
## Psalm 142:1–7

—⚬⚬⚬—

I cry aloud to the LORD; I plead aloud to the LORD for mercy.
I pour out my complaint before Him; I reveal my trouble to Him (vv. 1–2).

—⚬⚬⚬—

Few of us have been forced to find refuge in a cave, but all of us have felt some of the same emotions David experienced. The New International Version identifies Psalm 142 as a prayer of David when he was in the cave, and it offers a number of insights into David's heart. It also provides a worthy example for us. Note what David did when he was overwhelmed with unfair treatment and difficult circumstances.

First and foremost, *David prayed.* The psalm provides an unquestionable testament that David responded to his difficulty with prayer. Few of us would argue about prayer being the proper response in our crises, but we often don't perceive prayer as being the most practical response. We think, "God can save me from my sins but not from my situation."

Next we notice that *David cried aloud.* The scene touches my heart as I imagine this young man sobbing in the cave. I was nearby once when a teenage boy slammed his hand in a car door. He was in immense pain. I watched him as he struggled between his need to be reduced to a bawling baby and his external need to keep his dignity. I watched him try to control his quivering lip. David was probably no different from that young man. I wonder how much he wished for the old days when he was unimportant, unimpressive, and contentedly keeping sheep. He had not asked for God's anointing, yet he had met nothing but trouble since that day. We can only begin to imagine the thoughts, fears, and losses that brought him to tears.

I believe that crying "aloud" helped David maintain sound emotional, mental, and spiritual health. Sometimes there's just nothing like a good cry. It clears the air, doesn't it? David was a real man by anyone's standards, yet he knew no better outlet than crying aloud to his God. "Cry aloud to the Lord" when you feel overwhelmed. He can take it!

A third detail stands out: *David poured out his complaint to God.* He told God his troubles. I am convinced this is one of the major contributors to David's godlike heart: he viewed his heart as a pitcher, and he poured everything in it on his God, whether it was joy or sadness, bitterness or fear. David not only poured out his heart as a personal practice, he urged others to do the same.

David did not just pour out his emotion, he also *rehearsed his trust in God.* In Psalm 142:3, he said, "When my spirit grows faint within me, it is you who know my way." David was so exhausted that he feared he would become negligent in his alertness to the snares his enemies set for him. His prayer to God also became a reminder to himself: "God knows my way." Prayer is for our sake as much as it is for God's pleasure. When I see the words I've written in my journal extolling the mighty virtues of God, I am reminded of His constant activity on my behalf, and my faith is strengthened.

The text yields a fifth observation; did you notice how *David longed for God's presence?* Because we need God's presence, our feelings are worth sharing with Him whether or not they accurately describe the truth. In verse 4, David said, "Look to my right and see; no one is concerned for me." (Guards often stood to the right of their appointees, ready to take an arrow in their defense.) David was reminding God that he had no guard. He surmised from his aloneness that no one was concerned for him. His next words were, "I have no refuge; no one cares for my life." Although he had found a cave in which to hide, he felt he had no refuge because no one there was there who cared personally for him.

Certainly many people cared for David, but because they were not in his presence, he felt forsaken. His feelings were not an accurate assessment of the truth, but they were worthy to share with God. Feelings can be a little like our laundry. Sometimes we can't sort them until we dump them out.

We can see that God honored David's telling Him exactly how he felt because He brought David's brothers and his father's household to be with him. God knew David needed his daddy. Later, God would mature David and teach him to stand alone. He wouldn't always send David's father to him. But God always responded to David's cry for help.

For a sixth principle from the passage, notice that *David confessed his desperate need.* A wise man knows when those who stand against him are mightier than he! David had killed both a lion and a bear; even the mighty Goliath had become just "like one of them" in David's eyes (1 Sam. 17:36). So why did David feel overwhelmed on this occasion? It may have been because he had never battled a secret enemy. This time he had members of Saul's entourage pursuing him with secret schemes.

Does David's plight sound familiar? According to Ephesians 6, we also fight an entire assembly of unseen powers and principalities. Without the intervention of God and His holy armor, we are mud on the bottom of the enemy's boots. How wise to humbly seek God's aid by admitting, like David in Psalm 142:6, "rescue me . . . for they are too strong for me!"

# DAY 92
### Proverbs 6:20–35

———⟨∞⟩———

*For a commandment is a lamp, teaching is a light,*
*and corrective instructions are the way to life (v. 23).*

———⟨∞⟩———

We do not have the luxury of considering the events between David and Bathsheba a rarity. Unfortunately, many people of God allow their hearts to wander and fall into adultery. The threatened institution of marriage in our society, inside the church and out, beckons us to confront the actions of King David. His actions can teach us not only how adultery can happen but how it can be avoided or prevented. Let's consider a few places David went wrong.

1. *He was in the wrong place at the wrong time.* Notice the very first phrases of 2 Samuel 11: "In the spring, at the time when kings go off to war." David had once been a very effective administrator and delegator; however, he had exceeded the wise bounds of delegation and left himself with little responsibility and idle hands. David handed to Joab a baton he should have kept for himself. David should have been leading his troops just as the other kings were leading theirs. He was obviously restless. Second Samuel 11:2 says, "David got up from his bed." He had delegated so much responsibility that he left himself open to boredom and temptation.

2. *He failed to protect himself with a network of accountability.* At one time he had been sensitive to the thought of offending God. He sought the counsel of prophets and allowed himself to be held accountable. But we've reached a season in David's life when he was answering to no one, apparently not even God. All of us need to be surrounded by people who are invited to hold us accountable and to question the questionable. No one questioned David's actions, yet they knew he was wrong. I want people in my life who love me enough to offend me if necessary and help me not to fall.

3. *He was lonely.* He allowed himself to be placed so high on the throne that he found himself all alone. The words of 2 Samuel 9:1 hint at David's loneliness and lack of peers as he cried, "Is there anyone still left of the house of Saul to whom I can show kindness for Jonathan's sake?" Dave Edwards, a well-known Christian speaker, once said, "All rebellion begins in isolation."

How can we avoid making the same kind of mistakes?

# DAY 93
### Jeremiah 33:14–22

---

"This is what the LORD says: If you can break My covenant with the night
so that day and night cease to come at their regular time, then also
My covenant with My servant David may be broken" (vv. 20–21).

---

One unexpected day the clouds will roll back and the King of all kings will
burst through the sky.

> *"On that day his feet will stand on the Mount of Olives, east of*
> *Jerusalem, and the Mount of Olives will be split in two from east*
> *to west. . . . Then the LORD my God will come, and all the holy*
> *ones with him. On that day there will be no light, no cold or frost.*
> *It will be a unique day, without daytime or nighttime—a day*
> *known to the LORD. . . . The LORD will be king over the whole*
> *earth. On that day there will be one LORD, and his name the only*
> *name" (Zech. 14:4–7, 9).*

Christ Jesus will sit on the throne of David in the city of Jerusalem, and
hope will give birth to certainty! We will join the one who said, "You turned
my wailing into dancing; you removed my sackcloth and clothed me with joy,
that my heart may sing to you and not be silent. O LORD my God, I will give
you thanks forever" (Ps. 30:11–12). With David, we will sing to the One who is
worthy!

That day there just might be one who can't seem to stop singing.

Oh, yes, I believe David will dance once more down the streets of
Jerusalem—this time without an eye to despise him. Oblivious to anyone but
God—the focus of his affections, the passion of his heart.

David will dance his way to that same familiar throne, but this time it will
be occupied by Another. No one above Him. None beside Him. David will see
the Lord high and lifted up, and His train will fill the temple. He'll fall before
the One who sits upon the throne, take the crown from his own head and cast it
at His feet. He'll lift his eyes to the King of all kings and with the passions of an
entire nation gathered in one heart, he will cry, "Worthy!"

Surely God the Father will look with great affection upon the pair.

# DAY 94
## Matthew 1:1-17

⸻

This is the genealogy of Jesus the Messiah the son of David, the son of Abraham (v. 1).

⸻

The genealogy David and Christ shared was of obvious importance. In Matthew 1:3, we see that both David and Christ were descendants of Judah, one of the sons of Jacob. In the prophecy that Jacob spoke over Judah, he said, "The scepter will not depart from Judah, nor the ruler's staff from between his feet" (Gen. 49:10). You see, David was not a random choice. He was one of the most important figures in the genealogy of Christ, "the Lion of the tribe of Judah" (Rev. 5:5).

I never fail to be encouraged by Christ's heritage. How do you respond to the fact that the only perfect person in Christ's genealogy is Christ Himself?

To me, Christ's flawed family history serves as a continual reminder of the grace of God in my life. In my human desire for perfection, I want to be so good that I need no one and no thing. It may surprise you to know that this desire grows from a biblical base: the tower of Babel. The tower pictures graphically our human drive to take God's place.

But whenever my perfectionism kicks in, I run back to Scripture—to the only source of perfection:

> *For all have sinned and fall short of the glory of God, and are*
> *justified freely by his grace through the redemption that came by*
> *Christ Jesus (Rom. 3:23–24).*

God chose David. On the surface, the choice made no sense. But God doesn't work on sense; He works on grace. God called you, and God called me. He knew what He was doing.

In many ways David's life foreshadowed or pictured details of Christ's life. God illustrated the unknown about the Messiah through the known about David. David was not divine or perfect, but God has used him to teach us truths about the One who is.

# DAY 95
## Matthew 3:1–6

---

They were baptized by him in the Jordan River as they confessed their sins (v. 6).

---

We can almost picture John waist-deep in water with people streaming out to be baptized. They were confessing their sins, because they weren't being baptized unto salvation. John was baptizing them unto repentance, preparing them to encounter the Savior, the only One who could bring them salvation.

I believe they were quite specific confessing their sins. In all likelihood they were crying out these confessions, maybe even wailing them, weeping over their sins. Then came Christ. We know *He* was not coming to be baptized unto repentance. He was the spotless Lamb of God. Complete perfection. He was the only One who had no confessing to do that day in those waters. He came for John to baptize Him.

I just want you to get the picture here. I'm not trying to make a doctrinal statement or an interpretation of Scripture. I'm just asking you to see a picture. We know that God was baptizing His Son into ministry—the representation of the death, the burial, and the resurrection. But I also see something so precious in the fact that the people had confessed their sins standing in those same waters and then were baptized. Christ comes after they've made these confessions. He is baptized—drenched in the same waters where they had confessed their sins. I'm just talking symbolism here, but do you almost see Him wearing the sins they had confessed in those waters?

I love the practice of daily coming to the line with Christ and naming my sins. I don't practice a "Lord, forgive me for all of my sins." I don't see true biblical repentance in that. Repentance assumes we are naming the sin to acknowledge it. Then I like to discuss with God why it doesn't agree with His Word, why the sin isn't what He wants for me. That kind of repentance begins to get those precepts down into my soul.

I love Acts 3:19: "Repent, then, and turn to God, so that your sins may be wiped out, that times of refreshing may come from the Lord." Those of us who have already received Christ have been baptized into Him. Now daily confession is like refreshment to our souls. We come away from repentance cleansed. Ready to be filled. Ready to walk in the Spirit.

# DAY 96
## Matthew 3:13–15

—∞∞∞—

But John tried to stop Him, saying, "I need to be baptized by You,
and yet You come to me" (v. 14).

—∞∞∞—

Our gloriously deliberate God orchestrated the lives of two extraordinary
men, born six months apart, to converge waist-deep in the waters of the Jordan
River. For John the Baptizer, it was the beginning of the end. He had prepared
God's way, and now God was preparing his. For Jesus, it marked the end of the
beginning. His life would descend on Galilee, Judea, and Jerusalem like a desert
storm. That day in the river of promise, John baptized Jesus with water, and Jesus
baptized the Jordan with glory.

Just imagine what was going on in the mind of Christ as He was walking to
the river Jordan. I wonder if He stopped to watch the scene for a while, with the
people confessing their sins. Did He watch this mighty servant of God preaching
the Word with boldness? I'm just picturing somehow that horizon and His figure
overlooking the scene. Then He walks up to the shore, and John sees Him.

I've written something that is strictly fiction. I was just reflecting on what
might have been going through John's mind as Jesus approached him. Perhaps
these thoughts will help us see again what happens when very real people encounter the Son of God:

"My tongue had been like a flame that day. The Word of God came to me
in the desert like fire from heaven. If I hadn't preached it, it would have consumed me. I had no fear. No intimidation. God sent me to those Jordan waters,
and I knew they'd come. No prearranged meeting. Just the wind of the Spirit
wooing, drawing, then blowing away the debris of sin, preparing the way for the
Deliverer. No matter who came to the shore to hear or to jeer. The message was
immutable, "Repent! For the kingdom of heaven is near!"

"The fruit of repentance pierced the wind with cries of confession and
waves of grief. I hardly stepped out of those waters that day. My voice grew raspy
and hoarse but never quiet. Boldness was the marrow in my bones. Funny how
stunned we are when the future we prophesy suddenly becomes present. I had
told them I was unworthy to loose His sandals and that I would only baptize
with water for repentance. He would baptize with the Holy Spirit and with fire. I
spoke like an authority. Like an associate of the closest kind. Like someone who
knew it all. I didn't.

"I was just raising a repentant man from the waters when I saw someone
out of the corner of my eye walk to the water's edge. As I think back, how those
waters kept from parting that day, I'll never know. Numbers were gathered on

the shore. Others were waist-deep in the water. Suddenly I became oblivious to all but the overpowering presence of the One. There He stood, looking straight at me, through me. Oh, it was Him all right! I had been preparing for Him all my life, and yet I was not ready. All I could do was look at Him and shake my head, 'No. Please, no! Not me. I have need to be baptized by You!'

"Suddenly I was overcome by my own compulsion to flood the shore with waves of repentance, and He answered, 'Let it be for now. It is proper for us to do this to fulfill all righteousness.' So I consented, shaking all over. I placed my left hand on His back and my right hand on His chest. I felt the heartbeat of the Son of God. As if in slow motion, I leaned Him back into those waters, His weight submitting to my hands.

"All of a sudden the Jordan chilled me to the bone. I raised Him from the waters, and He stood before me drenched in the river of promise. The water dripping from His beard seemed to drop like diamonds, proclaiming His endless perfections. He alone had no confessions to make that day. Only one was made over Him, the confession of His holiness enthroned in heaven. 'This is my Son whom I love and with Him I am well pleased.' The blessing of the Father fell like a dove from heaven. He walked out of those waters and into our lives, interrupting a fallen world with grace and truth. My name is John. I am the son of a simple man and woman. I baptized the Messiah that day."

Can you imagine? He had prepared all his life. When we set apart our lives unto Him, He will do wonders with us the likes of which we cannot imagine.

# DAY 97
## Matthew 3:16-17

—∞∞—

The heavens suddenly opened up for Him, and He saw the Spirit of God
descending like a dove and coming down on Him (vv. 16–17).

—∞∞—

Back in Genesis 1, God created the heavens and the earth, He separated
the expanse from the waters, and He called that expanse the sky. I can't help but
think, then, "If He called it into being and put it in its place, He can open it if
He wants to!" On the day when Jesus was baptized, the Father opened up the sky
like a window, and showed Christ the vision through it.

This event makes me think of Stephen, the very first martyr, because heaven
was opened to him and he saw Jesus Christ standing at the right hand of God on
his behalf. What I want you to understand is that heaven is right there. We look
up at that sky at night and the expanse of the stars. He is literally just an open
window away from us, sitting on His throne. His presence is in us and on us. God
upon His throne is near. We just can't quite see it yet.

On this special occasion God did something unusual. He opened up that
window, and Christ looked straight into heaven. It had been a long time since
He had seen that vision. I believe part of God's purpose for sending Jesus here
was to experience life as we do. That means I don't believe He had X-ray vision
every single second into the throne room of God. I believe that many times He
prayed, meditated, and had relationship with His Father in the very same ways
we do today. So what a time this must have been to capture that moment when
He could see heaven open and the Holy Spirit descend.

And then to hear His Father's blessing. Again, I don't think God spoke
audibly to His Son every day He was on earth. I think maybe Jesus was called
here to sympathize with us and to take part in the kind of relationship we do. A
whole lot of His prayer was spent talking to God, knowing only in His own Spirit
and through God's Word what the Father was answering Him. So the audible
voice of His Father sounding forth at His baptism must have just fallen on Jesus
with the dearest of familiarity. This was the love of His life. I want to think that
through the night, He replayed that voice and blessing in His own mind a thousand times. "He loves Me. Life is hard here, but He's proud of Me. I have the
blessing. I have the blessing."

# DAY 98
## Matthew 4:18–22

———∞∞∞———

Going on from there, He saw two other brothers, James the son of Zebedee, and his brother John. They were in a boat with Zebedee their father, mending their nets (v. 21).

———∞∞∞———

The people we will come to know together in this book were Jews at a time when Judaism had perhaps never been more Jewish. By this expression I mean that although they were under Roman rule, they enjoyed significant freedom to live out their culture. They were firmly established in their land and had their temple. Every sect of religious life was functioning at full throttle: the Pharisees, the Sadducees, and the teachers of the law, to name only a few.

Life in the Galilean villages of Capernaum and Bethsaida must have seemed light-years away from the hub of religious life and Herod's temple in Jerusalem, but one thing varied little from Hebrew to Hebrew: YHWH was life. Provider, Sustainer, Sovereign Creator of all things. (YHWH is the divine name of God, never pronounced by the Jews; in English it is often referred to as Yahweh or Jehovah.) To them, to have little thought of God was to have little thought at all.

Our John the apostle came from the rural land to the north. If the more sophisticated Jew in the Holy City thought the simple settlers on the Sea of Galilee envied him, he was sorely mistaken. Neither was without the inevitable troubles that make living part of life. Each had his preferences. Each had a point of view. One awakened to the brilliance of the sun dancing off the gleaming walls of the temple. The other saw the sun strolling on the surface of the lake. A fisherman would have been hard to convince that the glory of God dwelled more powerfully in a building made of stone than in a bright pink and purple sunset over the Sea of Galilee. I know this for a fact. I live with a fisherman.

Two pairs of sons grew up not far from each other on the northern tip of the Sea of Galilee. Four pairs of feet earned their calluses on the pebbles of a familiar shore. From the time their sons were knee-high to them, Zebedee and Jonah were responsible not only for making sure their rambunctious offspring didn't drown but also for harnessing their insatiable curiosity with their trades. The fathers were the walking day-care centers for their sons, and their sons' mothers would be expecting them home in one piece before dusk or after a long night of fishing.

Peter, Andrew, James, and John. They were trees planted by streams of water being raised to bring forth their own fruit in season (Ps. 1:3). If those fathers had only known what would become of their sons, I wonder if they would have raised them any differently. Come to think of it, I doubt it. They were simple men with one simple goal: to teach their sons all they knew.

Our task is to piece together what John's life might have been like in childhood and youth before a Lamb came and turned it upside down. We first meet John on the pages of the New Testament in Matthew 4:21. There we read that the fishing boat contained "James the son of Zebedee, and his brother John" (HCSB). Scholars are almost unanimous in their assumption that John was the younger brother of James. In the earlier references, he is listed after his brother, James, which was often an indication of birth order in Scripture and other ancient Eastern literature.

In their world, if any name existed more common than James (a hellenized form of *Iakob* or Jacob), it was John. Since the family used the Hebrew language, they actually called him Jehohanan. It may sound a little fancier, but the name was as common as could be. I don't get the feeling James and John were the kinds of boys about whom the neighbors mused, "I can't wait to see what they'll turn out to be. Mark my word. They'll be something special!" Those who watched them grow up assumed the sons of Zebedee would be fisherman. Just like their father.

If we're right and James was the older brother, he held the coveted position in the family birth order. Special rights and privileges belonged to him as well as a birthright that assured him a double portion of his father's estate. The firstborn was a leader in the family, commanding a certain amount of respect for a position he did nothing to earn. John? He was just the little brother.

Most of us have experienced the ambiguity of being known by little more than our relationship to someone else. I can remember feeling lost in a whole line of siblings growing up. I have fond memories of my mother calling me every name in our big family but mine. I often grinned while she scrambled for the right one and then, exasperated, finally would say, "If I'm looking at you, I'm talking to you!" I'd giggle, "Yes, ma'am!" and run off while she was still doing her best to remember what my name was.

Some things about parenting must be universal. Surely Zebedee looked straight at Jehohanan and accidentally called him Iakob at times. If so, would young John have been the type to let it go unnoticed, or might he have said, "Abba! I am Jehohanan!" These are thoughts I love to explore imaginatively when studying a character.

Either way John was no doubt accustomed to being Zebedee's other son and James's little brother. However common his name, the meaning was extraordinary: "God has been gracious."[27] Growing up on the shore of Jesus' favorite sea, John had no idea at this point just how gracious God had been. He would soon get a glimpse.

# DAY 99
## Matthew 4:23

Jesus was going all over Galilee, teaching in their synagogues, preaching the good news of the kingdom, and healing every disease and sickness among the people (v. 23).

Luke's recap of this same event in chapter 4 concludes with a definitive statement: "He kept on preaching in the synagogues of Judea" (v. 44). *He kept on*—no matter how many directions He felt pulled. No matter how many needs remained in each town. No matter what others prioritized for Him—"He kept on." Why? Because every other need humanity possessed was secondary to the need to hear and receive the gospel. Not unimportant, mind you. Just secondary. Physical healing affects this life alone, but the kingdom is forever.

Then why did Christ spend time and energy performing miracles of healing on such temporal bodies? Probably for three primary reasons:

1. *Because He could.* He can do whatever He wants. Before that fact makes you nervous, remember: what He wants is always consistent with who He is. Among many other wonderful things, He is the healer. In one way or another, He heals every single person who comes to Him by faith.

2. *Because He is compassionate*—beyond anything we can imagine.

3. *Because the miracles helped authenticate the messenger.*

Preaching the good news of the kingdom of God was Christ's absolute priority. One of the biggest temptations even mature believers face is being sidetracked by the urgent. Many situations need our attention. They tempt us to let them steal our focus. Christ may have faced the same temptation when the people came to Him and tried to "keep him from leaving them" (Luke 4:42). The people's attempts to hold onto Christ may not have been limited to just the vocal and emotional. They may have hung onto Him physically too. How His heart must have broken for them. Yet He knew the best thing He could do for them was to stay true to His mission.

Can you imagine how Jesus longed for the time when His work would be accomplished and He could dwell within the hearts of all who would receive Him, never to leave them? Until then, He had a job to do. Christ ignored neither the urgent need nor the ultimate goal—but He never allowed the former to hinder the latter.

## DAY 100
### Matthew 4:24–25

———

They brought to Him all those who were afflicted, those suffering from various diseases and intense pains, the demon-possessed, the epileptics, and the paralytics (v. 24).

———

As I imagine all that happened that Saturday and all they saw, I know one of the thoughts I'd have had if I had been John. *Is there anything the man can't do?* He watched Jesus practically bring the house down with His teaching. He watched Him confront and cast out a demon. He watched Him not only heal Simon's mother-in-law but instantly restore her strength. Then every manner of distress landed on their doorstep.

I love Matthew Henry's words of commentary on the scene at the door. "How powerful the Physician was; he healed all that were brought to him, though ever so many. Nor was it some one particular disease, that Christ set up for the cure of, but he healed those that were sick of divers [various, diverse] diseases, for his word was a panpharmacon—a salve for every sore."[28]

His Word was a "panpharmacon." Ah, yes. I have yet to have an ailment God had no salve to soothe. What may be even more peculiar is that I have yet to have an ailment of soul that God's Word was not the first to point out, diagnose, then heal. His Word is far more glorious, powerful, and fully applicable than we have any idea. You very likely did not pick up this particular devotional book because you sought healing. You would surely have picked other titles. But based on my own experience and many references in Scripture, you will undoubtedly receive some fresh diagnoses and, if you cooperate, a new measure of healing. As will I. I'm counting on it.

That's the nature of His Word. As Psalm 107:20 says, "He sent His word and healed them; He rescued them from the Pit" (HCSB). How often God has had to send forth His Word and begin the healing to get me healthy enough to face the diagnosis!

I want you to revel in something wonderful. Every time God has prepared us with His Word and gotten us to a point that we can receive a hard "pill" to swallow from Him, healing has already begun. Once He confronts us, we never need to be overwhelmed by how far we have to go. If we've heard Him through His Word, healing has already begun.

Take heart. He is the Panpharmacon.

## DAY 101
### Matthew 10:5–10

—∞∞—

You have received free of charge; give free of charge (v. 8).

—∞∞—

Up until now, the Twelve had watched Christ at work and had witnessed His miracles, but they had not yet been empowered to exercise those wonders. I don't imagine the disciples expected to do anything but watch. But they were about to receive a very special welcome to the wild world of Jesus Christ. Jesus called the disciples together and gave them "power and authority to drive out all demons and to cure diseases" (Luke 9:1). Then He sent them out to preach and heal. He told them to take along no provisions but to stay where the people welcomed them.

Wouldn't you love to have eavesdropped on the conversations between the disciples as they prepared to go out? Like us, I'm not sure they had a clue what they had been given. They had the privilege to be the closest earthly companions to the Son of God. They were chosen to witness the most remarkable phenomenon in all human history: the Word made flesh and dwelling among us. They broke bread with Him, laughed with Him, and talked Scripture with Him. They knew the sound of His breathing when He slept. They knew His favorite foods. They watched Him heal the sick, deliver the demon-possessed, and raise the dead. If they had never received another thing, they had been granted a privilege beyond all others. But Christ didn't stop there. He also gave them power and authority.

Christ's words in Matthew 10:8 should inspire us to pour out our lives like drink offerings for the rest of our days. "Heal the sick, raise the dead, cleanse those who have leprosy, drive out demons. Freely you have received, freely give." The word for "freely" is *dorean*, meaning "freely, gratis, as a free gift." I think you might be very interested to see another way this same Greek word is translated into English.

In John 15:25 Jesus said, "They hated me without reason." The phrase "for no reason" is translated from the same word, *dorean*. What does that tell you about the things we've received from Christ? Unreasonable grace! Nothing is reasonable about the love of God or the gifts He so freely gives! Like me, I know you've received freely from God in ways you can't begin to count, but has that unreasonable grace caused you to freely give of yourself to others recently?

# DAY 102
## Matthew 11:2–5

---

When John heard in prison what the Messiah was doing, he sent a message
by his disciples and asked Him, "Are You the One who is to come,
or should we expect someone else?" (vv. 2–3).

---

People who seem to live out the faith almost flawlessly inspire me; but I am also moved to meditation by those who grapple and wrestle with it. I find that rather than give me "permission" to doubt, their stories usually give me permission to move through my doubt to a place of spacious faith. May God use today's reading toward such an end.

Both Luke and Matthew tell us that John the Baptizer sent messengers to Jesus asking if He was the Messiah. Jesus told them to return to John and tell him just what they had seen: "The blind receive sight, the lame walk, those who have leprosy are cured, the deaf hear, the dead are raised, and the good news is preached to the poor" (Luke 7:22).

Matthew, however, gives us one additional piece of information about the situation. John sent his disciples, all right . . . from his prison cell (Matt. 11:2). Mark 6:17–18 tells us that John was there because he confronted King Herod about his adultery. Do you suppose John's location may have influenced the question he sent his disciples to ask Jesus?

My heart is awash with compassion for a man who sat in prison two thousand years ago. Four walls closing in surely must limit your vision. The facts to support Christ's messiahship were all there. I'm pretty certain John knew it. Furthermore, the baptizer knew Jesus was the Messiah the moment he saw Him at the Jordan River. But time and circumstances can dull the image on your faith perception, and leave you feeling not sure *what* you believe.

I don't think John's sudden bout with doubt had anything to do with public merit. It was a private matter. John had heard the wonders Christ had done for others. I think maybe his faith was shaken because he could have used a wonder for himself, and he didn't appear to be getting it. John knew with his head that Jesus was the Messiah. Sitting in that prison cell, I think he was having a little trouble knowing it with his heart.

We don't have trouble relating here. Have you known Christ long enough to witness His marvelous works? Have you heard testimonies of His intervening power? Even after such evidence, has your faith ever been greatly shaken because of something He didn't do for you personally? Like John, have you ever found yourself waiting and waiting on Christ to come through? Have you ever endured long stretches of suffering on a certain matter while hearing all sorts of wondrous works He was doing elsewhere?

It hurts, doesn't it? We can be believers in Jesus for years, literally seeking Him, finding Him, and serving Him—then suddenly have a staggering bout with doubt. Overwhelmed with guilt and fear, we'll think, "How in the world could I be doubting after all this time?" It's a horrible feeling!

I'd like to suggest, however, that these kinds of doubts are probably not coming from our heads. They're coming from our hearts. Our feelings. Our emotions. Our hurts.

John was not like "a reed swayed by the wind" (Luke 7:24). Rather, he was a man of absolute conviction. That's exactly what faith means. *Pistis*, the Greek word translated "faith," means "firm persuasion, conviction." For our purposes today, "firm persuasion" or "conviction" represents head-faith! Perhaps John had questions, but they weren't enough to sway the reed! If John had truly harbored deeply embedded questions about Christ's authenticity, I don't believe Jesus would have hesitated to rebuke him. He certainly didn't hesitate with some others. Yet Christ was very gentle with John. He simply reminded him that He was fulfilling His job description to the letter.

I believe the root of John's question was, "Why am I sitting in prison while Jesus is going about His business all over the countryside?" Surely John was wondering how he was supposed to "prepare the way" for Him from prison. If Jesus were meeting all the criteria of messiahship, He was supposed to be proclaiming freedom for the prisoners (see Luke 4:18). And John knew a prisoner who could use a little freedom.

John's ministry had lasted only about a year. The baptizer could not have imagined that his purposes had been so quickly fulfilled. John couldn't have foreseen that he was a shooting star leading the way in the night until the dawn would rise.

Our discussion raises an important question: If a real difference exists between head-doubt and heart-doubt, is heart-doubt "no big deal"? When our emotions begin to override what our minds know is true, can we just surrender to our heart-doubts? I don't think so. Our heart-doubts can be very dangerous if we remain in them. But, if we wrestle through them with the Lord Jesus, when we get to the other side of our crisis, we will find ourselves spilled into a place of spacious faith!

# DAY 103
## Matthew 14:19–21

Everyone ate and was filled. Then they picked up 12 baskets
full of leftover pieces (v. 20).

I just have to share a thought with you about this astounding miracle of Jesus, this feeding of the five thousand with His disciples' mere fishes and loaves.

At the age of twenty, my older daughter was asked to speak to a group of teenage girls in Oklahoma. Of my two children she is the shy one. With horror on her face, she told me she was certain God was telling her to say yes. I cannot express to you how far outside her comfort zone this was at the time.

The butterflies never left her stomach from the time of the invitation until the day of the conference. What emotion flooded my heart as I put her on that plane to go speak—instead of the other way around. Contrary to her worst fears, she lived through it! And the young women received a sound message from the Word . . . even if the voice was a little shaky here and there.

The next morning she called me with such a tender heart, her voice cracking, and said, "Mom, I just had my time with the Lord . . . and He was so . . . sweet."

I knew exactly what she was talking about. I said, "Oh, my precious child, you have just experienced that which would be worth selling all your earthly possessions to gain, and yet it's a gift of grace: divine approval. The smiling nod of God. Nothing like it."

With the slightest whisper, my very humble, gentle child said, "Yes."

I'm fighting back tears at the thought. You see, this act of obedience was terribly difficult for her. She could have provided a list of other students, but she didn't. In effect she said, "All I have is this pitiful handful of fish and loaves," and Jesus said, "Bring them to me." When all was said and done, she wasn't sure what the girls had received, but God had given her bread from His Word and she had distributed it the best she knew how.

Amanda was glad to have survived . . . but imagine her surprise when she didn't just survive. The next morning as she sat before the Lord, He handed her a basketful of leftovers. She had been willing to be a disciple. A learner. A novice. He would not have dreamed of leaving her empty-handed.

You either, my friend. It's not His style.

# DAY 104
## Matthew 16:13–23

—— ∞ ——

Peter took Him aside and began to rebuke Him,
"Oh no, Lord! This will never happen to You" (v. 22).

—— ∞ ——

Try to picture Peter saying something like, "Jesus, can I see You just a minute right over here? Excuse me, brothers. We'll be right back," then commencing his rebuke of the "Son of the living God." In my opinion, Peter the rock was pretty fortunate he didn't get thrown into the nearest lake! A couple of thoughts surface as I look at this interchange:

1. *One minute we can be so "on target" and the next minute so "off."* Without a doubt, some of my better moments preceded my worst disasters. How about you? I mean, one moment Peter made a statement that Christ said could only have been revealed to him by the Father. The next thing we know he's made a statement Christ attributed to the devil. One minute a rock—the next minute a stumbling block. Whew! What a frightening thought! How on guard we must be.

I keep looking at Peter's words: "This shall never happen to you!" (Matt. 16:22). I wonder, based on Christ's response to him, if in Peter's heart he might have been thinking: "This shall never happen to *me!* I've given up everything to follow You! You can't go dying on us here! We've got a kingdom to build!" Peter didn't understand that Christ's suffering and death were the means by which He would indeed secure the kingdom.

2. *All Satan needs to have momentary victory over a disciple is for us to have in mind the things of men.* Satan doesn't have to get us blatantly thinking satanic thoughts to have victory over us. All he needs is to get us looking at life from man's perspective rather than God's. But if we surrender our minds to the things of God, we are safe! We don't have to constantly look out for our own best interests, because *He's* constantly looking out for them. What Peter didn't understand is that what may have seemed best in the short run would have been disastrous in the long run. Had Jesus saved His disciples the anxiety of His betrayal, trials, and death, He wouldn't have saved them at all.

On this earth I don't know that we will ever perpetually have in mind the things of God rather than the things of man. But if we don't make the deliberate choice to have in mind the things of God when faced with our biggest challenges, most of us will probably default back to our natural instinct—the things of man.

# DAY 105
## Matthew 18:1–9

—∞∞∞—

Woe to the world because of offenses. For offenses must come,
but woe to that man by whom the offense comes (v. 7).

—∞∞∞—

Let's state a serious fact based on Matthew 18: events or situations can actually cause people to sin. Before we attempt to interpret Christ's statements, let's make sure we understand what He didn't mean. Christ didn't mean that in some cases people have no choice *but* to sin. He didn't absolve the one who sins from the responsibility to repent. He did mean, however, that conditions can exist and things can happen that so greatly increase the tendency toward sin that a terrible woe is due the responsible party.

What are these offenses or "things that cause people to sin"? (Luke 17:1). The Greek word is *skandalon*. The idea of our English word "scandal" is present in the meaning. *Skandalon* is "the trigger of a trap on which the bait is placed, and which, when touched by the animal, springs and causes it to close, causing entrapment. It always denotes an enticement to conduct which could ruin the person in question."

If you apply this concept to Jesus' words, you see that the declaration of "woe" would apply to the one who set the trap or (figuratively speaking) became the trigger of the trap. But to be liberated we must not shift all responsibility to the trapper, because the truth remains that we did take the bait. To live consistently outside a trap, we must recognize our own responsibility in at least three ways. We are responsible for:

1. *repenting of the sin* of taking the bait;

2. *learning why* we took the bait;

3. *asking God* to mend and fortify the weak places in the fabric of our heart, soul, and mind so we will not continue life as a victim.

A critical part of my own personal freedom in Christ has been asking God to help me search my heart, soul, and mind for vulnerabilities to foolish decisions. Taking responsibility in these areas produced one of the greatest harvests of my life. I learned to willingly lay my heart bare before Him, to invite Him to reveal my weaknesses and handicaps, and to be unashamed. I also developed daily dependency upon Him because my old vulnerabilities had become such habits, practices, and ways of life.

This doesn't minimize, of course, the sin of the trapper. The ramifications of this are so great that he becomes the object of "woe," meaning "disaster, calamity." Christ issued a woe to anyone who causes another person to sin, but He pronounced a particular indictment against anyone who causes "one of these little ones" to sin (v. 6).

The word Jesus used to refer to "little ones" certainly includes literal children, because He actually "called a little child and had him stand among them" (Matt. 18:2). However, careful attention to the word suggests additional meaning. I believe Christ includes those who are childlike or inferior to the trapper in knowledge, experience, authority, or power—anyone of whom it might be easy to take advantage. A sixteen-year-old may have the body of an adult, but he or she most assuredly is not grown up. Seduction by an adult is entrapment even if the young person "sinned" in any level of willing participation. Similarly, in adult life, one person often wields authority over another in much the same way through rank or position.

That Christ holds the trapper greatly responsible is a gross understatement! He appears to be saying, "If you have entrapped a weaker, more vulnerable person in sin, you're going to wish you had drowned in the deepest sea rather than deal with Me."

Most of us have asked, "Why do these things happen?" Matthew 18:7 tells us that these atrocities "must come." "But why?" we ask. The original word for "must" means "compelling force, as opposed to willingness. As a result of the depravity and wickedness of men, there is a moral inevitability that offenses should come." Add the kingdom of darkness to the depravity of humans, and you have a formula for exactly the evil we see in our world. But a day of reckoning is coming. No trapper gets away with entrapment forever—either of the human kind or the spirit kind. Neither can escape the eyes of *El Roi*, the God who sees.

Most of us are not naïve enough to think that these kinds of offenses never happen in churchgoing families. I'd like to highlight one area that doesn't get much press but where people are at great risk for offense in the church: New believers are so impressionable. Sometimes their zeal far exceeds their knowledge. They sometimes believe virtually anything a more experienced Christian tells them. Biblical doctrines can be twisted into false teaching to entrap immature believers in all sorts of sins. If God would judge those outside His own household, I think we can rest assured He would discipline His own.

Let's not start feeling guilty for some atrocity we may not have committed, but by all means let's be on our guard never to cause another person to sin. The Word is clear we have that potential.

# DAY 106
## Matthew 23:1–36

⸻

"Woe to you, scribes and Pharisees, hypocrites! You clean the outside of the cup and dish, but inside they are full of greed and self-indulgence!" (v. 25).

⸻

Paul's father entrusted him to the finest rabbinic school, but he was not there alone. He was surrounded by good and bad influences. He saw people who were the real thing, and he saw people who were religious frauds.

We need look no further than the Word of God to see many of the influences Saul encountered among the Pharisees of Jerusalem. Saul was a contemporary of Jesus. Soon after Saul finished his education in Jerusalem and presumably headed back to Tarsus, John the Baptist began to "prepare the way for the Lord" (Matt. 3:3). In no time at all, Jesus was on the scene, teaching in the same synagogue where Saul had recently stood. Saul found influences like the wise teacher Gamaliel, but he also experienced influences like the ones Jesus so aptly described in the Gospels. In fact, many of the Pharisees and members of the Sanhedrin whom Christ encountered were Saul's instructors or classmates.

The term *Pharisee* was meant to represent genuine piety and deep devotion to God. Although exceptions certainly existed among the Pharisees, in the days of Jesus and Saul the term had become synonymous with hypocrisy and cynicism.

Matthew 23 is an entire discourse addressed to the teachers of the law and Pharisees. I hope you've taken the time to read the chapter carefully. Notice all the specific ways Jesus described the same people Saul encountered in Jerusalem. When I did this, I made a list. For example, I didn't just note that they were hypocritical, but described the *ways* they were hypocritical. My list looked something like this: they made demands of others that they themselves did not keep (v. 4); they made their religious actions into show to impress others (v. 5); they loved to be the center of attention (v. 6); and they not only wouldn't enter the kingdom of God, they prevented others from entering (v. 13). What a horrible description.

Take a thorough look at these characteristics and the others you see in Matthew 23. Do you see any that describe you as well? Godly people are valiant people. They are people with the courage to ask God to spotlight areas of weakness, sin, and failure. Then God can strengthen, heal, and complete what is lacking.

# DAY 107
## Matthew 26:26–30

—∞∞∞—

When they had sung a hymn, they went out to the Mount of Olives (v. 30).

—∞∞∞—

Tens of thousands of Jews celebrated the Passover that year in Jerusalem. For many, the year's observance was indistinct from the last. They had no idea that nearby the Lamb of God lifted the cup of redemption and offered it to all.

In the upper room the disciples' stomachs were full, their recollections rekindled, and their feet washed by the Son of man. "Having loved his own who were in the world, he now showed them the full extent of his love" (John 13:1). The One who created time submitted Himself to it. In the same perfect order that the heavens and the earth were created, salvation's story must unfold like a book already written . . . penned before the foundation of the world. The Spirit of God blew the next page open to the chapter called "Agony." The garden awaited.

"When they had sung a hymn, they went out to the Mount of Olives" (Matt. 26:30). Jesus singing! How I would love to hear that sound. When He sang, did the angels of heaven hush to His voice? Or did they cease their song and join in His? Did He sing tenor? Bass? Did Christ and His disciples sing in harmony, or did they all sing the melody? Did Jesus sing often, or was this a moment of rarity?

How fitting that on this very night Christ, the coming King, would give voice to songs penned centuries earlier just for Him. Traditionally, every Seder or Passover celebration ended with the latter half of the Hallel, Psalms 115–118. Very likely Christ and His disciples sang from these psalms. Imagine the Son of God singing these words as the seconds ticked toward the cross.

Whatever Christ sang as the Passover meal concluded that night, the words had significance for Him that the others could never have comprehended. I wonder if His voice quivered with emotion? Or did He sing with exultation? Perhaps He did both, just as you and I have done at terribly bittersweet moments when our faith exults while our sight weeps. One thing we know: Christ, above all others, knew that He was singing more than words. That night He sang the score of His destiny.

# DAY 108
## Matthew 26:36–46

---

Taking along Peter and the two sons of Zebedee,
He began to be sorrowful and deeply distressed (v. 37).

---

I have studied this scene many times before but never from the point of view of the disciples. Imagine that you are one of the three. Consider what Jesus had represented to them for the past three years. He certainly represented security and strength. Grown men don't follow for three years with virtually no income unless they are completely taken with the leader. I believe Jesus was their whole lives. In Him their pasts made sense. Their present was totally immersed in Him, and all their hopes for the future rested in His faithfulness to do what He promised. And indeed He would . . . but never in a million years would they have expected how.

"My soul is swallowed up in sorrow—to the point of death. Remain here and stay awake with Me" (Matt. 26:38 HCSB).

Wait a second! This was their Rock! Their Strong Tower! "What in the world is wrong with Him? Why is He on the ground like that? Why is He writhing in anguish? Why is His hair drenched in sweat? It's freezing out here! And why does His sweat look like blood drops falling to the ground? Why does He keep asking for a cup to be taken from Him? What cup? He's crying 'Abba!' What's He so upset about? Is it because one of us betrayed Him? Why won't He stop? I hate seeing someone cry like that. I thought nothing could get to Him. Why won't He stop?"

The disciples may not have realized that Jesus was no less God that moment than He was on the Mount of Transfiguration or when He raised the dead. Their Rock and their Strong Tower was not falling apart. He was falling on His knees. That takes strength. Christ knew what He was going to have to do when He came to earth. He is the Lamb slain from the foundation of the world. He was as good as dead from the beginning. Jesus lived for one purpose alone: to do the will of His Father. Yet He still felt.

We are not wrong to feel. We are only wrong to disobey. Ask for the cup to be removed, but resolve to do His will. That's why He drew the three close enough to see. To teach them to pray . . . not sleep . . . in their anguish. This time they slept. But a time would come when each would rise from his own Gethsemane and bear his cross.

# DAY 109
## Matthew 27:45–54

---

At about three in the afternoon, Jesus cried out with a loud voice, "Elî, Elî, lemá sabachtháni?" that is, "My God, My God, why have You forsaken Me?" (v. 46).

---

The curtain drops on our scene in the form of darkness, which lasted three hours. The Light of the world was about to be extinguished, if only for a brief time. Just before He breathed His last, Jesus cried out with a loud voice, "Father, into your hands I commit my spirit" (Luke 23:46). How appropriate that He would use His last breaths to utter the trust upon which His entire life had rested.

But I'm not sure we can properly appreciate those words of faith unless we consider the ones spoken by Him only moments before. I believe this cry, "My God, my God, why have you forsaken me?" marked the exact moment when the sins of all humanity—past, present, and future—were heaped upon Christ and the full cup of God's wrath poured forth. Somehow I believe that to bear the sin, Jesus also had to bear the separation. Though Christ had to suffer the incomparable agony of separation from the fellowship of His Father while sin was judged, I am moved that He breathed His last breath with full assurance of His Father's trustworthiness. The human body of the life-giver hung lifeless. It was finished. He gave up His last human breath so He never had to give up on humanity.

Several years ago, I had the privilege of participating in a solemn assembly of 30,000 college students gathered on a huge field in Memphis, Tennessee. After we heard a powerful message about the cross, two young men began to walk down the hill carrying a large wooden cross. The two students, bent under the weight, carried the heavy cross through the crowd to a place just in front of the platform and then erected it as a visual aid. We couldn't possibly have planned what happened next.

Students began running to the cross with an urgency I can neither possibly describe nor recall without sobs. They sprinted from every direction through the crowd. Their sobs echoed in the open air. They lifted the cross out of the ground and began to pass it with their hands lifted high above their heads all over the crowd. They passed it from hands to hands all over the crowd and up the hill. I am covered with chills as I recall the scene when the repentant found refuge in the shadow of the cross.

In our sophistication and familiarity, have we been away too long? Run to the cross.

# DAY 110
## Mark 1:16–20

Immediately He called them, and they left their father Zebedee
in the boat with the hired men and followed Him (v. 20).

I'm so glad God chose to include the name of James and John's father in Scripture. He wasn't just any man. He wasn't just any father. He was Zebedee. He had a name. He had feelings. He had plans. He was probably close enough to each of his sons' births to hear Salome, his young, inexperienced wife, cry out in pain. He probably wept when he was told he had a son. And then another. No doubt, he praised God for such grace. Daughters were loved, but every man needed a son to carry on the family line, after all.

Two fine sons. That's what Zebedee had. He named them himself. They played in his shadow until they were old enough to work; and if I know anything about teenage boys, they still played plenty behind his back even when they were supposed to be working. Just about the time Zebedee grew exasperated with them, he'd look in their faces and see himself.

At the time when Christ called James and John, I have a feeling they had never been more pleasure or more support. Life is curious. Just about the time you get to reap some of the fruit of your parenting labors, the young, flourishing tree gets transplanted elsewhere.

Keith and I experienced this season of life I'm describing. The summers of our daughters' college years were great fun, and we never secretly wanted to push them back to school or down an aisle. They had never been more delightful, never been easier to care for, and never had more to offer in terms of company and stimulating conversation. I wonder if Zebedee felt the same way about his young adult sons.

Just when Zeb was reaping a harvest of parental rewards, James and John jumped ship. All he had to show for it was a slimy fishing net. What would happen to the business? What about Zebedee and Sons? No matter how Zebedee felt, I have a pretty good feeling God had great compassion on him. After all, He knew how Zebedee felt when John had to be called away from his father's side in order to fulfill his destiny.

Chances are pretty good Zebedee thought their sudden departure was a phase and they'd get over it. Glory to God, they never did. Once we let Jesus Christ really get to us, we never get over Him.

# DAY 111
## Mark 1:21–28

—∞∞∞—

They were all amazed . . . saying, "What is this? A new teaching with authority! He
commands even the unclean spirits, and they obey Him" (v. 27).

—∞∞∞—

The disciples saw Christ perform some eye-opening miracles almost from
the start. Although we are saving further comments on the wedding at Cana for
later, we know that it was the location of Christ's first miracle and that John's reference to the time frame of the wedding was "the third day" (John 2:1). The next
occurrence in sequence was Christ's trip to Capernaum with His mother, brothers, and disciples (John 2:12). The events we will study next probably happened
during the same stay in Capernaum, so imagine them falling next in sequence.

Jesus had just called Andrew, Peter, James, and John. Mark tells us they went
to Capernaum (Mark 1:21). Picture these four fishermen mingling in the crowd
gathered that Sabbath in the synagogue. I have an idea Christ's new disciples
didn't just watch Jesus as He preached. I have a feeling they watched the reaction
of others who were listening to Him as well. Mind you, at least Peter and Andrew
lived in Capernaum at that time (v. 29). A town this size had only one Jewish synagogue, so they worshiped with virtually the same people week after week. They
knew them personally. Some were relatives. Others were neighbors or business
associates. Imagine the kinds of reactions the disciples saw on these familiar faces
as Jesus preached.

Talk about an interesting service! If an "amazing" message were not enough
excitement, just then a man in their synagogue who was possessed by an evil spirit
cried out, "What do You have to do with us, Jesus—Nazarene? Have You come to
destroy us? I know who You are—the Holy One of God!" (v. 24 hcsb). Suddenly
their heads turned toward the opponent, almost like spectators in a tennis match.

I wonder if the crowd knew this man had an evil spirit before this moment
or if they had been oblivious for years to the nature of his problems. Had they
known, I'm not sure they would have allowed him in the synagogue, so my feeling is that the man may have kept it covered to some extent. Goodness knows
Satan loves a good disguise. Somehow, however, when the authority of Christ was
released in that place, the demons lost their cover. Jesus has a way of bringing the
devil right out of some people, doesn't He?

Yes, the mere presence of Jesus had caused the man—or should we say the
demon?—to cry out at the appearance of divine authority. Jesus commanded the
demons to come out of the man, but He also added something more. He commanded the spirit to be quiet.

Picture John witnessing these events. Many scholars believe he was the
youngest of the disciples. One strong basis for this deduction is his positioning

and apparent role at the Passover meal just before Jesus' crucifixion. We'll examine those events later, but for now keep in mind that the youngest at the Passover meal usually sat nearest the father or father figure so he could ask the traditional questions. I will refrain from building any doctrines on this deduction (since I could obviously be off base), but I am personally convinced enough that John was the youngest that I'll adopt this philosophy. If he was, can you imagine his face in particular while Jesus encountered—then cast out—these demons?

I think he probably experienced an entire concoction of emotions. Young men dearly love competitions, so he must have savored seeing his new team "win," even if only one Player was involved in the match. I have to think the encounter also scared him half to death. One thing that might have offset his fear was that he had to be indescribably impressed with his new mentor.

He wasn't the only one. Mark 1:21 tells us the crowds were generally amazed and astonished by Christ's teachings, but Mark 1:27 intensifies the adjectives by saying they were "all amazed" by His demonstration of authority over the demons.

We do love a show, don't we? When I think how patient Christ has been with our human preference for divine fireworks, I am more amazed than ever. Christ knows us intimately. He knows how to get our attention, but He also desires that we grow up and seek His presence and glory more than the display of His might. John and the other disciples would see many miracles, but Jesus was after something more. He was out to build maturity into this group.

I have a feeling by the time the fishermen reached Capernaum with Jesus, something more tagged along—the news of their leaving Zebedee holding the net. I don't doubt for a minute that these young men whose reputations were on the line reveled in the grand reaction people in the community had to their new Leader. What could be more exciting than being associated with the most powerful and popular new man on the scene?

# DAY 112
## Read Mark 1:29–30

---

As soon as they left the synagogue, they went into Simon and Andrew's house
with James and John. Simon's mother-in-law was lying in bed with a fever,
and they told Him about her at once (vv. 29–30).

---

What a relief to know that God doesn't just go to church, He goes to our
homes! When I was a little girl, I was fairly certain God lived in our church
baptistry. My vivid imagination turned dressing-room doors into secret passages
that led into the mysterious dwelling of the divine boogie man. I am happy to
report, though, that God doesn't live in the baptistry. He lives in the hearts of
those who trust Him and in the homes of those who provide Him room.

Sometimes, though, we don't bother to summon Jesus Christ into our
homes until we are overwhelmed by threatening circumstances.

Do you have a sense of Christ's activity in your home? I've a good reason for
asking you this question. Almost every spiritual marker of Christ's heightened
activity in my home came as a direct result of some threatening situation. Right
now both my daughters are walking with God, but I assure you this did not
simply happen in the natural evolution of their lives. I watched their relationships
grow over the years they shared our home, through situations in which some
threat convinced them to cleave closer to Christ.

When Jesus went to help Simon's mother-in-law, Luke 4:39 tells us He
"bent over her." I don't think I'm reading too much into the picture to imagine
a close encounter suggesting deep concern. I always reacted in a similar way any
time one of my children was sick. I didn't remain upright and stoic, checking off a
list of symptoms. I bent over them and drew close. I had learned from my mother
that I could better gauge a temperature with my cheek on their foreheads than
with a thermometer. I could not keep my distance from a sick child, even if her
malady was contagious.

Christ could have healed Simon's mother-in-law from the front porch. He
didn't. He came to her and drew down close. After all, she was in no position to
seek help for herself. He involved Himself one-on-one with those He helped.

Our homes today are threatened by fevers of all sorts—far beyond the
physiological: unresolved conflict, unforgiveness, unfaithfulness, compromising
media communications, pornography, and more. We need Jesus in our homes.

# DAY 113
## Mark 1:31–34

———∞———

So He went to her, took her by the hand, and raised her up (v. 31).

———∞———

Think of events such as Jesus' birth, baptism, crucifixion, and resurrection as primary events that can indeed be placed in time sequence. Then consider the specific incidents from Jesus' life as secondary events. We won't often be able to put the secondary events of the four Gospels into an unquestionable chronological order. Each of the Gospel writers selected the events and stories for specific reasons. Matthew wrote to show that Jesus is the Jewish Messiah. Mark wrote to tell the Romans about what Jesus did. Luke wrote to show that Jesus came to be the Savior for all peoples, and John wrote to show the meaning of Jesus' ministry. The Spirit led them to write to convey the message, not to tell us the order of events.

Based on identical time sequencing in Mark and Luke and with nothing in Matthew or John to refute it, however, I believe we can rightly assume that the first healing of the sick ever witnessed by the disciples was in Simon Peter's home.

Before we talk about the healing, however, let's consider a bit about the order of events in the Gospels. Surely an early turning point came in the hearts and minds of the disciples when healing hit home. I know it did for me. Seeing Him work in a church service is one thing. Witnessing His healing in the life of your own family is another. That's when a person begins to get it through her head that Jesus doesn't just love church. He loves people.

By comparing Mark 1:21 and 29, we see it was the Sabbath day. Jesus had delivered the demon-possessed man in the synagogue. "As soon as they left the synagogue, they went into Simon and Andrew's house with James and John" (v. 29 HCSB). Christ raised the ire of the Pharisees on more than a few occasions by picking this particular day of the week for healings. It seems as if He were making a point. Later we're going to see that in many ways this was the perfect day of the week for healing.

I didn't realize until doing some research that even His first healing was on the Sabbath. Obviously, Christ saw the purpose of the day far differently than many of His contemporaries. Apparently Simon Peter's mother-in-law was healed just in time to rise from the bed and get ready for company. As soon as the sun set, the whole town gathered at her door. They brought Jesus the sick and demon possessed for healing.

Have you ever seen someone receive an instantaneous physical healing like those described in this text? I've known plenty of people God healed physically, but I haven't had many chances to watch the manifestation of an instant healing take place before my very eyes. Few of us choose to confront the suffering around us because we feel so helpless. Imagine the contrast between the agony of seeing human suffering and the ecstasy of seeing them healed. What would such an experience have been like for Mother Teresa, for instance, as she daily died to her own desire for personal comfort and confronted the unimaginable suffering in Calcutta? Then to see many healed? Somehow my mind can hardly even fathom the range of emotions.

John had observed hundreds of Sabbaths in his life. Imagine that he awakened on the morning prior to these miraculous events with a fresh wave of, "I can hardly believe what I've done! I wonder what my mom and dad are thinking right now." He must have been excited and unsure, and his soul was filled with the reality that something new was looming on the horizon.

He prepared to go to the synagogue for services just as he had done all his life, only this time he got a bit more than he bargained for. The scroll was unraveled, and the Scripture for the day's service was read. Then Jesus took the role of rabbi, sat down, and preached the curly locks nearly off their heads.

Just then a man possessed by demons started shouting, and John saw Jesus get stern, perhaps for the first time. In an astounding show of power, Jesus cast out the demons, causing the man to shake violently. John thought as long as he lived, he would never forget the sound of those demons shrieking. He and the other disciples then walked together to Simon Peter's house, whispering all the way about what they'd seen. Simon Peter's mother-in-law was sick with a fever, so Jesus took her by the hand, helped her up, and the fever left her so instantaneously she began to serve them. Then they began to hear sounds at the door. Murmurings. Shrieking. Crying. Sounds of moaning. Sounds of hope. What's that— hope? Yes, hope—hope which says, "What He did for her, He might do for me." And that He did.

When John had awakened that morning, his mind could not have conceived just how many mercies were new that particular sunrise. I can only imagine the kinds of things that went through the mind of the young disciple the following night. He probably tossed and turned, unable to clear his head and rest. Perhaps he and James whispered from their pallets until they were overtaken by exhaustion and finally fell asleep.

# DAY 114
## Mark 1:35

∽∞∽

Very early in the morning, while it was still dark, He got up, went out,
and made His way to a deserted place. And He was praying there (v. 35).

∽∞∽

Two times of day; two fascinating looks at our Jesus—the One and Only.

Luke 4:40 tells us that the sick and suffering came out to see Jesus "when
the sun was setting." To those of us who are Gentiles, the reason for this is not so
obvious. Christ had previously left the synagogue when He went to the home of
Simon, meaning it was the Sabbath day. Remember, at this point Christ primarily
had been ministering in various synagogues to Jews. It was unlawful for them to
carry the sick on the Sabbath. But God-fearing people counted the moments until
the sun set over the Sea of Galilee, marking the close of day. So as the darkness
fell, they bundled their sick and brought them to the Light. The thought almost
makes me cry. It was as if they watched the clock of the law tick until it finally
struck grace . . . and they raced to Him with their need. How blessed we are to
live in the liberty of a completed Calvary! The pharmacy dispensing God's grace
is open 24/7.

But a second snapshot of time also appears in our passage. Early the next
morning, Jesus rose and went out to pray (Mark 1:35). I wish I had words to
express the feelings such scriptural moments stir in me. The thought of Christ
ducking out the door while it was still dark to find a place to be by Himself with
God floods my soul with emotion. I love every glimpse of the unique relationship Father and Son shared while Christ was on earth and His Father was in
heaven. Never before had such a bridge connected the celestial and the terrestrial.
I always wonder what Christ said to His Father and what He heard in those intimate moments. Did God the Father speak audibly to Him? Or did He speak in
His heart like He does to you and me through His Word? I can't wait to find out
someday in glory.

We have no idea how often Jesus got to steal away with His Father, but
Scripture says He was soon interrupted by his disciples, excitedly shouting,
"Everyone is looking for you!" (v. 37). I'm convinced we don't give enough thought
to how challenging Jesus' prison of flesh must have felt to Him. Prior to His
advent, He was completely unencumbered by the natural laws governing the
human body. Suddenly He experienced for Himself the pull to be in many places
at once and the challenge to prioritize not just the good but the goal: proclaiming
the good news of the kingdom of God. "That is why I have come" (v. 38).

# DAY 115
## Mark 1:36–39

⸻

Simon and his companions went searching for Him.
They found Him and said, "Everyone's looking for You!" (vv. 36–37).

⸻

Ah, here we have an insight into the present state of mind of Jesus' first followers. Forget what Jesus did in private! They wanted to be seen in public with the popular Jesus! We're not going to be too hard on them, now, because they were demonstrating a normal part of adolescent Christianity. We're the same way in our spiritual immaturity. At first we are far more excited about corporate worship than we are private worship.

The terminology of the original language tells us they were tracking Jesus down, almost like a manhunt. The Greek word translated "to look," is often used in a hostile sense.[29] I'm not suggesting they were hostile toward Jesus but that they were quite anxious and maybe even a little put out with Him that He wasn't where all the people were. We see no indication from the text that they hesitated for a moment of respect or awe when they found Jesus praying. They barreled on the scene with, "Everyone is looking for you!"

I would like to offer a little conjecture that the companions tracking down Jesus may have been Peter, James, and John. Later in His ministry, these three men were chosen by Christ to watch Him on several different occasions in the inner places. Something caused Jesus to single them out, and it wasn't their spiritual maturity. I think two primary motivations compelled Christ to draw the three into several intimate places:

• The fact that they just didn't "get it" at times.
• The fact that Jesus knew once they did "get it," they'd really get it!

In other words, I wonder if Christ might have thought, "So you're not the boundaries types, are you? Okay, I'll take you behind some ordinary boundaries, but I'll hold you responsible for what you learn while you're there." Just food for thought.

I have a friend whose little boy thought he was the teacher's pet because she seated him in class right in front of her desk. He didn't realize for years that she was motivated by his discipline problems. Why didn't she just send him to the principal instead of expending so much energy on him? Because she knew the child had a student in him, and she was determined to find it. And she did. We're going to see Peter, James, and John get their desks moved to the front of the class. Just like children, they might be tempted at times to think the Rabbi moved them there because they were the Teacher's pets.

# DAY 116
## Mark 5:35–43

—∞∞∞—

He took the child by the hand and said to her, *"Talitha koum!"* (which is translated,
"Little girl, I say to you, get up!").... At this they were utterly astounded (vv. 41–42).

—∞∞∞—

I want to remind you of one of our objectives. You may otherwise be frustrated over my leapfrogging from place to place in Scripture. Although I wish we could go through every step the disciples took with Christ, one of the purposes of this journey is to draw riches from the life and letters of John. We've taken the first steps of his encounters with Jesus rather slowly because he was among those first chosen to follow Christ. For a time we will pick up the pace rather dramatically as we leapfrog from scene to scene. As we focus on the synoptic Gospels, our objective is to concentrate on the settings where John is named or known to be present.

Keep in mind that Jesus had many followers, but He chose twelve from the many to walk nearest to Him. Every moment the twelve spent with Jesus was significant, but over the next couple of days we're going to look at two scenes with some common denominators that no doubt had a profound effect on John. Try your best to view each occurrence from his point of view. Keep in mind that John was probably the youngest of the apostles and younger brother to one. Think of him as flesh and blood, and imagine what each experience might have been like for him.

We find scene one in this passage from Mark, chapter 5. The synagogue ruler named Jairus had requested that Jesus heal his daughter, and they were on the way to his home. Men met them and told Jairus not to bother the Rabbi because the girl had already died. Jesus told Jairus, "Don't be afraid. Only believe" (v. 36 HCSB).

I am fascinated by what Jesus did next. First, "He did not let anyone accompany Him except Peter, James, and John, James' brother" (v. 37 HCSB). This reduced number proceeded to the home. The mourners had already gathered. In fact, they laughed when Jesus said the girl was not dead. So He drove the crowd out of the house. He took the three disciples and the girl's parents into the room with Him. Jesus then raised the girl from the dead with a mere verbal command.

I can't help wondering what went through the minds of the three men when they were allowed to follow Jesus to a place the others weren't invited. I know what would have gone through my feminine mind. Women tend to be so relational. I hardly would have been able to enjoy the privilege without fretting over the others being left out. Then, of course, I would have worried about whether they would be mad at me when we got back. I would imagine for days that they were acting a little weird. In fact, knowing I would have fretted myself half to death, Jesus most likely wouldn't have bothered letting me come. No telling how many things I've missed because I make a knot out of the simplest string.

Oh, but how I would have hated to miss the eyeful the three got that particular day. Raising the stone-cold dead is nothing less than divine. This scene was not business as usual no matter how many miracles the three had seen and even performed.

I have been with several people right around their times of death, and I was utterly amazed each time how quickly the body grew cold. In spiritual terms, the soul is what keeps a body warm. Physical death occurs when the soul (meaning the immaterial part of a person—soul and spirit) departs the body. At its exodus, the warmth of life departs as well. We can be comforted by the fresh realization that the spiritual life is in the soul, and the soul continues living. We talk about the finality of death, but it has relatively little finality to the believer.

I'm so glad Jesus didn't listen to those who discouraged Jairus from "bothering" the teacher any more. Their reason was because the girl was dead. But the death of a loved one is no time to quit "bothering" Jesus. No, He's not very likely to raise our loved one from the dead, but He can do countless other things to get us through our losses. Comfort is the most obvious need, but we have others.

I often talk to people who remain hamstrung by a death that has left many issues or answers unresolved. If I may be so bold, sometimes the missing person is not a loved one but an unforgiven or unforgiving one with whom we needed to make peace. Hopelessness often ensues. Depression can result. Sometimes we are convinced that all parties must be alive and kicking for us to gain peace in a situation.

Needless to say, the ideal time to make peace with others is while everyone's still breathing. But if it's too late, bother the Teacher! He doesn't have our limitations or rationalizations. Has a death left you with unfinished business? Finish it with Jesus.

# DAY 117
## Mark 7:31–36

———ೲ———

They brought to Him a deaf man who also had a speech difficulty, and begged Jesus to lay His hand on him. So He took him away from the crowd privately (vv. 32–33).

———ೲ———

Sometimes when Jesus is about to do something really special in our lives, He will rearrange our surroundings. He will take us out of our element, just as He took this deaf man "away from the crowd" to give him a new perspective on God's glory and power.

This reminds me of a time when our daughter Amanda had begun dating a young man. They were just getting to know one another. It was that exciting stage of dating life when everything about this other person is fresh and new and interesting.

They were walking through a shopping mall together, and he turned to her and said, "I want so much to know you, Amanda. And I want you to know me. I want you to know what I love." He began describing to her how much he enjoyed mountain climbing and camping, just being out in the wild—a whole world away from anything that's the norm of everyday life. He went on and on about what it meant to him to be out in the middle of nowhere and to sense nature all around him.

"I'd say that's my element," he concluded. "What's yours?" She looked around the mall and motioned to the sights, sounds, and stores that enveloped her. "*This* is my element." She was dead serious. When she told me about it later, I had to go to my room, shut the door, and fall on the bed laughing. I thought, "Yep, that's her element, all right. She got it honest. Her mother raised her in it."

It's true. I remember how disappointed I was when I figured out that my spiritual gift wasn't shopping at the mall, as I had originally thought. After becoming a serious believer and trying to recognize what my gifts were, I discovered that "fashion" wasn't even on the list of biblical attributes. My theory was blown.

Instead, the Lord was calling me out of my element, growing in me the spiritual gift of love for the body of Christ. But to do that, He needed me in a new set of surroundings, out where He could show me that even if we speak with the tongues of angels, if we don't have love, we may as well be clanging brass.

Until He has us out of our element—and into His—we will never see His glory. We will always be deaf to what He was trying to say.

# DAY 118
## Mark 9:2–10

His clothes became dazzling—extremely white as no launderer on earth could whiten them. Elijah appeared to them with Moses, and they were talking with Jesus (vv. 3–4).

Although much time elapsed and many significant events occurred between the healing of Jairus's daughter and the transfiguration, what makes these two scenes priorities at this point in the book is the inclusion of only three disciples.

In Mark 5:37, the three were listed as "Peter, James, and John, James' brother" (HCSB). In this scene, John is no longer named like a tagalong brother. At this point, we see his identity in Scripture undoubtedly emerging. Also note that Jesus didn't just let Peter, James, and John come along. He *took* them. He "led them" there (Mark 9:2).

God's will always expresses divine intention. Just as Jesus was intentional toward the experiences and exposures of the three, Christ is intentional toward us. He never bosses us or appoints us to something for the sheer sake of presuming authority. His will always has purpose. Sometimes we go our own ways, and God still has mercy on us and shows us something there. Other times we beg Him to allow us to go a certain place and He consents. Still other times God takes us places we never intended to go. Those are places where He will reveal Himself to us in ways we didn't even know He existed.

All three synoptic Gospels record the transfiguration. Matthew's Gospel supplies the detail that the three disciples fell facedown to the ground. I am convinced that the people of God miss many appropriate opportunities to fall facedown to the ground, not in an emotional frenzy but in complete awe of God. We don't have a clue Who we're dealing with. I believe one of Jesus' chief reasons for transfiguring Himself before the three disciples was to say, "I am not like you. This is just a glimpse of who I am."

Remember, Jesus had equipped them with supernatural power to perform some of the same miracles He performed. What would keep these three from thinking that just maybe, in time, they might be His peers? God forbid the thought! Jesus is not a superhuman. He is God—the beloved, divine Son of Him who occupies the throne of all creation.

God says in Psalm 50:21, "You thought I was just like you. But I will rebuke you and lay out the case before you" (HCSB). One primary reason He takes us to places we've never been is to show us He's not like anyone else.

# DAY 119
## Mark 9:14–18

───◆◆◆───

I asked Your disciples to drive it out, but they couldn't (v. 18).

───◆◆◆───

We are often empowered to do far more than we exercise. In Luke 9:1 we read that Jesus gave the disciples "power and authority to drive out all demons." Had He taken it back? No, they still possessed the power but were unable to exercise it for some reason. What in the world happened to disable them? Let's explore a couple of possibilities.

1. *Their most positive influences were absent.* Keep in mind that not only was Christ out of sight, but so were the three leaders of the disciples. In moments like these, we learn where our confidence is. If we have boldness when certain empowered believers are close by, but we lose it in their absence, could it be that we've been sipping out of their power shaker of faith instead of filling our own? We'll never discover our strengths in the power of God if we keep drawing off another's.

2. *Their strongest negative influences were present.* The presence of the teachers of the law must have been terribly intimidating to these comparatively uneducated men. You and I aren't always surrounded by faith-encouragers either. But we can't afford to wait for all the atmospheric conditions to be right before we act on the power of God. In fact, I think God is teaching us that the worst conditions can often provide the best atmosphere to act in faith. He doesn't want our confidence regulated by our audience. If faith-discouragers can shake our confidence badly enough to disable us, our confidence may be in ourselves instead of God.

I remember a time when a critical letter from a seminary graduate shook my confidence. As I read the list of mistakes she was pointing out, I started thinking, "She's right! What in the world do I think I'm doing? I have no formal theological education. I shouldn't even be doing this!" But God reminded me during the following days that I was exactly right: I *shouldn't* be doing this. This ministry is God's. If my confidence is in myself, I'm in big trouble. God also assured me that I will always make mistakes, but they will serve as reminders to my readers never to think more highly of this teacher than they ought. Only One can be taken at His every word.

# DAY 120
## Mark 9:19–29

---

Many times it has thrown him into fire or water to destroy him.
But if You can do anything, have compassion on us and help us (v. 22).

---

After nearly four decades of knowing Christ, I am only beginning to realize the magnitude of the sin of unbelief. The word "unbelieving" in verse 19 means "not worthy of confidence, untrustworthy." This definition implies that when we are faithless, we are concluding that Christ is not worthy of our confidence, that He is . . . (I can hardly bring myself to write the word) . . . *untrustworthy*. The disciples' unbelief was their willingness to let the temperature of their faith rise and fall according to their surrounding dynamics rather than God's steadfast Word. The characteristic cause of all spiritual failure is lack of faith in God.

But the disciples weren't the only ones having a crisis of faith here. The boy's father had been through a lot watching his son suffer. He frequently feared for his son's life. We can sympathize with the despair he felt. But unfortunately, like many people, he was far more familiar with the power of the devil than the power of the Son of God.

Even in our churches, many are learning more about the power of the devil than the omnipotence of the living God! Like the father in this passage, many do not understand that surrounding dynamics, like the length and depth of defeat, have absolutely no bearing on Christ's ability to perform a miracle. Hear it again: *no bearing*.

Consider the dynamics of length and depth in our text today. We know from the father's response to Jesus' question that his son had suffered since childhood (Mark 9:21). Now, the reason Jesus asked how long the boy had been in his present state wasn't because the answer had a bearing on Christ's ability to free him. He asked the question for the purpose of framing a miracle against the backdrop of hopelessness. Then the father, after stating the hopelessness of the boy's condition, made a statement that probably provokes a host of emotions in each of us: "But if you can do anything, take pity on us and help us" (Mark 9:22). I'd like to break down this phrase into several pieces, then consider Christ's response.

• *"But . . ."* This one little word suggests the tiniest mustard seed of faith in the father—a seed Christ compassionately watered. I am continually moved by Christ's willingness not just to meet us halfway but, like the father of the prodigal, to run the entire distance once we take the first step in His direction. The Word of God is filled with accounts of hopeless situations followed by that wonderful little word: "but . . ."! Because of His great compassion, sometimes that little whisper is all the invitation Jesus needs to show His power.

• *"If You can."* Christ took exception to the father's use of the word "if," because when an action is consistent with the Word of God, the question is never *if* He can. It may be if He *wills*, but never if He can. When those who have access to Christ experience long-term defeat in their lives, it is often wrapped up in a continued "if You can" mentality. We who know Christ must always answer with a resounding: "Nothing is too hard for Him!"

In at least one way, you and I can't claim the ignorance of the father in this story. We assume he didn't know Christ personally. So Jesus didn't reprove the father the same way He reproved the disciples. Like them, you and I know Christ Jesus as far more than a teacher rumored to possess supernatural power. We call Him Lord. Consider the irony of addressing Him as Master of the universe, then asking Him to come to our aid—if He can. Notice the next words from this distraught dad:

• *"If You can do anything."* Contrast the two words from Mark 9 for a moment: "anything" (v. 22) and "everything" (v. 23). Dear one, Christ can't just do *anything*. Christ can do *everything!* Stop wondering if Christ can do "anything" in your situation, and start believing Him to do "everything" glorious!

Immediately the father exclaimed, "I do believe; help me overcome my unbelief" (v. 24). I can't describe the encouragement this father's honesty has given me through the years. First he cried out, "I do believe!" Then he confessed his unbelief. I believe the father changed his tune because he was looking straight into the face of truth. The closer we get to Jesus, the more difficult it is to stretch the truth.

The wonderful part of the father's exclamation is his realization that, although he lacked faith, he wanted to believe! Then he did exactly what he should have done: he asked for help to overcome his unbelief.

I can't count the times I've imitated this father's actions. In my earlier days with God, I viewed faith as my willingness to make a believing statement with my mouth rather than face the questions of my heart. If only I had understood how Romans 10:10 reverses that order: "For it is with your heart that you believe and are justified, and it is with your mouth that you confess and are saved."

It's time for a dramatic change of approach. If we don't have bold faith, let's start asking boldly for the faith we lack. Imagine the love of a God who says, "It's true that without faith it is impossible to please Me. But I am so anxious to reward you with blessing, I'm even willing to supply the faith you lack. Ask Me, My child! Ask Me for what you lack! I am the only One who can help you overcome your unbelief!"

# DAY 121
## Mark 10:35–45

❦

Whoever wants to become great among you must be your servant,
and whoever wants to be first among you must be a slave to all (vv. 43–44).

❦

James and John painted a pretty good picture of spiritual toddlerhood, didn't they? But let's face it. All of us have to go through spiritual toddlerhood and adolescence to get to a place of maturity. We don't ordinarily leap up. We grow up.

For a few moments, however, James and John did nothing but descend deeper and deeper into the quicksand of their own self-absorption. (And never doubt it is quicksand.) In this scene, James and John made only three statements: "Teacher, we want You to do something for us if we ask You" (v. 35 HCSB), "Allow us to sit at Your right and at Your left in Your glory" (v. 37 HCSB), and a third statement from verse 39 that we'll consider in a moment. Meditate on these. Try to capture the emotions and attitudes behind them. Do you see a growing audacity with each statement?

And don't think for a minute they wouldn't have dug themselves deeper if given the opportunity. Had Christ told them He might consider one on His right and one on His left, how long do you think it would have taken them to rumble over who would sit where?

Their famous last words almost slay me. After Christ asked, "Are you able to drink the cup I drink or to be baptized with the baptism I am baptized with?" they answered without hesitation: "We are able." They didn't have any idea what they were talking about because they didn't have any idea what Christ was talking about. Soon they would. One day in the distant future they would sip from the cup and know the baptism of His suffering. But in their present state they needed a baby bottle, not a cup.

Our problem is often the same as theirs. We let the human image of Christ mislead us into downsizing Him. "If He'd just stoop a little and we stood on our tiptoes, we'd be just about side by side. One at His left. One at His right." But I am convinced that if we, present company included, really "got" the concept of being chosen and called by the divine Son of God, His Spirit would have to set us on our feet for us to get off our faces (Ezek. 2:1). Yes, we've been chosen and, yes, we've been called, and we'll know we're grasping the concept when our humanity is cloaked in humility—not "Teacher, we want You to do something for us," but "Teach us to do for You whatever You ask."

# DAY 122
## Mark 14:32–42

⸺⸱⸺

*He said, "Abba, Father! All things are possible for You. Take this cup away from Me. Nevertheless, not what I will, but what You will" (v. 36).*

⸺⸱⸺

Without Mark's Gospel, we would not know Christ cried out to His Father using the name, "Abba." I don't often give you an extensive quote, but this one captured my soul with rich meditation; I hope it will yours.

> Abba is originally . . . a word derived from baby-language. When a child is weaned, "it learns to say 'abba (daddy) and 'imma (mummy)." . . . Also used by adult sons and daughters. . . . 'abba acquired the warm, familiar ring which we may feel in such an expression as "dear father." Nowhere in the entire wealth of devotional literature produced by ancient Judaism do we find 'abba being used as a way of addressing God. The pious Jew knew too much of the great gap between God and man to be free to address God with the familiar word used in everyday family life. . . . We find only one example of 'abba used in reference to God. It occurs in a story recorded in the Babylonian Talmud: "When the world had need of rain, our teachers used to send the schoolchildren to Rabbi Hanan ha Nehba [end of the 1st cent. B.C.], and they would seize the hem of his cloak and call out to him: 'Dear father ('abba), dear father ('abba), give us rain.' He said before God: 'Sovereign of the world, do it for the sake of these who cannot distinguish between an 'abba who can give rain and an 'abba who can give no rain.'"[30]

When Christ Jesus fell to His face and cried out, "Abba, Father," He cried out to the Abba who can give rain. The sovereign of the world was His Daddy. Everything was possible for Him . . . including removing the cup of dread.

Never minimize the moment by thinking God couldn't have removed the cup. Do not subtract God's freedom of choice from this picture. God could have chosen to reject the way of the cross. After all, He is the sovereign of the universe.

That God could have stopped the process yet didn't is a matchless demonstration of love. Can you think of anyone for whom you'd watch your only child be tortured to death? "'Abba, Father,' he said, 'everything is possible for you. Take this cup from me'" (Mark 14:36).

The request Christ placed before the Father ought to make us catch our breath. It ascended to heaven through wails of grief. God's beloved was overwhelmed with sorrow to the point of death. Luke's Gospel tells us His sweat dropped like blood, a condition almost unheard of except when the physical body is placed in more stress and grief than it was fashioned to handle. Do we think God sat upon His throne unmoved?

Our hearts ought to miss a beat. Christ could have walked past the cross. He could have—but He didn't. Luke 22:47 tells us, "While he was still speaking a crowd came up." Imagine the scene they walked into that night.

Please try to grasp Christ's physical condition just before the crowd headed up the Mount of Olives to seize Him. Like a body that rejects a transplanted organ, the human body of Jesus Christ was practically tearing itself apart. The full throttle of divine impact and emotion was almost more than one human body could endure. The stress had nearly turned Him inside out. I do not make this point to emphasize His weakness. Quite the contrary. In fact I find the scene recorded in John 18:6 portrays His incredible power. When Jesus told the crowd, "I am he," even overwhelmed with sorrow to the point of death, the proclaimed presence of Jesus Christ knocked the mob to the ground.

Dear sweet Jesus. We really have no idea who You are, do we? Your God-ness could not be diminished for a moment, in or out of that prison of flesh. Lord, don't let us forget. You, who submitted Yourself to the hands of sinful men, were very God.

# DAY 123
## Luke 1:26–33

—⊶∞⊷—

You will conceive and give birth to a son, and you will call His name Jesus (v. 31).

—⊶∞⊷—

Picture the omniscient eyes of the unfathomable *El Roi*—the God who sees—spanning the universe in panoramic view, every galaxy in His gaze. Imagine now the gradual tightening of His lens as if a movie camera were attached to the point of a rocket bound for planet Earth. Not a man-made rocket, but a celestial rocket—of the living kind.

Gabriel has been summoned once again to the throne of God. At least six months have passed since God last sent him to Jerusalem, to foretell another unexpected birth—this one to an elderly priest named Zechariah, whose equally aged wife, Elizabeth, was to bear a son, John—John the Baptist. This previous assignment took Gabriel to Herod's temple, one of the wonders of the civilized world. But this time heaven's lens focuses northward.

Imagine Gabriel plunging earthward through the floor of the third heaven, breaking the barrier from the supernatural to the natural world. Feature him swooping down through the second heaven past the stars God calls by name. As our vision "descends," the earth grows larger. God's kingdom gaze burns through the blue skies of planet Earth and plummets like a flaming stake in the ground to a backward town called Nazareth.

I love to imagine where Mary was when Gabriel appeared to her. I wonder if she was in her bedroom or walking a dusty path fetching water for her mother. One thing for sure: she was alone.

No matter where the angelic ambassador appeared to Mary, he must have stunned her with his choice of salutations: "Greetings, you who are highly favored! The Lord is with you." Prior to Zechariah's encounter, four centuries had passed since God had graced the earth with a heavenly visitation. I doubt the thought occurred to anyone that he would transmit the most glorious news ever heard in all the world to a simple Galilean girl.

How I love the way God works! Just when we decide He's too complicated to comprehend, He draws stick pictures.

I'm sure Mary wasn't looking for an angelic encounter that day. As the recipient of such news, she was totally unsuspecting. Humble. Meek. Completely caught off guard. Luke 1:29 tells us Mary was "greatly troubled" at his words. The phrase actually means "to stir up throughout." You know the feeling: when butterflies don't just flutter in your stomach but land like a bucket at your feet, splashing fear and adrenaline through every appendage. Mary felt the fear through and through, wondering what kind of greeting this might be. How could this young girl comprehend that she was "highly favored" (Luke 1:28) by the Lord God Himself?

The angel's next statement was equally stunning: "The Lord is with you." Although similar words had been spoken over men such as Moses, Joshua, and Gideon, I'm not sure they had ever been spoken over a woman. I'm not suggesting the Lord is not as present in the lives of women as He is men, but this phrase suggested a unique presence and power for the purpose of fulfilling a divine kingdom plan. The sight of the young girl gripped by fear provoked Gabriel to continue with the words, "Do not be afraid, Mary, you have found favor with God" (v. 30). Not until his next words did she have any clue why he had come or for what she had been chosen.

"You will be with child and give birth to a son" (v. 31). Not just any son—"the Son of the Most High" (v. 32). Probably only Mary's youth and inability to absorb the information kept her from fainting in a heap!

Then came my favorite line of all: "You are to give him the name Jesus" (v. 31). Do you realize this was the first proclamation of our Savior's personal name since the beginning of time? Jesus. The very name at which every knee will one day bow. The very name that every tongue will one day confess. A name that has no parallel in my vocabulary or yours. A name I whispered into the ears of my infant daughters as I rocked them and sang lullabies of His love. A name by which I've made every single prayerful petition of my life. A name that has meant my absolute salvation, not only from eternal destruction, but from myself. A name with power like no other name. *Jesus.*

What a beautiful name. I love to watch how it falls off the lips of those who love Him. I shudder as it falls off the lips of those who don't. *Jesus.* It has been the most important and most consistent word in my life. Dearer today than yesterday. Inexpressibly precious to me personally, so I am at a loss to comprehend what the name means universally.

*Jesus.* The Greek spelling is *Iesous*, transliterated from the Hebrew *Yeshu'a* (Joshua). Keep in mind that Christ's earthly family spoke a Semitic language closely related to Hebrew (called Aramaic), so He would have been called Yeshu'a. One of the things I like best is that it was a common name. After all, Jesus came to seek and to save common people like me. Most pointedly, the name Jesus means "Savior." Others may have shared the name, but no one else would ever share the role. We have much to learn about Jesus, the Savior. I can hardly wait!

# DAY 124
## Luke 1:34–35a

—∞∞∞—

Mary asked the angel, "How can this be,
since I have not been intimate with a man?" (v. 34).

—∞∞∞—

Luke 1:27 tells us that when the angel Gabriel appeared to Mary to
announce that she would bear the Son of God, she was a virgin "pledged to be
married to a man named Joseph." Actually, their betrothal compares more to our
idea of *marriage* than engagement. The difference was the matter of physical intimacy, but the relationship was legally binding. Betrothal began with a contract
drawn up by the parents or by a friend of the groom. Then at a meeting between
the two families, in the presence of witnesses, the groom would present the bride
with jewelry. The groom would announce his intentions to firmly observe the
contract. Then he would sip from a cup of wine and offer the cup to the bride.
If she sipped from the same cup, she was in effect entering covenant with him.

The next step was the payment of the *mohar*, or dowry, by the groom. This
occurred at a ceremony, ordinarily involving a priest. Other traditions were also
practiced, but these were the most basic and consistent. By the time a couple
reached this step, their betrothal was binding, though a marriage ceremony and
physical intimacy had not yet taken place. An actual divorce would be necessary
to break the covenant. Furthermore, if the prospective groom died, the bride-
to-be was considered a widow.

Betrothal traditionally occurred soon after the onset of adolescence, so it
is probably accurate to imagine Mary around age thirteen at the time of the
announcement. Remember, in that culture a thirteen or fourteen-year-old was
commonly preparing for marriage.

Mary's question, then, was a quite obvious one: She asked, "How will this
be . . . since I am a virgin?" (v. 34).

Gabriel met Mary's question with a beautifully expressive response. "The
Holy Spirit will come upon you, and the power of the Most High will overshadow you." The Greek word for "come upon" is *eperchomai*, meaning "to . . .
arrive, invade . . . resting upon and operating in a person." Only one woman in all
of humanity would be chosen to bear the Son of God, yet each one of us who are
believers have been invaded by Jesus Christ through His Holy Spirit (see Rom.
8:9). He has been invading the closets, the attic, and the basement of my life ever
since I accepted Him. How I praise God for the most glorious invasion of privacy
that ever graced a human life!

# DAY 125
### Luke 1:35b-38

———

"I am the Lord's slave," said Mary. "May it be done to me
according to your word." Then the angel left her (v. 38).

———

I wonder if Mary knew when He arrived in her womb. Brothers in the
faith might be appalled that I would ask such a question, but female minds were
created to think intimate, personal thoughts like these! I have at least a hundred
questions to ask Mary in heaven.

No doubt Mary would have some interesting stories to tell. Part of the fun
of heaven will be hearing spiritual giants tell the details of the old, old stories.
Mary certainly wouldn't have thought of herself as a spiritual giant, would she? I
would love to know the exact moment this young adolescent absorbed the news
that she would carry and deliver God's Son.

Gabriel ultimately wrapped up the story of the divine conception with one
profound statement: "So the holy one to be born will be called the Son of God"
(v. 35). The term *holy one* has never been more perfectly and profoundly applied
than in Gabriel's statement concerning the Son of God.

Could a teenager have fathomed that she was to give birth to the Son who
was the radiance of God's glory and the exact representation of His being? (Heb.
1:3). Perhaps Mary's age was on her side. When my two daughters were teenag-
ers, and when they would tell me something, I always had more questions than
they had answers. I'd say, "Did you ask this question?" to which they'd invariably
say, "No, ma'am. Never even occurred to me." I wanted to know every detail.
They were too young to realize any were missing!

Mary only asked the one question. When all was said and done, her solitary
reply was: "I am the Lord's servant. . . . May it be to me as you have said" (v. 38).
The Greek word for slave or servant is *doule*, which is the feminine equivalent
to *doulos*, a male bondservant. In essence, Mary was saying, "Lord, I am Your
handmaid. Whatever You want, I want." Total submission. No other questions.

We might be tempted to think: *Easy for her to say! Her news was good! Who
wouldn't want to be in her shoes? Submitting isn't hard when the news is good!* Oh,
yes, the news was good. The best. But the news was also hard. When the winds
of heaven converge with the winds of earth, lightning is bound to strike. Seems
to me that Gabriel left just in time for Mary to tell her mother. I have a feeling
Nazareth was about to hear and experience a little thunder.

# DAY 126
## Luke 1:39–44

—∽∞∼—

When Elizabeth heard Mary's greeting, the baby leaped inside her,
and Elizabeth was filled with the Holy Spirit (v. 41).

—∽∞∼—

Imagine that you are Mary, thirteen or fourteen years old, but in a very different culture. You awakened to the sun playing a silent reveille over the Galilean countryside. You dress in typical fashion, a simple tunic draped with a cloak. A sash wrapped around the waist allows you to walk without tripping over the long fabric. You are the virgin daughter of a Jewish father, so you have draped your veil over your head and crossed it over your shoulders for the duration of the day. You have never known another kind of dress, so you are completely accustomed to the weight and the constant adjusting of a six-foot-long, four-foot-wide veil. Beneath the veil, thick, dark hair frames a deep complexion and near-ebony eyes.

Without warning, a messenger from God appears and announces that you have been chosen among women to bear the Son of God. You can hardly believe, yet you dare not doubt. As suddenly as the angel appeared, he vanishes. You are flooded with emotions.

What do you imagine you would be thinking and feeling right now? What in the world does a young woman do after receiving such life-altering news?

Often God allows the space between the lines of His Word to capture our imaginations and prompt us to wonder. Not this time. He told us exactly what Mary did next.

Remember Gabriel's declaration. The most revolutionary news since Eden's fall: "the Savior is on His way." Announcing the soon-coming Messiah, he offered the stunned adolescent an almost out-of-place slice of information. By the way, "Elizabeth your relative is going to have a child in her old age, and she . . . is in her sixth month" (v. 36).

How like God! In the middle of news with universal consequences, He recognized the personal consequences to one girl.

For years the scene of Mary running to Elizabeth has tendered my heart. I'd like to share my thoughts on this moment from my first book, *Things Pondered: From the Heart of a Lesser Woman.* These words were never meant to provide doctrinal exegesis, but to invite us to the momentary wonder of being a woman:

"How tender the God who shared with her through an angel that someone nearby could relate. The two women had one important predicament in common—questionable pregnancies, sure to stir up some talk. Elizabeth hadn't been out of the house in months. It makes you wonder why. As happy as she was, it must have been strange not to blame her sagging figure and bumpy thighs on the baby. And to think she was forced to borrow maternity clothes from her friends' granddaughters. But maybe Elizabeth and Mary were too busy talking between themselves to pay much attention. Can you imagine their conversation over tea? One too old, the other too young. One married to an old priest, the other promised to a young carpenter. One heavy with child, the other with no physical evidence to fuel her faith. But God had graciously given them one another with a bond to braid their lives forever.

"Women are like that, aren't they? We long to find someone who has been where we've been, who shares our fragile places, who sees our sunsets with the same shades of blue."[31]

Elizabeth lived fifty to seventy miles from Nazareth. Mary had no small trip ahead of her and no small amount of time to replay the recent events. She probably joined others making the trip, but we have no reason to assume anyone traveled with her. Can you imagine how different she was already beginning to feel? How did it feel to finally enter the village Zechariah and Elizabeth called home? What do you imagine was going through Mary's mind as she passed village merchants and mothers with children?

Finally, Mary entered Zechariah's home and greeted Elizabeth. Mary's words of salutation may have been common, but Elizabeth's reaction was far from common. The infant John jumped within his mother's womb, and Elizabeth was suddenly "filled with the Holy Spirit" (v. 41). Elizabeth proclaimed Mary and her child "blessed" and asked a glorious question: "Why am I so favored, that the mother of my Lord should come to me?" (v. 43).

Mary and Elizabeth shared not only tender similarities but also vital differences. Elizabeth pointed out the most profound difference: she was expecting her son; Mary was expecting her Lord. The concepts seem almost unfathomable even with the complete revelation of the Word. Don't miss the riches that follow Elizabeth's inspiring question. She went on to announce: "As soon as the sound of your greeting reached my ears, the baby in my womb leaped for joy. Blessed is she who has believed that what the Lord has said to her will be accomplished!" (Luke 1:44–45).

# DAY 127
## Luke 1:46–55

—◦◦◦—

The Mighty One has done great things for me, and His name is holy (v. 49).

—◦◦◦—

Mary's wonderful words from her Magnificat offer us an opportunity to catch a glimpse of several facts about her:

*Her excitement.* Mary had probably been too scared to celebrate before, but Elizabeth's confirmation of God's miraculous work set her free! How do I know? Behold verse 47: "My spirit rejoices in God my Savior." The original word for "rejoices" is *agalliao*, meaning "to exult, leap for joy, to show one's joy by leaping and skipping denoting excessive or ecstatic joy and delight. Often spoken of rejoicing with song and dance." Whether or not young Mary began physically jumping up and down with joy and excitement, her insides certainly did! I am totally blessed by the thought. Nothing is more appropriate than getting excited when God does something in our lives. I think He loves it!

*Her love of Scripture.* Mary's song reflects twelve different Old Testament passages. She didn't just hear the Word; she held it to her heart and pondered it. Scripture draws a picture of a reflective young woman with an unusual heart for God. A young Hebrew girl believed nothing to be as important as motherhood. I believe she must have recalled a favorite Old Testament story when she received the news. Mary sang praises to God just as Hannah had done over the birth of Samuel.

*Her humility.* Her statement that "all generations will call me blessed" (v. 48) was not voiced in pride but from shock. Mary reminds me of David, who said: "Who am I, O Sovereign Lord, and what is my family, that you have brought me this far? . . . Is this your usual way of dealing with man, O Sovereign Lord?" (2 Sam. 7:18–19). In a way, the answer to his question is yes. God seems to love little more than stunning the humble with His awesome intervention.

*Her experience.* Please don't lose the wonder of it. Marvel with me at the fact that she was plain, simple, and extraordinarily ordinary. I always felt the same way growing up. Still do, deep down inside. That's part of the beauty of God choosing someone like you and me to know Him and serve Him. May we never get over it.

# DAY 128
### Luke 2:1–7

---

In those days a decree went out from Caesar Augustus that the
whole empire should be registered (v. 1).

---

I have heard the questions thousands of times: Why do we celebrate
Christmas on December 25? How do we know when the birth of Christ took
place? Why celebrate Christmas at a time originally set for ancient pagan
celebrations?

The Scrooges are right; we don't know when Christ was born. But I happen
to think His is a birth worthy of celebrating at some time of year. After all, God
didn't just tolerate celebrations and festivals commemorating His faithfulness—
He commanded them! His idea! Some were solemn; others were for the pure
purpose of rejoicing before the Lord.

On one such occasion Nehemiah said, "Go and enjoy choice food and sweet
drinks, and send some to those who have nothing prepared. This day is sacred to
our Lord. Do not grieve, for the joy of the Lord is your strength" (Neh. 8:10). The
Book of Esther also speaks of an annual day set aside for "joy and feasting . . . a
day for giving presents to each other" (Esther 9:19). The most concentrated list of
Old Testament feasts appears in Leviticus 23. The chapter describes seven different
feasts. In verse 5 we read, "The Lord's Passover begins at twilight on the fourteenth day of the first month."

The first month falls, according to the new moon, over the last half of
March and the first half of April. The timing has significance to all of us who
have carried children in our wombs. In the Jewish calendar, the fourteenth day of
the first month is called the day of conception. If our God of perfect planning and
gloriously significant order happened to overshadow Mary on the fourteenth day
of the first month of His calendar, our Savior would have been born toward the
end of our December. We have absolutely no way of knowing whether or not He
did, but I would not be the least bit surprised for God to have sparked His Son's
human life on one Passover and ended it on another.

No, I don't believe in Easter bunnies, and I don't have much of an opinion on Santa Clauses, but I'm a hopeless romantic when it comes to celebrating
Christmas, the birth of my Savior. Until a further "Hear ye! Hear ye!" comes
from heaven, December 25 works mighty fine for me.

# DAY 129
Luke 2:8–14

———

The angel said to them, "Don't be afraid, for look, I proclaim to you good news
of great joy that will be for all people" (v. 10).

———

Luke 2 identifies the first persons to receive the glorious announcement of
Christ's birth. Why do you think God first proclaimed the good news to a motley
crew of sheepherders? He seems to enjoy revealing Himself to common people
rather than to those who feel most worthy. He often uses the foolish things of
this world to confound the wise (see 1 Cor. 1:28). Maybe God had a soft place in
His heart for the shepherds watching over their flocks.

Don't miss the fact that the announcement came to the shepherds while
they were watching over their flocks "at night" (v. 8). Sometimes in the contrast
of the night, we can best see the glory of God. Verse 9 tells us that "the glory of
the Lord shone around them." Notice the Scripture does not say that the glory
of the Lord shone around the angel but around the shepherds. As you picture
the scene, keep in mind that only one angel, an angel of the Lord, appeared to
them first. The other heavenly hosts did not join the scene until after the birth
announcement. Most definitely, the glory shone around the shepherds.

Try to imagine for a moment what happened. How do you think the glory
of the Lord looked around the shepherds? We don't know for sure; I'm just asking
you to picture it in your mind right now.

I am convinced that God wants us to get involved in our Scripture reading. Using our imaginations and picturing the events as eye-witnesses can make
black ink on a white page spring into living color. No matter how the glory of
God appeared, it scared the shepherds half to death. The words of the angel are
so reminiscent of my Savior. Often He told those nearly slain by His glory not
to be afraid.

Oh, how I love Him. The untouchable Hand of God reaching down to
touch the fallen hand of man. "I bring you good news of great joy that will be for
all the people" (v. 10). I am convinced our witness would be far more effective if
we brought our good news with great joy.

# DAY 130
## Luke 2:15–20

∞

But Mary was treasuring up all these things in
her heart and meditating on them (v. 19).

∞

How do you suppose Mary felt on the night of nights after Jesus had been born? The following are just some thoughts that God gave me as I tried to imagine what it would have been like over those next couple of hours. But I want to be very clear here: this is strictly fiction. I just invite you to imagine with me what Mary's first moments might have been like as a mother:

Her body lay sapped of strength, her eyes were heavily closed, but her mind refused to give way to rest. She ached for her mother. She wondered if she yet believed her. She heard the labored breathing of the man sleeping a few feet from her. Only months before he was little more than a stranger to her. She knew only what she had been told and what she could read in occasional shy glances. She had been told he was a good man. Over the last few days, she found out he was far more than a good man. No man, no matter how kind, could have done what he had done. She wondered how long it had been since he'd really rested.

A calf, only a few days old, awakened hungry and could not find its mother. The stir awakened the baby who also squirmed to find His mother. Scarcely before she could move her tender frame toward the manger, He began to wail! She scooped Him in her arms, her long hair draping His face, and she quietly slipped out of the gate. She gingerly sat down and leaned against the outside of the stable, propped the baby on her small lap, and taking a strip of linen and tying back her hair, she began to stare into His tiny face. She had not yet seen Him in the light. She had never seen the moon so bright. The night was nearly as light as the day. Only hours old, His chin quivered, not from the cold, but from the sudden exposure of birth. His eyes were shaped like almonds and were as black as the deepest well. She held Him tightly and quietly hummed a song she'd learned as a child. She had been so frightened of this moment, so sure she would not know what to do. She had never held an infant so small, and He was God, wrapped in soft, infant flesh, with bones so fragile she felt like He could break. She had pictured this moment so many times. What would the Son of the Spirit look like? She never expected Him to look so normal, so common. Must have been the part He inherited from His mother. She was so sure she'd feel terribly awkward. So afraid she'd drop Him—the Messiah—and God would be awfully sorry He had given Him to her! Instead, every fear, every doubt, every inadequacy was momentarily caught up in the indescribable rapture of a mother's affection.

She remembered asking Elizabeth things she dared not ask her father and mother. Once when they were walking together at the end of the day, the wind blew her cousin's robes against her, and like a curious teenager, Mary tried her hardest to catch a good glimpse of Elizabeth's rounded middle. At the time she herself had no physical evidence that God's promise was true. But she had enough faith to ask endless questions. What am I to do when He comes? Her cousin's reply would remain etched upon Mary's heart long after He had saved the world. He will tell you what He needs from you. Beyond what He needs, all He wants is for you to embrace Him and talk to Him.

She looked back into His delicate face and watched Him closely as He seemed to stare deeply into the moonlit sky. And she began to talk. "Sweet baby boy. Do You know who Your Daddy is? Do You know Your name? Do You know why You're here? What do You see when You look out there? Can You see the stars? Do You remember their names? Do You think I'll do OK? Will You love me too?" A tear dropped from her chin to His. He yawned and made such a funny expression she grinned, wiping her face on the yellowed rags she'd draped around Him. The fussing calf had obviously found its mother. Not a sound was coming from inside the stable. The earth stilled. The infant slept. She held the babe next to her face, and for just a moment, all the world was silent to the breath of God.

She closed her eyes and listened, stealing time like a hidden metronome, as high and as wide as she dared to think, but she still could not begin to comprehend. She, a common child of the most humble means who had never read the Scriptures for herself, was embracing the incarnate Word. The fullness of the Godhead rested in her inexperienced arms, sleeping to the rhythm of her heart. This time she hummed a song she did not know, a song being sung by the choir of angels hovering over her head but hidden from her carnal senses. The deafening hallelujahs of the heavenly hosts were silent to mortal ears except through the sounds of a young woman's voice who had unknowingly given human notes to a holy score. The glory of God filled the earth. Heaven hammered a bridge, but one young woman sat completely unaware of all that swelled the atmosphere around her. The tiny baby boy had robbed her heart. "So, this is how it feels to be a mother," she mused.

She crept back into the stable, wrapped Him in swaddling clothes and laid Him in the manger. Just down the path, the sun peeked gently over the roof of an inn full of barren souls who had made Him no room.

# DAY 131
## Luke 2:21–24

—◦◦◦—

When the days of their purification according to the law of Moses were finished,
they brought Him up to Jerusalem to present Him to the Lord (v. 22).

—◦◦◦—

Jesus' parents had Him circumcised on the eighth day of His young life.
Then they presented Him at the temple and offered the sacrifices required of new
parents. Each of the steps Mary and Joseph took after Christ's birth was typical
of devout Jewish parents. What made these events atypical is that their infant
would ultimately fulfill the prophetic representation of each of these rituals. Let's
take a brief look at all three rites: circumcision, redemption, and purification.

*The Rite of Circumcision.* We read about circumcision in Genesis 17:1–14.
It was so important that verse 11 says it would serve as "a sign of the covenant
between me and you." Verse 14 says an uncircumcised male "will be cut off from
his people; he has broken my covenant." The rite of circumcision was God's way
of requiring the Jewish people to become physically different because of their
relationship to Him.

A careful reading of Colossians 2:9–15 sheds light on how the infant Jesus
would later be used to fulfill a different kind of circumcision in believers. Verse 11
says: "In him you were also circumcised, in the putting off of the sinful nature."
If you have walked with Jesus for any time, you can point to ways in which our
spiritual circumcision results in proof that we are different than the persons we
originally were.

When the infant Jesus was circumcised at eight days of age, I'm not sure
His parents could fathom that He was the physical manifestation of the covenant
God had made thousands of years earlier. Second Corinthians 1:20 says, "No
matter how many promises God has made, they are 'Yes' in Christ." The infant
that Joseph held during Jesus' circumcision was the very Yes of God to the promise of the covenant being symbolized.

*The Rite of Redemption.* In Luke 2:22–24 two distinct rites were observed
by Mary and Joseph. Before we research them, please note that a segment of
time has passed between the circumcision and the presentation. According to
Leviticus 12:1–8 a woman was to wait thirty-three days after the circumcision
before presenting a son at the temple. Exodus 13 tells us the reason why every
firstborn male was to be redeemed. The redemption was a reminder that "the
LORD brought us out of Egypt with his mighty hand" (v. 16).

Mary and Joseph went to Jerusalem in obedience to this command. Like all
devout Jewish parents, they presented their infant to the Lord to depict sacrifice
and redemption. When Jewish parents presented their firstborn son to the Lord,
they were symbolizing the act of giving him up by saying, "He is Yours and we

give him back to You." Then they would immediately redeem him or, in effect, buy him back.

Few teachings are more important and consistent in God's Word than the doctrine of redemption. The Hebrew word is *padhah*, meaning "to redeem by paying a price." The New Testament tells us Christ came to fulfill for us the very rite Mary and Joseph observed as they presented the Christ child to the Lord.

Ephesians 1:7 says, "In him we have redemption through his blood, the forgiveness of sins, in accordance with the riches of God's grace." Consider this verse from the apostle Paul's Jewish perspective. He drew a parallel to our entrance into the family of God. Since most of us are Gentiles, we are considered the "adopted ones" in God's family. What was true in a tangible sense after the birth of a Jewish son is true of us in a spiritual sense after our rebirth as "sons" of God. We all must be redeemed. The wonderful picture for us, however, is that we are not bought from God by our natural parents. Rather, Christ buys us from our natural parentage, which is sinful flesh, to give us to His Father. If the concept is too confusing, just celebrate that Christ has redeemed you!

*The Rite of Purification.* The rite of redemption was distinct from the rite of purification. This purification is described in Leviticus 12:1–8. The prescribed sacrifice included a lamb, but the law made provision for impoverished parents. Verse 8 says, "If she cannot afford a lamb, she is to bring two doves or two young pigeons." Luke told us that Jesus' parents offered the poverty version of the sacrifice.

Have you ever considered what Christ's earthly poverty has to do with us? Second Corinthians 8:9 proclaims that "though he was rich, yet for your sakes he became poor, so that you through his poverty might become rich."

Mary and Joseph offered the least sacrifice permitted by Jewish law for the rite of purification. How fitting that they held in their arms the greatest sacrifice a holy God could ever make for their eternal purification. Titus 2:14 tells us that Jesus Christ "gave himself for us to redeem us from all wickedness and to purify for himself a people that are his very own."

The Word made flesh first entered the temple wrapped in a baby blanket. His earthly parents lifted Him to His Father and, in essence, purchased Him from heaven—for a while—for a lost world. One day that baby would buy them from earth for the glory of heaven. Wow.

## DAY 132
### Luke 2:41–47

※

After three days, they found Him in the temple complex sitting among the teachers,
listening to them and asking them questions . . . and all those who heard Him were
astounded at His understanding and His answers (vv. 46–47).

※

I had the joy of raising my children alongside my best friend of twenty-plus
years. Numerous times we thought one of our children was with the other, only
to find the child in the dog bowl or splashing in the toilet. We feel fortunate we
didn't leave any of them while on a vacation somewhere.

I'm not sure anything prompts emotions like finding a lost child. Fear
surges through your heart during the search. Relief floods over you when you
find the child safe. Then if the child discounts parental concern, emotions surge
to vengeance!

Yet even though I feel compassion concerning Mary's and Joseph's fear, I
love what they found their son doing on the third day of their search—sitting in
the temple, conversing with the teachers:

*"Listening."* I'm so thankful Christ not only speaks, He also listens. We don't
know if God allowed the twelve-year-old Christ to exercise His full omniscience
or to unleash just enough wisdom to astound His listeners. But I love the fact
that Christ still listens—not just to learn, since He knows all things. Rather, He
allows us to pour out our hearts because He loves us and wants to hear us.

*"Asking them questions."* Contrary to popular belief, faith is not the avoidance
of questions. Our faith grows when we seek answers, and we find many between
Genesis 1:1 and Revelation 22:21. We may hear a gentle, "Because I said so,"
to those questions God chooses not to answer, but I don't believe our heavenly
Father is offended by questions. Part of Christlikeness is learning to listen and
ask appropriate questions, even of those you respect in the faith.

*"His answers."* As we go along in this devotional journey, we will see several examples of Him posing a question only He could answer. Christ certainly
uses that teaching method with me. Sometimes He'll cause me to dig through
Scripture for a question He seemed to initiate. Other times the question may
come as a personalized whisper in my heart. Then as He reveals my insecurities
and fleshly defense mechanisms, He gives me new understanding. He answers
me, so that I don't have to live off my own answers.

# DAY 133
### Luke 2:48–50

—∞∞—

"Why were you searching for Me?" He asked them.
"Didn't you know that I had to be in My Father's house?" (v. 49).

—∞∞—

Mary, understandably hurt that Jesus had chosen to hang back in Jerusalem and leave them to worry about His safety, asked Him a question in verse 48: "Son, why have you treated us like this?" Christ's response in verse 49 suggests He was as mystified that they'd expect to find Him anywhere else as they were mystified to find Him there: "Didn't you know I had to be in my Father's house?"

The words "had to" come from the Greek word *dei*, meaning something that is "inevitable in the nature of things." Likely this word has never been used more literally. After all, the Father and the Son had the same nature. Christ was drawn to God, not as a devout believer, but as an overpowering magnet—as two pieces of the same whole.

Still, the fact remains that Mary had asked a question, and Jesus had given an answer. But verse 50 tells us that she didn't understand the answer He supplied.

This remains part of our experience today. I believe we are always free to ask Jesus questions. And I believe He is always faithful to answer, even though his answer may not be speedy in coming. But even if it does come immediately, we may not *understand* the answer until later. Maybe much later.

In my opinion, Christ's response was quite interesting. I've searched every Greek translation I can find, and none of my resources have an original word that directly translates to "house" (NIV) or "business" (KJV) in verse 49. From what I can gather, a more precise translation of Christ's response might be: "Didn't you know that I had to be about my Father?"

That question implies the desire of my heart more than any other I can imagine. I just want to be about God. Not about ministry. Not about my own agenda. Not about writing Bible studies. Not about me at all. When all is said and done, I would give my life for people to be able to say, "She was just about God." That would be the ultimate legacy. "Not that I have already obtained all this . . . but I press on" (Phil. 3:12). May we live lives that would cause others to be surprised to find us any other place than to "be found in him" (Phil. 3:9).

# DAY 134
## Luke 2:51–52

—∞—

Jesus increased in wisdom and stature,
and in favor with God and with people (v. 52).

—∞—

Luke 2:52 appears brief and to the point but actually broadens dramatically our concept of Christ during those years when He went from boy to mature man.

*Jesus grew in wisdom.* The Greek word for "wisdom" is *sophia.* Consider two segments of the definition: (1) *Sophia* is skill in the affairs of life, practical wisdom, and wise management as shown in forming the best plans and selecting the best means, including the idea of sound judgment and good sense. (2) In respect to divine things, *sophia* is wisdom, knowledge, insight, deep understanding. So as you seek to formulate an impression of what Christ was like in His earthly form, please view Him as both completely practical and deeply spiritual. In fact, Christ came to show us that the deeply spiritual is very practical.

I encourage you to avoid imagining Christ as so deep you'd have to dig to find Him or so spiritual His head is in the clouds. He came bringing heaven to earth. In today's terms, He was a man who could preach an anointed sermon, then change a flat tire on the way home from church.

No wonder Christ became such a rare teacher! Believing people are starving for a wisdom that is both deeply spiritual and vastly practical. Christ embodied every dimension of wisdom in His earthly life, even before He officially began His public ministry.

*Jesus grew in stature.* This phrase tells us the obvious: Christ grew physically (and mentally) in the vigor and stature of a man. What is, of course, less obvious is what He grew to look like. God's Word lets us use our permanent markers only once as we try to imagine Christ's appearance, even though our solitary source happens to be one of my least favorite verses. God knows my heart and why I feel this way.

Isaiah 53:2 predicts about the coming Messiah: "He had no beauty or majesty to attract us to him, nothing in his appearance that we should desire him." I simply cannot imagine Christ not being beautiful, but I also believe beauty is in the eye of the beholder. All of us can think of people who are beautiful to us but whose faces might never be chosen for a magazine cover. Don't read more into Isaiah 53:2 than is there, however. The intent of the original terms is that He didn't have a magnificent, godlike physical appearance that attracted people to Him. The descriptions don't necessarily imply that Christ was unattractive but that His looks were most likely ordinary.

*Jesus grew in favor with God.* Oh, how I love picturing the relationship Christ shared with His heavenly Father. I will limit my comments for now because I don't want to steal the joy of discovery as we search out dimensions of their relationship in the days to come.

For now, note what the word *favor* means. The Greek word is *charis*, which is often translated "grace" in the New Testament. *Charis* means "grace, particularly that which causes joy, pleasure, gratification, favor, acceptance." Jesus' growing in favor with God basically implies that their relationship became an increasing delight to both of them. Without a doubt, the relationship between God the Father and God the Son is totally unique. Indeed Jesus is the One and Only—the only begotten of the Father. And the relationship the two of them shared while Christ was earthbound is unparalleled.

*Jesus grew in favor with men.* As we attempt to formulate a picture of Christ's stature and personality, this description is extremely important. Isaiah 53:3 tells us that He was despised and rejected by men. But understand that He was not despised and rejected until He became a complete threat to the establishment. Actually, His popularity was the driving force behind Jesus' opponents' lust for His blood.

In Luke 2:52, God states Christ's favor with men, but throughout the Gospels He demonstrates it. Fishermen don't leave their nets to follow someone void of personality. People didn't just respect Him—they liked Him. The word *favor* is undeniably related to the word *favorite*. I don't believe we are stretching the text in the least to say that Christ was a favorite of many who knew Him.

Think for a few moments of the different characteristics of people who tend to capture your favor. Unless those characteristics are inconsistent with godliness, in all likelihood Christ possessed them. I can readily share a few of my favorite characteristics in people: godly, warm, and personable, at least somewhat demonstrative, knowledgeable in a specific area so I can learn from them, trustworthy, and funny! Although God's Word tells us that we are not to show favoritism, all of us have favorite characteristics we enjoy in people. You can safely assume that Christ possessed many of the dimensions you would favor most.

I simply want you to be reminded that He was real. His sandals flapped when He walked down the road. His hair was misshapen when He awakened. He had to brush the bread crumbs off His beard after He ate. The muscles in His arms flexed when He lifted His little brothers and sisters. He had hair on His arms and warmth in His palms. He was the Son of God and the Son of man. Fathom the unfathomable.

# DAY 135
## Luke 4:1–13

——∞∞——

Jesus returned from the Jordan, full of the Holy Spirit, and was led
by the Spirit in the wilderness for 40 days to be tempted by the Devil (vv. 1–2).

——∞∞——

Christ's experience in the desert represented an intense season of temptation that was tailored by the enemy for the challenges of messiahship that lay
ahead. God placed Jesus with His adversary in a lab of sorts to establish the
ground rules from the very beginning. With this idea in mind, let's briefly consider each temptation:

1. *"Tell this stone to become bread" (v. 3)*. Could Christ turn a stone into bread?
Undoubtedly! So why shouldn't He? After all, He was famished. Matthew 4:2
tells us He had been fasting for forty days. Nothing is wrong with eating when
a person is hungry—unless a greater issue is involved. Most likely Jesus' intent
in fasting was to seek God and refrain from all distractions, much the same way
Anna, the prophetess, was said to serve God "night and day, fasting and praying"
(Luke 2:37). Since we know Jesus was filled with the Spirit and led by the Spirit,
we can assume the Spirit prompted the fast; therefore, the fast wasn't over until
God said so.

What did this temptation have to do with Christ's imminent ministry?
Robert Stein says the issue was whether or not Christ would use His power for
His own ends. "Would He live by the same requirements of faith and dependence
on God as everyone else in the kingdom?"[32] Satan's strategy wasn't all that differ-
ent from what he used when tempting Eve in the garden (see Gen. 3:1). In both
cases, Satan wanted to sow doubt, but not because he had any. He knew what
God had said to Adam and Eve, and he definitely knew Christ was the Son of
God. Why in the world would Satan have tried sowing doubt in Christ?

We see a second similarity between the Garden of Eden and the wilderness,
in that both temptations involved food. Christ was hungry. Eve was hungry, too,
even though her hunger was for something different. Our appetites are ferocious.
They are fodder for much temptation. I find Paul's description of the enemies of
the cross of Christ very interesting in Philippians 3:19 when he said their minds
are on earthly things and "their god is their stomach." Although you and I are not
enemies of the cross, we certainly know the temptation of making our stomachs
gods. But Christ didn't fall to this temptation. Instead He responded with two
critical phrases.

Christ's first phrase of response was universal, because Scripture applies to
every temptation we can ever face. He said, "It is written" (Luke 4:4). In those
words He clarified the matter of authority. Jesus subjugated Satan's words to
God's Word.

The second phrase of Jesus' response was issue-specific. "Man must not live on bread alone." Christ applied the specific word from Scripture to meet His need. So Satan moved on to the next temptation.

2. *"If you worship me, it will all be yours" (v. 7).* We cannot imagine Christ ever being the least bit tempted to worship Satan, but can we not imagine that He might have been tempted to rip Satan's authority out of his hands?

Christ didn't challenge Satan's ability to *make* such an offer. We can assume Satan must have had the authority as the prince of this world. It's true the authority God has allowed Satan is limited and temporary, but it is nonetheless very real.

Yet can you imagine how Christ must feel as He watches the state of the world under the influence of the evil prince's authority? Oppression, violence, and deception characterize the world God loves. Surely Christ is counting the days until He grabs the deed restriction to the world and reigns without rival in righteousness.

Satan was hoping Christ would be so anxious to secure the world that He'd worship him. Needless to say, Satan was wrong. Christ will most assuredly reign over this world, but not until all things have happened according to God's kingdom calendar.

Once again Christ called on Scripture, this time with the specific application: "Worship the Lord your God, and serve him only" (v. 8). Christ adamantly resisted worshiping Satan as a way to gain the world. So Satan moved to his third temptation.

3. *"Throw yourself down from here" (v. 9).* Based on Christ's response to this temptation, we know that at least one of Satan's intentions was to tempt Christ to put God to the test. But Satan may have had a second intention in this particular temptation. The placement of the temptation at the temple suggests that the enemy may have been hoping a dramatic scene would cause the Jews to hail Jesus as their king before He faced the cross. If Christ had foregone the cross, He would have been no less God, but we would be lost.

In conclusion, it's clear that these were no ordinary temptations. They appear to be direct assaults on the messiahship of Christ. We can, however, draw a few applications from them:

• Seasons of intense temptation are not indications of God's displeasure.

• Satan is tenacious. Don't expect him to give up after one or two tries.

• Scripture is the most powerful tool in our fight against temptation. Don't fight back with *your* words. Fight back with God's!

# DAY 136
## Luke 4:14–21

—∞∞—

He began by saying to them, "Today as you listen,
this Scripture has been fulfilled" (v. 21).

—∞∞—

I was a mess before the Savior set me free. That's why my dearest life passages are the ones found in Isaiah 61:1–2 and quoted again in the Gospel of Luke. Jesus went to His home synagogue in Nazareth and declared both the fact and the nature of His call and ministry—to preach good news to the poor . . . to heal the brokenhearted . . . to proclaim freedom for the prisoners . . . sight for the blind . . . to release the oppressed . . . and to proclaim the year of the Lord's favor (Luke 4:18–19). Let's briefly discuss each part of that description:

1. *"The Spirit of the Lord is on me, because he has anointed me to preach good news to the poor" (Luke 4:18).* Christ didn't mean the financially destitute. The Greek word for "poor" is *ptochos*, indicating "utter helplessness, complete destitution, afflicted, distressed." I think God is far too faithful to let anyone make it through life without confronting seasons of utter helplessness. Sooner or later, any healthy individual discovers that autonomy doesn't cut it. Like beggars we go from person to person with our empty cup, crying, "Can't you add anything to my life?" They might throw in a coin or two. But when we shake the cup, the tinny echo reminds us how empty we remain. Until we allow Jesus to fill our cups daily, we simply subsist. Sooner or later, God will make sure we confront the poverty of living on the alms of others so that we may learn to feast on Him.

2. *"To heal the brokenhearted" (Luke 4:18 KJV).* Some New Testament translations include this phrase, while others don't. Either way, it is worthy of our consideration. The original word for "brokenhearted" is *suntribo*, meaning "to break, strike against something . . . to break the strength or power of someone." The Greek word for "heal" is *iaomai*, meaning "to heal, cure, restore." I love the Hebrew word translated "heal" in Exodus 15:26 when God introduced Himself by a new title: "I am the Lord who heals you." The word *raphah* means "to mend (by stitching), repair thoroughly, make whole." I picture God focusing steadily on the object of repair. One stitch follows another. It takes time. I picture painful penetrations of the healing needle. I don't know about you, but I'm quite sure if my healing processes had been painless, I would have relapsed.

3. *"To proclaim freedom for the prisoners" (v. 18).* Long after my salvation, I was in many ways like the prisoners in Psalm 107:10–16, 20, suffering "in iron chains, for they had rebelled against the words of God" (vv. 10–11). Many people sincerely love God, but I don't think anyone stands to appreciate the unfailing love of God like the believer finally set free from failure. I know this captive can undoubtedly testify: He sent forth His Word and healed me. Stitch by stitch.

But please notice that Christ *proclaimed* freedom. He didn't impose it. It remains an offer.

4. *"Recovery of sight for the blind" (v. 18)*. Although Christ would heal many from physical blindness, I believe His intent here was a far more serious kind of blindness. Second Corinthians 4:4 says, "The god of this age has blinded the minds of unbelievers, so they cannot see the light of the gospel of the glory of Christ, who is the image of God."

I find the original word for "blind" in both Luke's Gospel and Paul's second letter to the Corinthians to be so interesting. *Tuphlos* means "to envelop with smoke, to be unable to see clearly." Perhaps none of the enemy's attempts to cloud our vision compare to our fiery trials. His job is to keep us blinded to the One who walks with us through the fire. Oh, believer, God is there whether our spiritual eyes discern Him or not.

5. *"To release the oppressed" (v. 18)*. I looked up every definition for "oppressed" in the Greek and Hebrew dictionaries. A half dozen original words are translated in the Bible with our single word "oppressed," and all but one have the word "break" in the definition. I'm becoming more and more convinced that heavy-duty oppression is Satan's counterfeit for biblical brokenness.

At times I've fought back the tears as I've heard testimonies of people who had been utterly unable to function, describing themselves as broken by God. I don't think God's brand of brokenness is total emotional wreckage. God's intent in breaking us is to bend our stiff knees so that we will submit to His authority and take on His yoke. His aim is our abundant and effective life. Being totally unable to function because the mind and emotions are in shambles is Satan's counterfeit. Praise God, Christ can certainly use Satan's counterfeit brokenness to bring us to a place of accepting His own, but I think we credit some things to Christ that He doesn't do.

6. *"To proclaim the year of the Lord's favor" (v. 19)*. Those who gathered that year in the Nazarene synagogue were staring in the face of the Lord's favor—His blessed gift of grace, Jesus Christ. The word "year" can be translated as "any definite time." God places before each of us a definitive period of time to accept the Lord's favor. He wills for none to perish but for all to come to repentance (see 2 Pet. 3:9). The world has until His return. The individual has a definitive period of time known by God alone. I am not past begging people not to wait too long for salvation, because eternal life in heaven is at stake. Neither am I beyond begging them to embrace His freedom, because abundant life on earth is at stake. He longs to be your champion now.

# DAY 137
## Luke 4:22–30

———

They were all speaking well of Him and were amazed by the gracious words
that came from His mouth, yet they said, "Isn't this Joseph's son?" (v. 22).

———

The translation "spoke well of" in Luke 4:22 comes from the Greek word
*martureo*, meaning "to be a witness, bear witness . . . to be able or ready to testify." "Amazed" is the Greek word *thaumazo*, meaning "struck with admiration."
Either of these words could be used by spectators after attending any rock concert
and being impressed by a talent. The wording suggests that they were impressed
by Christ's delivery—not so much what He said, but how He said it.

Let me draw on my experience and offer a possible explanation. After delivering a message, nothing hits me like cold water more than someone saying, "You
are a great speaker." First of all, I know better than that. I have a thick accent
and use tons of country colloquialisms. Far more importantly, though, if someone makes a statement like that, I know either I failed miserably or the person
didn't get it. In the case of Jesus' teaching, we know He can't fail, so obviously,
they didn't get it. In Jesus' seemingly harsh words (vv. 24–27), He may have been
responding to their grading His speech rather than receiving His message.

Notice also a second consideration: the velocity of the crowd's change of
mood. The crowd's mood went from admiration to a murderous rage in the
moments of Christ's confrontation. Luke describes them as furious (v. 28). The
word in the text for "furious" comes from the word *thuo*, meaning "to move
impetuously, particularly as the air or wind, a violent motion or passion of the
mind." The north wind of their admiration suddenly reversed into a south wind
of tornadic proportions. When a mood can change in a matter of moments from
admiration to murderous fury, something is amiss.

The types of crowds Christ encountered two thousand years ago still fill
many churches today. Many congregations want to hear impressive A+ messages,
but the messenger better keep his confrontational thoughts to himself. The same
committee that throws out the red carpet to a new preacher may eventually roll
him out the door in it! Meanness at church sometimes exceeds anything that
occurs in secular surroundings. As James 3:10 says, "My brethren, these things
ought not so to be" (kjv).

# DAY 138
## Luke 4:31–37

———∞∞———

In the synagogue there was a man with an unclean demonic spirit
who cried out with a loud voice, "Leave us alone!
What do You have to do with us, Jesus—Nazarene" (vv. 33–34).

———∞∞———

Christ's earthly ministry had hardly been launched before the demonic world confronted Him—in a synagogue, no less. Thank goodness, Christ isn't spooked by the demonic world. No matter what authority Satan and his subjects have been temporarily allowed in this world system, Christ can pull rank any time He wants. On that day in Capernaum, He wasted no time. A demon-possessed man shouted loudly and declared Jesus to be the Holy One of God.

The demon appeared to desire attention. We can assume the demon was loud because Christ adamantly told him to "Be quiet!" I'm certainly not suggesting that all demonic activity is loud. I am asking you to consider that when allowed to penetrate a place meant for practices of devotion to God, one of the chief tactics of demons is to divert attention.

I've seen this tactic. At a recent conference a woman began to shriek right after someone prayed and before I was to speak. The wise and godly woman leading the conference immediately went to the microphone and dealt graciously but firmly with the outburst. Although I've not often observed that type of behavior, the few times I've experienced it, I discerned a tactic of the demonic world to divert attention.

Note that the demon seemed to be telling some semblance of the truth, but we see a distortion or misuse of the truth in the demonic testimony. He was acting as a counterfeit preacher of sorts. He could not stop the truth so he hoped to disqualify the message by the instability or insanity of the apparent messenger.

Some years ago, a strange thing happened at our church. Each Sunday, for six or seven weeks, a man who appeared to be mentally ill would stand outside the main doors and "preach" to us using a megaphone as we left the building after worship. Some of the statements he made were technically scriptural, but his appearance and his approach demonstrated such instability that he did more to distract people from the truth than attract. The typical listener's tendency would be to disbelieve anything he said simply because he was the one saying it.

Noise and distraction. These remain some of the enemy's stock-in-trade.

# DAY 139
## Luke 5:1–7

❧

When He had finished speaking, He said to Simon,
"Put out into deep water and let down your nets for a catch" (v. 4).

❧

At the time when Andrew, Peter, James, and John were casting their nets into the Sea of Galilee, a vigorous fishing industry was booming all over the lake. Many villages populated the shores of this body of water. Not only was it the food basket of the region; the sight was breathtaking. It still is. The surrounding hills cup the lake like water in the palm of a large hand. I've seen with my own eyes how the early spring sunrise hangs lazily in the clinging winter mist. Since the first time I saw the Sea of Galilee, I understood why Christ seemed to favor the villages near its shore over the metropolis of Jerusalem.

Bethsaida lies at the northern tip where the Jordan River feeds the lake. The name Bethsaida means "house of fishing,"[33] and it lived up to its name. We know for a fact that Andrew and Peter were from Bethsaida, and we can safely assume Zebedee also raised his sons in the village, since they were all partners. As we will soon discover, at some point Andrew and Peter moved to nearby Capernaum where Peter lived with his wife and mother-in-law (Mark 1:21, 29). We don't know for certain which of the two villages housed James and John at this point in their lives, but we do know they all continued to work together.

Obviously Zebedee was the one who owned the fishing enterprise. We read in Mark 1:20 that James and John "left their father Zebedee in the boat with the hired men." While I don't want to intimate that Zebedee was wealthy (since few villagers were), we'd probably be mistaken to think him poor. The reference to the hired servants tells us that he owned his own business and was profitable enough to have servants in addition to two healthy and able sons. Both boats might easily have been in his ownership. Peter and Andrew could have fished from one (which was considered theirs in Luke 5:3) while a little farther away (Mark 1:19) James and John fished from another.

God wisely equipped us with four Gospels because we learn far more from hearing several accounts of anything especially noteworthy. The facts one writer included may not have been noted by another because each point of view was tinted by the individual's perspective and priorities. While writing *Jesus the One and Only*, I learned I could almost always expect Luke to be a little more specific than the other Gospel writers, which made perfect sense to me. He was a doctor, and a good doctor pays attention to details. You'll find this principle to hold true in the passage at hand.

In his fifth chapter, Luke recorded the call of Peter, Andrew, James, and John. Simon Peter told Jesus that they had fished all night. Obviously our little band of fisherman worked the graveyard shift at times. I can only think of one thing worse than fishing in the cold. That would be not catching anything. It happens to the best of fisherman. When it happens to my husband, Keith, I always ask him the typical sanguine woman question: "But did you have fun with your friends anyway?" My personality is given to the philosophy that the question is not so much whether you succeeded or failed but if you had fun in the process. I wish I had a picture of Keith's face when I ask him that question. I'd put it in the margin for your amusement.

I can go no further without musing over Christ's divinely uncanny ability to waltz right into a life and turn it upside down, inside out, and every which way but loose. Just think how many times those fishermen had prepared and cast their nets together. Picture how many years they had practiced a routine. They weren't fishing for the pure enjoyment of it as my husband does. Fishing was their job. I don't doubt they loved it as most men would, but don't think for a moment it wasn't work. Hard work.

Hear them declare it so. Upon Jesus' suggestion that they "put out into deep water and let down your nets for a catch," Peter answered Jesus, "Master, we've worked hard all night long and caught nothing" (Luke 5:4–5 HCSB).

Yes, they worked hard. Day in. Day out. Then one day Jesus walked up. And everything changed.

Oh, beloved, isn't that exactly like Him? Jesus walks right up, catches us in the act of being—again today—exactly who we were yesterday, and offers to turn our routine into adventure. Hallelujah! Have you allowed Christ to do that for you? If you're bored with life and stuck in a rut of routine, you may have believed in Christ, but you may not yet have agreed to follow Him. Christ is a lot of things, but boring? Not on your life! Life with Him is indeed a great adventure.

You don't necessarily have to leave behind what you do if He proves your present course to be His will, but I assure you He will have you leave the boredom and routine of it behind. When Jesus Christ takes over our lives, things get exciting!

# DAY 140
## Luke 5:8–11

—∞∞∞—

He and all those with him were amazed at the catch of fish they took, and so were
James and John, Zebedee's sons, who were Simon's partners (vv. 9–10).

—∞∞∞—

Today we celebrate a fact that continually staggers my imagination: Christ
calls mere mortals to join Him in His work. Trust me, He doesn't *need* our help.
Christ could save the world through dreams and visions if He chose to. But He
doesn't. He delights in asking us to join Him. I am convinced that every believer
is summoned by Christ to work with Him here on earth. In fact, we learn a lot
about how and why He does it by observing this encounter between Jesus and
Peter on the lake in Luke 5:

1. *Christ knows more about our jobs than we do.* Jesus told Peter how to fish.
Now, had Peter not already known Christ, he might have thought: "Me fisherman, You carpenter. I won't tell You how to build, and You don't tell me how to
fish." Instead, he submitted with only one brief disclaimer: "We've done this all
night and caught nothing."

One of the most critical reasons believers experience defeat is because we
categorize only a few areas of our lives as Christ's arena. Many Christians think
Christ's jurisdiction doesn't extend into certain areas. So, as if to save Him the
extra trouble of dealing with things that don't concern Him, they leave Christ at
church to deal with areas related to His expertise.

Satan is greatly defeated when we start living the truth that every area is
Christ's specialty. Whether you're a homemaker, steelworker, or CEO, Christ
knows every detail associated with your job. Jesus knows accounting, movie-the-
ater managing, banking, drafting, engineering, nursing, real-estate brokering,
and anything else we could do. For crying out loud, the One who knows the
numbers of hairs on your head could also style them if He wanted. Not one of us
does anything for a living that He can't do better.

2. *Christ honors our submission even when our only motivation is obedience.* If
there was one phrase I wasn't going to say as a parent, it was "Because I said so."
I heard those words from my Army captain dad more times than I could count. I
wasn't about to repeat them. After all, I had studied child development. I vowed
to explain things to my children as if they were little adults. I almost got away
with it too. Then I had Melissa—the proverbial "But, why?" child. One day she
pushed me too far, and something in me snapped. I suddenly exploded, "Because
I said so!" Not just once. I screamed it over and over like a mad bull on a rampage.
I even screamed it at the dog. Four-year-old Melissa shrugged her shoulders, said
"OK!" and skipped off happily.

I called my dad and thanked him. Sometimes God allows us to explore the "whys" of His instructions. Other times He wants us to obey "because He said so." Then wait on the Lord to bless your act of obedience, no matter how long it takes. He is faithful.

3. *The same job subjected to Christ's authority can yield entirely different results.* Peter surely had fished in every level of water in the lake. The key to his enormous catch was not the deep water Jesus had instructed him to fish in. It was simply the authority of Christ. Beloved, if your job has grown stale, you may not need a new occupation. You may just need a new partner. "Whatever you do, work at it with all your heart, as working for the Lord, not for men, since you know that you will receive an inheritance from the Lord as a reward. It is the Lord Christ you are serving" (Col. 3:23–24).

Every hour you do your job as working for the Lord gets punched on a time clock in heaven. You get paid by God Himself for the hours you work as unto the Lord. I'm not being cheesy. Our future inheritance is real, and it far exceeds minimum wage. As you partner with Christ at your job, you will be more efficient. No matter whether your new efficiency increases your earthly dividends or not, it most definitely will increase your *eternal* dividends, where moth and rust cannot destroy or thieves break in and steal (see Matt. 6:19).

4. *Christ's willingness to empower us can overwhelm us.* Simon Peter already knew Jesus possessed extraordinary power, but he felt the real impact of Christ's power when that authority worked through his own hands. Suddenly the fisherman fell at Jesus' knees and said, "Go away from me, Lord; I am a sinful man" (Luke 5:8).

What blessed condescension that the God of glory would use us! And what humility this realization should bring! Peter was not prepared to receive his call until he had been confronted by his sin.

I have assuredly faced moments of such stark realization of my own sin that I felt unbearable pain. Interestingly, those moments did not come during times of rebellion, but rather, they came during close encounters with God when I drew close enough to get an eyeful of myself. Those realizations were both harrowing and liberating. The surrender resulting from the realization of my own innate unholiness did more to activate the holiness of God in me than anything I've ever experienced. How like God! Even our painful realizations of sinfulness are to mortify us to new life.

# DAY 141
## Luke 5:12–16

⎯⎯∞⎯⎯

A man was there who had a serious skin disease all over him. He saw Jesus, fell face-down, and begged Him: "Lord, if You are willing, You can make me clean" (v. 12).

⎯⎯∞⎯⎯

This miracle from Luke 5 reveals a great deal of insight into God and His complex ways, helping us grapple with some challenging issues that question the hearts of men—questions we shouldn't be afraid of exploring as good students of the Word.

In essence, the leper was saying, "Lord, I know You possess the power to heal me. And if You in Your wisdom and plan see purpose in it, then please do it." So first, we see that the diseased man humbly approached Christ in absolute belief. Although he suffered from a horribly debilitating skin ailment, he did not suffer from a lack of faith. He believed Jesus could heal him. He just didn't know if he would.

This brings us, then, to a second consideration: was it in God's will to perform this miracle that the leper was asking for?

I believe with all my heart that the central issue involved in whether or not God heals a believing (see Matt. 9:28) and requesting (see James 4:2) Christian's physical illness is found in His eternal purpose. Although I don't pretend to understand how or why, some illnesses may serve more eternal purpose than healing would, while other healings serve more purpose than illnesses do.

Try as I might, I cannot imagine what purpose some illnesses and premature deaths serve. But after years of loving and seeking my God, I trust who He is, even when I have no idea what He's doing. Above all things, I believe God always has purpose in every decision He makes. Jesus healed people many times, but His healings were always with purpose and intent.

How much like the leper are you? Are you convinced (first of all) that Christ can do absolutely anything? And secondly, are you also seeking His purposes in everything? Are you more desirous of His work and will being done through your life than you are to be healed of your hardship or handicap? If so, don't lose courage. As long as this remains the desire of your heart, come to Christ as the leper did—humbly making your request while seeking His purposes for your life.

# DAY 142
## Luke 5:17–26

———∞———

"But so you may know that the Son of Man has authority
on earth to forgive sins"—He told the paralyzed man—"I tell you: get up,
pick up your stretcher, and go home" (v. 24).

———∞———

Jesus came as the Son of Man to rescue us from the great plight of man: we have a sin problem, and we are powerless to help ourselves. Given the right set of circumstances and the wrong state of mind, each of us is capable of just about anything. Even if we could get our external lives under perfect and legalistic control, we'd probably rot on the inside with the heinous sin of pride. Let's face it, we're all hopeless—except that Jesus came as the "Son of Man" with the "authority on earth to forgive sins."

I can remember being so devastated over a sin I had allowed to ensnare me that I repeatedly begged God to forgive me. I confessed my sin with great sorrow and turned radically from it. Still I continued to plead for forgiveness. Then one day in my Bible reading, God revealed these Scriptures to me from Luke 5. He spoke to my heart and said: "Beth, My child, you have an authority problem. You think you can do your part, which is repent. You just don't think I can do My part, which is forgive."

I was stunned. I began to realize that my sin of unbelief was as serious as my prior sin of rebellion. I wept and repented for my failure to credit Him with the authority He possessed to forgive my sins. It was eye-opening!

In his book *I Should Forgive, But . . .*, Dr. Chuck Lynch says when we keep confessing the same sin over and over, "each subsequent time the sin is confessed, rather than the confession bringing relief, it only reinforces the false belief that it has not been forgiven. Double, or re-confession, only deepens the false belief that we have not been forgiven."[34] I know he's right, because my constant re-confessions did not bring me relief. They only made me more miserable and self-loathing. Relief came only when I decided to take God at His Word.

If you have truly repented—which means you have experienced godly sorrow and a subsequent detour from the sin—bathe yourself in the river of God's forgiveness. The Son of Man has authority to forgive sins right here on earth. You don't have to wait until heaven. You can experience the freedom of complete forgiveness right here. Right now. Fall under Christ's authority and accept His grace.

## DAY 143
### Luke 6:1–11

———∞∞∞———

The scribes and Pharisees were watching Him closely, to see if He would
heal on the Sabbath, so that they could find a charge against Him (v. 7).

———∞∞∞———

Back in Luke 5:17, the Pharisees and doctors of the law were seen "sitting
by" while Jesus was teaching (KJV). Matthew Henry wrote, "How many are there
in the midst of our assemblies, where the gospel is preached, that do not sit *under*
the Word, but sit *by!* It is to them as a tale that is told them, not as a message that
is sent them; they are willing that we should preach *before* them, but not that we
should preach *to* them."[35]

Can you recall a time when you attended a Bible study or church service that
profoundly affected a few of the people you were with, while others in attendance
were completely unmoved? Like the Pharisees and teachers of the law, sometimes
the unaffected can be the most "religious" people in the room. Could the difference be that they were sitting *by* rather than sitting *under* God's Word?

One of the stories in today's passage is proof positive of this.

On the Sabbath day, Jesus encountered a man with a withered right hand.
Think of all the jobs that would have been difficult if not impossible for this man.
A shepherd had to be adept at using a rod and a staff. A farmer needed both
hands to plow. A carpenter had to hold a hammer in one hand and a nail in the
other. A merchant would have had a difficult time securing and displaying goods
with only one hand. Even a tax collector needed his right hand! So in the context
of this event from Jesus' life, in which He would give a discourse on the issue of
rest versus work, I don't think it was a coincidence that the man involved had
lived a humiliating life of unwelcome "rest" from effective labor. Christ granted
him rest on this day from his incapacity and futility. The One who created the
Sabbath used it to bring restoration to a man weary of uselessness.

Meanwhile, however, the Pharisees and teachers of the law were "sitting
by," watching Jesus, just looking for some basis to condemn Him. Their primary
reason for attending was to see if Jesus would heal.

(By the way, I love the fact that they were convinced Christ would heal if He
encountered someone in need—even on the Sabbath. What a healer He is! No
amount of laws could keep Him from being Himself! The Pharisees and teachers
of the law caught Christ in the act of being God. Hallelujah!)

But by coming with the expressed intent of finding fault with Jesus, they
proved that the most merciful people are those who have been sitting under the
faucet of God's mercy instead of sitting by with a critical eye. Please note this sad
fact, which was emphasized by the events following the Pharisees' and teachers'

speculations: those who look for reasons to accuse will undoubtedly find some. They quickly found basis to accuse Jesus.

In my own life and ministry, I've accepted the fact that anyone looking hard enough to condemn will sooner or later be accommodated. I really do believe that more people in the body of Christ are generally accepting than accusing, but one mean-spirited person is practically enough to ruin anyone's day. Francis Frangipane wrote something so powerful on this subject, I immediately committed it to memory. He said of the Lord:

> To inoculate me from the praise of man, He baptized
> me in the criticism of man, until I died to the control
> of man.[36]

Beloved, one thing I know for sure on this subject: nothing will squelch our efforts to seek the approval of others like not receiving it! Furthermore, those who approve of us one day can be the same ones who accuse us the next. I encourage you to break free from the traps set by approval and accusation. We are called to live our lives above reproach but to expect reproach anyway. Christ was blameless yet was blamed continually. I think you can trust me on this one: blameless people are rarely those who cast blame.

When the man with the shriveled hand stood before Him on the Sabbath, Jesus knew the Pharisees and teachers of the law were looking to accuse Him. But He did not allow Himself to be controlled by potential accusations nor even by the law that He Himself instituted. He was indeed the Lord of the Sabbath.

His public question to His accusers made them look terribly foolish: "I ask you, which is lawful on the Sabbath: to do good or to do evil, to save life or to destroy it?" (v. 9). Picture the scene described in verse 10 as Jesus "looked around at them all." Eye to eye. Just waiting for someone to give Him an answer. They were struck dumb. Or maybe dumber. Then He said to the man, "Stretch out your hand." And he did. Right there in front of all those perfect and pious-looking people, the man who all his life had probably hidden his handicap under the sleeve of his garment stretched forth his humiliating infirmity—and was healed. It was enough to make those who were sitting by to be "filled with rage," off to their own little corners to discuss "what they might do to Jesus" (v. 11).

It's a question we must answer every time we hear or read a message from His Word. What will we do with Jesus? Will we sit under His teaching? Or just sit by?

# DAY 144
## Luke 7:1–10

—∞∞—

Jesus heard this and was amazed at him, and turning to the crowd following Him,
He said, "I tell you, I have not found so great a faith even in Israel" (v. 9).

—∞∞—

Jesus almost seems delightfully shocked in this encounter with the centurion, as though He was caught off guard by such faith. I'm so glad God purposed for Christ to know all things yet also to know the thrill of sudden amazement.

Perhaps you've bought into the "wretched worm that I am" mentality enough to be uncomfortable thinking about Christ being impressed by anything wretched man can do. But since we're attempting to develop God's taste in us—to love what He loves, hate what He hates, and marvel at what He finds marvelous—perhaps we could all use a little adjustment in our perception of the divine.

A word God used in Isaiah 66:2 blows my mind. The verse says, "This is the one I esteem: he who is humble and contrite in spirit, and trembles at my word." The word *esteem* means to "regard with pleasure, . . . have respect." God is clearly saying that He respects certain people.

Our difficulty imagining that God could have respect for a mortal is because we confuse attitudes of respect with feelings of inferiority. We tend to view respect as a feeling we have for those we perceive as being superior to us. And on our best day, we are so inferior to Christ that, if not for the Lord's great love (see Lam. 3:22), we would be consumed by holy fire.

If we're to have a balanced perception of all this, however, we must keep in mind that God created us. We are His "workmanship" (Eph. 2:10). He loves us. At times, He actually delights in us. God could have created us void of weakness and with a complete inability to sin. He didn't. He purposely created us with free will and affections so that we could choose Him and love Him in the midst of many options and much opposition.

God didn't create robots. He created humans. So when God sees humans cooperate with His good work and fulfill what they were created to be, He sees something very good. Perfect? No. But respectable? Yes. When the Father sees a human who is prone to selfishness, pride, and arrogance humble himself or herself and tremble at His Word, He esteems that person. Hallelujah! Oh, how I want to be someone God could respect!

## DAY 145
### Luke 7:11–17

—❧—

When the Lord saw her, He had compassion on her and said, "Don't cry" (v. 13).

—❧—

How hard must it have been for Christ to possess all authority but stick to a kingdom plan requiring its timely exercise? Even now, He could sneeze on Satan and blow him to oblivion, but that's not the plan. Satan's prompt demise would spare us trouble, but it would also spare us growth resulting in many rewards. So until the right time for Satan's disposal, Christ restrains Himself.

Other areas of restraint must have also been challenging for Jesus as He walked on this pavement. For example, imagine the thoughts this funeral procession must have provoked in the mind of the author of life.

I think the very lordship of Christ overwhelmed Him at that moment in Nain. No one else in the crowd could do anything about the widow's plight. They possessed no power. Christ was the only one present who had lordship over the living and the dead. His heart went out to her. He felt deeply. He spoke only two words to her: "Don't cry." We've all said those two words to someone who was brokenhearted, but I believe Christ probably meant something a little different.

I don't know about you, but most of the time when I've said to someone, "Don't cry," my heart was saying, "Please stop crying. I can't bear to see you in so much pain!" Usually the words come from one who can't stand to see the hurt because she is powerless to help. Christ, on the other hand, is never helpless. When He said, "Don't cry," He meant, "Not only do I hurt for you, but I'm also going to do something about the cause of your hurt."

Verse 14 records Jesus' initial action: "He went up and touched the coffin." Picture the structure more like a stretcher than our Western concept of a coffin. The body was placed on a board and shrouded with burial linens. Now imagine Christ walking up and touching this burial slate.

The first thing we read after Christ touched the bier is that the ones who were carrying it stood still. They probably stood there bug-eyed. You see, for anyone unnecessary to the interment process to risk touching the dead body was a serious no-no. Jesus was ritually defiling Himself. What they couldn't have realized is that the Son of God could not be defiled no matter what He touched. One day soon He would literally take on the sins of the entire world while still remaining the perfect Lamb without spot or blemish.

We've already seen that Christ did not need to touch to heal. He didn't even need to be present. He seemed to touch because it came natural to Him. I'm anxious to share with you what "touched" means in today's context. The word is *haptomai*, from the word *hapto*, meaning "to connect, bind." *Haptomai* means "to apply oneself to, to touch." The word "refers to such handling of an object as to exert a modifying influence upon it." Christ Jesus literally connected Himself to the situation. We apply all sorts of medication for hurts. Christ took one look at this woman's grief and applied Himself.

I hope you'll also be blessed by the Greek antonym or opposite term for "touched"—*egkrateuomai*. You will find the English translation of this word listed at the very end of the fruits of the Spirit in Galatians 5:22–23. The word is "self-control."

In today's text, imagine Christ acting out of exactly the opposite of self-control. Stick with me here until you grasp the meaning. When Christ saw the woman in such agony and faced with such hopelessness, I'm suggesting He literally cast off self-restraint and *reacted!* The difference between Jesus and us is that He doesn't sin even when He casts off self-control! Christ does not depart from the Spirit whether He responds or reacts.

Herein lies the most profound difference between the miracle in Nain and the previous miracle of the centurion's servant in Capernaum. In the widow's case, the only prerequisite was her pain. Unlike the centurion, she made no request. She exhibited no faith. In fact, we have no idea if the grieving mom even realized Christ existed. She was probably too enveloped in her own agony to notice. He awaited no conditions nor apparently had any intention of using the moment for instructional purposes.

Jesus ran into a woman in hopeless despair and just reacted with what came most naturally to Him—healing mercy. Oh, how I praise Him! I believe we possibly have a small glimpse into what Christ would do in every one of our despairing situations if a greater plan was not at stake. I believe what comes most naturally to Christ every time He encounters need is to instantly fix it. Is it possible He exercises great restraint to work any other way in the face of devastation? I think so.

A plan of profound importance exists that sometimes overrides the miracle we desperately desire. But I am comforted to know that instantaneous healing and resurrection power come even more naturally to our Christ than waiting and working through long but necessary processes. The biggest reason why I can trust in the sovereignty of God is because I am so utterly convinced of the sweetness of God.

# DAY 146
## Luke 7:23–30

⸺∞⸺

Blessed is the man who does not fall away on account of me (v. 23 NIV).

⸺∞⸺

It is a real challenge to work through our doubts and not let them imprison us like John's were threatening to imprison him! Christ stated the biggest risk of doubt in verse 23: "Blessed is the man who does not fall away on account of me."

The original word for "blessed" is *makarios*. Revel in this definition of the term: "Biblically, one is pronounced blessed when God is present and involved in his life. The Hand of God is at work directing all his affairs for a divine purpose, and thus, in a sense, such a person lives *coram Deo*, before the face of God."[37] Luke 7:23 tells us these words apply to the person who doesn't fall away on account of Christ.

What does "falling away" mean? The Greek word, *skandalon*, means "a cause of stumbling." Add the meanings of these two definitions and we arrive at the following sum total in Luke 7:23: "The Hand of God is at work directing divine purpose, or blessing, in all the affairs of the one who doesn't let the perceived activity or inactivity of Christ trap him or make him stumble." It's a mouthful, but chew on it awhile!

I don't think Luke 7:23 is talking about falling away from Christ. It's talking about falling over a stumbling block into a trap. One of Satan's most effective devices for causing a devout believer to stumble is to trap him over a matter of faith. Satan even tries to use Christ Himself against us. The most effective faith-trap Satan could set for a Christian is to tempt him or her to doubt the goodness, rightness, or mightiness of Christ.

Note that Christ held John in highest esteem even after being questioned. John was under a terrible strain, and his martyrdom was imminent. Christ knew that! He could handle John's questions because He knew the heart and mind from which they came. After proclaiming that no one born of women was greater than John, Jesus said the "least in the kingdom of God is greater than he" (v. 28).

Please understand that this statement in no way diminished John. Christ simply meant that a new era was unfolding in the kingdom calendar, and to be a part of it would be greater than being a prophet under the old Covenant. Thank God every day that you live this side of Calvary!

# DAY 147
## Luke 7:36–38

—∞∞∞—

Then one of the Pharisees invited Him to eat with him.
He entered the Pharisee's house and reclined at the table (v. 36).

—∞∞∞—

Our scene unfolds in the dining area of one of the more prestigious homes in the village. The Pharisee's home was large enough to accommodate Jesus and an undisclosed number of other guests. The Pharisee's wife and any other women involved probably ate separately. They would not have considered this a slight since the men customarily practiced segregated fellowship in many social settings. Incidentally, their manly discussions often turned into passionate theological debates that they thoroughly enjoyed. Such conflict tends to make me nervous, so I would happily have stayed in the kitchen with the dessert and coffee.

Do you have difficulty picturing Christ in this scene? Do you imagine Him never fitting into a Pharisee's home? I think God desires to broaden our understanding and fine-tune some of our mental footage of Christ. The more I study His earthly life, the more I'm grasping that He could fit in anywhere . . . and nowhere.

Remember, Christ is void of all prejudice. He was no more likely to stereotype all Pharisees than He was to stereotype all who were poor, blind, or ill. Furthermore, He was just as anxious to save them from their sins. The obvious difference was how anxious the individual was to be saved.

Before we are too harsh in our view of the Pharisees, we are wise to remember that their negative tendencies resemble those of anyone—even someone in our day and age, someone you could name without thinking twice—who values religion and ritual over relationship with the Savior. Interestingly, in the Gospels not once do we see a Pharisee who is confronted in the stronghold of legalism and self-righteousness ever admit to seeing it in himself. My point is that no one is likely to see him or herself as pharisaical without an honest and courageous look inside. In fact, our story never indicates that Christ's host received the message delivered to him through these events.

But it doesn't mean that Jesus would automatically thumb his nose at an invitation just because of what this man stood for. Jesus is willing to reach into anyone's life, no matter how sinful they are or how sinless they think themselves to be.

# DAY 148
## Luke 7:39–48

—&infin;—

When the Pharisee who had invited Him saw this, he said to himself,
"This man, if He were a prophet, would know who and what kind of woman
this is who is touching Him—she's a sinner" (v. 39).

—&infin;—

I am learning so much in my journey with Christ Jesus—lessons I wish I
had learned long ago. I am learning that my heart and mind are of greater importance to Him than my words and deeds. Our innermost places desperately need
daily purification. Part of the process is recognizing and confessing judgmental,
impure, or critical thoughts before they can make their way to our mouths and
our actions. But God really can change our negative thought processes, attitudes,
and motives. The process takes time and cooperation, however, because these
thought patterns are just as much habitual sin as the transgressions of the woman
of ill repute.

We certainly see how deep-seated this tendency is by hearing the Pharisee
talking "to himself." This phrase and Christ's response have great importance
because they force us to realize that He holds us responsible for the things we say
to ourselves. (Ouch.) Yes, He reads our minds. And sometimes, our minds need
a viewer rating.

Don't overlook the fact that Christ's willingness to allow the woman to
wash His feet caused the Pharisee to question whether or not Jesus was a prophet.
The Pharisee implied that Jesus obviously did not know what kind of woman
she was. The original wording is quite interesting. The English "what kind" is
derived from two Greek words: *poios*, meaning "what," and *dapedon*, meaning
"soil." The Pharisee's comment that Christ did not know where she came from
literally meant "He has no idea the dirt she comes from."

You know what, beloved? Dirt is dirt, and we've all got it no matter where
we come from. I'm not sure Christ sees one kind of dirt as dirtier than another.
One thing is for sure: His blood is able to bleach any stain left by any kind of dirt.
Oh, thank You, Lord.

I like the King James Version of Christ's first response after He read the
Pharisee's thoughts: "Simon, I have somewhat to say unto thee" (v. 40). Lest you
think I'm feeling pious in my deep compassion for the habitual sinner, please
know I'm presently shuddering over the times Christ has had "somewhat" to say
unto me! I also love the King James Version response of the Pharisee: "Master,
say on" (v. 40) makes me grin. I wonder what he was expecting the Master to "say
on"? I have a feeling it wasn't what Christ said.

Christ told a parable of canceled debts. Two men owed money to a moneylender. One owed much, the other only a little, but neither had the money to

pay what he owed, so the moneylender canceled the debts of both. Then Jesus asked Simon to summarize which debtor loved the moneylender most. The answer was obvious, but Simon's words "I suppose" revealed his reluctance to acknowledge it. After Simon pinpointed the one with the bigger debt canceled, Christ said, "You have judged correctly" (v. 43). Interestingly, Simon had been judging throughout the whole ordeal. It was just the first time he had judged correctly.

Christ then brought the parable to life. He compared the way Simon and the sinful woman had responded to Him. All three times Christ's description of the Pharisee's actions began with the unsettling words, "You did not." How poignant. You see, one of the surest signs of an ancient or modern-day "Pharisee" is a life characterized far more by what he or she does *not* do than what he or she does. "No, Simon. You did not sleep around. You did not take bribes. You did not externalize your depravity. But as well, you did not give Me any water for My feet. You did not give Me a kiss. You did not put oil on My head. You did not see yourself as a sinner, and you did not receive My gift of grace—but she did."

He packs the punch into the living parable in verse 47: "Therefore, I tell you, her many sins have been forgiven—for she loved much. But he who has been forgiven little loves little." Not because that's the way it has to be, but because that's the reality of our human tendency.

A couple of additional truths strike a chord in me. First, I see that Christ never downplayed nor minimized her sin. Human sympathy makes excuses like, "What you did wasn't that bad" or "After all you've been through, no wonder . . ." But Christ never calls sin less than it is. To picture Christ minimizing the woman's sinful past is to miss the entire point of the encounter. The point is that even though her sins had been many, heinous, and habitual, she had been forgiven, saved, and liberated to love lavishly. Of all the commandments the Pharisee had kept, she (rather than he) had observed the most important one. "Love the Lord your God with all your heart and with all your soul and with all your mind and with all your strength" (Mark 12:30).

The exquisite beauty of loving Christ is that it makes it impossible to keep only one commandment. The Word tells us that the person who truly loves God will pursue the obedient life (see John 14:21) and be far more likely to persevere in trials (see James 1:12). Loving God is the vital lifeline to all the other commandments.

Christ never preached the annihilation of affection. Instead He taught the *redirection* of affection. Human affection first directed to God and filtered through His hands returns to us far healthier and fit for others.

# DAY 149
## Luke 7:49–50

He said to the woman, "Your faith has saved you. Go in peace" (v. 50).

During the writing of my book *Breaking Free*, the enemy used every trick in the book to break me. He is our accuser (see Rev. 12:10) and a shameless opportunist (see Luke 4:13). He knew that *Breaking Free* necessitated very deep scrutiny of my history because the study is based on my journey to liberty. My whole life has forever been laid bare before God, but it had never been so vividly laid bare before me. At the taunting of the enemy, I found myself at one point so grieved over the "yuck" in my history that I could not imagine how God could possibly use me. I literally questioned my own calling.

During this painful time, I had a speaking engagement in Louisiana. Customarily someone from the host church delivers a devotional to the team before the conference begins. That day a woman who did not know me, had never heard me speak, had never read a single word I'd written, walked in the door and pulled up a chair in front of me. The entire group could hear her, but the devotional she delivered was for me.

She sat only inches away and never took her eyes off mine. With obvious anointing, she told the story of the sinful woman in the Luke 7 passage, then she said, "I don't know you, Beth. I have no idea why God sent me with such a message to give you, but He told me clearly to say these words to you: 'Tell her that her many sins have been forgiven—for she loved much.'" I cannot describe my feelings then or my feelings now.

This Scripture is the only one framed on my desk. It sits only inches from my computer. As I sit at my desk, I stare at the reminder of God's unreasonable grace, and I'm reminded that I'm forgiven. Indeed, how could someone like me not love Him much?

Perhaps, as it did for me, this passage causes you to picture yourself in this sinful woman's place. If you, too, have been in this scene with Jesus, perhaps you know the inner struggle of a sinful past. Oh, how I would love to be for you today what that woman in Louisiana was to me during that difficult time. Allow me to pull up my chair right in front of you, look you in the eye, and tell you what He told me to say: "Your many sins have been forgiven—for you love much." Go in peace.

## DAY 150
### Luke 8:4–15

—∞∞—

He said, "The secrets of the kingdom of God have been given
for you to know, but to the rest it is in parables" (v. 10).

—∞∞—

The parable of the sower helps us understand the obstacles that limit us
and the elements that would free the Spirit to teach us the deep things of God.
But before we look at the differences in each type of "soil," let's address a critical
common denominator: all four heard the Word, yet only one produced a harvest.

It is not enough to hear the Word! We have just stumbled on my greatest burden for the body of Christ. How many people sit in church services
where Scripture is never taught? They're not even hearing the Word of God!
Furthermore, what masses of believers hear the Word but continue to live in
defeat because they don't apply it?

I was one of them. I desperately wanted to change. I was miserable in my
captivity. I just didn't understand that the power to be transformed was in the
authentic application of Scripture. Our obedience is not to make God feel like
the boss. Trust me. He's the boss and He knows it. Our obedience to apply the
Word of God is so we can live victorious lives that glorify our Father in heaven.
Hearing it is simply not enough.

Now let's consider each of the types of soil the seed of God's Word fell on.

1. *The seed along the path.* Luke 8:12 tells us Satan possesses the ability to
come and take away the word from a hearer's heart, although not the *believing*
hearer's heart. Once we've received the Word, it's out of his reach. He can try to
distort our understanding of it, but he cannot steal it. As we'll soon see, however,
we can give it up by our own volition.

The Greek word for "take away" gives the image of an owl swooping down,
snatching its prey in its claws, and soaring back victoriously to its perch. Scripture
implies countless reasons why Satan desires to snatch the Word from us before
we've internalized it. Imagine the evil nature of one who seeks to keep people
from being saved.

2. *The seed on the rock.* The rocky soil doesn't just receive the Word. It receives
the Word with joy! How eye-opening to realize that we can hear the Word and
receive it joyfully, yet never let it penetrate the depths. Listen, some of the words
of God are hard! I think He'd rather see us receive a Word, wrestling over it with
tears and letting it take root, than to jump up and down with ecstatic joy for only
a while.

The shallow hearer only believes until the "time of testing" (v. 13). What
a shame! We miss one of life's most awesome experiences if we don't see God's
Word stand up under trial. He wants to show us it works. He wants to show us

He works! If we stop believing, we will never know the power and faithfulness of God.

3. *The seed that fell among thorns.* These hearers are defeated by the distractions of the world: worries, riches, and pleasures. You don't have to be rich to be distracted by riches. You don't have to have much to want more. Working ourselves into the ground to afford more things is symptomatic of this.

The word for "pleasures" is *hedone*, from which we get our term "hedonism." Hedonism views "pleasure, gratification, and enjoyment" as the chief goals of life. Please take caution before you view all forms of pleasure as an enemy of the faithful believer. Few things frustrate me more than people who picture the Christian life as entirely sacrificial and for martyrs only. Walking with Christ is the greatest pleasure of my life. But even this sacred pleasure cannot be my goal. Knowing and pleasing Christ must be my goal. Luke 8:14 says they also don't "mature," which is far more than unfortunate. It's a tragedy. The word "mature" comes from two Greek words: *telos*, meaning "end, goal, perfection," and *phero*, meaning "to bring, bear." The hearers of the Word who are distracted by the constant call of the world will never fulfill God's awesome plan for their lives. According to 1 Corinthians 2:9, distracted individuals miss life's greatest treasure. No mind has even conceived "what God has prepared for those who love Him."

4. *The seed on good soil.* The good soil represents the one who hears the Word and retains it. "Retains" pictures chewing the Word up and swallowing it until it occupies a place in us. When God's Word is deliberately internalized, it will be authentically externalized because it's no longer what we do—it's part of who we are.

Isaiah 55:11 declares that God's Word will not return void or empty. It will accomplish the purposes for which He sent it. That's a fact. But I want it to accomplish and achieve in me, don't you? When this generation asks who Christ's brothers and sisters are, I want Him to point us out joyfully. For our kinship to be obvious, we've got to hear God's Word and do it. When He sends forth His Word, may He find fertile soil in each of us.

Then, when we've reached our lives' intended goals, we will go out in joy and be led forth in peace, the mountains and hills will burst into song before us, and all the trees of the field will clap their hands. Persevere, doer of the Word. A harvest is coming.

# DAY 151
## Luke 8:1–3, 19–21

———∞∞∞———

He replied to them, "My mother and my brothers are
those who hear and do the word of God" (v. 21).

———∞∞∞———

One of my chief goals in this journey is for us to feel as if our feet have felt
the warmth of the sand in every place where Jesus stood. In Luke 8, we have a
fresh opportunity to adjust our mental images to include a few new people on
the scene. In addition to the Twelve, Jesus had other companions. "Women who
had been cured of evil spirits and diseases: Mary (called Magdalene), from whom
seven demons had come out; Joanna . . . Susanna, and many others" followed
Him (v. 2).

Whether or not these received a verbal invitation the way the Twelve had,
a powerful force drew them. After everything Christ had done for them, these
women could not help but follow Him. You don't have to talk many freed captives
into serving Christ. Like Paul in 2 Corinthians 5:14, the love of Christ compels
them.

But it didn't seem to compel some of those who might have seemed most
suited to cling to Him—His physical family. When His mother and brothers
came to see Him but could not get to Him because of the crowd, Jesus had some
strong words for them.

But Jesus was not *rejecting* His family as much as He was *redefining* it. His
statement reflected inclusion more than exclusion. Christ's family probably came
to take Him home to keep Him from appearing foolish. They surely weren't there
to encourage Him. John tells us "even his own brothers did not believe in him"
at this time (John 7:5).

Of course, we know that Mary certainly believed Jesus was the Son of God,
but the pressure of family members can be quite forceful. Perhaps her other sons
were intent on confronting Jesus, and she came along to act as a peacemaker.
Sound familiar, moms? You don't have to be a mother to imagine how she felt in
her present position.

Christ's revolutionary words that redefined His family dynamics are as critical for us today as they were for those who heard them then. Don't miss the
profound importance of God's Word. According to Luke 8:21, our kinship to
Jesus Christ is directly revealed through what we do with the Word of God.
What you are doing right now—studying His Word—is not just a good idea. It
is the very warmth and vitality of the family bloodline—proof that we are family
to Jesus Christ.

## DAY 152
### Luke 8:26–39

—∞∞∞—

When he saw Jesus, he cried out, fell down before Him, and said in a loud voice,
"What do You have to do with me, Jesus, You Son of the Most High God" (v. 28).

—∞∞∞—

After rebuking the waves—and a boatload of disciples—Jesus arrived in the territory of the Gerasenes where they promptly encountered a memorable individual. The man they met was naked, lived among the tombs, possessed superhuman strength, and—did I mention—provided rent-free housing for a legion of demons. This demon-possessed man not only had the power to break ropes and chains; he also supernaturally recognized Jesus as the Son of God. We want to consider several points coming from the encounter.

1. *Our God is even God over the godless.* The second that Christ stepped His foot on their "turf," the demons knew He carried His authority with Him. As hard as the demonic world tries to keep Him out, no one can keep Christ out of any place He is determined to go. Verse 28 tells us that when the demoniac saw Jesus, he cried out and fell at his feet. While I certainly wouldn't confuse the demoniac's trip to His knees with worship, it definitely was a sign of the demon's acknowledgment that Christ was the Son of the Most High God.

2. *The demons may have anticipated Christ's coming.* Even my most conservative commentaries entertained the idea that the storm on the way could have been an attempt by the kingdom of darkness to discourage Christ's arrival. We see a hint toward the possibility of this idea in the way Christ rebuked the wind and waters as if they were disobedient. Could they have been temporarily acting under the instruction of the god of the air (see Eph. 2:2)? Just food for thought, but it would help to explain why the demoniac met Christ on the shore, knowing for certain who He was.

3. *The demons know their time is limited.* Luke focused on only one of the demoniacs, but Matthew tells us that there were actually two. He also tells us that they begged Jesus not to torture them "before the appointed time" (Matt. 8:29). The demons knew something we may sometimes forget. Satan, too, is filled with fury because he knows that "his time is short" (Rev. 12:12).

I don't believe the plan for the Son of God to come to earth was any secret. I believe Satan knew what was going to happen. I just don't think he knew when. Seeing the Word wrapped in flesh reminded him that his time allotment was getting shorter and shorter. In the same way, the demons controlling the man on the Gerasene shore knew a day of reckoning had been appointed for them.

4. *Demons can enact supernatural strength.* Matthew tells us that "they were so violent that no one could pass that way" (Matt. 8:28). Luke tells us that the demons enabled the man to break chains (see Luke 8:29). I feel the need to stress

something about supernatural power: not all of it comes from God! I have felt chills run down my spine when I've heard someone say: "It had to be God! It was totally supernatural!" At times Satan is able to display signs and wonders. But remember, ours is the Prince of Peace. All conflict He ordains is for the ultimate purpose of peace under His righteous rule. Oh, for the government that will be on His shoulders! (see Isa. 9:6–7).

5. *Solitary places can be used by God or Satan.* This man "had been driven by the demon into solitary places" (v. 29). Jesus also valued solitary places. In Mark 6:31, He said to the disciples, "Come with me by yourselves to a quiet place and get some rest." We all need times of solitude to spend with God. But our times of isolation can be used by the enemy as well. If we isolate ourselves from the support of others, Satan can have a field day.

Only Christ can defeat demonic powers. Without Christ, a "legion" of humans cannot take authority over a single demon. However, Jesus the One and Only can instantly take authority over legions of demons. The climactic point of the story reveals an almost laughable irony. The demons begged to be cast into the swine rather than into the abyss. (If you think I'm going to say a word about deviled ham, you're mistaken!)

The villagers came out of the woodwork only to find the talk of the region sitting at Jesus' feet, dressed and in his right mind. The people allowed fear to eclipse the life-changing facts, and they begged Jesus to leave. He could have healed them, saved them, taught them, sanctified them, and, for heaven's sake, delighted them. But all they wanted Him to do was to leave them.

Jesus left the Gerasenes, all right. But not without a vivid reminder of who He was and what He could do. Long after they recovered from the swine-at-sea incident, there would still be a man about town with a restored mind and real dignity who couldn't seem to hush. Christ told him, "Return home and tell how much God has done for you" (v. 39). How long do you think it had been since he had been home? Not back to the tombs, but home. Clothes on his back. Roof over his head. Soundness in his mind. A message on his tongue. So the man went and told all over town how much Jesus had done for him. All the demons in the air couldn't stop him, for his knees had bowed to a new authority.

# DAY 153
## Luke 8:40–42a, 49–56

———∞———

Just then, a man named Jairus came. He was a leader of the synagogue.
He fell down at Jesus' feet and pleaded with Him to come to his house (v. 41).

———∞———

I long to sit at Jesus' feet in heaven and hear Him describe personally His earthly experience. I want to hear all the missing details. I want to hear what He was thinking when certain things happened. And when I do, I think He'll have plenty to say about the text we're observing today.

Upon Jesus' return from across the lake, a crowd greeted Him. Luke 8:40 says they were all expecting Him. (I do dearly love surprise encounters with Jesus, but I think He is quite pleased when we live our lives in expectancy.) Verse 41, however, re-introduces us to a major player who didn't come just to welcome Jesus. He came *desperate* for Jesus. Jairus was a ruler of the synagogue, but this day no ritual dignity stood in his way. His daughter lay dying, and he threw himself at the feet of Jesus pleading for her life.

Jim Cymbala, in his book *Fresh Wind, Fresh Fire,* wrote, "I discovered an astonishing truth: God is attracted to weakness. He can't resist those who humbly and honestly admit how desperately they need him."[38] This certainly described Jairus on this day. Jairus also reminds me of the centurion in Luke 7. He seemed to understand the concept of authority because of his authoritative position. He seemed to grasp that one ruler existed before whom all others should bow, even if one of those "others" was a ruler of the synagogue.

If you were to ask any set of parents how much they focus on their child when he or she is sick or in some kind of serious danger or distress, they'd tell you they can hardly focus on anything else. This was certainly the case with Jairus. Jesus was his last hope. Who else could heal his little girl from the throes of death?

Whom do you know that is possibly down to his or her very last hope? Perhaps, like me, you even know several. Think of these people and keep them in your peripheral vision today, as well as tomorrow when we look at the story this passage is sandwiched around—Jesus' healing of a woman who had been bleeding for twelve years. He is there for the desperate. He specializes in the hopeless. Every time you think of those who are suffering, think of Jesus, who knows the path through dire need.

# DAY 154
## Luke 8:42b–48

—⟨∞⟩—

In the presence of all the people, she declared the reason
she had touched Him and how she was instantly cured (v. 47).

—⟨∞⟩—

We read in verse 42 that the crowd pressed so closely to Jesus they were almost crushing Him. Yet a woman behind Him touched only the edge of His cloak, and He discerned the difference. Please keep in mind, she never even touched His skin. Amazing! Notice, too, that when Christ asked, "Who touched me?" they all denied it. Odd, isn't it? The people were so close they were nearly crushing Him, but no one admitted to touching Him. Their response reminds me of children too afraid of getting into trouble to admit to something. Did they not realize He wanted few things more than for them to reach out to Him?

When the woman realized she could not go unnoticed, she "came trembling and fell at his feet" (v. 47). Beloved, no one goes unnoticed by Christ—least of all a person acting on faith. I love the fact that the woman came trembling, even though she had exercised enough faith to draw forth the healing power of Jesus. It's good to know that the faithful still come trembling. In fact, their reverence is a critical part of their faith. The truly believing will most certainly also be the bowing.

Why do you think Christ asked her to identify herself? I think one reason might have been so that she could enjoy the healing she had received. Most modern Bible translations don't record one phrase found in the King James Version of verse 48: "Daughter, *be of good comfort:* thy faith hath made thee whole; go in peace." In this way I believe Christ was saying, "Do not go forth as someone who feels like they have stolen a gift! Be of good cheer! I freely give it to you!"

Verse 42 also tells us Jesus was on His way to heal the dying child of Jairus when the woman in the crowd touched the edge of His cloak. Christ Himself described what happened: "Someone touched me; I know that power has gone out from me" (v. 46). The primary point I want to make is that Christ released enough power to heal a woman of a twelve-year hemorrhage, but still had plenty to raise Jairus's daughter from the dead! Let that sink in! I know that you know it with your head, but I want you to receive it in your heart. Christ's power supply is limitless. He's not the Wizard of Oz with a limited number of wishes to grant. His power and mercy are infinite. He can take you much farther than Kansas, Dorothy.

One night at Bible study, I asked the entire group to come to their feet for a time of intercessory prayer. I then asked anyone with an "overwhelming need" that seemed absolutely "insurmountable" to sit down. I don't mind telling you, few people were left standing. And based on their tears, I don't think they were just being dramatic. I had anticipated having enough intercessors left standing to lay hands on all those who sat down. Boy, was I mistaken! For a split second I didn't know how to proceed. Then the Spirit of God seemed to speak to my heart. What joy flooded my soul that very moment as God called upon me to come boldly before His throne and ask for a miracle for every life because He had plenty of power to go around. That's exactly what I did. The testimonies written to me the next week were unforgettable. Virtually everyone witnessed some type of wonder that week.

Now hear this: Jesus has more than enough power! Does He seem to be on His way to another need, one that you perceive may be more important than yours? More a matter of life and death? No problem! Reach out and grab that hem! You are not going unnoticed—not even if He's on His way to raise the dead!

Oh, friend, would you dare to believe that He is completely able? If He doesn't grant you what you ask in faith, it is never because He lacks the power. I believe it's because He wants to release an all-surpassing power and reveal an even greater glory through another answer. Will we laugh at the thought like the foolish mourners outside Jairus's home? Or will we be invited into the house to behold a miracle?

# DAY 155
## Luke 9:1–6

———

So they went out and traveled from village to village,
proclaiming the good news and healing everywhere (v. 6).

———

I find it interesting that Christ's instruction to His disciples to go and min-ister was for a specific mission or task. I believe the concepts of calling and task are often confused in the body of Christ. I know that I confused the concepts in the early years of my surrender to ministry.

When I was in my mid-twenties, my wonderful ministry mentor, Marge Caldwell, helped me to see that God had equipped me with some of the speak-ing gifts. Once I began to exercise those gifts, I assumed that speaking was my calling. God soon made very clear, however, that my calling was to surrender my life every day to His will, to be His woman, and to do what He asked, whatever that was. I remember sensing Him speak to my heart saying, "Beth, I do not want you surrendered to an assignment. I want you surrendered to Me." I realized that God did not want me "hung up" on the kind of assignment He would give me. He didn't want it to matter to me whether He asked me to teach the Word of God to a hundred people or to rock one baby in the church nursery. My calling was to be abandoned to Him.

The Twelve were called to be Christ's learners or pupils. They also were designated apostles, meaning they would be sent forth. What would His pupils be sent forth to do? Whatever He told them. In our human need for the security of sameness, we tend to want one job assignment from God that we can do for the rest of our lives. He's far more creative than that!

You may ask, "Isn't it possible for God to assign a lifelong task such as preaching at one church for forty years?" Absolutely! But we are wise not to make assumptions by surrendering to the assignment! Our calling is to surrender to God. Think of the pitfalls we could avoid if we were more abandoned to God than to a particular kind of service.

Remember the meaning of *disciple*: pupil, learner! We can't keep skipping class—our time with God in the Scripture and in prayer—and expect to know when He's scheduled a field trip!

# DAY 156
## Luke 9:10–17

∞

"We have no more than five loaves and two fish," they said,
"unless we go and buy food for all these people" (v. 13).

∞

Any of us who have ever been exhausted by an intense time of ministry can deeply appreciate the opening scene in Luke 9:10. The apostles returned from their preaching and healing mission. Mark pictures the Twelve gathered around Jesus reporting all they had done and taught. What affection floods this setting! We can assume He omnisciently knew everything they had done and taught, yet I love how He celebrated their news with the same excitement as someone at a surprise party.

Sometimes I'll be busy telling God every detail of something exciting that happened, a thousand words a minute, when suddenly I will stop and say, "But I guess You already knew that." Every single time I sense Him saying, "Don't let that stop you, child! Tell on!" Beloved, I so much hope that you feel free to talk to Him with the excitement of a friend.

But Christ not only sees our excitement, He sees our exhaustion. I love the way the King James Version says it: "They had no leisure so much as to eat" (Mark 6:31). He saw their need for leisure over a refreshing meal. His invitation to them is so warm and intimate that my affection for Him swells every time I read it: "Come with me by yourselves to a quiet place and get some rest."

Wouldn't you know it? In the middle of their private getaway, the public showed up. Yet Christ's response to the crowd touches me: "He welcomed them" (Luke 9:11); "They were like sheep without a shepherd" (Mark 6:34). Desperate, vulnerable, without direction, without protection, and He had compassion on them. According to Matthew 14:21, we are safe to picture at least ten thousand people gathering all over the countryside. Christ "healed those who needed healing" (Luke 9:11). The day wore on, and the sun rested again on a western hill. Then about that time, some interesting things began to happen. Consider the following observations with me:

1. *Christ sometimes provokes a question so that He can be the answer.* I love how John's version tells us Christ prompted the question to Philip, "Where shall we buy bread for these people to eat?" (John 6:5). Verse 6 tells us, "He asked this only to test him." I think Christ might have been testing His disciples to surface what they had learned or, like me, what they had *yet* to learn! Think of the miracles they had seen Christ perform by this time. Yet they couldn't imagine how they were going to feed all these hungry people. I think Jesus may have been testing them to see if they were beginning to think in a "faith mode." Their response proved they still practiced fragmented faith. While they had seen Christ cast out

demons and heal the sick, it had not yet occurred to them He could feed the masses. They still had much to learn about Christ's complete jurisdiction. He can meet our spiritual needs, our emotional needs, and our physical needs. He is both deeply spiritual and entirely practical. Christ was teaching them to see Him, His power, and His authority in every area of life.

2. *Christ wants us to be open to what He can do through us.* I love the way He tossed the responsibility for feeding the crowd right into His disciples' laps. "You give them something to eat" (Luke 9:13). Mind you, they had received power and authority to heal the sick and cast out demons, yet they looked helplessly at two fish and five loaves as the totality of their resources.

I believe Christ was saying, "Think bigger, boys!"—not only about what *He* could do, but also what *they* could do *in His name.* Where the disciples were concerned, I believe this event was all about stretching their thinking. His words are entirely absent of rebuke. Don't miss the fact that He used the disciples to distribute the meal. He wanted them to feel the weight of the baskets and see the hands of those reaching to be fed. Real power. In real forms. In real life.

3. *Christ can perform astounding wonders when we bring Him all we have.* Matthew 14:17 records the disciples saying, "We have here only five loaves of bread and two fish." Christ responded, "Bring them here to me." Beloved, I want you to hear something loud and clear: no matter what your "only" is, when you bring all of your "only" to Jesus, it's huge! When we bring Him everything we have, He multiplies it beyond our wildest imagination. On the other hand, we can surrender Him "some" of our lot, and it can dwindle to virtually nothing.

4. *Christ saved a basket-load of leftovers for each disciple.* The disciples picked up twelve baskets of leftovers. I just can't make myself think that was a coincidence. I'm no mathematician, but the numbers work for me. The people were fed. The disciples each wound up with a basketful of leftovers. That's what happens when you take part in God's provision.

# DAY 157
## Luke 9:23–27

〰️

He said to them all, "If anyone wants to come with Me,
he must deny himself, take up his cross daily, and follow Me" (v. 23).

〰️

Don't miss the fact that Peter was invited to "follow" Jesus even after the horrible *faux pas* of rebuking His Master. I am intrigued that Peter actually heard this invitation three times before Christ ascended to the right hand of the Father: once in Matthew 4:19, again in this passage, and finally in John 21:19. It's almost as if he were getting a crash course in Follow 101, Follow 202, and Follow 303. The first one was to follow Him as a *disciple*. The second one was to follow Him with a *cross*. The third one was to follow Him to *death*. Not coincidentally, tradition teaches that Peter indeed ended up following Christ to the death . . . on a cross.

In Christ's invitation I see two key concepts: *denying self* and *taking up the cross daily*. Those who accept this invitation are called to deny themselves. I don't believe Christ was talking about the things we typically consider self-denial. The issue here wasn't fasting from food, nor was it denying self a single extra. It wasn't about self-loathing either, because Christ commanded us to love our neighbor as ourselves. I believe the primary issue involved in this kind of self-denial is denying our right to be our own authority.

This passage brings us to the sobering realization that what we might think of as being under our own authority—having in mind the things of men—could easily be transferred to Satan's authority. I've learned the hard way that denying my right to be my own boss is what keeps me from getting slaughtered by Satan in warfare. Let's face it: this "be-your-own-boss" stuff is nothing but a myth.

But the second concept is just as vital: the key to true "follow-ship" with Christ is the recommitment to take up the cross daily. One reason I am drawn to Luke's version of this invitation over Matthew's is because he includes that all-important word—*daily*.

In my opinion, Dr. Luke wrote the prescription for the victorious life, and he wrote it for all of us who would desire to become Christ's disciple: live life one surrendered day at a time. Eyes to the East. Hands to the cross. Feet to the path.

# DAY 158
## Luke 9:28–36

Peter and those who were with him were in a deep sleep, and when
they became fully awake, they saw His glory (v. 32).

God has often chosen to unveil His glory on the top of a mountain. In
Exodus, He beckoned His servant Moses to climb the mount and see His glory.
Elijah also had a mountaintop view of the greatness of God. So when Christ
summoned Peter, James, and John to the top of a certain mountain, there was
precedent for it, yet they could never have imagined what awaited them. I think
we can rest assured, though, that it was worth the climb.

*They saw His glory!*

When was the last time you saw Christ transfigured before you? We grow
comfortable with the Christ we know. Then suddenly He shatters the box we've
put Him in, leaving us asking, "Who is this man?" Christ reserves the right to
bring us to places that force us to ask that question again. At those times, if we're
willing, Christ will show us a glimpse of His glory, and we will be changed as He
transfigures Himself before us.

Jesus regularly seeks to readjust our vision of Him. And I believe the more
we are willing to receive from Him, the more He is willing to reveal to us. I think
the reason Jesus took Peter, James, and John to the mountain was because they
were willing to receive greater revelation. How blessed we truly are when we have
eyes that are willing to see and ears that are willing to hear. In the words of Jesus:
"Whoever has will be given more, and he will have an abundance. Whoever does
not have, even what he has will be taken from him" (Matt. 13:12).

How blessed we are when we want to see Him. How blessed we are when
we begin to make our chief cry to Him, "Lord, I want to know You. I want to
know the reality of You. I want to know who You really are. Shatter my present
perspective and show me the reality of You."

We are a direct by-product of who we believe and who we see Christ to be.
I believe He blesses the prayer, "Father, daily show me the reality, the greater
reality of Your Son Jesus Christ. Transfigure Him before my very eyes, and then
give me the courage to adjust my life to what I see."

# DAY 159
### Luke 9:46–48

⸻⸺⸻

An argument started among them about who would be the greatest of them (v. 46).

⸻⸺⸻

The latter part of Luke 9 contains several seemingly disjointed snapshots of the disciples. First we see Jesus attempting to penetrate their thick skulls with the message of His soon-coming suffering and death. "Listen carefully to what I am about to tell you: The Son of Man is going to be betrayed into the hands of men" (v. 44). Hard to make it much clearer than that, wouldn't you say? But we read that the Twelve didn't understand, and that they were afraid to ask Jesus what He meant. Instead, an argument broke out among them about which of them would be greatest. Can you imagine?

Of course we can. We are not much unlike Christ's original disciples. They thought their argument had been a private matter, but Christ knew their thoughts, just as He does ours. We may never have argued with someone openly about our own greatness, but Christ knows our hearts, as well as the attitudes that inhabit them. He knows our society thrives on ambition. And He knows that if we're not extremely discerning, we will bring these same ambitions into the church. He knows our biggest hindrance to greatness as Christians is our desire to be great.

Don't miss the contrast of Christ and His disciples at this point in His earthly tenure. Christ was on the road to greatness, but His road would take Him through betrayal, rejection, suffering, and death. Philippians 2:6–8 tells us Jesus "did not consider equality with God something to be grasped, but made himself nothing, taking the very nature of a servant, being made in human likeness. . . . He humbled himself and became obedient to death—even death on a cross."

How different this is from our own chosen path to greatness. And yet the Scripture uses Christ's model to urge us not to grow weary and lose heart, since Jesus "endured the cross, scorning its shame" for the "joy set before him" (Heb. 12:2–3). He "tasted death" on our behalf. God the Father chose to "make the author of [our] salvation perfect through suffering" (Heb. 2:9–10).

Don't be confused by the idea that the "author of our salvation" became perfect through suffering. He was always perfect in terms of sinlessness. The word "perfect" in this verse is *teleioo*, meaning "to complete, make perfect by reaching the intended goal." Christ reached the goal (our salvation and His exaltation) through suffering. His road to greatness was a rocky one. A painful one. He knew it in advance, and yet He set His face resolutely toward the goal and accomplished it for all time. Simply put, we were worth it to Him.

And no matter how resistant we may be to this call, our road to true greatness will be the same as His—the highway of humility. At times it too will involve suffering, rejection, betrayal, and, yes, even death—to self. The question becomes, "Is He worth it to us?"

Without a doubt, one of the primary works God has sought to accomplish in me is to help me get over myself. The process has been excruciating and will no doubt be lifelong, but I have never been more thankful for any work in my life. I know no other way to say it: God finally got me to a place where I made myself sick. Oh, I still get plenty of glances at my self-centeredness, but never without a good wave of nausea. God and I now have a term for it in our prayer time. Don't expect something deeply intellectual or theological. We just call it my "self-stuff." Almost every day I ask God to help me address any active "self-stuff" and nail it to the cross. I literally name anything He brings to mind and look it straight in the face, even if it makes me cry. The following terms fall under the category of "self-stuff." Give them a good look:

- self-exaltation, self-protection,
- self-righteousness, self-will,
- self-loathing, self-worship,
- self-serving, self-promotion,
- self-indulgence, self-absorption,
- self-delusion, self-pity, self-sufficiency.

Did I leave anything out? Is that some stuff, or what? If you think of others, by all means, add them to my list. Self, self, self! May it be enough to make a "self" sick! Here's the big lie: Satan has convinced us that putting down our self-stuff is some huge sacrifice. Oh, beloved, what deception! Our self-stuff is what makes us most miserable! What an albatross our self-absorption is.

I cannot stress strongly enough that getting over the self-stuff is a daily challenge. As long as we inhabit this tent of flesh, it will rise up in us. We must choose to "deny [ourselves] and take up [our] cross daily" (Luke 9:23). The challenge demands total honesty before God. Remember, He never convicts us to condemn us. He wants to liberate us. Oh, God, so deal with self in each of us that when You read our thoughts, You will find stronger and stronger evidences of Your own.

# DAY 160
## Read Luke 9:49-50

---

John responded, "Master, we saw someone driving out demons in Your name,
and we tried to stop him because he does not follow us" (v. 49).

---

We saw John, his brother, and his buddy Peter as they viewed sights the others could hardly have imagined. They beheld revelations of His glory both in raising the dead and conferring with those long supposed dead. One might say you'd have to be dead to be unaffected by such sights, but obviously in both cases the dead were highly affected! No one remained unchanged. But how were the disciples changing? That's the question.

In yesterday's passage from Luke 9, we saw the disciples arguing about which of them would be greatest, now we see John—not once but twice—snapping the suspenders of his perceived superiority, bringing a sense of entitlement to the inner circle.

I'm sitting here shaking my head. Oh, not just at *them*. At myself. At the whole lot of us. Sometimes I wonder why God doesn't give up on us when we cop attitudes like these. I am so grateful that God is both nearsighted and farsighted. He sees us as we really are, and He sees how we'll really be. I'm pretty convinced that only the latter keeps the former alive.

Perhaps John's age didn't help. Life simply hadn't had time to beat him over the head with humility—not like Moses, who had all of forty years on the far side of the desert followed by a flock of aggravating people to humble the exclusivity right out of him.

In a wonderfully peculiar account in Numbers 11:24–30, Moses faced a similar situation. He took the elders of Israel into the tent of meeting. There the Spirit of God came upon them and they prophesied. Two of the elders, however, did not come with the group. Yet these two also began to prophesy in the camp. When Joshua heard what was happening, he asked almost the exact question as John in our incident above. He asked if he should stop the two. Moses responded, "Are you jealous on my account? If only all the LORD's people were prophets, and the LORD would place His Spirit on them" (Num. 11:29 HCSB).

I'll never forget standing in the resource room of my office with a friend who asked, "What does it feel like to look at all these books with your name on them?" My face screwed up into a knot, and I said, "All they represent to me is one holy beatin' after another!" I am sad to say that much of what I've learned has come with the rod of God, but things are beginning to change, aren't they, Father? I hope so.

## DAY 161
### Luke 9:51–56

———

When the disciples James and John saw this, they said,
"Lord, do You want us to call down fire from heaven to consume them?" (v. 54).

———

James and John remind me of two little boys holding their popguns, jumping up and down, pleading: "Let me shoot! Let me! Let me!" The difference is, this was no game. They wanted to call down the fire of God. They were eagerly asking for permission to be agents of massive, irreversible destruction.

Nothing is more permanent or terrifying than the destruction of the lost. We ought to be scared to death to wish such a thing on anyone. Eternity is a long time. So even when punishment comes to the terribly wicked, we are wise to remember with deep sobriety, humility, and thankfulness that only grace saves us from a like sentence.

We know this world is filled with wickedness. As Christ's present-day disciples, we will no doubt be offended when people reject the Savior the way the Samaritan village did on this day. God's desire, however, is for us to pray for His mercy, for His Holy Spirit's conviction, and for their repentance rather than their judgment. Christ said even of those who hammered the nails into His flesh, "Father, forgive them, for they do not know what they are doing" (Luke 23:34).

God is indeed the righteous Judge. When Christ returns, those who rejected Him will literally cry to the mountains, "'Fall on us!' and to the hills, 'Cover us!'" (Luke 23:30). Judgment is coming, but may the thought of it cause us to weep, plead, and pray. Never boast about being saved while others are not. Only one thing stands between us and the lost: a blood-stained cross.

Dear one, I know this may be coming across to you as quite harsh. But please know that this message was written with such love. I have been the worst of transgressors in so many ways. No matter how common these attitudes are, they are terribly offensive to Christ. May we humble ourselves before Him, repent, and daily choose to lay down the albatross of our own egos.

Oh, God, give us a longing—not for the sin of this world to be judged—but for the sinners of this world to be forgiven.

# DAY 162
## Luke 10:1–16

───❄───

Whoever listens to you listens to Me. Whoever rejects you rejects Me.
And whoever rejects Me rejects the One who sent Me (v. 16).

───❄───

This concept Jesus taught in verse 16 is something else I love so much about Him. In many ways, He says to those who belong to Him and who seek to do His will: "Don't take rejection personally. Let me take it for you."

We see this principle at work in Acts 9. Saul set out to persecute Christians, but Jesus came along and knocked him off his donkey. "Falling to the ground, [Saul] heard a voice saying to him, 'Saul, Saul, why do you persecute me?'" (Acts 9:4). Beloved, can you accept that Christ takes very personally the unfair things that happen to you? Consider a couple of reasons why we are wise to let Christ assume our rejections:

1. *Only Christ can take rejection without being personally incapacitated or hindered by it.* Who can begin to estimate the mileage Satan gets from rejection? We have an overwhelming tendency to take it personally. From a bit of rejection Satan can get anything from a mile of discouragement to a thousand miles of despair. But Christ says to us, "Let Me take it personally for you. It can *hurt* Me, but it can't hinder Me." David had it right when he wrote, "Contend, O LORD, with those who contend with me; fight against those who fight against me. Take up shield and buckler; arise and come to my aid" (Ps. 35:1–2).

2. *Only Christ can properly respond to rejection.* We are often powerless to do anything about it. In fact, our attempts at responding to it often make the situation worse. We don't fully understand what lies at the heart of rejection. We cannot judge another person's intention or motive. But Romans 2:2 assures us that "God's judgment against those who do such things is based on truth."

I love to hear Keith say, "Elizabeth, let me worry about that." In essence, Christ says the same thing to us. If we suffer rejection, let Him worry about it. Let Him take it personally so we don't have to. Besides, even Jesus has Someone to shield Him from the blow of rejection. Take one last look at Luke 10:16. "He who listens to you listens to me; he who rejects you rejects me, *but he who rejects me rejects him who sent me.*" Trust His big shoulders, beloved, to be strong enough to take whatever others dish out.

# DAY 163
## Luke 10:17–24

---

In that same hour He rejoiced in the Holy Spirit and said,
"I praise You, Father, Lord of heaven and earth" (v. 21).

---

Jesus sent out seventy-two disciples to teach and heal, instructing them to "ask the Lord of the harvest . . . to send out workers" into His harvest field (Luke 10:2). He sent these disciples out "two by two." The original language phrase for this is *ana duo.*

I love the fact that Christ sanctions companionship in the work of the gospel! The point is not the magic number of "two" (as opposed to three or four). The point is simply togetherness. Exceptions to this exist, of course, when we are called to stand alone, but the standard rule of our lives in Christ is far more often the fellowship, protection, accountability, and double dividends of joint service.

I can hardly describe the joy my coworkers in the gospel bring me. My best friend and I met each other by serving together in Mothers' Day Out over twenty years ago. God called us to work *ana duo,* and we've been a duo ever since! Few things can add to our lives like the fellowship of serving together. I didn't want you to miss that point in this passage.

But today, I want to look more carefully at what happened when the seventy-two returned, rejoicing with something that resembled amazement. In verse 17 they essentially said, "Wow! It happened just like You said it would, Jesus! Even the demons were subject to us in Your name! What a rush!"

Sandwiched between expressions of jubilation, Christ took a quick moment to remind them that they had a greater motivation for rejoicing than this: *their names were written in heaven.* So although we see Him celebrate their victories, we also see Him teaching them to base their joy on something far more reliable than accomplishments and abilities. He wanted them—and he wants us—to understand that the greatest cause we have for joy is not what we do but who we are. We are children of the eternal *El Elyon.* Our names are recorded in heaven. We are very wise to find our joy in who we are because of Him, rather than what we can do because of Him.

But now let's enjoy these two awesome moments of celebration. Verse 21 tells us Jesus was "full of joy through the Holy Spirit." Here's a place where the original language is so much fun. In verse 17, the word for the joy of the disciples is *chara,* meaning essentially what you'd assume: "rejoicing" and "gladness." The word switches in verse 21, however, to a far more intense original word. The word for Jesus' joy is *agalliao,* meaning "to exult, leap for joy, to show one's joy by leaping and skipping, denoting excessive or ecstatic joy and delight." In the

Septuagint of the Psalms, this idea often spoke of "rejoicing with song and dance."

Someone may ask, "Do you expect me to believe Christ jumped up and down with ecstatic joy?" I don't have one bit of trouble believing it!

"Could the word simply mean He rejoiced in His heart?" Possibly, but the essence of the word *agalliao* is what happens when the word *chara* gets physical! You may apply it either way, but I prefer to jump up and down with Jesus. With all my heart, I believe Christ Jesus was and is demonstrative.

But what would cause Jesus to leap with ecstatic joy in this scene (whether physically or internally)? At least two catalysts for colossal joy appear in these verses:

1. *Satan's defeat.* "I saw Satan fall like lightning from heaven" (v. 18). According to Revelation 12:10–12, Satan was cast out of heaven for pride, rebellion, and his desire to usurp the Most High (see also Ezek. 28:16–17; Isa. 14:12–13). At the risk of oversimplification, Satan has attempted to get back at God ever since by targeting those He loves.

But we who are in Christ possess the power through God's Word and His Spirit to avoid being defeated by the evil one. Problem is, we don't always exercise that power. The disciples in Luke 10 did. They exercised the authority He had given them, and Christ was ecstatic! At the end of the contest, the scoreboard read: Believers 72, Satan 0. That was a score Jesus could have spilled His popcorn over! When was the last time you got excited over the defeat of the devil? Notice, too, the other side of the equation:

2. *The servants' victory.* "I praise you, Father, Lord of heaven and earth, because you have hidden these things from the wise and learned and have revealed them to little children" (v. 21). You see, the wise and learned of this world are often too sophisticated to throw caution to the wind and believe they're capable of doing something they've never thought possible. If we stay in our neat little perimeters of safe sophistication where we walk by sight and not by faith, we'll never have room to leap and skip with Jesus in ecstatic joy.

Oh, beloved, give Him a chance to leap and dance over you! Dare to do what He's calling you to do! And don't always be so reasonable. I have a feeling there's one thing Christ likes better than leaping and skipping and dancing over you. How about *with* you? When you hear that victory music playing, get up out of that chair and shake a leg.

# DAY 164
## Luke 10:25–37

Just then an expert in the law stood up to test Him, saying,
"Teacher, what must I do to inherit eternal life?" (v. 25).

Scripture describes Jesus' questioner as an expert in the law. His job was to interpret the law of Moses the way modern lawyers interpret the constitution. He considered himself such an expert that he intended to make Jesus look foolish. The problem is, you can't find a subject on which Christ isn't the ultimate expert. The expert in the law didn't know that Christ knew the drill far better than he did.

So Jesus responded to him with a question that means little to us but was very familiar to the lawyer. He asked, "How do you read it?" This question was used constantly among scribes and lawyers. One would ask the other his interpretation on a certain matter. Before he would give his answer, he would say, "How do you read it?" This way, the one who asked the question ended up having to "go first."

(Of course, you and I know what the scribe didn't know. Christ not only wrote the law, He came to fulfill it. The resident expert in the law was way over his head when he threw a pop quiz at the author of the Book.)

Being forced to "go first," the legal mind delivered the correct answer according to Old Testament law: "'Love the Lord your God with all your heart and with all your soul and with all your strength and with all your mind'; and 'Love your neighbor as yourself'" (Luke 10:27). The conversation could have stopped when Jesus said, "Do this and you will live" (v. 28). Instead, the lawyer had to ask one more question: "And who is my neighbor?" (v. 29).

Do you hear a change in tone? The man wanted to justify himself—to show himself righteous—but why? Who said he wasn't? Christ didn't say a single condemning word to him. Jesus simply told him his answer was correct and to go live his answer.

But the man couldn't let the matter go. In Christ's presence, the lawyer felt condemned by his own words. He knew God intended for His people to help those in need. So the lawyer attempted to justify himself by splitting hairs with his definition of a neighbor. His immediate defense mechanism was to try to start an argument. Not an unfamiliar tactic, is it? We've all been experts at that one!

Jesus answered the man's question with one of the most repeated stories in the New Testament, telling of a priest and a Levite on their way home to Jericho from Jerusalem who both ignored a man that had been beaten and robbed along the road. But the irony in their unwillingness to help would have been more obvious to the lawyer than to us. He would have quickly understood that they were on their way home from the most important life work they would ever do—performing their brief tenure of service in the temple. We would expect that at no time would they have been more humbled, grateful, or willing to meet someone's needs. But that's not what happened. In fact, both the priest and the Levite passed by on the other side.

The words of the law in Exodus 23 make the actions of the priest and Levite even more incriminating. Moses wrote, "If you come across your enemy's ox or donkey wandering off, be sure to take it back to him. If you see the donkey of someone who hates you fallen down under its load, do not leave it there; be sure you help him with it" (vv. 4–5).

Don't you praise God, though, for the third passerby in the scene? Our common name for this parable would have been an oxymoron to many Jews of that era. Most would have believed there was no such thing as a "good" Samaritan. They were considered little more than mongrels. Half-breed dogs. That's precisely why Christ interjected the Samaritan into the play.

Scripture tells us the Samaritan saw the man and took pity on him. You would think that at least the priest and the Levite would have done the right thing because of their positions, even if they *felt* the wrong thing. In sharp contrast, the Samaritan came upon the scene with no obligation whatsoever, and everything within him was deeply moved with compassion. He didn't just do what was right. He felt it.

Sometimes good at its best is when the law of the heart eclipses the law of the land. Stepping across a boundary to help is sometimes our first introduction to the commonality of humanity on the other side. Offering help in a time of need can be the first step to overcoming God-dishonoring prejudice.

Don't forget the reason Jesus told the story. Whom did He say was our neighbor? I am reminded of an Old Testament verse that describes a neighbor at Passover. Because all of the lamb was required to be consumed at the Passover observance, Exodus 12 explains that a family was to share with their nearest neighbor if their household was too small for a whole lamb.

From Jesus' parable we can see that our neighbor is the person with a need—the broken one. In terms of Exodus 12, our neighbor is one with whom we can share the Lamb. As people who have been passed over by the angel of death, we are called to share the Lamb.

# DAY 165
## Luke 10:38–42

—◦◦◦◦—

The Lord answered her, "Martha, Martha, you are worried and
upset about many things, but one thing is necessary. Mary has made
the right choice, and it will not be taken away from her" (vv. 41–42).

—◦◦◦◦—

This passage is not a contrast between good and bad. It's a contrast between
good and better. Martha was a good woman. Jesus loved her very much, apron and
all, as confirmed in John 11:5—"Jesus loved Martha and her sister and Lazarus."
Her joy and satisfaction, however, were sacrificed on the altar of self-appointed
service. Recognizing Martha's positives and negatives, let's explore some applications together.

1. *Martha opened her home, but Mary opened her heart (vv. 38–39).* Don't miss
the fact that Martha opened her home to Jesus. Not Lazarus, the head of the
house. Nor Mary, the depth of the house. It was the "hands" of the house that
invited Jesus in. Otherwise, Mary wouldn't have had a set of feet at which to sit,
nor would Lazarus have had a friend with which to recline. Martha's hospitality
brought Him there. If only Martha had understood that Christ wanted her heart
more than He wanted her home.

2. *Distraction is the noble person's biggest hindrance to listening (vv. 39–40).*
Martha wasn't stopping her ears and refusing to listen. She was simply "distracted." In this way, we've all been Marthas! How many times have we reached
the car after a church service only to realize that we missed half the message due
to a distraction?

Now imagine that the church service was meeting in your den while you
were preparing lunch! Talk about distracting? The Greek word for "distracted"
in verse 40 is *perispao*, meaning "to draw different ways at the same time, hence
to distract with cares and responsibilities." Can we relate? You see, our culture
may be entirely different, but women have had the same challenges since the
beginning of time.

3. *Sometimes ministry can be the biggest distraction to the pursuit of true intimacy
with God (v. 40).* I've heard the saying many times, "If Satan can't make us bad,
he'll make us busy." Actually, he can't make us anything, but he gets a lot of
cooperation. I am reminded of our study on the good Samaritan. How wise of
our God to place these two accounts back-to-back in Scripture. First we saw an
incriminating look at servants of God who ministered in the temple but refused
to help a dying man. Now we catch a look at a servant who was so busy helping,
she couldn't hear from the heart of God.

4. *Martha forgot to keep the "pre" in preparation (v. 40).* Understand that the
preparations she made were not frivolous. They were important! By doing them,

Martha served Christ appropriately and enhanced the atmosphere in which He taught. Very likely she served a meal and made sure all the arrangements were made for His comfort and the exercise of His own ministry. These preparations were important. They just weren't limited to the "pre." The issue is that she continued all her duties when the time came to sit at Christ's feet and listen.

I speak at many conferences during which the event's leadership either never makes it into the sanctuary or, when they do, they never lose that harried and distracted look. Recently, however, I spoke at a conference where the leadership was truly the most participatory, involved group during the Bible study. When I inquired later, they said, "Oh, we worked really hard in advance to get everything finished so we could relax when the time came." They made all the preparations, but when the time came, the men of the church and several hired caterers served while they attended. What wisdom we find in keeping the "pre" in preparation!

5. *Those distracted by service are often those who miss how much Jesus cares (v. 40).* I have a feeling if someone had asked Mary at the end of the day if Christ cared about her, she would have answered affirmatively without hesitation. But Martha came to Christ and asked, "Don't You care?"

Beloved, Christ's love for us never changes. However, our sense of His loving care can change dramatically from time to time. And I believe the determining factor in whether we sense His love or not is our willingness to abide in Him, to seek to practice a relationship in which we develop a keener awareness of His presence.

Sometimes we are so shocked when a seasoned servant of God confesses that he or she is struggling with belief and awareness of God's loving care. We might think, "You of all people! You are such a wonderful servant of God. How can you doubt for a moment how much He cares for you?" Could it be that somehow service has distracted them from abundant, life-giving intimacy? Don't neglect to give Him ample opportunities to lavish you with the love He always feels for you.

6. *Many things are important, but only one thing is necessary (v. 42).* In our fight for right priorities, many things vie for the top of the heap, but only one is necessary. Ultimately, our relationship with Christ is the one thing we cannot do without. Christ's message is not that we should neglect family and other responsibilities to pray and to study the Bible. His message is that many things are important, but one thing is essential: Him. Incidentally, Mary turned out to be one of the greatest servants of all, lavishing Christ with her most expensive offerings (see John 12). She learned. So can we.

# DAY 166
## Luke 11:14–23

---

When a strong man, fully armed, guards his estate, his possessions are secure. But when one stronger than he attacks and overpowers him, he takes from him all his weapons he trusted in, and divides up his plunder (vv. 21–22).

---

Just as God is possessive over His holy house, you can be sure Satan is possessive over his unholy house. Therefore, we can't help but deal with the reality of Luke 11:21, assuming that he is the "strong man" in Jesus' parable. But thank God we have verse 22 to follow it up, where we learn some valuable things about our Jesus, our One and Only:

1. *Satan may be strong, but Christ is "stronger."* We are wise neither to overestimate nor underestimate Satan's power. But even though we are no match for him, he is no match for God. We may be at war with a very powerful enemy, but we who are in Christ are at peace with a far more powerful God. As Paul taught, we can now take our stand against the enemy because we are "strong in the Lord and in his mighty power" (Eph. 6:10).

2. *Christ will attack and overcome Satan.* Satan is a defeated foe. The defeating blows actually came through a hammer on the nails of the cross. Christ finished the work when He willingly gave His life for our sins. So God is now biding His time until His kingdom calendar has been accomplished and all who will receive His salvation are redeemed. Then one day, God's finger is going to point right at the strong man, and Satan is going to wish he'd never existed.

3. *Our someone stronger is going to take away Satan's armor and divide up the spoils.* Do you know what this means to us? Jesus Christ is going to take back what Satan has stolen from us! And not all the spoils have to wait until we're in heaven!

I can readily cite a personal example. Even though Satan stole many things from me through my childhood victimization, I am finally ready to say that God has given me back more than my enemy took. The enemy has fought against me with his weapons of shame, secrecy, and deception, but the plunder my Lord has won back for me has finally tipped the scale. Through the many response letters I've received from my book *Breaking Free: Making Liberty in Christ a Reality in Life,* I believe I can now say that the grace gift of seeing others helped through the power of the Holy Spirit has begun to outweigh the many years of pain that resulted from the abuse. The strong man may have put up a good fight, but his fight was no match for my stronger Man's muscle.

# DAY 167
## Luke 11:24–28

—∞∞∞—

When an unclean spirit comes out of a man, it roams through
waterless places looking for rest, and not finding rest, it then says:
"I'll go back to my house where I came from" (v. 24).

—∞∞∞—

Satan is a lot of things, but creative is not often one of them. He ordinarily sticks to what has worked in the past. I've experienced this personally when he has attempted to return to an area in my life where he held a previous stronghold—even though he's already been forced to leave.

Beloved, listen carefully. We were created by God to be inhabited by His Spirit. We were not created to be empty. The vacuum in every human life does not yearn to be fixed. It yearns to be filled. God can deliver us from a terribly oppressive stronghold, but if we don't fill the void with Him, we are terribly susceptible to a relapse.

My Sunday school class has what we call VIPs—Victors in Process. Every quarter, members who need extra prayer and accountability come before our class for special notice. Throughout the quarter, they can hardly get through the door without lots of hugs and direct questions about how they're doing. One of our recent VIPs was a beautiful young woman recovering from a fierce cocaine addiction. How wise she was to realize that she couldn't just "get clean." If she was going to be safe, she had to fill the cavernous void left behind by cocaine with the satisfying, liberating filling of the Holy Spirit.

I'm telling you, a second round of the same demonic stronghold can be more powerful than the first. What a frightening prospect for someone who isn't sealed by the Holy Spirit (see Eph. 1:13; 4:30). Sure, most of us are at higher risk of *oppression* than *possession*, but the principle still applies: once we've been delivered from a stronghold, if we make ourselves vulnerable to it again, our second encounter may be far worse.

This is because Satan hates to lose. If he was defeated once, given the opportunity, he'll try harder the next time. Furthermore, a second onslaught can cause such discouragement and feelings of hopelessness within the victim, she feels weaker than ever. Satan also knows that the empty space—if left uninhabited by Christ—leaves the victim with a voracious appetite. So let's repeat this concept until it's engraved in our cranium: victory is not determined as much by what we've been delivered *from* as by what we've been delivered *to*. It's not enough to be swept clean and put in order. We must be filled full of God.

# DAY 168
## Luke 12:1–34

⚬⚬⚬

The Gentile world eagerly seeks all these things, and your Father knows that you need them. But seek His kingdom, and these things will be provided for you" (vv. 30–31).

⚬⚬⚬

If we truly believe what God says about our value to Him, our lives will be dramatically altered. Based on this long segment of Scripture from Luke 12, which includes a wide mix of teachings and parables and different kinds of audiences, I want to suggest five ways such a belief makes a difference.

1. *Believing our great value to God frees us from much hypocrisy.* Christ opened His bold declarations in Luke 12 with a warning against hypocrisy. The primary meaning of the word is "pretending." Please give special attention to His specific audience. Although He was surrounded by crowds of unbelievers and religious leaders, Jesus began to speak "first to his disciples" (Luke 12:1). True disciples who follow Christ and lead others to do likewise face great temptation to be hypocritical. Christ warned, "Be on your guard" (v. 1). In other words, if we're going to live free of hypocrisy, we must proactively guard against it. The bottom line of hypocrisy is the need for people to think more highly of us than we really are. Let's face it. It's easier to act than to clean up our act.

Hypocrisy has so much to prove. Ironically, it seeks to prove that which is not even true. But when we accept our real value to God, we don't have anything left to prove. We can be real because we are of great value to the only True Judge.

2. *Believing our great value to God frees us from unnecessary fear.* Luke 12:4 comes like a shock wave to our systems: "I tell you, my friends, do not be afraid of those who kill the body and after that can do no more." Why do we have such difficulty grasping Jesus' point of view? Because we are far more convinced of the "here and now" than the "after that." Eternity is a far greater reality than this short breath of time. If we are in His fold and are called His friends, Christ's word to us is, "Don't be afraid; you are worth more."

Keith and I keep a bird feeder on the back porch. I watch the sparrows scatter the seed and flutter their wings. They are not beautiful like other birds that grace our yard. They are plain and ordinary. But I love knowing that God never forgets a single one of them. When fear seeks to assail me, I go to the window and am reminded again—if He cares for them, He most assuredly cherishes me. After this short breath is a long "after that."

3. *Believing our great value to God frees us to acknowledge Him shamelessly.* Verse 8 assures us that Christ Jesus can hardly wait to acknowledge us before the very "angels of God"—even after all our frailties and failures! (Check out Jude 24.) If He is unashamed of us in all our imperfections, how can we be ashamed of Him, our Redeemer and our Deliverer?

Yet at one time or another, all of us have faced the temptation to shrink away from openly acknowledging Christ. I've learned one of the best ways to get over these attacks of shame. Do it over and over until it loses its intimidation! Just be honest with Him and *tell* Him you're afraid. Tell Him all the reasons why. Then ask for the power of the Holy Spirit to come upon you and make you a powerful witness (see Acts 1:8). He will! Then one day, He'll acknowledge you before the angels!

4. *Believing our great value to God frees us from the need for riches.* In verse 15, Christ warns us to also "be on [our] guard" against all kinds of greed. Then He reminds us of a powerful truth: "a man's life does not consist in the abundance of his possessions." Aren't you thankful for that? I'm reminded of a friend's statement: "We act out what we believe, not what we know." If we believe our value to God and believe our life does not consist in the abundance of our possessions, why then do we have such an abundance of possessions? Perhaps we know Luke 12:15 with our heads, but we really don't believe it with our hearts.

James 1:17 tells us our Father is the giver of all good gifts. Throughout all of eternity, we will be lavished in the limitless wealth of the CEO of the universe. Until then, we show ourselves to be sons and daughters of the one true God when we give, give, and give. Let's keep shoving that abundance out the door to help others in need, and God will lay up treasures for us in His own divine storage lot.

5. *Believing our great value to God frees us from much worry.* "Life is more than food" (v. 23). I need a needlepoint of that for my kitchen! How about you? The issue of food, however, is not the point. The point is *worry*. I'm not sure many things compare to the challenge of ceasing to worry. Maybe one reason why is because we have so many prime opportunities to practice it! But you know what? We're never going to overcome worry by eliminating reasons to worry. Rest assured, life isn't going to suddenly fix itself. God wills that we overcome worry even when overwhelmed by reasons to worry.

Christ summed up the futility of worry in verses 25 and 26. We can't add a minute to our life by worrying. Simply put, worry is useless—even when we're worrying about the lives of our children. I am prone to worry somewhat about myself but endlessly over them. Yet all our worry, even when done in the name of love, can accomplish absolutely nothing. When will we learn to turn our worry effort into prayer?

# DAY 169
## Luke 12:35–40

❦

You must be like people waiting for their master to return from the wedding banquet
so that when he comes and knocks, they can open the door for him at once (v. 36).

❦

Jesus told the disciples a set of interlaced parables in Luke 12 about being
ready for His return. We'll look at the first one today. The point of each dealt
with watchfulness and doing what Christ assigns us to do. Christ wants His
people to be ready and waiting. No matter whether you're a pretribulationalist, a
post-tribulationalist, an amillennialist, a dispensationalist, or have no clue what
any of these terms even mean, Christ is coming back. Every eye will see Him.

Some things about God's ways make me grin . . . like the way He knows
our tendency to play amateur prophet. He puts all of us in our date-setting places
by basically saying, "The only thing I'll tell you about My next visit is that you
won't be expecting Me." The urgency is to be ready at all times. "Keep your lamps
burning" (Luke 12:35).

Our version of keeping our lamps burning is leaving a light on at night
for someone out late. One of the shocks of the empty nest is no longer having
someone to "wait up for." Those of us who have older children have experienced
the late-night difficulty of falling into a deep sleep before they get home. We
can doze perhaps, but we don't fully sleep until they're safe inside. Even though
waiting up is exhausting, it's a reminder of close family relationships and responsibility. At this particular season in my life, my heart is encouraged to know that
we still have Someone for whom to "leave the light on."

Several years ago a precious friend of mine lost her only son, a young adult.
Five years later she lost her husband. I have ached for her aloneness. But I am so
grateful that those of us in Christ always have Someone for whom we can wait
expectantly at all times. Christ calls on us to be watching for Him when He
returns—not inactively, mind you, but as servants (v. 37). Luke 12:38 tells us, "It
will be good for those servants whose master finds them ready, even if he comes
in the second or third watch of the night."

Christ's desire is that we live in such close involvement with Him that all
we lack is seeing Him face-to-face. Oh, that God would create in each of us such
an acute awareness and belief of His presence that we won't be caught off guard!
That our faith will simply be made sight! That we'll be gloriously shocked but
unashamed!

# DAY 170
## Luke 12:41–48

———

*That slave who knew his master's will and didn't prepare himself
or do it will be severely beaten (v. 47).*

———

For those with a knowledge of God, the cost of wickedness during our wait for Jesus' return is astronomical. I'm not sure we ever hear stronger words out of His mouth than these: "He will cut him to pieces and assign him a place with the unbelievers" (v. 46).

I believe Christ was most likely addressing His remarks to the people He described in Luke 11:52: "Woe to you experts in the law, because you have taken away the key to knowledge. You yourselves have not entered, and you have hindered those who were entering." I'd like to suggest that the picture of the head servant beating the menservants and maidservants while the master was away (Luke 12:45) could easily represent spiritual abuse at the hands of religious leaders. God will hold those of us who are leaders responsible for this.

I can think of many examples, but one instantly raises its ugly head in my mind—the preacher who beats and bangs hellfire and damnation on his pulpit, piously condemning his flock for all manner of evil, while abusing his wife and children at home. I wish I could tell you that I've only heard such a testimony once or twice. Let me stress that I still believe the far greater population of Christians resist that kind of hypocrisy, but spiritual abuse of this nature exists far more than we want to believe.

Another form of spiritual abuse is using Scripture or the name of God to manipulate others. I have very little doubt we will be called to account for the times we have used God's name to get what we want. Christ despises all forms of human oppression. A huge penalty awaits those who possess a knowledge of God yet persist in meanness and self-indulgence. Forgive me if my temperature on this matter is showing. If not for the authentic examples of godliness, I would despair over all the abuse I've seen in the religious community.

But I also know the future punishment of the unfaithful will be fair: "From everyone who has been given much, much will be demanded" (v. 48). That's fair. But that's serious. I have been given so much. I must accept the fact that much is also required. Here is our joy and security in the midst of much required: Christ is never the author of spiritual abuse. Every single thing required of us will be amply rewarded far beyond our imagination.

# DAY 171
## Luke 13:31–33

He said to them, "Go tell that fox, 'Look! I'm driving out demons and performing healings today and tomorrow, and on the third day I will complete My work'" (v. 32).

I love Christ's last five words in verse 32 (HCSB): "I will complete My work."

• Not "I will complete My work if all the conditions are right."
• Not "I will complete My work if you cooperate with me."
• Not "I will complete My work if I'm still alive."

"I will complete My work." It's that simple. The New International Version renders His statement, "I will reach My goal." No ifs, ands, or buts.

"I will." Period.

Beloved, find security in the fact that nothing is haphazard about the activity of God. He has a goal, and He has a definitive plan that is to be executed precisely according to His will.

You no doubt noticed Christ's symbolic phraseology in this verse, as well. In a sense, Christ spoke in the style of a parable. When He spoke of the miracle activity He would be doing "today and tomorrow," followed by "the third day," He spoke not in the immediate sense but in a future tense. Because of our hindsight advantage, we hear the unmistakable hint of the three days beginning with the cross and ending with His resurrection. In essence, Christ said, "I have a goal. I have work to do *today* toward that goal. I have work to do *tomorrow* toward that goal. But very soon that goal will be accomplished."

Perhaps Christ's use of the words "today," "tomorrow," and "the third day" suggest three segments of time in *our lives* as well. Today is our now. The third day could represent the ultimate fulfillment of God's goals for our lives. And tomorrow could represent every moment between now and then. He will complete His work in us, too.

Christ's return message to Herod emphasized that nothing could turn Him from His goal. Neither Herod nor any other power posed a threat to the plan. They would be used only as puppets to fulfill it. When we live our lives according to God's will, no Herod in the world can thwart our efforts at reaching God's goal. Not a Herod of sickness nor a Herod of crisis. Not even a Herod that seems to hand us over to death.

# DAY 172
## Luke 13:34–35

—∞∞∞—

Jerusalem, Jerusalem! The city who kills the prophets and stones those
who are sent to her. How often I wanted to gather your children together,
as a hen gathers her chicks under her wings, but you were not willing (v. 34).

—∞∞∞—

I want us to look today at a spiritual principle I call *immunity*—meaning,
shelter from all evil imposition on God's plan. One dramatic example of this
principle is found in the account of the two witnesses in Revelation 11. The elements of immunity in their experience are easy to identify:

1. The witnesses get their power from God (v. 3).
2. When they are opposed, God dramatically defends them (v. 5).
3. When they have finished their testimony, the beast kills them (v. 7).

*But* . . . notice that the two witnesses cannot be killed until they have finished their testimony. And even at that, their deaths are by no means a tragic end
to the story. God raises them from the dead and makes a mockery of their enemy
(see Rev. 11:11–12).

Although the prophecy of the two witnesses is far more dramatic than the
story of our lives, they illustrate a principle God applies to us as well. When we
live under the umbrella of God's authority and seek to obey His commands, the
enemy may oppose us and even oppress us, but he cannot thwart the fulfillment
of God's plan for us. Any permission he receives to oppose us will be issued only
for the greater victory of God. Death cannot come to the obedient children of
God until they have finished their testimony. When we surrender our wills to
the will of the Father, we find a place of blessed immunity. Strengthened by His
power and shielded by His protection, we are assured of reaching our goal.

This principle is beautifully illustrated in Luke 13:34, where we see the
heart of God on display as His Son cries out for the citizens of Jerusalem to come
under His sheltering wings of protection. The Old Testament paints a similar
portrait in Psalm 91. These words fall around us like a down comforter from
heaven. The psalmist wrote: "He who dwells in the shelter of the Most High will
rest in the shadow of the Almighty" (Ps. 91:1). The implication of this verse is
that a place of safety—a certain level of immunity from evil onslaughts—exists
for those who choose to dwell there. The concept of *dwelling* in Psalm 91:1 is virtually synonymous with the concept of *obeying* or *remaining* in John 15:10, where
Jesus tells us we abide or remain in Him and His love through our obedience.

Obedience to our Father's commands is the key to immunity from the
enemy. Obedience is what positions us in the shadow of the Almighty. When
we are living in obedience, any evil that comes against us will have to go through
God first. Christ lived for one purpose: to do the will of the One who sent Him

(see John 6:38). And because He was entirely surrendered to the will of His Father, Herod's threat in Luke 13:31 had no power over Him. When the time came, the rulers and the chief priests could be used only as puppets by God in His pursuit of greater glory.

I am convinced the same is true for us. We gain the place of immunity through obedience to His will. This explains why Christ longed to gather the children of Israel into His arms the way a hen gathers her chicks under her wings, but He did not. Why? Because they weren't willing. They chose their own will over Christ's, forfeiting the shelter of His wings. The result was desolation and defeat (see Luke 13:35; 19:43).

The same unwillingness can have similar results in our lives today. As believers in Christ, two different forms of immunity apply to us. All who personally receive the grace gift of God have the first kind of immunity: protection from eternal judgment. We stand in the shadow of the cross. The judgment that should have come to us came to Christ instead.

But the second kind of immunity does *not* come automatically upon our salvation. It results only when we surrender our will to the Father's will. When we bow to His authority, we become immune to defeat and all other threats to the plan of God for our personal lives. I don't mean we're immune from trouble, tribulation, or even a certain amount of oppression, but they won't be able to defeat us. Through obedience, we will possess and practice the God-given power to overcome them, and God's plan will be uninterrupted.

I know these principles are true because I've experienced them. I have complete assurance of my salvation. I am convinced that the cross has immunized me against all judgment for sin. However, I have without a doubt been temporarily defeated by the enemy and done things that were not part of God's plan for my life. By surrendering to my own will in certain seasons, I have stepped outside the shelter of the Most High. And although the enemy could not overtake me, he certainly had a field day with me.

Today, I am a living, breathing, grace-filled Plan B. But I'm a Plan B who has learned some painful lessons that have changed my practices. I presently jump out of bed with one primary plan of attack for the day: ducking under the sheltering wing of the Most High so the enemy will have to get through Him to get to me.

He yearns to lavish us with His possessive, protective love—to cover us from so many unnecessary harms. There is a secret place. Go, beloved, and hide.

# DAY 173
Luke 15:11–32

~∞~

While the son was still a long way off, his father saw him
and was filled with compassion (v. 20).

~∞~

At times I've descended from the place of appropriate repentance where I was sorry for my sins, to the place of inappropriate self-loathing where I was sorry Christ was "forced" (as if He could be) to save me. I'd find myself wishing I had been a nicer sinner. More pleasant to save.

Emotion washes over me today as I remember again: Christ came for sinners like me. He *wanted* to save me. He didn't come for the pious and perfect. Our Savior came to seek and to save the lost. The hopeless. The foolish. The weak. The depraved. In His own words: "It is not the healthy who need a doctor, but the sick. I have not come to call the righteous, but sinners to repentance" (Luke 5:31–32).

I have no idea how many times I've read and even taught the story of the prodigal son, yet it still brings me to tears. I am such a product of this kind of father love. Perhaps you are too. I've watched God take a young woman I love very much and restore her to the right road after a prodigal detour. She has cried out to me, "When will all these painful repercussions end?"

I have answered her, "Not until the very idea of straying causes you such painful flashbacks that you're hardly ever tempted to depart His will again." God wants to whisper to our hearts, "Are you sure you want to go back there again?" and hear us say, "No way do I want that kind of pain!"

Luke 15:17 tells us that the son considered the abundance of his father's hired hands and realized the insanity of starving to death. He waited to go home until his desperation exceeded his pride. That the prodigal planned what he would say hints at the difficulty of his return. I wonder if the son was pacing. And pacing. And pacing. He could see his home in the distance, but perhaps he could not bring himself to walk that last mile. He looked at his father's vast estate and glanced down at his own poor estate. His clothes were worn and filthy. Dirt under every nail. His hair long and matted or shorn to the skin to defend against lice. All at once, he became aware of his own foul smell. He was destitute. Degraded.

But the prodigal's father was looking for his son in the distance. I imagine that every day since his son's departure, his father had studied the horizon in search of his son's silhouette. Just as the starving son had longed for food, his father had yearned for him. His was a yearning so deep that no amount of work could assuage it. Family members could not replace it. No distraction could soothe it. Oh, friend, can you glimpse the heart of God? Do you realize that when you run from Him, He yearns for you every minute and cannot be distracted from His thoughts of you?

When God sees our poor estate and the ravaging effects of our foolish decisions, He doesn't just sit back and say, "She got what she deserved." He is filled with compassion and longs to bring us back home. Yes, we face consequences, but those consequences are a loving summons back to the Father.

In one of the most moving moments in all of Scripture, Luke 15:20 records that the father "ran" to his son. Scripture often employs anthropomorphisms—descriptions of God as if He had a human body. We sometimes read that God walked (in the midst of His people) or that He rode (on the clouds like chariots), but this is the only time in the entire Word of God when He is described as running.

What makes God run? A prodigal child turning his face toward home! How can we resist Him? How can we not reciprocate such lavish love?

When was the last time you saw an older man, the father of adult children, run? Would you picture it now? Can you feel his heart pounding in his chest? Can you hear him catching his breath? Nothing could keep him from his son.

When he reached the son, the son tried his best to give the speech he had planned, but to no avail. In all his talk of unworthiness, he didn't realize he was unworthy even before he left. He was a son not because he earned the right to be, but because he was born of his father. He could exceed the realm of his father's shield, but he could not exceed the reach of his father's love. "Quick! Bring the best robe and put it on him. Put a ring on his finger and sandals on his feet. Bring the fattened calf and kill it. Let's have a feast and celebrate. For this son of mine was dead and is alive again; he was lost and is found" (vv. 22–24). The father literally kissed the son's past away.

Merciful Savior! Graceful God! You have kissed this prodigal's past into forgetfulness! Though mockers may accuse me, though gossipers may make sport of me, though brothers may jealously despise me, I will celebrate! Let all hear music and dancing! For I once was dead and now I'm alive again. I once was lost and now I am found.

# DAY 174
## Luke 17:1–4

⊶⊷

If he sins against you seven times a day, and comes back to
you seven times, saying, "I repent," you must forgive him (v. 4).

⊶⊷

After dealing with the subject matter of the first two verses of Luke 17—things that cause people to sin—Christ suddenly switched to a subject that seems to have no relationship to this. I'd like to suggest, however, a powerful connection between the two. Few things cause people to sin like unforgiveness. Difficult-to-forgive circumstances can set a trap. And Satan is very adept at using unforgiveness as bait to entrap us in sin (2 Cor. 2:10–11).

Please note that Christ's specific prescriptive in Luke 17:3–4 is to fellow believers when we sin against one another. Someone might ask, "Does this mean I have to forgive only other Christians?" No, indeed. Luke 11:4 clearly tells us we are to forgive "everyone" who sins against us. The difference may not be in the forgiveness but in the rebuke. I believe Christ suggests a different method of dealing with a brother's or sister's sin. He issued a directive to "rebuke" a fellow believer (v. 3). When dealing with the unsaved, we are still called to forgive—but not necessarily to rebuke.

We were called to be different in the body of Christ. If we are functioning as a healthy body, ideally we should be able to bring issues that affect us to the table with one another to dialogue and, when appropriate, even to rebuke or receive a rebuke. This type of approach demands the maturity expressed by Ephesians 4:14–15. Paul told us we are no longer to be infants but are to "speak the truth in love" to one another.

Needless to say, a tremendous burden of responsibility falls on the one *giving* the rebuke. An appropriate rebuke is speaking the truth in love "with great patience and careful instruction" (2 Tim. 4:2). We may not be off base in concluding that a rebuke which invites anger and bitterness might fall under the category of entrapment to sin. Obviously, a huge responsibility also falls on the recipient to rightly *accept* the rebuke. I am learning that an important part of maturing as a believer is knowing how to receive a rebuke.

If we would learn the art of giving and receiving an appropriate rebuke in the early stages of wrongdoing, we would guard ourselves more effectively against offenses of "millstone" magnitude (Luke 17:2). I don't know about you, but I'll be chewing on this lesson long into the night.

# DAY 175
## Luke 17:11–19

———∞∞∞———

Jesus said, "Were not 10 cleansed? Where are the nine?
Didn't any return to give glory to God except this foreigner?" (vv. 17–18).

———∞∞∞———

While I ministered in India, I was often stunned by what God empowered me to do. He seemed to raise me above my fleshly senses and allow me to minister in extreme circumstances. Only one thing was I unable to do, and it has haunted me ever since. I had confidently planned to minister in a leper colony. The opportunity didn't readily arise, but after passing very close to several colonies, I deliberately did not pursue it.

The reason was not unconcern. Rather, I feared I would dishonor them by becoming physically ill. I almost became ill just passing by. Nothing could have prepared me for the sight or the smell. I had been in one squalid village after another without hindrance, but the smell of diseased and decaying flesh was more than I could handle.

I don't know if God was upset with me, but I was definitely upset with myself. My experience helps me to appreciate this story. Let's highlight several significant pieces of information shared about the lepers in Luke 17.

1. *The lepers were outside the city gate.* What could be worse than forced isolation? I can hardly stand the thought of the emotional results of this dreadful disease, especially in an ancient society. The law of Moses said, "As long as he has the infection he remains unclean. He must live alone; he must live outside the camp" (Lev. 13:46).

Try to imagine what this was like. Oh, beloved, I'm so grateful we never have to stand at a distance from Christ. Not only is He incapable of catching our "disease," He is never reluctant to embrace us. Who could be more brokenhearted, more crushed in spirit, than these outcasts? Yet in the words of Psalm 34:18, "The LORD is close to the brokenhearted and saves those who are crushed in spirit." He drew near them with His soothing balm.

2. *The lepers cried out in a loud voice.* Don't miss the fact that every word attributed to the lepers is in a "loud voice" (vv. 13, 15). The distance explains their initial volume, but why did the one who returned and fell at Jesus' feet also cry out in a loud voice?

I'd like to suggest that they were accustomed to having to shout. Leviticus 13:45 is probably as hard for you to read as it is for me: "The person with such an infectious disease must wear torn clothes, let his hair be unkempt, cover the lower part of his face and cry out, 'Unclean, unclean!'"

Because of the nature of this ministry and my own testimony, I encounter many people who live like the ten lepers. They are in bondage either to sin or to the aftereffects of sin. Their voices may be silent, but their expressions cry out: "Unclean! Unclean!" They feel excluded from the pretty part of the body of Christ. Yet they feel their shame is displayed for all to see. My heart breaks every time. These lepers were not just asking for sympathy. They needed someone to change their lives, and Jesus was the One and Only who could.

3. *The common condition of the lepers eclipsed their differences.* The lepers had to have been a mix of Samaritans and Jews. Christ never would have commented that only a "foreigner" returned with thanks if none of the ten had been Jews. Yet the tragic plight of the lepers gave them far more in common with each other than their differences as Jews and Gentiles. Aren't we the same way? Before we are redeemed, not one of us is better than the other. We are all in the same sad state—lepers outside the city gate. Lost and isolated. Marred and unclean—whether we've lied or cheated, devalued another human being, or committed adultery. Lost is lost. Furthermore, found is found. All of us in Christ have received the free gift of salvation in one way only: grace. When we judge a brother's or sister's sin as so much worse than our own, we are like lepers counting spots.

4. *The lepers were cleansed during their faith-walk to the priest.* I love the way Scripture refers to their healing as being made clean (v. 14). Oh, dear sister or brother, that's what healing has meant to me. Being made clean! Do you know why I recognize those who wear shame like a cloak? Scarlet letters on their chests? Because I did. But I don't anymore. Acts 10:15 tells us so clearly, "Do not call anything impure that God has made clean."

You can be fairly certain the village priest had never practiced the purification ritual to pronounce a leper clean. I can almost picture him reading the instructions in Leviticus 14 step by unfamiliar step—like we read a new recipe. What a story he had for the Mrs. that night! Then again, it wouldn't have been like a woman to miss the parade of ten former lepers dancing their way down Main Street. Finally, note the punch line of the event:

5. *One leper returned to give praise to God.* I wonder if he tried to get the other nine to come with him. Or if he suddenly stopped in his tracks realizing he hadn't said thanks, then darted impulsively from their presence to find Christ. The point is, his healing made him think of his healer, not just himself. Sadly, the rest of them never knew Christ except from a distance. When the one returned, he was unrestrained—falling at Christ's feet and thanking Him.

Just one last thought. I wonder if he was the one with the most spots?

# DAY 176
## Luke 17:20–36

—∞∞—

As the lightning flashes from horizon to horizon and lights up the sky,
so the Son of Man will be in His day (v. 24).

—∞∞—

Let's emphasize a few facts concerning the end of the age and Christ's return:

1. *Christians will long for Christ's return before the world ever sees it.* Luke 17:22 intimates that one of the signs of His return will be a heightened longing. Christ is most assuredly returning, but not as soon as believers may hope as they look upon the tragic state of the earth. I experience that longing every time I watch a documentary on a starving, suffering people group or hear a horrific report of violence and victimization. My only answer is to pray, "O, Lord Jesus, come quickly!" I don't doubt that you also have overwhelming moments when you deeply long for Christ to return and right all wrongs.

2. *Many will come claiming to be Christ.* In Luke 17:23, Jesus warned that as the end of time hastens, the incidence of false-messiah claims will increase. But the sheer visibility of Christ's return is enough reason why believers should never be susceptible to this kind of deception. When Christ returns, people won't have to read about it in the paper. Every eye will see Him. Any rumor of His return is automatically false. When He comes back, the whole world will know it.

3. *The world will display dramatic increases in depravity.* One key word characterizing the hastening conclusion of this age is *increase*. God's Word describes end-time events like birth pains (see Matt. 24:8), meaning the evidences increase in frequency and strength. Matthew's version plainly characterizes the end of the age as marked by the increase of wickedness. "Because of the increase of wickedness, the love of most will grow cold" (Matt. 24:12).

Luke 17:25–28 states that the time of Christ's return will be like that of Noah or Lot. The Old Testament lends some important insight into the condition of the societies surrounding both of these men. I believe the end of time will parallel the days of Noah and Lot in many ways, but among them will be dramatic increase in perversity. Can anyone deny that we are living at a time of dramatic escalation in sexual sin? I believe our society is presently being sexually assaulted by the devil. I am convinced based on multiple characteristics of the last days that they have already begun. However, I'm certainly not date-setting Christ's return. Luke 12:40 makes it plain that forecasting a time of Christ's return is a waste of time. Jesus said, "the Son of Man will come at an hour when you do not expect him." So if we're going to be, like Noah, righteous people surrounded by a sea of unrighteousness, we have no other recourse than to radically refuse to cooperate and proactively choose to fight back. If we're going to be victorious in a latter-day society, we must become far more defensive and offensive in our warfare.

4. *The latter days will show a notable increase in violence and cataclysmic events.* Luke 21:10 tells us "nation will rise against nation, and kingdom against kingdom." Luke 21:12, 16 and Matthew 24:9 warn of the escalation in the persecution and martyrdom of Christians. Those of us who live in the United States like to think persecution and martyrdom are not characteristic of our generation of believers, but we are mistaken. Parts of our body are suffering terribly in many areas of the world.

Had enough bad news for now?

Me too! There's good news, too!

5. *The worldwide witness of the gospel of Jesus Christ will increase.* Ours is such a God of mercy! He will not judge the wickedness of the earth until the testimony of His Son has reached every nation. Jesus said, "The gospel of the kingdom will be preached in the whole world as a testimony to all nations, and then the end will come" (Matt. 24:14).

What kind of simultaneous increase does this prophecy necessitate? An increase in missionaries! Dr. Jerry Rankin of the Southern Baptist International Mission Board told me that the number of people surrendering to foreign missions is increasing so dramatically, it can be explained no other way than as God fulfilling prophecy. Rejoice in the fact that there will be a soul harvest that no man can count of every tribe, tongue, and nation (see Rev. 7:9)!

6. *The activity of the Holy Spirit will increase.* Acts 2:17 proclaims, "'In the last days, God says, I will pour out my Spirit on all people. Your sons and daughters will prophesy, your young men will see visions, your old men will dream dreams." I believe God was hinting at an insatiable appetite to know and share God's Word! Beloved, your love for Scripture is evidence of that harvest. We haven't simply "wised up" in this generation by getting into God's Word. It's the outpouring of the Holy Spirit! Unprecedented numbers of people are becoming armed with the sword of the Spirit because we're entering an unprecedented spiritual war!

I'm so grateful to live during this awesome season on the kingdom calendar. In some ways we live in the worst of times to date. But in other ways we live in the best of times. The winds of true worship are blowing. The Spirit of God is moving. I don't want to hold on to my church pew and sing, "I shall not be moved." I want to move with Him!

Don't you?

# DAY 177
### Luke 18:18–21

※

"I have kept all these from my youth," he said (v. 21).

※

Consider the abbreviated list of commandments Christ mentioned—each of which concerned man's relationship with man—and then let's play a game together. Take a look at each command the ruler claimed to have kept since boyhood. Give each a mental check mark for his probable obedience, or a mental X for those that seem a little less probable.

• *"Do not commit adultery."* Okay, this one may have been a pretty easy check mark—that is, if he knew nothing about lust being the same thing as committing adultery in his heart (Matt. 5:27–28). Let's give him a check mark here.

• *"Do not murder."* Of course, there's that little "anger" issue that Christ discussed in Matthew 5:21–22, but let's go ahead and give him a check mark on this one, too.

• *"Do not steal."* Maybe we've never mugged someone on the street or even swiped candy from the convenience store, but did we ever secretly defraud or steal anything of a less tangible nature from another person? Perhaps so. I'm still willing to give him a check mark, but let me just say I'm impressed!

• *"Do not give false testimony."* This command is simple: never tell anything false or untrue. Any exaggeration would fall under the category of false testimony. Picture us at age seventeen, talking to our friends on the telephone, giving our version of this story and that. The rich young ruler's protection may have been that he had never been a seventeen-year-old girl nor owned a phone. Hopefully he never had time to fish either. We can give him a check mark if he insists, but you better give me an X.

• *"Honor your father and mother."* Let's see. I hardly ever dishonored mine to their faces, but does it count if, behind their backs, I did a few things they told me not to do? Oops. Go ahead and give the wonder boy a check mark, but I get another X.

How did you fare? Shall we call you perfection personified? Or is your halo slipping a bit? As for me, am I thankful for a Savior! The rich young ruler needed one too. His good track record had certainly fogged up his mirror. Don't get me wrong. I like him. I'm even impressed with him, but I'd rather be saved than be like him!

# DAY 178
## Luke 18:22–30

—⚬⚬⚬—

When Jesus heard this, He told him, "You still lack one thing:
sell all that you have and distribute it to the poor, and you will
have treasure in heaven. Then come, follow Me" (v. 22).

—⚬⚬⚬—

If this were a game show, the bell indicating the mention of the secret word would have just sounded. Eternal life with God demands perfection. Someone has to be perfect. Either us or someone who stands in for us. This man wanted so badly for it to be him. But as good as he had been and as hard as he had tried, he was still lacking. Christ then stuck a pin in the rich young ruler's Achilles' heel: his possessions.

One of the primary purposes of this divine pinprick was to show the man he wasn't perfect nor would he ever be. I really believe a second purpose may have been to offer an authentic invitation for the searching young man to follow Him. Remember, Jesus didn't have only twelve disciples. He had twelve *apostles* among a greater number of disciples. If the rich young ruler had done what Christ suggested, could he have followed Him? Certainly! He simply needed to lighten his load and be free of wealth's encumbrances. A truckful of possessions would have proved cumbersome.

I also believe Christ had a purely benevolent purpose for the seemingly harsh demand. Jesus looked at this young man and saw a prisoner. The man wasn't really the ruler. His possessions were. Jesus pointed him to the only path to freedom. Sometimes when our possessions have us, we have to get rid of them to be free.

Of course, Christ knew in advance what the young man would choose. When it comes right down to it, we all follow our "god." The ironic part about this story, however, is that the rich young ruler was grief stricken over his own choice. He walked away very sad or in Greek, *perilupos*: "severely grieved, very sorrowful." Unless his heart changed somewhere along the way, he lived the rest of his life with all that wealth and an empty heart. The question would have haunted him forever: "What do I still lack?" (Matt. 19:20).

Perfection or a perfect substitute. He had neither. He lacked Jesus.

I wonder if the man stuck around long enough to hear the rest of the conversation between Christ and His disciples (vv. 24–30). Jesus said something like: "Yes, an eternal inheritance involves sacrifice here on earth, but whatever you lay down here for My sake, you will receive a hundred times as much in eternity." How sad to believe anything less.

# DAY 179
## Luke 19:1–10

———

When Jesus came to the place, He looked up and said to him, "Zacchaeus, hurry and come down, because today I must stay at your house" (v. 5).

———

Can you imagine what the title of the next day's headline would have been if there had been a newspaper called *The Jericho Chronicle*? As a means of creative exploration, let's try to capture a few of the newsiest statements that might have appeared in their morning editions. The lead story might have read:

• *The Renowned Jesus of Nazareth Passes through Jericho.* Jesus couldn't seem to pass through anywhere without getting involved. He seemed to attract the dust of every village in His sandals no matter how resolved He was to reach Jerusalem. I wonder if His disciples were ever frustrated that He couldn't go anywhere without encountering one commotion after another. I'm sure His followers were thrilled and amazed by all He did, but I'm also sure they were often tired, hungry, and famished—and wouldn't have minded going unnoticed every once in a while.

• *Chief Tax Collector Seen Scurrying Up Tree.* Zacchaeus wanted to see Jesus so badly, he went to considerable lengths for a grown man. Picture him running ahead of the parade of people, looking for a tree with a view. Did he have to jump to reach a sturdy branch, or did the sycamore spare him a nice, low rung? Can you hear him huffing and puffing his way up that tree? Clad in a robe, no less? Nothing like climbing a tree in a long dress. How long has it been since you climbed your last tree?

• *Traveling Man Requests Chief Publican's Hospitality.* I can almost picture Christ working His way through the crowd as if totally oblivious to the short man in a tall tree. He suddenly looked up with complete familiarity. "Zacchaeus," He said. How in the world did Jesus know his name? Maybe the same way He knew Nathaniel's a few years earlier. "Zacchaeus, come down immediately. I must stay at your house today" (Luke 19:5). Why must He? Perhaps because the Son lived to do the will of His Father, and His Father simply could not resist a display of interest in His Son. The Father and Son have an unparalleled mutual admiration society. That day Zacchaeus may have had a pair of skinned knees and elbows that endeared a special dose of the Father's affections.

Luke 19:6 says, "So he came down at once and welcomed him gladly." At once. I'm not sure God honors anything more in a man than a timely response to His Son. No doubt the chief tax collector had many regrets in life, but among them wasn't the time he wasted between Christ's invitation and his welcome.

• *Chief Publican Caught in the Act of Rejoicing.* I don't think we're off base to imagine that his sudden display of glee was slightly out of character. The Word doesn't paint tax collectors as campus favorites. Don't you love how Christ can change an entire personality? Not only can He make the blind man see, but He can also perform a much greater feat: He can make the grump rejoice! Our church pews might not have so many empty seats if we'd invite Him to display such a feat in us! The good news coming from people in a bad mood undermines the message a tad.

Don't you think Christ delights in our glad responses, when we rejoice to obey Him? Let me be clear that God honors obedience even when we're kicking and screaming. But can you imagine how blessed He is when we're eager to do His will?

• *Noted Preacher Goes to Dinner with Sinner.* I think you'll enjoy the definition of the Greek word for "guest" in Luke 19:7. The word means "to loose or unloose what was before bound or fastened. To refresh oneself, to lodge or be a guest. It properly refers to travelers loosening their own burdens or those of their animals when they stayed at a house on a journey." In effect, Zacchaeus's hospitality said to Jesus: "Come to my house and take a load off. Lay Your burden down and be refreshed. I'd be honored to have You." What an awesome thought that at the same time, Christ was saying to Zacchaeus: "Let Me come into your house and take your load. Lay your burden down and be refreshed. I'd be honored to have you."

• *Jericho's Richest Resident Gives Half His Possessions to the Poor: Also Repays Debts with Heavy Interest.* Luke 19:8 says Zacchaeus stood up and said, "Look, Lord! Here and now I give half of my possessions to the poor, and if I have cheated anybody out of anything, I will pay back four times the amount." Here and now! The moment the Holy Spirit moves, I often sense a greater empowerment to respond generously. The more time I allow to pass, the more my selfishness is apt to well up.

One short man had never stood taller than he did on this day. I don't hear a single shred of resistance, do you? He almost seemed anxious to get rid of some things. Perhaps the wealth had been less a blessing and more a curse. Proverbs 15:27 tells us, "A greedy man brings trouble to his family, but he who hates bribes will live." Maybe Zacchaeus had come to see the trouble of valuing wealth over God.

Either way, it was a big news day in Jericho . . . and for the little guy in the headlines.

# DAY 180
## Luke 19:28–48

~~~

*Every day He was teaching in the temple complex. The chief priests, the scribes, and the leaders of the people were looking for a way to destroy him (v. 47).*

~~~

We have arrived at a most critical juncture in our journey. Having accelerated through the parables, we now slow to a crawl, with magnifying glass in hand, to move through the final three chapters of Luke's Gospel. We will spend every remaining moment attempting to become eyewitnesses to the events at the conclusion of his account.

Luke 9:51 records that "Jesus resolutely set out for Jerusalem." He performed many miracles and delivered vital messages along the way. But Luke 19:28–48 indicates that Christ's presence was finally becoming more than His opposition could stand. His triumphal entry into Jerusalem, His cleansing of the temple. To the religious establishment, these were the proverbial straws that broke the camel's back.

I wish we could all sit together on the Mount of Olives and look at the Holy City for a while. Picture it in your mind. The garden where Christ retreated was on the hill directly across from the altar of sacrifice on the temple mount. Jesus taught at the temple during the day, then at night He retreated to the Mount of Olives, which overlooked the temple.

Not long ago, I sat near this place where Jesus retreated. I couldn't help wondering what went through His mind during those days. On that temple mount God had provided the substitutionary offering for Isaac (see Gen. 22:1–19; see also 2 Chron. 3:1). Paul wrote that through Abraham, God had provided an "advance" showing of the gospel of grace (Gal. 3:8). Fast forward, now, two thousand years to the scene where Christ was camped on the mountain parallel to the place of sacrifice at the temple. He resolved to fulfill the gospel that had been preached to Abraham. The time was imminent.

And, oh, by the way—"The Passover was approaching" (Luke 22:1). God's timing is never coincidental, but it was perhaps never more deliberate than in the events that unfolded in the opening lines of Luke 22. A new year on Israel's sacred calendar had just begun. The most sacred and critical year in all of human history was beginning—"the year of the Lord's favor" (Luke 4:19). The age of the completed redemptive work of God was unfolding. Can you imagine the anticipation in the unseen places? The kingdom of God and the kingdom of darkness were rising to a climactic point on the divine calendar.

# DAY 181
## Luke 21:5–28

---

When these things begin to take place, stand up and lift up your heads,
because your redemption is near! (v. 28).

---

I love eschatology—a fancy word for end-time events. Few subjects are more exciting to study than the glorious future awaiting us. Just don't lose your head over it! Bible topics are not meant to become our focus—not even critical themes like holiness and service. *Jesus* is our focus. Remember, the enemy's primary goal is to disconnect us from the Head. Colossians 2:19 describes the kind of person who becomes more interested in spiritual things than the Spirit of Christ: "He has lost connection with the Head." That's why we must be very careful when dealing with exciting subjects like eschatology.

Among the many facts we know about Christ's return, the one that is most clear is this one: *it will be unmistakable.* Luke 21:27 tells us that people "will see the Son of Man coming in a cloud with power and great glory."

Revelation 1:7 also makes it clear that Christ's return to this earth will be impossible to miss: "Look, he is coming with the clouds, and every eye will see him, even those who pierced him; and all the peoples of the earth will mourn because of him. So shall it be! Amen."

If you carefully compare Luke 21:7 with Matthew 24:3, you will see that the disciples asked Jesus about two events. I believe the disciples thought they were asking only one question. In reality they asked about two events separated by millennia—the destruction of the temple and the return of Christ. The temple was destroyed in AD 70. We await Jesus' return today.

I confess that I would like to shake those disciples and tell them to ask better questions. Parts of Jesus' discourse fit the events surrounding the destruction of the temple. Some of His words can apply only to the Second Coming. Some leave us wondering. Why do you suppose Jesus didn't choose to be more clear about these events? Wouldn't you like to have a clearer road map or timetable?

But whether or not we can answer all the questions that come to our mind, you and I can be sure we are living in an era on the kingdom calendar that will climax with the visible return of Jesus Christ. It's unmistakable.

# DAY 182
## Luke 22:1–3

———

The chief priests and the scribes were looking for a way to put Him to death. . . . Then Satan entered Judas, called Iscariot, who was numbered among the Twelve (vv. 2–3).

———

Few things startle and shake us to the core like the sudden revelation of a Judas. Maybe because we can't believe we didn't see it coming. Maybe because we're terrified that if one of us could be Judas, couldn't we all? We are terrified by our similarities! And rightly we should be. But one thing sets us apart. Judas sold his soul to the devil.

John 13:28 tells us no one at the meal understood. But over the course of years and countless replays of the scene in the mind of the apostle John, he knew the devil entered into Judas at that table right before their very eyes. How did he know?

Christ taught in John 14:26 that the Holy Spirit is also the Holy Reminder. He can reveal the truth even in something past and remind us what He was teaching us, though we were unable to grasp it at the time. Jesus often teaches us lessons that He knows we won't fully assimilate until later.

Try to grasp that Judas was not inhabited by any old demon from hell. Satan is not omnipresent. He can only be one place at a time. And for that time, he was in Judas. The prince of the power of the air flew like a fiery dart into the willing vessel of one of the Twelve. This proves that we can follow—closely—and still not belong to Jesus. We can talk the talk. We can blend right in. We can seem so sincere.

I believe through the videotape of his own retrospect, John saw the devil in Judas's eyes. I think he saw Satan in Judas's hands as he reached for the dipped bread. Think about it. For the briefest moment, two hands held the same bread. One soiled by silver; the other only a thin glove of flesh cloaking the hand of God. John saw the devil in Judas's feet as he walked away . . . for if we are ever truly with Christ, we cannot leave Christ.

Two-thirds of a century later, John would write, "They went out from us, but they did not belong to us; for if they had belonged to us, they would have remained with us. However, they went out so that it might be made clear that none of them belongs to us" (1 John 2:19 HCSB). We learn some of our best, and worst, life lessons at the table. John learned this lesson at the table. He learned all too well.

# DAY 183
## Luke 22:4–6

᳁

He went away and discussed with the chief priests and temple police
how he could hand Him over to them (v. 4).

᳁

I wonder if Judas knew he was inhabited by Satan the moment it happened. Perhaps the entrance of the unholy spirit has counterfeit similarities to the entrance of the Holy Spirit. Most of us do not remember "feeling" the Holy Spirit take up residency within us the moment we trusted Christ as our Savior, yet He soon bore some sign of witness through the fruit in our lives. We have no way of knowing if Judas "felt" the unholy spirit take up residence within him, but it certainly wasn't long until the fruit of wickedness was revealed.

If you are new to the study of Scripture, the thought that Satan could enter a disciple might be terrifying. Please understand that just because a person appears to follow Christ doesn't necessarily mean he has placed saving faith in Him. Keep in mind that Satan entered Judas as opposed to Peter, James, or John, even though at times each of them had certainly revealed weakness of character. Satan was able to enter Judas because he was available. Judas followed Christ for several years without ever giving his heart to Him. The authentic faith of the others protected them from demon possession, albeit not oppression, just as it protects us. Judas proved to be a fraud, whether or not his tenure began with better intentions.

The evil one methodically seeks to work in your life and mine. Satan's planning counterfeits the awesome work of God. Just as our God has a holy plan that He executes in an orderly fashion, the enemy of our souls has an unholy plan he also executes in an orderly fashion.

Satan is not stupid. When I recall the technical procedures he's enacted in my life, I am stunned at his working knowledge of my fairly well-disguised vulnerabilities—even those I didn't know I had. He possesses a surprising amount of patience to weave seemingly harmless events into disasters, while his subject often never sees it coming.

What is our defense? The Word tells us not to be ignorant! Wising up to what the Word has to say about Christ's authority and the devil's schemes has empowered me to throw some holy kinks into Satan's unholy plans for my life.

## DAY 184
Luke 22:7–8

———∞∞∞———

Jesus sent Peter and John, saying, "Go and prepare
the Passover meal for us, so we can eat it" (v. 8).

———∞∞∞———

Christ's appointments are never haphazard. He can accomplish anything He desires by merely thinking it into existence. That He assigns men and women to certain tasks implies that the experience of the servant or beneficiary is often as important as the accomplishment. Sometimes more so. God can do anything He wants. He sovereignly chooses to employ mortals to flesh out an invisible work in the visible realm . . . even Jesus the perfect Word made flesh.

I believe that Peter and John were not only chosen for the job of preparing the Passover but that the job was chosen for them. When I considered this scene in *Jesus the One and Only*, I shared what I believe is far more than a coincidence: Peter and John's repetitive references in their letters to Christ as the Lamb. They seemed to have understood the concept of the Paschal Lamb like none of the other writers of the New Testament. I believe a tremendous part of their understanding came in retrospect after their preparation for the last Passover with Christ.

But God added another fresh insight to this as I became more deeply aware of the early influence John the Baptist had upon Peter and John. We know that each was either directly discipled by the Baptizer or indirectly influenced through their brothers. John 1:29 tells us that these disciples first encountered Jesus through the words of the Baptizer: "Look, the Lamb of God, who takes away the sin of the world!"

Jesus would not rest until He taught Peter and John exactly what that title meant. The pair didn't run by the Old City market and grab a saran-wrapped package of trimmed lamb for a buck fifty a pound. No, they picked out a live lamb and then had the sweet thing slaughtered. Very likely they held it still for the knife. Most of us can hardly imagine all that was involved in preparing for a Passover, but you can be sure that none of it was wasted.

That's one of the things I love about Christ. He's not into waste management. If He gives us a task or assigns us to a difficult season, every ounce of our experience is meant for our instruction and completion if only we'll let Him finish the work.

The other day I came across a verse that causes me to stop, meditate, and ask big things from God every time I see it. Psalm 25:14 says, "The LORD confides in those who fear him; he makes his covenant known to them." I desperately want God to be able to confide in me, don't you? The King James Version puts it this way: "The secret of the LORD is with them that fear him." I want God to tell me

His secrets! I believe these hidden treasures are not secret because He tells them only to a chosen few, but because not many seek to know Him and tarry with Him long enough to find out.

I believe as Peter and John prepared the Passover meal that day, they were privy to many secrets that became clearer and clearer to them as time passed. Ecclesiastes 3:11 says that God makes everything beautiful in its time. I truly believe that if we're willing to see, God uses every difficulty and every assignment to confide deep things to us, and that the lessons are not complete until their beauty has been revealed. I fear, however, that we have such an attention deficit that we settle for bearable when beauty was just around the corner.

Surely many years and Passover celebrations passed before Peter and John fully assimilated the profound significance of the one in which Jesus became the Lamb. John never could get over it. From the pen of an elderly, shaking hand, we find over twenty references to the Lamb in the Book of Revelation. And it was Peter, his sidekick, who wrote:

> *For you know that you were redeemed from your empty*
> *way of life inherited from the fathers, not with perish-*
> *able things, like silver or gold, but with the precious*
> *blood of Christ, like that of a lamb without defect or*
> *blemish (1 Pet. 1:18–19 HCSB).*

Look at that opening expression of 1 Peter 1:18 again: "from your empty way of life inherited from the fathers." When I think of a Jewish heritage, I imagine it to be anything but empty! We Americans are such a hodgepodge of cultures that many of us lack the rich traditions of other less alloyed cultures. And who could have enjoyed richer ways of life and more tradition than those handed down by Jewish forefathers to their sons and daughters? Yet Peter called them empty. Why?

I think because once He saw their fulfillment in Jesus Christ, he knew that these "inheritances" were empty without Him. Once he knew the true Passover Lamb, an Old Testament Passover meant nothing without its fulfillment in Jesus. Christ became everything, and all former things were empty without Him.

# DAY 185
## Luke 22:9–13

───◈───

So they went and found it just as He had told them,
and they prepared the Passover (v. 13).

───◈───

I don't believe Christ simply glanced up, saw Peter and John, and decided they'd be as good a choice as anyone to prepare for the Passover. Quite the contrary, this profound work was prepared in advance for them to do (see Eph. 2:10). It's likely the two men may have wished someone else had been chosen for the tasks, some of which were usually assigned to women. The Passover involved a fairly elaborate meal with a very specific setting. They may have grumbled, as we often do. Why? Because we may have no idea as to the significance of the work God has called us to do.

Give some thought to the preparations Peter and John made. You can read about the original Passover in Exodus 12:1–14. The meal involved three symbolic foods to be eaten during every observance: "meat roasted over the fire, along with bitter herbs, and bread made without yeast" (Exod. 12:8).

While every part of the meal was highly symbolic, it had no meaning at all without the lamb. The most important preparation Peter and John made was the procuring and preparing of the Passover lamb. The detailed preparation involving the lamb would soon be fulfilled in Jesus Christ, of course. They may not have grasped the significance of it at the time, but eventually they "got it."

Peter and John are the only two of the Twelve who were recorded referring to Jesus as the Lamb. Many years later Peter would write of Jesus that we were redeemed "with the precious blood of Christ, a lamb without blemish or defect. He was chosen before the creation of the world, but was revealed in these last times for your sake" (1 Pet. 1:19–20). For John's part, you can read Revelation 5 for what I think is the most majestic passage in Scripture about the Lamb of God.

Is it coincidence that only these two apostles wrote about Jesus as the Lamb? Not on your life. Christ's ultimate goal in any work He assigns to us is to reveal Himself, either through us or to us. The Holy Spirit used the tasks He assigned Peter and John that day to reveal to them the Lamb of God, to deeply engrave these images and remembrances in their minds. Beloved, the tasks God gives you are never trivial.

## DAY 186
### Luke 22:14–22

———∞∞∞———

He took bread, gave thanks, broke it, gave it to them, and said,
"This is My body, which is given for you. Do this in remembrance of Me" (v. 19).

———∞∞∞———

When the hour came, Jesus and His apostles reclined at the table. The Passover was a celebration for families and those closest to them. Christ was surrounded by His closest family. They may have been weak, self-centered, and full of unfounded pride, but they were His. He desired to spend this time with them.

Capture this meal with your imagination. I think we've inaccurately pictured the last meal as moments spent over the bread and the wine. Christ and His disciples observed the entire Passover meal together. Then He instituted the new covenant, represented by the bread and the wine.

As they gathered around the table at sundown, Christ took the father role in the observance. Soon after they gathered, He poured the first of four cups of wine and asked everyone to rise from the table. He then lifted His cup toward heaven and recited the Kiddush, or prayer of sanctification, which would have included these words or something very close: "Blessed art Thou, O Lord our God, King of the universe, Who createst the fruit of the vine. Blessed art Thou, O Lord our God, Who hast chosen us for Thy service from among the nations . . . Blessed art Thou, O Lord our God, King of the universe, Who hast kept us in life, Who hast preserved us, and hast enabled us to reach this season."[39] This is very likely the blessing He recited in Luke 22:17.

If Christ and His disciples followed tradition, they took the first cup of wine, asked the above blessing, observed a ceremonial washing, and broke the unleavened bread. These practices were immediately followed by an enactment of Exodus 12:26–27. The youngest child at the observance asks the traditional Passover questions, provoking the father to tell the story of the exodus. Early church tradition cited John as the youngest apostle.[40] In all likelihood, John assumed the role of the youngest child in the family, asking the traditional questions that provoked Christ to tell the story of the Passover. Many scholars believe John may have been the one who asked the questions at the last supper because of his position at the table. John 13:23 tells us John was reclining next to Christ.

The four cups of wine served at the Passover meal represented the four expressions, or "I wills" of God's promised deliverance in Exodus 6:6–7. At this point in the meal, Christ poured the second cup of wine and narrated the story of Israel's exodus in response to the questions. Oh, friend, can you imagine? Christ, the Lamb of God, sat at their table and told the redemption story! He recounted the story as only He could have—and then, at the very next sundown—He fulfilled it! Oh, how I pray He will tell it again for all of us to hear when we take it together in the kingdom!

They ate the meal between the second and third cups. Although all four cups would have been observed at the last supper, not all four cups are specified in Luke's Gospel. We know, however, exactly which cup is specified in Luke 22:20 because of its place of observance during the meal. The third cup was traditionally taken after the supper was eaten. It is represented by the third "I will" statement of God recorded in Exodus 6:6: "I will redeem you with an outstretched arm and with mighty acts of judgment."

This is the cup of redemption. I am convinced this cup is also the symbolic cup to which Christ referred only an hour or so later in the garden of Gethsemane when He asked God to "take this cup from me" (Luke 22:42). This was a cup of which He could partake only with outstretched arms upon the cross.

The imminent fulfillment of the cup of redemption signaled the release of the new covenant that would be written in blood. We know Christ did not literally drink this third cup because He stated in Luke 22:18 that He would not drink of another cup until the coming of the kingdom of God. Instead of drinking the cup, He would do something of sin-shattering significance. He would, in essence, become the cup and pour out His life for the redemption of man.

Christ never took anything more seriously than the cup of redemption He faced that last Passover supper. His body would soon be broken so that the Bread of life could be distributed to all who would sit at His table. The wine of His blood would be poured into the new wineskins of all who would partake. It was time's perfect night—a night when the last few stitches of a centuries-old Passover thread would be woven onto the canvas of earth in the shape of a cross. Sit and reflect.

> *O perfect Lamb of Passover,*
> *Let me not quickly run.*
> *Recount to me the blessed plot,*
> *Tell how the plan was spun*
> *That I, a slave of Egypt's lusts,*
> *A prisoner of dark dread,*
> *Could be condemned unto a cross*
> *And find You nailed instead.*

# DAY 187
## Luke 22:24–30

Who is greater, the one at the table or the one serving? Isn't it the one at the table? But I am among you as the One who serves (v. 27).

Are you like me? Do you want to be made like Him—but more through His victories than His sufferings? Thankfully, we have a Savior who is willing to steadfastly walk with us even when we take three steps forward and two steps back. We'll see the colors of His willingness painted like a mural on the walls of the upper room.

If we often find ourselves in contrast to Jesus' perfect character, we're not so unlike His original disciples. Their inability at the Passover table to pinpoint who was the worst among them led to a dispute over who was the greatest. Had not Christ already dealt with them over this issue? However, being declared "guilty as charged" only condemns us. Left alone, it does nothing to change us. Like the apostles, we are slow to learn.

When we recognize that the disciples' sandals fit our feet, let's allow Christ to kneel in front of us, slip them off, and wash our feet. Oh, how we need Jesus to minister humility to us. Without it, He will vastly limit how much He ministers through us. John 13 tells us how Jesus laid aside His garments and washed the disciples' feet.

As effective as the lesson was, Christ still hadn't settled the issue of greatness. He knew that the matter was so critical that He would need to prove on a field trip what He had taught in class. I could kick myself for forcing lessons into field trips instead of learning them in the classroom, but I don't mind telling you, field trips are effective! I fear the lesson on greatness is rarely learned in the classroom alone.

Within hours, each of these disciples would encounter just how "great" they were. All would desert Christ and flee (see Matt. 26:56). However, the lesson taught and demonstrated in the upper (class)room, then confirmed during the field trip, would eventually "stick." Christ turned these eleven status-seekers into humble servants.

Again I find myself so amazed at the character of Christ. Just when we wouldn't have blamed Him if He had thrown water all over them, He washed their feet. And just when they argued over who was the greatest, He paid them their greatest compliment. Luke 22:28 records His words, "You are those who have stood by me in my trials."

# DAY 188
## Luke 22:31–34

---

Simon, Simon, look out! Satan has asked to sift you like wheat.
But I have prayed for you that your faith may not fail.
And you, when you have turned back, strengthen the brothers (vv. 31–32).

---

As surely as Christ knew Judas would betray Him, He knew the rest of His disciples would desert Him. He knew every move each disciple would make. The implication from Luke 22 is that Satan asked to "sift" the disciples "as wheat" in verse 31, and that Christ specified Peter's own encounter in verse 32. I tend to think the Scriptures imply Christ permitted Satan to attack Peter with greater force than the others. If so, we might want to ask ourselves why. I believe these few verses intimate several reasons.

1. *Peter was the natural leader among the disciples.* Christ seemed to be singling him out as a leader in Luke 22:31 as He directed the statement concerning all the disciples (plural "you") to Peter: "'Simon, Simon, Satan has asked to sift [all of] you [disciples] as wheat.'" Very likely, Christ thought that Peter, as a leader among the disciples, could either take or needed the extra heat. I have a hunch both apply. Please be encouraged that Satan can't just presume to sift a believer like wheat. I believe this precedent suggests he must acquire permission from Christ. (Compare Job 1.) Christ will not grant the devil permission to do anything that can't be used for God's glory and our good—if we let it.

But those in critical positions like Peter aren't the only ones who can benefit from a good sifting. Please know, if ever I put on a shoe that fits, it would be this one. I, too, as a servant, badly needed a sifting. And I assure you, God was faithful to permit it. Being sifted like wheat is not your regular brand of temptation. It's an all-out onslaught by the enemy to destroy you and cause you to quit. It surfaces what you detest most in yourself and reveals the ugliness of self. Not everyone has or needs such an experience.

The horror of my sifting season remains as real as yesterday, but (I pray) so is the grain left behind. The method of sifting wheat is to put it through a sieve and shake it until the chaff, little stones, and perhaps some tares rise to the surface. The purpose is that the actual grain can be separated and ground into meal. Satan's goal in sifting is to make us a mockery by showing us to be all chaff and no wheat. Christ, on the other hand, permits us to be sifted to shake out the real from the unreal, the trash from the true. The wheat that proves usable is authentic grain from which Christ can make bread.

Praise Christ's faithful name! Satan turned Peter's field trip into a field day, but he still couldn't get everything about Peter to come up chaff. Satan's plan backfired. He surfaced some serious chaff, to be sure, but Christ let Peter have a good look at it. Then Christ blew the chaff away, took those remaining grains, and demonstrated His baking skills. But Christ had a few other reasons for allowing Peter to be sifted like wheat.

2. *Christ knew that Peter would turn back.* "But I have prayed for you, Simon, that your faith may not fail. And when you have turned back . . ." (Luke 22:32). Not *if*, but *when*. We're somewhat like books Satan can read only from the outside. His book review is limited to assumptions he makes about what's inside, based on what he reads on our "book jackets." He cannot read the inside of us as Christ can.

Satan observed Peter's overconfidence and propensity toward pride. He surmised that, when the sifting came, every page would come up chaff. He was wrong. Christ knew Peter's heart. He knew that underneath Peter's puffed-up exterior was a man with a genuine heart for God. Jesus knew that Peter could deny Christ to others, but he could not deny Christ to himself. He would be back—a revised edition with a new jacket.

3. *Christ knew how Peter's return and "revision" could be used for others.* "And when you have turned back, strengthen your brothers" (v. 32). From falling, Peter was about to learn how to stand. Peter would indeed fall, but his faith would not fail. He would use everything Christ taught him to strengthen his brothers.

Christ didn't want to take the leader out of Simon Peter. He just wanted to take Simon Peter out of the leader. His goal was to let Satan sift out all the Simon-stuff so Christ could use what was left: a humble jar of clay with no confidence in his flesh.

Not everyone has to learn to stand by falling. Better ways to learn exist, but I'm afraid that I learned a similar way. I finally learned to stand on Christ's two feet because my feet of clay turned out to be so unstable.

I was not so unlike Peter. I was young when I surrendered my life to Christ and was completely confident that nothing could shake my commitment. Excuse my bluntness, but I was an idiot. I cannot recall ever learning a more difficult lesson than that which my own sifting season taught me, but neither can I recall a lesson more deeply ingrained. Many years have passed, and I still do not live a day without remembering it and fearing another departure from Christ's authority more than I fear death.

I wouldn't wish a sifting on a single soul, but if that's what a life of harvest requires, may God use it so thoroughly that the enemy ends up being sorry he ever asked permission. Beloved, commitments can be shaken, but Christ cannot. When the shakedown comes, may the fresh winds of God's Spirit blow away the chaff until all that is left is the bread of life.

# DAY 189
## Luke 22:47–62

---

Peter said, "Man, I don't know what you're talking about!"
Immediately, while he was still speaking, a rooster crowed (v. 60).

---

I am convinced that one reason God placed the account of Peter's denial in all four Gospels is so we'd sober to the reality that if Peter could deny Christ, any of us could. Never lose sight of the fact that Peter was certain he could not be "had." Yet he denied Christ not once. Not twice. But three times.

Denying Christ is huge. Do you think the blows Jesus later endured from the whip stung any more than Peter's denial? Don't minimize his sin in that courtyard. As we look at this again, I hope we'll recognize those factors that set Peter up for failure so we can avoid similar pitfalls.

1. *Peter was willing to kill for Jesus, but he was reluctant to die for Him.* Keep in mind the time element. Only an hour or so before Peter denied Christ to save his own skin, he had drawn a sword and cut off a man's ear. Maybe Peter's haste to use the sword was not just motivated by his desire to defend Jesus but by his concern to defend himself.

Nothing displays our self-love like a crisis. But Christ's disciples, both then and now, are called to live above that human baseline of self-importance. Remember that Christ had called Peter and His disciples to deny themselves and take up the cross daily (Luke 9:23). If Peter had denied himself, he would not have denied Christ.

The reason we can "forget" about ourselves is because Christ never forgets us. We can afford to be less important to ourselves because we are vastly important to God. Biblical self-denial will never fail to be *for* us rather than *against* us, whether here or in eternity. When Peter chose to deny Christ rather than himself, he really chose human limitations over divine intervention.

2. *Peter followed Jesus, but at a distance.* Obviously, if Peter had been holding onto Jesus' robe, he probably wouldn't have denied Him. Even though Christ asked the soldiers to let His disciples go (see John 18:8), why didn't even one insist upon staying, especially after all the miracles and proofs the Twelve had seen? From a divine standpoint the answer is most likely God's sovereignty in fulfilling prophecy that Christ would be deserted and forsaken. From a human standpoint, however, the answer is pure fear.

The scene reminds me of 2 Kings 2, when God was about to take His prophet, Elijah, up into a whirlwind. Elijah had several stops to make on his way to the Jordan River, and he continued his attempt to say farewell to his servant, Elisha. But all three times, Elisha said to him, "As surely as the LORD lives and as you live, I will not leave you" (2 Kings 2:2, 4, 6). If Peter had been as insistent as

Elisha, Satan would not have had the room to come between him and his master with a sieve to sift him like wheat. Elisha's actions showed sheer determination to follow his master to the ends of his earthly life.

When we tiptoe to keep from being too obvious or to obscure ourselves in safe places and remain unidentifiable, we are already bounding toward denial.

3. *Peter sat down with the opposition and warmed his hands by the same fire.* I've been in Jerusalem in the early spring, so I can assure you the night was indeed cold. The semidesert climate may heat a spring day, but the temperature drops dramatically when the sun goes down. Since fear also has a way of quickening the senses, we're probably picturing Peter accurately as a young man who trembled nearly uncontrollably as he stood at that fire.

But I believe he made a very poor choice of company in the courtyard. John 18:18 tells us Peter joined "the servants and officials" at the fire in the middle of the courtyard. However unintentionally, he ended up surrounding himself with others who, in effect, denied Christ. The risk of failure heightened dramatically at that moment. Can we ever note a point of application here! Being sent by God to be a witness to those who "deny" Christ is one thing. Warming our hands by the same fire is another.

I cannot help but relate some of my own seasons of defeat to Peter's. I will regret some of my choices every day of my life. Like Peter, I also made some choices in my past that went beyond rationalization. How thankful I am now that I couldn't just make excuses for my behavior! Any part of me I could have "excused" would still be "alive and kicking." Listen to my heart carefully: I want no part of myself. None. I want Jesus to so thoroughly consume me that I no longer exist. I am far too destructive. I would do far too much to deny His lordship. One regret I will never have is that God got me "over myself" by letting me confront this truth: in me dwells no good thing.

I do not doubt that Christ's face was painted with pain when His and Peter's eyes met in the courtyard, but I think the conspicuous absence of condemnation tore through Peter's heart. I wonder if Christ's fixed gaze might have said something like this: "Remember, Peter, I am the Christ. *You* know that and *I* know that. I called you. I gave you a new name. I invited you to follow Me. Don't forget who I am. Don't forget what you are capable of doing. And, whatever you do, don't let this destroy you. When you have turned back, strengthen your brothers."

# DAY 190
## Luke 22:63–71

---

They all asked, "Are You, then, the Son of God?"
And He said to them, "You say that I am" (v. 70).

---

I remember a childhood game I tried to avoid at all costs. It was called King of the Mountain. The players established a high place of some kind as the "mountain." The "king" was the one who could defend his territory by kicking or pushing anyone who came near him. It was a mean game. But it was nothing compared to the real-life King of the Mountain contest that took place between Pilate, Herod, the self-promoting religious leaders . . . and the true King Jesus, the One and Only.

As you picture every moment of these "mock court" proceedings in Luke 22, don't lose sight of these words in verse 70: "Are you then the Son of God?" Imagine every event unfolding on a large-screen TV, and during the entire ordeal these words scroll boldly across the bottom of the scene: "THE SON OF GOD." The irony is this: the only reason Christ was standing in front of them was because He was exactly who they "tried" Him for being. Though His accusers couldn't see the truth for themselves, Christ was found guilty of being the Son of God. They would end up releasing the insurrectionist and crucifying the Savior of the world.

Aren't you thankful humanity can "try" Christ for being anything they choose, and yet He is who He is? No amount of disbelief can change Him or move Him. Why did the chief priests and teachers of the law disbelieve? Why couldn't they accept their Messiah? Because they wanted to be king of the mountain.

And so our Savior was stripped. Mocked. Spat upon. Struck . . . again and again. Flogged. Beyond recognition. The fullness of the Godhead bodily. The bright and morning Star. The Alpha and Omega. The anointed of the Lord. The beloved Son of God. The radiance of His Father's glory. The Light of the world. The Hope of glory. The Lily of the valley. The Prince of peace. The Seed of David. The Son of righteousness. The blessed and only potentate, the King of kings, and Lord of lords. Emmanuel. The With of God.

The most terrifying truth a mocking humanity will ever confront is that no matter how Jesus is belittled, He cannot be made little. He is the King of the mountain.

# DAY 191
## Luke 23:26–31

---∞∞∞---

A great multitude of the people followed Him,
including women who were mourning and lamenting Him (v. 27).

---∞∞∞---

According to ancient custom, the cross, or at least the crossbeam, was placed upon the ground, then Christ was stretched out upon it. I cannot imagine being the one who actually targeted the nail to the proper place in the skin and struck the blow. Do you think he at all costs avoided Christ's eyes?

They probably secured His hands before His feet so that His arms would not flail when His feet were nailed. We often picture that the nail wounds were in the palms, but the delicate bones in the hands could not hold a victim to the cross. The nails were usually driven through the wrists. In Hebrew, the wrist was considered part of the hand rather than the arm.

Without becoming more graphic than necessary, crucifixion, almost always preceded by a near-to-death flogging, was unimaginably painful and inhumane. This kind of capital punishment was targeted as a deterrent for rebellious slaves and was forbidden to any Roman citizen, no matter how serious his crime. Crucifixion was a totally inhumane way for even the two criminals to die. But this was the King of glory! They took a hammer and nails to the "Word made flesh."

I want you to sit and "listen" to the sound of the hammer striking. I'm not trying to be melodramatic. I just want us to come as close as possible to being eyewitnesses. You don't have to open your eyes and "look," but I want you to open your spiritual ears and listen. Move close enough to hear the conversation of the marksman as he positions the nail at the wrist of Christ. You'll have to fight the crowd to get close enough. Then listen to the hammer hit the nail—several times at each hand and foot to make sure the nails are securely in place. I'm not trying to make you wince. I only want you to hear the sound as the nails are driven securely into the wood.

As painful and horrendous as the pounding hammer sounds to our spiritual ears, Colossians 2:13–14 says that while we were dead in our sins, God made us alive with Christ. He "canceled the written code, with its regulations, that was against us and that stood opposed to us; he took it away, nailing it to the cross."

I will never fully grasp how such human atrocities occurred at the free will of humanity, while God used them to unfold His perfect, divine, and redemptive plan. Christ was nailed to the cross as the one perfect human. He was the fulfillment of the law in every way.

# DAY 192
## Luke 23:32-33

---

When they arrived at the place called The Skull, they crucified Him there,
along with the criminals, one on the right and one on the left (v. 33).

---

If you study the Old Testament prophecies of Jesus, you will find that they come in a dazzling variety of forms. In some places the predictions were clear. They obviously pointed to the coming Messiah. In other instances they were veiled. Join me now as we look at an absolutely fascinating passage—these words that apply so beautifully to Christ at this moment. In their immediate sense, they were written about Eliakim, the palace superintendent during the Assyrian invasion of Israel, but you can see their ultimate significance in terms of the cross of our Christ. In the passage God said,

> *"I will clothe him with your robe and fasten your sash around him and hand your authority over to him. He will be a father to those who live in Jerusalem and to the house of Judah. I will place on his shoulder the key to the house of David; what he opens no one can shut, and what he shuts no one can open. I will drive him like a peg into a firm place; he will be a seat of honor for the house of his father"* (Isa. 22:21–23).

Note how God said He would give His servant the key to the house of David, opening a door no one can shut. He said He would "drive him like a peg into a firm place." As unfathomable as the process is to you and me, the cross was the means by which God chose to position Christ in the seat of honor for the house of His Father. The cross is the open door no man can shut.

Isaiah 22:23 says, "I will fasten him as a nail in a sure place" (KJV). The original word for "firm" in the NIV and "sure" in the KJV is *aman*: "in a transitive sense to make firm, to confirm . . . to stand firm; to be enduring; to trust."

Nothing was accidental about the cross of Christ. The Son of God was not suddenly overcome by the wickedness of man and nailed to a cross. Quite the contrary, the cross was the means by which the Son of God overcame the wickedness of man. To secure the keys to the house of David and open the door of salvation to all who would enter, God drove His Son like a nail in a sure place. A firm place. An enduring place.

When God drove His Son like a nail in a firm place, He took the written code, finally fulfilled in His Son, and canceled our debt to it. With every pound of the hammer, God was nailing down redemption.

# DAY 193
## Luke 23:34–43

Jesus said, "Father, forgive them, because they do not know what they are doing" (v. 34).

As if the physical wounds Christ suffered were not enough, they were not the killers in crucifixion. Death crept in slowly through exhaustion and asphyxiation from an increasing inability to hold oneself up to draw breath. If you've ever experienced anything close to "excruciating" pain, can you imagine how difficult talking would be?

Regardless of how many times you've heard sermons preached on Christ's next words, don't hear them casually. The moment words formed on His tongue and His voice found volume, He said, "Father, forgive them, for they do not know what they are doing" (Luke 23:34).

Not "Father, consume them," but "Father, forgive them." This may be the most perfect statement spoken at the most perfect time since God gave the gift of language. As unimaginable as His request was, it was so fitting! If the cross is about anything at all, it is about forgiveness. Forgiveness of the most incorrigible and least deserving.

I don't believe the timing of the statement was meaningless. It was the first thing He said after they nailed Him to the cross and hoisted it into view. His immediate request for the Father's forgiveness sanctified the cross for its enduring work through all of time. His request baptized the crude wood for its divine purpose.

Please understand, the cross itself had no power. Neither was it ever meant to be an idol, but it represents something so divine and powerful that the apostle Paul said, "May I never boast except in the cross of our Lord Jesus Christ, through which the world has been crucified to me, and I to the world" (Gal. 6:14).

Dr. Luke was the only one God inspired to record the forgiveness statement. How appropriate that a physician would be the one to pen such healing words. Surely, in the days to come, many involved were haunted by their consciences. No doubt many in the crowd at the crucifixion were saved on the Day of Pentecost, since both events occurred in Jerusalem only weeks apart and on major feast days. The main reason to believe these were the same people, however, is because God doesn't ordinarily refuse the request of His Son.

## DAY 194
### Luke 23:50–56, Luke 24:1–8

————⚬⚬⚬————

The women were terrified and bowed to the ground.
"Why are you looking for the living among the dead?" asked the men (v. 5).

————⚬⚬⚬————

How the Sabbath hours must have dragged for these women. They had prepared the spices and perfumes but were forced to rest on the Sabbath. They had come with Jesus from Galilee, so we can assume they were guests in others' homes. Surely the time seemed to be an eternity. Women two thousand years ago were not so unlike we are today. We want to do something. Feeling needed is sometimes the very thing that keeps a woman going. For months they "had followed him and cared for his needs" (Mark 15:41). Now all that was left to do was to serve Him in memorial. They needed to get to the tomb and do the one last thing they could for their Lord.

As the moments crawled by, I'm sure these women recounted with horror the last few days' events. Surely at times they sat in silence, each one weeping in painful solitude as she remembered every encounter with Him. Jesus had a way of making a person feel like the apple of His eye. He still does.

The women "rested" through a Sabbath dusk that frustratingly gave way to night. More waiting. They probably never slept a wink and were on their way to the tomb before a cock could crow. John 20:1, spotlighting Mary Magdalene, tells us "it was still dark."

Mark tells us that the women were hoping the officials would allow someone to roll away the stone so they could apply the spices and perfumes to the body. To their astonishment, they saw that the "very large" stone had been rolled away. The women had no way of knowing at that moment what Matthew 28:2–4 records. I love the wording in Matthew 28:2: "An angel of the Lord came down from heaven and, going to the tomb, rolled back the stone and sat on it." Can you fathom the angels' horror when humans mocked, spat on, beat, flogged, and crucified the Son of God?

Imagine the joy of the angel whose thunderous arrival caused the ground to shake. God chose him to be the one who rolled back the stone—not to *free* Jesus, but to reveal Him already missing! Can you picture the angel's gleaming face as he perched on that stone? The guards were so afraid that they shook and became like dead men. The graveyard *needed* a few folks acting like dead men, since a number of the formerly dead were suddenly walking the streets (see Matt. 27:52–53). I'm about to have to shout hallelujah! The women entered the tomb, but they did not find the body.

Acts 2:24 tells us exactly why Christ was raised from the dead: "God raised him from the dead, freeing him from the agony of death, because it was impossible for death to keep its hold on him." Some things are simply impossible—and death keeping its hold on Jesus is one of them.

Mind you, the women didn't yet understand. Luke 24:4 tells us "while they were wondering about this, suddenly two men in clothes that gleamed like lightning stood beside them." John's version hints at these two celestial ambassadors' assignment. He tells us the two angels were seated where Jesus' body had been, "one at the head and the other at the foot" (John 20:12).

Quite possibly, these angels also guarded the body of Jesus while it lay "in state" in the sepulcher. The Old Testament tabernacle contained a marvelous picture foreshadowing this moment. The ark of the covenant represented the very presence of God. In Exodus 25:17–22, the very specific instructions for the "mercy seat" (KJV) or "atonement cover" (NIV) on the ark of the covenant demanded the cherubim to be in exactly that position. Do you see the picture? No, I can't be dogmatic that the cherubim prefigured the angels at Christ's head and feet—but I am personally convinced. Jesus has always been the means by which God would "meet with" humanity (Exod. 25:22).

If the cherubim prefigured the angels in the tomb, can you imagine how they guarded the body through the wait? With their wings overshadowing Him, they faced each other, looking toward the cover. Picture their reactions when the glorified body of Jesus sat up from the death shroud and walked out of the tomb, right through the rock. Wouldn't you have loved to hear as Christ thanked them for their service?

Glory to God! Though the news echoed throughout the heavenlies at the moment of Christ's resurrection, the angels probably longed for God to turn on their volume in the earthly realm and announce it to the mortals. At the sight of the angels, the women fell on their faces. The celestial guards announced to them, "Why do you look for the living among the dead?" The what? The living! "He is not here; he has risen!" (Luke 24:5–6).

Oh, glorious, merciful, omnipotent God! He is risen indeed! I cherish the next five words of the angels: "Remember how he told you" (v. 6). Beloved, have you forgotten something He told you? Christ, our Lord, is faithful to His promises. If you're not presently "seeing" Him at work in your situation, do not live as if He's lifeless and you're hopeless. Believe Him and expect Him to reveal His resurrection power to you!

# DAY 195
## Luke 24:9–12

Mary Magdalene, Joanna, Mary the mother of James, and the other women
with them were telling the apostles these things (v. 10).

If I may say with a chuckle, one possible reason God chose to reveal the
resurrection first to women is because He can trust us to get the word out! Telling
what we've been told is our specialty! However, nothing can deflate the spirits of
an enthusiastic woman like an apprehensive audience. Luke 24:11 records that
the apostles "did not believe the women, because their words seemed to them
like nonsense."

Sisters, don't be insulted by this scene in Luke 24:11. Rather, be blessed that
God was up to something awesome even in this seemingly insignificant detail.
You see, "the witness of women was not [even] acceptable in that day."[41] They
couldn't testify as witnesses.

Now isn't this just like our Jesus! He threatened the status quo in countless
ways, not the least of which concerned women. He invited them into Bible class
(see Luke 10:39) after they had spent centuries learning what little Scripture they
could from their husbands. He honored their service during a time in which men
were the only ones who ministered publicly (see Mark 15:41). He healed, forgave,
delivered, and made whole the very ones society shunned. Women of ill repute.

Appointing these women as the first to share the news of Jesus' resurrection
was a definite "custom shaker." Jesus knew the apostles wouldn't believe them,
but perhaps He felt that the pending discovery of their authenticity would breed a
fresh respect. After all, at the first roll call in the post-ascension New Testament
church, you'll see women listed as part of the first New Testament cell group (see
Acts 1:13–14).

For centuries the synagogue had kept men and women separate. Suddenly
they would be working, praying, and worshiping shoulder-to-shoulder. Christ
built His church on a foundation of mutual respect. Don't misunderstand. Christ
wasn't prioritizing women over men. He simply took the ladder down to the
basement where society had lowered women. And with His nail-scarred hands,
He lifted them to a place of respect and credibility.

The last thing we women should want to do in the body of Christ is to
take men's places. They have far too much responsibility for my taste! But by all
means, let's take *our* places! We have also been called to be credible witnesses of
the Lord Jesus Christ.

# DAY 196
## Luke 24:13–35

He asked them, "What is this dispute that you're having with each other as you are walking?" And they stopped walking and looked discouraged (v. 17).

Imagine that God has decorated your mansion in glory with a number of framed pictures of you and Christ. The pictures capture the two of you during momentous earthly occasions. You could not see Him with your eyes, but He was there every moment in living color. Hopefully, we've each walked with Him long enough to have a few treasured photos with expressions suggesting we chose to see with the eyes of faith rather than the eyes of humanity. I can almost imagine Christ sitting around heaven with small groups of us, pulling out the photo album, pointing out a few sour expressions. Picture us covering our faces with good-humored embarrassment, turning as red as beets.

No doubt the still shot of Cleopas in Luke 24:17 is one that would spur a little good-natured, heavenly ribbing. Christ, however, didn't find it nearly so amusing this side of heaven. Note that the events surrounding Christ's crucifixion were so well publicized, Cleopas implied that Jesus must have been a visitor to be unaware of the recent happenings. He then proceeded to tell Christ . . . about Himself! Can you imagine being in Cleopas's sandals? Wouldn't you hope you got the facts straight?

If Christ had been a teacher grading Cleopas on his oral report, what grade do you think He would've given him? If I were doing the grading, I wouldn't have subtracted points until the "kicker" in Luke 24:21: "But we had hoped that he was the one." Picture the downcast face, the sagging posture. Listen to the tone in his voice. For a clue, see Christ's indignant response in Luke 24:25: "He said to them, 'How foolish you are, and how slow of heart to believe all that the prophets have spoken!'" Cleopas seemed to be saying, "We had hoped . . . but He let us down."

The Word of God often couples a downcast soul with feelings of hopelessness. In Greek the word for "hope" encompasses far more than wishful thinking. It means "confident expectation." Christ told His followers what to "expect" and reminded them that a victorious ending would follow the tragic means. When Christ gives us His Word, He wants us to live in absolute expectation of it, trusting that whether it happens sooner or later, it will happen.

Cleopas and his friend had allowed the very evidence that could have ignited them with hope to make them hopeless instead. Remember now—the women had shared the testimony that Christ was alive. I realize I'm taking the next statement out of context, but I get a kick out of Cleopas's words in Luke 24:22: "In addition, some of our women amazed us." There you have it. Women are amazing.

It's absolutely scriptural. Of course, *amazing* can mean many things. The most common colloquialism we have that matches the word for *amazing* is to say something has "blown our minds." I blow Keith's mind all the time—but it's not always something for me to be proud of. Sometimes he just stands there and gives me that "she's blonder than she pays to be" look.

Christ clearly showed His displeasure over the men's disbelief. He rebuked them, but He followed the rebuke with some of the most amazing moments in Scripture: "Beginning with Moses and all the Prophets, he explained to them what was said in all the Scriptures concerning himself" (v. 27). What I would give to hear that comprehensive dissertation! Christ began with the books of Moses, went straight through the prophets, and explained what was said in all the Scriptures concerning Himself. Part of heaven for me will be hearing a replay of this sermon! The entire Old Testament was written about or toward Christ. Imagine Jesus Himself explaining the hundreds of ways the Scriptures predict and prepare for His coming. I could teach on this subject for hours, and I don't know even a fraction of the ways Christ is taught in the Old Testament.

Luke's use of "explained" (v. 27) in reference to Christ's teaching means "to interpret, translate. To explain clearly and exactly." I can't wait to know exactly what some Scriptures mean. Unlike me, Christ never had to say, "I think . . ." or "I believe this means . . ." He knew. What a Bible lesson those two men heard! A lesson that would have taken forty years of wilderness wanderings for me, Christ delivered with glorious precision over a few Emmaus miles. No wonder the two men hated to part with Jesus! "Jesus acted as if he were going farther. But they urged him strongly, 'Stay with us'" (vv. 28–29).

Don't you love the part in a movie when the surprise is revealed? We have now arrived at that climactic moment. Allow me to set the stage for you. The men invited Jesus into one of their homes. A simple meal was prepared. They reclined at the table. Christ took the role as server. He broke the bread and called down divine favor through a benediction. He handed each of them a portion of the small loaf. As if the veil of the Holy of Holies was torn again before their very eyes, they recognized Him! Then He disappeared.

Talk about a photo I want to see in a heavenly album! Can you imagine those expressions? I have a feeling "downcast" wouldn't be an adequate description.

# DAY 197
## Luke 24:36–49

——∞∞∞——

He said to them, "Peace to you!" But they were startled and terrified
and thought they were seeing a ghost (vv. 36–37).

——∞∞∞——

I have to laugh out loud from the delightful irony that Christ's greeting
of peace nearly scared the disciples to death (see Luke 24:37). John 20:19 helps
explain why Christ's surprise visit incited such fear. The disciples were locked in
for fear of the Jews.

Luke 24:37 translates two very strong original words to describe the terror
of the disciples. Suffice it to say, they could not have been more frightened. I
think they would have run for their lives if they could have moved. Notice that
just minutes earlier they were cheering, "It is true!" But somehow when they
came face-to-face with Jesus, the sight was almost more than they could bear.

I delight in knowing our future will be somewhat similar. You and I have
banked our entire Christian lives on the fact that Jesus is very much alive, yet I
have a feeling when we actually behold Him, it will only be eternal life that keeps
us from dropping like dead men. Christ responded to the fright of His disciples
by asking, "Why are you troubled, and why do doubts rise in your minds?" The
original word for "troubled" implies a sudden disturbance of all sorts of emotions.

The original word for "doubts" in Luke 24:38 is *dialogismos*. You see in it
the word *dialogue*. The Greek word means "thoughts and directions" and can also
mean "debate." I think the disciples' minds went on instant overload, dialoguing
all sorts of debates between what their eyes suddenly saw and what their brains
could not rationalize. I can almost hear Christ saying, "Boys, you don't have a
mental file already prepared to stick this information in. This one won't compute
intellectually. Quit trying. Just behold and believe."

Christ's willingness to continue to draw us to belief totally astounds me.
At no time did He say, "You bunch of idiots! I'm sick of trying to talk you into
believing me!" When the sight of Him wasn't enough, Jesus said, "Look at my
hands and my feet. It is I myself! Touch me and see; a ghost does not have flesh
and bones, as you see I have" (v. 39).

We have often seen His hands through constant provision and glorious
intervention. We have often seen His feet as He's gone before us. Surely we have
beheld the hands and feet of Christ with eyes of faith. Let us not be afraid, but
only believe.

# DAY 198
## Luke 24:50–53

—◦◦◦◦—

While He was blessing them, He left them and was carried up to heaven. After worshiping Him, they returned to Jerusalem with great joy (vv. 51–52).

—◦◦◦◦—

Luke's Gospel pen, filled by the ink of the Spirit for twenty-four glorious chapters, appropriately runs dry on a priceless scene. A small band of motley men, whose lives had been turned every which way but loose by Jesus of Nazareth, strained for their last earthly glimpse of Him.

Thirty-three years earlier, the feet of God toddled their first visible prints on earth, a young mother's footprints chasing close behind. The walk grew rough, the path strewn with stones and thorns. Now God incarnate stepped off this planet with feet scarred and bruised. As God predicted at the fall, the ancient serpent struck Christ's heel, but on the day He ascended, all things were under Christ's feet. Jesus Christ walked the way of humanity so that humanity could walk the way of God. How beautiful the feet that brought good news.

Not one of those disciples was sorry He had come their way. Their losses were incalculable. Most of their friends. Much of their family. Their jobs. The blessings of their fathers. Physical safety. And now, a leader they could see. Yet they left the Mount of Olives with great joy, continually praising God, for their ordinary lives had been interrupted by glory.

The sufferings of this world simply could not compare to the glory He had revealed to them. It sustained and swelled them long after the visible became invisible. You and I are the spiritual descendants of Peter, James, John, and all the others who offered their lives, not for what they thought or what they hoped, but for what they knew. Whom they knew. Our faith is based on fact, beloved. Never let anyone convince you otherwise.

Jesus the One and Only—the title is His forever. He was the One and Only long before He breathed a soul into humanity, and He will continue to be the One and Only long after the last soul has been judged. He is changeless. But you and I were destined for change. So determined is God to transform us, we cannot draw near Him and remain the same. May our tenure on this planet be characterized by one simple word . . . *Jesus!*

# DAY 199
## John 1:1–5

⟨⟩

Life was in Him, and that life was the light of men.
That light shines in the darkness, yet the darkness did not overcome it (vv. 4–5).

⟨⟩

Many inspired men in Scripture confessed the glorious gain of pursuing God, but few can compete with our very own apostle John. In the totality of John's writings and in a comparison of his Gospel with the three synoptics, John has more to say about the concepts of life, light, love, truth, glory, signs, and belief than anyone else in the entire New Testament.

John has overwhelmingly more to say about God as Father than any other inspired writer. In fact, out of 248 New Testament references to God as Father, John penned 130. In impressive balance, John also has more to say about God and the world than any other inspired writer. Of the New Testament references to the world, 103 out of 206 are John's. I could go on with many examples.

My point? It's certainly not that his Gospel is better than others. Each was inspired just as God perfectly intended. The point is that in length of life and depth of love, John discovered the concept of "more." In fact, I'm convinced that a nutshell explanation for John's entire experience and perspective is intimated in one of the most profound statements of Christ ever dictated to him. Jesus said, "I have come that they may have life and have it in abundance" (John 10:10 HCSB).

Do you realize that Christ wants you to have a great life? Don't confuse great with no challenges, hardships, or even suffering. In fact, the greatest parts of my life experience have been overcoming the overwhelming in the power of the Holy Spirit. When we lay down these lives of ours, God wants us to be able to say we lived them fully. We didn't miss a thing He had for us. We had a blast with God. Just like John.

Jesus offered a lot of life; John took Him up on it. Jesus shed a lot of light; John chose to walk in it. Jesus revealed a lot of glory; John chose to behold it. Jesus delivered a lot of truth; John believed it. Jesus shed a lot of blood; John felt covered by it. Jesus lavished a lot of love; John received it. Jesus is full of everything we could ever need or desire. Thankfully, many receive, but others receive more abundantly. John was one of those.

# DAY 200
### John 1:6–13

——∞——

But to all who did receive Him, He gave them the right to
be children of God, to those who believe in His name (v. 12).

——∞——

John's Jesus is the same One who is meant to be ours: the preexistent, miracle working, only begotten Son of the Father of all creation. Years ago God revealed to me that I believed in my childhood church's Christ, who (thankfully) was a Savior for sinners, but I had hardly begun to believe in the Bible's Christ. Yes, He is a Savior for sinners and so much more! We have derived a staggering amount of our impressions of Christ from vastly incomplete if not totally unreliable sources, as sweet and respectable as they may be!

We are blessed beyond measure for every time one of these human instruments extended us reliable impressions of Jesus. I derived most of my early impressions about Jesus based not so much on what I *learned* at church as what I *saw* at church. I certainly believed Jesus saves, and that belief led me to my own salvation experience. But I believed Him for little more because I saw evidence of little more. The few marvelous exceptions marked me forever, but I wonder why so many believers believe so little of Jesus. I'm just going to say it like I see it. Either Jesus no longer does what the Bible says He did, or we don't give Him the chance.

John went out of his way to present us an all-powerful Son of God who speaks and His Word is accomplished. A Savior who not only saves us from our sins but can deliver us from evil. A Great Physician who really can heal and a God of glory who reveals His magnificence to mere mortals. And, yes, a God of signs and wonders. We've already seen John testify that one of his chief purposes in his Gospel was to testify to the signs Jesus performed so that readers would believe—not in the miracles themselves, mind you, but in the Christ who performed them.

Many claim, "The day of miracles has ceased." I don't doubt that God may employ miracles less frequently in cultures where the Word of God is prevalent, but I know Jesus Christ still performs miracles. The first reason I know this to be true is from the claims of Hebrews: "Remember your leaders who have spoken God's word to you. As you carefully observe the outcome of their lives, imitate their faith. Jesus Christ is the same yesterday, today, and forever" (Heb. 13:7–8 HCSB).

The second reason I know Jesus Christ still performs miracles is because I'm one of them. I'm not being dramatic. I'm telling you the truth. The only excuse for an ounce of victory in my life is the supernatural, delivering power of Jesus Christ. I was in the clutches of a real, live devil, living in a perpetual cycle of defeat.

Only a miracle-working God could have set me free then dared to use me. Scripture suggests no greater work exists. According to the apostle Paul in Ephesians 3:20, God "is able to do above and beyond all that we ask or think—according to the power that works in you" (HCSB). Do you see, Beloved? The most profound miracles of God will always be those within the hearts and souls of people. Moving a mountain is nothing compared to changing a selfish, destructive human heart.

Third, I know Jesus Christ still performs miracles because I've witnessed them. I have seen Him do things most people I know don't even believe He does anymore. Jesus healed a woman I know personally from liver cancer and a man I know personally from pancreatic cancer. I've seen women bear healthy children who were diagnosed inside the womb with debilitating conditions. I was in a service with a dear friend in his eighties who has been legally blind for years when God suddenly restored a remarkable measure of his sight—right on the pew of a Baptist church! Hallelujah!

Like you, I have also seen many who have not received the miracles they hoped for. I can't explain the difference except to say that God often defers to the greater glory. Sometimes the far greater miracle is the victory He brings and the character He reveals when we don't get what we thought we wanted.

On the other hand, sometimes we see little because we believe little. That's the obstacle you and I want to overcome so that we can live in the abundant blessing of Jesus Christ. When my life is over, I may not have seen Jesus perform some of the miracles the Word says He can—but let it be because He showed His glory another way and not because I believed Him for so pitifully little that I didn't give Him the chance!

When we received Christ as our Savior, you might picture that a pipe of power connected our lives to God's throne. Unbelief clogs the pipe, but the act of believing clears the way for the inconceivable! As much as John's Gospel has to say about believing, I'm not sure anyone recorded a more powerful statement than Mark. He tells us Jesus said, "Everything is possible to the one who believes" (Mark 9:23 HCSB).

Through His work on the cross and His plan before the foundation of the world, Christ has already accomplished so much for your life in heaven! But if His work is going to be accomplished here on earth where your feet hit the hot pavement, you're going to have to start believing Him—the Jesus of the Scripture.

# DAY 201
## John 1:14–18

———∞∞———

Indeed, we have all received grace after grace from His fullness (v. 16).

———∞∞———

John 1:16 introduces a key concept that will carry us through this vital part of our journey. I encourage you to memorize it! If you will receive what this verse is saying to you, your entire life experience with Jesus will be transformed.

The original word for "blessing" is *charis*, often translated "grace." This explains the King James rendering: "And of his fulness have all we received, and grace for grace." *Charis* is "that which causes joy, pleasure, gratification, favor, acceptance . . . a benefit . . . the absolutely free expression of the loving kindness of God to men finding its only motive in the bounty and benevolence of the Giver; unearned and unmerited favor."[42]

Based on John 1:14 and 1:16, then—and this definition—I believe we can accurately draw the following conclusions:

1. *Jesus is full of grace and truth.* He's the One and Only.

2. *All of us get to receive from His fullness!* Not just John the apostle. Not just John the Baptist. Jesus is full and overflowing with everything any of us who believes could possibly need or desire, and we get to receive from it!

3. *These grace gifts flowing from Christ's fullness* are not only beneficial, but they are expressions of God's favor that cause joy and pleasure!

It's high time I made a blatant confession. I am a Christian hedonist. Have been for years even before I knew what the term meant. I wish I had better words for it, but let me just say it like it is: Jesus makes me happy! He thrills me! He nearly takes my breath away with His beauty. As seriously as I know how to tell you, I am at times so overwhelmed by His love for me, my face blushes with intensity, and my heart races with holy anticipation. Jesus is the uncontested delight of my life.

I never intended for this to happen. I didn't even know it was possible. It all started with an in-depth study of His Word in my late twenties and then surged oddly enough with a near emotional and mental collapse in my early thirties. At the end of myself I came to the beginning of an intensity of relationship with an invisible Savior. No one had ever told me such a relationship existed. Now I spend my life telling anyone who will listen.

I thought I was just weird. I knew so many believers who wore Christ like a sacrifice that I thought I missed something somewhere. Don't get me wrong. Plenty of believers in the world make huge sacrifices in the name of Jesus Christ, but I'm not sure American believers can relate . . . and we can be a little nauseating when we try.

By far the biggest sacrifices I've ever made were times I chose to pursue myself and my own will over Jesus and His. I'd be a liar to tell you Jesus has been some big sacrifice for me. He is the unspeakable joy and love of my life. In crude terms, I think He's a blast.

While still in the closet, I began stumbling on other Christian hedonists. Perhaps Augustine is the most blatant historical example. Of his conversion in 386, Augustine wrote, "How sweet all at once it was for me to be rid of those fruitless joys which I had once feared to lose! . . . You drove them from me, you who are the true, the sovereign joy. You drove them from me and took their place, you who are sweeter than all pleasure."[43] My heart leaps as I read words that I, too, have lived!

Jonathan Edwards was another. In 1755 he wrote, "God is glorified not only by His glory's being seen, but by its being rejoiced in. When those who see it delight in it, God is more glorified than if they only see it."[44]

C. S. Lewis was also a fine Christian hedonist. He wrote:

> If there lurks in most modern minds the notion that to desire our own good and earnestly to hope for the enjoyment of it is a bad thing, I submit that this notion has crept in from Kant and the Stoics and is no part of the Christian faith. Indeed if we consider the unblushing promises of reward and the staggering nature of the rewards promised in the Gospels, it would seem that our Lord finds our desires not too strong, but too weak. We are half-hearted creatures, fooling about with drink and sex and ambition when infinite joy is offered us, like an ignorant child who wants to go on making mud pies in a slum because he cannot imagine what is meant by the offer of a holiday at the sea. We are far too easily pleased.[45]

Beloved, I don't care who you are or how long you've known Jesus, I am convinced we have hardly scratched the surface. So much more of Him exists! So much more He's willing to give us! Show us! Tell us! Oh, that we would spend our life in furious pursuit!

# DAY 202
## John 1:35–42

---

When Jesus turned and noticed them following Him, He asked them, "What are you looking for?" They said to Him, "Rabbi . . . where are You staying?" (v. 38).

---

Peter, Andrew, James, and John knew Christ at least by reputation based on John the Baptist's faithful ministry, and at least several of them knew Him by a prior encounter. We know from John 1, for example, that two disciples were nearby and heard John the Baptist declare Jesus to be "the Lamb of God" as He passed by (vv. 35–36). Verse 40 identifies one of these men as Andrew. Many scholars believe that John the disciple was the other, since as a rule John did not identify himself in his writings. We know for certain that Peter met Christ at this earlier time because John 1:42 tells us Andrew brought him to meet Jesus.

So when Jesus approached them at their boats, they were primed and readied by God—even if through a short period of time—to leave everything behind and follow Christ anywhere.

In fact, I'd like to suggest that just as James and John were preparing their nets, they themselves had been prepared. The word "preparing" in Mark 1:19 can also mean "repairing." The exact same word is used in Galatians 6:1 for restoring a fallen brother—"If someone is caught in a sin, you who are spiritual should restore him gently." Oh, how thankful I am that the same God who prepares also repairs and restores.

Joshua 3:5 contains a wonderful challenge: "Consecrate yourselves, because the LORD will do wonders among you tomorrow" (HCSB). God can perform a miracle in any one of us at any time, but amazing things happen when you and I are willing to get prepared for a mighty work of God. Included in that mighty work will most assuredly be what we need most—whether a fresh work, a repair, or a full-scale restoration.

As we get to know John and see events through his eyes, I trust God will be preparing us also. Let's allow God to consecrate us and lay the groundwork for something spectacular. I pray that by the time we reach the end of this book, God will be amazing and astonishing to us. Right this moment, let Jesus look you straight in the eyes and tell you that He knows who you are and who He wants to make you. That's the only way you and I will ever discover the One who calls us and the one we were born to be. Child, a great adventure awaits you.

# DAY 203
## John 2:1–5

———∞∞———

On the third day a wedding took place in Cana of Galilee. Jesus' mother was there, and Jesus and His disciples were invited to the wedding as well (vv. 1–2).

———∞∞———

I believe Jesus didn't have to have His arm twisted to attend a wedding. I happen to think He loved a good party. Still does. I am convinced Jesus' basic personality in His brief walk in human flesh was delightful and refreshingly relational.

You remember, for example, that Jesus made the disciples allow children to come to Him (Matt. 19:14). It's pretty obvious that children aren't drawn to cranky people. The Scripture also tells us that Jesus' critics complained about His eating with tax collectors and "sinners" (John 5:30) and about seeing Him partying rather than fasting (Matt. 9:14).

Why in the world have we let "partying" become associated with licentiousness? God created man and formed within him an authentic soul-need to feast and celebrate. In fact, God deemed celebration so vital, He commanded His people to celebrate at frequent intervals throughout the calendar year (Lev. 23). Let me say that again: He *commands* that we celebrate His goodness and His greatness!

So I say it's time we take the whole idea of partying back. I'm always mystified that many nonbelievers think Christians must be dull, bored, and wouldn't know a good time if it socked them in the noggin. Boy, do we have a secret! No one laughs like a bunch of Christians! My staff and I roll with laughter together at times.

I even remember a time when three of my dearest friends and I scrunched on one couch together, all holding hands. One of us had lost a daughter several days earlier to a drunk driver. But as we held on to one another for dear life, God gave us the sudden gift of the hardest belly laugh any of us had enjoyed in a long time. Unbelievers might be insulted to know that when we go to their parties, we wonder why they think they're having such a good time. (Lean over here closely so I can whisper: *I think they're boring.*)

The primary reason why celebrations around Christ's presence are so wonderful is because they are the kind intended to be sparkling refreshment to a world-worn soul. We get to attend Christ's kind of parties without taking home a lot of baggage. We don't have a hangover later or a guilty conscience. Christ-centered celebrations are all the fun without all the guilt. That's real partying.

# DAY 204
### John 2:6–11

———∞———

Jesus performed this first sign in Cana of Galilee. He displayed His glory,
and His disciples believed in Him (v. 11).

———∞———

This miracle performed in the physical realm was meant to reveal something far more glorious in the spiritual realm. Though Jesus certainly met an immediate need at the wedding, the wine represented something of far greater significance.

I believe this new wine is beautifully implied in Ephesians 5:18. Paul wrote, "Don't get drunk with wine, which leads to reckless actions, but be filled with the Spirit" (HCSB). The passage implies that the filling of the Holy Spirit does in full measure what we try to accomplish when we desire to be drunk with wine.

You see, one reason people drink too much wine is because it changes the way they feel and the way they behave. The "new wine" of Christ does the same thing, but His effects are always good. Jesus came to bring the new wine of the Spirit! Something we can drink our fill of without all the negative side effects of wine and the emptiness it leaves behind in the wake of the temporary fix.

Throughout the Old Testament, only handfuls of people had the Holy Spirit in them or upon them because under the old covenant God gave the Spirit for empowerment more than fulfillment. John's Gospel will reveal later that one of Christ's primary purposes for coming and laying down His life was to send the Holy Spirit to us—not just to walk beside us but to dwell in us. At the first revelation of Christ's glory in Cana, they had no idea that the true New Wine was on its way! The Master of our banquet saved the best of the wine for last.

Beloved, do you realize that joy and gladness are among the many gifts and services Christ brought His Holy Spirit to grant? Check it out for yourself. "The fruit of the Spirit is love, joy, peace, patience, kindness, goodness, faith, gentleness, self-control. Against such things there is no law" (Gal. 5:22–23 HCSB).

Just think! No matter how much you drink of His Spirit, against such things there is no law. Further, the more you drink, the more fully satisfied you are with love, joy, peace, and all sorts of side effects we're so desperate to achieve. To top off the goblet, instead of losing self-control, we gain it. You can't beat a drink like that!

# DAY 205
## Read John 2:12

※

After this, He went down to Capernaum, together with His mother, His brothers,
and His disciples, and they stayed there only a few days (v. 12).

※

I love the fact that Jesus talks in words and images His listeners can understand. When He said, "I will make you fishers of men" (Matt. 4:19), He obviously used terminology Andrew, Peter, James, and John could understand. He didn't use the same terminology with Philip, Nathanael, or Matthew, but I am convinced one part of the sentence applies to every single person Jesus Christ calls. "Come, follow me and *I will make you* . . ." Decades later when God had used these men to change the face of "religion" forever, they still could not boast in themselves. Christ made them the men and the influences they were.

I can't express what these thoughts mean to me. I was such a broken and scattered mess. So emotionally unhealthy. So insecure and full of fear. I am not being falsely modest when I tell you that when Christ called me, He had pitifully little to work with. I was a wreck . . . and stayed that way for longer than I'd like to admit. I have such a long way to go, but this I can say: I followed Christ, and anything that I am or have of value is completely from Him.

So how does Christ "make" a man or a woman? We will explore many ways, but the most immediate way He began building His new followers into the people He wanted them to be was by spending intense time with them and showing them how He worked.

Piecing the Gospels together in a precise chronological order is a task far too challenging for me. I'm relieved to know that it is also a little too challenging for other Bible commentators. What we do know is that Christ and His small and yet incomplete band of followers attended a wedding in Cana together very soon after their union. In fact, John 2:1 says on the third day a wedding took place in Cana in Galilee, but we can't be entirely sure what he meant. It sounds like the third day after John began to follow Jesus.

We already explored the wedding more fully when we studied the uniqueness of John's Gospel, so now I'd like you to view the verse immediately following the celebration. John 2:12 says, "After this he went down to Capernaum with his mother and brothers and his disciples. There they stayed for a few days."

Christ's family and His disciples obviously enjoyed at least a brief season of peace and harmony. I didn't give that idea any thought until researching for this study. The schism in Christ's family didn't develop until a little while later (John 7:3–5). Eventually we will behold the reconciliation brought by the power of the resurrection. For now, however, picture Christ surrounded by both His family and His new disciples.

I am fairly convinced that we don't really know people until we stay with them for a few days. Can I hear an amen? Although I'm grinning, I have almost always been more blessed than less. Not long ago, Amanda and I got stranded in Tennessee after a conference due to a serious flood in Houston. When I learned the airport was closed, I frantically called Travis, my dear friend and worship leader, and asked if he had room for two more in his van back to Nashville. Without making a single preparation for us, his young family of four graciously received us into their home for two nights. Although we were already very close friends, we bonded for life. The treasure of having part of my ministry family and part of my natural family in fellowship together was priceless.

The disciples were new on the scene. They probably didn't have quite the comfort level interacting with Christ's family for those several days that I enjoyed with my worship leader's family. Still, they got to see Christ interact with His own family—an opportunity that I think was critical. Soon they would see Him perform all manner of miracles. They already had witnessed the changing of water to wine, but the sights they would soon see would nearly take their breath away. You see, people are much harder to change than water.

As they watched this man named Jesus—this carpenter's son—as they fellowshipped with Him then witnessed His work, what do you think they saw? Consistency? Versatility? Unwavering passion? Or a lamb as often as a lion? The center of all attention? Or a teacher that became a student of all those around Him? We know they saw absolute authenticity, but how do you imagine they saw it portrayed?

Don't think for a minute that thinking about such matters is a waste of time. The more we grasp the flesh-and-blood reality of these encounters and try to imagine the intimate details the disciples witnessed in Christ the better! What we're studying isn't religious fiction or simple Christian tradition. Christ walked into people's lives and transformed them. You and I want nothing less.

# DAY 206
John 3:16–21

◦◦◦

For God loved the world in this way: He gave His One and Only Son,
so that everyone who believes in Him will not perish but have eternal life (v. 16).

◦◦◦

One of the most astonishing statistical comparisons between the Gospel of John and the three synoptics is how much more God inspired him to tell us about the world. Based on a word count comparison, Matthew mentions the world ten times, Mark five times, and Luke seven times. The Gospel of John? A whopping seventy-three times! In fact, the totality of John's New Testament contributions informing us about the world constitutes almost half the mentions in the entire New Testament. Obviously we will miss a very important concept in John's Gospel if we overlook what he tells us about the world.

Perhaps the most overwhelming is a concept to which we've grown inordinately casual: Jesus was sent by God to the world.

John 17 tells us that the Father and Son had fellowship and shared glory before the world even existed. Jesus said, "Father, glorify Me in Your presence with that glory I had with You before the world existed" (John 17:5 HCSB). In fact, I am absolutely convinced that mankind exists out of the holy passion of the Trinity to draw others into their fellowship. Thus, the plan of salvation was already completely intact before the creation of the world. Then when the Holy Trinity was ready, each member participated in the creation.

Genesis 1:1: "In the beginning God created the heavens and the earth." Stay with me here. The Word of God delineates between one little planet He called the earth and the entire rest of the universe. We have no idea what is out there. What little science documents and hypothesizes makes Genesis 1:1 inconceivably impressive.

Our solar system is in a galaxy called the Milky Way. Scientists estimate that more than 100 billion galaxies are scattered throughout the visible universe. Astronomers have photographed millions of them through telescopes. The most distant galaxies ever photographed are as far as 10 billion to 13 billion light-years away. The Milky Way's diameter is about 100,000 light-years. The solar system lies about 25,000 light-years from the center of the galaxy. There are about 100 billion stars in the Milky Way.[46] Imagine, 100 billion stars estimated in our galaxy alone, and Psalm 147:4 tells us God "counts the number of the stars; He gives names to all of them" (HCSB).

Impressive, isn't it? In the beginning God created the sun, the moon, every star, all their surrounding planets, and the earth. You and I have no idea what God's activities may have been elsewhere in the universe, but according to the Bible and as far as He wanted us to know, He picked out one tiny speck upon which to build a world. Our world. And He picked it out so that when the time had fully come, He could send His Son (Gal. 4:4).

# DAY 207
## John 4:27–38

∽∾∽

Just then His disciples arrived, and they were amazed that
He was talking with a woman. Yet no one said,
"What do You want?" or "Why are You talking with her?" (v. 27).

∽∾∽

Hear me clearly: I am pro-men. And (not but) I am also pro-women. What may come as a news flash to some is that these pros are not exclusive. I believe the biblical roles and responsibilities of men and women differ sometimes to complement and complete each other, but our places in the heart of God are the same.

Yes, Jesus speaks to women who listen. Always has. Always will. Anyone who wants to believe Christ didn't have profound encounters with women might want to skip the Gospel of John, because it supplies many detailed accounts that are abundant in meaning.

John 4:1–39, for example, introduces us to the woman from Sychar. You probably know her by the label "the woman at the well," but do you realize she was the first person to whom Jesus declared His messiahship? He led their conversation from His request for a drink to His gift to her of Living Water. The woman then became an evangelist as she returned to Sychar to proclaim: "Come, see a man who told me everything I ever did! Could this be the Messiah?" (John 4:29 HCSB).

John 8:1–11 tells of the religious leaders grabbing a woman who was taken in the act of adultery and bringing her before the Lord. There they demanded that Jesus judge her, but He refused to play their game. He knelt and drew on the ground until their consciences began to accuse them. When the crowd melted away, Christ asked the woman, "Where are they? Has no one condemned you?" When she replied, "No one, Lord," Jesus responded, "Neither do I condemn you. Go, and from now on do not sin any more" (vv. 10–11 HCSB).

John 11:17–44 recounts Jesus arriving in Bethany after the death of his friend Lazarus, and we see him dealing with the two sisters, Mary and Martha, as individuals. Martha went to meet Jesus with combined words of reproach and hope. "If You had been here, my brother wouldn't have died. Yet even now I know that whatever You ask from God, God will give You" (vv. 21–22 HCSB). Jesus calmly accepted her words and revealed Himself to her in a fresh way. "I am the resurrection and the life. The one who believes in Me, even if he dies, will live. Everyone who lives and believes in Me will never die—ever. Do you believe this?" (vv. 25–26 HCSB).

Mary met Jesus differently. She also stated her belief that Jesus could have healed her brother, but she fell at His feet weeping. In this case Jesus "was deeply moved in spirit and troubled" (v. 33). He asked where they had laid Lazarus, and

Christ wept. Then to the joy of both sisters He called Lazarus from the grave.

John 12:1–8 continues the story of Martha and, particularly, Mary. Six days before the Passover when Jesus would die, the sisters gave a dinner in Jesus' honor. Overcome by her love for Jesus and, I suspect, both motivated by a premonition of what was to come and driven by the Spirit, Mary poured perfume on Jesus' feet and wiped them with her hair. Judas Iscariot declared the gesture an extravagant waste of what could have gone to the poor. But Jesus declared Mary's action sacred in anointing Him for His burial. Matthew 26:13 wraps up this scene best with Jesus' words: "I tell you the truth, wherever this gospel is preached throughout the world, what she has done will also be told, in memory of her." Our very words at this moment continue the fulfillment of His promise.

Based on these segments—and many others we could list—three things about Christ astound me and make me fall even more in love with Him:

1. *Jesus was not ashamed to be seen with a woman.* This may not seem like a big deal, but how many of us have dated someone or even married someone who seemed ashamed at times to be seen with us? Beloved, Jesus Christ isn't ashamed to be seen with you. In fact, He wants nothing more! He's also not ashamed to talk to you. I meet so many women who are timid about sharing what they've gleaned in Bible study because they don't have much education and they're "probably wrong." Listen, the One who spoke the worlds into being has chosen you for a bride! Study His Word like someone being spoken of and spoken to! He wants your life to radiate proof that He's been talking to you. He's proud of you!

2. *Though very much a man, Jesus understood the needs of a woman.* I despise that ridiculous feminist "theology" that tries to make a woman out of God or at least make Him feminine so we can feel like we have an advocate—"someone who understands." Beloved, Christ understands us better than we do! Of course, He has a decided advantage over every other man. He wove us together in our mother's womb. Still, I'm relieved to know that I am never too needy for Christ—particularly when I'm feeling a tad high maintenance. Did you notice how personal He got in almost every scenario? He was totally unafraid of intimacy then—and He still is.

3. *Without exception, Jesus honored women and gave them dignity.* Do you see a single hint of second-class treatment? In any stretch of the imagination, can you make a woman-hater out of Jesus? Not on your life.

# DAY 208
## John 5:16–23

—∞—

"My Father is still working, and I am working also.". . . Not only was He breaking
the Sabbath, but He was even calling God His own Father (vv. 17–18).

—∞—

One of the first passionate words out of a toddler's mouth is, "Mine!" I'm not
even sure this word has to be taught. No one will argue where two-year-olds get
"No!" but where in the world do they get "Mine"? I'd like to suggest that posses-
siveness is one of the most intrinsic elements embedded in the human psyche. No
one has to learn a "my" orientation. It's intertwined in every stitch of our DNA.

God created us with a need to know that something belongs to us. From
the time we are toddlers, we begin testing what is ours by process of elimination.
Everything is "mine" until we learn from our parents what doesn't belong to
us and what can be taken from us. "No, child, that's not yours, but here's this
blanket. It is yours." In fact, perhaps we could say that maturity is not so much
disregarding our "my" orientation as learning how to appropriately recognize and
handle what is and isn't ours.

I don't know about you, but I need to know that a few things really do
belong to me. I am convinced that a certain need to possess is so innate in all
of us that if we could truly not call anything our own, our souls would deflate
with hopelessness and meaninglessness. Please hear this: ours is not a God who
refuses us the right to possess anything. He's simply protective enough of our
hearts not to encourage a death grip on things we cannot keep. He's not holding
out on us. He's not dangling carrots in front of our noses, then popping us in the
mouth when we lunge to bite the bait. Contrary to much public opinion, God is
not playing some kind of sick "I-created-you-to-want-but-will-not-let-you-have"
game with us. Quite the contrary, the Author of Life will only encourage us to
call "mine" what is most excellent. Most exquisite. So to those who receive, God
gives Himself.

Part of the human condition means that to live in any semblance of order,
we must confront a never-ending influx of "no's." In the midst of so much we
cannot have, God says to His children, "Forsake lesser things and have as much
as you want of . . . Me." While God is the owner and possessor of all things, He
freely invites us to be as possessive over Him as we desire. He is my God. And
your God. He's the only thing we can share lavishly without ever decreasing our
own supply.

# DAY 209
## John 8:48–59

◈◈◈

The Jews replied, "You aren't 50 years old yet, and You've seen Abraham?" Jesus said to them, "I assure you: Before Abraham was, I am" (vv. 57–58).

◈◈◈

We are going to examine seven claims Christ made in the Gospel of John about who He is. These seven titles are by no means the totality of His claims. They simply share several common denominators in John's Gospel that we don't want to miss. In so doing, we will find that the Gospel of John tells us more about the self-proclaimed identity of Christ than the others. Note Christ's claims of identity in the following Scriptures. No matter how many times you've seen these titles, I pray you will approach them with freshness.

• "I am the bread of life. . . . No one who comes to Me will ever be hungry, and no one who believes in Me will ever be thirsty again." (John 6:35 HCSB)

• "I am the light of the world. Anyone who follows Me will never walk in the darkness but will have the light of life." (John 8:12 HCSB)

• "I am the door of the sheep. All who came before Me are thieves and robbers, but the sheep didn't listen to them. I am the door. If anyone enters by Me, he will be saved and will come in and go out and find pasture." (John 10:7–9 HCSB)

• "I am the good shepherd. The good shepherd lays down his life for the sheep." (John 10:11 HCSB)

• "I am the resurrection and the life. The one who believes in Me, even if he dies, will live." (John 11:25 HCSB)

• "I am the way, the truth, and the life. No one comes to the Father except through Me." (John 14:6 HCSB)

• "I am the vine; you are the branches. The one who remains in Me and I in him produces much fruit, because you can do nothing without Me." (John 15:5 HCSB).

In fairly rapid succession, Jesus made a point of defining Himself a perfect seven times. I see three basic common denominators in these seven titles. Consider each with me:

1. *All seven titles are preceded by "I am."* I want you to consider the impact of these two words when emitted from the mouth of Jesus the Messiah. That's why I wanted you to look at John 8:48–59 in its entirety, focusing on verse 58, where Jesus said to His accusers, "I assure you: Before Abraham was, I am" (HCSB). The reason they reacted so violently and wanted to stone Him for blasphemy was because they knew exactly what He meant. He was identifying Himself as God. Either Jesus came as the incarnate God, or He is a liar. He cannot be anything in between.

Notice John 18:6, for example. After Judas betrayed Jesus in the garden of Gethsemane, the gathered mob asked Jesus' identity. Christ responded, "I am He," and the entire troop fell backward to the ground. I believe the reason they collapsed before Him is intimated in the original language, where the Greek word for "he" is conspicuously missing. The Interlinear Bible translates it like this: "When He said to them, I AM, they departed into the rear and fell to the ground."

You see, the rest of us could say "I am," and it would mean nothing more than a common identification. When Christ says the words "I am," they are falling from the lips of Him who is the Great I Am!

2. *The word "the" is included in each title.* Go back and read each of the seven "I am" titles, and you will find in every case Jesus said "I am *the*" rather than "I am *a*." This may seem scholastically elementary, but nothing could be more profound theologically. Just think about your own approach to Jesus Christ. Is He *a* light to you, or *the* Light? Is He *a* way for you to follow—perhaps here and there in life—or is He *the* way you want to go? Is He *a* means to the afterlife in your opinion? In other words, deep down inside do you think that several world religions probably offer a viable way to life after death and Jesus is but one of them? Or is He *the* resurrection and the life?

3. *Each of Christ's seven "I Am" statements in John's Gospel is relational.* Christ is many things. He is truly the Great I Am. He is the Savior of the world. He fulfills numerous titles in the Word of God, but I believe the spiritual implication of the seven "I am" sayings in the broad approach of John's Gospel is this: Jesus Christ is everything we need. Every one of these titles is for us! Remember, He is the self-sufficient One! He came to be what we need—not just what we need but what we desire most in all of life. The "I Am" came to be with us.

We will never have a challenge He can't empower us to meet. We will never have a need He can't fill. We will never have an earthly desire He can't exceed. When we allow Christ to be all He is to us, we find wholeness. One piece at a time. Every time you discover the reality of Christ fulfilling another realm of your needs and longings, His name is written on a different part of you, and you are that much closer to wholeness.

# DAY 210
## John 13:1–5

⸻

Jesus knew that the Father had given everything into His hands,
that He had come from God, and that He was going back to God (v. 3).

⸻

When Christ came to this planet, He forsook many of His intrinsic divine rights in order to accomplish His earthly goals. Philippians 2:7 says he "emptied Himself by assuming the form of a slave, taking on the likeness of men" (HCSB). John 1:3–4 tells us "all things were created through Him, and apart from Him not one thing was created that has been created. Life was in Him, and that life was the light of men" (HCSB). Yet Christ didn't walk around saying, "Hey, bud, do you see that dirt you're walking on? Who do you think made that?"

To our knowledge, Christ didn't sit with the disciples in the moonlight and tout His ownership over the heavens by giving them all the proper names of the stars. In alphabetical order. When we consider that Jesus Christ came to earth as the fullness of the Godhead bodily, He actually showed amazing restraint in exercising His divine rights. Matthew 26:53–54 offers one example. As the mob was arresting Him, He told Peter to put away his sword. "Do you think that I cannot call on My Father, and He will provide Me at once with more than 12 legions of angels? How, then, would the Scriptures be fulfilled that say it must happen this way?" (HCSB).

Jesus made a point of fully exercising one right, however, to the constant chagrin of the Jews. Jesus freely claimed His Sonship to the Father. None of the comparative statistics between Gospels is more staggering than the number of references to God as Father. Approximately 110 times out of 248 references to God as Father in the New Testament occur in the Gospel of John. No other New Testament book comes close.

Never lose sight of the fact that relationship came to mean everything to the apostle John. When you think about John from now on, immediately associate him as one who was wholly convinced of Jesus' love. In turn, John had much to say not only about reciprocal love but love for one another. We will see the concept only swell over the remaining course of this book. I don't believe we're off base in assuming that the priority of relationship with Christ is exactly what fitted him to receive the great Revelation.

To John, identity came from association. He very likely absorbed this philosophy from tagging along with Jesus.

Christ knew His constant references to God as His Father incited the Jews riotously, yet He was so insistent, He had to make a point. Through His actions and expressions, Christ seemed to say, "I've set aside My crown, My position, My glory, and soon I'll set aside My life for all of you. But hear me well: I will not lay down my Sonship. God is My Father. Deal with it."

Dear child of God, if you and I were as unrelenting in exercising our rights of sonship (or daughtership), our lives would be transformed. Satan would never be able to dislodge us from God's plan and blessing. You see, Christ had to make the decision to lay aside many rights, but because He retained the most important one of all, His right of Sonship, Satan could not win. Christ led many sons to glory and got to once again pick up every right He laid aside.

And as those who have received Christ's Spirit of Sonship, the same is true for us. Times may arrive when God asks us to lay down the right to be acknowledged in a situation. Or the right to give our opinion or take up for ourselves. The right to a promotion we think we deserve. The right to leave a spouse even though we might have biblical grounds. The right to withhold fellowship when the other person has earned our distance. The right to be shown as the one who was right in a situation. The right to our dignity in earthly matters. The right to our basic human rights.

But let this truth be engraved on your heart: You will never be required to lay aside your rights of sonship, nor must you ever fall to Satan's temptation to weaken your position. As long as you exercise your rights of sonship, constantly reminding yourself (and your enemy) who God is and who you are, Satan will never be able to defeat you or thwart any part of God's plan for your life. Any loss or other right God permits or persuades you to lay aside is temporary. You will ultimately receive a hundredfold in return.

Hold your position, beloved! Never let anything or anyone talk you out of exercising your rights of sonship! The very reason Satan targets us is because we are the sons (or daughters) of God. He is defeated when we refuse to back off from our positional rights. The last thing he wants to hear from you is, "I am a born-again, justified child of God, and I exercise my right to rebuke you! You, devil, are defeated. You can't take me from my Father nor my Father from me." So, say it!

God will never turn a deaf ear to you or look the other way when you are treated unjustly. As His child, you have 24/7 direct access to Him. You aren't left to "hope" He hears you, loves you, or realizes what's going on. Know it, Sister. Never view your situation in any other context than God as your Father and you as His child.

# DAY 211
## John 13:21–30

---∞∞∞---

One of His disciples, the one Jesus loved, was reclining close beside Jesus. Simon Peter
motioned to him to find out who it was He was talking about (vv. 23–24).

---∞∞∞---

John's location at the Passover meal constitutes one of the chief reasons
many scholars believe John was the youngest disciple. At the traditional Jewish
Passover, the youngest child at the table who is able to talk often sits nearest the
father or father figure and asks the traditional questions that prompt the father to
tell the story of deliverance from Egypt. The room was small enough for Peter to
ask Jesus a question even if he was seated at the opposite end of the table. The fact
that he prompted John to ask the question suggests that John may have assumed
the role as the official petitioner that evening.

I also love imagining that the youngest among them might have had the
least protocol and acted as he felt, not just according to what was proper. Hence
his leaning against Jesus. Glory! You see, there's just nothing doctrinal about
John's leaning on Jesus. It wasn't the law. It wasn't in the proverbial Passover
book of rules. John didn't have to lean on Jesus to talk to Him. Christ could hear
him just fine. John leaned on Him because he wanted to. Because he loved Him.
Because He was . . . leanable. Approachable. Downright lovable.

Both of my daughters are very affectionate, but my older is without a doubt
more proper. My youngest wouldn't know the word "protocol" if it were tattooed
on her forehead. (I hope I don't give her any ideas. She's threatened a tattoo
before.) From the clues we gather here and there, I like to think that John was
somehow the same way with Jesus. Very likely, he was the baby of this family.
And his affection for Jesus wasn't encumbered by silly things like protocol. I love
that about him.

One of our primary tasks through this journey is to explore the deep affection that flowed like a teeming brook between Jesus and John. I'll just be honest
with you. I want what they had. I want what God and David had. I want what
Christ and Paul had. If a mortal can experience it with the Immortal Invisible, I
want it. I want to know this love that surpasses knowledge so that I may be filled
to the measure of all the fullness of God (Eph. 3:19). All else is just an empty way
of life handed down by bored and unmotivated forefathers. No thanks. Give me
Jesus. If I make someone else uncomfortable, well . . . that's just too bad.

# DAY 212
## John 14:15–18

—∞—

The world is unable to receive Him because it doesn't see Him or know Him. But you
do know Him, because He remains with you and will be in you (v. 17).

—∞—

Without exception, John's Gospel equips us with more information about
the Holy Spirit than any of the synoptics. I wish somehow I could write the next
statement in neon lights upon this page to catch the eye of every reader: *The Holy
Spirit is the key to everything in the life of the believer in Christ!*

I have testified many times to my defeated Christian life through my teenage years and early twenties, even though I rarely missed a church service or
activity. I take full responsibility for my own defeat because I could have read
for myself what the churches I attended at those times did not teach me. But
although I received many wonderful treasures from the churches of my youth, I
did not learn two of the most vital keys to a victorious life: how to have an ongoing, vibrant relationship with God through His Word and how to be filled with
the power and life of the Holy Spirit. Both of these are vital concepts that the
enemy does everything he can to make us miss. The Word and the Holy Spirit
are by far his biggest threats.

One of the most revolutionary truths Christ told His disciples is in John
14:17. He told them that the Spirit of Truth at that time was living with them
but would soon be in them. Think about the repercussions of that promise. What
difference could the Spirit of God make living *in* a person as opposed to *with* a
person? Beloved, that very difference turned a band of fumbling, fleshly followers
into sticks of spiritual dynamite that exploded victoriously on the world scene in
the book of Acts. The difference is enormous! Impossible to overestimate! He
then filled them in a far more powerful expression at Pentecost in Acts 2:1–4.
These glorious events unleashed a new revolutionary economy of the Holy Spirit
for the "Church Age" and onward until the return of Christ.

The Holy Spirit now indwells every person who receives Christ as his or
her personal Savior (Rom. 8:9). Oh, that we would absorb the magnitude of that
spiritual revolution! Dear believer in Christ, the Spirit of the living God—the
Spirit of Jesus Christ Himself, the Spirit of Truth—dwells inside of you! Have
we heard these concepts so long that we've grown calloused to them?

# DAY 213
## John 14:19–21

———∞∞∞———

The one who loves Me will be loved by My Father.
I also will love him and will reveal Myself to him (v. 21).

———∞∞∞———

God has never revealed Himself to me in flames of fire from within a bush like He did to Moses in Exodus 3:2; nor have I ever seen chariots of fire like Elisha; but I have often beheld God's glory through nature. My soul is as drawn to a certain chain of mountains in the Northwest as a river is drawn to the sea. At least several times a year I feel the wooing of God to come and meet Him there. I confer with Him every day at home, but occasionally our souls crave a display of His glory that can best be seen against a less common backdrop, don't they?

Not too long ago I stayed by myself in a small place in the national park overlooking "my" mountains. Every night when I got into bed, I reminded myself that I had come for rest as well as inspiration. I'd try to talk myself into sleeping past dawn, but I never could. I rose every morning long before light, threw on a heavy coat, and drove to find a front-row seat to behold the sunrise. I rolled down my window to hear the mighty beasts of the field bugle their presence. In perfect covenant consistency, every morning God caused the rays of sunlight to baptize the tips of the mountain—then I watched until He bathed the valley as well. I was so overcome by the majesty such awesomeness suggested that I thought my heart would leap from my chest. At such a moment, Habakkuk 3:3–4 invaded my thoughts:

> *His splendor covers the heavens, and the earth is full of His praise. His brilliance is like light; rays are flashing from His hand. This is where His power is hidden* (HCSB).

God's Word suggests He can reveal Himself in numerous ways, but His ultimate revelation to man was through His very own Son, Jesus. He came to show us God in an embraceable, visible form. I believe a very important part of Christ's promise in John 14:21 is that after His departure, He would continue to reveal, manifest, or make Himself known to His followers through the witness of His Spirit and the power of His Word.

# DAY 214
### John 14:22–26

---

If anyone loves Me, he will keep My word. My Father will love him,
and We will come to him and make Our home with him (v. 23).

---

One of the most significant qualities found in God's brand of love is that
it is demonstrative. Christ directed His followers to love as He loved them. This
implies that the more we obey and love God, the more vividly we may see, experience, and enjoy demonstrations of His love. But like His disciples, we are often
unable to recognize the demonstration until we obey the wooing of the Spirit in
repentance and sprout the firstfruits of love.

I've lived an illustration that might help: God brought a darling young
woman into my life who had been through untold turmoil. Abused and misused,
she didn't trust anyone. She needed love as badly as anyone I had ever known, but
she was terribly suspicious and hard to show love to. God, however, kept insisting
that I show her the love of Jesus.

One day I said to Him, "Lord, I'm trying to be obedient, but she is just like
trying to hug a porcupine!" Over the months and years, God turned my beloved
porcupine into a puppy. I loved her throughout our relationship, but the softer
and more loving she became, the more love I was able to show her. As she grew
more loving, she could better receive the love I had for her.

On a much greater scale, I believe the principle applies to God's demonstration of love to us. I am convinced that the more we obey and love Christ
Jesus, the more He will disclose Himself to us. We are perpetually surrounded
by means through which He could show us His worth, His providence, and His
presence. But we must open the eyes of our spirit to see it—by loving Him and
obeying Him.

I am persuaded that the truth God inspired in the apostle John became the
apostle's virtual philosophy and approach to life. We have already concluded that
John forsook ambition for affection. Love became his absolute center. He was a
man who pursued obedience even when no one was watching. With his whole
being, He lived the divine conditions of John 14.

Years down the road, then, is it any wonder our immortal Savior and Lord
handpicked him when He determined to deliver the incomparable book of
Revelation? How fitting. John himself represents the ultimate human example
of his own penmanship.

# DAY 215
## John 15:1–8

—∞∞∞—

My Father is glorified by this: that you produce
much fruit and prove to be My disciples (v. 8).

—∞∞∞—

What I'm about to say is not to your pastor, your teacher, your mentor, your hero in the faith, your best friend at church, or anyone else. It's to you. Beloved, the God of all the universe has ordained that your precious life bear much fruit.

For several days we've been talking about "more." Now we're going to talk about "much." And I will repeat it as many times as I must. God hasn't appointed you to mediocrity but to a life of profound harvest. I weep for the body of Christ I love so dearly because I am overwhelmed with Paul's godly jealousy (2 Cor. 11:2) that each of you receives, savors, and celebrates what your God has for you.

I am sick of the enemy's subtle scheme to convince the masses in the body of Christ that only a few lives in each generation are truly significant. Your life was set apart for significance! Get up right this second, look in the nearest mirror, and say it out loud to that image in front of you. And while you're at it, say, "God has chosen you, and He wants to be glorified by you bearing much fruit."

I'm not saying another word until you go to that mirror. My friend, sometimes what you and I need is a good fussing at. We are not yet fully believing God! If we were, we'd be so astounded and delighted in Him and living so far beyond ourselves that we wouldn't be able to contain our joy. We somehow continue to entertain those things that hold us back from immensely productive lives.

I hope we clear a few of those obstacles out of the way through the course of this book, but I'd like to address one right away. Many think that the sins of their pasts have exempted them from tremendously fruit-bearing lives. First, if that were true, I assure you I would not be writing to you right now. Second, if we haven't repented and allowed God to restore us and then redeem our failures, we will tragically fulfill some of our own self-destructive prophecies. God is not the one holding us back from "much fruit" after failure. In tandem with the devil, we are the ones. God's primary concern is that He is glorified. Few unmistakable evidences glorify Him more than powerfully restored lives that humbly and authentically proclaim His faithfulness to the death.

# DAY 216
## John 15:9–17

—◦◦◦—

If you keep My commands you will remain in My love, just as I have kept
My Father's commands and remain in His love (v. 10).

—◦◦◦—

The Father is so adamant that we bear much fruit, He has extended practically inconceivable offers to us. As I share them with you, pardon my excitement
as I dangle a few happy participles. He offers to us:

1. *A love we can live in.* When will we get through our heads how loved we
are? Take a look at perhaps the most astounding verse in this entire segment of
Scripture: "As the Father has loved me, I have also loved you" (John 15:9 HCSB).
Try to grasp this truth as tightly as you can: Christ Jesus loves you like the Father
loves Him. He loves you like His only begotten—as if you were the only one!
Christ then follows His statement with a command: "Remain in My love." I
love the King James word for "remain"—*abide*. The term means exactly what it
implies: to dwell in His love, remain in it, tarry in it, soak in it. For heaven's sake,
live in it!

Even the most steadfast among God's servants make mistakes and foolish decisions of some kind along the way. We will always give Satan plenty of
ammunition to discourage us. But if we don't literally camp in the love of Christ,
we will talk ourselves out of untold fruit by dwelling on our own unworthiness.
Accept the fact that we are unworthy and yet lavishly loved by a God of redemptive grace.

2. *A source we can draw from.* If we were to list the kinds of things that hold
us back from immensely fruit-bearing lives, we might include "a lack of talent
or ability." But conspicuously missing in this dissertation on lives bearing much
fruit is any reference whatsoever to ability. The one requirement for a profusely
fruit-bearing life is that we abide in Christ the same way a branch remains physically attached to the vine. All we have to do is embed ourselves in Him, let
the power source flow, and He'll do the work through us. That's the secret! The
branch must remain open to the flow of the vine's life. If the branch were simply
wound around the vine tightly, it would still die without producing any fruit.

We so often have our own agendas about how we want to serve God. We
spend untold energy but never produce lavish and God-glorifying fruit. We
have to be open to the power flow and the purposed work the Vine wants to
accomplish.

3. *A Gardener we can depend on.* You've heard of personal trainers. Our
Gardener is so determined for fruitful lives to bear even more fruit, He commits
Himself as their personal pruner! Notice verse 2: "Every branch in Me that does
not produce fruit He removes, and He prunes every branch that produces fruit so

that it will produce more fruit" (HCSB). I believe this verse suggests that God works all the harder on the child who is producing fruit so she or he will produce even more.

If you are a true follower of Jesus Christ, I bet you sometimes feel like God is picking on you. Have you ever exclaimed in exasperation, "God never lets me get away with anything"? Have you ever noticed, though, that God seems particularly jealous with you? That He extracts from your life those mindless and meaningless activities that He seems to "put up with" in other believers' lives? That, dear one, is because you have proved to be a cooperative fruit-bearing child and He knows He has a prime branch through whom He can be all the more glorified.

Do you see the progression suggested in verses 2 and 5? God desires for those who bear fruit to bear *more* fruit—and for those who bear *more* fruit to bear *much* fruit! As nervous as the thought may make us, God can be trusted with a pair of shears in His hand.

4. *Joy we can revel in*. The fact of the matter is that we have been called to lives of obedience. Yes, the grace of God covers our sins as we trust in Christ's finished work on the cross. But we will not bear much fruit without obedience to our Father's will. In fact, according to John 15:10, if we don't walk closely to Him in obedience, we will never draw near enough to abide in His love. He loves us no matter what we do, but we will not be able to pitch our spiritual tents in His presence when we're disobedient. Does all this sound like a life of just serving and sacrificing?

Then you'd better read John 15:11 again. Jesus said, "I have spoken these things to you so that My joy may be in you and your joy may be complete" (HCSB). What an amazing thought! God is sovereign and could have rigged the plan to serve Him only. He could have demanded our obedience and service—or else. He didn't. Our heavenly Father is the giver of all good gifts (James 1:17). God longs to bless us with abundant life and joy. And not just any joy—Christ's joy! Perfect, full, magnetic, and contagious!

The joy of Jesus comes to the believer only one way: transfusion. Like an intravenous drip from Vine to branch! God doesn't just have more for you. He has much. Much love. Much fruit. Much joy. And in the process, the God of the universe derives much glory from one measly mortal. Who can beat a deal like that?

## DAY 217
John 16:5–11

—∞—

"When He comes, He will convict the world about
sin, righteousness, and judgment" (v. 8).

—∞—

You and I need nothing on this earth like more of the Holy Spirit. Do we need to love an unlovely person? Do we need extra patience? Could we use a little peace in the midst of chaos? Do we need to show an extra measure of kindness? Could anyone stand a little more faithfulness to God? Could anyone use a strong dose of self-discipline? How about a heaping soulful of joy? Take a look at Galatians 5:22–23. They all come with the fullness of the Holy Spirit! You see, we don't just need more patience. We need more of the Holy Spirit filling us and anointing us!

Now before anybody starts writing me letters, let me go on to explain. I realize the Holy Spirit is a person. When He comes into a believer's life at salvation, He moves in personally. We believers have the Spirit, but the infinite Spirit of God continues to pour Himself into our lives. Any given day I may enjoy a greater portion of His Spirit than I did the day before. He continues to pour out more of His Spirit from on high.

Does anyone need deep insight from God's Word? An added measure of understanding? Anyone need the eyes of her heart enlightened to know the hope of her calling? Does anyone want to fulfill God's eternal purposes for her life and think with the mind of Christ instead of the misleading mind of mortal flesh? All of these come with "more" of the Holy Spirit! (see 1 Cor. 2).

Child of God, don't just absorb this truth! Get up and celebrate it! God gives the Spirit without measure! He has all that you need. Or more properly stated, He is all that you need. Our fulfillment and greatest joy are in the flooding of the Holy Spirit of God in our lives. He is how we understand God's Word and will for our lives!

Here's a good one: Could anyone use a sharper memory? Take a look at John 14:26. "The Counselor, the Holy Spirit—the Father will send Him in My name— will teach you all things and remind you of everything I have told you" (HCSB). The Holy Spirit is the blessed Reminder. Have you ever noticed we have a very sharp memory about destructive things but a far duller memory over instructive things? We need more of the Holy Spirit! He is your key to memorizing Scripture or retaining anything biblical. Take Him up on it!

Since I began to learn what God made available to me through His Holy Spirit and what He is not only willing but eager to do for me, the level of supernatural power in my life in comparison has skyrocketed. I want the same for you! I am so jealous with a godly jealousy for you that I can hardly stand it!

# DAY 218
### John 16:12–15

—∞∞∞—

When the Spirit of truth comes, He will guide you into all the truth. . . . He will glorify Me, because He will take from what is Mine and declare it to you (vv. 13–14).

—∞∞∞—

Beloved, every one of these books and Bible studies as well as any message of value God has given me has come directly from the power of the Holy Spirit! I know better than anyone else that I am incapable of any such thing. Years ago I came face-to-face with my own self-destructive humanity, surrendered my life to be crucified with Christ, and determined to live henceforth through the resurrection power of the Holy Spirit. I certainly don't always live my days filled with the Holy Spirit, but the rule (with obvious exceptions) has become the daily pursuit of the Spirit-filled, Christ-empowered life. The difference is night and day. Do I ask for more and more of God's Holy Spirit? You bet I do! And He gives Him without measure! The beauty of His endless supply is that my portion does not take an ounce away from yours!

Now here's a word of warning. Don't confuse asking for more of the Holy Spirit with asking for more manifestations of the Holy Spirit. James 4:2–3 gives us two reasons why we don't receive: We fail to ask, and we ask with wrong motives.

We may not have experienced the fullness of God's presence and empowerment in our lives because we haven't asked. However, sometimes we ask with wrong motives or what the King James Version calls asking "amiss, that ye may consume it upon your lusts." We can have wrong motives for asking for more of the Holy Spirit. Here are a few of my own examples of wrong motives.

• If I want more of the Holy Spirit so that people will be impressed with me or so that I will feel powerful, then my motives are self-glorifying and dishonoring to God.

• If I desire a manifestation of the Holy Spirit as proof that God exists, then my motive is to prove (or to test) God rather than glorify God.

A right motive for asking for more of the Holy Spirit is that God be glorified in you and me through our effective and abundant Spirit-filled lives. Matthew coined it best: "Let your light shine before men, so that they may see your good works and give glory to your Father in heaven" (5:16 HCSB).

Remember what we learned earlier about Christian hedonism? God is most glorified in us when we are most satisfied in Him.[47] Our soul's satisfaction for God's glorification is a wonderful motive for requesting more of the Holy Spirit.

What do you need most from the Holy Spirit? Are you actively praying for more of Him toward that end?

# DAY 219
## John 19:17–27

───∞───

When Jesus saw His mother and the disciple He loved standing there,
He said to His mother, "Woman, here is your son" (v. 26).

───∞───

Have you ever looked around you at circumstances you could never have
imagined experiencing and thought, "How did we get here?"—days that you desperately wish you could drop off the calendar so you can just go back to life as it
was?

I believe that such experiences give us some concept of the way John must
have felt in the scene depicted in the nineteenth chapter of his Gospel.

Can you imagine how John's head must have been spinning? Don't you
know he wished someone would wake him up from his nightmare? Then came
a profoundly tender and emotional interchange between Jesus, John, and Mary.
Jesus assigned John to care for Mary, but be sure that you don't tag it as a warm
and fuzzy moment and try to snuggle up to it. The events John observed were
horrific. We can only appreciate the depth of the tenderness against the backdrop
of the horror.

After beating Jesus within inches of His life, they held His hands and feet
against the crude wood and fastened Him there with a hammer and three long
nails. Whether or not John saw the pounding of the hammer, heaven could hear
the pounding of his heart. At a time when any thinking man would want to run
for his life, the youngest of all the disciples stayed.

Near the cross. That's what the Gospel of John says. Above the young man
hung his world. His hero. His attachment. His future. His leader. Love of his
life. Three years earlier he had been minding his own business trying to gain his
daddy's approval with a boat and a net. He hadn't asked for Jesus. Jesus had asked
for him. And here he stood. Isaiah's startling prophecy tells us that by the time
the foes of Jesus had finished with Him, His appearance was disfigured beyond
that of any man, and His form marred beyond human likeness (Isa. 52:14).

"When Jesus therefore saw his mother and the disciple standing by, whom
he loved, he saith unto his mother, Woman, behold thy son!" (John 19:26 kjv).
Don't take it lightly. Hear it. Not the way the passion plays do it. Hear the real
thing. Hear a voice erupting from labored outburst as Jesus tried to lift Himself
up and draw breath to speak.

Every word He said from the cross is critical by virtue of the fact that Jesus'
condition made speaking harder than dying. Chronic pain is jealous like few other
things. It doesn't like to share. If a man is in pain, he can hardly think of anything
else, and yet Jesus did—perhaps because the pain of His heart, if at all possible,

exceeded the pain of His shredded frame. The look of His mother's face. Her horror. Her suffering.

Jesus gazed straight upon the young face of the one who was standing nearby. John's face. Less than twenty-four hours earlier, this face had nestled against His chest in innocent affection. John, like our Melissa, was the baby of the family . . . and he knew it. He no doubt reveled in its privilege. If anyone had an excuse to run from the cross, perhaps it was John, and yet he didn't.

Jesus saw the disciple whom He loved standing nearby. I believe indescribable love and compassion hemorrhaged from His heart. "Then saith he to the disciple, Behold thy mother! And from that hour that disciple took her unto his own home" (John 19:27 KJV).

If the cross is about anything, it is about reconciliation. "For he himself is our peace, who has made the two one and has destroyed the barrier, the dividing wall of hostility" (Eph. 2:14). The unbelief of Christ's brothers had raised a wall of hostility between them and His disciples. As Christ gazed upon His beloved mother and His beloved disciple, He saw His own two worlds desperately in need of reconciliation and a woman who no doubt was torn between the two. Simeon's prophecy to Mary was fulfilled before Jesus' very eyes: "A sword will pierce your own soul" (Luke 2:35 HCSB). How like Jesus to start stitching a heart back together even as the knife was tearing it apart. One day soon His family and His disciples would be united, but the firstfruit of that harvest stood beneath the cross of Christ. "From that hour the disciple took her into his home."

How perfectly appropriate! Right at the foot of the cross we discover the very quality that set the apostle John apart from all the rest.

I am reminded of an Old Testament saint about whom God said, "My servant Caleb has a different spirit and follows me wholeheartedly" (Num. 14:24). God didn't mean a different Holy Spirit. All of us who are redeemed have the same Holy Spirit. No, God was referring to something wonderful about Caleb's own human spirit that made him unique. I believe John had something similar. These were fallible men prone to the dictates of their own flesh just like the rest of us, but they had something in them that was almost incomparable when overtaken by the Holy Spirit. They were simply different.

# DAY 220
## John 19:28–37

—∞∞∞—

He who saw this has testified so that you also may believe.
His testimony is true, and he knows he is telling the truth (v. 35).

—∞∞∞—

You and I have arrived at a red-letter moment on which much of the remainder of our journey hinges. I am convinced we've stumbled on the thing that set John apart and made him the fertile soil into which God could sow the seeds of such a Gospel, such epistles, and such a revelation.

John remained nearby Jesus whether his leader was on the Mount of Transfiguration or in the deep of Gethsemane's suffering. John leaned affectionately upon Him during the Passover feast but also followed Him into the courts for the trials. John clung to Jesus when He raised the dead, and he clung to Jesus when He became the dead.

John was found nearby when human reasoning implied his faithful Leader's mission had failed. He could not have comprehended that the plan of the ages was going perfectly. Yet he remained. He who looked upon a face that had shone like the sun (Matt. 17:2) was willing to look upon a face bloody and spit upon. He stayed nearby during both Christ's brightest and darkest hours. The young disciple knew Jesus in the extremities. John was willing to look when others would have covered their eyes, and he beheld Him. How can we behold what we are unwilling to see?

We cannot claim to know anyone intimately whom we've not known in the intensity of both agony and elation. Anyone with eyes willing to truly behold Jesus will at times be confused and shocked by what he sees. You see, if we're willing to be taken to the extremes of His glory where intimate knowledge is gained, we will undoubtedly see things of Him we cannot explain and that sometimes disturb.

Then comes the question: Will we walk away from Jesus when from human understanding He looks weak and defeated? Do you know what I mean by that question?

When based on earthly evidence, human reasoning is left to one of two harrowing conclusions: He is either mean or weak. Think, beloved, about what I'm saying. Will we cling when our human reasoning implies evil has defeated Him? Or that evil seems to be found in Him? Will we stand by faith when human logic says to run? That's what will make us different.

# DAY 221
## John 19:38–42

There was a garden in the place where He was crucified.
A new tomb was in the garden; no one had yet been placed in it (v. 41).

Sometimes violent circumstances shake the earth beneath our feet. We feel as if a canyon has suddenly appeared and we've been hurled into it. Our emotions swing wildly, and we think we'll be torn in two. Those like Mary and John who loved Jesus most must have felt such a dichotomy of emotions at the finality of His death.

Watching someone suffer violent pain causes most loved ones to feel relief when it ends, even if death bid it cease. Then true to our self-destructive, self-condemning natures, relief often gives way to guilt. To add to the heap, the finality of the death ushers in feelings of hopelessness. Why? Because humanity has bone-deep indoctrination in the following statement: Where there is life, there is hope.

Not in God's strange economy. That day of all days, where there was death, there was hope. And strangely, even now for those of us in Christ, our greatest hope is in what lies beyond our deaths. We stand on the edge of our cliff-like emotions looking into the deep cavern of our grief, and we're sure that the jump will kill us. Yet for those of us who entrust our feeble selves to our faithful Creator, in ways I can neither explain nor describe, it doesn't. When death of some kind comes and we are willing to take it to the cross, to remain nearby, and to suffer its grief, we will also experience the resurrection.

We say, "But part of me has died with it." And indeed it has. Hear the words of Christ echo from the grave: "I assure you: Unless a grain of wheat falls into the ground and dies, it remains by itself. But if it dies, it produces a large crop" (John 12:24 HCSB). As a child bearing the name of Christ, if a part of you has died, in time it was meant to produce many seeds. Oh, Beloved, don't give up!

We hear so much talk about the phases of grief: the shock, the anger, often depression, then, finally, acceptance. We're led to believe that acceptance of death is the final stage of grief. But if we are in Christ, the final stage has not come until we've allowed God to bring forth resurrection life and many seeds from the kernel of wheat that fell to the ground. Yes, we have to come to acceptance, but not just acceptance of the death. Acceptance of the resurrection life. Don't stop until you experience it. Though it tarry, it shall come!

# DAY 222
John 20:24–31

∞∞

These are written so that you may believe Jesus is the Messiah, the Son of God, and by believing you may have life in His name (v. 31).

∞∞

In his book *Encountering John*, Andreas J. Köstenberger wrote:

> Apart from "Jesus" and "Father" there is no theologically significant word that occurs more frequently in John's Gospel than the word "believe" (*pisteuo*; 98 times). . . . Another interesting observation is that while John uses the verb "to believe" almost a hundred times, he does not once use the corresponding noun (*pistis*, "faith"). It appears therefore that John's primary purpose is to engender in his readers the act of believing, of placing their trust in Jesus Christ.[48]

Glory to God! John's Gospel doesn't just call us to belief, as if it were in the past tense and complete. In Christ we are called to be living verbs, Beloved! We are called to the ongoing act of believing! Yes, for many of us the belief that secures our salvation is past tense and complete. In other words, we have already trusted Christ for salvation, and we are now and forever secured. But tragically too many live in past-tense belief, believing God for little more from that time forward.

Believing in Christ and believing Christ can be two very different things. We begin with the former, but we certainly don't want to end there! We want to keep believing what Jesus says about Himself, His Father, and us until we see Him face-to-face.

Think of the roll call of the faithful in Hebrews 11. As eternally vital as faith is, none of these were commended for the initial faith that enabled them to enter a relationship with God. Rather, they were commended for ongoing acts of believing at times when their physical eyes could not see what God told them they could believe.

It's by no coincidence either that the same Gospel that speaks so often about the act of believing also includes the word "life" more than any other. Any of those in the great cloud of witnesses of Hebrews 11 would tell us that really living the Christian life is synonymous with really believing the God who created it.

# DAY 223
### John 21:1–7a

———∞∞∞———

"I'm going fishing," Simon Peter said to them. "We're coming with you," they told him. They went out and got into the boat, but that night they caught nothing (v. 3).

———∞∞∞———

Peter, Thomas, Nathanael, James, John, and two other disciples were all gathered in a fishing boat. My husband would tell you that seven men in your average boat is at least five too many, but Peter and the others had obviously returned to the commercial vessel where Peter had earned his living for years. He seems to have ascribed to this philosophy: when you don't know what to do, do what you used to do.

Even though the disciples must have been ecstatic to have Christ in their midst, I believe He purposely let those days become an identity challenge for them. Notice Jesus didn't hang around with them every minute He was back. He had appeared to the disciples only twice before this encounter (John 21:14).

The fact that Jesus didn't bind Himself to them during His brief post-resurrection tenure must have been confusing to them. I'm not sure they knew how they fit into Christ's plans from this side of the grave. Surely the thought occurred to them, "What need does anyone powerful enough to walk out of a tomb have for the likes of us?" They didn't understand that Christ's primary purpose during those forty days was for people to understand that He was God. Therefore, Jesus had more on His agenda than appearing only to the apostles. First Corinthians 15:5–7 lets us know Jesus appeared to over five hundred disciples.

But Psalm 46:10 tells us what to do when we're not sure where we fit in God's action plan. The psalm says, "Cease striving and know that I am God" (NASB).

Yep. Be still and know it ourselves. Don't default into our past. Don't jump the gun for our future. Just behold and know. Instructions will come when the time is right. In the meantime, just *be*—even though *being* is so much harder than *doing*, isn't it?

Thankfully, Jesus knew where to find His disciples anyway, and He interrupted their doing with His own being. John seemed to have a better grasp of what Christ had come to be than any of the others at this point. He is only attributed four words in this scene: "It is the Lord." Oh, that you and I would come to recognize what is the Lord and what is not.

# DAY 224
## John 21:7b–14

—∞—

When Simon Peter heard that it was the Lord, he tied his outer garment
around him (for he was stripped) and plunged into the sea (v. 7b).

—∞—

The second that John announced the stranger along the shoreline was
indeed Jesus, Peter jumped from the boat and swam to Him with all his might. I
realize our primary attentions have been on John in his Gospel, but I can't let this
moment pass without putting the flashlight on one of Peter's sterling moments.

In our Christian circles we so often surround ourselves with people of similar practice of faith. We have our unspoken codes. Spiritual practices that we
consider acceptable. We also agree on things that are not. Things that are weird.
Behaviors that are just, well, overboard. Then someone jumps ship and decides
he or she doesn't care what the rest of us think. Nothing is going to get between
him and Jesus.

Glory! As much as I love John, in this scene I want to be Peter!

Actually, I remember well when I began to break the unspoken code of just
how far my church compadres and I would go with this "spiritual thing." Years
ago, those closest to me charged me with going overboard far more disapprov-
ingly than others. Do you know what, though, Beloved? I wouldn't climb back in
that boat for anything. How about you? Have you jumped out of the boat of what
is most comfortable and acceptable and decided you want Jesus even if you have
to make a fool of yourself to get to Him? If not, are you ready? What's holding
you back?

Let me warn you. Intimacy with Christ doesn't always feel warm and fuzzy.
Just ask Peter. That water was cold! This scene would have taken place during the
latter part of our month of May. The days are very warm in that part of Galilee,
but the temperature drops dramatically during the night. Mind you, this fishing
trip took place before breakfast (John 21:12). No wonder the rest of the disciples
followed in the boat!

I believe Jesus esteemed Peter's impetuous determination to get to his Lord. I
am also convinced that this act was an important part of Peter's restoration. Notice
he didn't ask to walk on water. He was willing to dog paddle in ice water to get to
Jesus this time.

# DAY 225
John 21:15–23

⁂

When Peter saw him, he said to Jesus, "Lord—what about him?" "If I want him to remain until I come," Jesus answered, "what is that to you?" (vv. 21–22).

⁂

Ambition could not supply the motivation to follow Jesus where Peter would have to go. In John 21, Jesus repeated the one motivation that would suffice. Jesus said to him three times, "Simon, son of John, do you love Me?" (John 21:17).

Oh, beloved, can you see the significance? No other motivation will last! We might feed the sheep or serve the flock based on other motivations for a while, but only one thing will compel us to follow the Lord Jesus Christ faithfully to the death: *love!*

You see, our callings may differ, but if we're going to follow Jesus Christ in the power of the crucified life, our compellings will be the same. Only love compels to the death. Circumstances will inevitably happen in all our lives that will defy all discipline, determination, and conviction. Opposition will happen. Life will get hard. Only love will keep burning when everything else disintegrates into an ashen heap. Pray for this one thing more than you pray for your next breath. I am convinced love is everything.

But I wasn't the first one convinced. I simply follow in a long line of believers who failed their way into the discovery that love is the highest priority and motivating force in the entire life of faith. Generations before any of us wised up, a young disciple named John was so drawn to Christ's discourse on love that he couldn't help but listen as Jesus and Peter walked away from the others to talk.

I am convinced the conversation recorded in John 21:15–23 began in the group of eight. Perhaps in the course of the question and answer, however, Jesus quite naturally stood up, brushed Himself off, and took a few steps away from the small circle of men. Peter, unnerved by his own interpretation of the repetitive question, probably jumped to his feet and followed.

Verse 17 tells us that Peter was "grieved" because Jesus questioned his love a third time: "Lord, you know everything! You know that I love you" (HCSB). Mind you, he was still drenched to the bone from his zeal. Jesus then prophesied the reason why Peter's love for Him would be so critical. Peter would be asked to glorify God by giving his own life. Only love would make him willing. Then, as if to say, "Knowing all this and with your eyes wide open," Christ reissued the call, "Follow me!" Don't downplay it for an instant. The cost of the call was huge.

We don't know what caused Peter to suddenly look behind him and see John following them. Perhaps John stepped on a branch that had fallen to the ground. Perhaps he groaned audibly when he heard Christ foretell his closest friend's future. But I don't believe John trailed them out of selfish curiosity. I think he sensed the enormity of the concept the risen Teacher was teaching through this emotional interchange.

This was no tiptoed eavesdropping. I think he was drawn to the conversation like a magnet. I believe Scripture will prove that John, perhaps like no other disciple in that circle, assimilated the profound implications of what his beloved Savior was saying. "You are My called ones. You have tough futures ahead of you, but the glory God will gain will be immeasurable. Love is the only motivation that can afford this kind of cost."

When Peter saw John, he asked, "'Lord—what about him?'" Oh, at times like these, how I wish we had the Bible in its completely inspired and original form on videotape! We would be far better equipped to interpret a scene accurately if we could see the expressions on the face of the speaker and hear his tone of voice. Since we have no such help, words like Peter's may have as many different interpretations as I have commentaries. I'm looking at two different commentaries right this moment, and each says something different about Peter's motivation for asking this question.

No matter what your interpretation may be, I think we all can admit that the question plagues each of us at times, whatever our reason for asking. Perhaps God has called you to suffer some pretty difficult circumstances while another seems to flourish in relative ease. Or perhaps your heart has broken for someone who works so hard and serves so diligently, but difficulty is her constant companion. Maybe one of your children has seemed so blessed and gifted by God and you keep looking at the other and asking, "Lord, what about him?"

Beloved, over and over Jesus tells us, "You can trust Me!" In this scene He is saying to His present-day disciples, "You can trust Me with you, and you can trust Me with them. I am the same God to all of you, but I have a different plan for each of you. You won't miss it if you keep following. Remember, I've been a carpenter by trade. Custom blueprints are My specialty. God's glory is My goal. Now fill your canteen to the brim with love and follow Me."

# DAY 226
### John 21:24–25

—∞∞∞—

There are also many other things that Jesus did, which,
if they were written one by one, I suppose not even the world itself
could contain the books that would be written (v. 25).

—∞∞∞—

In the very early years of the New Testament church, Eusebius penned the following statement from Clement of Alexandria: "John, last of all, conscious that the outward facts had been set forth in the Gospels, was urged on by his disciples, and, divinely moved by the Spirit, composed a spiritual Gospel."[49] If Clement was accurate, John was familiar with the synoptic Gospels and had neither the desire nor a compelling of the Holy Spirit to repeat the biographical approach of Matthew, Mark, and Luke. The Gospel of John shares only about 10 percent of its content with the other Gospel writers. Clement did not mean all four were not equally inspired. He simply suggested that the last Gospel can draw us further into spiritual truths.

Though John's approach is vast and deep, my Greek teacher tells me that John's Greek is the most easily read of all the New Testament books. Perhaps Augustine had these facts in mind when he wrote, "John's Gospel is deep enough for an elephant to swim and shallow enough for a child not to drown."[50] So whether we're elephants or children in our relationship to the Word, you and I can splash to our delight in the living water of this Gospel.

Like several other New Testament books, the end of this Gospel explains why the book had a beginning. I never hear this verse (John 21:25) without thinking about my first guide in Israel who told me that the ancient Hebrews often spoke in pictures and images. He said, "For instance, we would read John's intent in this final verse like this: 'If all the trees of the forest were quills and the oceans ink, still they could not record all Jesus did.'" Ah, yes! That's my kind of wording!

Whatever your preference in rhetoric, we can conclude from John's ending that the elements shared in the pages of his Gospel were purposefully selected by the leadership of the Spirit working through the personality and priorities of John. No other Gospel writer surpasses his determination to express Jesus' absolute deity. John wrote his Gospel so that the reader would behold truth from an utterly convinced eyewitness that Jesus Christ is the uncontested Christ. The Messiah. The Son of God.

# DAY 227
## Acts 1:1–11

—⧲—

*Why do you stand looking up into heaven? This Jesus,*
*who has been taken from you into heaven, will come in the same way*
*that you have seen Him going into heaven (v. 11).*

—⧲—

Luke begins the Book of Acts, the companion volume to the Gospel of Luke, at the end of Christ's earthly tenure. Luke tells us Jesus had showed Himself to be alive "by many convincing proofs, appearing to them during 40 days and speaking about the kingdom of God" (Acts 1:3 HCSB). Now at the end of that time, Christ and His disciples gathered at the Mount of Olives.

Try to imagine being one of the eleven on the hillside that day. Verse 11 seems to imply they were all standing, so imagine that they were basically eye to eye with Jesus, not letting a single word from His mouth fall to the ground. Jesus promised them the power of the Holy Spirit. Then without warning the disciples realized that they were glancing somewhat upward as He seemed a tad taller. As He rose a head above them, surely some of them looked down and saw that His feet were no longer on the ground. Luke 24:50 tells us Christ was blessing them as He lifted off the ground. Can you imagine what they were thinking and feeling?

Perhaps by now your imagination has drawn a rough sketch of the apostle John on the canvas of your mind. Picture him and the others bug-eyed with their mouths gaping open. Had my grandmother been one of the disciples (a frighteningly funny thought), she would have stood there saying, "Now, don't that just beat all?" I feel sure they said something comparable in Aramaic.

Just about the time they might have tried to rub the supernatural sight out of their eyes, God threw a cloudy cloak of *shekinah* glory over His beloved Son and swept Him home. Oh, don't you know the Father had been watching the clock of earth for that precious moment to finally arrive? While Christ was no prodigal, He was most assuredly a son who had journeyed to a foreign land. I can almost hear the Father say to His servants, "Quick! Bring out the best robe and put it on him; put a ring on his finger and sandals on his feet. Then bring the fattened calf and slaughter it, and let's celebrate with a feast, because this son of mine was dead and is alive again" (Luke 15:22–24 HCSB). Had the angels not broken the stare, the remains of eleven stiff carcasses might still be on the Mount of Olives today.

## DAY 228
### Acts 1:12–14, 2:1–8

—∞∞∞—

When the day of Pentecost had arrived, they were all together in one place.
Suddenly a sound like that of a violent rushing wind came from heaven (vv. 1–2).

—∞∞∞—

You are probably very familiar with the scene described in these verses, but sometimes overfamiliarity can be the biggest treasure thief of all. Rewind the verses again, and let's play them in slow motion.

Scripture tells us the disciples' return to the city after observing Christ's ascension on the Mount of Olives was a "Sabbath day's journey" (Acts 1:12), which would have been about three-fourths of a mile. I have walked that brief trek a number of times, and it is straight downhill until you ascend back up the temple mount to the city gates. You can hardly keep from walking fast due to the incline, but somehow I'm imagining their mouths were traveling faster than their feet. (You're imagining that mine was too!)

We read that the disciples went upstairs to the room where they were staying (Acts 1:13). The definite article and the emphatic arrangement of the words in the Greek sentence structure indicate that the location was well-known and highly significant to the disciples.[51] In the days that followed, the now eleven apostles were joined for prayer by several women, Mary, and Jesus' siblings. Acts 1:15 shows Peter speaking to that first New Testament cell group that numbered 120 people.

You may attend a church about this size and wonder with frustration what God could do with such a small group of people. Dear One, when the Holy Spirit falls on a place, it doesn't matter how small the group—things start happening! Remember, the Holy Spirit comes in order to get results! And in light of Acts 2, we know what can happen when the Holy Spirit interrupts a prayer meeting.

Now I want you to come with me on one of my favorite journeys. Open your Bible to Leviticus 23—(I'll wait on you)—and look at the headings that appear there, if your Bible contains those. This awesome Old Testament chapter records the annual feasts God appointed to Israel. I am convinced every one of them is ultimately fulfilled in Jesus Christ. In the context of this chapter, we'll emphasize three.

The most important of the Jewish feasts was (and is) Passover (Lev. 23:4–8). I so love the last few words in 1 Corinthians 5:7—"Christ our Passover has been sacrificed" (HCSB). We can easily see the connection that Jesus is the fulfillment of all the Passover lambs slain in history. What a glorious connection between the Old and New Testaments!

The feast that immediately followed Passover was Firstfruits, when a sheaf of the first grain of the harvest was waved before the Lord for His acceptance

(Lev. 23:11). This was the day after the Passover Sabbath, obviously falling on a Sunday. First Corinthians 15:20 clearly says that the resurrection of Jesus was the firstfruits. "Now Christ has been raised from the dead, the firstfruits of those who have fallen asleep" (HCSB).

Fifty *(pente)* days after Passover came the Feast of Weeks, later called Pentecost. It was the celebration of seven weeks of harvest. The one sheaf waved on Firstfruits turned into an entire harvest celebrated seven weeks and one day later. "But each in his own order: Christ, the firstfruits; afterward, at His coming, the people of Christ" (1 Cor. 15:23 HCSB). The Feast of Weeks was the presentation of an offering of new grain to the Lord (Lev. 23:16). In other words, it was the celebration of harvest reaped.

Now do you see the significance of what happened on Pentecost? Fifty days earlier, Christ the Passover Lamb had been crucified. On the day of Firstfruits—that very Sunday morning—His life was waved acceptable before God as the firstfruit from the dead. Fifty days after Pentecost, the Holy Spirit came just as Christ promised. And He came to show off! He revealed His all-surpassing power in simple jars of clay that day. The Holy Spirit never comes just to show off, however. He comes to show off and bring results: "Every day the Lord added to them those who were being saved" (Acts 2:47 HCSB).

Beloved, I present to you the first harvest reaped by the life, death, and resurrection of Jesus Christ our Lord. That's Pentecost! And even now I believe we are still living in the continuing harvest of Pentecost. Christ tarries only so that the harvest can reach its peak ripeness and be reaped to the glory of God. He does not will for any to perish but for all to come to repentance (2 Pet. 3:9). He desires everyone. He forces no one. He will not wait forever.

One day the ultimate Feast of Trumpets (Lev. 23:23–24; 1 Thess. 4:16) will come, and we will meet Jesus in the air. Then one day the books will be opened and closed for the last time, and the final judgment will take place (Rev. 20:11–15). The Day of Atonement will be past (Lev. 23:26–27; Rom. 3:23–25). Those who were covered by the blood of the Passover Lamb will tabernacle (Lev. 23:33–34) with God forever and ever . . . and so shall we ever be with the Lord (1 Thess. 4:17).

I feel like getting started a little early. I'm going to go put on some praise music, and I may just slip on my dancing shoes!

# DAY 229
## Acts 3:1–10

—⊶⊷—

When he saw Peter and John about to enter the temple complex, he asked for help.
Peter, along with John, looked at him intently and said, "Look at us" (vv. 3–4).

—⊶⊷—

What you have in this chapter of Scripture is a pair of mighty fine servants. Allow me to highlight a few things I love about Peter and John in this scene.

1. *They cherished their heritage.* Please don't miss the fact that the New Testament church was Jewish! According to Acts 2:46 the believers met daily in the temple courts. Acts 3 opens with Peter and John on their way to the three o'clock prayer time at the temple, which coincided with the evening sacrifice. The thought never occurred to them to cast off their Judaism for their new faith in Christ. For heaven's sake, Jesus was Jewish! Nothing could have been more absurd. Their Messiah had fulfilled their Jewish heritage. They were no longer obligated to the letter of the Law because Christ had met its righteous requirements. They were free, however, to enjoy its precepts and practices as expressions of their faith in Jesus.

Can you imagine how belief in Christ and their newfound knowledge of Jesus as the answer to every symbolic practice spiced up their participation? Suddenly the black-and-white of their ritual prayer services turned Technicolor with the life of the Spirit. I snicker when I think of observers at Pentecost thinking the disciples must have been drinking. Don't you know they secretly wanted a sip of whatever the believers were having?

Try to grasp this, though: God cherishes your heritage, too. You may balk, "What are you talking about? My past is horrible!" Listen carefully, Beloved. We are no longer under the law and authority of our pasts, but like Peter and John we are also free to use them as they lend expression to our faith in Jesus. As much as you might not want to hear this, you couldn't become the servant God is calling you to be without the threads of your past being knitted into the Technicolor fabric of your future.

Still not convinced? Perhaps you're thinking, "I'd take Peter and John's Jewish heritage over mine any day!" Wonderful! Because in addition to your own, you have their heritage, too! Behold what Galatians 3:29 says about you: "If you are Christ's, then you are Abraham's seed, heirs according to the promise" (HCSB). I love that Peter and John cherished their heritage.

2. *Peter and John understood true religion.* They were not so busy getting to prayer meeting that they missed the beggar at the gate. Don't miss the significance of the location at the gate called Beautiful. Leave it to God to appoint a bitter reality in our "beautiful" scene. Try as we may to avoid the misery, misfortune, and injustice around us, they will find us, even in cities filled with gated, extravagant

"planned communities" with walls around them to keep the niceties in and the unpleasantries out.

Peter and John could have glanced at the nearest sundial and said, "Oops! We're almost late for prayer meeting. Beg on, brother!" Instead, Peter looked straight at the man as did John (Acts 3:4). Refreshing, isn't it? I'm not much for looking suffering and poverty straight in the face. I'll face it, all right. But I like to look slightly to one side or the other. Not Peter and John. They looked straight at him and likewise demanded that he look straight at them.

3. *Peter and John gave what they had.* I love the words in the King James: "Silver and gold have I none; but such as I have give I thee: In the name of Jesus Christ of Nazareth rise up and walk" (Acts 3:6). God never asks us to give what we don't have! Somehow I'm relieved by that assurance.

4. *Peter took him by the hand and helped him up.* Peter and John knew better than anyone that the power to heal the man came solely from the Holy Spirit. The man wasn't healed because Peter took him by the hand and helped him up. To me, the tender representation here is that Peter offered the man a handful of faith to help him get to his feet. After all, this man had been crippled all his life. What reason did he have to believe he could be healed? All he thought he wanted was a little money. When the beggar grabbed on to Peter's hand, he felt the strength in his grip. The confidence of his faith. In one clasp, Peter offered a handful of faith, and that was all the man needed to come to his feet.

Oh, Beloved, can you see him? Close your eyes and watch! Watch the beggar jump to his feet, his tin cup tumbling down the temple steps and the few measly coins spinning in the afternoon sunshine. Look at the expression on his face! Watch him dance on legs thin from atrophy. Look! Look straight at him! That's him jumping and praising God through the temple courts. Laugh over the horrified expressions on pious faces. Look for the others in the crowd who are ecstatic with joy and decide to grab a handful of faith for themselves.

5. *Peter and John took no credit for the miracle.* After all, if man can do it, it really isn't a miracle, now is it? Miracles are from God . . . for the likes of crippled man. Someone reading today has been begging God for trivial things like silver and gold when God wants to raise her to her feet to jump, dance, and praise Him. Why do we want God to help us stay like we are? Grab a handful of faith and be changed!

# DAY 230
## Acts 5:27–42

—∞∞—

Gamaliel, a teacher of the law who was respected by all the people . . . said to them, "Men of Israel, be careful about what you're going to do to these men" (vv. 34–35).

—∞∞—

One of the most wonderful concepts in the Word of God concerns the plan He has for our lives. In Galatians 1:15, Paul described God as the One "who from my mother's womb set me apart and called me by His grace" (HCSB). Yes, God had a plan for Saul from birth. Nothing in the young man's life would be a waste unless he refused to let God use it.

In hindsight, then, it's no wonder that Saul took a seat in the classroom of the rabbi Gamaliel, grandson of the great Hillel—names of considerable importance in the history of Judaism. Gamaliel continues to be so highly esteemed in Judaism that even the rabbi I interviewed for this writing spoke of him with genuine familiarity. So highly revered was Gamaliel that the Jews referred to him as "the beauty of the law."[52]

All of Saul's religious training, his countless hours spent in Scripture and study, and his brilliance in spiritual matters would all be parts of God's ornate plan. God would use what Saul learned at the feet of Gamaliel, who was "clearly a remarkable man—the first to whom the title Rabban (Master) was given."[53]

He was almost liberal in comparison to many of his contemporaries. Bighearted, wise, and open-minded, Gamaliel had been raised on the teachings of his grandfather Hillel, whose words often had a remarkable similarity to the Greatest Rabboni who would ever live, Jesus Christ. "Judge not thy neighbour until thou art in his place; . . . my abasement is my exaltation; he who wishes to make a name for himself loses his name; . . . what is unpleasant to thyself that do not to thy neighbour; this is the whole Law, all else is but its exposition."[54] Do those words sound familiar? God in His wonderful wisdom made sure that the law was taught to Saul with a touch of rare grace.

God included a sample of Gamaliel's teachings in the passage you read from Acts 5. During the early days of the young church, the Jewish officials wanted to put the apostles to death, but Gamaliel advised them: "Stay away from these men and leave them alone. For if this plan or this work is of men, it will be overthrown; but if it is of God, you will not be able to overthrow them. You may even be found fighting against God" (vv. 38–39 HCSB). Obviously Saul sat at the feet of one of Judaism's most grace-filled teachers.

# DAY 231
## Acts 6:8–15

---

Some from Cilicia and Asia came forward and disputed with Stephen. But they were unable to stand up against the wisdom and the Spirit by whom he spoke (vv. 9–10).

---

No messenger could run quickly enough to satisfy Saul's curiosity about events in Jerusalem. I suspect he kept abreast of the growing menace facing his fellow Pharisees. Finally the sightings of Jesus ceased, but His followers circulated a preposterous account of His ascending into the heavens. The Pharisees really didn't care how He left. They were just glad He was gone. "If only we'd come up with that body," they must have fretted. You can be sure students and teachers debated every conceivable theory.

A few no doubt wondered, "What if Jesus really did come back from the dead?" After all, they remembered that unfortunate Lazarus incident. How convenient it would have been for the Pharisees if the stir had simply died down. Instead, as the months passed, the number of Jesus' followers grew, as did their boldness.

Saul was probably disgusted over the way the Pharisees had mishandled the problem. If he wanted it done right, he'd obviously have to do it himself. So Saul packed his things and headed for Jerusalem, salivating for the chance to be the hero. Saul arrived in Jerusalem just in time to hear an infuriating speech from a man named Stephen.

Acts 6:8 says Stephen was a man full of God's grace and power who "was performing great wonders and signs among the people" (HCSB). When Saul arrived, his fellow Jews were trying to debate the follower of Christ, but Stephen's passionate love for Jesus was tying a group of empty, legalistic Pharisees in knots.

Many of us remember our own agony of emptiness. And right here on earth's miserable sod, Stephen was full—not just because he'd accepted Jesus as Savior, but because he had surrendered his whole life to Christ's will and purpose. The more Stephen poured out his life for Christ, the more Christ poured His life into Stephen.

Stephen was full of faith, full of God's grace and power. Only a person full of the Holy Spirit can possess the kind of power Stephen displayed and yet remain full of God's grace. You see, a person full of the Holy Spirit cannot be full of self. Pride never accompanies power in the fully yielded life.

Stephen showed biblical meekness—the power of God in a loving package—but his witness infuriated Saul's fellow Jews. So they cooked up some false charges against Stephen, much as they had against Jesus.

They brought Stephen before the Sanhedrin and confronted him with false witnesses. When those sitting in the Sanhedrin looked at Stephen, they got a shock. "His face was like the face of an angel" (Acts 6:15).

I wonder if they thought of Moses. Scripture says when he came down from Mount Sinai, "his face shone as a result of his speaking with the Lord" (Exod. 34:29 HCSB). Or did they recognize the marks of wisdom as indicated by King Solomon: "A man's wisdom brightens his face, and the sternness of his face is changed"? (Eccles. 8:1 HCSB).

Whatever the Jewish leaders thought, I doubt they expected what they got next. Stephen stood accused. His life literally hung in the balance. But instead of placating his accusers or defending himself, Stephen preached one of the most classic sermons in history. He rehearsed his and their Jewish history, showing at every point how God had prepared for and sent His Son. Read Acts 7:1–53, and you can join Saul in the crowd as he listened to Stephen's speech before the Sanhedrin.

Obviously Stephen was not playing the part of a politician. He referred to those in his audience as "stiff-necked" with "uncircumcised hearts and ears" (v. 51). Finally they covered their ears, dragged him out of the city, and began to stone him.

Before we leave Stephen, don't miss a final detail that may have planted the seed of the gospel even in a zealous young Pharisee's heart. While they were stoning him, Stephen cried out, "Lord, do not hold this sin against them" (Acts 7:60). As we walk through the ministry of Paul the apostle, remember the forgiveness voiced by a dying believer. In a human sense, that one sentence may have borne more fruit than any from that day to this. Stephen's words of forgiveness were to have a permanent impact on Saul. The seed might have taken a while to germinate, but the rabbi from Tarsus would never escape the witness of Stephen.

When I think of my life, I think of all the Christians whose witness has shaped me. When I get to heaven, I know I want first to see my Savior, but when I've spent a few centuries at His feet, I wonder who else I'll want to see. I'd like to take a basin and a towel to wash the feet of those who have meant so much to me here. I think Stephen has a high place on the "wash list" of Saul of Tarsus.

# DAY 232
## Acts 7:54–8:1

—∞∞∞—

They threw [Stephen] out of the city and began to stone him.
And the witnesses laid their robes at the feet of a young man named Saul (v. 58).

—∞∞∞—

The Bible mentions Saul for the first time in Acts 7:58. "The witnesses laid their robes at the feet of a young man named Saul" (HCSB). Remember him in this role of coat-watcher, because it's the last time you'll see it. Saul's zeal quickly took him on to active persecution of the followers of Jesus.

Yes, Saul was there, giving approval to Stephen's death. The original Greek word for approval is *suneudokeo*. Are you ready for this? It means "to take pleasure with others." It is a word sometimes used of both parties in a marriage who are mutually pleased with something (see 1 Cor. 7:12–13). Applying the original meaning to Saul's actions, the scene becomes clearer. He was pleased with their actions, and they were pleased with his approval. A mutual admiration society. To provide further startling clarity, consider that the verb tense of the word describing Saul's action expresses continuous or repeated action. In other words, Saul was virtually cheering throughout the entire exhibit. He didn't just give his approval when Stephen breathed his last. He cheered at every blow, like points on a scoreboard.

As Jesus watched, He didn't miss a single nod of Saul's phylacteried head. Remember, Christ was up on His feet at the time (see v. 56). Can you imagine the alloy of emotions He must have experienced as He looked on the two key players in the kingdom that day? One *for* Him; one *against* Him. One covered in blood; the other covered by prayer shawls. One who could not save himself from men; the other who could not save himself from sin. One dead in body but alive in spirit; the other alive in body but dead in spirit. One loved by God; and the other loved by God. Grace, grace, God's grace.

Just a day in the life of a man named Stephen. A shooting star. He had one brief performance. One chance on stage. But it was absolutely unforgettable. As the curtain fell on his life, he received a standing ovation from the only One who really mattered. I have a feeling that seconds later the two of them hadn't changed positions much. Christ was still on His feet. Stephen was still crumpled to his knees. How sweet to imagine the first heavenly words he heard that day: "Welcome, Stephanos, My joy and My crown."

# DAY 233
## Acts 8:1–13

---

So those who were scattered went on their way
proclaiming the message of good news (v. 4).

---

Earlier in the book of Acts, we witnessed the New Testament church gathering often for prayer in the temple courts. But the disciples soon faced a virtual end to their freedom to practice their faith unafraid on temple grounds, as the religious leaders threatened Peter and John "not to preach or teach at all in the name of Jesus" (Acts 4:18 HCSB).

Over the next several chapters, persecution increased like stones pummeled from the fists of a crazed mob. The reality of the religious establishment's intentions rose frighteningly to the surface as Stephen fell to his knees. I am convinced he was bloodied and bruised by a gnawing and growing paranoia in their souls: What if they were wrong about Jesus of Nazareth? What if they did crucify the Son of glory? They would do everything they could to silence the mouths of those who made them question their own actions.

But the Sanhedrin underestimated the tenacity of Christ's unschooled and ordinary followers, who in effect inverted their muzzles and made them megaphones. Acts 8:1–4 tells of God's unusual method of spreading the gospel. In *The Two St. Johns of the New Testament*, James Stalker wrote, "Not infrequently it was by persecution that the new faith was driven out of one place into another, where, but for this reason, it might never have been heard of; so that the opposition which threatened to extinguish the fire of the Gospel only scattered its embers far and wide; and wherever they fell a new fire was kindled."[55]

What amazing providence! When Christ told His disciples that they would receive power and become witnesses not only in Jerusalem but to the uttermost parts of the earth, they never expected His means! No, His ways are not our ways. Our ways would always be comfortable. Convenient. Certainly without hurt or harm. We would always ask that God use the favor of man to increase our harvests. Not the fervor of opposition.

If you've walked with God very long, I have little doubt He has used what you perceived as a very negative means to achieve a positive result. I suspect that God has allowed you to experience a fence pushed down painfully in your life to expand His horizon for you. God is faithful, isn't He? Even when He turns the ignition on a holy bulldozer to plow down a confining fence.

# DAY 234
## Acts 8:14–25

---

When the apostles who were at Jerusalem heard that Samaria
had welcomed God's message, they sent Peter and John to them (v. 14).

---

Does the location of Samaria and its relationship to John ring a bell of any
kind to you? The first bell this reference probably rings is the word Christ spoke
over the eleven disciples in Acts 1:8 before His ascension. I'd like to suggest that
when Christ made the proposal that His disciples would be witnesses in Samaria,
He raised a few eyebrows. Jerusalem? No problem. Judea? Absolutely. Ends of
the earth? We're Your men, Jesus. But Samaria? Jews despised the Samaritans!
If Gentiles were the target of the Jews' prejudices, then the Samaritans were the
bull's-eye. And the feelings were mutual. Samaritans were considered by most
Jews to be a mongrel breed. They were border people who lived in the strip of land
between the Jews and the Gentiles. The Jews didn't associate with the Samaritans
(John 4:9).

The idealists among us might be thinking, "But surely since they followed
Christ, the disciples didn't have those kinds of prejudices toward people." Luke
9:51–56 gives a far more realistic picture. Our friends James and John wanted to
call down fire on a Samaritan village because of a small slight. Don't assume they
were being overdramatic and didn't really mean what they were saying. That Jesus
took great offense to their suggestion is clear as He turned on His heels and gave
them a swift rebuke.

Yes, Jesus saw something lethal in James and John's hearts that day. But
instead of threatening His childish followers with a dose of their own medicine,
Jesus chose a far more effective route. In Acts 8:14, Jesus arranged to assign John
to be an ambassador of life to the very people he volunteered to destroy. Don't
think for an instant John's assignment was coincidental. Even as the words fell
from Jesus' lips in Acts 1:8, He may very likely have looked straight at John when
He said, ". . . and Samaria."

Earlier I mentioned our naïveté to think followers of Christ are automatically void of prejudices. Whether our preferred prejudices are toward denominations, people of other world religions, colors, or economics, they are usually so
deeply ingrained in us that we just see them as "the way we are" rather than as
sin. But make no mistake—prejudice is sin. The prejudgment and stereotype of a
grouping of people is sin. Plain and simple.

One of God's redemptive tools for dealing with prejudice is appointing His
guilty child to get to know a person from the group she or he has judged. I was
reared in one denomination and had very few if any relationships in my young
life with anyone outside of it. Much prejudice evolves from pure ignorance, and

I grew up judging some groups of people that I simply didn't understand. But God wasn't about to let me stay in my bubble, because He intended to develop in me a heart for the entire body of Christ. His redemptive way of accomplishing His goal was to place me in the position of getting to know others who practiced their Christian faith in ways that differed from mine.

The most obvious work God did in my life involved a woman from one of those churches that my old church would have considered maniacal and unsound. I was in my twenties and "accidentally" developed a friendship with her before I knew where she went to church. I fell in love with her heart for God. She had such a love for His Word, and we boasted in Him often and developed a deep friendship.

When I found out her denomination, I was stunned. She wasn't crazy. She wasn't a maniac. She wasn't unsound. When my other friends would make fun of people from that church, I couldn't bring myself to join in anymore. The jokes weren't funny.

I don't think for a second John missed the point when the apostles sent him and Peter to the Samaritans. He came face-to-face with them. They, too, were created in the image of God. They, too, loved their children and worried over their welfare. They, too, bruised when they were hit and wept when they were sad. They seemed so different from a distance. Somehow, up close and personal, they didn't seem nearly so . . . weird. Then something really amazing happened. "Peter and John laid their hands on them, and they received the Holy Spirit" (Acts 8:17 HCSB).

Well, well, well. They got their wish after all. They *did* call down fire on the Samaritans. The kind of fire that destroys things like hate. Meanness. Prejudice. For those who let this Holy Fire consume them. The kind of fire that destroys the old and births the new. Our God is a consuming fire, and that day He lit the hearts of Samaritans at the hands of Jews.

I want to say something that sounds simple, but it is so profound to me right at this moment: How I praise God that we—sinful, selfish, ignorant mortals—can change. John wasn't stuck with his old prejudices. God neither gave up on Him nor overlooked the transgression. God was gracious enough to push the envelope until change happened. Acts 8:25 concludes the segment by saying that Peter and John "traveled back to Jerusalem, evangelizing many villages of the Samaritans" (HCSB). How like Jesus. He turned John's prejudice into a fiery passion.

# DAY 235
### Acts 9:1–9

Saul got up from the ground, and though his eyes were open, he could see nothing.
So they took him by the hand and led him into Damascus (v. 8).

If you asked me today what I question most at this point in my journey with Christ, my answer would not be, "Why do bad things happen to good people?" Nor would it be, "Why have You allowed me this suffering?" It would most definitely be, "Why did You call me? With all my failures and frailties, why do I have the privilege of loving You, of knowing You the little that I do?"

As the blinding light falls suddenly on a murderous persecutor, we may be left in the dark to understand why we each have been called; but our eyes will be opened to the One who called. And we will sigh and confess, "How very like Him."

Dr. Luke's account of Saul's conversion is probably quite familiar to you. In my mind's eye I can just see young Saul strutting around Jerusalem, determined to make a name for himself as a hotheaded rabbi seeking authorization to arrest followers of Jesus in Damascus and return them to Jerusalem. He was on his journey when God intervened and knocked him off his donkey. Jesus asked Saul, "Why are you persecuting Me?" (Acts 9:4 HCSB). This encounter left a blind and very chastened Saul being led into Damascus where he would hear about Jesus from a courageous believer named Ananias.

Would you agree that no example could much better illustrate the statement that a person can be sincere in his beliefs yet be sincerely wrong? Saul knew it all, and yet he knew nothing.

I remember some of my first experiences when this formerly dogmatic, closed-minded woman unwillingly discovered the shade of gray. I used to see everything in black and white. I've concluded that for those who only see gray, God often emphatically and lovingly paints portraits of black and white so they are forced to acknowledge the contrasts. For those who only see black and white, He introduces situations when answers aren't so easy, where lists "A to Z" cannot be found, and when points one, two, and three don't work. Gray.

Life is full of grays, but in Saul's dramatic conversion, you and I get to enjoy a little black and white—the evil of a sinner's heart, the purity of a Savior's mercy.

# DAY 236
## Acts 9:10–22

---

All who heard him were astounded and said, "Isn't this the man who, in Jerusalem, was destroying those who called on this name?" (v. 21).

---

Few things are more precious than the expressions on a newborn's face as he or she is suddenly cast from the darkness of the womb into the bright lights of the delivery room. I remember both laughing and crying at my daughters' faces screwing up indignantly as if to say, "Would the same wise guy who turned on that light mind turning it off?"

Many years ago when a grown man was born again on the dusty road to Damascus, a light came on that no one was able to turn off. We will soon discover many who tried.

The Lord told Ananias to look for Saul praying at a certain house. The Bible doesn't tell us the content of Saul's prayer, but it does tell us what happened next. Ananias came to Saul, and . . .

> *Then he placed his hands on him and said, "Brother Saul, the Lord Jesus, who appeared to you on the road you were traveling, has sent me so you may regain your sight and be filled with the Holy Spirit." At once something like scales fell from his eyes, and he regained his sight. Then he got up and was baptized (Acts 9:17–18 HCSB).*

Paul's version of these events appears in Galatians 1:14–18. He was careful to tell the reader that he did not consult any man but went immediately into Arabia following his conversion. Apparently Saul thought he'd better get to know the One who obviously knew him so well. He had already learned more about Scripture in his young years than most learn in a lifetime. What he needed now was to come to grips with the Author.

When his quiet exile with the Savior was over, he once again approached the ancient city of Damascus. What strange thoughts must have clouded his mind. He first came to Damascus to profane the name of Christ. Now he returned to *preach* the name of Christ. He first came to Damascus to take prisoner the followers of the Way. Now he would stay in their homes. He had to know he would be the talk of the town, yet the inevitable mockery did not slow him down.

In fact, we read that "Saul grew more and more powerful and baffled the Jews living in Damascus by proving that Jesus is the Christ" (Acts 9:22). This verse tells us two wonderful things about Saul:

1. *He grew more powerful.* The Greek word for "powerful" is *end-unamoo*, also used in Hebrews 11:34 as a description of Samson. The supernatural power Samson possessed physically, God gave to Saul spiritually! Saul was probably a man of small physical stature. A writer in the second century described him as "a man rather small in size, bald-headed, bow-legged, with meeting eyebrows, a large, red and somewhat hooked nose."[56] Little about his physical appearance was intimidating, but when the Spirit of God fell on him, he became the spiritual heavy-weight champion of the world!

2. *He proved to the Jews that Jesus is the Christ.* The word translated as "proved" or "proving" means "to cause to come together, to bring together . . . to join or knit together." Let's insert one of these phrases in the Scripture so we can see the picture God is drawing for us. "Saul . . . [knit together to] the Jews . . . that Jesus is the Christ" (Acts 9:22). What did he knit together? The old with the new! He knit the teachings of the Old Testament Law and Prophets with their fulfillment in Jesus Christ.

His speech to them was probably much like Christ's speech to the two travelers on the road to Emmaus. Luke tells us that Christ appeared to the men on the road, but they did not recognize him. "Then beginning with Moses and all the Prophets, He interpreted for them the things concerning Himself in all the Scriptures" (Luke 24:27 HCSB). Both Christ and Saul proved He was the promised Messiah by knitting the promises of the Old Testament to their fulfillment in Jesus. The proof was there. All they needed to do was believe. Unlike the Gentiles, the Jews knew Scripture. They just hadn't recognized the One about whom the Scriptures were written!

Saul was hardly the kind of man to be ignored. Saul with the gospel was like a teenager with the radio. He kept turning up the volume. Inevitably, ironically, the Jews conspired to kill him, so Saul took the first basket out of town. According to his personal testimony in Galatians 1:18, Saul wanted to get acquainted with Peter anyway. From the look of things, this was a perfect time for a visit to Jerusalem.

Can you imagine how differently Saul must have approached the city this time? Every step he took had new significance. Damascus was northeast of Jerusalem, so Saul walked past the Mount of Olives and the Garden of Gethsemane. He walked through the Kidron Valley, dodging the hardened ground over ancient graves. He walked through the city gates where his face was recognized instantly. The chief priests expected him to return with prisoners. Instead, only one prisoner returned: a prisoner of Jesus Christ.

# DAY 237
## Read Acts 9:23-26

---

*When he arrived in Jerusalem, he tried to associate with the disciples,*
*but they were all afraid of him, since they did not believe he was a disciple (v. 26).*

---

You may wonder what the persecutor-turned-preacher named Saul had to do with our John. Actually, Paul's testimony will offer us several important insights into the apostle John and also will supply us with a very valuable time line.

In Galatians, Paul tells that after his conversion he went to Arabia and then returned to Damascus. Only after three years did he travel to Jerusalem. The three years encompassed his original stay in Damascus, his flight to the desert, his return to Damascus, and his travel time to Jerusalem. Position John among the disciples in Jerusalem at this time.

But don't miss the words in Acts 9:1, where Saul was "still breathing threats and murder against the disciples of the Lord" (HCSB). Peter, John, and the others had plenty of reasons to take Saul's actions personally. Furthermore, they hadn't received the same vision God had given to Ananias in Damascus concerning the validity of Saul's conversion. Saul could have faked his conversion as a means of getting close to them and exposing their unrelenting evangelism after the warning to cease.

Fast-forward your thoughts on the time line now to the events surrounding the death of James, John's beloved brother. We have no reason to believe much time passed between Paul's conversion and the martyrdom of James. We know that Stephen was martyred before Paul's conversion and that Paul in fact gave approval to his death. James was martyred after Paul's conversion. Even though several years had passed, don't you imagine that if John were anything like most of us, he had some pretty strong feelings about Paul?

Even though Paul dramatically gave his life to Christ before James was seized and killed, had I been John, I would have had a fairly difficult time embracing him. I'm afraid I might have had thoughts like, "If not for people exactly like you, my brother might still be alive." Maybe John felt none of what I'm describing, but I believe Christ's first ragtag band of followers were like us. Yes, the Holy Spirit had come to them and, yes, they had matured somewhat, but grief and loss don't always perpetuate extremely rational feelings. None of the rest of the apostles had lost a blood brother at this point. I just have to wonder how John felt about Paul those first several years.

# DAY 238
## Acts 9:27–31

———∞∞———

Barnabas, however, took him and brought him to the apostles and explained to them
how, on the road, Saul had seen the Lord, and that He had talked to him (v. 27).

———∞∞———

God had issued Saul an undeniable apostolic calling. He probably assumed
his place was with the other apostles. But when he arrived in Jerusalem and tried
to associate with them, "they were all afraid of him, since they did not believe he
was a disciple" (Acts 9:26 HCSB). As despicable as he had been, our hearts sting
for him a little, don't they? Perhaps each of us can relate to the unique stab of
loneliness.

Two wonderful words begin the next verse: "But Barnabas." We will meet
many people through our study. Some will be honorable. Others will not. A
few will be heroes. Without a doubt Barnabas was a hero. Few things touch my
heart more than Christian men who risk vulnerability in obedience to Christ.
Barnabas reached out a helping hand to a discouraged man. Saul took that hand.
Two lives bonded in that moment.

Barnabas offers us an example we don't want to miss. His name had been
Joseph, but the disciples renamed him "son of encouragement." God used
Barnabas over and over to give others the courage to be the people He had called
them to be. When Barnabas brought Saul before the other apostles, they may
have remembered how each of them had been the focus of his encouragement at
one time or another. Now he encouraged them to accept a new brother. Many
probably criticized Barnabas for being gullible concerning Saul. Barnabas was
willing to give people a chance even when others weren't.

Barnabas persuaded the apostles to accept the new convert, and the most
powerful preacher in all Christendom was set loose in Jerusalem. Consequently,
Saul did such a fine job of debating the Grecian Jews, he nearly got himself
killed. The brothers pushed Saul on a boat to Tarsus to keep him from losing his
head. I can't help but chuckle at the words that follow Saul's departure: "So the
church throughout all Judea, Galilee, and Samaria had peace" (Acts 9:31 HCSB).
Saul had a way of stirring things up. No doubt, Tarsus had enjoyed her last breath
of peace for a while. Saul was on his way.

Meanwhile, the church he left behind "was strengthened; and encouraged
by the Holy Spirit, it grew in numbers" (v. 31). Sounds like Barnabas still hung
around awhile, doesn't it? Let's look for ways to be a Barnabas in another's life.

# DAY 239
## Acts 10:9–28

—∞∞—

"You know it's forbidden for a Jewish man to associate with or visit a foreigner. But God has shown me that I must not call any person common or unclean" (v. 28).

—∞∞—

One of the main differences between Peter and Paul was the contrast in their callings. Peter was entrusted with the Jews; Saul was entrusted with the Gentiles (Gal. 2:7). I suspect that Peter often thought of Saul's calling and was relieved it wasn't his! Imagine how many times he must have thought about Saul's being called to minister to the Gentiles and thought, "Better him than me!" Saul might as well have been called to lepers. Peter may have even wondered if Saul's punishment for persecuting the church was to get the leftovers. But in no time at all, God taught Peter a very important lesson through the vision we read about in Acts 10. God always dishonors prejudice.

Peter probably not only saw himself as *different* from the Gentiles, but *better*. His attitude is nothing new. Like most of us, his prejudices were handed down through the generations. Many otherwise strong, God-serving, Bible-believing Christians are steeped in prejudice. Peter was one of those. Yet his willingness to have his closed mind pried open was testimony to his godly sincerity.

Having our minds pried open is rarely easy, but vision is rarely given to those who refuse. We are challenged to overcome prejudice on many levels, certainly not just race. Economics divide. Denominations divide. Ministries divide. Differences will always exist, but division doesn't always have to result. Although God chose Peter and Saul to minister to different groups of people, He intended for each of them to see the importance of the other in the overall vision. Saul later wrote, "He who was at work with Peter in the apostleship to the circumcised was also at work with me among the Gentiles" (Gal. 2:8 HCSB). God had driven the point home to Peter through a series of visions in which He commanded, "What God has made clean, you must not call common" (Acts 10:15 HCSB). Praise God that all who are in Christ have been made clean.

We must be careful to avoid spiritual elitism. Everything we are and anything we possess as believers in Christ is a gift of grace. Pure hearts before God must be cleansed from any hint of spiritual pride. We must aggressively fight the enemy when he seeks to nullify our growth and good works by making them invitations for pride and prejudice.

# DAY 240
## Acts 11:19–26

———∞———

But there were some of them, Cypriot and Cyrenian men,
who came to Antioch and began speaking to the Hellenists,
proclaiming the good news about the Lord Jesus (v. 20).

———∞———

Persecution scattered the early Christians as far as Phoenicia, Cyprus, and Antioch. But some gutsy believers who had traveled to Antioch broke the mold. They began to share with Gentiles also. As a result of their testimony in Antioch, "a large number who believed turned to the Lord" (Acts 11:21 HCSB).

When God desires to do "a new thing" (Isa. 43:19), He purposely seeks out a few righteous renegades who don't have a problem breaking the mold! Mold-breakers are usually people who don't care much about popularity or tradition.

I have a good friend at church who is a mold-breaker. He has been used of God to help make our church a viable presence in this generation. I don't mind telling you, he has had as many enemies as friends. These men from Cyprus and Cyrene were mold-breakers too. The soil across the street from the synagogue looked awfully fertile to them—so they scattered and spoke!

I have to smile as I read the words in Acts 11:22, "The report about them reached the ears of the church in Jerusalem" (HCSB). Antioch was about three hundred miles north of Jerusalem, but juicy news travels faster than a speeding bullet! Barnabas was dispensed to Antioch immediately. When he arrived in Antioch, he "saw the evidence of the grace of God" (v. 23). Reality superseded rumor, and he was glad!

According to verse 23, Barnabas "encouraged all of them to remain true to the Lord with a firm resolve of the heart" (HCSB) to plan in advance to remain faithful to Him! I cannot overemphasize the importance of this exhortation. This principle is one I diligently sought to teach my children, to make them understand that the point of temptation or the pinnacle of pain is not the ideal time to decide whether to stick with Christ. The most effective time to resolve to obey Christ is in *advance* of difficulty. Planning to stay faithful can greatly enhance victory.

I wish I could say I always resolved in advance to "remain true to the Lord." Certainly there were times I didn't. But I finally learned the wisdom of Barnabas's good advice and have been thankful for the fruit of safety it bears. Barnabas had seen the cost of believing in Christ firsthand. He was teaching these new believers the kind of resolve that would hold up even against the threat of death. And under his faithful tutelage, a great number of people were brought to the Lord.

Although Barnabas was overjoyed at the great harvest the scattered seeds had ultimately produced, these missionaries were obviously in a situation over their heads. They needed a specialist, an expert discipler. They needed Saul. And right about then, he probably needed them. Barnabas headed for Tarsus, looking for him. So for a whole year Barnabas and Saul met with the church and taught great numbers of people. What a team they must have made—Saul the teacher, Barnabas the encourager. One taught the principles of a godly life. The other assured them they could do it with God's help.

The next phrase in Acts 11:26 conjures up many emotions in me: "The disciples were first called Christians in Antioch" (HCSB). What a great word: *Christian*—

• An emotional word causing one man joy and another man fury—one man peace and another man turmoil.

• A dividing word unceasingly drawing a line. Either a man *is* or he is not; he is either for or against.

• A uniting word, drawing together unlikely pairs in workplaces and neighborhoods over one single bond.

• A defining word for which countless people have lived and, likewise, countless people have died.

The Greek word the believers were called was *Christianos*. It does not occur in the New Testament as a name commonly used by Christians themselves. Christian was a label coined by unbelievers as a form of ridicule. Once again, how beautifully God stole the victory from Satan. The very word used as a mockery became the greatest privilege a man could boast.

The apostle Peter gave a different twist to this insult directed at believers: "If anyone suffers as a Christian, he should not be ashamed, but should glorify God with that name" (1 Pet. 4:16 HCSB). Christians have been beaten, whipped, starved, humiliated, mutilated, hung, tortured, burned at the stake, crucified, and fed to lions. Yet two thousand years after a man called Jesus of Nazareth walked the streets of Jerusalem, two billion people alive on this earth today call themselves by the ever-dividing, ever-uniting word: Christian. God is still scattering the seeds a few righteous renegades planted in a city called Antioch. Had they only known what they were starting.

## DAY 241
### Acts 12:1–5

———— ∞∞∞ ————

About that time King Herod cruelly attacked some who belonged
to the church, and he killed James, John's brother, with the sword (vv. 1–2).

———— ∞∞∞ ————

I have studied and even taught Acts 12 many times. I love the story of
Peter's deliverance from prison, but I had never before regarded the events from
John's point of view. How devastated he must have been!

By this time in the Book of Acts, the disciples all knew the Jews could make
good on their threats. They had crucified Christ and stoned Stephen. They told
Peter and John to stop speaking in the name of Jesus or else.

They chose "or else." Acts 8:1 tells us that a persecution had scattered the
believers, but the apostles remained in Jerusalem. Yes, John and Peter trekked to
Samaria, but the ministries of the apostles remained intact in Jerusalem for this
period of time. I assume that they simply did not yet feel released by the Holy
Spirit to center their ministries elsewhere.

Now in a terrible wave of persecution, James was arrested. I wonder if John
saw them seize his brother. If not, who broke the news to him? Can you imagine
the sear of terror that tore through his heart? Remember, John was the apostle who'd had connections when Jesus was arrested and was able to get into the
priest's courtyard. Don't you know he tried to pull every favor and call on every
connection he had? He probably couldn't sleep. He couldn't eat. He no doubt fell
facedown on the floor and begged God to spare his brother's life.

Beloved, don't hurry past this scene. James was John's flesh and blood. All
the disciples were terrified, but none of them could relate to John's horror. Surely
prayer meetings took place. Don't forget, these were men with the power and
authority of the Holy Spirit to heal diseases and cast out demons. No doubt they
named and claimed James's release and demanded his life in prayer. For all we
know, James claimed his *own* life before his jailers and forbade them to harm one
of Jesus' elect. After all, the disciples were promised power and were told they
would be Christ's witnesses all over Jerusalem, Judea, Samaria, and the uttermost
parts of the earth. His ministry had just begun! No, this couldn't be the end. He
would surely be delivered!

Then they killed him.

I pity the person who came to John with the news. In 2 Samuel 1, David was
so horrified by the report of Saul and Jonathan's deaths that he had the bearer
of bad news slain. Although John had no such authority or desire, don't you
imagine he wanted to shake the bad news out of the bearer's mouth and demand
a different ending? Don't you also imagine that he tried his hardest to shake the
reality out of his own head? James was the first of the disciples martyred. Reality

must have hit like an unsuspected tidal wave, crashing on the shores of servant lives.

More than any of the other ten, John must have replayed the events a thousand times in his mind, wondering if his big brother had been terrified or calm. Did he think of their parents? Hadn't Zebedee been through enough? How was he going to tell his mother? Had James felt any pain? Was it quick? Was he next? Then before he had time to steady from reeling, he learned he was not next. Peter was.

Have you ever felt like a percussionist had just slammed king-size cymbals on both sides of your head? "Not Peter! This was too much! Not James *and* Peter! Not both of them, Lord! Please, please, no, Lord!"

Perhaps John's mind flew back to that time on the lake shore when "Peter turned around and saw the disciple Jesus loved following them. . . . When Peter saw him, he said to Jesus, 'Lord—what about him?'" (John 21:20–21 HCSB).

"Yeah, Lord! What about me? How will I go on through all of this without James and Peter? What are You doing? What *aren't* You doing? Will You let them kill all of us?"

John had good reason to believe Peter might never make it out of that prison. But then he did. God granted him a miracle . . . scarcely before they had mopped the blood of John's big brother off the floor. Can you imagine the mix of emotions John must have felt if he was anything like the rest of us?

When you grapple with questions like, "Why did God let the blood of my brother spill but performed a miracle for my best friend?" the explanations of others only frustrate you more. In fact, often we only bother asking so we can release a little anger in the demand of a better answer. Rarely will it come.

Solitude is not so much the place we find answers. It's the place we find our own square foot of earth from which to grapple with heaven and decide if we're going on—possibly alone—without our answers. And many of us will. Why? Because the privilege of wrestling with such a holy and mysterious God still beats the numbness—the pitiful mediocrity—of an otherwise life. Sometimes we don't realize how real He is until we've experienced the awesomeness of His answerless Presence. He knows that what we crave far more than explanations is the unshakable conviction that He is utterly, supremely God.

# DAY 242
## Acts 13:1–3

—∞∞—

As they were ministering to the Lord and fasting, the Holy Spirit said, "Set apart for
Me Barnabas and Saul for the work that I have called them to" (v. 2).

—∞∞—

The first church in Antioch remains such an example to us. We've already
seen willing evangelists, willing recipients, and effective discipleship revealed in
the readiness of this infant church to give. Acts 13 unfolds with another mark of
an effective church body: strong leadership.

Barnabas, Simeon, Lucius, Manaen, and Saul were prophets and teachers
in the church. Notice that Saul was listed last of the five at this point of his ministry. These five prophets and teachers didn't just hold important positions; they
each had a personal passion for God. While they were worshiping and fasting,
the Holy Spirit instructed them to send Barnabas and Saul on a mission to other
cities and regions, spreading the Good News into uncharted Christian territory.
The leaders of the church in Antioch were constantly ready to hear from God;
therefore, when He spoke, they were listening!

Again and again in Scripture we see God's perfect timing. In Galatians
1:15, the apostle explains that he was set apart from birth (about AD 10). He did
not receive salvation until around AD 36. He was not set apart for his signature
ministry until around AD 46. Not one minute was wasted. God was training Saul
during those formative years. Meanwhile, Barnabas the encourager was proving
his effectiveness among both Jews and Gentiles. When God's time came, both
men were ready for the Holy Spirit to send them out. "Then, after they had fasted,
prayed, and laid hands on them, they sent them off" (Acts 13:3 HCSB).

I grew up in a denomination that prioritized missions and spurred a love
and appreciation in my heart for missionaries. That's one reason why this Acts
13 moment is so precious to me. Meet the first international missionaries: Saul
and Barnabas! Set apart to be sent off—just like so many other faithful ones who
have followed in their footsteps, forsaking the securities of home and family to
follow Christ anywhere. As of this writing, more than eighty thousand evangel-
ical missionaries presently serve overseas.[57] I have no greater admiration for any
group of people.

# DAY 243
Acts 13:4–12

---

"You son of the Devil, full of all deceit and all fraud, enemy of all righteousness!
Won't you ever stop perverting the straight paths of the Lord?" (v. 10).

---

Next we pack our bags and join Paul on his first missionary journey! You'll soon see that the apostle's life was anything but boring. His many experiences will prove that living and moving in the center of God's will does not mean we avoid opposition. To the contrary, we often meet challenges because of our choice to follow God! Being a sold-out servant of Jesus Christ requires courage, but—praise His name—He who requires it also supplies it. Throughout this book we have the privilege of learning from the example of a man who knew opposition intimately. His key to victory was knowing the One in charge far more intimately.

Indeed, Saul met some interesting characters in his travels! He got no farther than his second stop when he met a man I'm sure he never forgot. His name was Bar-Jesus (or Elymas). He was the attendant to Sergius Paulus, the proconsul or governor of Cyprus.

Bar-Jesus committed a serious offense against both his supervisor and the kingdom of God. "The proconsul . . . summoned Barnabas and Saul and desired to hear God's message" (Acts 13:7 HCSB). Bar-Jesus did everything he could to oppose them and keep the proconsul from believing. The apostle rebuked the sorcerer, and God struck him blind.

Here we read that Saul was also called Paul! What a relief! I have tried to refer to him by the name used in whatever Scriptures we were studying. But we are least familiar with his Hebrew name, Saul, and most familiar with his Roman name, Paul. The Scriptures call him Paul from this point on, and so will we.

Paul called Bar-Jesus a "son of the Devil" (Acts 13:10 HCSB). He was actually using a play on words because the name Bar-Jesus in Aramaic means "son of Jesus." In effect, Paul was saying, "You're no son of Jesus. You're a son of the devil!" He not only meant the term to be taken figuratively; he meant it literally, as I hope you will see. The three descriptions given in Scripture (v. 10) support Paul's accusation against him. Consider how the following phrases Paul used apply to Elymas as well as to Satan:

• *Full of deceit*. The Greek word means "bait, metaphorically and generally fraud, guile, deceit." Remember, Bar-Jesus or Elymas was a sorcerer, which meant he was a *magus*, or presumed wise man, who "specialized in the study of astrology and enchantment."

• *Full of trickery*. The word is often used for theft achieved through "wicked schemes or plots."

• *Perverted the right ways of the Lord.* The word means "to turn or twist throughout; to distort, pervert, seduce, mislead; to turn away."

So Paul's accusation that Bar-Jesus was a "son of the Devil" was quite appropriate. You can imagine Paul came up against the schemes of the enemy many times as he sought to do the will of God. As we study his life, we too can learn to identify the works of darkness and be equipped to stand against them.

Acts 13:11 records the first miracle we see God perform through the apostle Paul. He struck Bar-Jesus blind. Satan is powerful, but he is no match for the Son of God. The proconsul "believed and was astonished at the teaching about the Lord" (Acts 13:12 HCSB). This Greek definition is a favorite. The word "astonished" or "amazed" is the Greek word *ekplesso*, which means "amazed" only in the sense of knocking one out of his senses. I can't count the times God has knocked me out of my senses through something He has taught me about Himself.

God wants to amaze us with the wisdom of His Word. He wants to blow our minds and widen our vision! He wants to show us how relevant He is. How can we do our part so He can do His? Serguis Paulus, the proconsul, revealed to us a marvelous link. Ultimately he was "astonished at the teaching about the Lord" (v. 12) because he "desired to hear God's message" (v. 7 HCSB). He was ready to receive, and God honored the desire of his heart! Let's learn to pray like the psalmist who said, "Open my eyes so that I may see wonderful things in Your law" (Ps. 119:18 HCSB). He may just blow our minds.

Think of times you've picked up your Bible and were interrupted, distracted. How often when you attend a worship service are you distracted while preparing to go, on the way, or at the service? Does your annoyance become anger directed at a child, spouse, or friend? Our anger needs to be directed at the source. When you desire to study God's Word, Satan will do everything to distract. Ask the Holy Spirit to empower you to recognize the source of your distractions and to channel your anger where it belongs—toward the evil one.

# DAY 244
## Acts 13:13–41

---

"Let it be known to you, brothers, that through this man forgiveness of sins is being proclaimed to you, and everyone who believes in Him is justified" (vv. 38–39).

---

Barnabas and Paul traveled on to Pisidian Antioch (not the Antioch in Syria where believers were first called Christians). On the Sabbath they attended the synagogue worship and received a wonderful invitation. Sometimes we yearn for God to crack open a receptive door to share our faith. We scramble to grab an opportunity that never seems to come. Other times God swings open a door so quickly, we're too stunned to walk through it! God swung the door open so quickly in Pisidian Antioch that He almost blew the beard off the rabbi! Practically by the time Paul and Barnabas found a chair, they were asked to share a message of encouragement.

Paul was not about to miss a golden opportunity. Like any good orator, he shaped his style and material to fit his audience. As he stood in the synagogue, he addressed Jews and those who believed in the God of Israel. He presented the gospel by rehearsing for them their history.

I am convinced that Paul had a very specific purpose as he introduced Christ to the Jews through their own history. Remember when Paul went to Arabia after his conversion and spent some solitary time trying to sort things out? You may recall that he returned to Damascus and "baffled the Jews . . . proving that Jesus is the Christ" (Acts 9:22). As we saw earlier, the word "proving" means "knitting together." In Arabia, Paul had been knitting together the old and the new and found the two strands of yarn to be a perfect match. Paul's intention was to give the Jews in Pisidian Antioch a knitting lesson! He urged them to see how perfectly Christ knit the past with the present. They did not have to forsake their history. They just needed to accept the rest of the story!

But Paul was such a prodigy of grace, he could not preach a sermon without it. He charged the Jews with having executed their own Messiah with "no grounds" for what they did (v. 28), yet he extended the invitation to any "brothers" (v. 38)—fellow Jews—to receive forgiveness through Christ. What glorious news! If a person who had shared the responsibility for Christ's death could be forgiven, can any person be beyond forgiveness?

# DAY 245
## Acts 13:42–52

---

The Jews incited the religious women of high standing and the leading men of the city.
They stirred up persecution against Paul and Barnabas and expelled them (v. 50).

---

Acts 13:43 shows that Paul and Barnabas's first experience in Galatia was positive. "Many of the Jews and devout proselytes" met with them after the message and received their encouragement. But although the initial reception was so positive, can Satan be far behind when God is at work? The Jewish leaders "were filled with jealousy and began to oppose what Paul was saying by insulting him" (v. 45 HCSB).

This group of ancient Jews was privileged to receive the ministry of the apostle Paul himself, but in a flash they went from being subjects of ministry to being sources of opposition, inciting other men and women of influence to give additional weight and volume to their criticism. Ultimately, of course, the enemy of salvation was the one using these Jews, just as they used the leading women and men of the city. All were puppets on his strings. Little has changed. Satan still takes advantage of women and men, seizing their powers of influence for his own purposes.

I want to ask the Holy Spirit to help us with a special assignment. Meditate on your last seven days for several moments. Picture yourself in your usual roles as well as specific encounters. Think of ways you exerted the power of influence, whether rightly or wrongly. I will get you started with a few questions I am asking myself: Did you influence your spouse in a decision at work? Did you influence a friend who was upset with someone? Did you influence a class or a group of people in a meeting? Did you influence your boss or employees? Did you influence your children in situations they were in? Consider every point of influence you can remember, and add to your list as the Holy Spirit reminds you of others.

You're probably more influential than you thought. If you had lunch with friends this week, you probably influenced someone in some way. If a friend shared a problem with you, you influenced him or her somehow with your response. If you gave your opinion on a matter recently, you very likely affected someone else's. We are constantly exerting influence. Influence is a gift, a trust. We must be careful how we use it. Take heed. Satan can affect masses of followers through a few leaders.

## DAY 246
### Acts 14:1–7

—◦◦◦◦—

When an attempt was made by both the Gentiles and Jews, with their rulers,
to assault and stone them, they found out about it and fled (vv. 5–6).

—◦◦◦◦—

Between Paul's tenacity and Barnabas's encouragement, neither lacked motivation, even after leaving Pisidian Antioch in a cloud of dust. By the time they could see Iconium in the distance, they were spilling over with the kind of joyful anticipation that can only come from the filling of the Holy Spirit. A new challenge awaited them. Perhaps more of a challenge than they expected!

When they got to Iconium, the missionary pair again began at the synagogue. They "spoke in such a way that a great number of both Jews and Greeks believed" (Acts 14:1 HCSB). But like Pisidian Antioch before, the Jewish leaders' jealousy led them to poison the minds of the people against Paul and Barnabas.

Interestingly enough, just as the Pharisees and the Herodians overcame their mutual dislike of each other to oppose Jesus, some of the Jews and Gentiles temporarily overcame their aversion to one another for a common cause. They joined in opposing the gospel message and messengers. But in spite of the opposition, Paul and Barnabas "stayed there for some time and spoke boldly, in reliance on the Lord, who testified to the message of His grace by granting that signs and wonders be performed through them" (Acts 14:3 HCSB).

Then things took a dark turn for our heroes. They learned of a plot to stone them. So naturally our miracle-working pair confronted their accusers, right? Wrong.

They ran for their lives!

You may be surprised to hear that they fled in the face of the plans set against them. Shouldn't they have stayed and trusted God to guard them from attack since they were doing His will and preaching His message? Couldn't the same power used to perform signs and miracles be used to stifle their enemies?

I believe their actions offer us a fitting description of this dynamic duo: they were smart! I don't believe they were reacting out of pure fear. They were responding out of pure wisdom—and quickly! Proverbs 22:3 says that "a sensible person sees danger and takes cover, but the inexperienced keep going and are punished" (HCSB).

Christ Himself often chose prudence. "Jesus traveled in Galilee, since He did not want to travel in Judea because the Jews were trying to kill Him" (John 7:1 HCSB). On another occasion Christ's enemies picked up stones to stone him, "but Jesus hid himself, slipping away from the temple grounds" (John 8:59).

No reasonable person could mistake Christ's prudence for cowardice. Look at the words of Matthew 26:1–2: "When Jesus had finished saying all this, He told His disciples, 'You know that the Passover takes place after two days, and the Son of Man will be handed over to be crucified'" (HCSB).

Why didn't Christ slip out of their hands *this* time? John's gospel gives us the answer on an earlier occasion when they tried to seize Jesus: "No one laid a hand on Him because His hour had not yet come" (John 7:30 HCSB). The reason Christ did not resist His accusers when they came to arrest Him was that the time had come for Him to give His life as a sacrifice for sin.

Paul and Barnabas responded to impending danger the way Christ did on several occasions. Supernatural power could have changed things. Christ could have opened the earth and commanded it to swallow His pursuers in Palestine or the pursuers of His beloved ambassadors in Iconium. Yet He chose to use another method. Christ *did* deliver Paul and Barnabas from an evil attack. He just used their heads and feet to do it! I see two general principles at work regarding miraculous intervention in the New Testament:

1. Miracles were used more often for authenticity than intervention.

2. Miracles were used most often when natural means were either not available or were not conceivable.

Jesus ordinarily used natural means of provision. When He and His disciples were hungry, they usually found something to eat. When they were thirsty, they went to a well and drew water to drink. He could have supplied anything they wanted supernaturally, but He chose natural means whenever available. He responded the same way to impending danger. He used His feet or sometimes a boat, and He departed.

Whether God uses natural means or supernatural means to deliver us from danger, both are divine provisions. God supplied the healthy legs that Paul and Barnabas used to flee. God provides the car we drive to the nearest public place when we're being followed. The person who walks on the scene out of nowhere and frightens off an attacker is an ambassador of God! Thank God for His natural forms of provision!

# DAY 247
## Acts 14:8–20

—❦—

When the crowds saw what Paul had done, they raised their voices, saying in the Lycaonian language, "The gods have come down to us in the form of men!" (v. 11).

—❦—

Do you ever wonder why God doesn't more often perform miraculous works? Have you thought, "Just one good miracle would turn this place upside down"? If so, consider what happened here. Paul and Barnabas proceeded to the city of Lystra and began to preach the good news. There they encountered and healed a man who had been crippled from birth. Because of the miracle, the crowd began to declare: "The gods have come down to us in the form of men!" (Acts 14:11 HCSB). Not exactly the result the pair desired.

The crowd brought bulls and wreaths to the city gates of Lystra to offer sacrifices to Barnabas and Paul as gods. Because of an old Greek myth, the people of Lystra were afraid not to honor Paul and Barnabas. For generations a story about two Greek gods who visited earth had circulated among the people of Lystra. The two gods were met with scorn except for one poverty-stricken couple who showed them hospitality. According to the myth, the gods cursed the people but gave the couple an opulent palace. The people of Lystra were taking no chances in case these gods had returned.

We have already seen a vital fact about Paul and Barnabas: they were smart! Now we witness a second description of both men at critical moments: they were sincere. They rushed into the crowd, tearing their clothes, declaring themselves mere men.

The sincerity of Paul and Barnabas is refreshingly obvious. They not only tore their clothes in grief because the people had made such a preposterous assumption, but they wasted no time in setting the record straight. They did not capitalize on a moment's glory. They did not use their attentions to get a good home-cooked meal. They rushed out to the crowd, shouting, "Men! Why are you doing these things? We are men also, with the same nature as you" (v. 15 HCSB).

We all know that human beings are indescribably fickle. One minute we are laying palm branches in the road and crying, "Hosanna in the highest." The next minute we are crying, "Crucify Him," or, "I never knew Him." So it was with the adoring crowd at Lystra. One minute they were preparing to worship Paul and Barnabas. "Then some Jews came from Antioch and Iconium, and when they had won over the crowds and stoned Paul, they dragged him out of the city, thinking he was dead" (v. 19 HCSB).

That didn't take long, did it? Think about this carefully: Barnabas and Paul could have used the crowd's wrong impression that they were gods, but they maintained their integrity. A flashy miracle at just the right time, and not one stone would have been thrown. The crowd would have bowed at their feet. Paul and Barnabas could have slipped out of town without a scratch. Instead, Paul was stoned so severely that they dragged him outside the city thinking he was dead.

Can you imagine the pictures flashing in Paul's mind with every blow of a stone? I'm sure his memory replayed Stephen's radiant face. Paul probably could not bear to think of himself worthy to die for the name of Christ in the same way. He probably fell unconscious thinking he was about to breathe his last, but this was not Paul's time.

Paul and Barnabas had arrived in Iconium with joyful anticipation, only to have to depart quickly under threat of stoning. They had escaped one of the most painful forms of punishment ever devised. They wiped their brows, gave a sigh of relief, and headed into Lystra. But before they knew what had happened, the stones were flying. They had no place to run, nowhere to hide.

Many years later Paul still remembered the events in Iconium and Lystra and shared a peculiar testimony. He said, "You, however, know all about . . . what kinds of things happened to me in Antioch, Iconium and Lystra, the persecutions I endured. Yet the Lord rescued me from all of them" (2 Tim. 3:10–11).

Any person in his or her right mind would prefer to be rescued before the first stone is thrown, not after the last! Yet Paul described both his experience in Iconium (where he departed prior to suffering) and his experience in Lystra (where he departed *after* suffering) as the Lord's divine rescue. Perhaps his inspired choice of words will intensify your appreciation of his exquisite testimony. The original word for "rescue" in 2 Timothy 3:11 is *rhuomai*, which is derived from a word meaning "to drag along the ground." *Rhuomai* means "to draw or snatch from danger, rescue, deliver." Please read the remainder of the definition with great care and meditation: "This is more with the meaning of drawing to one-self than merely rescuing from someone or something."

You see, God wasn't only interested in drawing Paul out of difficulty or danger. He wanted to draw Paul closer to Himself. Every time God delivers us, the point is ultimately to draw us closer to Himself. Whether we get to avoid pain and suffering or we must persevere in the midst of it, our deliverance comes when we're dragged from the enemy of our souls to the heart of God.

# DAY 248
## Acts 14:21–22

∞

They returned to Lystra, to Iconium, and to Antioch . . . telling them, "It is necessary to pass through many troubles on our way into the kingdom of God" (vv. 21–22).

∞

This next portion of Scripture unfolds in Derbe. In just a few short verses, we see Paul and Barnabas backtrack through a number of cities on their way to Syrian Antioch, where they had been commissioned. But why did they take the long route? Why in the world would they go back through Lystra (where Paul had been stoned and left for dead), Iconium (where they narrowly escaped being stoned), and Pisidian Antioch (where they were persecuted and expelled)? Acts 14:22 tells us exactly why they walked back into potential peril: to strengthen the disciples and encourage them to remain true to the faith. Paul and Barnabas considered this message about inevitable hardships such a priority that they risked everything to go back through those three cities and tell it.

Their message of encouragement by warning of hardship may seem to be a paradox to us. We may not find a message about unavoidable troubles very strengthening! But we must first recognize that the inevitable nature of hardships can motivate us to redirect our energies. *Fear* of trials sometimes depletes more energy than *facing* trials! Once we accept the inevitability of hardship, we can redirect our focus from fear of trials to faithfulness. In the face of tribulations, we often sense a heavenly strength filling our souls right on time.

Second, realizing the inevitability of hardship encourages us in the faith. I would be pretty discouraged if I thought hardships in the lives of surrendered Christians were unusual and were always signs of disobedience. Yes, hardship sometimes comes as a direct result of sin and disobedience. We usually are aware when consequences of sin have caused us deep suffering, but many other times trials have nothing at all to do with disobedience. Believing a heretical prosperity gospel can leave us terribly discouraged, wondering what we've done wrong. We wonder why we can't seem to muster enough faith to be healthy, problem free, and prosperous.

Be encouraged to know that difficulty is not a sign of immaturity or faithlessness. The Holy Spirit will do His job and let you know if you are suffering because of sin. Otherwise, remember—we must go through many hardships to enter the kingdom of God.

# DAY 249
## Acts 14:23–28

—⊗⊗⊗—

When they had appointed elders in every church and prayed with fasting, they committed them to the Lord in whom they had believed (v. 23).

—⊗⊗⊗—

I hope we have shared some of the strength and encouragement Paul and Barnabas gave to the believers in Lystra, Iconium, and Pisidian Antioch. Those new converts saw living examples of perseverance through suffering. Paul and Barnabas departed from each city under difficult circumstances. They went out of their way to return so they could say, "We're OK! We've survived! And we're still believing and serving!" In seeing the joy and commitment of God's suffering servants, they knew they could survive too.

The time came, however, for Paul and Barnabas to leave. But they did something to ensure an ongoing strengthening and encouraging of their new disciples.

Acts 14:23 tells us they appointed elders in each church. The Greek word is *presbuteros*, which means "older, a senior." The *Holman Bible Dictionary* tells us the "elders in the Pauline churches were probably spiritual leaders and ministers, not simply a governing council."[58] Not coincidentally, Paul and Barnabas wanted to leave the new believers with ongoing strength and encouragement, so they carefully appointed elders who were not only spiritually mature but also (if I may say so gently)—old! However, older men were not the only ones charged with responsibility.

In Titus 2:3–6, Paul also charged older women, younger women, and younger men to faithful service. Sounds to me like God values the wisdom and life experience of older men and women. It also sounds to me like He chooses to use people of every age whose hearts are turned to Him.

Life is difficult. The converts in Lystra, Iconium, and Pisidian Antioch were surely strengthened and encouraged as they saw living examples of people who were surviving hardships with victory and joy. Listening to Paul and Barnabas testify must have greatly impacted their ability to endure. We don't have Paul and Barnabas, but we have hosts of older people who are more than happy to tell us about the faithfulness of God—if we'll just stop, ask them, and listen.

# DAY 250
## Acts 15:1–21

---

"Why, then, are you now testing God by putting on the disciples' necks a yoke that neither our forefathers nor we have been able to bear?" (v. 10).

---

Legalism. This one little word—more than any other—is probably responsible for causing more churches to die, more servants to quit, and more denominations to split. Like a leech, legalism saps the lifeblood out of its victim. It enters the door in the name of righteousness to vacuum out all the dirt and ends up vacuuming out all the spirit. Don't confuse legalism with recognition and pursuit of godly standards.

Two sets of legalists emerge in this portion of Scripture: 1) Judean visitors to Antioch who told Gentile Christians they must be circumcised to be saved, and 2) the believers in Jerusalem from the party of the Pharisees who told them they must also obey the law of Moses. The statement of the Pharisees became the basis of the Jerusalem Council.

Let's offer the legalists more grace than they offered Gentile believers. I'll assume they weren't acting out of pure meanness. But even in giving them the benefit of the doubt, I see at least three mistakes they made in behalf of the new Gentile converts.

1. *They drew a universal standard from their personal experience.* Since they had been circumcised prior to salvation, they decided everyone else should be as well. Through the ages people have struggled with the same wrong assumption based on their own personal experience. If God worked one way in their lives, any other way must be invalid. Let me illustrate with the story of two men.

The first man lives a godless, depraved life. The Spirit of God convicts him. He falls on his face, surrenders to Christ as Lord of his life. He serves faithfully and never goes back into the old patterns of sin. He becomes a preacher and boldly proclaims the message that people are not saved unless they instantly surrender their entire lives to the lordship of Christ. If they have ever fallen back, they were never saved at all.

The second man received Christ at a very early age and then fell away in rebellion for years. He returns to Christ as the penitent prodigal, slips into his old ways several times, and finally reaches freedom in Christ. In his opinion a person's state of salvation cannot in any way be judged by his actions. He believes a man can live like the devil for a season of his life and still be saved.

Both men are born again, but both men are mistakenly applying their experience to every other believer. Each of these men could find some degree of scriptural support, so who is right? God is. He is right and justified in saving whomever He pleases. There is only one way to be saved: by grace through faith in the Lord Jesus Christ (see Eph. 2:8–9). God uses many methods to draw people to Himself. He is far more creative than we want to think. Only He can judge the heart.

2. *They tried to make salvation harder than it is.* James delivered a strong exhortation to the Jerusalem Council in Acts 15:19: "We should not cause difficulties for those who turn to God from among the Gentiles" (HCSB). What a frightening thought! We must ask ourselves a very serious question: Do we make it difficult for people around us to turn to God? Do we have a list of rules and requirements that turns people away?

Part of the exquisite beauty of salvation is its simplicity. Any man, woman, or child can come to Christ with absolutely nothing to offer Him but simple faith—just as they are. Salvation requires nothing more than childlike faith—believing that Jesus Christ died for my sins and accepting His gift of salvation. The heart and the life sometimes turn instantaneously like the first example. Other times the heart turns instantaneously but the life adjusts a little more slowly like the second example. Let's not make salvation more difficult than it has to be.

3. *They expected of others what they could not deliver themselves.* In Acts 15:10, Peter was asking in essence, "Why are you expecting of someone else what you know you can't deliver yourself?" The question is one every believer should occasionally ask him or herself. Do we have almost impossible expectations of other people? Do we expect things of our mates we wouldn't want to have to deliver ourselves? Do we expect near perfection in our children and tireless commitment from our coworkers? Are we yoke brokers just looking for an unsuspecting neck?

Yoke brokers are miserable people because they are never satisfied with less than perfection. Their obsession with everyone else's lack of perfection helps them keep their minds off their own. Yoke brokers are selling a yoke no one wants to buy—their own. If anyone has ever expected of you something you knew he or she couldn't do, then you have an idea how it feels to be the hapless victim of a yoke.

Let's return to the simplicity of salvation. Not adding to. Not taking away. When we paint the picture of our salvation for others to see, we may use different colors, textures, and shapes on the edges of the parchment. But in the center can only be a cross. Anything else cheapens grace and cheats the believer. Paul wasn't about to let that happen to his beloved flock.

# DAY 251
## Acts 15:22–35

———∞∞∞———

It was the Holy Spirit's decision—and ours—to put no greater burden
on you than these necessary things.... If you keep yourselves
from these things, you will do well (vv. 28–29).

———∞∞∞———

God can break any yoke, even those we don't realize we're wearing. Thank
goodness, the message of freedom prevailed at the Jerusalem Council. Paul and
Barnabas departed with a letter personalized for the Gentile believers in Antioch.

But at first glance the letter seems somewhat contradictory. Gentile believers didn't have to be circumcised to be saved, but they were urged to abstain
from several practices forbidden under Jewish law. So were they free from the
law or not? Yes and no. They were free from the law of Moses but not free from
the life-giving laws of God. The freedom God gives is to come out and be separate from the practices of the former worldly life. The letter to the believers in
Antioch was a declaration of liberty. The four areas of abstinence would help
them remain free.

Let's pinpoint one of the four areas that offers an important learning opportunity for us: the believers in Antioch were told to abstain from food sacrificed to
idols. Gentile believers might have reasoned that although they would not dream
of sacrificing to idols anymore, what harm could be done by simply buying the
leftover food at a good price after it was offered?

Satan sometimes tempts us the same way. We don't desire to go back to our
old lifestyles, but certain parts of it seem so harmless—some of the old friends,
the old hangouts, and the old refreshments. But the elders wisely warned the
early believers that nothing is harmless about the practices of the old life. Eating
foods sacrificed to idols could weaken them to former practices or cause someone
else to stumble.

The Gentile believers would not forfeit their gift of grace by eating foods
sacrificed to idols, but they would risk their freedom and compromise their sep-
arateness. They were wise to avoid anything that would place them close enough
to the vacuum to be sucked back in. Safety and freedom are found in staying so
far away that you can't even hear the vacuum cleaner running.

Paul and Barnabas were now back home. Back with their beloved flock.
They returned to tell them they were free . . . and to show them how they could
stay that way.

# DAY 252
## Acts 15:36–38

⸙

Paul did not think it appropriate to take along this man who had deserted
them in Pamphylia and had not gone on with them to the work (v. 38).

⸙

Sailors speak of the call of the sea, but something stronger than the sea
called Paul. He relished his days in Antioch. How beautifully the garden had
grown from a few seeds scattered six years earlier! He enjoyed the privilege of
returning to the same quarters every night and laughing over a meal with good
friends. He busied himself with the work of a pastor. He loved these people and
his partner, Barnabas. But filled with the Spirit of God, Paul felt compelled to
go where the Spirit led.

We may plan to stay forever and commit with noble intentions to do one
thing for the rest of our lives. But when the Spirit of God moves within us, we
must move with Him or be miserable. Paul knew God had called him to Antioch
only to send him out again. He had learned to obey both the abiding and the
moving of the Holy Spirit. He had been allowed by God to abide in the comforts
of Antioch for a season. Now the Spirit of God compelled him to move again.

I love being drawn into the story line and relationships of Scripture, but
involvement also increases the disappointment when our heroes show their
humanity. We are about to see how God uses flawed people like you and me.

Remember John Mark, who bailed out on Paul and Barnabas in the middle
of their first missionary journey? Barnabas was one of those men willing to take
a risk on a young missionary who had failed on his first attempt—the same way
he had once taken a risk on a hotheaded young Pharisee who had come to Christ.
Paul, on the other hand, was hard and tough. So when the two prepared to revisit
the churches from their first journey, Barnabas said John goes. Paul said John
stays.

John went. With Barnabas. Paul took Silas as Barnabas's replacement.

Barnabas had been the first to accept Paul and welcome him among the
brothers in Jerusalem. Together they had faced the kind of peril and persecution
that bonds two people for a lifetime! They were a team. So when the Holy Spirit
compelled Paul to return to the towns where they had preached, he wanted his
dear friend and partner to go with him. Imagine how difficult this severance
must have been for them.

But they each had had strong emotions about John Mark, as well as toward
each other. And obviously, both of them were upset by their differing opinions. I
think Paul and Barnabas were simply that different, but according to Colossians
4:10, John Mark was more than just a fellow believer to Barnabas. They were also
cousins. Strong emotions can spawn sharp disagreements.

But disagreements between people have a strange way of inviting observers to pick sides. I've caught myself trying to decide who was right and who was wrong. I feel a strange need to make up my mind and get in one camp or the other. But let's start becoming aware of our tendency to get involved (at least emotionally) as judge and jury when people disagree. Next time we're in a similar situation, perhaps we should ask ourselves, Does someone always have to be right and another wrong?

Paul and Barnabas both were Spirit-filled servants of God, yet they differed vehemently on whether John Mark should join them. We might assume that either Paul or Barnabas was not under the leadership of the Holy Spirit; after all, the Spirit could not possess two opinions. Or could He? I believe both men could have been under the direct influence of the Holy Spirit and yet still have differed. How? The Holy Spirit might have been saying yes to Barnabas and no to Paul. He might have wanted Barnabas, not Paul, to take John Mark. Why? So God could divide and multiply. Paul had matured so effectively under Barnabas's help and encouragement, they had grown equally strong. Though they might have preferred to serve together the rest of their lives, God had a more practical plan. He had other young preachers He wanted each man to train. As a result of their differing convictions, two preachers became four, and soon we'll see another. Paul and Barnabas went their separate ways—two mentors, each with a new apprentice. The empty place in Paul's ministry left an appropriate space for a man named Silas to fill.

Scripture tells us most divisions are not of God, but Acts 15 suggests that sometimes God wants to divide and multiply. Can you imagine how much simpler church life could be if we accepted that God could place two people under different convictions to multiply ministry? I've seen this phenomenon occur at my own church. Two very strong leaders in our church differed over whether we should have traditional worship or contemporary worship. Who was right? Both of them. God divided one worship service into two, and we now reach more people.

Often differences erupt due to less noble motivations—two opinionated people unwilling to budge. And unless we invite God to come to the rescue, the results can be disastrous. Ministries and partnerships often divide and dwindle rather than divide and multiply. On the other hand, when God leads two people who have walked together to a fork in the road, He can do something wonderful—*if* they and their constituents are mature enough to deal with it!

# DAY 253
## Acts 15:39–41

―∞―

There was such a sharp disagreement that they parted company,
and Barnabas took Mark with him and sailed off to Cyprus (v. 39).

―∞―

Like Paul and Barnabas, we may sometimes find ourselves strongly differing with someone about matters related to church or ministry. But differing convictions don't have to become razor-sharp contentions. Here is a four-step plan for dealing with conflicts between believers:

1. *Identify the real source of the argument.* Job 16:3 asks a relevant question: "What ails you that you keep on arguing?" Ask the Holy Spirit to shed light on the true source. Sometimes we believe that conviction is the motivation for our differing views until we allow God to reveal our selfishness or unwillingness to change. Part of spiritual maturity is risking our position in favor of the will and glory of God. Let's be willing to allow Him to shed light on any selfish or worldly motive.

2. *Submit the issue to God.* James 4:7 exhorts, "Submit to God. But resist the Devil, and he will flee from you" (HCSB). An important part of giving anything to God is taking everything from Satan. Ephesians 4:26–27 tells us not to sin in our anger and thereby give the devil a foothold. Satan has a field day with our arguments and quarrels. When we ask God to remove all selfish, worldly motives and influences of the enemy, issues often either disappear or downsize to a workable level.

3. *Resist the temptation to sin in your anger.* Anger in and of itself is not sin. It is an emotion, and sometimes a very appropriate emotion. But unfortunately, anger heightens the risk of wrong actions or words. Each of us regrets something we've said or done in anger. Let's ask God's help when we are angry at another believer so that our feelings do not turn into wrong actions.

4. *Pray for (and if possible, with) the other person involved.* Prayer changes things and people! Philippians 4:6 invites us to pray about everything. Can you imagine how defeated the enemy would be if two divided church leaders or laymen got down on their knees together and prayed for God's glory? We don't have to be together on every issue, but we can be together in prayer!

# DAY 254
## Acts 16:1–3

―❦―

He went on to Derbe and Lystra, where there was a disciple named Timothy,
the son of a believing Jewish woman, but his father was a Greek (v. 1).

―❦―

One of my favorite parts of studying Paul's life is exploring some of his friendships; yet as many as he had, one would differ from all the rest. Many years later I'm sure his heart was washed with emotion as he recalled his return to Lystra and the risk he took on a young man named Timothy. From the very beginning, Timothy was special. Allow Scripture to shed some light on his distinctives.

1. *Timothy was a unique choice because of his youthfulness.* In 1 Timothy 4:12, Paul counseled Timothy not to let anyone look down on him because of his youth, yet even this piece of advice came a full fifteen years after Timothy had joined Paul. Paul's words in 2 Timothy 3:15 demonstrate that in spite of his youth, Timothy was fertile soil from which ministry grew: "From childhood you have known the sacred Scriptures, which are able to instruct you for salvation through faith in Christ Jesus" (HCSB). I believe Paul saw Timothy's tremendous potential for fruit bearing. The opportunity to train him while he was still young and teachable was probably a benefit to Paul's ministry, not a hindrance.

Do you know any young people who are trying to be genuine servants of God? If so, they may be discouraged because no one is taking them seriously. Why not make a point of encouraging a young servant through a note, a call, or a pat on the back?

2. *Timothy had a unique upbringing.* He came from a family with a Jewish mother and a Greek father. You may have an insight into Timothy's childhood because of differences in your own parents' belief systems. Growing up in a home with one believing and one unbelieving parent is hard. In those days, having a Jewish mother who had accepted Christ and a Greek father who didn't believe would have been both difficult and different.

My generation was the first to be raised on films and fairy tales in living color. Movies like *Cinderella, Snow White*, and *Beauty and the Beast* redefine romance as two people from different worlds falling deeply in love. Typically their only problem is their unyielding family. Love ultimately overcomes and they live happily ever after. We need to teach our children the truth about real romance and love that lasts. The sparks that fly from two different worlds converging in one couple usually end up burning someone!

Paul delivered a strong exhortation in 2 Corinthians 6:14: "Do not be yoked together with unbelievers." The Greek word for "yoked" is *zugos*, which means "a yoke serving to couple any two things together and a coupling, a beam of a balance which unites two scales, hence a balance." In the next verse Paul asked a question to make his point: "What harmony is there?" When two completely different belief systems are joined together, the result often is a lack of balance and harmony.

You may have grown up in this kind of home, so you know how rocky this life can be. Perhaps you may presently be in a home where spiritual beliefs differ drastically. If so, I hope you receive some encouragement from Timothy's experience. God can prevail and bear wonderful fruit from an unequally yoked couple as we will see, even though their lives are often more complicated than they had to be.

3. *Timothy had a unique perspective.* He had been intimately exposed to three practices he and Paul would encounter in ministry: agnosticism because of his father's unbelief, Judaism because of his mother's heritage, and Christianity because of his mother's acceptance of Christ as Messiah and Savior. Even though he did not have the security of two believing parents, he gained an insight that would prove valuable in ministry. God wasted nothing in either Paul's or Timothy's background. He won't waste anything in your background either, if you will allow Him to use you.

4. *Timothy had a unique maturity.* In our society we've almost become convinced that bad influences are stronger than good. Timothy certainly is evidence to the contrary. We have a wonderful biblical precedent proving that godly influence can carry a much heavier weight than ungodly influence.

The words of 2 Timothy 1:5 offer strong encouragement to anyone married to an unbeliever. Paul wrote of the "sincere faith that first lived in your grandmother Lois, then in your mother Eunice, and that I am convinced is in you also" (HCSB). Yes, you can rear godly children in spite of imperfect circumstances. Lois and Eunice lived their faith. Timothy saw genuine examples of faithfulness. Their lives were devoted to God even when the company left. They were genuine—not perfect, but real. Their sincerity won Timothy to the truth.

Hang in there, parent! Let your children see the sincerity of your faith. Let them see you praying and trusting. Nothing carries the weight of sincere faith!

For Christ, Paul sacrificed many things dear to the Jew: marriage, children, strong extended family. God honored Paul's sacrifice by giving him other priceless gifts. Timothy was one of those gifts. He filled a void in Paul's life that no one else ever matched. Years later Paul described Timothy as "my dear son." Perhaps God thought a crusty old preacher needed a young whippersnapper as much as Timothy needed him.

# DAY 255
## Acts 16:4–8

⸺⸎⸺

When they came to Mysia, they tried to go into Bithynia, but the Spirit of Jesus
did not allow them. So, bypassing Mysia, they came down to Troas (vv. 7–8).

⸺⸎⸺

Romans 8:9 tells us God has placed His Spirit within each person who has
received Christ. One reason His Spirit takes up residence inside us is to tell us
things only believers can understand, leading us in areas of obedience to Christ.
The Holy Spirit always leads believers in Christ, but we don't always recognize
His leadership. A few basic practices can help us follow the leadership of the
Holy Spirit.

1. *Study God's Word.* God will never lead us in any direction contrary to His
Word.

2. *Yield to the Holy Spirit's control.* Being yielded to God's authority keeps us
pliable and open-minded to a possible change of plans.

3. *Pray for clear leadership.* Adopt David's approach to prayer in Psalm 27:11,
asking God to teach you His ways and lead you in a straight path.

4. *Pray for wisdom and discernment to recognize specific directions.* Paul asked
God to give believers "a spirit of wisdom and revelation" (Eph. 1:17) to know
Him better. This request is a good guideline for us too.

5. *Make plans, but hold on to them loosely!* I don't believe God intended for
Paul, Silas, and Timothy to travel haphazardly through the countryside. Paul was
a very intelligent man. He probably formulated an itinerary just like most of us
would, but he kept his plans open just in case God had different ideas!

6. *Learn to recognize peace as one of God's prompters.* Peace is one of the most
obvious earmarks of the authority of Christ. A sense of peace will virtually
always accompany His will and direction—even when the direction might not
have been our personal preference. On the other hand, a lack of peace will often
accompany a mistaken path—even when the direction is definitely our personal
preference. Remember, Christ is the Prince of Peace. His peace will accompany
His authority.

More than any other disciple, Paul was used of God to teach about the
activity of the Holy Spirit. But Paul could not teach what he had never learned.
He learned to follow the leadership of the Holy Spirit one day at a time, one city
at a time. Let's learn from his example and be willing to change our course when
we sense God has different plans.

# DAY 256
## Acts 16:9–15

⚬⚬⚬

Lydia, a dealer in purple cloth from the city of Thyatira,
who worshiped God, was listening. The Lord opened her heart
to pay attention to what was spoken by Paul (v. 14).

⚬⚬⚬

Paul and his small band of missionaries did not have to wait long for redirection after God removed their sense of peace and approval, prompting them not to enter the province of Asia. Following their willingness to allow God to change their plans, He used a vision to lead them into uncharted territory—a vision of a man from Macedonia begging Paul, "Cross over to Macedonia and help us!" (Acts 16:9 HCSB). As a result, the missionary band traveled to Philippi where Paul found no synagogue, so he preached at a gathering place outside the city.

There by the river he encountered a woman named Lydia. We've seen Paul have more thrilling encounters. Nothing outwardly dramatic happened. Almost seemed ho-hum, didn't it? Was this all that God had in mind—one woman's reception of the gospel—when He resisted their plans to preach His Word in the direction they were headed? But after temporarily closing a door in the province of Asia, God strained their eyes to see a much wider vision. The gospel of Jesus Christ went to Europe! Within a couple hundred years, Christians numbered in the tens of thousands in Europe. We hear people say, "When God closes a door, He opens a window." Sometimes we might just be underestimating Him. We just saw Him close a door and open a continent.

And it all started with a businesswoman named Lydia.

No one would ever suspect some of the feelings of spiritual inferiority professional Christian businesswomen harbor at times. For everyone who ever wondered if God could use a professional businesswoman, meet Lydia. She was a city girl, a salesperson. A homeowner with enough room to house a host of people. Yet her professional life was balanced by the priorities of her spiritual life. She worshiped God. She didn't see the Sabbath as an opportunity to catch up on some sleep and straighten up the house. She gathered with other believers. She found a place of prayer (v. 13). She opened her home. She made herself available to God. Because she did, "the Lord opened her heart" to hear Paul's message. And God gave birth to the gospel in Europe. I'd say that businesswoman had a pretty important ministry, wouldn't you?

# DAY 257
## Acts 16:16–24

—∞∞∞—

They said, "These men are seriously disturbing our city. They are Jews, and are promoting customs that are not legal for us as Romans to adopt or practice" (vv. 20–21).

—∞∞∞—

You may be wondering why four men preached the gospel in Philippi but only two of them were punished. Where were Luke and Timothy when the sparks started flying? The Roman world had recently experienced a fresh surge of anti-Semitism, and Emperor Claudius had expelled all Jews from Rome. Because few things are more contagious than prejudice, Philippi (a Roman colony) quickly caught the virus. Timothy and Luke may have been considered Gentiles by the Roman authorities. Since the governors of Philippi knew virtually nothing about Christianity, Paul and Silas were dragged before a strongly anti-Semitic magistrate and persecuted because of their Jewish heritage.

Imagine how the foursome felt: divided over their backgrounds, two were freed, and two were carried away maliciously. I'm not at all sure which two had the easier sentence. The book of Hebrews acknowledges the kinds of roles both pairs played: "Remember the earlier days when, after you had been enlightened, you endured a hard struggle with sufferings. Sometimes you were publicly exposed to taunts and afflictions, and at other times you were companions of those who were treated that way (Heb. 10:32–33 HCSB).

God is very aware that standing close to someone who is hurting hurts! He does it every day. But whether we are the ones suffering or we're alongside another, His grace is sufficient for our need. So you can cry out for help, even when you're hurting for someone else. He'll hear you and acknowledge your need!

Luke and Timothy deeply needed God's comfort as they watched the severe flogging of their partners. First, Paul and Silas were stripped—an incomprehensible humiliation to anyone with a Jewish background. Then they were mercilessly beaten with rods.

Paul probably suffered in both ways. He suffered his own blows, but he also stood by Silas as he was stripped and severely whipped. Can you imagine how Paul ached for his new assistant? Did he wonder if Silas could take it? If so, he found that no one needed to underestimate Silas. Luke and Timothy strained for a last look at their partners as the authorities dragged them to prison, wondering if they would ever see them again. In some ways, Luke and Timothy's night may have been longer than Silas and Paul's.

# DAY 258
## Acts 16:25–34

—◦◦◦—

About midnight Paul and Silas were praying and singing hymns to God,
and the prisoners were listening to them (v. 25).

—◦◦◦—

The two bloodied servants of God—Paul and Silas—had been taken to a
dungeon and placed in stocks, unable to move, pain wracking their bodies. Yet
though they were bound in iron chains, they found freedom to sing.

We cheat the faithful servants from showing us God's glory if we believe
God chose to anesthetize their pain. The awful truth is that death would have
been a relief. The challenge of their moment was living until the pain became
bearable—pain that is never more vivid than in the midnight hour. The night
lacks the kindness of the day when demands and activities distract. Each time
their hearts beat, every nerve ending throbbed with pain. In spite of their
anguish, their prayers ascended before the throne, and God gave them "songs in
the night" (Job 35:10).

Prayers come naturally when we are distressed—but songs? Finding notes
is difficult when your body is gripped with pain. Nonetheless, these few notes
found their way into a melody, and their melodies turned into hymns. Every
stanza issued a fresh strength and their voices were unchained—penetrating
walls and bars.

The most difficult part of my service as a Sunday school teacher has been
watching my members bury loved ones. Several years ago one of my members lost
her fifteen-year-old son in an automobile accident. I will never forget accompanying our friend to the funeral home and helping her choose a casket. All four of
us walked to the car and drove away without saying a word. Within a couple of
blocks, one of us began to cry, and then the rest joined her without saying a word.
Then after several minutes of silence, another began to sing with broken notes, "I
love you, Lord . . . and I lift my voice . . . to worship You . . . O, my soul rejoice."
I could hardly believe the nerve of my fellow member to sing at a time like that.
But before I could look at her with proper horror, the mother's best friend joined
in, "Take joy, my King, in what You hear . . . may it be a sweet, sweet sound in
Your ear."

The words fell from their lips a second time and to my shock, the brokenhearted mother began to sing. If *she* could sing, I knew I could not remain silent.
So we sang the rest of the way home that day. Not one of us had a solo voice, and
yet I wonder if I will ever hear a sound so beautiful again. I knew then what God
meant when He told us to lift up the sacrifice of praise. When praise is the last
thing that comes naturally to us and we choose to worship Him anyway, we've
had the privilege of offering a genuine sacrifice of praise.

When we sing a midnight song or speak praises in the darkest hours, the chains of hopelessness not only drop from our ankles but sometimes from the ankles of those who listen. We can preach the gospel in many ways, but the message is never more clear than when God's people refuse to cease their praises during intense suffering.

In their bondage, Paul and Silas were free to sing. They were also free to stay. Finally their songs were eclipsed by the rumblings of an earthquake. The foundations of the prison trembled before an awesome God. The prison doors flew open, every chain was loosed, and the jailer drew his sword to kill himself. Paul's words to him penetrate my heart: "Don't harm yourself!" (Acts 16:28 HCSB). How many people have felt compelled to harm themselves over hopelessness? The jailer knew he would be held responsible for their escape. "Don't harm yourself, because all of us are here!" shouted Paul.

Sometimes God frees us from chains so we can turn our backs on our slavery and walk away like Peter in Acts 12. He was free to leave. As a result, the church that was praying for his release was edified. Other times God frees us from chains so we can remain where we are to share the message of freedom with other captives. Paul was free to stay, not to leave. Because he did, a man asked, "'What must I do to be saved?'" (16:30). And an entire household found sweet liberty.

I met a young man who had experienced freedom from the bondage of homosexuality. Although he was a dedicated servant, God had never appointed him to share that part of his testimony nor minister to those still chained in that lifestyle. Like Peter, he had been freed to leave. Yet after God delivered me from the bondage of my childhood victimization, He called me to share my basic testimony and reach out to other survivors of abuse. I had been freed to stay. Both my friend and I experienced the glorious freedom of Christ. One was free to leave and one was free to stay, but we each trust God with His perfect plan for our lives.

God reserves the right to use His servants and their experiences in different ways. Let's try to resist copying a blueprint from another person's ministry. God is very creative, and He always has purpose in the specific ways He chooses to use us. Be willing to allow Him to put some things to public use and other things to private use. As life draws us to extremes, may we pass our tests as Paul and Silas did—with a song.

# DAY 259
## Acts 17:1–9

⎯⎯∞⎯⎯

As usual, Paul went to them, and on three Sabbath days reasoned
with them from the Scriptures (v. 2).

⎯⎯∞⎯⎯

Our next passage takes us to another stop on Paul's second missionary
journey—the Greek city of Thessalonica. We know Luke had accompanied the
missionaries to Philippi, but his terminology suggests that their paths parted for
awhile, presumably for the sake of the gospel. Luke's references to "we" rather
than "they" will pick up again several chapters later in the book of Acts. For now
we see Paul and Silas in Thessalonica.

Before we proceed, let's highlight a few points from this passage at the
beginning of Acts 17. Paul and Silas had traveled one hundred miles from
Philippi to Thessalonica without the benefit of a motorized vehicle. They seemed
to know exactly where they wanted to go and certainly did not lack the stamina
to get there!

You may be wondering what criteria made one city more of a priority than
another. Obviously the first criteria was the leadership of the Holy Spirit. If He
did not lead, they did not go. Paul cited another criteria in Romans 15:20, when
he declared, "My aim is to evangelize where Christ has not been named, in order
that I will not be building on someone else's foundation" (HCSB).

God used both of these principles: the leadership of the Holy Spirit and
Paul's desire to go into territories untouched by the gospel. And in each new
venue, not only did Paul customarily preach in the synagogues first, he employed
the same method each time. He sought to prove that Jesus was the Christ with
the Old Testament Scripture. I believe he used this method with them because
God had used it so effectively on him in the desert of Arabia. He knew this tech-
nique could work on the hardest of hearts because it had worked so well on his.

As a result, some Jews and many Greeks believed. But wherever there is
an awakening, you can always expect opposition. It wasn't long before the seed
of jealousy was planted in other Jews. They incited a riot, storming the house of
Jason, Paul's host in Thessalonica, searching in vain for a crack at "these men who
have turned the world upside down" (v. 6 HCSB). We see method. We see message.
We see patterns and expectations. We see a man serving God with a perfect
blend of spiritual sensitivity and dogged determination.

# DAY 260
### Acts 17:10–14

———— ⟨⟩ ————

They welcomed the message with eagerness and examined
the Scriptures daily to see if these things were so (v. 11).

———— ⟨⟩ ————

The Christians in Thessalonica got Paul out of jail and sent him to Berea. Only twenty miles from the sea, Berea had everything to offer: warm coastal breezes tempered by snowcapped mountains. What could be more inviting than a city set between the mountains and the ocean? Exceeding the noble sight, however, was the nobility of the people. The Bereans possessed characteristics that provide an excellent standard for believers today:

1. *They were willing to receive.* Acts 17:11 tells us the Bereans received the message. The Greek word for "receive" is *dechomai*, which means "to accept an offer deliberately and readily." The Bereans accepted the offer to come and hear what Paul had to say.

Many churches work overtime to offer opportunities for Christian growth and encouragement: conferences, retreats, Bible studies, discipleship training, and other methods. Often a relative few attend. And sometimes the ones who don't are the very ones who criticize the church for not doing enough. Many times we don't lack opportunities; we lack willingness. The Bereans accepted the offer to hear Paul teach and preach, and the fruit was bountiful.

2. *They were ready to receive.* The Bereans not only accepted the offer to hear Paul; they were eager to receive what he said. The original word for "eagerness" is *prothumia*, which indicates a predisposition for learning (Strong's). Our experiences in Bible study, worship services, and other discipleship opportunities are greatly enhanced when we approach each one with a predisposition for learning. We need to prepare ourselves with everything we can to have a receptive disposition before we arrive.

3. *They cross-examined the message with the Scriptures.* Paul was a very effective communicator, yet the Bereans did not take his word for everything. They measured the accuracy of his message against Scripture through their own personal examination of the Word. The original word for "examined" in Acts 17:11 is *anakrino*, which means "to ask, question, discern, examine, judge, search" (Strong's).

We all need to learn to study the Scriptures for ourselves. All believers have the right to ask questions and examine the Scriptures to check the accuracy of the teaching they hear. Congregations can be easily misled if they do not feel or exercise the freedom to double-check teaching and preaching against the Word of God. A savvy communicator can use the Scriptures taken out of context to teach almost anything! Any portion of Scripture must be compared with Scripture as a whole.

Some years ago a national forest had to close off a portion of its park to tourists. A number of bears starved to death during the time the park was closed. They had grown so accustomed to being fed by the tourists, they had ceased feeding themselves. We can likewise grow so accustomed to being spoon-fed the Word of God that we forget how to examine the Scriptures for ourselves. We can cease checking the nutritional value of what we're being taught!

But the Bereans not only performed the right practices, I believe they possessed the right heart. They didn't examine the Scriptures to see if they could find error in how Paul had dotted an "i" or crossed a "t." Their motive was not to argue. Some people double-check their pastors and teachers on every issue just to find an error so they can feel superior. The Bereans had no such motive. So a wonderful and sometimes rare combination occurred in Berea: the best kind of preacher met the best kind of audience. And a great awakening of faith resulted.

But soon the Jews in Thessalonica found out Paul was preaching in Berea and were vindictive enough to travel fifty miles to agitate and stir up the people! The original word for "stir up" has an interesting meaning. *Saleuo* means "to rock, topple, shake, stir up" (Strong's). The enemy of our souls will use every means and every human agent he can to topple us. And if all we have going for us are the opinions of men through sermons or lessons, little will be left when life shakes us up. But when we've learned to examine the Scriptures for ourselves, we have a few things nailed down when life starts to rock.

As you continue to study the Word of God, one nailed-down, personally discovered truth will turn into many, and you will be better equipped to face anything that comes your way. Nothing will profit you more than learning to examine the Scriptures for yourself. Let every preacher and teacher be a catalyst to your own personal journey through the Word. Spend time exploring. Invest in an exhaustive Bible concordance, a good Bible dictionary, and a sound set of commentaries. Accept opportunities to get into in-depth Bible studies and really get to know the Word. Be ready and willing to receive from the many opportunities available, but with the ability to discern truth from error through deep personal examinations of the Scripture. Imitating the noble practices of the Bereans will be your safety as teachers come and go—and your sanity when life rocks and rolls.

# DAY 261
## Acts 17:15–23

——⊗⊗⊗——

I even found an altar on which was inscribed: TO AN UNKNOWN GOD.
Therefore, what you worship in ignorance, this I proclaim to you (v. 23).

——⊗⊗⊗——

Come along as we see a lesson in contrasts. The next audience Paul encountered differed drastically from the noble Bereans. Meet the ancient Athenians. They will make you wonder how people who knew so much could understand so little.

Paul had a fruitful ministry at Berea until troublemakers came from Thessalonica. Then at the urging of the believers, Paul once again found himself moving on. This time the destination was Athens. Some of the believers escorted Paul there and left him, where he awaited the arrival of Silas and Timothy.

So Paul had to encounter the imposing city of Athens all by himself. And according to Acts 17:16, he reacted strongly to the sight of a city full of idols. Imagine going on a mission trip to a city like Varanasi, India—a Hindu holy city filled with temples and images depicting hundreds of gods. Yet here we have a tender opportunity to see the sincerity of Paul's heart, for "he reasoned in the synagogue with the Jews and with those who worshiped God, and in the marketplace every day with those who happened to be there" (v. 17 HCSB). He had no emotional or spiritual support and probably little physical support. None of the others would have known if he had simply been too intimidated to preach. No one would have blamed him anyway. Yet day by day he tried to reason with any Athenian who would listen, because he was so concerned that they needed Jesus Christ.

This audience of philosophers lived to hear some new idea and invited Paul to their meeting of the Areopagus on Mars Hill. There he preached an unusual sermon. He reached across the gulf of culture and beliefs that separated his hearers from Christ, finding an object lesson from their culture that he used to share the gospel with them. He found that they had an altar with this inscription: "to an unknown god." Beginning from that point, Paul shared the gospel with the philosophers. He said in effect, "Let me tell you about this God you don't know."

I believe Acts 17 contains one of the best sermons he ever preached. He used the perfect illustration (the unknown God) and drew his audience to the perfect invitation.

# DAY 262
Acts 17:24–34

⸺❦⸺

Some began to ridicule him. But others said, "We will hear you about this again."
So Paul went out from their presence (vv. 32–33).

⸺❦⸺

Paul never mentions a church resulting from his work in Athens. Only a few people became believers there, and he never made contact with them again as far as we know. Based on the information in Scripture, the few believers never multiplied into more.

And yet notice that he was not persecuted in Athens, nor was he forced to leave the city. Acts 18:1 tells us he simply left. Glance back over the previous chapters of the book of Acts. Compare this trip to the many others in Paul's ministry. Count the times he ran into very little opposition or persecution. You will search in vain to find another experience exactly like the one he had in Athens.

Why didn't they lift a hand to persecute him? Because they were too cold to care. Paul's experience in Athens is a perfect example of a situation in which people were open-minded to a fault. Their motto was "anything goes." Everyone was welcome to his own philosophy. Live and let live! If it works for you, go for it! Athens was the birthplace of the tolerance movement.

Often persecution is not nearly the enemy that indifference is. The Athenians did not care if Paul stayed or left. They believed virtually everyone was entitled to his god. A few sneered. Others were polite enough to say they would be willing to listen to his strange teachings again. But most never realized Paul was escorted into town by the one true God. And most never cared.

Acts 17 has changed the way I pray about the nations. I cannot count the times I've asked God to crumble the spirit of opposition and persecution in many nations where Christians are a small fighting force. I will still continue to ask God to strengthen and protect those facing opposition and persecution. However, I now find my heart drawn across the map to places where a quieter dragon of perhaps equal force has made its den—the spirit of indifference. Christianity can grow and flourish under some of the most difficult opposition, but it will prosper very little where people refuse to be changed by it. Paul's experience in Athens proves that the best of sermons will never change an unwilling person's heart.

# DAY 263
## Acts 18:12–18

—∞∞∞—

Paul, having stayed on for many days, said good-bye to the brothers and sailed away to Syria.... He shaved his head at Cenchreae, because he had taken a vow (v. 18).

—∞∞∞—

Dr. Luke seems to have included a sentence of pure trivia in Acts 18; yet in it we may discover a hidden treasure. At first glance, Acts 18:18 seems strange. When Paul left Corinth, he had his hair cut off at Cenchreae because of a vow he had taken.

Luke's writing is so tight, so succinct, his inclusion of Paul's quick stop by the barbershop is almost comical. Why in the world would we need to know Paul got a haircut? Actually, this verse holds a primary key to understanding Paul's visit to Corinth. The point is not the haircut. The point is the reason for Paul's haircut.

Paul's haircut resulted from a vow he had made. Remember, Paul was a Jewish Christian. His Jewish heritage was deeply rooted. He understood that Christ did not save him to make him *forget* his heritage but to *complete* his heritage. At times he still applied some of the former practices of the Jew, not as legalities but as wise choices. Virtually without a doubt, the vow to which Luke was referring was the Nazirite vow.

Numbers 6:1–8 describes the Nazirite vow. The second verse explains the nature and purpose of it: "If a man or woman wants to make a special vow," he or she could employ the Nazarite vow as "a vow of separation to the Lord."

The word "wants" identifies the first crucial element of the Nazirite vow—it was strictly voluntary. The word "special" points to the second element. The Nazirite vow was special because of its voluntary nature and because it was offered to men and women alike (v. 2)—unusual in ancient Judaism. Third, notice that the purpose of the Nazirite vow is "separation." The Hebrew word is *pala*, indicating something consecrated to God, distinguished from others, something marvelous and even miraculous often coming from something difficult (Strong's).

Now let's see if we can put this definition into understandable terms. If an Israelite man or woman was going through a time when he or she felt the necessity to be extraordinarily consecrated to God—usually a time of extremely difficult circumstances or temptation—the person would voluntarily take this vow. They knew that in order to be victorious or obedient, they needed extra help and concentration on God.

Paul's recent experiences in Athens were not the only problems he faced in coming to Corinth. He had to confront incredible depravity in this cosmopolitan city. Even by today's standards, Corinth was extremely sexually explicit. The most significant pagan practice was the cult of Aphrodite. Aphrodite represented lust and every kind of sexual perversion. Her followers literally worshiped her through acts of immorality—often in plain sight. Paul had never seen anything remotely like the perversion he would encounter in Corinth.

The haircut in verse 18 is not the beginning of the vow. The haircut signaled the end. Before he entered Corinth's gates, Paul wisely committed himself to the vow of the Nazirite so he could maintain consecration to and concentration on Christ, the only One who could lead him to victory (see 2 Cor. 2:14).

Paul's actions teach us an important lesson. We obviously need to avoid temptation, but when we can't help but face it, we can prepare ourselves.

Numbers 6:3 commands anyone taking the Nazirite vow to abstain from wine or strong drink. I have chosen to abstain from alcohol not because I believe alcohol is forbidden, but because I believe it could become a distraction to me. No one told me to abstain from alcohol. I voluntarily made the decision after an honest self-evaluation. I do not believe I could deal with both alcohol and the serious devotion God has asked of me. I can think of too many ways Satan could use it to trap me.

Another practice of the Nazirite provides our clue to understanding the message of Acts 18:18. Those who took the Nazirite vow were to allow their hair to grow long as a physical sign of special devotion to God. That way, if they temporarily forgot their vow, the quickest glance in a mirror would remind them. Also, others would ask why they let their hair grow so long, and this would give them an opportunity to testify about their devotion to God. Once Paul's need for extraordinary consecration to God was over, he went to Cenchreae and got a haircut!

I am impressed with Paul at this point. How about you? His weaknesses, insecurities, and temptations were the same as ours, but he was wise in dealing with them.

Matthew 10:16 is one of my favorite verses. Jesus told His followers to be as "shrewd as serpents and as harmless as doves" (HCSB). Innocence or harmlessness does not mean naïveté. In fact, had Paul approached Corinth naively, he could have gotten into serious trouble. The kind of innocence Christ described was righteousness in spite of reality! That's the kind of righteousness Paul lived. It's the kind we can live as well.

# DAY 264
## Acts 18:19–23

---

He himself entered the synagogue and engaged in discussion with the Jews. And
though they asked him to stay for a longer time, he declined (vv. 19–20).

---

When Paul completed his long stay in Corinth, he sailed for Syria, accompanied by a couple he had met and stayed with in Corinth—Priscilla and Aquila.
(Their names sound good together, don't they?) Once again the apostle to the
Gentiles made a beeline to the synagogue to reason with the Jews, but in Ephesus
he found a different reception. The Jews at the synagogue asked him to spend a
while with them. This time, however, Paul declined. He went on with his journey
to Antioch, leaving Priscilla and Aquila behind.

Do you find Paul's return to the synagogue interesting? Recall his last experience with the Jews in the synagogue of Corinth. He became so frustrated with
them, "he shook out his clothes and told them, 'Your blood is on your own heads!
I am clean. From now on I will go to the Gentiles'" (Acts 18:6 HCSB). I thought he
had finished preaching to the Jews altogether. But in Ephesus he went right back
to the synagogue and reasoned with them again. Paul's ministry was far more
productive among the Gentiles, so why did he continue to return to the Jews in
virtually every city he visited?

In Romans 9:2–5, Paul answered this question. He so desperately wanted
his fellow Jews to know Christ that, if possible, he would have died for them. He
could hardly bear for the Jews to miss Christ. He must have been ecstatic over
the favorable response of the Jews at the synagogue in Ephesus, but again we see
why Paul was such an effective minister and servant. He had surrendered his life
to the leadership of the Holy Spirit. He was not driven by his own desires and
rationalizations. In his position, I might have convinced myself I was supposed
to remain in Ephesus, at least for a while, based on my own desires to see God
do a work among a people I loved and an apparent open door. They were begging
for more! Yet Acts 18:20 tells us he declined. Paul firmly and lovingly said no.

I have a difficult time saying no. Do you? Paul probably had a difficult time,
too, but he was careful to remain focused on God's priorities for him. Paul's
example teaches us a timely lesson. The fact that a need exists does not mean God
has called me to meet that need. We are wise to trust Him when He seems to be
leading us contrary to those things we want to do or those things that seem to be
so rational and fitting.

# DAY 265
## Acts 18:24–28

———◦∞◦———

*Being fervent in spirit, he spoke and taught the things about
Jesus accurately, although he knew only John's baptism (v. 25).*

———◦∞◦———

We now get to discover one reason why God did not lead Paul to remain
in Ephesus. A Jew named Apollos came there. He was a powerful, passionate
preacher with a thorough knowledge of the Scripture. So while Paul may not
have known it, his void left an opening for a dazzling preacher. When we can't
say no even when God does not give His approval, two unfortunate repercussions
often result: we don't do a good job and we don't leave an opening for God's
chosen person to fill.

But the account of Apollos gives us one more lesson before we move on. He
traveled to Achaia to preach. Corinth was the capital of Achaia, so he walked
into exactly the same audiences the apostle Paul had. Initially Apollos only knew
part of the gospel. But "after Priscilla and Aquila heard him, they took him home
and explained the way of God to him more accurately" (Acts 18:26 HCSB). With
his newfound knowledge, Apollos preached the same kind of message but with
his own style.

We get a good glimpse into human nature as Paul later addressed the
believers in Corinth. They responded to those who came and preached to them
by forming warring camps. The people then reacted much like we react today. We
tend to compare Christian leaders and fall into camps behind our choices. We
must make a concerted effort to avoid doing so. Each of us could cite an example,
but every branch of in-depth Bible study has loyal supporters who swear by that
particular method or teacher. Some would rather fight than switch.

God is wooing people to His table for the meat of His Word like never
before. He is joyfully using many different methods and styles to accomplish His
goal of equipping His church to be effective and holy during difficult days. God
has raised many fine teachers and preachers for our day. Let's reap the benefit of
as many as possible and value their contributions whether they are magnetic like
Apollos, analytical like Luke, forthright like Paul, or warm like Priscilla and
Aquila. Paul's style may have been one reason some of the Corinthians preferred
Apollos: Paul didn't mince words. But his answer to those who were camping
around certain speakers? "Oh, grow up!" (see 1 Cor. 3:3–4).

# DAY 266
## Acts 19:1–7

——— ∞ ———

"Did you receive the Holy Spirit when you believed?" "No," they told him,
"we haven't even heard that there is a Holy Spirit" (v. 2).

——— ∞ ———

Acts 19 begins with Paul's meeting an interesting group of believers. They did not know about the Holy Spirit, and they had received only the baptism of John. These people were in a strange situation—in limbo between the Old and New Testaments. Paul told them of Christ with the result that they received the Holy Spirit, spoke in tongues, and prophesied.

These original converts knew virtually nothing about the Holy Spirit. Even their knowledge of the Old Testament didn't help much because the Spirit's activity was so different after the coming of Christ. Remember, only about a hundred people in the Old Testament were ever described as having the Holy Spirit in or on them. Prior to Christ and the birth of the New Testament church, the Spirit's purpose was not to mark salvation but to empower certain individuals for designated tasks. Since the birth of the church, the Holy Spirit takes up residence in every believer in Christ (see Rom. 8:9). John's baptism was a sign of repentance in anticipation of the coming Christ. Christian baptism is a mark to demonstrate the salvation Christ has given and the receipt of the Holy Spirit.

God knew the concept of the Holy Spirit would be difficult for new believers to understand as He raised up His church, so God made His Spirit obvious. He sometimes accompanied His Spirit with a sudden physical evidence such as speaking in tongues. Few topics have caused division like speaking in tongues. But no matter what you believe about tongues, Paul was clear on at least two points concerning the activity of the Holy Spirit:

1. All believers are baptized by the Holy Spirit. The Spirit resides in all believers equally (see 1 Cor. 12:13).

2. Not all believers spoke in tongues (see 1 Cor. 12:30).

Many believe God never uses the gift of tongues today. Many others believe God always gives the gift of tongues to every true believer. I believe we are wise to avoid words like *always* and *never*. He told us to love one another, not judge one another.

# DAY 267
Acts 19:8-10

---

When some became hardened and would not believe, slandering the Way in front of
the crowd, he withdrew from them and met separately with the disciples (v. 9).

---

Acts 19:8–10 summarizes Paul's ministry in Ephesus, where he preached
in the synagogue for three months until stiff opposition arose, persuading Paul
to move his ministry to a lecture hall where he could concentrate on discipling
believers, with the result that "all the inhabitants of the province of Asia, both
Jews and Greeks, heard the word of the Lord" (v. 10 HCSB).

Interestingly, it was the same group in Ephesus that had previously asked
Paul to spend more time with them (see Acts 18:20) who quickly got over him
when he returned! "Some became hardened and would not believe" (19:9 HCSB),
which is why Paul took a group of the followers aside and began discipling them
daily. Can you imagine being part of that Bible study? But again, don't miss the
bountiful fruit produced from Paul's discipleship group: within two years the
message of Jesus Christ and His gospel had spread throughout the entire region.
The churches of Laodicea, Colosse, and Hierapolis were all founded as a result of
this great and supernatural movement of God.

Like Gideon's army (see Judg. 7), a few well-trained soldiers in the Lord's
service can be more effective than hundreds who have never been discipled. God
honors His Word and often overtly blesses discipleship with fruit far beyond
human effort. Paul was an effective teacher, but God still produced fruit far
beyond his labor. When a few seeds produce a huge crop, God's up to something
supernatural! Acknowledge it and praise Him! He makes obvious His blessing
on true discipleship.

God performs His work in countless ways we cannot see. He remains active
in our lives even when we are unaware, even when we feel defeated, unwelcome,
and misunderstood. Sometimes, however, He makes Himself entirely obvious—as He would go on to work through Paul in the passage we'll consider
tomorrow—so that what we see will strengthen our faith in what we cannot see.
The early church was learning concepts completely new to most. God purposely
showed His visible handprints so that many would place their lives in His invisible hands.

# DAY 268
## Acts 19:11–20

—∞∞—

This became known to everyone who lived in Ephesus, both Jews and Greeks. Then fear fell on all of them, and the name of the Lord Jesus was magnified (v. 17).

—∞∞—

My oldest daughter, Amanda, was very frightened of storms when she was little. Loud peals of thunder sent her into near panic, even when we were in the safety of our home. One day when the sky seemed to be falling, I held her in my arms and said, "Honey, the heavens are just displaying the glory of God (see Ps. 19:1). They are showing us how mighty He is." Her little forehead furrowed as if she were really thinking over what I had said. Some weeks later, she was upstairs playing when a storm hit. I heard her feet scurry like lightning down the stairs. Then she yelled at the top of her lungs, "Mommy! God's really showing off today!"

God seemed to work overtime on Paul's stop in Ephesus as He revealed His power in extraordinary ways. God used special demonstrations to authenticate His ambassadors and persuade belief. More than anywhere else in the apostolic era, it was a time when God chose to display His power. The accent of Acts 19 appears in verse 11: "God was performing extraordinary miracles by Paul's hands" (HCSB).

One reason God showed His marvelous power to such a degree in this particular city was because Ephesus was a renowned center for magical incantations. In his book *Paul the Traveller*, Ernle Bradford wrote, "Ephesus was the centre of occult studies, indeed it has been called 'The Home of Magic.'" He also tells us, "Ephesus was full of wizards, sorcerers, witches, astrologers, diviners of the entrails of animals, and people who could read one's fortune by the palm of the hand or the fall of knucklebones."[59] Many of the Ephesians were neck deep in the occult, but virtually the entire population was extremely interested in supernatural phenomena and the powers of the unseen world. This is one reason Paul was most outspoken to them about spiritual warfare in his letter to them, the book of Ephesians. While Paul was in their midst, God intentionally got their attention by surpassing anything they had ever seen.

I believe God revealed His power there to make true repentance obvious. The activity of the Holy Spirit in Acts 19:18–19 is perhaps my favorite of those that God performed in Ephesus—only slightly more awe-inspiring than the power in Paul's facecloths and work aprons, or the hilarious story of the seven sons of a Jewish priest named Sceva in verses 14–15. (I can hardly read that story without laughing. I'm sure God has a great sense of humor. This account makes me wonder if the devil may even have one.) Some works of God are more subtle but not necessarily less supernatural. According to John 16:8, one of the most important activities of the Spirit is to "convict the world about sin, righteousness, and judgment" (HCSB). Matthew 3:8 tells us to "produce fruit consistent with repentance" (HCSB). And when the new converts burned their sorcery books, they brought forth some impressive fruit!

God can reveal Himself through both natural or supernatural means. Both are at His complete disposal. Although God also worked in subtle ways, He apparently chose to reveal Himself through several phenomenal means while Paul was in Ephesus. Why did He make His activity so obvious among the Ephesians? Because Satan had made his work so obvious there. Satan is powerful, but he is no match for the Almighty God.

Sometimes I am completely perplexed by God's willingness to humor us. His mercy knows no bounds. When He wanted to lead the Magi to the Christ child, He did not lead them by a mark in the sand. He led them through a star because they were stargazers—then He went beyond anything they had ever seen. In the same way, when God wanted to lead the Ephesians to the Savior, He did not lead them through a cloudy pillar. He got their attention through supernatural phenomena, because that's where they were looking. God wants to be found. He does not will for any to miss Him, and He is so gracious to show up right where we are looking—so He can take us beyond anything we've ever seen.

God sometimes reveals Himself to a homeless man hiding under a bridge through a blanket brought to him by a caring minister. He sometimes reveals Himself to a drunk through a servant who cares for him and offers him Living Water. He sometimes reveals Himself to a prostitute through a godly police officer who tells her Christ can set her free.

If we're waiting for the needy to walk through our church doors, we may wait a long time. God doesn't wait for people to come to Him. He goes to them and desires to intervene right at the point of their need. He's looking for a few brave people, like the apostle Paul, who are willing to go rather than wait for them to come. He's not looking for show-offs. He's looking for people through whom He can show off His Son. May we be some of those people. We might end up agreeing with Amanda: "God's really showing off today!"

# DAY 269
## Acts 19:21–31

―――∞∞∞―――

"So not only do we run a risk that our business may be discredited,
but also that the temple of the great goddess Artemis may be despised" (v. 27).

―――∞∞∞―――

While Paul was in Ephesus, the Emperor Claudius was poisoned and the Roman Empire fell into the hands of a seventeen-year-old boy named Nero. Christians soon suspected he was the Antichrist. Rome would ultimately be an important part of Paul's life. His wisdom told him to go there. God did not want him to miss it either, so He placed a virtually irresistible compulsion in Paul. And just in case the motivations of wisdom and burden were not enough, we are about to see a third: trouble—lots of trouble.

In the passages we've read so far, Paul was opposed only once before by the Gentiles. The first case of opposition occurred in Philippi (Acts 16:16–19) when Paul cast the demon from the fortune-telling girl. Now here in Acts 19 a silversmith named Demetrius stirred up opposition because the Christian revival was a threat to the income of those who sold idols. In both Philippi and Ephesus, it was profit that motivated Gentiles to oppose Paul.

Obviously a person does not have to be entirely genuine to be effective! Demetrius appealed to the people of Ephesus both financially with the claim that Paul was hurting trade, and spiritually with the idea that he was robbing Artemis of her majesty. Demetrius apparently reasoned that one of those two needles would surely hit a vein in everyone within earshot. He may have lacked integrity, but he didn't lack intelligence. His approach worked better than he could have dreamed. The people began shouting, "Great is Artemis of the Ephesians!"

In Greek mythology Artemis was believed to be the daughter of Zeus. The temple the Ephesians had built in her honor was so mammoth, it was later considered one of the Seven Wonders of the Ancient World. The Ephesians exceeded the size of her temple, however, with their ability to make a buck in her name. The silver craftsmen were making a fortune off silver charms and statuettes of her likeness. You can be fairly certain most of the merchants cared very little about robbing Artemis of her majesty. You can also be certain the outspoken apostle had assured them she had none.

This scene must have been something to behold. The crowd shouted "Great is Artemis of the Ephesians" for hours. Paul wanted to go into the theater to speak to the crowd, but his friends persuaded him not to go. In the situation I find a number of fascinating clues into the person and personality of Paul.

1. Based on Paul's willingness to address the crowd (v. 30), we may assume that he sometimes had more courage than sense! He was going to speak out in behalf of Christianity no matter what! The theater in Ephesus held twenty-five

thousand people! When God gives us good sense, He expects us to use it. I believe the only time we are to walk into a dangerous or risky situation is when we have crystal clear leadership from God.

2. Also based on verse 30, I believe Paul's disciples were not afraid to disagree with him. He was not a religious dictator who surrounded himself with yes-men. Times obviously existed when his colleagues said no. He was not only a preacher and teacher, he was a discussion leader (see v. 9). Leaders who are afraid of others disagreeing with them usually don't leave much room for discussion.

3. I am fairly impressed by a third assumption we can make: Paul sometimes let the wisdom of others take precedence over his own desires. We read that Paul's friends would not let him go. If I know anything at all about the apostle, he had to let them not let him! Short of being physically tied down, I can't imagine how they could stop him from going unless he submitted to their wisdom. He could have rebuked them for not believing that speaking up was worth the risk of dying. Instead he obviously listened to them and relented. I am refreshed by leaders who do not think they always have to be right.

4. One more assumption I would like to make is based on verse 31. Paul obviously had many good friends. When we began our journey together, I'm not sure any of us pictured Paul as friendly. Although he possessed a passion for Christ and a perseverance in servitude, I never really thought of him as being genuinely gracious. I assumed he was respected far more than he was liked. But Paul obviously had good friends from every walk of life: Jews, Gentiles, rich, and poor. Aquila and Priscilla did not leave their home and travel with Paul because he was unpleasant! Obviously he possessed a genuinely likable personality. Many people surrendered to serve Christ as a direct result of Paul's influence. Had he been an ogre, people would not have been so ready to follow his example.

Verse 31 describes another group of people who were extremely fond of Paul: officials of the province. They loved him enough to beg him not to venture into the theater. Let's learn something about judging others. We tend to describe people in brief phrases: he's always funny; she's always so bossy; he's such a controlling person; she never fails to be upbeat. God created human beings to be the most complex creatures alive. None of us can be wrapped up in a single phrase. Yes, Paul could be unyielding, but he could also be persuaded. He could be tough, and he could be very gracious. He was not so different from the rest of us, perhaps, on any given day!

# DAY 270
## Acts 19:32–41

───⊶✧⊷───

Meanwhile, some were shouting one thing and some another, because the assembly was in confusion, and most of them did not know why they had come together (v. 32).

───⊶✧⊷───

The crowd of twenty-five thousand Ephesians was a madhouse. That's when the Jews pushed a man named Alexander to the front, hoping to provide a defense, a disclaimer for them. They wanted him to tell the crowds that Paul's teaching was separate from theirs, that they were not responsible for the financial harm done to the silver craftsmen. "But when they recognized that he was a Jew, a united cry went up from all of them for about two hours: 'Great is Artemis of the Ephesians!'" (Acts 19:34 HCSB).

The Jews knew without a doubt that the silver craftsmen were profiting off the ignorance and sinful practices of pagans. They certainly had a stake in confronting idolatry. Exodus 20:3–4 unmistakably forbids it. Because of their opposition to Paul, however, they violated their own consciences and belief system.

Consider, though, the beliefs of the Ephesians. They believed the image of Artemis had fallen from heaven. Some scholars assume they were describing a meteor that had hit Ephesus, one that the people had thought to look like a multi-breasted woman. Therefore, they assumed it was the goddess Artemis and hailed her as the deity of childbirth. I am sometimes amazed at the things people believe.

A number of years ago, I prepared to teach the book of Genesis in Sunday school. In an attempt to be prepared for questions and rebuttals, I thought I'd study the theory of evolution. I was somewhat intimidated by the prospect, but I checked out a few books and started my research. I only had to flip a few pages before my chin dropped to the ground. At times I even laughed out loud. I couldn't believe that this theory is taught as fact in many public schools. After a fairly in-depth comparison, I decided it took far more faith to believe in evolution than creation!

When Paul came to Ephesus, he brought the message of a Messiah sent from God who offers eternal life to every individual who believes. I'm no rocket scientist, but I find Paul's message far more believable than a goddess falling out of heaven in the form of a meteor. Yes, God requires faith—but not as much as a number of other belief systems falling out of the skies today. Go ahead and believe Him. He's very believable.

## DAY 271
### Acts 20:1–12

---

A young man named Eutychus was sitting on a window sill and sank
into a deep sleep as Paul kept on speaking. . . . Overcome by sleep
he fell down from the third story (v. 9).

---

I am so amused by this text. God used my desire to be like Paul to motivate
me to write an entire book about him. So far, I've noticed that most of the characteristics I share with him are those of his human rather than his spiritual nature.
A common colloquialism states, "If the shoe fits, wear it." I don't know what size
shoe you wear, but I can tell you in advance: this lesson is a size 7 medium. Just
my size. Read on. It just may come in your size too.

In two verses Luke tells us that after leaving Ephesus, Paul then traveled
through Macedonia and into Greece where he stayed three months. The Jews
again plotted against him as he prepared to sail for Syria, so he took the land
route back through Macedonia once more. Counting Luke, eight people accompanied Paul back through Macedonia.

The group spent a week in Troas, culminating in the event I find so humorous and convicting. Paul taught, and because they were going to leave the next
day, he talked until midnight. Luke tells us that the upstairs room where they
were meeting contained many lamps. A young man named Eutychus fell asleep,
fell out the window, "and was picked up dead" (Acts 20:9).

You know you aren't having a good day when you fall asleep in church and
are picked up dead. Unlike most of us, however, Eutychus stayed dead for only
a short while.

Luke wrote meticulously without inclusion of unnecessary details. What
bearing do you suppose the lamps had on the account of the midnight meeting?
And while we are supposing, can you think of any reasons why God made certain
Luke joined Paul in time for this strange set of circumstances?

We want to grasp as accurately as possible the kind of man Paul was. The
love of Christ so compelled him that his energy seemed to have no bounds. We
will do his memory no harm, however, by pointing out that sometimes his energy
exceeded that of his audience. Like many other preachers and teachers, Paul
preached longer than his audience was prepared to listen!

Figuratively speaking, at this point I am pulling the shoe out of the box
and putting it on my guilty foot. A woman once said to me after one of my lec-
tures, "I'm going home and taking a nap. You've worn me out." Sometimes those
of us in teaching, preaching, and speaking positions talk too long. Mind you,
we can have the best of intentions. I can entirely relate to the apostle for being

so long-winded; this was his last chance, and he was determined to say everything he could before he departed. He didn't want to leave a single thing unsaid.

In Paul's defense, I must explain one of the pitfalls accompanying the gift of teaching. Teachers often feel that whatever they learn, they must teach—every last word of it! I have forty-five minutes on Sunday mornings during which I often try to teach everything I learned in hours of preparation. Sometimes I've tried to teach all I knew—plus a lot of things I didn't! Paul obviously didn't always know when to wrap up a message either. Don't you get a kick out of Luke's words: "Paul talked on and on"? (v. 9).

I believe God purposely gave us the opportunity to giggle over a fairly typical event: a preacher or teacher outlasting the audience. However, God provided a very effective eye-opener by doing something quite atypical. He gave Paul a chance to raise the dead!

Picture the scene with me a moment. A large group of people were gathered in one room, and the lamps provided just enough heat to make the atmosphere cozy and warm. Most of the listeners had awakened with the rising sun, and the time was now approaching midnight. Eutychus was sitting in the windowsill, trying to stay attentive. The young man's eyelids would drop; then he would force them open. He finally fell into a deep sleep, probably had a dream that caused him to jump, and out the window he flew. This story would not be humorous without the happy ending. Since you know God raised Eutychus from the dead, wouldn't you have loved to see Paul's face when the boy fell out of the window? He ran downstairs as fast as his legs could carry him. "Paul . . . threw himself on the young man and put his arms around him. 'Don't be alarmed,' he said, 'He's alive!'" (v. 10). What a relief! A wonderfully rare phenomenon took place that day.

I find myself amused once again as the scene ends. Paul went back to business as usual. He climbed three flights of stairs, broke bread with them, and talked until daylight. All in a day's work. I have a feeling no one fell asleep this time. In fact, they may have been wide awake for days! Here is my moral to the story: may God bring back to life whom man hath put to sleep.

So make me one promise as we conclude: never sit close to a window when working on one of my lessons, listening to one of my teaching series, or reading one of my books. Meanwhile, I'll see if I can get this size 7 shoe off my foot and back in the box where it belongs.

# DAY 272
## Acts 20:13–21

---

"I testified to both Jews and Greeks about repentance toward
God and faith in our Lord Jesus" (v. 21).

---

After his eventful night in Troas, Paul set sail on his journey toward
Jerusalem. He purposely sailed past Ephesus, yet he summoned the elders to
come to Miletus and meet with him. Paul had little time, so he left the Ephesian
elders the basic necessities.

Like a father with only a few moments left to share his heart with his children, Paul shared things that were priority to him. He reminded them of the
attention he had given to their needs. He shared his assumptions, his ambition,
his heartfelt admonition, and his deep affection. He said, "You know, from the
first day I set foot in Asia, how I was with you the whole time—serving the
Lord with all humility, with tears, and with the trials that came to me through
the plots of the Jews—and that I did not shrink back from proclaiming to you
anything that was profitable, or from teaching it to you in public and from house
to house" (Acts 20:18–20 HCSB).

I believe Paul was personally attentive to the Ephesians because he became
involved with them emotionally as well as spiritually. Remember, he remained
among these people for several years. I believe he poured himself out among
them as much or more than any other group to whom he ministered. They saw
his "humility." This word involves "the confession of his sin and a deep realization
of his unworthiness to receive God's marvelous grace." He was open with them
about his past sin and his feelings of unworthiness in the ministry God had given
him. They not only saw his humility; they saw his heart. He did not hide from
them his tears or the pain of his hardships.

The Ephesians knew Paul was genuine. He approached them withholding
nothing. He did not hesitate to preach anything that would be helpful. He loved
them enough to teach them anything and everything that would be of benefit,
even if they didn't like it. He was willing to hurt their feelings momentarily if it
would help their hearts eternally.

Paul had given them everything he had while he was there. In verse 27, he
restated: "I did not shrink back from declaring to you the whole plan of God"
(HCSB). He didn't just teach them the many wonderful things God wanted to do
for them. He also taught them the truth about hardships that would inevitably
come and the calling of the crucified life.

# DAY 273
## Acts 20:22–24

⸺✹⸺

In town after town the Holy Spirit testifies to me that
chains and afflictions are waiting for me (v. 23).

⸺✹⸺

In his attentiveness Paul withheld nothing from the Ephesians. He assumed he was bound to have difficulties when he got to Jerusalem because the Holy Spirit had warned him of hardships in every other city. He couldn't imagine Jerusalem being any exception. In fact, he probably assumed he would have more problems than ever as he returned to Jerusalem.

He also assumed he would never see the Ephesians again. I have a feeling he might have feared he would be put to death in Jerusalem. Some scholars believe he did see the Ephesians once more. Others believe he did not. At this point he spoke to them as if he would never see them again.

Next he shared with them his chief ambition: "I count my life of no value to myself, so that I may finish my course and the ministry I received from the Lord Jesus" (Acts 20:24 HCSB). He was so determined to be faithful to the task God had assigned him, his certainty of suffering could not dissuade him.

Fear is a very powerful tool. Don't think for a moment Satan did not try to use fear to hinder the apostle from fulfilling God's purposes, and don't think Paul was not terrified at times. Of course he was. To think otherwise would be to minimize his faithfulness. Paul was afraid, but his love for Christ exceeded his fear of suffering and death. His primary ambition was finishing his task faithfully. Notice the phrase in verse 24: "the ministry I received from the Lord Jesus." Paul felt no responsibility to complete the task Christ had given Peter or Barnabas or Timothy. He believed and taught that God has specific plans for each believer. He expressed the concept clearly in Ephesians 2:10: "We are His creation—created in Christ Jesus for good works, which God prepared ahead of time so that we should walk in them" (HCSB).

God has a task for you—one He planned very long ago and suited for our present generation. Remember you are not responsible for completing anyone else's task, just yours. God desires for us to encourage one another in our tasks (see Heb. 10:24–25), but we are responsible only for completing our own.

# DAY 274
## Acts 20:25–31

———

"Be on guard for yourselves and for all the flock . . ." (v. 28a).

———

Believing he would never see the Ephesians again, Paul had an urgency to share with them an admonition. He warned the Ephesian elders about the vulnerability of the young church. He told them to expect savage wolves to try to devour the flock. Paul considered the warning so vital, he repeated it over and over during the three years he was among them.

Don't miss an important part of his admonition. In verse 28, Paul named two groups the elders were to keep watch over: themselves and the flock God had given them. What an important message Paul's words send to us! We can hardly keep watch over a group if we don't keep watch over ourselves! The Greek term for "keep watch" is *prosecho*. "As a nautical term, it means to hold a ship in a direction, to sail towards . . . to hold on one's course toward a place." Many leaders have seasons when their lives seem temporarily out of control. Most people who have served God for decades have had a season in which they got off course. Those who never depart from the course in many years of service deserve our highest commendations, but they are rare.

I do not believe a leader who temporarily veers away from the course should never be allowed to lead again. I can't find a biblical precedent for such thinking. On the other hand, we are wise leaders to step out of leadership when we are having a difficult time staying on the course. We simply cannot lead others to a place to which we are not steering our own lives. Yes, leaders must watch over their own lives very carefully, but Paul also told them they must act like shepherds keeping watch over their flocks.

We don't have to be church elders for these words and warnings to apply to us. If God has assigned you a flock, you have a serious responsibility to keep a close watch over your own life and to care deeply for theirs. A crucial part of keeping watch over our flocks is knowing the Word of God! In verse 30, Paul warned that "men will arise and distort the truth." The word "distort" denotes an action of twisting or turning. Satan is a master at twisting and turning the Word of God. He's been honing his twisting skills since his first successful attempt in the Garden of Eden. He subtly twists the Word in hope that we won't realize we've been misled until after he wreaks havoc. Paul had very little time to address the Ephesian elders, yet the warning to watch over themselves and their flocks was an absolute priority. Paul shared one last element with the Ephesians, which we will see tomorrow. He shared his sincere affection for them.

# DAY 275
## Acts 20:32-38

---

"And now I commit you to God and to the message of His grace . . ." (v. 32a).

---

The final picture painted at the end of Acts 20 touches my heart so much. Paul was a man of many words, but the primary message of his affection for the Ephesians came more in action than in words. Any man as beloved as Paul had most assuredly loved. He was the very one who taught others, "Love never fails" (1 Cor. 13:8). I wonder if at this moment he thought love also never fails to hurt. He committed them to God, said a few last words, then knelt with them and prayed.

Don't quickly pass by this moment. Let it take form in your mind. Imagine a group of men, replete with all the things that make them men—size, stature, strength, controlled emotions—on their knees praying together. Thankfully this is not a picture I have trouble imagining. My pastor often asks the men of our church to join him at the altar down on their knees in prayer. As a woman in the church, nothing makes me feel more secure. To me, a man is his tallest when he is down on his knees in prayer.

Imagine this next scene between Paul and the elders: "There was a great deal of weeping by everyone. And embracing Paul, they kissed him" (v. 37 HCSB). One by one each man hugged him and said good-bye. With every embrace I'm sure he remembered something special—a good laugh shared, a late night over a sick loved one, a baptism in a cold river, a heated argument resolved. He had been their shepherd. Now he would leave them to tend their flocks on their own. In the midst of painful good-byes, perhaps Paul thought the same thing I've thought a time or two when my heart was hurting: "I will never let myself get this involved again." But of course, he did. And so will we, if we continue to walk in the footsteps of our Savior. To extend hands of service without hearts of love is virtually meaningless.

The chapter concludes with Paul and his friends walking side by side down the path to the docks, beards still wet with tears. Had I been Paul, I would have gotten on that ship as quickly as possible and dared not look back. That's not what happened. Luke opens the next chapter by reporting, "We tore ourselves away from them and set sail" (21:1 HCSB). I think Luke, who was waiting at the boat (see 20:13), literally had to go and tear the apostle away from them.

Obviously the Ephesians had some idea how blessed they were to have the kind of leader Paul was to them. He was a leader who kept watch over himself and his followers. In nautical terms, he was the best kind of captain—one who kept the vessel on course even if his compass took him far from those he loved. He had given them all he had. The best kind of good-bye is the kind with no regrets.

# DAY 276
## Acts 21:1–6

——∞∞∞——

All of them, with their wives and children, escorted us out of the city. After kneeling
down on the beach to pray, we said good-bye to one another (vv. 5–6).

——∞∞∞——

Although Paul had the opportunity to stretch his legs at several ports on his
way to Jerusalem, he disembarked twice for a number of days. His first lengthy
stop was not by choice. Because the first boat made so many stops, the traveling preachers sought out a vessel going straight across to Phoenicia (Acts 21:2),
hoping to save time. To their dismay the ship docked in Tyre for seven days
to unload cargo. Have you ever noticed how often God has a blessing on the
unscheduled stops along our way? God had a blessing waiting for Paul and the
others on their unscheduled stop.

Verse 4 tells us that Paul sought out the Christian disciples in Tyre so that
he and his men would have a place to stay. Acts 11:19 tells how Christians had
been planted in Phoenicia, the region in which Tyre was located. They were scattered by the same wave of persecution in which Stephen was martyred.

Don't forget how deeply Paul, then known as Saul, had been involved in
the persecution that caused these believers to scatter. Had they heard about the
amazing convert, or did they believe he was still a terrible threat? Either way,
they were surprised to lay eyes on the sea-weary travelers. I never cease to be
amazed at the hospitality of believers in the New Testament church. Even in
my grandmother's day, she and many others often opened their homes to total
strangers who needed a place to rest for a night on their long travels. I am saddened by our loss of hospitality today. The disciples in Phoenicia opened their
homes to Paul and his fellow travelers. Their hearts were so instantly bound with
his, they begged him not to go to Jerusalem.

This time, entire families of believers accompanied him to the harbor.
Can you imagine what a sight this scene must have been for others to behold?
Men, women, and children kneeling in the sand praying with one heart and
mind for the apostle and his beloved associates. Just picture what the sand must
have looked like after Paul boarded the ship and the crowd went back home.
Footprints leading to and from the shore. Then nothing but knee prints clustered
together in the damp sand. A sight for God to behold. Long after the tide washed
away every print, the power of those prayers was still at work.

# DAY 277
## Acts 21:7–14

—◦◦◦—

Since he would not be persuaded, we stopped talking and simply said,
"The Lord's will be done!" (v. 14).

—◦◦◦—

Acts 21:8 tells us Paul and the others disembarked in Caesarea and stayed in the house of Philip. Philip is first mentioned in Acts 6:5 in the list of the seven original deacons. Not only was he a Spirit-filled Christian and a very wise man, he was also an extremely effective evangelist. We can compile something of a profile based on Acts 8:26–40. When we see his faithfulness, it is no wonder he had four daughters who prophesied. We considered the rich heritage Timothy received from his mother and grandmother. Philip's faithfulness obviously had a similar effect on his daughters.

Young people are far more likely to surrender their lives to serve God when they've seen genuine examples firsthand. Many are touched by the faithfulness of youth ministers, Sunday school teachers, and pastors, but nothing can match the lasting impact of a faithful parent. If my children don't think I'm genuine, no one else's opinion matters to me. On the front page of my Bible, I've written a reminder I'm forced to see every time I open it: "No amount of success in ministry will make up for failure at home."

What do you think Paul made of these four women who prophesied? You may be wondering if he had to be resuscitated when he met them. In his defense I would like to say that Paul was the first to recognize women with the gift of prophecy (when he taught spiritual gifts in 1 Cor. 11). A study of the entire life and ministry of Paul reveals an interesting fact. He had a vastly different outlook and attitude toward women than many people suppose. Unfortunately many people have based their thinking about him on a couple of excerpts from his writings. Knowing Paul, if he had disapproved of Philip's four daughters, he would have been the first to tell him!

What exactly were Philip's daughters doing anyway? What does prophesying mean? The original word is *propheteuo*, which means "to declare truths through the inspiration of God's Holy Spirit . . . to tell forth God's message." A prophet is a "proclaimer, one who speaks out the counsel of God with clarity, energy, and authority." In ancient days, prior to His completed revelation, God often used prophets or "proclaimers" to warn people about the future. Virtually all God wanted foretold, He ultimately inspired in His written Word, the Bible. So the gift of prophecy is most often used today as the proclamation of God's truth. Whether or not they foretold any part of the future, Philip's four daughters—in today's terms—were Christian speakers!

In Acts 2:18 God said He would pour out His Spirit on both men and women. I believe the growing numbers of strong Christian men and women speakers are examples of God's fulfillment of His promise. I am convinced we are living in the midst of a significant work of God on His kingdom calendar.

Speaking of prophets, Paul encountered another at the house of Philip. His name was Agabus. And like Ezekiel of old, Agabus delivered his message through an enacted parable. By tying his own hands and feet, Agabus predicted that imprisonment awaited Paul in Jerusalem.

Agabus must have been extremely convincing because his actions had a far greater impact than the disciples' words in Tyre. On his last stop, although Luke and the others accompanied Paul to Tyre, only the Phoenician disciples urged him not to go to Jerusalem (see 21:4). In Caesarea, after Agabus's prophetic performance, Luke, the other missionaries, and the people *all* urged Paul not to go (see v. 12).

In turn, Paul also responded with strong emotion. Though he could hardly tear himself away from the Ephesian elders in Acts 20:37, he never wavered in his resolve. He also remained unmoved when the disciples in Tyre urged him not to go. Yet we see him respond with enormous emotion when his beloved associates—Luke, Timothy, and the others—wept and pleaded with him not to go. Let's try to capture an accurate picture. These men were not just crying. The original word for "weeping" is the strongest expression of grief in the Greek language. These men were sobbing. Paul responded tenderly, "What are you doing, weeping and breaking my heart?" (Acts 21:13 HCSB).

Paul's beloved friends were so crushed over what awaited him that their strength dissolved, their noble sense of purpose disintegrated, and they begged him not to go. Had he not been so convinced of the Spirit's compelling him to go, he surely would have changed his mind. He voiced his determination to each of them: "I am ready not only to be bound, but also to die in Jerusalem for the name of the Lord Jesus" (v. 13b HCSB).

We sometimes feel as if we're playing tug-of-war with God. In bitter tears we sometimes let go of the rope, tumble to the ground, and cry, "Have your way, God! You're going to do what You want anyway!" God is not playing a game. He doesn't jerk on the rope just so He can win. In fact, He doesn't want us to let go of the rope at all. Rather than see us drop the rope and give up, He wants us to hang on and let Him pull us over to His side.

God's will is always best even when we cannot imagine how. Surrendering to His will doesn't mean you lose. Ultimately it means you win. Keep hanging on to that rope and let Him pull you over to His side. One day you'll understand. And you'll see His glory.

# DAY 278
## Acts 21:15–25

———

How many thousands of Jews there are who have believed.... 
But they have been told ... that you teach all the Jews who are among 
the Gentiles to abandon Moses (vv. 20–21).

———

Over the objections of the other believers, Paul set his face to go to Jerusalem. But if his arrival in Jerusalem had been a performance, he certainly would have received mixed reviews.

1. *Paul met acceptance.* What blessed words these are: "When we reached Jerusalem, the brothers welcomed us gladly" (v. 17 HCSB). Don't miss Luke's terminology: "When *we* reached Jerusalem." After being unsuccessful in their attempt to plead with Paul to avoid going there, one would not be surprised if Paul's companions had said, "You go ahead if you want. The rest of us refuse to be so foolish."

Nearly thirty years earlier, Christ's disciples also tried to talk Him out of going back to Judea when they knew trouble awaited Him. When He could not be dissuaded, Thomas said, "Let's go so that we may die with Him" (John 11:16 HCSB). Neither group was called to give their lives in association with their leader at this point, but surely God acknowledged their willingness.

What a sigh of relief must have come when Paul and his associates were greeted with warmth and approval by the believers in Jerusalem. Only one verse attests to Paul's testimony to James, the elders, and the others (Acts 21:19 HCSB), but you can assume he talked for some time as "he related one by one what God did among the Gentiles through his ministry." The hearts of James and the others are evident in their reception of his testimony: "they glorified God" (v. 20 HCSB). Notice, they did not praise Paul. Unfortunately acceptance was not the only response Paul met.

2. *Paul met apprehension.* After hearing Paul's wonderful news, James and the elders had good news of their own, and a little bad news. They gave Paul the good news first: "how many thousands of Jews there are who have believed" (v. 20 HCSB). What glorious words! What could Paul have wanted more? According to Romans 9:3, absolutely nothing! He would have agreed to be cursed forever if the Jews would accept Christ. I wonder if Paul immediately began shouting hallelujah and dancing and praising God. Regardless, they jumped quickly to the bad news.

They almost seemed to be sparing his dignity. Yes, many had believed in Christ, but James and the elders observed, "All of them are zealous for the law.... But they have been informed that you ... [tell] them not to live according to our customs" (vv. 20–21). In other words, they're saved—but they're mad. Talk about throwing a bucket of ice water on a warm reception.

This dilemma draws compassion from my heart for both James and Paul. I feel compassion for James. We have all been in his position. He was caught in the middle of anger and disagreement between people he cared about. Just imagine the gnawing in James's stomach as Paul was giving a detailed account of all God was doing among the Gentiles. James knew he would have to tell Paul about the Jews.

I also feel compassion for Paul. He expected opposition from unbelievers, but to be hit immediately in Jerusalem by the disapproval of fellow believers must have drained his energy and excitement. Furthermore, much of what they were saying about him wasn't even accurate. He never told Jewish Christians not to circumcise their children. He told them not to insist that Gentile Christians circumcise theirs! He was trying to make the point that circumcision had nothing whatsoever to do with salvation.

Perhaps you know how Paul felt when he met disapproval among his own and found he had been misunderstood. Have you ever thought, "I expected this kind of thing from unbelievers, but I wasn't expecting this from my own fellow believers"? If so, you are part of a large fraternity, with Paul as a charter member.

James and the elders immediately suggested that Paul join four men in their purification rites, so that all would see he still respected the customs. Paul submitted to their authority and did as they asked. His point regarding the ancient Hebrew customs was to practice them when wise or observe them as a reminder but not to live under them as a burden and a means of salvation.

Several times in Paul's ministry he was placed in a similar position with both Jews and Gentiles. He explained his actions in 1 Corinthians 9:19–23. He said that though he was free in Christ, he made himself a slave to everyone so that he could win as many as possible. He said he became like a Jew to the Jews in order to win the Jews, and like a Gentile to the Gentiles in order to win the Gentiles. Paul's great summary statement challenges every believer: "I have become all things to all people, so that I may by all means save some" (1 Cor. 9:22 HCSB).

Like Paul, each of us must seek common ground with those who do not know Christ. We can respond legalistically and shun harmless practices, but if we do, we risk alienating the very people we want to reach.

# DAY 279
### Acts 21:26–36

---

When Paul got to the steps, he had to be carried by the soldiers because of the mob's violence, for the mass of people were following and yelling, "Kill him!" (vv. 35–36).

---

As we saw in yesterday's reading, Paul met welcome acceptance from some of the believers in Jerusalem. He met discouraging apprehension from others. Sadly, he also met a third reception: *accusation.* Imagine the moment. Paul and the Asian Jews, who had given him so much trouble in Ephesus, saw each other. I have a feeling Paul thought, "Oh, no!" and the Asian Jews thought, "Oh, yes!" They stirred up the crowd in the temple, the entire city fell into an uproar, and they grabbed Paul and tried to beat him to death. Can you imagine what the apostle was thinking? Surrounded by such a mob, I'm sure he thought he was about to draw his last breath. I can hardly imagine being beaten by *one* person. What would it be like to be beaten by a gang?

Did Paul recall the image of the prophet Agabus tied up with his belt? Paul had expected to be seized, but I'm not sure expectation and preparation are always synonymous. I don't think Paul was prepared for a mob to keep shouting, "Wipe this person off the earth—it's a disgrace for him to live!" (Acts 22:22 HCSB). Was he ready for hatred and wholesale rejection by the people he would have given his life for? I'm not sure how adequately a person can prepare for such pain.

Later, in his letter to the Philippians (3:10), Paul made a reference to wanting the fellowship of sharing in Christ's sufferings. Paul received Christ by faith, knew Christ by name, but came face-to-face with Christ through experience. He spoke to Him through prayer. He grew in Him through the Word. But this particular day, Paul experienced a fellowship in His sufferings unlike any he had ever encountered.

Both Christ and Paul knew suffering was inevitable. Both Christ and Paul knew they would end up giving their lives—One as the Savior of the world, the other as His servant. Both grieved over Jerusalem. Both felt compelled to return to the holy city. Both knew the horror of being swept up in an angry mob. Both experienced the newness of every rejection. But no matter how many times it comes, one can hardly prepare for people who wish you dead. Paul did not know what would happen to him, but he did know Christ. As the apostle fellowshipped in His sufferings, he had never known Jesus better.

## DAY 280
### Acts 21:37–22:3

———∞∞∞———

"I am a Jewish man, born in Tarsus of Cilicia, but brought up in this city at the feet of
Gamaliel, and educated according to the strict view of our patriarchal law" (v. 3).

———∞∞∞———

Although Saul's education in a Pharisee's home was probably typical, his
response to this instruction was certainly atypical. We might say, "He took to it
like a duck to water."

Saul was an exceptional student. Hebrew fathers were not notorious gush-
ers, so his father probably didn't brag on him a lot. Yet he no doubt considered
the wisest approach for Saul's future, not unlike a modern father looking for the
best university for his gifted son. In the search for the best continuing Jewish
education, he set his sights on Jerusalem, the homeland—the fountain of Jewish
learning.

Mixed emotions must have filled the heart of the young man as he prepared
for the journey to Jerusalem. Like most teenage boys, his emotions probably
swung to the same extremes as his changing voice. Like any thirteen-year-old
going so far from home, he was probably scared to death. Yet as a Jewish thirteen-
year-old, he was considered a man. He packed his bags with articles foreign to
us but common to the ancient Jew: prayer shawls, phylacteries, sacred writings,
and customary clothing. He probably didn't gaze with affection over familiar
contents in his room prior to leaving. The Jew was not given to domestic decor
and did not believe in images on the walls.

All his life Saul had heard about Jerusalem. His father probably made the
journey often. Three annual feasts beckoned Jewish men from near and far to
the city of Zion. A proper Pharisee traveled to Jerusalem for the annual Passover
Feast. Saul likely stayed home and watched over the family affairs while picturing the busy streets and solemn assemblies of the sacred city. Saul probably
devoured every story his father told about Jerusalem upon his arrival home. Now
it was his turn.

Most assuredly, Saul's father sought a Jewish traveling companion for his
young son, someone who could provide proper supervision as the young student
traveled from Tarsus to Jerusalem. As Saul boarded the boat at the docks of
Tarsus, he had no idea just how familiar the nauseating heaving of a sea vessel
would ultimately become to him. The boat sailed almost due south as Saul gazed
at the ancient coastal cities of Sidon and Tyre in the distance. After several rather
unpleasant days on board, he probably arrived at the port of Caesarea with a
chronic case of sea legs. There he exchanged rubbery limbs for the peculiar sore-
ness of riding on the back of a beast over rough country. Thirty-five miles later, he
caught the first glimpses of the city set on a hill—Jerusalem, the City of David.

Young Saul's eyes beheld a far more cosmopolitan city than had his ancestors. Just a few decades prior to Saul's visit, Herod the Great sought the favor of the Jewish populace by rebuilding not just the temple but the entire city of Jerusalem. The desert sun danced on city walls built of Jerusalem limestone. Saul probably dismounted just before the city gate. The elders sitting at the gate looked up only long enough to notice the young traveler. No heathen was he. Noting his age, they probably nodded with approval over his father's obvious choice of further education—a budding rabbi, no doubt.

Just inside the gate, Saul cast his eyes on the impressive fruit of Herod's labors: a large theater, a palace, an amphitheater, a hippodrome for horse and chariot races, imposing fortified towers, and perfectly blended architecture. But all this paled in comparison to the structure on top of the hill—Herod's temple. Herod rebuilt the temple bigger and better than its predecessor. Huge, richly ornamented white stones mounted one upon another created a lavish feast for the eyes. Young Saul witnessed one of the most magnificent buildings in the entire world.

Saul probably ran up the main street of Jerusalem to the house of the Lord. He surely conjured up pictures of King David dancing down that very street. He hurried up the many stairs to greet magnificent porches surrounding the entire enclosure. Then he walked to a wall, one that held tremendous significance for the Jew, but one that would hold far more significance for a Jew who would ultimately become the world's most renowned missionary to the Gentiles.

When, from a prison cell in Ephesus, Paul wrote that Christ had broken down the wall that separates Jew and Gentile, the apostle was not simply referring to a figurative wall of partition. He was referring to an imposing structure he had faced on the temple grounds as an adolescent many years before. Being raised in a Gentile city, young Saul had no problem reading the notices inscribed in Greek and Latin. This literal middle wall of partition in the temple forbade access of the defiling heathen into the inner sanctuaries of the house of God. As a young man born into a position of religious privilege, he stood a little taller—chest a little broader—as he read those words. What a contrast of emotions he would feel many years later as he came to despise the prejudice of those who would not recognize the walls crumbled by the cross. To them Saul would write, "For he is our peace, who hath made both [Jew and Gentile] one, and hath broken down the middle wall of partition between us" (Eph. 2:14 KJV).

## DAY 281
### Acts 22:1–21

---∞∞∞---

"Brothers and fathers, listen now to my defense before you." When they heard that he
was addressing them in the Hebrew language, they became even quieter (vv. 1–2).

---∞∞∞---

Acts 22 contains Paul's account of his own Damascus-road conversion. His
approach contains several elements that build a powerful testimony. We can learn
from the following four elements in sharing our own testimonies.

1. *Paul communicated simply and clearly.* Paul spoke in Greek to the commander and in Aramaic to the Jews. Few of us are fluent in several languages,
as Paul was, but we can apply his example, learning to communicate more effectively by speaking the language of our hearers.

I grew up going to Sunday school and church. I spent much of my early
social life with other Christians, so I had a difficult time learning to speak a
language an unchurched person could understand. My speech was so laced and
interwoven with church terms that those unacquainted with church life could
hardly understand me. I practically needed an interpreter!

I still have to remind myself to resist assuming every listener knows the
lingo. I'm learning to use figures of speech and expressions that lost people will
more likely understand. I'm also, like, you know, learning to use more contemporary expressions when speaking to youth. Of course, learning to speak understandably does not mean adopting any level of vulgarity. It means speaking with
a greater level of clarity.

2. *Paul honestly described his former conduct.* We lose our listeners the moment
they sense an attitude of superiority in us. Paul spoke with honesty and humility.
As he explained his background and his persecutions of the church, he related
with them as one who had been exactly where they were. Not all of us have a
background as dramatically different from our present lifestyles as Paul did, yet
we have all been lost. Lost is lost.

Remember an important principle about sharing our former conduct.
Generalizations usually are best. I try to avoid becoming specific about ungodly
actions in my past. I want the listener to focus on my Savior, not my behavior.
Sometimes we glorify ungodly behavior by highlighting how bad we were. This
method can dishonor God, and it can dishonor the listener by stirring unnecessary mental images of sin. Share past conduct with caution!

3. *Paul related his experience of conversion.* Few of us have experienced the
dramatic conversion Paul described in Acts 22:6–16, but we can tell how we
accepted Christ. Don't think your testimony is meaningless if you didn't have a
dramatic conversion. Every conversion cost the same amount of Christ's blood

shed on the cross. Yours is just as meaningful as the most dramatic conversion ever told.

In the parable of the prodigal son, the elder brother felt insulted because the father accepted his brother after a season of wild living (Luke 15:29–30). He didn't understand the biggest difference between the two brothers was that the prodigal son had to live with the personal loss and suffering. If your conversion was less sensational than others, praise God for less drama! With it probably came less pain! You don't have to see a bright light from heaven to have a story to tell. The determining factor is not how exciting your conversion was but how excited you are now about your conversion.

4. *Paul shared how he received his commission.* He was very clear that God had a purpose for his life. The people we talk to need to know that there is life after salvation! Salvation is not only about eternity. Salvation is also the open door to a rich earthly life in which we enjoy the love and direction of an active God.

Many unbelievers are repelled by Christianity because they are afraid they'll have to give up so much in order to live for Christ. As we share our testimonies, we can help them see all we've gained since Jesus came into our hearts, all the ways our lives have been blessed and enhanced by His presence within us. Make your sense of ongoing purpose a part of your testimony. We often have no idea how much people are struggling to find a reason to live and to persevere through difficulty.

# DAY 282
## Acts 22:22–29

꘠

The commander ordered him to be brought into the barracks, directing that he be examined with the scourge, so he could discover the reason they were shouting (v. 24).

꘠

On a human scale we cannot judge Paul's visit to Jerusalem a success. Perhaps his experiences in places like Athens and Jerusalem will teach us to think differently about success and failure. Hopefully we will come to understand that in our Christian lives, success is obedience to God, not results we can measure.

I'm sure Paul wanted to bear fruit in Jerusalem more than any place on earth. Yet we see him face greater opposition and struggle in Jerusalem than virtually anywhere in his ministry. In the holy city Paul was forced to measure his ministry strictly on his obedience to the Spirit, not outward results.

Unfortunately the Jews didn't think much of Paul's purpose on this earth. Once he acknowledged the importance of the Gentiles to God, he lost his audience. Sadly their personal need to feel superior exceeded their spiritual sensibilities.

Paul desperately wanted the Jews to receive Christ. Was he a failure because they rejected him? Was his testimony shared in vain? Absolutely not. God had compelled Paul to go to Jerusalem. He had warned him of hardships. He had given Paul an opportunity to share his testimony with the very people who had just tried to kill him.

Did they hear Paul's message? Oh, yes. Otherwise, they would not have responded so emotionally. Few of those in hearing distance that day forgot Paul's testimony. We cannot judge effectiveness from immediate results. According to John 14:26, the Holy Spirit can remind a person of truth taught long ago. When we obey God, we find great comfort in leaving the consequences up to Him.

Paul avoided a flogging because God equipped him with Roman citizenship even before his birth. God used every ounce and detail of Paul's past, even his unique citizenship. I want God to use every ounce of me too. Paul poured himself out like a drink offering in Jerusalem. He received little encouragement to preach while he was there—but he continued. Paul's certainty of what he had been called to do was exceeded only by his certainty of who called. Paul considered Him who called worth it all.

# DAY 283
## Acts 22:30–23:1

———— ◦◦◦ ————

Paul looked intently at the Sanhedrin and said, "Brothers, I have lived
my life before God in all good conscience until this day" (v. 1).

———— ◦◦◦ ————

We learn volumes about Paul by noting his priorities. A clear conscience
was no doubt one of them, since he spoke of it often in his letters. The Greek
word for "conscience" is *suneidesis*, which means "to be one's own witness, one's
own conscience coming forward as a witness. It denotes an abiding consciousness
whose nature it is to bear witness to one's own conduct in a moral sense. It is
self-awareness." In lay terms we might say the conscience is an inner constituent
casting a vote about the rightness of our behaviors.

God's Word helps us compile several facts concerning the conscience:

1. *People without a spotless past can enjoy a clear conscience.* What wonderful
news! Paul spoke of possessing a clear conscience numerous times, yet he considered himself one of the worst possible offenders. His conscience was clear even
though he had wronged many people in the past. A clear conscience is possible
for those of us who have sinned.

2. *Good deeds cannot accomplish a clear conscience.* Have you ever tried to worship or serve God when your conscience was bothering you after an unsettled
argument with your spouse or a coworker? Or perhaps after telling a lie to someone? Hebrews 9:9 tells us of two things that will never clear the conscience of
the worshipper: gifts and sacrifices. We've all probably tried to soothe our consciences with good works. God's Word tells us we cannot offer enough gifts or
sacrifices to clear a guilty conscience. Take heart! The Bible does give us some
steps to a clear conscience.

3. *The Holy Spirit works with the believer's conscience.* The Holy Spirit plays a
critical role in creating and maintaining a clear conscience. In Romans 9:1, Paul
said the Holy Spirit confirmed his conscience. Once we have received Christ and
the Holy Spirit resides within us, the Holy Spirit will work with our consciences.
The Spirit works both to confirm a clear conscience and to convict a guilty conscience. We all naturally prefer to ignore our sin. The one part of us that does not
ignore sin is our conscience. For that reason the Holy Spirit deals with conscience
first, not with our intellect or emotions. You might think of the relationship this
way: the Holy Spirit plants conviction in the soil of the conscience. If ignored,
that conviction will usually grow and grow.

4. *The conscience is an indicator, not a transformer.* Only the Holy Spirit can
change us and clear our consciences. By itself, all the conscience can do with a
guilty person is condemn. My conscience may lend an awareness of what I ought
to do, but it supplies little power to do it. The believer possesses something far

greater. The Holy Spirit who resides in us supplies abundant power not only to recognize the right thing, but to do it!

Can we really have clear consciences? The Bible says we can. Considering Paul's past, if he can have a clear conscience, any of us can. Like me, you may have discovered that asking God for forgiveness doesn't always make you feel better. Sometimes we know we're forgiven, but we still feel a load of guilt. How can we discover the freedom of a clear conscience? I believe Hebrews 10:22 holds several vital keys: "Let us draw near with a true heart in full assurance of faith, our hearts sprinkled clean from an evil conscience and our bodies washed in pure water" (HCSB). Consider these steps to a clear conscience:

*Bring your heavy conscience to God.* When we have a guilty conscience, we shy away from the presence of God. We tend to resist what we need most: an awareness of God's love! Draw near to God!

*Approach God with absolute sincerity.* Come entirely clean before Him. Spill your heart and confess everything you feel. Tell Him about the guilt that continues to nag at you. You'll not only clear your heart and mind, you'll tattle on the evil one who has no right to keep accusing you after repentance.

*Ask God to give you full assurance of His love and acceptance.* In His Word, God tells you over and over how much He loves you. He assures you of His forgiveness. He also tells you He forgets your confessed sin. Ask God to give you faith to take Him at His Word. You needn't fear rejection or ridicule. Let Him reassure you of His love and forgiveness.

Picture the cross of Christ once more. Really take a good mental look at it. Was Christ's death on the cross enough to cover your sin? Enough to take away your guilt? Yes. He gave everything He had for everything we've said, done, or thought. Then picture yourself at the foot of His cross, close enough to have your heart cleansed by His redemptive blood. No sin is too grievous. No load is too heavy for Christ to carry. Walk away free, and leave with God that old condemning tape you've been playing over and over on your mental "recorder"!

Like the apostle Paul, we can enjoy a clear conscience even after a guilty past. Don't wait another moment. "Draw near to God" (Heb. 10:22).

# DAY 284
### Acts 23:2–10

⎯⎯∞⎯⎯

"God is going to strike you, you whitewashed wall!
You are sitting there judging me according to the law,
and in violation of the law are you ordering me to be struck?" (v. 3).

⎯⎯∞⎯⎯

During his stay in Jerusalem, Paul had no need to make a living. God had already booked him a room in the city jail. God did not allow the apostle to be jailed to his harm but to provide a means of safety for him while allowing him to share his testimony in the highest courts, as in the case of Acts 23 and his appearance before the Sanhedrin and Ananias, the high priest.

Why was Ananias so insulted at Paul's confession about living before God "in all good conscience" (Acts 23:1)—insulted enough to have Paul struck in the mouth? Was it because Paul referred to them as "brothers"? Or could it have been because Paul was indirectly suggesting a conscience check for everyone listening?

Unfortunately we don't have the benefit of hearing Paul's voice inflection. But his response instantly following the slap suggests he might have been ready for an altercation. "God is going to strike you, you whitewashed wall!" (v. 3). I'm quite sure the temperature in the room rose dramatically. After Paul called Ananias a name, those standing close to him said, "Do you dare revile God's high priest?" (v. 4 HCSB). Don't miss Paul's response. "I did not know, brothers, that it was the high priest" (v. 5 HCSB).

If we could have heard Paul's voice, I believe his inflection might have contained a little sarcasm. No doubt Paul knew he was insulting the high priest. He was far too knowledgeable not to have recognized Ananias's robes and obvious position of honor. I believe he knew he was insulting the high priest and probably offended him further by saying, in effect, "Sorry, but I never would have recognized this guy as a high priest."

I'm suggesting Paul may have been in an interesting mood, and if I may be so bold, even a touch of an insolent mood. I mean absolutely no disrespect to the apostle, but I believe he sometimes struggled with a temper. And when dealing with a foe like Ananias, whom history records as a very insolent, hot-tempered man, the sight of his false piety and that of the other religious leaders probably made Paul's stomach turn—especially because he had been one of them. Sometimes the ugliest picture we see of ourselves is the one we see in others. And even a great man like Paul can find it to be more than he can take.

# DAY 285
## Acts 23:11–22

The following night, the Lord stood by him and said, "Have courage! For as you have
testified about Me in Jerusalem, so you must also testify in Rome" (v. 11).

Sometimes we must read between the lines in the book of Acts to see Paul
the man and not just his travels. Acts 23:11 offers us a perfect opportunity to read
between the lines without stretching the text. I hope Christ's tenderness toward
His willing captive touches you. He stood near Paul and said, "Have courage!"

Why did Christ draw so physically close to Paul at this particular moment?
I believe Paul was overcome with fear and may have been convinced he would not
live much longer. He had looked straight into the eyes of rage. He was separated
from his friends. He was imprisoned by strangers. I believe he was terrified.

Later Paul wrote from another prison cell, "My God will supply all your
needs according to His riches in glory in Christ Jesus" (Phil. 4:19 HCSB). He could
make such a claim because God had been so faithful to meet his needs. In Acts
23:11 God looked on His servant Paul imprisoned in Jerusalem, and He didn't
just see emotions. He saw the need they represented. Paul was afraid. He needed
courage. Just like Philippians 4:19 said, God literally met his need in Christ
Jesus. That day in Paul's prison cell, Christ stood near and said, "Have courage!"
He meant, "I'm right here. Take courage from Me!"

The Lord gave Paul great motivation for courage by giving him confirmation: Paul was going to Rome. His life could not be taken until the mission
was complete. Paul surely knew that Christ's confirmation did not mean Paul
wouldn't suffer or be greatly persecuted. He simply knew he could not be killed
until he had testified about Christ in Rome.

God timed Paul's injection of courage perfectly to offset the conspiracy to
kill Paul. Overnight in Jerusalem Paul became the center of a dangerous whirlwind of rage that rapidly gained force. By morning, forty men bound themselves
with an oath to kill him. The original terminology tells us they were binding
themselves to a curse if they didn't carry out their plans. They may not have
realized they had bound themselves to a curse already! In the words of Micah
the prophet: "Woe to those who dream up wickedness and prepare evil plans on
their beds! . . . Therefore, the Lord says: 'I am now planning disaster against this
nation; you cannot free your necks from it'" (Mic. 2:1, 3 HCSB).

# DAY 286
## Acts 23:23–35

———∞∞∞———

"Get 200 soldiers ready with 70 cavalry and 200 spearmen to go to Caesarea at nine tonight. Also provide mounts so they can put Paul on them" (vv. 23–24).

———∞∞∞———

We have already had a number of occasions to consider God's creativity in terms of His methods of delivery. He can shake the foundations of a prison, or He can employ the Roman cavalry to accompany a servant out of town. But note one constant that Paul addressed in his second letter to the Corinthians: "We have placed our hope in Him that He will deliver us again. And you can join in helping with prayer for us" (2 Cor. 1:10–11 HCSB). Never underestimate the effects of intercessory prayer lifted for our deliverance. Never underestimate the effects of your prayers for others.

The year I began working on this study of Paul, my heart was torn to pieces over a devastating loss. For several months no one outside our family and friends knew about it. Because the wound was so fresh, we were not yet able to tell the story. Letters poured in from all over the nation saying something like this: "God has placed a heavy burden on my heart for Beth and her family. I do not know what is wrong, but I'm praying for them." I could hardly believe it. Once we shared more openly about our loss, we learned that literally thousands of people were praying for us. I am absolutely certain those prayers delivered us from the pit of despair. Many times my soul would sink in grief. I'd feel like I was about to descend into depression. But each time I began to slip, I sensed something like a supernatural net disallowing me to descend another inch.

God can deliver anyone from anything at any time. He doesn't need any help. Yet He invites us to be part of His great work through prayer. If we don't intercede for one another, we miss opportunities to see His deliverance and thank Him for His faithfulness. I like to call this God's profit-sharing plan. When we pray for one another, we share the blessings when deliverance comes because we've been personally involved. Their thanksgiving becomes our thanksgiving.

Many scholars believe Paul wrote 2 Corinthians on his third missionary journey, prior to his arrest in Jerusalem. If so, the Corinthians' prayers were actively involved in Paul's deliverance. He rode in style to Caesarea, surrounded by soldiers, horsemen, spearmen, and the prayers of the Corinthian Christians.

# DAY 287
## Acts 24:22–27

---

As [Paul] spoke about righteousness, self-control, and the judgment to come, Felix became afraid and replied, "Leave for now, but when I find time I'll call for you" (v. 25).

---

As we begin today's reading, my mind drifts back over the many stops we've made with the apostle Paul. I suppose none of us wants to trade times, places, and lives with him; but each of us must admit that Paul's tenure on this earth was extremely fascinating. He could write about "the breadth, and length, and depth, and height" (Eph. 3:18 KJV) because he experienced each of those extremes. This man we're studying in God's Word was flesh and blood. But he was extraordinary.

Acts 24 unfolds with Paul incarcerated in Caesarea after being escorted by a grand cavalry. Ananias the high priest arrived with an entourage, including a lawyer named Tertullus who brought the charges against Paul before the governor. Few things are more disgusting than a political spiel that bears no resemblance to the truth. Tertullus began by flattering Felix, the governor. Judging by the lawyer's words, Felix deserved his own holiday for being a peacemaker, a reformer, a tireless officer, and a noble man! Tertullus knew better. Felix was vile and incompetent. Nero had him recalled only two years later. He was a former slave who had cunningly gained favor with the imperial court, "known for his violent use of repressive force and corrupt self-aggrandizement."[60]

After blatantly flattering Felix, Tertullus delivered his charges against Paul. He said that Paul was a troublemaker who stirred up riots among the Jews and that he had tried to desecrate the temple (see vv. 5–8). Paul responded to the charges with a forthright description of his journey to Jerusalem and the events there.

Felix obviously viewed the conflict as a no-win situation. The size of the Jewish community and the Roman citizenship of Paul left Felix in a dilemma. He lacked the wisdom to make an appropriate decision, so he did nothing. He left Paul in prison. God, however, was clearly up to something. Several days after the hearing, God gave Paul an interesting opportunity. He sent the preacher to a congregation of two: Felix and Drusilla. Drusilla was the third wife of the governor, and both of them had deserted previous spouses to marry. God equipped Paul with a tailor-made lesson for the two. Verse 25 tells us Paul "discoursed," which means "to speak back and forth or alternately, to converse with." He didn't just give a sermon. He led Felix and Drusilla in an interactive study. The core of Paul's message was "faith in Christ Jesus" (v. 24).

The apostle's message contained three points: "righteousness, self-control and the judgment to come." We could summarize his message like this: salvation by grace teaches us to live self-controlled lives. Paul risked bodily harm when he preached such a forceful message to Governor Felix and his wife. Christ had assured the apostle he would go to Rome, so he knew he wouldn't be killed; but torture can be a more difficult prospect than death! You can be sure Paul didn't bring the message Felix was expecting. He and Drusilla, a Jewess, most likely expected a message of mystical divinity. Instead they got a message of practical clarity, and every point stuck.

Felix was not amused by the outspoken preacher. Verse 25 tells us he "was afraid and said, 'That's enough for now! You may leave.'" I see some irony in his choice of words. History describes him as a man with a gross lack of self-control.[61] I have a feeling he rarely applied the words "That's enough for now" to himself. Felix told Paul he would send for him at a more convenient time.

I'm not sure confrontation with personal sin is ever convenient. Some of the messages I've needed to hear most were those I wanted to hear least. Like Felix, we in our human natures often resist what is best for us. But unlike Felix, we can dare to accept a truth and find freedom.

While Felix felt fear, Luke tells us of no reaction from Drusilla. We might surmise she was also convicted and frightened, but Scripture only tells us Felix was afraid. I would like to offer a different theory. Perhaps Drusilla simply did not humble herself enough to be afraid. She had quite an interesting heritage—one plagued with pride.

Remember Herod Agrippa I from Acts 12:19–23? He was Drusilla's father. He bestowed on himself the glory due only to God. As a result he was eaten by worms and then died. You might think having a father who was eaten alive by worms would have some impact. Instead, Drusilla led an adulterous life in spite of all she knew about morality and reverence for God from her Jewish heritage. The generational bondage of pride could have been broken with her father's dreadful demise. Instead she resisted the message, willingly picked up the chain of pride, and carried on.

God in His mercy reaches out to the immoral, ill-tempered, and boastful. Many hear but run the other way. Others hear but never apply. But some listen and are set free. God not only sent Felix and Drusilla a fitting message, He sent them a fitting messenger. Paul could not stand before them as one who had never experienced a terrible lack of self-control. He was once puffed with pride. His only righteousness was in the law. Then one day Jesus confronted him in the middle of his sin. He'd been running straight to Him ever since.

# DAY 288
## Acts 25:13–22

---

Agrippa said to Festus, "I would like to hear the man myself."
"Tomorrow," he said, "you will hear him" (v. 22).

---

Acts 25 begins with the arrival of a new leader of the province. Festus replaced Felix, but Paul remained in prison. The Jewish leaders immediately appealed to the new governor to have Paul returned to Jerusalem for trial. Though two years had passed, and they were either very hungry or had abandoned their vow not to eat until Paul was dead, they still harbored such hatred of the apostle that they could think only of killing him. Rather than be returned to Jerusalem, Paul appealed to Caesar. Why he did remains a mystery.

After Festus heard Paul's defense, he said in effect, "I would turn him loose, but since he appealed to Caesar, I send him to Rome as a prisoner." We cannot judge from the words of Festus whether Paul might have been freed. What we do know is that the apostle is about to travel to Rome at last, but first he has one more chance to present the gospel.

King Agrippa and his wife Bernice came to Caesarea to pay respects to the new governor. Festus told them about Paul, and they decided to hear from the apostle. As Paul had done with Felix and Drusilla, he preached to the new trio. Festus's response contains a fascinating statement. He "was at a loss how to investigate" Paul's claims that a dead man named Jesus was alive (Acts 25:20).

I remember sharing with a loved one how I know Christ is alive. He said, "I believe in reincarnation," and, "I believe a spiritual presence exists rather than a certain God." He continued by repeating the words "I believe" over and over. Suddenly God gave me such a strange insight, and I was overwhelmed at the difference between my loved one and me. He believed the things he had been taught through New Age philosophy. I didn't just believe. *I knew.* I gently said to him, "My God is not just Someone I believe in. He's Someone I know. I've felt His presence. I've seen His activity. I've experienced His deliverance. I've been touched by His healing. I've witnessed answered prayer. I've 'heard' Him speak straight to me through His Word. Yes, I believe. But more than that, I know."

My loved one said nothing more, but I knew he heard my heart. Dead prophets simply don't save, guide, heal, deliver, answer prayers, or speak through an ancient text with the relevance of this morning's newspaper.

# DAY 289
## Acts 26:24–32

———∞∞∞———

"King Agrippa, do you believe the prophets? I know you believe." Then Agrippa said to
Paul, "Are you going to persuade me to become a Christian so easily?" (vv. 27–28).

———∞∞∞———

My advice to anyone who is investigating the matter of Christ's existence
would probably be these two suggestions:

1. Open your heart to the possibility of Christ's authenticity by coming to
church and getting to know Christian people.

2. Ask Christ if He's real, then be honest and open enough to watch for Him
to reveal Himself.

Good investigators ask certain questions: who? what? where? when? how?
The context of Acts 26 shows what we may know: who is in control and even
what He's doing and where He's leading—but we'll rarely guess when and how!
Let's take the Jewish leaders and Paul as an example of our inability to know
these things.

1. *Neither Paul nor the Jewish leaders understood when.* Paul didn't know when
God would fulfill His promise. Paul knew who had called him and what Christ
had called him to do. He even knew where: God was going to send him to Rome.
But Paul might never have guessed he would still be sitting in jail two years
after the promise. That's why he probably asked God many times—When? Time
means so much to you and me. When God sheds light on ministries He wants us
to fulfill or promises He plans to keep, we usually assume He means right now!
A study of the Jewish patriarchs, however, proves that years may separate God's
promise and its fulfillment. Not one minute is wasted, but God rarely seems to
fulfill His revealed plan when we expect.

Likewise, the Jews didn't know when God would fulfill His promise. They
believed God would send the Messiah. That was the answer to who. They also
knew what He would come to do: bring salvation. They were certain where:
Israel, then to all parts of the world. But they didn't understand when. They were
still looking for a Messiah, even though He had already come. Sometimes we can
keep asking when God is going to do something He's already done!

2. *Neither Paul nor the Jewish leaders understood how.* God had assured Paul
He was sending him to Rome, but Paul would never have guessed how. In Acts
25:25 Festus announced, "When he himself appealed to the Emperor, I decided
to send him" (HCSB). Actually it was God who had decided to send Paul to Rome,
but He was about to use Festus as the vehicle. Paul may have wondered over
and over how he would ever get to Rome while under arrest. He probably asked
his associates many times to pray for his release so he could fulfill his calling in

Rome. I wonder if Paul ever imagined his arrest would be the tool God would use to give him an all-expenses paid trip to his destination.

I recently heard a famous actor share his testimony before a secular audience. He said when he was a boy, God revealed to him that he would reach out to thousands and thousands of people. All his life he had waited for God to call him to preach. God never did. Instead the young man developed into an Academy Award–winning actor. He was thankful for his opportunities to act, but he could not understand what had happened to his calling. The evening he was honored, he said he realized God had fulfilled His promise. The young boy never would have guessed how God would do what He said.

God is the Deliverer, but we never know how He might deliver us. We see that God always fulfills His promises, just not always the way we imagine.

If Paul was occasionally shocked by how God fulfilled His promises, he was not the only one. God had assured the Jews He would send the Messiah, but they never would have guessed how. They were expecting great pomp to accompany their king's arrival. They were not expecting someone who looked so ordinary, so common. They unfortunately wanted a prestigious king more than a servant Savior.

Praise God, He gives us what we need, not what we want. If Christ had come to immediately wear His crown, we would be hopelessly lost. A crown of thorns and a splintered cross had to precede a crown of jewels and a hallowed throne. If they hadn't, Christ would still have a throne but no earthly subjects to approach it.

God calls us to be good investigators. We don't have to be at a loss on how to investigate such matters. When we don't know what, when, where, or how, we can trust in who. We won't always find our answers, but we can always find our God when we seek Him with all our hearts. And He will love and comfort us until all other answers come.

# DAY 290
## Acts 27:9–12

———— ∞◦∞ ————

*But the centurion paid attention to the captain and the owner
of the ship rather than to what Paul said (v. 11).*

———— ∞◦∞ ————

We ordinarily think of the apostle Paul as deeply spiritual, but Acts 27 reminds us he also could be rather practical. He had spent much time on ships traveling the Mediterranean. Winter was approaching. In ancient days few vessels risked the sea during the winter months.

Although Paul was no expert seaman, he also wasn't a man to keep his opinion to himself. He warned the pilot, the centurion, and the ship's owner, "Men, I can see that this voyage is headed toward damage and heavy loss" (Acts 27:10 HCSB). Can you picture this little bearded man licking the end of his index finger and holding it up to check the direction of the wind? Paul might have been perceived as a know-it-all at times. This was one of those times when someone probably should have listened.

The pilot and owner insisted on sailing regardless of difficulty. Like a plot from a disaster movie, they put profit above safety. They let their ledgers eclipse their good sense. The Alexandrian ship serviced Rome with expensive grain. They took advantage of the first gentle breeze and headed out, running a risk that would eventually catch them right between the eyes, driving them helter-skelter on the open seas.

This particular peril in the apostle's life struck a chord in my heart for reasons I couldn't quite identify at first. I finally realized why: he and the others met great difficulty because of someone else's poor judgment.

I've gone through storms as a direct result of my own rebellion. I've also gone through storms as a result of spiritual warfare. Others were ordained directly by God for His glory. But sometimes the most difficult storms of all can be those that result from another person's poor judgment. A wrong decision by a business partner, a boss, a driver, a jury, a teacher, a child, or a spouse can have devastating repercussions on other lives.

Of the four origins of personal storms I just identified, the one caused by someone else's poor judgment has its own unique difficulty because we have someone else in flesh and blood to blame! We feel much greater potential for bitterness and unforgiveness. If you find yourself in that position, keep your eyes (as Paul did) on God's greater purpose.

# DAY 291
## Acts 27:13–26

———∞∞∞———

For many days neither sun nor stars appeared, and the severe storm kept raging; finally
all hope that we would be saved was disappearing (v. 20).

———∞∞∞———

The sailors on board with Paul took steps to deal with the storm that enveloped their ship. In their actions I see practical behaviors we can also apply in our
lives for surviving our personal storms. Although the points I am about to make
might not apply to a literal ship on an angry sea, they will be helpful in the storms
we encounter when someone close to us exercises poor judgment.

1. *Don't pull up the anchor* (see v. 13). The ship's masters were ill advised to
attempt to sail, but they decided to weigh anchor anyway. Jesus Christ is our
anchor beyond the veil (see Heb. 6:19–20). When gentle breezes blow in our lives
and all seems calm and peaceful, we often become less attentive to Him. We're
not as aware of our need for the One who secures our lives and holds us steady
until the storms begin to rage. Don't let a few calm breezes give you a false sense
of security in yourself and your surroundings. Stay anchored in Christ in gentle
times too.

2. *Don't give way to the storm* (see v. 15). Peril caused by another person's
poor judgment can often cause feelings of immense helplessness. Don't give way
to the storm. Give way to the Master of the seas.

3. *Do throw some cargo overboard* (see v. 18). As the storm worsened, the crew
began to jettison cargo to keep the ship afloat. Raging storms have ways of identifying some old stuff we're still hanging on to. When we're upset over someone's
poor judgment, we have a tendency to drag up memories of other times we've
been wronged as well. Storms complicate life enough. Ask God to simplify and
clarify a few things in your life by helping you throw some old cargo overboard.

4. *Do throw the tackle overboard* (see v. 19). After jettisoning the cargo, the
crew still needed to further lighten the ship. The tackling on a ship included all
kinds of gear: ropes, pulleys, spars, masts, and planks. These objects were man-
made provisions needed to master the storm. Storms are seldom pleasant, but
they can serve an important purpose. They help us to see the man-made solutions
we're substituting in place of depending on and getting to know God.

5. *Never give up hope* (see v. 20). Luke uses the word "we" when identifying
those who gave up hope. This is a man who wrote one of the Gospels! How could
he lose hope? He had witnessed miracles! This text reminds us that anyone can
lose hope when a storm rages. The original word for "gave up" in verse 20 is the
same one translated "cutting loose" in verse 40. We might say Luke and the
others cut loose their hope when the storm continued to rage day after day. The

psalmist offers us a lifesaver in our raging storms in Psalm 62:5: "Rest in God alone, my soul, for my hope comes from Him" (HCSB).

The "hope" in Psalm 62:5 is the word *tiqvah*, which literally means "a cord, as an attachment" (Strong's). The psalmist contrasted the disappointment he often experienced in man with the security he found in his faithful God. His cord or rope was attached to God alone. We're all holding on to a rope of some kind for security, but if anyone but God is on the other end, we're hanging on by a thread! Hang on to Christ for dear life when the waves break harshly against you. He will be your survival no matter what the storm may destroy. Only He can keep you from becoming bitter. Only He can rebuild what gale-force winds tear apart.

6. *Listen for God to speak* (see v. 24). Incline your ear to the Master of the seas when the storms rage. He will not be silent. Just when the passengers and crew had lost hope, Paul stood to testify. He told them, "This night an angel of the God I belong to and serve stood by me, saying, 'Don't be afraid, Paul. You must stand before Caesar. And, look! God has graciously given you all those who are sailing with you'" (vv. 23–24 HCSB).

God will probably not send an angel from heaven to speak audibly to you, but He may send a fellow believer, a neighbor, a pastor, or friend. You can also hear Him speak through His Word anytime you are willing to open the Bible and receive.

Job also suffered for reasons outside his control, in ways we will never experience. He had plenty of places to lay blame. I believe one reason he survived such tragedy was because God proved not to be silent as Job had feared. The place in which He spoke to Job is very applicable to us today. Job 40:6 tells us, "The Lord answered Job from the whirlwind" (HCSB). God will speak to you too—straight to your heart. Sometimes others can make decisions that are devastating to our lives. I cannot promise you everything will be OK. It may be; it may not be. But I promise you based on the faithfulness of God that *you* can be OK. Just don't pull up that anchor. And never let go of the rope.

# DAY 292
## Acts 27:27–44

---∞∞∞---

The soldiers' plan was to kill the prisoners so that no one could swim off and escape. But the centurion kept them from [it] because he wanted to save Paul(vv. 42–43).

---∞∞∞---

Let's allow God to open our eyes to the importance of faithfulness and obedience through a study in contrasts, by seeing that the umbrella of protection or destruction in one man's hand can often cover many heads. The kind of cover these figurative umbrellas provide is not only determined by belief in God versus unbelief, but also by faithfulness versus unfaithfulness.

In Acts 27 God gave Paul an umbrella of protection because of Paul's obedience in ministry. Whether or not the others on board his sinking ship realized it, many were gathered under the umbrella and found safety. But let's take a look at another kind of umbrella in the storm, on display in the familiar account of the prophet Jonah. You'll recall that God called the prophet to go preach deliverance to Nineveh, Israel's bitter enemy. But rather than preach to the people of Nineveh, Jonah ran the other way, booked passage to Tarshish, and wound up in a fishy situation. Consider these similarities between Jonah and Paul:

• Both were Hebrews, had Jewish backgrounds, and believed in the one true God.

• Both were preachers.

• Both were called to preach unpopular messages in pagan cities.

• Both boarded a ship.

• Both experienced a terrible, life-threatening storm.

• Both greatly impacted the rest of the crew.

• Both knew the key to the crew's survival.

Paul and Jonah had many similarities, didn't they? But let's consider a few contrasts between Paul and Jonah. They differed in at least the following ways:

• Paul was compelled to go to Rome; Jonah was repelled by his calling to Nineveh.

• Paul faced many obstacles on his way to Rome, including imprisonment, injustices, inclement weather, and other difficulties; Jonah's only obstacle was himself!

• Paul had to sit and wait for the Lord; Jonah stood and ran from the Lord!

• Paul felt responsibility for the crew, although the calamity was not his fault; Jonah slept while the others worked to survive the calamity he had brought on them.

Paul and Jonah are great characters to compare and contrast because we can relate to both of them! Sometimes we respond with obedience like Paul. Other times we run from God with a sprinter's stride like Jonah, who revealed an amusing cowardice when in Jonah 1:12, the fugitive preacher told the ship's crewmen, "Pick me up and throw me into the sea so it may quiet down for you, for I know that I'm to blame for this violent storm that is against you" (HCSB). Notice he never offered to jump in!

Let's ask a fair question based on their examples: Does prompt obedience really make much difference? When all was said and done, didn't Paul suffer through a terrible storm although he had been entirely obedient? Didn't Jonah get another chance to obey, and an entire city was spared? So . . . what difference does prompt obedience or faithfulness make anyway?

God loves us whether or not we are obedient, but the quality of our Christian lives is dramatically affected by our response. Allow me to point out a big difference between the obedient Christian and the disobedient one, between obedient times and disobedient times. Jesus said, "If you keep My commands you will remain in My love, just as I have kept My Father's commands and remain in His love. I have spoken these things to you so that My joy may be in you and your joy may be complete" (John 15:10–11 HCSB).

Although Jonah was ultimately obedient and surprisingly successful, you will search in vain for a single hint of joy in his life. Although Paul seemed to suffer at every turn, he had more to say about joy than any other mouthpiece in the Word of God.

An attitude of obedience makes a difference both to the servant himself and to those close by. Servants of God can dramatically affect the lives of others positively or negatively. Under Jonah's umbrella in the storm, many experienced calamity. Under Paul's umbrella, however, many found safety.

Is the sky rumbling? Are clouds darkening? Is a storm rising in the horizon? If you are a child of God, you will hold an umbrella in the storm. You will not be under the umbrella alone. Neither will I. Our children will be under there with us. Our coworkers may be too. The flocks God has entrusted to us will be there. Even the lost are often drawn to people of faith when hurricane winds begin to blow. Child of God, you and I are centered on the bow of the ship when storms come and the waves crash. May the rest of the crew find an umbrella of blessing in our midst.

# DAY 293
## Acts 28:1–6

---

They expected that he would swell up or suddenly drop dead. But after they waited a long time and saw nothing unusual happen to him, they changed their minds (v. 6).

---

One of the vipers indigenous to the region where Paul and his shipmates crashed is a small but poisonous snake. Interestingly, it looks similar to a dead branch when immobile, so in all likelihood Paul picked up the snake as he was gathering brushwood. (Doesn't that just give you the creeps?) When he put the branches in the fire, the viper took the first way out: Paul's hand. Can you imagine what Paul was thinking as the snake dangled from his hand? "Five times I received from the Jews 40 lashes minus one. Three times I was beaten with rods. Once I was stoned. Three times I was shipwrecked" (2 Cor. 11:24–25 HCSB), *and now this!*

God used the creature, however, to reveal the beliefs of the islanders. Their response to Paul's snakebite was, "This man is probably a murderer, and though he has escaped the sea, Justice does not allow him to live!" (Acts 28:4 HCSB). Even though their assumption was incorrect, they revealed a limited knowledge of the one true God. Depending on the Bible translation you have, you may have noticed the word "Justice" was capitalized as a proper noun. The original Greek word *dikastes* actually means "a judge, one who executes justice, one who maintains law and equity." Although the island of Malta had presumably never been evangelized, its inhabitants revealed an awareness of a divine judge who maintains justice in the world.

Out of love for the world, God makes Himself known even in the most remote places on earth. Some call this self-disclosure "natural revelation." God desires for people to seek the unknown through the known, discovering a greater knowledge leading to salvation. Paul penned the clear words verifying God's universal declaration of His existence: "From the creation of the world His invisible attributes, that is, His eternal power and divine nature, have been clearly seen, being understood through what He has made. As a result, people are without excuse" (Rom. 1:20 HCSB).

God is so merciful, isn't He? He doesn't just want people to be without excuse. He doesn't want people to be without a Savior. Justice was the natural light through which the people of Malta first perceived the one true God.

# DAY 294
## Acts 28:7–10

The rest of those on the island who had diseases also came and were cured.
So they heaped many honors on us (vv. 9–10).

When God performed His awesome, miraculous work on the island of Malta, healing all the sick, I believe His main purpose was to meet their spiritual needs. Three details suggest God worked in the physical realm for spiritual reasons.

First, *Paul prayed* before he healed the chief official's father, not wanting the people of Malta to think he was a god. Prayer helped redirect their attention to the source of all healing—Jesus Christ, the Great Physician.

The second detail that suggests God used physical needs to shed light on spiritual realities was His *means of healing*. He used Paul to heal, yet Luke was a physician. Why? I believe God wanted the people of Malta to recognize God (instead of some well-educated professional) as the source of their healing. No doubt God used Luke many times to tend the sick, but when He wanted to leave no room for doubt, He used someone with no knowledge of medicine.

The last detail that suggests God was up to something spiritual was *wholesale healing*. Sadly, an evangelist may not pack the house with good preaching and Spirit-filled worship, but he can draw large crowds with rumors of healing. Yes, God cares about the sick. He cares deeply. And He often heals physical illnesses, but seldom in Scripture did He use a servant to bring physical healing to an entire land. God used the physical needs of those in Malta to draw attention to the only One who could meet their spiritual needs. He trusted Paul not to take credit for a work only God can do.

We, too, must be careful to give God the glory when He uses us to accomplish things only He can do. Every time you exercise a spiritual gift, God is accomplishing His work through you. If you are a servant of God and you have known Him long, He has used you to do something only He can do.

Think of a work He has accomplished through you. If you're uncomfortable with this request, you may still be taking too much credit. I'm asking you to boast in God, not in yourself. Pray about your availability for any work He might use you to accomplish. Then commit to give Him the glory.

# DAY 295
## Acts 28:11–14

꙰

*There we found believers and were invited to stay with them*
*for seven days. And so we came to Rome (v. 14).*

꙰

In the early spring of AD 61, God fulfilled His promise to Paul. The apostle arrived in Rome. Our text in Acts is very brief and may leave some of us yearning for details. Although Luke wrote about the shipwreck in detail, he did not include Paul's reaction when he reached Rome. Surely he was overwhelmed by the imposing sight, yet more so by his faithful God.

Paul had never seen anything like Rome. At the time of his arrival, Rome was inhabited by one million citizens and approximately the same number of slaves. By even today's standards, the city was gigantic. Rome shared a number of characteristics with many current overcrowded inner cities. Although magnificent buildings and luxurious villas begged to steal the onlooker's attention, he would have to tear his focus from the seas of tenements on the verge of collapse. These four- to five-story *insulae*, with no running water or sanitary restrictions, housed most of the city's population.

As Paul approached the gargantuan city, I believe God knew he would be overwhelmed by a great sea of strangers and the certainty of enemies. Not coincidentally, God met him at each stepping stone to Rome with brothers. Keep in mind that brotherhood in Christ is not a term related to masculinity. It refers to the unique fellowship shared by brothers and sisters in Christ.

Scripture refers to a natural sibling of Paul's only once, yet I counted ninety-nine times in his epistles when the apostle referred to other Christians as brothers. The Greek word for "brothers" is *adelphos*. In reference to fellow believers in Christ, the term "came to designate a fellowship of love equivalent to or bringing with it a community of life." As Paul approached Rome, God knew he needed "a fellowship of love" or "a community of life."

Paul's need was not unique. People are desperate for a sense of community today. We all want to feel like we belong somewhere. God recognizes our need for community and desires to meet the need through His church—the body of believers God organized to offer a community of life.

# DAY 296
## Acts 28:15–16

The believers from there had heard the news about us and had come to meet us. . . .
When Paul saw them, he thanked God and took courage (v. 15).

Many people believe in Christ as Savior yet never sense a brotherhood or sisterhood with other Christians. In Paul's life, however, I see three strands that formed the cord of brotherhood he felt with other believers.

1. *Paul believed in the power of prayer and in our spiritual poverty without it.* Over and over in his letters, Paul assured churches of his prayers. He didn't just ask God to bless them. Paul jealously sought God's best for them. He asked big things of God because he knew God had big things to give. Paul had experienced the riches of an intimate relationship with Christ. He wanted other believers to experience those same riches.

2. *Paul believed that part of his calling was to share his gifts and faith with other Christians.* He truly believed that Christians have an obligation to one another as well as to the lost. In 1 Corinthians 12:12 he said, "The body is one and has many parts, and all the parts of that body, though many, are one body" (HCSB). Without apology, Paul instructed believers, as "parts" of the "body" of Christ, to recognize their obligation to one another—and their need for one another. Generally speaking, my spiritual gifts were given for your edification; your spiritual gifts were given for mine.

3. *Paul desired to see all people come to Christ.* He preached to anyone who would listen, and he considered any convert a brother or sister. All were equally in need of salvation, and all were equally loved by God. At first consideration we may fully believe we share his attitude, but sometimes we struggle with the equality of all believers. We may desire to see all people saved regardless of their race and position, but we don't necessarily want them to attend church with us.

Paul was greatly encouraged by the brothers who met him in Rome. Their faces were unfamiliar, but they each had been washed in the blood of Jesus Christ. They were family. God used prayer, a sense of mutual obligation, and a sense of equality to bind their hearts. Paul's example teaches us that a sense of community is not derived from the actions and attitudes of others toward us, but from our actions and attitudes toward them. As we imitate his approach to other believers, we will form cords of love not quickly broken.

# DAY 297
## Acts 28:17–29

—∞∞∞—

*"Therefore, let it be known to you that this saving work of God*
*has been sent to the Gentiles; they will listen!"* (v. 28).

—∞∞∞—

How terribly we cheat ourselves when we have as much as we want from God. Although many of us have received the gift of salvation, in other ways we are not unlike some of the Jews that Paul encountered. We mimic the words of Felix, holding up our hand to God and saying, "That's enough. That's all I'm comfortable with" (see Acts 24:25).

Whatever the reason for our resistance, we may suffer from our own rendition of Paul's diagnosis of many Jews. Based on my own experience, I recognize the danger. At times I've resisted what God wanted to do in me or through me. I seemed to hear Him less, see His activity less, and, tragically, love Him less. Thankfully, when I finally relented and became receptive, my spiritual abilities to hear, see, and love were restored to me.

Let's examine the expressions Paul used and consider the abilities at risk when God desires to give and we continue to resist.

1. *"You will listen and listen, yet never understand"* (Acts 28:26 HCSB). By the word "listen," Paul referred to the basic physical ability. By the phrase "never understand," he referred to a crippling inability. The Greek word for "understanding" is *suniemi*, meaning "the assembling of individual facts into an organized whole, as collecting the pieces of a puzzle and putting them together." *Suniemi* is exercised when "the mind grasps concepts and sees the proper relationship between them." Do you see the tragedy at stake?

When we continue to resist what God has for us, we may cripple our ability to understand how the pieces of our puzzle fit together. We will constantly single out our experiences rather than understand them as parts of a whole. The things we go through may never make any sense to us. Preachers and teachers may tell us God is at work in our lives, but although we physically hear, we have little ability to understand.

Although we will not understand everything until we see Christ face-to-face, God often blesses us by letting many things make sense during our lifetimes. Most things I've encountered eventually made sense as I developed a more cooperative spirit and a greater understanding of God's purposes. Many of those experiences still hurt, but I find comfort in seeing their eventual usefulness as parts of the whole.

You might think of the process this way: God is faithfully putting a puzzle together in each life so that the final picture will resemble Christ (see Rom.

8:28–29). If we continue to resist this further work, we will be less likely to see the pieces fit.

2. *"You will look and look, yet never perceive"* (Acts 28:26 HCSB). Again Paul referred to a basic physical ability as he used the word "look" to mean human vision. "Perceive" is translated from the Greek word *eido*, which merges the ability to see with the ability to know. *Eido* is "not the mere act of seeing, but the actual perception of some object." If we continue to resist the further blessings and works of God in our lives, we may lose some ability to see past the obvious and the physical. Those who allow God to unleash His Holy Spirit in their lives are those who often perceive spiritual and eternal works in the physical and temporal realm. People who never see with spiritual eyes can't comprehend how others claim to see God at work.

I'll never forget the time Amanda's seat belt in our old station wagon wouldn't fasten. Five years old at the time, she pushed and pushed on it to no avail, so I finally told her to crawl into the front seat. Seconds later, the window where she had been sitting inexplicably imploded and pieces of glass embedded into the seat she had just left. I exclaimed, "Thank You, dear God!"

Later she asked, "Do you really think that was God?"

I said, "No, baby. I *know* that was God." Every now and then God blesses us with a good dose of *eidos*. We not only see—we know! When Paul tried to point out Christ's fulfillment of Old Testament prophecy, many Jews chose to close their eyes and refuse to see. God wants to give us supernatural sight. Let's not resist Him. Our lives are so much richer when we not only see but we also perceive!

3. *"This people's heart has grown callous"* (Acts 28:27 HCSB). I was surprised when I discovered the meaning of the word "calloused." You may be too! The original word is *pachuno*, meaning "to make fat . . . calloused as if from fat." According to this verse, people who continue to resist God can develop fat around their hearts. In the physical realm, one reason fat develops around the heart is a lack of exercise. In spiritual matters many of the Jews had ceased exercising their hearts. Religion for them involved more of a state of mind and intellect than the heart.

At one time or another, we've all been hurt in love relationships. But if we cease to exercise our hearts by loving God and loving others, getting involved, and taking risks, our hearts will become diseased and hardened.

Through the prophet Isaiah and the apostle Paul, God revealed three dangers and three opposite blessings. By heeding Paul's warning, we can have ears willing to hear, eyes willing to see, and hearts willing to be exercised.

# DAY 298
## Acts 28:30–31

---

*He welcomed all who visited him, proclaiming the kingdom of God and teaching the things concerning the Lord Jesus Christ with full boldness (vv. 30–31).*

---

We now conclude our studies in the fascinating book of Acts. I've relished every second of our journey. In a blinding light on the Damascus road, I saw God's mercy. In a midnight song from a dungeon, I heard authentic worship. In every miracle on the island of Malta, I felt hope. The book of Acts has quickened my senses and involved me. I pray that you've also gotten involved. Much more awaits us, but not from the pen of Luke. Our upcoming days will take us to the letters Paul wrote during the last six years of his earthly life. But Luke's final account provides a fitting conclusion to the book of Acts.

Recently a friend asked me what impressed me most from my research about Paul. I didn't hesitate to answer. God used the apostle's unparalleled passion for Christ to woo me into the study, then used his inconceivable perseverance to sustain me.

When I was a child, someone gave my brother an inflatable clown with sand in the base. No matter how we socked that clown, he always came back up for more. The apostle was no clown, but every time he got hit, he bounced back up for more. Of course, the reason for his perseverance was his deep passion for Christ.

In these last moments from the book of Acts, we've gotten a glimpse of the risk we take when we put our hand up to God and say, "No more. I'm comfortable this way." We've also realized how much we have to gain by remaining receptive to God. He has so much to give us. Yet His greatest riches are those things that are conformable, not comfortable.

As we conclude the book of Acts, I pray we've each had our eyes unveiled to the extra-ordinary works God can do in ordinary lives. As we've sojourned from chapter to chapter in Luke's wonderful book, we've met Stephen, Paul, Barnabas, John Mark, Timothy, Silas, Aquila, Priscilla, Philip the evangelist, his four daughters, and many more. They all shared one thing in common: they were simple flesh and blood infiltrated by the awesome power of the Holy Spirit—all because they didn't resist.

We may never leave our native land or travel by sea, as Paul did. But if we love and serve God, our lives will be a great adventure. He'll never take you anywhere He has not already prepared for your arrival. Keep trusting Him. There are more Acts to be performed.

# DAY 299
## 1 Corinthians 1:26–31

———∞∞———

God has chosen the world's foolish things to shame the wise,
and God has chosen the world's weak things to shame the strong (v. 27).

———∞∞———

God often proves Himself when we feel we have the least to offer. And in our passage for today, Paul explained why God sometimes uses this method: so we can be clear that the power comes from Him and not from us. He concluded, "The one who boasts must boast in the Lord." Perhaps Paul's words mean more to you now that you know how he felt when he left Athens.

Just before the taping of my first video series, God allowed me to go through a very difficult time. My confidence took a severe beating. I was so emotionally exhausted that I did not know how I would get through the taping. I sat before the Lord very early the morning we were to begin, and I told Him I did not think I was going to make it. I had worked so hard in preparation; yet as the time arrived, I had nothing to offer.

Thousands of dollars worth of equipment had been shipped to Houston. An amazing number of personnel had worked to prepare. Six cameras had been set in place. An audience had gathered. Everything and everyone was ready—but me. I walked out on that set with only enough strength to get on my knees and pray. But when I got up off my knees to teach, a stream of strength seemed to pour from heaven. Not in buckets. It was more like an intravenous drip. Just enough for me to know He was sustaining me minute by minute. I never felt a rush of adrenaline. I never felt a sudden gust of mighty wind. All I know is that many demanding hours of work took place over the days of that taping, and never did I lack the strength necessary to complete the task. Never in my adult life have I had less confidence, yet He gave me enough of His to keep my knees from buckling.

You may wonder why God allowed me to go through such a difficult season of inadequacy just before that task. I wondered myself until I received the first letter from a viewer of the video series. I wept as I read her words of thanks, and I whispered back, "It was God. Not me." Perhaps God has opened a door for you, but you have no confidence. Is insecurity holding you back from the ministry God has for you? Each of us struggles with insecurities and the loss of confidence. No one has ever been used more mightily than the apostle Paul, yet he was so scared at times he made himself sick!

# DAY 300
## 1 Corinthians 2:1–5

—∞∞∞—

When I came to you, brothers, announcing the testimony of God to you,
I did not come with brilliance of speech or wisdom (v. 1).

—∞∞∞—

I suspect that Paul's visit to Athens affected him far more than we realize. Few people believed and received Christ. Paul was overwhelmed by the polytheistic beliefs of the residents. They wanted to argue philosophies rather than consider the truth. The Athenians did not throw Paul out of the city or persecute him in any obvious way. The few converts appear to have produced little fruit. Apparently no church was established. Paul spent most of his days in Athens alone. Although 1 Thessalonians 3:1 indicates Timothy and Silas might have come as he asked, they were quickly sent elsewhere. After a brief stay in Athens, he simply moved on in frustration.

Paul had plenty of time to think on his way to Corinth. He spent several grueling days alone. During those long hours, I believe he convinced himself that every effort in Athens had failed. As we often do, I suspect he became so focused on the negative that he lost sight of the positive.

Have you ever noticed how lengthy times of solitude affect us differently depending on our state of mind? Aloneness exaggerates our emotions and sensitivities. For example, we can sometimes sense the presence of God and hear His voice far more clearly when we have several days alone. But on the other hand, solitude can also exaggerate negative feelings. We find ourselves almost thinking too much! We look back on a situation and decide nothing good came from it at all. Insecurity turns into immobilization, and intimidation turns into terror! If you have ever had a lengthy time alone in which your mind "ran away with you" on the wings of negative thoughts, then you probably understand something of what Paul was feeling.

I believe the more Paul thought about his experiences in Athens, the worse he felt. First Corinthians 2:1 may suggest that Paul felt intimidated by the Athenians, and these feelings accompanied him to Corinth. Athens attracted intellectuals who could debate eloquently and were eager to flaunt their knowledge. As he tried to preach to them, the Epicurean and Stoic philosophers disputed with him. Some sneered, "What is this pseudo-intellectual trying to say?" (Acts 17:18 HCSB).

Paul had been the pride of his graduating class—the child prodigy! You can imagine the beating his ego took in Athens. I think Paul felt like a failure. First Corinthians 2:2 says by the time he reached Corinth, he had "determined to know nothing . . . except Jesus Christ and Him crucified" (HCSB). Thank goodness, he knew the only thing he really had to know! He determined to base his life and ministry on Christ—his one certainty!

In 1 Corinthians we see an insight Paul eventually gained from his experience. Are these words evidence that he may have been thinking back on the Athenians? "For to those who are perishing the message of the cross is foolishness, but to us who are being saved it is God's power. For it is written: 'I will destroy the wisdom of the wise, and I will set aside the understanding of the experts'" (1 Cor. 1:18–19 HCSB).

God used this entire experience to show Paul an important lesson. In 1 Corinthians 2:14 he wrote, "But the natural man does not welcome what comes from God's Spirit, because it is foolishness to him; he is not able to know it since it is evaluated spiritually" (HCSB). Paul ultimately gained the insights he wrote about in 1 Corinthians, but as he traveled to Corinth he was still in turmoil. On the miles between Athens and Corinth, Paul probably hashed and rehashed his experiences. He wished he had said this or that. Sometimes we can't explain exactly what we believe. Other times we think of just the right answer when it's too late. We end up feeling foolish because we weren't persuasive.

Obviously Paul's experience had a great impact on his next opportunity. He entered Corinth "in weakness, in fear, and in much trembling" (1 Cor. 2:3 HCSB). The word "weakness" comes from an original word used for a sickness. It suggests that Paul was so scared he was physically ill. The word for "trembling" indicates something we've all experienced: hands shaking from nervousness. The opposite word is "confidence." By the time Paul reached Corinth, he had lost his confidence. Possibly he wondered if the fruit he had seen in other cities had come from God's blessings on Barnabas or Silas.

Does seeing Paul's experience in this light help you to relate to him as a fellow struggler on the road to serve Christ? You probably didn't know the apostle Paul shared the same feelings. Neither did I. I hope you can find encouragement in his experience.

The enemy would have enjoyed preventing Paul from ministering in Corinth because of feelings of inadequacy, but Satan was unsuccessful. God instead used Paul's feelings to give a great "demonstration of the Spirit and power" (1 Cor. 2:4 HCSB). The word for "demonstration" in this passage is *apodeixis*, meaning "proof." What a wonderful term! Do you see what Paul meant? He was so intimidated by the time he reached Corinth, the abundant fruit ultimately produced through his preaching was proof of the Holy Spirit's power! God sometimes uses us most powerfully when we feel the least adequate.

# DAY 301
## 2 Corinthians 11:22–33

—◦◦◦—

I faced dangers from rivers, dangers from robbers, dangers from my own people,
dangers from the Gentiles, dangers in the city, dangers in the open country (v. 26).

—◦◦◦—

After the Grecian Jews tried to kill him in Jerusalem, Saul boarded a boat for Tarsus, his homeland (see Acts 9:29–30). Through Paul's own testimony in Galatians 1:21, we know that he went to Syria and Cilicia. Five years passed between his departure to Tarsus and his next appearance in Scripture. Many scholars refer to these as the "missing years." Although we have no details of Saul's life during this time, we can be sure the inhabitants of the cities he visited didn't describe him as missing! Probably the reason the events of those five years are missing from the book of Acts is because Luke, the writer, was not an eyewitness.

But consider a few things that might have happened during the interim years. In Acts 9:16, the Lord told Ananias that He would show Saul how much he must suffer for His name. I believe God began fulfilling this prophecy almost immediately. Figuratively speaking, he was thrown into many fires during his ministry, yet few would have been any hotter than those in Tarsus. He was the local hero among the Jewish community in his hometown. Most people probably knew that Saul had left Tarsus years before for the express purpose of dealing with the followers of the Way. Now he returned as one of them. I doubt anyone threw him a homecoming party.

We have no reason to assume his father had died, yet we see no reference to his reaction to Saul's conversion. His father may have acted as if his son had never been born. Even today when a Jew from an orthodox family turns from Judaism, parents sometimes consider the defector to be dead. Some observe an event akin to a funeral. Others prefer to blot them from their lives and consider them never born. Many families do not react so harshly and permanently, yet remember— Saul's father was a Pharisee! His son's defection was a fate worse than death.

God wasn't kidding when He said Saul would suffer for His name, was He? Yet many of the perils mentioned are not recorded in the book of Acts. The most likely time these sufferings took place was during the interim period not detailed in Acts. As Saul reenters the picture, however, we should assume his life had been anything but uneventful!

# DAY 302
## Galatians 2:1–10

—∞∞∞—

When James, Cephas, and John, recognized as pillars, acknowledged the grace that had been given to me, they gave the right hand of fellowship to me and Barnabas (v. 9).

—∞∞∞—

Picture the five men mentioned in Galatians 2:9 conferring together and giving approval to one another: James, the unbelieving mocker turned preacher; Peter, the one sifted like wheat, denying Christ three times, then having enough faith to return and strengthen his brothers; John, the Son of Thunder, who asked if he could sit at Christ's side in the kingdom and destroy the Samaritans with fire from heaven; Paul, a former religious madman who approved the murder of Stephen and helped fuel a persecution that resulted in James's death; Barnabas, the son of encouragement, who risked getting hammered by the early church by building a bridge between unlikely brothers.

That's just it. We're all unlikely brothers. In Christ's church, the pillars were never designed to match. Each one is distinct. What need would cookie-cutter disciples meet? None of us were meant to match. We were meant to fit together. Two identical puzzle pieces don't "fit." Oh, that we would celebrate that difference.

Do you remember what Paul said James, Peter, and John recognized in him that caused them to extend the right hand of fellowship? They "acknowledged the grace that had been given to me" (Gal. 2:9 HCSB). First Peter 4:10 echoes the same concept: "Based on the gift they have received, everyone should use it to serve others, as good managers of the varied grace of God" (HCSB). Beloved, we don't have to agree on every single point of doctrine. We don't even have to always get along. We just need to recognize that grace has been given to us all.

To fulfill our kingdom purposes on earth, we could all use a right hand of fellowship from others, couldn't we? When I think back on those that God so graciously appointed to extend such a hand to me, I am deeply humbled and awed. I have been asked countless times how John Bisagno, the longtime pastor of my home church, handled this ministry coming out of his church. Beloved, he didn't just handle it. He pushed it! For years the only reason people invited me to come to their church was because they trusted him!

Did Brother John know I had a lot to learn? Perhaps more than anyone else. So did my mentor, Marge Caldwell. Did he agree with everything I taught or did? I doubt it. Yet they both continued to work with me, give me a chance to grow, and let me develop into my own person and not cookie-cutter images of them. They each extended me the right hand of fellowship for one reason. They recognized the grace of God in my once broken life.

When LifeWay approached me with a contract to tape the first series, *A Woman's Heart: God's Dwelling Place*, I was pitifully wet behind the ears. I don't know much about what I'm doing now, but I assure you I knew nothing then. I was petrified. The enemy came against me with such conflict and fear, I think I would have backed out had I not signed a contract. I felt like I needed advice desperately and needed someone to tell me whether my feelings were normal.

I still feel like an idiot over what I did next, but I was desperate. I called Kay Arthur's office and asked to speak to her. I had no idea what I was doing. I had never seen her in person or had the privilege of taking one of her courses. Don't get the idea that I in any way saw a comparison. I just wanted to talk to a woman who had taught the Word on videotape no matter what gulf of knowledge and experience separated us.

But God wasn't about to let me get in touch with Kay Arthur. First of all, He wanted me to rely on Him alone. Furthermore, He knew He had already extended the right hand of fellowship to me through sufficient people. I also believe God knew how extremely impressionable I was at that time and that I had not yet allowed Him to fully develop my style. I have so much respect for Kay that if I could have, I would have wanted God to make me just like her. What need whatsoever would God have had for such a thing? Kay does an excellent job of being Kay, so why on earth would God have wanted me to approach Bible study in exactly the same way? He already had her!

Today I could pick up the phone and call Kay, and we could laugh and talk for an hour if we had the time. But through the years both of us felt the call of God to do something far more public. Each of us has gone out of our way to demonstrate that we are united in Christ Jesus and we serve the same God . . . albeit with different styles. I have taught some of her books. Kay has invited me to several of her conferences to lead prayer and to speak. She has extended to me something more precious than gold: the right hand of fellowship. She knows I have a lot to learn. We wouldn't agree on every interpretation. She is simply a woman who recognizes grace when she sees it. I am so grateful.

Fourteen years lapsed between the time Paul first tried to fit in with the apostles and when he finally received the right hand of fellowship. I'd like to suggest the hand didn't come a moment behind schedule. What use would God have had for Paul if he simply turned out to be another James? Another Peter? Another John? His mission was distinct. And so, Beloved, is yours. God knows what He's doing! Trust Him. God is busy making you someone no one else has ever been.

# DAY 303
## Galatians 4:3–7

——∞∞——

But when the completion of the time came, God sent His Son,
born of a woman, born under the law, to redeem those under the law (vv. 4–5).

——∞∞——

God purposed that His Son would come out of Nazareth but be born in Bethlehem. So He caused a census to require everyone in the Roman world to return to the place of his or her family's origin. Probably the timing was too close to the birth of the child for Joseph to leave Mary behind. One commentary tenderly suggested that Joseph may not have wanted Mary left behind and subjected to gossip.

Bethlehem is about five miles south of Jerusalem, quite a distance from Nazareth, with chains of hills and mountains in between. Theirs was no easy trip. Women could be tempted to picket the New International Version for leaving out one little detail that had a profound influence on Mary's trip: "Mary . . . being great with child" (Luke 2:5 KJV). We have to appreciate the fact that the verb tense indicates a continuous action. We might say she was getting greater by the minute.

I certainly remember feeling that way. I'll never forget catching a glimpse of myself, great with child, in the distorted reflection of the stainless-steel faucet on the tub. My stomach looked huge, and my head and arms appeared like nubs. From then on I took showers. Taking "great with child" on the road is no easy task.

Whether or not Mary and Joseph planned Christ's birth this way, God certainly did. One of my favorite phrases in the birth narrative is humbly tucked in Luke 2:6: "While they were there, the time came for the baby to be born." The time. The time toward which all "time" had been ticking since the kingdom clock struck one.

These words refer to the most important segment of time since the first tick of the clock. The second hand circled tens of thousands of times for thousands of years, then finally, miraculously, majestically—the time came. God's voice broke through the barrier of the natural realm through the cries of an infant, startled by life on the outside. The Son of God had come to earth, wrapped in a tiny cloak of human flesh. "She wrapped him in cloths and placed him in a manger, because there was no room for them in the inn" (v. 7).

## DAY 304
### Ephesians 5:22–24

———— ∞ ————

Wives, submit to your own husbands as to the Lord, for the husband
is head of the wife as also Christ is head of the church (vv. 22–23).

———— ∞ ————

For the next few days, we will concentrate on the letter to the Ephesians.
Most scholars believe Colossians and Ephesians were written early in Paul's two-
year imprisonment in Rome because he never hinted of a possible release as he
did in Philemon (see v. 22) and Philippians (see 1:19–26).

The letter to the Ephesians differs from his letter to the Colossians. Paul
never warned of deceptive philosophy; rather, he wrote about a greater knowledge and experience in Christ. We can easily deduce the reason for the omis-
sion of several basics. Remember, the Christians at Colosse had never met Paul,
while the people of Ephesus had benefited from his teaching and an unparalleled
demonstration of power for several years.

Paul found receptive soil in Ephesus, even in the midst of terrible hardships.
His lengthy and effective ministry in Ephesus not only resulted in deep bonds of
love and brotherhood (see Acts 20:37–38); it also freed him to proceed to great
depths in his letter. Space limits me to choose only one or two subjects from the
book of Ephesians, but among the most important are the biblical roles of three
distinct figures intimately involved in marriage: wives, husbands, and Christ.
Ladies, let's get the painful part over first!

First, look back to verse 21, where Paul speaks of "submitting to one another
in the fear of Christ" (HCSB). The attitude of all Christians is to be submissive
to one another. No discussion of this topic can stay on track apart from that
spirit. Paul's primary directive to women dealt with submission, while his primary directive to men dealt with love. Could it be that he was targeting the areas
most likely to be our weaknesses? Before we learn what submission means for
Christian wives, let's learn what it does not mean:

1. *Submission does not mean women are under the authority of men in general.*
I love the King James Version's rendition of Ephesians 5:22: "Wives, submit
yourselves unto your own husbands." Guess what? Wives aren't asked to submit
to anyone else's husband—just their own! While I make this point somewhat
tongue-in-cheek, many women assume the Bible teaches their general inferiority and subjection to men. Untrue. Paul is talking about marriage as a matter
between each husband and wife.

2. *Submission does not mean inequality.* Paul, the same man who taught submission, made a statement in Galatians 3:28 pertinent to our subject: "There is
no Jew or Greek, slave or free, male or female; for you are all one in Christ Jesus"
(HCSB). Spiros Zodhiates' definition of the Greek word *hupotasso* explains that

submission "is not due to her being inferior to her husband, for they are both equal before God."

3. *Submission does not mean wives are to treat their husbands like God.* One commentary explains: "'As to the Lord' does not mean that a wife is to submit to her husband in the same way she submits to the Lord, but rather that her submission to her husband is her service rendered 'to the Lord.'"[62] I think most husbands would be relieved to know they are not called on to be God to their wives!

4. *Submission does not mean slavery.* Let's release a few old notions and fears here! Paul uses an entirely different word in Ephesians 6:5 when he instructs slaves to obey their masters. This Greek word for "obey," *hupakouo*, embraces more of the meaning people often mistakenly associate with marital submission. *Hupakouo* means "to obey, to yield to a superior command or force (without necessarily being willing)." The term draws a picture of a soldier saluting his commander, not a wife submitting to her husband!

Now that we've learned a few things submission does not mean, just exactly what *does* it mean? The Greek word for "submit" is *hupotasso*. *Hupo* means "under" and *tasso* means "to place in order." The compound word *hupotasso* means "to place under or in an orderly fashion." Paul didn't dislike women; he liked order! He advocated order in the church, order in government, order in business, and, yes, order in the home. I'm convinced he even kept his cell in order! Galatians 3:28 and Ephesians 5:22 could spill from the same man's pen because Paul regarded husbands and wives as spiritual equals, though with certain obvious and functional differences.

The concept of a submissive wife really used to go against my grain until I began to learn more about God. Two realizations have changed my entire attitude:

• *God is good and loving.* He would never give approval to meanness or abuse. Any misuse of submission by either the husband or wife is sin.

• *God granted women a measure of freedom in submission that we can learn to enjoy.* It is a relief to know that as a wife and mother, I am not totally responsible for my family. I have a husband I can look to for counsel and direction. I can rely on his manly toughness when I am too soft, and I can rely on his logic when I am too emotional.

Certainly I haven't just delivered the definitive dissertation on submission, but I do believe I'm offering you sound doctrine. I hope it helps.

# DAY 305
## Ephesians 5:25–33

⸺∞⸺

Husbands, love your wives, just as also Christ loved the church and gave Himself for her, to make her holy, cleansing her in the washing of water by the word (vv. 25–26).

⸺∞⸺

In light of what we considered yesterday, Paul probably had the Ephesian Christians nodding their heads in agreement. Submission of the wife to the husband was codified Hebraic law. Nothing new here. Now Paul raised eyebrows in a hurry. He told husbands to love their wives.

For a society where women were little more than property, passed from father to husband, this command to love their wives was a radical idea. Paul knew few role models existed for the men to follow. He gave them the best role model possible: Jesus Christ.

1. *Husbands should love their wives sacrificially.* Just as a husband must be careful not to abuse his wife's exhortation to submission, a wife must not abuse her husband's exhortation to sacrifice. Some men work several jobs sacrificing time at home in a continual effort to raise the standard of living for their families.

2. *Husbands should love their wives in ways that encourage purity.* Christ encourages purity in His bride, the church, desiring for her to be holy and without stain. God calls upon husbands to treat their wives as pure vessels even in physical intimacy.

3. *Husbands should "love their wives as their own bodies"* (v. 28 HCSB). I have to snicker when I think about verses 28 and 29. I wonder if Paul might have been thinking, "If you love yourself at all, mister, then love your wife—because life will be far more pleasant under the same roof with a well-loved woman!" I also have to wonder if Paul's reference to a man treating his wife as he does his own body, such as feeding and caring for it, implies that husbands are supposed to cook for their wives. I'm not certain about that interpretation, but I would submit to my husband's cooking any day!

Think of marriage as a three-legged stool—a submissive wife, a loving husband, and Christ. All three must be in place for marriage to work as God intended. A wife submitting to an unloving husband is as lopsided as a loving husband sacrificing for a domineering wife. When Christ is not the head of the marriage, the stool falls indeed. Sadly, many Christian women are trying to keep their stools balanced with only one leg in place—their submission. Pray that your husband would love you out of his devotion to Christ.

# DAY 306
### Ephesians 6:10–13

———

Our battle is not against flesh and blood, but against the rulers, against the authorities, against the world powers of this darkness, against the spiritual forces of evil (v. 12).

———

We approach this day as a battalion of soldiers in the middle of a heavenly war. Lives are at risk. Casualties may be high. Our Commander in Chief issues orders. The victory is sure, but the fight will be difficult. Hear the voice of your Commander as He exhorts you to do the following:

1. *Realize your natural limitations.* We cannot enjoy spiritual victory without actively calling on the power of God. We are only strong when we are "strengthened by the Lord and by His vast strength" (v. 10 HCSB).

2. *Remember the "full armor"* (v. 11). Paul exhorted us to use every weapon available. Picture your Commander in Chief standing behind a table displaying six tools or weapons. He says, "I've tailor-made each of these for you. You may take only some of them if you choose, but they were designed to work together. Your safety and effectiveness are only guaranteed if you use them all." Trust me when I tell you that after at least six thousand years of practice on human targets, your enemy won't waste arrows on well-armed places. He will aim for the spots you and I leave uncovered. I know it from experience.

3. *Recognize your real enemies.* The struggles of warfare you and I experience do not originate in spouses, in-laws, neighbors, coworkers, or any earthly foe. Spiritual forces of evil exist. Not every problem we have is warfare, of course. Sometimes the prescription is repentance from sin. Other times, however, it is fortification against the evil one.

4. *Realize our enemies' limitations.* Satan and his powers and principalities cannot do anything they want with us. They have certain limitations. We can "resist" them, as Paul says in verse 13. Demons can oppress, but they cannot possess, for "when you heard the word of truth, the gospel of your salvation—in Him when you believed—[you] were sealed with the promised Holy Spirit" (Eph. 1:13 HCSB). He has "sealed you for the day of redemption" (Eph. 4:30 HCSB). Therefore, Satan cannot read your mind (though he can often guess what you're thinking from past behavior). Walk in the freedom of knowing that when you received Christ, God dropped His Holy Spirit into you, slammed on the lid, and tightened the cap. Nothing can get in. Not even the enemy of your soul.

## DAY 307
### Ephesians 6:14–20

❈

In every situation take the shield of faith, and with it you will be able
to extinguish the flaming arrows of the evil one (v. 16).

❈

When we stopped reading at Ephesians 6:13 yesterday, we were left with
the encouragement to "take your stand" (HCSB). Satan definitely wants to force us
off our property and make us feel like we're getting nowhere. But God has given
us the privilege of standing in the victorious space He desires for us. And He has
given us His mighty armor with which to join together with one another in spiritual combat against the enemy. You've most likely studied this list of weaponry
before, but as Peter believed, it is valuable to "remind you about these things,
even though you know them and are established in the truth you have" (2 Pet.
1:12 HCSB). May we continue to learn while we live, and fight while we have
strength.

*The belt of truth* represents not living a lie in any part of our lives, living free
of secret areas of hypocrisy. Satan loves to blackmail believers who have a secret
they want to keep hidden.

*The breastplate of righteousness* is the protection we receive when we choose
the right thing even when we feel like choosing the wrong thing. Not only will
we find protection from disaster, God will honor our obedience by changing our
hearts if we'll let Him. We will find great protection in learning to pray Psalm
141:4: "Do not let my heart turn to any evil thing" (HCSB).

*Feet readied with the gospel of peace.* The word for "readiness" is *hetoimasia*,
meaning "firm footing." Roman soldiers' boots had cleats on the soles to give
them firm footing. Our feet give our bodies balance. We can remain balanced
because, although we are at war with Satan, we are at peace with God. Sink your
feet into "the gospel of peace"!

*The shield of faith* is our protection when Satan tempts us to disbelieve God.
A big difference separates doubting what God may do and doubting God. Even
when you have no idea what God is doing, your protection is in never doubting
God is God. We're not called to have faith in our faith. We are called to have
faith in God and never doubt Him.

*The helmet of salvation* protects our minds. The best way to protect our mind
is to fill it with the Word of God and things pertaining to godliness. We need to
deliberately avoid destructive influences.

*The sword of the Spirit.* You've probably noticed the defensive nature of all
five previous weapons. The sword of the Spirit is our only offensive weapon
against the evil one. Christ demonstrated how to be an expert swordsman. In

His wilderness temptation Jesus attacked Satan with the Word of God until the enemy gave up. Know and use the Word of God persistently!

*Active, anytime prayer.* Retain an active prayer life. "Pray at all times in the Spirit" (v. 18 HCSB). Prayerless lives are powerless lives. Active prayer lives equip us with the power and motivation to put on the full armor of God. Because Paul mentioned praying for others next, I believe this first exhortation was primarily about praying for ourselves.

*Prayer for other believers.* Remember one another in warfare prayer "with all perseverance and intercession for all the saints," (v. 18 HCSB). Power results from collective prayer. God delights in our petitions for each other. Soldiers depend on one another to watch their backs! Not long ago I realized I was having an internal problem with anger. I was caught off guard because ordinarily I do not struggle with anger. I prayed many times; finally I shared my struggles with a friend. She began to join me in prayer, and the anger ceased immediately. I cannot explain why. I only know that Satan's secret was out, prayer doubled, and God acted.

*Prayer for spiritual leaders.* Notice Paul ended by asking for prayer— "Pray also for me" (v. 19 HCSB). Again, I believe he was talking about warfare prayer because he asked specifically for intercession regarding fearlessness. According to 2 Timothy 1:7, God does not give us a spirit of fear. Satan is the one who fuels fear in an attempt to keep people from serving God effectively. If the great apostle needed prayer to fulfill his calling fearlessly, we all need prayer! Our missionaries, pastors, leaders, and teachers need our prayers. The enemy wants to destroy ministries. Our prayers help build a hedge of protection around them.

The following list includes each of the exhortations about warfare we've considered today. As you read the list, mentally evaluate yourself on each of the actions.

- I reject personal hypocrisy (the belt of truth).
- I resist snares of unrighteousness (the breastplate of righteousness).
- I remain balanced (feet readied with the gospel of peace).
- I refuse unbelief (the shield of faith).
- I reinforce my mind (the helmet of salvation).
- I raise my sword (the sword of the Spirit).
- I retain an active prayer life.
- I remember others in warfare prayer.
- I specifically remember spiritual leaders in warfare prayer.

What a set of goals! Warfare is a reality for the Christian life. We can do nothing to change that. We can, however, decide whether to be victims or victors.

# DAY 308
## Philippians 3:2–11

———— ✺ ————

A Hebrew born of Hebrews; as to the law, a Pharisee; as to zeal, persecuting the
church; as to the righteousness that is in the law, blameless (vv. 5–6).

———— ✺ ————

Saul himself was a Pharisee and probably returned from Jerusalem to Tarsus
to serve as a teacher of the law. Imagine how his thinking was influenced by his
contemporaries. I believe Saul had set sail to Jerusalem as a young adolescent
with a pure heart; but somewhere along the way the negative influences out-
weighed the positive, and his purity began to erode. The law became his god.
That's what happens when you take the love out of obedience. The result is the
law. Without love for God and His Word, we're just trying to be good. Nothing
will wear you out faster.

Have you been there? I have! Trying to obey God and serve Him before
we've come to love Him can be exhausting.

Recently a friend shared a term that helps to explain what happened to the
once-noble ranks of the Pharisees. The term is "identity boundaries." These are
the walls we put up to separate our group from other groups. Gangs wear certain
colors to show who is in and who is out. Churches and denominations develop
distinctive teachings to accomplish the same goal. The first-century Jews became
so obsessed with identity boundaries that they forgot their purpose. They argued
endlessly about washing hands or observing the Sabbath, but they forgot about
loving God.

Saul epitomized such pharisaic obsession. He packed his diploma and
headed for a place to serve. Whether he divided his time between teaching and
his father's business is unknown. But one thing you can count on: he was absolutely miserable. How do I know? In Philippians 3:6, he said his zeal was so
great that he persecuted the church, and that his legalistic righteousness was
"blameless."

We cannot begin to comprehend what Saul's life was like as he sought to
live by the letter of the law because most of us do not have a Jewish background.
Daily rituals determined the first words out of Saul's mouth in the morning, the
way he took off his nightclothes and put on his day clothes, and how he sprinkled
his hands before breakfast. He carefully avoided eating or drinking quickly and
never ate while standing.

Saul pronounced numerous benedictions throughout the day. His entire day
was filled with ritual, and at night he took off his shoes and garments in the
prescribed order. He avoided certain sleeping positions and chose others. For the
sake of his heart and liver, he probably attempted to begin the night on his left
side and end the night on his right. He purposely kept his turning to a minimum.

Tossing and turning through the night is misery to us, but to Saul it could have been sin!

These daily rituals paled in comparison to all the laws regarding the Sabbath. Restrictions existed for almost everything. For instance, prior to the Sabbath a Pharisee cut his fingernails and toenails not in consecutive order but alternately. He then burned the nails. He avoided spitting in a place where the wind could scatter the saliva so he would not break laws concerning sowing on the Sabbath.

Do you get the general idea of what Saul's life was like as he attempted to live by the law "blamelessly"? These examples are just a few of hundreds of man-made laws. I do not cite them in order to ridicule the Jewish people. I share a few of the written traditions with you to point out man's overwhelming tendency to tax God's instruction. The Sabbath observance could not have been further from God's intent by the time Christ "became flesh and took up residence among us" (John 1:14 HCSB). The day of rest was hardly recognizable to the One who ordained it.

Saul was strangled by the letter of the law. He tried desperately to keep all the outward acts of obedience while his heart slowly eroded. Saul gradually became the model for Isaiah 29:13: "These people approach Me with their mouths to honor Me with lip-service, yet their hearts are far from Me, and their worship consists of man-made rules learned by rote" (HCSB). Inevitably, Saul's faraway heart would turn to faraway actions.

Oh, God, forgive us when we act like modern-day Pharisees. Convict us at the very moment of our departure from the law of love You have written on our hearts. Give us hearts of devotion, not heads full of religion.

# DAY 309
## Philippians 3:12–21

---∞∞∞---

One thing I do: forgetting what is behind and reaching forward
to what is ahead, I pursue as my goal the prize promised by
God's heavenly call in Christ Jesus (vv. 13–14).

---∞∞∞---

After such noble beginnings, such strict following of God's laws, incomparable attainment of the knowledge of Scripture, and every external mark of righteousness—what happened? How did a brilliant young rabbi become a relentless persecutor of men and women? He certainly did not develop into a murderous zealot under the instruction of Gamaliel, his highly esteemed teacher. Under similar circumstances, Gamaliel counseled his fellow leaders: "I tell you, stay away from these men and leave them alone. For if this plan or this work is of men, it will be overthrown" (Acts 5:38 HCSB).

Saul was not unlike others—the young and inexperienced—those who think they have all the answers. The obvious difference is that Saul's answers were lethal. Saul thought he was smarter than his teacher. No sense in waiting to see if the people of the Way would finally dissipate. He took matters into his own hands and tried to give them a much-needed shove. Acts 26:11 describes Saul's mental state perfectly: he had become obsessed. "Many a time I went from one synagogue to another to have them punished, and I tried to force them to blaspheme. In my obsession against them, I even went to foreign cities to persecute them" (Acts 26:11).

I'm certainly no counselor, but I suspect that most obsessions rise from a futile attempt to fill a gaping hole somewhere deep in a life. Saul's external righteousness and achieved goals left behind an itch he could not scratch. Can you imagine how miserable he must have been? Religiously righteous to the bone, inside he had nothing but innately wicked marrow. All that work, and it hadn't worked. All his righteous passion turned into unrighteous zeal, and he became dangerous.

The Greek word for "obsessed" is *emmainomai*. The root word is *mainomai*, which means "to act like a maniac." Our best attempts at homegrown righteousness are still but a moment from the unspeakable. Passions can turn a new direction with frightening speed. May none of us forget it. The prophet Isaiah said, "All our righteous acts are like filthy rags" (Isa. 64:6). If all the righteousness we have is our own, it's just an act. And acts don't last very long.

In this story we also get to see the purity of a Savior's mercy. Saul himself would later say, "God proves His own love for us in that while we were still sinners Christ died for us!" (Rom. 5:8 HCSB). Christ met Saul on the path to his darkest, most devious sin. For that very moment, for the depths of Saul's depravity, Christ had already died. Christ literally caught him in the act.

Toward the end of his life, he would sit in a jail cell and write: "Not that I have already reached the goal or am already fully mature, but I make every effort to take hold of it because I also have been taken hold of by Christ Jesus" (Phil. 3:12 HCSB). The Greek word translated "take hold" means "to lay hold of, seize, with eagerness, suddenness . . . the idea of eager and strenuous exertion, to grasp." Christ literally snatched Saul by the neck. This persecutor turned apostle would later write to Timothy, his son in the faith: "This saying is trustworthy and deserving of full acceptance: 'Christ Jesus came into the world to save sinners'—and I am the worst of them" (1 Tim. 1:15 HCSB).

Jesus sent Saul to open the eyes of many and turn them from darkness to light so they could receive forgiveness of sins. No greater calling exists, as well as no room for pride. God's chosen servant was never more than a flashback from humility. No one can teach forgiveness like the forgiven. Thank goodness, Saul ultimately became a zealous proponent of forgiveness of sin.

Let's end with some important thoughts about zeal. In the conversion of Saul, we see demonstrated that: a) we can wholeheartedly believe in something and be wholeheartedly wrong, and b) sincerity means nothing if it is misdirected. Saul believed in his cause with all his heart, yet it led him down the path to destruction. Saul was sincere. As he stated in Acts 26:9, "I myself supposed it was necessary to do many things in opposition to the name of Jesus the Nazarene" (HCSB).

Christ not only snatched Saul from Satan that pivotal day; He also snatched Saul from himself—from his own misguided zeal, his own obsessions. He can snatch you from yours too. I'm living proof. I couldn't count the times during any given month that I thank God for saving me not only from Satan but from myself.

Having studied the life of Saul, how can we ever doubt that Christ can save? Is anyone too wicked? Anyone too murderous? Grace never draws a line with a willing soul. His arm is never too short to save (see Isa. 59:1). He can reach into the deepest pit or down the dustiest road to Damascus. Yes, some things are gray such as, "Why did He choose us?" But some things are still black and white—I once was lost, but now I'm found, was blind but now I see.

# DAY 310
### Philippians 4:1–13

—◦◦◦◦—

Do what you have learned and received and heard and seen in me,
and the God of peace will be with you (v. 9).

—◦◦◦◦—

How many truly contented people do you know? They are rare gems, aren't they? The enemy loves to see our discontentment because contented Christians live a powerful and effective testimony. Their lives are walking witnesses, proving that Christ can deliver what the gods of this world can't. You can be sure of this: wherever one of these rare gems exist, a jewel thief is lurking close by.

We can identify the following five thieves of contentment based on Philippians 4:

1. *Pettiness.* To everyone who thought the apostle Paul did not believe in women in ministry, allow me to introduce Euodia and Syntyche: "I urge Euodia and I urge Syntyche to agree in the Lord. . . . Help these women who have contended for the gospel at my side" (Phil. 4:2–3 HCSB). They worked right beside him. They were fellow workers! They had just one little problem: they couldn't get along. Let's admit it: people can be petty!

God intentionally made women sensitive. But I believe the counterfeit of sensitivity is pettiness. We tend to get our feelings hurt easily and take things personally. God gave us a special tenderness and sensitivity to lend a sweetness to our service. Pettiness, however, sours a servant's heart and steals contentment.

2. *Anxiety.* I personally can't think of a more successful jewel thief. Paul counters, "Don't worry about anything, but in everything, through prayer and petition with thanksgiving, let your requests be made known to God" (Phil. 4:6 HCSB). No anxiety—what a thought! How do we turn off the valve that is pumping anxiety into our souls? Paul proposes an answer: prayer. You might say, "A better solution to fighting anxiety must exist. I've prayed—and still been anxious." I want to suggest gently that you haven't necessarily been practicing the kind of prayer Paul was describing as a prescription for anxiety.

Verse 6 describes an intimate and active prayer life. Notice Paul's words for prayer and supplication. The word "prayer" refers to a very general kind of prayer. The word "petition" or "supplication" is translated from the Greek word *deesis,* describing a very personal kind of prayer. *Deesis* is "the petition for specific individual needs and wants." Paul exhorted believers to come to God with general requests and needs as well as the details that cause us anxiety. And don't give up! Persist until peace comes. Keep praying not only about your critical needs but about everything! An open line of communication with God reminds you He is real and active in your life, and the peace that overflows lends contentment.

3. *Destructive thinking.* Proverbs 23:7 describes man with the words, "For as he thinks within himself, so he is" (HCSB). We might say a person feels like he or she thinks. Our human natures tend toward negative and destructive thoughts. If ten people complimented you today and one person criticized, which would you go to bed thinking about tonight? Probably the criticism!

Destructive, negative thinking is a habit that can be broken, but this thief takes diligence to overcome. God knows the tendency of the mind to think and rethink on a certain subject, meditating on things. Paul gave us a wonderful checklist for determining whether our thoughts are worth thinking! "Whatever is true, whatever is honorable, whatever is just, whatever is pure, whatever is lovely, whatever is commendable . . . dwell on these things" (Phil. 4:8 HCSB).

I struggle with destructive thinking just like you do. God has used Scripture memory and Bible study to set me free. I continue to make His Word a daily priority, but He also blesses the refreshment I gain from the occasional decent movie, a wholesome magazine, a good documentary, or a funny book. Worthy thought patterns are a key to contentment.

4. *Resistance to learn.* Paul said, "I have learned to be content in whatever circumstances I am" (v. 11 HCSB). No one was born with contentment. Paul learned from experience that God was faithful no matter what circumstance he met. Had he never been in want, He never would have learned! Often we're in no mood to learn when we're in difficult circumstances, but God desires to show us that we can't meet a circumstance He can't handle. We handcuff a sly thief of contentment when we ask God to give us hearts willing to learn.

5. *Independence.* Refusing to rely on God robs us of some of God's most priceless riches. Through countless ups and downs, Paul learned he could do everything God called him to do, but only "through Him who strengthens me" (v. 13 HCSB). Through the multitude of needs Paul encountered, he learned that "God will supply all your needs according to His riches in glory in Christ Jesus" (v. 19 HCSB). I believe Paul considered reliance on God a secret because everyone has to discover it for themselves. I can tell you God will meet your every need. I can say that you can do all things through Christ; but until you find out for yourself, it's still a secret. I can tell you, but He will show you. Let Him. He is so faithful.

Contentment is a rare gem. Because Paul ceased letting thieves steal his contentment, his testimony was powerful. Even many who belonged to Caesar's household were compelled to know Christ! (see v. 22). Paul had a secret they wanted to know.

# DAY 311
## Colossians 2:1–3

———◦◦◦◦———

I want their hearts to be encouraged and joined together in love,
so that they may have all the riches of assured understanding,
and have the knowledge of God's mystery—Christ (v. 2).

———◦◦◦◦———

I want you to consider two words for "knowledge" in these verses from Paul's letter to the Colossians. They help us learn something very significant about Christ and about our relationship with Him. The word "knowledge" in verse 2 comes from a wonderful word in the Greek language, *epiginostos*. It means a recognition of who Christ is, with particular emphasis on how this relationship requires participation on the part of the learner. It defines somewhat the security that's found in relationship with Him. Paul is saying, "I want these people to be secure, to have full assurance in their knowledge of Christ."

Now let me point you to the *second* word for "knowledge," which appears in verse 3: "Christ, in whom are hidden all the treasures of wisdom and knowledge." *This* word for "knowledge" is a different word entirely. It is a word that means "present and fragmentary knowledge." Now hang with me a second, because I think this will thrill you. What Paul is saying is that God is the fullness of all security *and* mystery. He meets all our emotional needs as well as all our mental needs.

Something in each of us just loves a relationship that is both secure and mysterious all at the same time. Let me give you a very personal example:

My relationship with Keith is my most personal earthly relationship. I love knowing that I have security—full assurance—in my relationship with my husband. I believe I can tell you, after many, many years of marriage, that I know this man.

But I remember a time when a friend of mine saw my husband having lunch with another woman. She saw that Keith was fairly affectionate to her. He often touched her in a tender way. He even put his arm around her as they walked out of the restaurant.

Well, this sight troubled my friend. But when I found out from her that she had seen him with another woman, I said, "I want to tell you something. I don't know what the explanation is, but I can tell you right now, it isn't what you're thinking."

How fun it was for me when Keith came in later that day and said, "You know who I had lunch with today? Tina. We had the neatest time together."

(Tina, by the way, is my husband's little sister.)

Now I'm not telling you that something bad could never happen to my marriage. However, I have assurance in him and our relationship. For Keith to cheat on me would be so out of character for him, it would never enter my mind.

In fact, I don't know how in the world I could be this blessed, but I don't think I have lived a day of my married life that my husband hasn't told me at least once—maybe even two or three times—how much he loves me. He'll pick up the phone in the course of a very busy, very difficult day and say, "I love you," even if he only has fifteen seconds and then hangs up the phone without saying good-bye. I know at this point in my life that I have security in my relationship with my husband.

Yet not too long ago, I was sitting in the company of some of our friends, and my husband began telling them a story. I watched his almost childlike face. He was so animated! It was a story about a fish fry he had given for his fraternity in college. (We had gone to the same school together; that's where we met and fell in love.)

In recalling this event, Keith said, "I told them all that I was going to have a big fish fry and that we'd have all the fish we could eat." But he ran out of time before he could go out fishing. So he went to the federal game reserve on that campus—which was very well guarded—and did his fishing there.

Now I realize this was illegal, but it was twenty-two years ago and fortunately the statute of limitations has expired.

I want to tell you something, though. As I was watching Keith reminisce that story, I just fell in love with him all over again. When we got in the car to drive home, I laughed and said, "I've never heard that story before!" It was so cute hearing him tell it.

You know what thrills me? Even after all these years, I am still discovering things about my man. I have security in him—yes—but if I had security and no mystery, that wouldn't be any fun, would it? And if all I had was mystery, where would the security be? But in my husband, I have both security *and* mystery.

That's what the Word of God is telling us we all have in Christ.

Don't you just love how Jesus meets our emotional and mental needs? He said, "You have knowledge of Me with security, with full assurance, in relationship with who I am. But you also have constant mystery as I give You these little fragments of knowledge one at a time to open your eyes to My greatness."

Jesus has taught us so much about Himself. There is so much we can be absolutely sure of. But we will never learn it all while we're here. No matter how often we seek Him, we will always be stunned by His greatness.

# DAY 312
## Colossians 2:4-7

◇◇◇

I am saying this so that no one will deceive you with persuasive arguments.
For I may be absent in body, but I am with you in spirit (vv. 4–5).

◇◇◇

During Paul's first imprisonment in Rome, he was under what we would
call house arrest. Acts 28:30, remember, tells us that "he stayed two whole years
in his own rented house. And he welcomed all who visited him" (HCSB). The
openness of Paul's first imprisonment in Rome enabled him to receive ample
information about the churches. One of the letters he wrote during this two-year
period became the book of Colossians. Though as far as we know, Paul never visited the Asian city of Colosse, he obviously received word about the false teaching there and wrote his epistle as both a warning and an encouragement. You
would benefit most by reading all four chapters of Colossians. If you choose one
chapter, the primary purpose for Paul's epistle appears in Colossians 2.

Paul made one primary purpose for the letter clear in verse 4: "so that no
one will deceive you" (HCSB). Have you, or someone you know, ever been taken
captive through some deceptive philosophy? Our world is replete with those who
seek to control others through false and deceptive beliefs.

Try to capture Paul's frame of mind as he wrote the Christians in Colosse.
He described himself as being in a great "struggle" (v. 1). The Greek word is *agon*,
from which we derive the English word "agony." *Agon* means "strife, contention,
contest for victory or mastery such as was used in the Greek games of running,
boxing, wrestling, and so forth." By using the word *agon*, Paul implied that he
was figuratively boxing or wrestling with Satan for the minds and hearts of the
Colossians and Laodiceans. No sooner had the people of Colosse and Laodicea
received the Word of God than Satan began infiltrating them with deceptive
doctrines. Satan used at least four "isms." Let's briefly consider each one.

1. *Gnosticism.* The word *gnosis* means "knowledge." Followers of the gnostic
belief system believed that knowledge, rather than faith, led to salvation. We risk
something of the same problem if we focus on knowledge instead of Christ. We
need to study the Bible to know and glorify Jesus rather than to impress others
with our knowledge. I once heard a friend utter a prayer I have not forgotten. She
said, "Lord, we know You desire followers who have hearts like a cathedral rather
than minds like a concordance."

Since the gnostics prioritized intellect and reason, they tried to force God
into humanly understandable form. They could not accept both the deity and the
humanity of Christ, so they tried to reduce Him to the status of an angel. Paul
responded to gnosticism clearly in verse 9: "For in Him [in Christ] the entire
fullness of God's nature dwells bodily" (HCSB).

2. *Legalism.* Paul addressed the fruitlessness of keeping endless laws that condemn rather than liberate the believer to pursue godliness. We humans constantly attempt to replace a love relationship with legalistic requirements such as:

• seeking to be more spiritual than others by keeping man-made, extrabiblical rules

• believing that God requires harsh treatment of the body

• elevating one Christian above another

• refusing to accept those who have committed certain sins

• attempting to restrain sin by lists of dos and don'ts

No matter how ingeniously humans pursue legalism, it will never work. Only a love relationship with Christ can change the human heart and bring about genuine piety.

3. *Mysticism.* This is the belief that we can obtain direct knowledge of God from our internal thoughts, feelings, or experiences. It conflicts with biblical faith because Jesus Christ is the source of our knowledge about God. In verses 18 and 19, Paul addressed a mystical belief that has recently infiltrated our own society—the worship of angels. Angels certainly have important positions in God's creation, but Paul helps us find the balance. Angels were created to praise God and act as messengers and ministering servants. We worship angels when we disconnect them from their original purpose, focusing on them alone outside of their place in God's created order.

4. *Asceticism.* In verses 20 through 23, Paul addressed the practice of denying the body and treating it harshly in an attempt to achieve holiness. Followers of asceticism do not stop at the wise denial of dangerous, perverse, or unhealthy practices. Ascetics deny the body unnecessarily. In Paul's day, as in ours, some people branded, burned, starved, or cut themselves in an attempt to force the body into submission. Most of us have discovered that unnecessary denial arouses more desires.

We still battle many of the same destructive philosophies faced by the early believers. Though the list of "isms" may change, Satan is still up to the same old tricks. He seeks always to infiltrate the church with his false teaching.

# DAY 313
### Colossians 2:6–15

---

As you have received Christ Jesus the Lord, walk in Him, rooted and built up
in Him and established in the faith, just as you were taught (vv. 6–7).

---

Once we accept Christ as Savior, we become joint heirs with Christ (see
Rom. 8:17), and God becomes our Father (see John 20:17). Satan may try to
kidnap us by enticing us away from the truth, but no matter what he does, he
cannot make us his. Let's discover how to protect ourselves from being lured
away by "empty deceit" (Col. 2:8).

1. *Remember how you received Christ.* None of us entered God's family
through our own effort. We received Christ as a gift of grace. Now Paul tells us
that the way we got in is the way we go on. We must not believe any teaching or
philosophy that replaces God's grace with our performance.

2. *Continue to live in Christ.* The best way for a child of God to avoid being
kidnapped is to stay close to home. Children in natural families cannot live
their entire lives in their yards, but children in the spiritual family of God can!
Continuing to live in Christ means remaining close to Him and retaining a focus
on Him. Any other focus can lead to deceptive doctrine, even if the focus is a biblical concept. Remember, any doctrine that loses connection with the Head has
been twisted into deception. Many of us have probably let something temporarily
become a greater focus than Christ Himself. I've seen people make a specific
belief or detail of doctrine such a focus. We are less likely to be kidnapped when
we stay close to home by staying focused on the Head, Jesus Christ.

3. *Grow deep roots in Christ.* The more we feel like family, the less likely
we'll be enticed. An important part of feeling like family is knowing your family
history and the belief systems handed down through the generations. Spiritually,
we have difficulty growing up until we've grown down. We form deep roots by
knowing the basics of our faith. We can receive Christ and be enthusiastic and
still fall into confusion the first time someone confronts us with strange doctrine.
Our roots are our basics.

4. *Grow up in Christ.* In verse 7, the apostle exhorted believers to be "rooted
and built up in Him" (hcsb). After we've grown roots, we're ready to grow up.
Hebrews 6:1 strongly exhorts believers to a progression in Christ: "Therefore,
leaving the elementary message about the Messiah, let us go on to maturity"
(hcsb). All of these keep us from being easy targets.

# DAY 314
## 1 Timothy 1:12–17

∞

He considered me faithful, appointing me to the ministry—one who
was formerly a blasphemer, a persecutor, and an arrogant man (vv. 12–13).

∞

Paul and Timothy spent years together, yet oddly the apostle had hardly
greeted the young preacher in this first letter before he repeated his testimony.
Twenty-six years had passed since a blinding light had opened the eyes of a persecutor named Saul, but he was still repeating his testimony because he never
forgot. He remembered like it was yesterday.

I don't know how you feel about Paul or the journey we've shared, but I
know I want his unquenchable passion! Fortunately, it's contagious. We catch it
by imitating what he did to get it. I see at least six reasons in 1 Timothy 1:12–17.

1. *He never forgot the privilege of ministry* (v. 12). Unlike most of us, Paul's
conversion and subsequent ministry took him from a life of relative ease to almost
constant pressure and turmoil. He was beaten, stoned, whipped, jailed, and
starved in the course of his ministry; yet he considered his calling to serve God
to be the greatest privilege anyone could receive.

A host of reasons probably existed for Paul's continued gratitude. One possibility stands out most in my mind. His chief desire was "to know Christ" (Phil.
3:10). I believe the more he knew Christ, the more he saw His greatness. The
more Paul saw His greatness, the more amazed he was to have the privilege to
serve Him. We will also become more amazed over our privilege to serve as we
seek to know Christ better.

2. *He never forgot who he had been* (v. 13). God used Paul to perform more
wonders and birth more churches than any other human in the New Testament.
In a quarter of a century, Paul had plenty of time to forget who he had been,
taking pride in his powerful ministry. One reason God leaves our memories of
past repented sin intact is because a twinge of memory is indeed profitable to us.
Pride is the archenemy of ministry.

I think one reason Paul continued to remember who he had been was
because his love for Christ continued to grow. The more he loved Christ, the
more he wondered how he could have sinned against Him so horrendously in his
past. I've personally experienced this. Even though I know I am fully forgiven,
the deeper my love for Christ has grown, the more I regret past sins.

3. *He never forgot the abundance of God* (v. 14). Paul discovered God's intent
was not just for us to get by. He is not the God of barely enough. Paul encountered a God who supergave! Paul wrote, "The grace of our Lord overflowed, along
with the faith and love that are in Christ Jesus" (HCSB). Paul never forgot the
abundance of God. Greater still, God never forgets the abundance of our need.

Isaiah described God's devotion to His children: "Can a woman forget her nursing child, or lack compassion for the child of her womb? Even if these forget, yet I will not forget you" (Isa. 49:15 HCSB). He sees our needs like a mother sees her helpless infant's needs. Like a loving mother, He will never forget one of His children.

4. *He never forgot the basics* (v. 15). Can you imagine the wealth of knowledge Paul gained in his quest for God? Still he never lost sight of the most important truth he ever learned: "Christ Jesus came into the world to save sinners" (HCSB). May we also never forget! We don't have to lose touch with our most basic belief to press on to maturity.

How long has it been since tears stung your eyes when someone received Christ? Or how long has it been since you felt deep gratitude for the simplicity of your salvation? I beg you, never stop thanking Christ for coming into the world specifically to save you.

5. *He never forgot his primary role* (v. 16). According to the apostle, God saved "the worst" of sinners to "demonstrate the utmost patience as an example" (HCSB). The Greek word for "example" means "to draw a sketch or first draft as painters when they begin a picture." Paul saw himself drawn in that picture. You are painted in the portrait. I am painted in. The worst of sinners—the spiritually blind, lame, and lost—find unlimited patience in our God! If we look on the era of Paul's life and his contemporaries to be the last great movement of God, then we have tragically misunderstood. If our conclusion is "Wow! Those were the days," we've missed the point. God is still painting the portrait of His church. Paul was only an example of what God can do with one repentant life. God hasn't finished the picture—but one day He will.

6. *He never forgot the wonder of God* (v. 17). Twenty-six years after he fell to his knees, Paul still felt so overwhelmed by the awesome work of God that he exclaimed, "Now to the King eternal, immortal, invisible, the only God, be honor and glory forever and ever" (HCSB). I wish I could have seen Timothy's face while reading Paul's words. Perhaps he thought, *How has he kept his wonder?* The answer? He never forgot who he had been. He relished the abundance of God. He never lost sight of the basics.

When my oldest daughter was little and I offered her a treat that had lost its luster to her, she responded politely, "No, thank you, Mommy. I'm used to that." The apostle Paul had known Christ for twenty-six years. Still he looked back on his salvation and the privilege to serve and never got "used to that." May God grant us a memory like Paul's.

# DAY 315
## 1 Timothy 2:8–15

———— ∽∾∽ ————

A woman should learn in silence with full submission. I do not allow a woman
to teach or to have authority over a man; instead, she is to be silent (vv. 11–12).

———— ∽∾∽ ————

Glancing through the book of 1 Timothy, you'll notice a continuing exhortation for order in the churches. In stressing this, Paul made some statements about women that raise controversy. Although he used far more ink to address deacons and overseers, I don't want to be charged with cowardice by omitting any mention of his instructions to women.

When he said, "A woman should learn in silence," (HCSB) he did not use a Greek word that meant "complete silence or no talking. [He used a word] used elsewhere to mean settled down, undisturbed, not unruly."[63] Paul's primary ministry was geared toward Gentiles who had never been trained to have respect and reverence in worship. Paul encouraged women to observe traditional customs lest the young churches suffer a bad reputation.

The Christian movement was new and fragile. Any taint of adverse publicity could greatly hinder the mission of the church and mean persecution for believers. Women had to restrain their new freedom in Christ (Gal. 3:28) so as not to impede the progress of the gospel. Paul's "weaker brother" principle (1 Cor. 8:9) applies, where he said, "Be careful that this right of yours in no way becomes a stumbling block to the weak" (HCSB). Thus, women were to learn quietly, without calling attention to themselves.

In regard to instructing women not to teach men, you must understand that most women in Paul's day were illiterate. They were not taught in synagogue schools or trained by a rabbi. Paul goes on to say in verse 12 that women should not usurp authority over men. The Greek word *authenteo*, "one who claims authority," is used only this one time in the Greek translation of the Bible. This word refers to an autocrat or dictator. Paul says women were not to come in and take over!

We cannot regard verses 11 and 12 as a prohibition against women opening their mouths in church or men learning anything biblical from women. For instance, Paul gave instructions for how women are to pray and prophesy (1 Cor. 11:5). He was fully aware of Priscilla's role in teaching Apollos in Ephesus (Acts 18:26). Paul issued differing instructions for churches based on their cultural settings and his desire for order in the church.

# DAY 316
### 1 Timothy 4:6–16

———

Practice these things; be committed to them, so that
your progress may be evident to all (v. 15).

———

Midway through my preparation for writing this book, I began to realize
that one of God's priority goals is to raise up and encourage passionate, perse-
vering servants who are completely abandoned to His will. Paul's exhortations
to Timothy stand as timeless words of advice to every servant of the living God,
regardless of generation or gender. I'd like to look at a few of these today, a few
more tomorrow.

*"Train yourself in godliness"* (v. 7 HCSB). Godliness does not instantly accompany salvation. Remember, salvation is a gift. Godliness is a pursuit. The word
meaning "to train" is *gumnazo*, from which we derive the word "gymnasium." The
apostle drew a parallel between an athlete preparing for the Greek games and a
believer pursuing godliness. An athlete who is preparing for intense competition
makes frequent visits to the gym.

*"Be an example"* (v. 12 HCSB). Although Timothy was young, Paul exhorted
him not to let others who were older intimidate him. Rather, he should set an
example "in conduct, in love, in faith, in purity" (HCSB). God is practical. His
Word works. He wants us to be living proof by our example. If we're leading but
we're not closely following Christ, we are misleading.

*"Do not neglect the gift that is in you"* (v. 14 HCSB). When we receive Christ,
God gives us spiritual gifts, but they must then be developed, cared for, and
cultivated. For example, I received Christ as a young child, but I did not use the
gift of teaching until I became an adult. Then God opened a door for me to teach
Sunday school. Although He gave me the spiritual gift and opened the door for
me to use it, God expected me to accept the opportunity and fan the gift into a
flame. Every week I had to study. I also spent numerous hours listening to other
teachers. I asked one to disciple me personally. I had to develop a consistent
prayer life. I also had to learn from my blunders and lessons that flopped! Still
I kept asking God to teach me His Word so I could be obedient. These are a
few ways God directed me to fan into flame one gift He gave me. God honors a
beautiful blend of gift and grit! He gives the gift, and He expects us to have the
grit to practice and learn how to use it effectively.

# DAY 317
## 1 Timothy 5:19–25

——∞∞∞——

Some people's sins are evident, going before them to judgment. . . . Likewise, good works are obvious, and those that are not obvious cannot remain hidden (vv. 24–25).

——∞∞∞——

We spent some time yesterday looking at several imperatives for strong ministry that Paul identified for Timothy. Today we consider two others that were part of his instruction to his son in the faith.

*"Keep yourself pure"* (5:22 HCSB). Nothing marks the erosion of character or has the potential to destroy ministries and testimonies like impurity. Paul told Timothy to "keep" himself pure. The original word for "keep" comes from the word *teros*, meaning "a warden or guard." Paul told Timothy to stand as a guard over purity in his own life. I must take responsibility for purity in my life. You must take responsibility for purity in your life. If you are trying to keep yourself pure but you continue to fall, I encourage you to seek godly counsel. A mature and discerning believer can help you identify reasons why you continue to be drawn to impurity. It is not too late to consecrate your life to God and find victory.

*"Turn away from godless chatter"* (6:20). The word for "godless" is *bebelos*, which speaks of "a threshold, particularly of a temple." This "threshold" separates the profane from the holy. If we are believers in Christ, we are sacred temples of His Holy Spirit. We have a choice as to what crosses the threshold and finds a place in our temples. Paul exhorts believers to discern a line in conversation that should not be crossed.

Sometimes we have to think of ways to turn away from godless chatter without deeply offending another person or disrespecting someone in authority. Pursuing godliness isn't always pleasant. Sometimes we are forced to make difficult decisions. He will direct us how to turn away appropriately. If we turn away proudly and self-righteously, we ourselves have crossed an important threshold. Humility is the earmark of God's genuine servant. Even when we turn away, we should be humble.

I pray that Paul's life has compelled you to be an active part of God's agenda. I hope you will never again be satisfied to sit on the sidelines. I pray that you desire for your life to leave footprints someone else could follow straight to Christ. None of these things will happen accidentally or coincidentally. Godliness and effective ministry take attention, but nothing you could pour your energies into will ever have a greater payoff.

# DAY 318
## 2 Timothy 2:1–13

———∞∞∞———

Keep in mind Jesus Christ, risen from the dead. . . . For this I suffer, to the point of being bound like a criminal; but God's message is not bound (vv. 8–9).

———∞∞∞———

We now approach the final letter from the pen of the apostle Paul. He wrote his second letter to Timothy during his last imprisonment in Rome, shortly before his death. Our goal is to capture the state of mind and physical conditions of the great apostle in the final season of his life. The letter reveals several descriptions of Paul's condition and state of mind during his final imprisonment.

1. *He was in physical discomfort.* Some criminals were simply incarcerated behind locked doors with no chains. Paul was held under conditions like those of a convicted killer, bound by heavy chains—the type that bruise and lacerate the skin. He was almost sixty years old and had taken enough beatings to make him quite arthritic. The lack of mobility greatly intensified any ailments or illnesses. He most likely was reduced to skin and bones. The cells where the worst prisoners were chained were usually filthy, wet, and rodent-infested dungeons. The beauty and articulation of Paul's final letter cannot be fully appreciated without realizing how physically uncomfortable he must have been when he wrote it.

2. *He was probably humiliated.* Captors in ancient prisons often thought of ways to shame their captives. Perhaps the least of their inhumanities was not allowing prisoners to wash and dress themselves adequately. Their confines doubled as bedroom and bathroom. In 2 Timothy 1:12, Paul said, "That is why I suffer these things. But I am not ashamed" (HCSB). Paul's words may hint at the attempts of his captors to shame him. He told Timothy several times not to be ashamed of him. As much as Paul had suffered, he was unaccustomed to the treatment he received in the final season of his life.

3. *He felt deserted and lonely.* No one came forward at Paul's first hearing. Can you imagine the loneliness he must have experienced as the bailiff called for defense witnesses, and silence fell over the courtroom? I don't think they deserted him because they didn't love him. Many grieved because they did not come to his defense, but they were frightened for their lives. As far as most of them were concerned, Paul was on death row anyway. They couldn't save him. After all, he was certainly guilty of denying the deity of Nero. Even in these extreme straits Paul still said, "May it not be counted against them" (4:16 HCSB).

4. *He longed for normalcy.* Although Paul's life was seldom normal in our terms, I believe he longed in his last season for things that were normal to him. He wanted his oldest friends. He asked for Mark. He spoke of Luke at his side. He sent greetings to Priscilla and Aquila. He begged Timothy to come quickly. His request for his scrolls, especially the parchments, also tenders my heart. His

scrolls were probably copies of Old Testament Scriptures. Very likely he had also recorded on parchments facts about the earthly life of Christ, based on the stories of Peter and Luke.

I can't begin to put myself in Paul's position, but if I were away from loved ones and facing certain death, I would want several things. I have stacks of journals where I've recorded prayers too private to allow anyone to read, yet I cannot bring myself to throw them away. During uncertain times when I'm called to walk by faith, I can turn back to my personal records of God's faithfulness and find strength again. My Bible and my journals are my most treasured tangible belongings. During difficult days, even holding my Bible close to my chest brings me comfort. No doubt Paul longed for these things.

A person confined and facing death inevitably turns the mental pages of the past. Surely Paul was no different. He must have thought about Tarsus. His mother's face. His father's voice. His childhood in a Jewish community. His first impressions of Jerusalem. The classroom debates he enjoyed. The way people whispered about his genius behind his back. His bright future. His return to Tarsus and the respect he commanded. His drive to persecute the people of the Way. The blinding light that sent him to his knees. He traded a life of respect and honor for one of rejection and tribulation. If his childhood friends could have seen him in that horrendous dungeon, they might have surmised that he had traded everything for nothing.

So, what do you have when you have nothing left? You have what you know. Faced with humiliation, Paul proclaimed, "But I am not ashamed, because I know whom I have believed and am persuaded that He is able to guard what has been entrusted to me until that day" (1:12 HCSB). Paul's sanity was protected by his certainty. He knew the One in whom he had believed.

Paul had entrusted everything to Christ. No matter how difficult circumstances grew, he never tried to take it back. As the chains gripped his hands and feet and the stench of death assailed him, he recalled everything he had entrusted to his Savior. With chained hands, Paul could still touch the face of God.

# DAY 319
## 2 Timothy 4:1–8

—∞∞—

I am already being poured out as a drink offering, and the time
for my departure is close. I have fought the good fight,
I have finished the race, I have kept the faith (vv. 6–7).

—∞∞—

Paul wasn't just pulling a word picture out of a hat when he uttered the statement, "I have fought the good fight, I have finished the race, I have kept the faith" (2 Tim. 4:7 HCSB). Anyone in the Roman Empire would know exactly what he was talking about. I wouldn't be the least bit surprised, in fact, if these words spread and ultimately hastened his death.

In AD 67, the year of Paul's death, Nero had the audacity to enter himself in the Olympic games. Mind you, Olympic athletes trained all their lives for the games. The thirty-year-old, soft-bellied emperor used medications to induce vomiting rather than exercise to control his weight.[64] He was in pitiful shape and ill prepared, but who would dare tell him he could not compete? He cast himself on a chariot at Olympia and drove a ten-horse team. "He fell from the chariot and had to be helped in again; but, though he failed to stay the course and retired before the finish, the judges nevertheless awarded him the prize."[65]

Nero did not finish the race. Nevertheless, a wreath was placed on his head, and he was hailed the victor. He showed his gratitude for their cooperation in the ridiculous scam by exempting Greece from taxation. For his processional entry into Rome he chose the chariot Augustus had used in his triumph in a former age, and he wore a Greek mantle spangled with gold stars over a purple robe. The Olympic wreath was on his head. "Victims were sacrificed in his honour all along the route."[66] You can be fairly certain they were from a despised group of people commonly called *Chrestiani*, or Christians.

Needless to say, word of the humiliating victory spread faster than the fire of AD 64. Soon after Nero returned to Rome, the apostle wrote his stirring final testimony. The edict was signed for his execution.

Yet God did not allow the deaths of His beloved apostles to overshadow their lives. Their departures were intimate encounters between themselves and the One for whom they laid down their lives. Teaching handed down through the ages tells us two soldiers by the name of Ferega and Parthemius brought Paul word of his death. They approached him and asked for his prayers that they might also believe in his Christ. Having received life from his instruction, they then led Paul out of the city to his death.[67] Traditional teaching claims he prayed just before his execution. At this point I would have trouble believing anything different. Wouldn't you?

After praying, the apostle Paul gave his neck to the sword. But before his earthly tent had time to collapse to the ground, his feet stood on holy ground. His eyes, possibly scarred and blurred from a glorious light on a Damascus road, saw their first crystal-clear vision in thirty years. Paul himself had written, "For now we see indistinctly, as in a mirror, but then face to face" (1 Cor. 13:12 HCSB). Faith became sight, and the raptured saint saw Christ's face. He beheld the ultimate surpassing glory.

No thought of beatings. No questions of timing. No pleas for vengeance. No list of requests. Just the sight of unabashed, unhindered, unveiled glory. And he had not yet looked past His face—"God's glory in the face of Jesus Christ" (2 Cor. 4:6 HCSB). He was seeing the face he had waited thirty years to see. The Righteous Judge raised a wreath of righteousness and placed it on the head of His faithful servant. He had finished the race. And more impressively, he had kept the faith. Never doubt the difference.

Paul once wrote, "Now I know in part, but then I will know fully, as I am fully known" (1 Cor. 13:12 HCSB). The partial knowledge of Christ that Paul had acquired in his lifetime was the same knowledge he claimed to be worth every loss (see Phil. 3:8–10). Oh, my friend, if partial knowledge of the Lord Jesus is worth every loss, what then will full knowledge be like? I cry out with our brother Paul, "Oh, the depth of the riches both of the wisdom and the knowledge of God!" (Rom. 11:33 HCSB). One day the prayer of the apostle will be answered for all of us. We will indeed "grasp how wide and long and high and deep is the love of Christ . . . and know this love that surpasses knowledge" (Eph. 3:18–19).

Until then, may God find us faithful, unstoppable servants of the One who saved us, waiting to hang our hats on heaven's door. "For I am persuaded that neither death nor life, nor angels nor rulers, nor things present, nor things to come, nor powers, nor height, nor depth, nor any other created thing will have the power to separate us from the love of God that is in Christ Jesus our Lord!" (Rom. 8:38–39 HCSB).

> *Most Worthy Lord,*
> *make me a drink offering*
> *and take me not home*
> *until the cup is overturned*
> *the glass broken*
> *and every drop loosed*
> *for Your glory.*

# DAY 320
## 2 Timothy 4:9–18

⸺∞⸺

The Lord will rescue me from every evil work and will bring me safely into
His heavenly kingdom. To Him be the glory forever and ever! (v. 18).

⸺∞⸺

Paul knew without a doubt he was soon to die. Yet he was no masochist. He
wasn't begging for the guillotine. He simply looked at life through the window
of these words: "For to me, to live is Christ and to die is gain" (Phil. 1:21). Our
journey together has been an effort to study the heart of a man who could sincerely make such a statement. Christ had profoundly transformed Paul's attitude
toward life and death.

1. *Paul saw death as a departure.* He did not say, "The time for my death is
close." He said, "The time for my departure is close" (2 Tim. 4:6 HCSB). His entire
life was a series of departures. He followed the leading of the Spirit through
Judea, Syria, Cilicia, Galatia, Pamphylia, Asia, Macedonia, Achaia, and Italy.
He never knew what awaited him as he entered a city, but one result was inevitable—as surely as he arrived, he would depart. God never let him hang his hat for
long. "Our citizenship is in heaven," he had said (Phil. 3:20 HCSB). To him, settling in would be pointless until then. Paul had faithfully done his time in Rome
and, predictably, another departure awaited him. This time, he was going home.

2. *Paul saw death as a rescue.* Paul didn't see death as a defeat. He did not
believe the enemy finally had his way. He saw death as a rescue! We tend to define
the word "rescue" an entirely different way. God certainly rescued Paul many
times on this earth, just as He has rescued us, yet Paul knew the greatest rescue
of all awaited him. Death was not God's refusal to act; death was God's ultimate
rescue. Oh, if we could only understand this difficult truth, how different our
perspectives would be. Paul not only saw death as the ultimate rescue from evil;
he saw death as a rescue from frail, limited bodies.

3. *Paul saw death as a safe passage.* Remember the words of 2 Timothy 4:18.
God will not only rescue us, but He will bring us safely to His heavenly kingdom.
Earlier we learned the original Greek meaning for the word "rescue." *Rhuomai*
means "to draw or snatch from danger, rescue, deliver. This is more with the
meaning of drawing to oneself than merely rescuing for someone or something."
God is not simply trying to snatch us from danger. He desires to draw us to
Himself spiritually, then one day physically. When our ultimate rescue comes,
God's purpose is to deliver us to Himself—safely.

# DAY 321
## Titus 2:1–3

---

*Older women are to be reverent in behavior, not slanderers,
not addicted to much wine. They are to teach what is good (v. 3).*

---

I wish I had the space to share about the older women who have mentored me as a Christian woman, wife, mother, and servant of God. If you are fortunate to have benefited from some godly mentors, you know that none of them were in your life accidentally. God brought you into their sphere of influence to fulfill His purposes. Paul, in his charge to older women, points out certain qualifications for a mentor to younger women.

1. *Reverent in the way she lives.* Her actions are to be those of a woman who respects God. Each of the women who have mentored me were quite different in personality, but they all shared one common denominator: their lives were replete with a reverence for God. Those I respect most are those who respect God.

2. *Not slanderous.* I believe older women may have more opportunities to remain active today than in Paul's day. One of my eighty-three-year-old friends told me one day that she was too busy to die! Still, for some who have grown idle, slanderous talk can become a means to keep life interesting. Younger women struggle with temptation to slander too. Slanderous people thrive on conflict and division. The godly mentor sets an example by edifying others through her speech—rejoicing over their victories and hurting with them in defeat.

3. *Not addicted to much wine.* The original word for "addicted" is *douloo*, meaning "to enslave." In Paul's generation, wine was the primary substance to which a woman might become addicted. Today we could fill a grocery aisle with potentially enslaving substances. I have two very dear friends whose mothers were alcoholics. They still struggle with the painful results. So many people in our society are enslaved to different substances. Alcohol, prescription and non-prescription drugs, diet pills, sleeping pills, and illegal drugs are readily available to anyone the least bit desperate or vulnerable.

The general purpose for older women mentoring younger women is stated at the end of Titus 2:3: "to teach what is good" (HCSB). The original Greek word for "good" is *kalos*, which "expresses beauty as a harmonious completeness, balance, proportion." Older women are to teach younger women about genuine beauty: God's idea of a beautiful woman.

# DAY 322
## Titus 2:4–5

Encourage the young women to love their husbands and children, to be sensible,
pure, good homemakers, and submissive to their husbands (vv. 4–5).

In his letter to Titus, Paul mentions three distinct ways in which older
women are to help younger women. Let's see what we can learn from these.

1. *Love your husband.* Interestingly, the original word used for "love" is not
*agape* this time. It's *philandros*, which speaks of "loving [someone] as a friend."
Romantic love is so important in a marriage, but we also need to learn to be a
friend to our mates. Women often have several good friends, but men tend to
have fewer close friendships. A man often needs his wife to be a friend as well as
a lover. *Phileo* love, which is central to *philandros*, grows from common interests.
By our feminine natures, women don't often share the same interests as men. But
we can learn to share their interests! I want to be a better friend to my husband.
If you're married, let's make this commitment together. We can be a friend to our
spouses. Let's start working on it right away.

2. *Love your children.* You may be thinking, *Who needs to be taught how to love
her children?* Lots of wounded people, that's who. I would make four suggestions
to those who have difficulty loving their children: 1) Seek a mentor who can help
train you to be a loving parent. 2) Seek sound, godly counsel to discover why your
heart is hindered and how you can find freedom in Christ. 3) *Do* the right things
until you *feel* the right things. In other words, hug your children and tell them
you love them whether or not these actions come easily for you. 4) Take up your
children's interests. Attend their school functions, go to their games, have their
friends over for pizza! Hang in there and seek some good support!

3. *Be busy at home.* The original word for "busy" means "one who looks after
domestic affairs with prudence and care." I believe Paul wanted older women to
teach younger women that homes and families do not take care of themselves.
Someone has to watch over the priorities. Children don't raise themselves.
Someone has to watch over them and be involved. A marriage doesn't improve
itself. Someone has to watch over it and encourage growth and intimacy. Even if
we work, wise women still remain very involved in their homes and families. The
wife and mother has something to give her home and family that no one else can
supply as effectively: tenderness, nurturing, a personal touch.

# DAY 323
## Philemon 1–10

---

I, Paul, as an elderly man and now also as a prisoner of Christ Jesus, appeal to you for my child, whom I fathered while in chains—Onesimus (vv. 9–10).

---

In the last years of the apostle's life, four out of five of his letters were written to individuals rather than to bodies of believers. One of these was addressed to Philemon, a believer from Colosse whom Paul probably met while ministering in a nearby city. Quite possibly Paul had been the one who had personally introduced Philemon to the Savior. They developed a friendship, and Paul saw Philemon become an active worker for the gospel. Philemon must have been a wealthy man to own a home large enough to serve as a meeting place for the church (see v. 2) as well as being a slave owner.

At some time in the intervening years, one of these slaves—Onesimus—had run away, apparently stealing from Philemon in the process. And by the providence of God, he had found himself in Rome, where he met Paul. We have no way of knowing for certain, but perhaps while he was on the run, Onesimus may have stolen again and been incarcerated with Paul. Either way, imagine how strange their meeting must have been once they realized they both knew Philemon. You can be sure their meeting wasn't a coincidence. God had ordained the fugitive slave to have a heart-to-heart collision with the most well-known slave of grace in all Christendom. Paul told him about Christ, and the runaway slave became a brother. Then Paul sent Onesimus back to Philemon with the letter that bears his name.

I am a hopeless romantic. I hate conflict, and I love happy endings. Of all the encounters we've studied, the conflict between Paul and Barnabas was one of the most difficult. I had grown to love the partnership between them so much. My heart ached over their disagreement about John Mark. Twelve years after that event, Paul was placed under house arrest in Rome. Now we see Mark with him once again (see v. 24).

You may be wondering why I am focusing on Paul and Mark when this letter is so obviously about Paul and Onesimus. I think Mark may have been Paul's inspiration for seeking restoration between Philemon and Onesimus. A dozen years earlier Paul had been hard and unyielding. But time heals and, if we're the least bit cooperative, it matures us. Sometimes we live and learn. Perhaps he had since learned a more excellent way.

# DAY 324
## Philemon 11–22

—∞∞—

Perhaps this is why he was separated from you ... so that you might
get him back permanently, no longer as a slave, but more than a slave—
as a dearly loved brother (vv. 15–16).

—∞∞—

Paul could have dealt with this situation between Philemon and Onesimus
in one of several different ways, but the wise apostle chose the most excellent way,
portraying a beautiful example of Micah 6:8: "He has showed you, O man, what
is good. And what does the Lord require of you? To act justly and to love mercy
and to walk humbly with your God."

More than sacrifices or offerings, God desires these three things from us: to
act justly, to love mercy, and to walk humbly with Him. The solution Paul sought
in the conflict between Philemon and his fugitive slave, Onesimus, met all three
requirements.

1. *Paul acted justly.* One way Paul might have handled this was to consider
Onesimus absolved from all responsibility after he repented and accepted Christ.
But Onesimus had wronged Philemon in several ways. He had run away from
his legal owner and possibly had stolen from him. In Paul's estimation the restoration of two Christian men was priority. The issue could not be resolved fully
unless Onesimus returned to Philemon and unless Philemon was repaid for all
Onesimus owed.

For justice to prevail, someone had to take responsibility for Onesimus's
actions, and someone had to pay his debt. Paul insisted that Onesimus take
responsibility for wrong-doing, yet Paul took on the debt (see v. 18). Likewise
we must take responsibility for our sins, but thankfully Christ has paid the debt!

2. *Paul loved mercy.* Paul did more than preach to people. He lived the concepts he taught. When he met Onesimus, he saw a man in need of a Savior.
Paul didn't just preach to him about the mercy of God, he showed it to him.
He took Onesimus's debt not only out of justice but also out of mercy, because a
sinner needed grace. Paul wanted Philemon to show mercy as well. According to
the original language, Onesimus was a slave bound into permanent servitude to
Philemon. His return to Philemon would mean the return to slavery.

Critics of God's Word often protest that the Bible seems to support evils
like slavery, but in fact the opposite is true. Jesus and Paul could have come
preaching against the specific evils of their day, such as slavery. If they had done
so, the message of heart transformation through forgiveness of sin would have
been lost. Instead both Christ and Paul concentrated on getting people into a
right relationship with God. They knew that evil social institutions would fall
before the force of people with the heart of the Father beating in their chests.

Although Paul had to deal with slavery realistically as a part of his society, he believed in absolute equality. He believed that slaves must be obedient to their masters just like citizens must obey the law, but he was definitely not an advocate of slavery. He told Philemon he was returning Onesimus to him "no longer as a slave, but more than a slave—as a dear loved brother" (v. 16 HCSB).

God has strong feelings about mercy. In the Old Testament God demanded mercy on slaves. God required His people to remember they also had been slaves and to have mercy on others. As Christ's ambassador, Paul did not violate the Old Testament principle. He had the full cooperation of Onesimus, who was willing to return so restoration would ensue. Paul also asked Philemon to be an ambassador of Christ by abolishing Onesimus's slavery and receiving him as a brother. Paul's proposal was to let mercy reign.

3. *Paul walked humbly with God.* The closer we draw near to God and the more we behold His majesty, the more we relate to the psalmist who said, "What is man that you are mindful of him?" (Ps. 8:4). Like the psalmist, Paul recognized the pit from which God had pulled him. Both enjoyed an intimate relationship with God, yet neither of them viewed Him as a chum or a running buddy. They each knew grace had bridged the wide gulf fixed between them. To walk with God is to walk humbly. We cannot help but confront His holiness. Paul's proposal for restoration between Philemon and Onesimus required both men to walk humbly with God.

Paul had to humble himself as well by resisting the temptation to be bold and order Philemon to do what he ought to do (vv. 8–9). Instead, he appealed to him on another basis, which brings us to our final point. When God sent His Son to be an atoning sacrifice for our sins, He fulfilled the law with love (see Rom. 5:8). Paul could have demanded certain actions from Philemon, but he appealed to him on the basis of love.

The hollowness of works without love becomes evident to all who seek to serve God. We cannot serve God wholeheartedly without the whole heart. Even though many years earlier Paul and Barnabas had probably made the right decision to divide and multiply, I'm not sure Paul responded to the conflict with John Mark in love. I think a hollowness accompanied Paul everywhere he went until the gulf was bridged with grace. He showed it by personal example to others like Philemon and us.

# DAY 325
## Hebrews 10:32–39

---

We are not those who draw back and are destroyed,
but those who have faith and obtain life" (v. 39).

---

I don't remember a whole lot about my life before salvation, because I was very young. But I can tell you that Christ's authority over my life has dramatically changed both my demeanor and life practices. I was once overly sensitive and very fearful. I would ten times rather have watched television than studied His Word. My character showed it too. Oh, I have a long way to go; but change is not only possible, it's also gloriously inevitable, "being confident of this, that he who began a good work in you [and in me] will carry it on to completion until the day of Christ Jesus" (Phil. 1:6).

I have waited until now to ask you to reflect on some words of Jesus from a previous story we read of the rich young man, so that we can compare this guy with Zacchaeus. Please observe Luke 18:24–25: "How hard it is for the rich to enter the kingdom of God! Indeed, it is easier for a camel to go through the eye of a needle than for a rich man to enter the kingdom of God."

A rich young ruler. A chief publican. Both wealthy men. One walked away lost, while salvation lodged at the other's home. Salvation was not impossible for either one of these rich men. Both had the Son of God standing right there in front of them . . . willing and able to deliver. The difference was that one saw how much he had to lose. The other saw how much he had to gain.

Notice, Christ did not ask Zacchaeus to sell everything he had and give to the poor, as He did to the younger man. Maybe because once Zacchaeus regarded Christ as life's true treasure, his wealth didn't mean nearly as much to him—which I believe is probably God's primary point to the rich.

A cynic might say, "Why did he only give away half to the poor?" Maybe because it took every other shekel to pay back all the folks he had cheated! Anyway, God isn't looking to take away our possessions. He is looking to make His Son our greatest possession.

"My righteous one will live by faith. And if he shrinks back, I will not be pleased with him" (Heb. 10:38). If you're facing a choice right now between pressing forward and drawing back, look at these two men. Which one do you want to be more like?

# DAY 326
## 1 John 1:1–4

⬦

*What we have seen and heard we also declare to you, so that you may have fellowship along with us . . . with the Father and with His Son Jesus Christ (v. 3).*

⬦

Years passed. John's beard grayed. The skin once leathered by the sun's reflection off the Sea of Galilee bore the deeper creases of age. His voice rasped the telltale signs of a fiery evangelist. The calluses on his feet became thick with age and country miles. The wrinkles around his eyes folded and unfolded like an accordion as he laughed and mused. While some scholars believe that John's Gospel and his letters were written within just years of one another, few argue that the epistles slipped from the pen of anything other than an aging man. Most believe 1 John was written around AD 85–90.[68]

John had celebrated many Passover meals since the time he leaned his head against the Savior's strong shoulder. So much had happened since that night. He'd never get the picture of Christ's torn frame out of his mind, but neither would he forget his double take of the resurrected Lord. The last time John saw those feet, they were dangling in midair off the tip of the Mount of Olives. Just as quickly, clouds covered them like a cotton blanket. The fire of the Holy Spirit fell . . . then the blaze of persecution seared. One by one the other apostles met their martyrdom. Just as Christ had prophesied, Herod's Temple, one of the wonders of the ancient world, was destroyed in AD 70.

Along the way, the winds of the Spirit had whisked John from all that was familiar—to the city of Ephesus. Decades separated him from those early days of water turned to wine and fishes turned to feasts. For most of us, age means sketchy memories and vague details. Not John. He recorded his clear memories with indelible words. He didn't climb gradually to a pinnacle in writing these epistles. He started at one. His letters seem to open with the mouth of a crescendo as if he had waited until he was about to explode to write it all down. I'm not sure the Holy Spirit as much *fell* on John as *leaped*.

Yes, you would think John's certainty might have waned or weakened with time and distance, but perhaps the most distinguishing mark of a true partaker of the riches of God and Christ is that the partners cannot hoard the treasures. They want everyone else to enjoy them too. Authentic partners and partakers of "fellowship"—*koinonia* in the Greek—simply cannot be selfish. Their joy is only complete as others share in it.

# DAY 327
## 1 John 1:5–10

—∞∞∞—

*If we confess our sins, He is faithful and righteous to forgive us our sins
and to cleanse us from all unrighteousness (v. 9).*

—∞∞∞—

First John 1:9 tells us the secrets to sharing a life of fellowshipping with Christ and walking in the light. "If we confess our sins . . ." The basic Greek word for "confession" is *homologeo*, which is derived from two other words. *Homou* means "at the same place or time, together."[69] *Lego* means "to say."[70]

In essence, confession is agreeing with God about our sins. But the portion of the definition that holds the primary key to remaining in *koinonia*—in "fellowship"—is the expediency of "the same place or time." I have confessed and turned from some sins in my life that profoundly interrupted *koinonia*. Why? Because I waited too long to agree with God about them and turn. I still found forgiveness, but *koinonia* was broken through the delay. As God began to teach me to walk more victoriously, I learned to often respond to the conviction of the Holy Spirit at the "same place or time," thereby never leaving the circle of fellowship or the path of "light."

You see, some of us think fellowship with God can only be retained during our "perfect" moments. I want you to see how 1 John 1:8 refutes that philosophy. "If we say, 'We have no sin,' we are deceiving ourselves, and the truth is not in us" (HCSB).

You might ask, "How can a person sin grievously and still remain in fellowship?" Please understand, all sin is equal in its demand for grace, but not all sin is equal in its ramifications (see Ps. 19:13). A person who commits robbery, adultery, or vicious slander departed *koinonia* when he or she refused to agree with God over the sin involved in the thought processes leading up to the physical follow-through. Think of *koinonia* like a circle representing the place of fellowship. We don't just walk in and out of that circle every time a flash of critical thinking bolts through our minds. I don't even think we leave that circle if a sudden greedy, proud, or lustful thought goes through our minds.

If we're in *koinonia* with God, the conviction of the Holy Spirit will come at that "place and time" and tell us those thoughts or initial reactions aren't suitable for the saints of God. Confession without delay not only helps *keep* us in *koinonia*; it is *part of* our *koinonia*!

# DAY 328
## 1 John 2:15–17

—∞∞∞—

Do not love the world or the things that belong to the world.
If anyone loves the world, love for the Father is not in him (v. 15).

—∞∞∞—

I stumbled upon a quote that I can't shake out of my head. "Saints . . . die to the world only to rise to a more intense life."[71] I've turned the quote over in my mind a hundred times, and I'm convinced it's true. John may be the perfect example. I believe God had something so divinely unique to entrust to this chosen apostle that He had to slay the call of the world in him. Mind you, not the call *to* the world but the call *of* the world.

I don't think John was so unlike Abraham or Moses. God chose these men but refined them for their tasks through the crucible of time and challenged trust. The obvious difference is that God used John mightily soon after his calling, but I'd like to suggest that his latter works fall into the category we'll call "greater works than these." As God sought to kill the world in His chosen vessels and crucify them to their own plans and agendas, their terms in waiting were not emptied and lifeless. Rather, their lives greatly intensified.

Our callings are not so different. We will never be of great use to God if we do not allow Him to crucify us to ourselves and the call of the world.

Our consolations, however, are exceedingly great! We trade the pitifully small and potentially disastrous for the wildest ride mortal creatures could ever know. We don't just die to self to accept nothingness. We lay down our lives and the call of the world to receive something far more intense. The call of God! The time spent awaiting further enlightenment and fuller harvest are meant to bulge with relationship.

Months then years then even decades may have blown off the calendar of John's life in biblical obscurity, but don't consider for an instant that they were spent in inactivity or emptiness. No possible way! Please do not miss the following point: During the interim years of biblical obscurity in John's life, one of the most intense relationships in the entire Word of God developed. Yes, Christ used John to cast out demons, heal the sick, and spread the good news through word of mouth. But somewhere along the way God built a man to whom He could entrust some of the most profound words ever recorded on parchment—all by a man once simply known as the "brother of James."

# DAY 329
## 1 John 2:24–27

——◦◦◦——

If what you have heard from the beginning remains in you,
then you will remain in the Son and in the Father (v. 24).

——◦◦◦——

Acts 12:2 is the last mention Luke makes of John as he refers to his brother's death. I am very intrigued by the fact that Luke mentions John only a handful of times in the annals of the early church—and never quoted him. Our dear John appears only as an aside to Peter. While the book of Acts traces almost every move of a converted persecutor named Saul, John's ministry continues with very little notice after James's death.

I wonder what the apostles thought about Paul gaining so much of the spotlight. I think we'd be pretty naïve to think they didn't notice. John may also have felt that Peter at least had an important future, even if it ultimately required his life. John, on the other hand, knew nothing about his own. All he may have known was that Peter's ministry was skyrocketing, and no one would argue that Paul was a household name.

John? Christ simply asked him to take care of his mother. Goodness knows he loved her. He took her into his home just like he promised, but somehow in the midst of the responsibility, neither Scripture nor traditions give us any indication he ever had a family of his own. Of course, to have known Mary so well was to gain priceless insight into Christ. After all, who knew Him better? Surely she recounted stories as the evening oil in the lamp grew scarce. Scripture paints John as curious, so I can't imagine that he failed to ask a thousand questions through the years. "What did Gabriel look like when he brought the news? Did you know instantly he was an angel? What was his voice like?" Or, "Did you almost lose hope that James and your other sons would ever believe?" If Mary was like most aging mothers, I imagine she told the stories all the more and perhaps even repetitively as her life hastened toward its end.

Many of the early church historians agree that John resided in Jerusalem until Mary died. I wonder what Mary's home-going was like. If John and Christ's half-brothers had any notion she was dying, they were no doubt by her side. A natural death must have been so different to the eyewitnesses of the resurrected Lord Jesus. They knew firsthand the reality of life beyond the grave. Can you imagine how anxious Mary was to see her firstborn son?

I have little doubt that those nearby reassured her through her final hours with words of their imminent encounter. Like all of us, God counted her steps and kept her tears in a bottle. Both were full and it was time. As He narrowed that solitary life to an earthbound close, He could easily see beyond the weathered face lined by time.

I like to think Mary was surrounded by loved ones as she inhaled her last ounce of earthly air. I imagine her sons gathered around her. All of them. The one she adopted at the cross and the One she surrendered to the grave. I wonder if they knew their Brother was right there among them . . . more present in His invisibility than they could ever be. Mary bid farewell to mortality and was ushered to immortality on the arm of a handsome Prince. Her Son. Her God.

John's job was done. What now? Perhaps he did what we sometimes do. When I am confounded by what I don't know, I rehearse in my mind what I do know. He knew that the last thing Christ told the apostles was that they would be witnesses in Jerusalem, Judea, Samaria, and the uttermost parts of the earth. I am of course offering supposition, but I wonder if he thought to himself, "I've served here in Jerusalem for years. I've preached to Samaritans, and I know Judea like the back of my hand. I'm no longer a young man. Who knows how much longer I have? I'm heading to the uttermost."

Beloved, listen. Christ's early followers were adventurers! They were pioneers! If they listened to us sit around and decide whether we had time to work in a Bible study with prison inmates around our nail appointments, they'd be mortified. In our postmodern era, church life is associated with buildings and programs. Church life to them was moving in the adrenaline and excitement of the Holy Ghost at the risk of life and limb. They were willing to do things we would reason couldn't possibly be the will of God (i.e., risking our necks) for the sheer joy of what lay before them. They ran the race. They didn't window shop.

I'm not meaning to be harsh, but I fear they might look at all of us and think virtually none of us looked like disciple material to them. But you know what I'd want to say to that first motley crew? "None of you looked like disciple material either when Christ dragged you from your safe little lives." My point? We can still become disciple material! I desperately want to! I want to live the Great Adventure. Don't you? Even if that Great Adventure leads me into virtual obscurity for a while.

# DAY 330
## 1 John 3:1–3

—∞∞∞—

Look at how great a love the Father has given us, that we should
be called God's children. And we are! The reason the world
does not know us is that it didn't know Him (v. 1).

—∞∞∞—

One of our greatest needs as we try to live sanely in our tornadic culture is simplicity—surrendering ourselves to the "one thing" that ensures everything else of great value. We see a perfect example of this concept in the apostle John. As the "disciple Jesus loved," John chose to believe and fully receive the love of Christ above all other things. What was the result? Just as Solomon asked for wisdom and became the wisest man in history, John prioritized love and became a flooding wellspring of affection. When God esteems our prayers, we get what we asked and far more.

I originally learned 1 John 3:1 in the King James Version: "Behold, what manner of love the Father has bestowed upon us." Keep in mind that all the major Bible translations still trace back to the Greek for accuracy. By using the word "behold," I think the apostle John was saying, "Can't you see it? Don't you perceive it? The love of God surrounds us with evidences! Just look!"

If we asked God to help us more accurately grasp the true disposition, character, and exquisite quality of His love for us, our lives would dramatically change! Because John chose to prioritize love, God opened his eyes to behold it and his soul to perceive it. Paul discovered something similar and prayed for all of us to do likewise. His prayer thrills me that we might "know this love that surpasses knowledge" (Eph. 3:19). I think Paul wanted us to experience God's love to the full measure of our capacity through the Spirit of God within us, then try to comprehend that its true measure and nature are far beyond that very experience. Just a taste. Just a glimpse. We are invited to know a love that is beyond human knowledge.

Beloved, God's love for you exceeds all reason—yes, His love *for you!* First John 4:16 says, "We know and rely on the love God has for us." The word for "know" in this verse is the same one Paul employed in Ephesians 3:19. You see, we can't define God's love, but we can behold it, experience it, and rely on it. Is 1 John 4:16 a reality for you? His love for you and me is an absolute reality, *but*—we can be so emotionally unhealthy that we refuse to experience it and absorb it into our hearts and minds.

First John 3:19–20 is powerful in this regard: "This then is how we know that we belong to the truth, and how we set our hearts at rest in his presence whenever our hearts condemn us. For God is greater than our hearts, and he knows everything." Ironically, many people are resistant to God because they imagine Him to be very condemning. In reality, humans are *far* more condemning and often emotionally dangerous. I am intrigued by a statement about Christ recorded in John 2:24: "Jesus would not entrust himself to them, for he knew all men."

I can almost imagine Christ saying to humanity, "I am perplexed with all your talk about whether or not you can trust Me. Actually, your heart can be at complete rest in My presence. My love is perfectly healthy. The greater risk is in My entrusting Myself to you." You see, our unhealthy hearts not only condemn us; they condemn others. I have seen marriages destroyed because one spouse refused to accept the reality of the other spouse's love for him or her. Our hearts sometimes even condemn God as we decide for ourselves that He can't be trusted and that He doesn't really love us unconditionally. Our natural hearts are very deceitful and destructive on their own.

I have had the privilege of getting to know many believers over the course of this ministry. And based on what I've seen, I am convinced that few people possess a virtually whole heart who have not pursued it deliberately in Christ. We don't have to be raised in severely dysfunctional homes to develop unhealthy hearts. All we have to do is expose ourselves to life. Life can be heartless and mean. Purely and simply, life hurts. We can't check ourselves out of life, however. Instead, God hopes that we'll turn to Him to heal us from the ravages of natural life and make us healthy ambassadors of abundant life in an unhealthy world.

Please know that God can heal your heart no matter what got it in such a condition. First John 3:20 tells us that God is greater than our hearts! And He knows everything! Yet knowing all things, God loves us lavishly. Perfectly. Unfailingly. If He can heal my shattered, self-destructive heart, He can heal anyone's.

Beloved, Satan is a liar! He knows if you and I take this thing about God's love seriously, we might become a John or a Paul in our generations. Oh, let's glorify God, spite the devil, and do it! It's not too late. Take your pulse. If your heart is still beating, it's worth healing! Here's the catch, however: God's method of healing a condemning heart is to love it to death . . . then create in us a new heart. A healthier heart. A heart filled with faith instead of fear. His perfect love is the only thing that will drive out that fear of ours.

# DAY 331
## 1 John 3:18–22

—∞∞∞—

If our hearts condemn us, God is greater than our hearts and knows all things (v. 20).

—∞∞∞—

Did John start doubting his identity and his significance somewhere along the way? Peter was no doubt the front-runner in Jerusalem and the early church. Next to him, the book of Acts implies James, the half-brother of Christ, was most prominent. Furthermore, John went to Ephesus and built on the foundation laid by none other than Paul, the former persecutor and latecomer onto the scene.

You may be thinking, "But what difference does that make?" In an ideal world, none. But this is no ideal world. In the dead of the night when insecurities crawl on us like fleas, all of us have terrifying bouts of insecurity and panics of insignificance. Our human natures fall pitifully to the temptation at times to pull out the tape measure and gauge ourselves against people who seem far more gifted and anointed by God.

John went on to outlive every other apostle while all of them were counted worthy to give their lives for the sake of Christ. Did he ever wonder if he were too unimportant to even be considered a threat enough to kill?

We may want to think he was surely too mature and filled with the Holy Spirit to have such thoughts, but keep in mind this is the same disciple who asked to sit at one of Jesus' sides in the kingdom. Yes, John was a new creature, but if Satan worked on him anything like he works on me, he targeted his weak times and hit him again with the same brand of temptations that worked in the old days. John's old fleshly desires for significance had been goliath. I can't imagine Satan not trying to pinpoint them again.

One way we have to respond is by choosing to believe what we know rather than what we feel. If John struggled with his identity in the era of the early church, that's exactly what he must have done. We know because of the virtually incomparable fruit produced after years of relative obscurity. In spite of others seeming more powerfully used by God and in the midst of decades hidden in the shadows, John remained tenacious in his task.

No doubt remains in my mind that God spent this time testing and proving John's character so he could be trusted with the greatest revelation. The answers God is willing to give us in our tomorrows often flow from our faithfulness when we have none today.

# DAY 332
1 John 4:7–12

———— ∞ ————

No one has ever seen God. If we love one another,
God remains in us and His love is perfected in us (v. 12).

———— ∞ ————

Somehow I don't find loving God quite as challenging as loving a few others I've known. I fear they'd say the same thing. It's with good reason that "Oh, brother!" is a common figure of speech for frustration. Our most serious challenges are usually not with circumstances. They're with people.

But exercising and strengthening the weak muscles of what I'll call "otherly affection" is paramount to God. If I may be simplistic, it's why we're still here. So what's a believer to do with all the challenges to love people we find difficult? Forget faking it. You and I are called to the real thing. While loving others God places in our paths will never cease to be challenging, the key is learning to draw from the resource of God's own *agapao* rather than our own small and selfish supply of natural *phileo* or fondness. *Agapao* is many things we imagine as love, but two primary elements set it apart.

*Agapao* begins with the will. It is volitional love. In other words, the beginning of true love is the willful decision to agree with God about that person and choose to love. Secondly, when Scripture makes a distinction between *agapao* and *phileo*, *agapao* love is based on best interest while *phileo* love is based on common interests. *Phileo* love often originates through preference and taste, as in a naturally developed friendship or sisterly relationship. *Agapao* tends to be the more "expensive" love because the element of sacrifice is part of its nature. It's simply harder. It necessitates will over emotion.

God's chief goal is to deepen each of our relationships with Him. And He knows that if we don't see our need for Him, we will never understand how sufficient and wonderful He is. Therefore, He continually challenges us to live beyond our natural abilities. He knows that challenges like loving someone we find difficult will place the obedient in the position to come to Him constantly for a fresh supply of His love. We have to pour out our own toxic and preferential affections so our hearts can be filled with His affections. As we ask for our cups to overflow with *agapao*, the liquid, living love of God will not only surge through our own hearts; it will splash on anyone nearby. Glory!

# DAY 333
## 1 John 4:13–19

———∞∞∞———

We have come to know and to believe the love that God has for us. God is love, and
the one who remains in love remains in God, and God remains in him (v. 16).

———∞∞∞———

Do you find it at all peculiar that John alone called himself "the one Jesus
loved"? (John 13:23 hcsb). If we believe the Gospel of John was inspired, however, then we must accept that the detail of John's self-identity was also inspired.
Not because Jesus' love for John exceeded the others but because God purposed
the reader to know how John saw himself. At first glance we might be tempted to
think John a bit arrogant for terming himself such, but God would never allow a
man who received such revelation to get away with that kind of self-promotion.

I'd like to suggest that John's evolving identity over the course of those
decades came out of the opposite kind of heart. God is far too faithful not to
have greatly humbled John before giving him such surpassing revelation. (See a
parallel concept in 2 Cor. 12.)

I believe quite possibly the heightened positions of Peter and Paul in the
era of the early church coupled with the impending martyrdom of each apostle
fed abasement in John rather than exaltation. Surely he struggled with terribly
perplexing feelings of fear that he, too, was doomed to martyrdom—and yet fear
that he wasn't. Does that make sense?

But as the years went by and the virile, youthful fisherman grew old and
gray, I am convinced that John's weakening legs were steadied and strengthened
on the path by the constant reassurance, "Jesus, You chose me. You keep me. And
above all else, You love me. You love me! No matter what happens or doesn't,
Jesus, I am Your beloved."

If any of us had been John during the years conspicuously silent in Scripture,
we might have given up. Or at least dropped into a lower gear. Not John. He
knew two things, and I believe he grabbed on to them for dear life. He knew
he was called to be a disciple. And he knew he was loved. Over the course of
time, those two things emerged into one ultimate identity. "I, John, the seed of
Zebedee, the son of Salome, the brother of James, the last surviving apostle am
he: the one Jesus loves." Beloved disciple. Somewhere along the way, John, that
Son of Thunder, forsook ambition for affection. And that, my friend, is why he
was sitting pretty when some of the most profound words ever to fall from heaven
to earth fell first like liquid grace into his quill.

# DAY 334
## 1 John 4:20–5:5

———⊶∞⊷———

Everyone who believes that Jesus is the Messiah has been born of God,
and everyone who loves the parent also loves his child (v. 1).

———⊶∞⊷———

My favorite account from the early church fathers concerning John was preserved by Clement. It begins with the statement, "Listen to a story which is not a story but a true tradition of John the Apostle preserved in memory."

While visiting a new bishop and his congregation in Smyrna, John "saw a young man of strong body, beautiful appearance, and warm heart. 'I commend this man to you,' [John] said, 'with all diligence in the face of the church, and with Christ as my witness.'"

John returned to Ephesus and, as promised, the bishop took the young man under his wing and baptized him. Time passed, and the bishop "relaxed his great care and watchfulness. . . . But some idle and dissolute youths, familiar with evil, corrupted him in his premature freedom." Before long, the young man had given himself entirely to a life of sin, committed crimes, and even renounced his salvation. Eventually John was summoned back to Smyrna and asked for a report of the young man. Somewhat taken aback, the bishop answered, "He has died"— meaning he had abandoned his faith.

John replied, "Well, it was a fine guardian whom I left for the soul of our brother. But let me have a horse, and someone to show me the way." When the elderly John found the young man, he started to flee. John called out to him, "Why do you run away from me, child, your own father, unarmed and old? Pity me, child, do not fear me! You have still hope of life. I will account to Christ for you. If it must be, I will willingly suffer your death, as the Lord suffered for us; for your life, I will give my own. Stay, believe; Christ sent me." (John knew better than anyone else that only Christ could ransom a man's life.)

The young man wept bitterly, embraced the old man, and pleaded for forgiveness. The account says that John led the young man back and "baptized him a second time in his tears. . . . He brought him to the church, he prayed with many supplications, he joined with him in the struggle of continuous fasting, he worked on his mind by various addresses and did not leave him, so they say, until he restored him to the church, and thus gave a great example of true repentance and a great testimony of regeneration, the trophy of a visible resurrection."[72] Truly, John practiced what he preached.

# DAY 335
## 2 John 1–6

To the elect lady and her children, whom I love in truth . . . because of
the truth that remains in us and will be with us forever (vv. 1–2).

Most days of the year, I can look at my life through a telescope and sit in utter amazement. God has fulfilled dreams I couldn't have had sense enough to dream. He delivered me from a life of recycling defeat and deeply embedded bitterness. He saved my marriage. He has allowed a former pit-dweller like me to serve someone like you. Oh, He has been indescribably gracious to me . . . just as He has to you.

But then I have these microscope days—days when I am determined to slap the most upsetting thing I can think about on a slide and stare at it for hours, to throw a pity party and resent any loved one who refuses to come.

Let me warn you, Satan will rarely refuse to attend a good pity party. Don't think for a moment that Satan won't confront you on the "day of [your] disaster" (Ps. 18:18)—whatever that may be. Sometimes we give him credit for having a heart and respecting when something should be off limits. After all, fair fighters don't hit a person when she's down.

Satan is not a fair fighter. He confronts us on our worst days and approaches us with his specialty: lies. You can't imagine the lies he tries to tell me on my microscope days. Other times he tries a different approach. But just about the time I want to default back to my old coldness, the Spirit of God within me whispers warm breath upon my cooling heart.

Many of us have been loved by unhealthy people who proved deceptive in other ways. We were left injured and confused. Incidentally, if we didn't let God heal us, we likely became unhealthy people ourselves who continued the process. Unhealthiness is contagious, and deceived people deceive people.

But truth sets us free. God, the great I Am, is the totality of wholeness, completeness, and self-existence. He is both truth and love! While Satan approaches us with hate and lies, we can be "loved in the truth" by God and by those His Spirit fills. Our God will only tell us the truth, and one of His chief truths is that loving is always worth doing.

I feel much better. Sometimes I just have to talk it out. I'm ready to put up my microscope and go back to my bifocals.

# DAY 336
## 2 John 7–13

---

*Watch yourselves so that you don't lose what we have worked for,
but you may receive a full reward (v. 8).*

---

No sooner does God reveal truth than Satan goes on the warpath with lies. Deception is his specialty, and his obvious goal is to get us to believe the lies. Therefore, they can't be blatant or we'd recognize them.

Notice John said nothing in this passage about these false teachers refuting every single doctrine concerning Christianity. Some of the false teachers in John's day did not refute that Jesus was divine, for instance. They simply said He wasn't man as well as God. John focused on this exact false teaching in his first letter: "Every spirit who confesses that Jesus Christ has come in the flesh is from God. But every spirit who does not confess Jesus is not from God." (1 John 4:2–3 HCSB). The issue of Christ coming in the flesh is so vital because we "enter the Most Holy Place by the blood of Jesus, by a new and living way opened for us through the curtain, that is, his body" (Heb. 10:19–20). Satan is ever trying to undermine the issue of salvation.

Think about this with me. God created man in His image. John 4:24 says, "God is spirit." You and I were created in three parts: body, soul, and spirit. I believe the "spirit" part of us is that which is created most pointedly in God's image. The spirit—when distinguished in Scripture from the soul—is the part of each human being that has the capacity to know and have a relationship with God. Our Maker literally equipped us with an inner longing to find Him.

First Corinthians 6:17 says that "anyone joined to the Lord is one spirit with Him" (HCSB). When we receive Jesus as our Savior, our spirit (that part of us with the capacity to know God) unites with the Holy Spirit, and they become one. So because I am a believer in Christ, when I refer to the spirit within me, I am talking about the Holy Spirit. But Satan wants to do anything he can to keep people blinded to the truth and lost. He knows all of us are created with a longing for God that we often confuse with a longing for anything "spiritual." But not every spiritual teaching is Christian, and he knows it.

The good news of Jesus Christ was running rampant all over the Middle Eastern part of the world in John's day and heading north, south, east, and west. Jesus was a hot topic of conversation. Once Satan established that he couldn't squelch spiritual hunger or stop the talk about Christ, he determined to supply a new story that made best use of both. He suggested through false teachers that Christ indeed came but not in the flesh. Therefore, the spiritually hungry could still have a belief system involving God but remain, as my relatives would say, as lost as a goose. Why? Because our access to God is through the torn flesh of

Jesus Christ. To deny the incarnation is to deny the one and only means of salvation.

I imagine you know someone at work or elsewhere that may be very "spiritual" but doesn't believe in the incarnate death of Christ as the means to salvation. Do you see what Satan has done? He has tried to feed their need for the spiritual and still keep them blind to the truth. Clever and terribly destructive, isn't he? Don't judge them. Pray like mad for them! Pray for the veil to be removed and the torn veil of Jesus' flesh to be made clear! Just take note that this is Satan at work.

John warned "the chosen lady" not to take any such teacher into her house. In those days, of course, most gatherings of believers met in what we now call "house churches." In many countries they still do. Though John's directive is certainly important for any individual believer, you can imagine how vital it would be for an entire church gathering. Traveling teachers were very common. I think John was saying, "Don't even consider giving anyone who teaches such false doctrine freedom to speak in your gatherings!"

Recently I spoke in a denominational church I haven't often had the privilege to serve. The pastor stood in the back of the sanctuary and listened to every word I taught. Someone asked me if I was bothered by his presence. I assured them I had nothing but respect for a pastor who watched over his flock so carefully. I also was quite relieved when I passed his test!

Pastors aren't just the shepherds of the men of the church. I have met pastors who I could tell were totally unconcerned about what their women were studying or to whom they were listening. Some of them think we're all just sipping tea and talking girl talk. I find myself thinking, "Mister, with all due respect, if your women catch a fire of false doctrine, they can burn down your whole church! Watch who you take into your "house." Watch *me*, for heaven's sake! Watch all of us!" Many would never knowingly teach deception or distortion, but all are dreadfully human.

Well, well, well. In his second letter John certainly said volumes in so few words. If only I could do the same. One of the things I like best about him is his balance. "Love one another!" And while you're at it, "Test the spirits!" Now that's a fine teacher.

# DAY 337
### 3 John 1–4

---

*Dear friend, I pray that you may prosper in every way*
*and be in good health, just as your soul prospers (v. 2).*

---

God has taught me serious lessons about the impact my physical body has on both my soul and my spirit. Think about the soul for a moment. If my body is completely exhausted, my soul is deeply affected and over time can absorb the physical weariness and translate it into depression or feelings of hopelessness. If we eat poorly, we can fuel anxiety and fear. Most of us know that stress is linked to heart problems, high blood pressure, and many digestive problems. As long as our souls and spirits are imprisoned in these physical bodies, they are greatly affected by their condition.

You and I live stressful lives. I've heard many of your testimonies, and I am astounded at some of your challenges. Some of you work all day, then tend a sick loved one all night. Others of you hold down several jobs as you try to keep your children in college. I often hear from young mothers who have three or four children under five years old. Now that's stress! I can't even imagine some of your challenges. I never dreamed I would have the challenges I face today. I am so grateful and humbled by God's present calling on my life to minister to women, but I will not kid you. It is work! Yes, God does most of it all by Himself, but the little He requires from me is everything I've got!

My dear co-laborer, you and I cannot effectively fulfill our callings if we don't watch after our health. Our bodies are temples of the Holy Spirit. Each of us faces a life beyond our natural capabilities. My calendar is overwhelming, and I take each scheduled date very seriously. If I end up with a virus and can't make a conference that was scheduled a year earlier, I am devastated. If I'm going to be faithful to you, I've got to cooperate with God and do my part.

Listen, we live in a hard world. That's why I'm convinced that one of our severest needs is pure rest. Not only sleep, but refreshment and recreation. So if you have guts enough not to disconnect and hide from the overwhelming needs out there, you need to add some Sabbath moments into your life to help you keep your head on straight. Start taking them! Hear me, dear friend—"I pray that you may prosper in every way and be in good health, just as your soul prospers" (HCSB).

# DAY 338
### 3 John 5–14

*I wrote something to the church, but Diotrephes, who loves to have
first place among them, does not receive us (v. 9).*

John drops several names in this one-chapter letter of his. Gaius appears as
John's dear friend. Diotrephes is seen as one who loved to be first and excluded
others. Demetrius bears a good name so that not only others but even the truth
speaks well of him.

Imagine being named in a letter that turned out to be inspired Scripture for
all the world to see! Whether in commendation or criticism, having your name
immortalized in Scripture is a heavy thought!

When I see a portion of Scripture with brief testimonials, I almost shiver.
A number of times in my life, I would have been anywhere from devastated to
humiliated over what might have been written in a one-sentence statement about
my life. That's why I love knowing that as long as we're kicking and breathing,
we can still change our testimonies. God hasn't put a period at the end of our
sentences yet.

But take note: that tiny little dot doesn't take long to jot. We may think
we're only mid-sentence when we're not. Attending as many funerals as I do is a
constant reminder to me. Let's not put off working toward what we hope God's
testimonial for our lives will state. As the writer of Hebrews said, "Today, if you
hear His voice, do not harden your hearts as in the rebellion" (3:15 HCSB).

Like poor Diotrephes. You'd think with a name like that, he wouldn't have
wanted to be first. Can you imagine such a one-sentence testimonial? "Beth loved
to be first and didn't like to have anything to do with the common folks." Egads!
The hair on the back of my neck is standing up!

Notice John didn't say the man was lost, however. Diotrephes was obviously
a member of the church. Though his actions weren't loving, he could easily have
been a Christian. Let's admit, if gossip and divisiveness are unquestionable signs
of "lostness," the few folks who do go to heaven are liable to have considerable
elbow room.

Thank goodness we won't have hard feelings and conflict in glory.
Otherwise, I could almost imagine Diotrephes saying to John, "Did you have to
go and write it down? Why couldn't you have just gossiped like I did?"

# DAY 339
## Revelation 1:1–3

—⚬⚬⚬—

The revelation of Jesus Christ that God gave Him to show His slaves what must quickly take place. He sent it and signified it through His angel to His slave John (v. 1).

—⚬⚬⚬—

For the remainder of our journey together, we will join John in exile on the island of Patmos in the Aegean. Don't bother packing your swimsuit. This six-mile-wide, ten-mile-long island is not exactly paradise. In John's day its rocky, barren terrain attracted the eye of the Romans as a perfect place to banish criminals. Under the rule of the Roman emperor Domitian (AD 81–96), Christianity was a criminal offense, and the apostle John had a fierce case of it.

I am curious why John, an undeniable Son of Thunder, was exiled rather than killed under the authority of Roman rule like the other apostles. Scholars agree we can assume he was harshly treated—even at his age—and forced into hard labor in the mines and quarries on the island. I still wonder why the Romans bothered since they publicly and inhumanely took the lives of so many other Christians. Ultimately, God wasn't finished with John's work on earth, and no one was taking him without his Father's permission. I wonder if the traditional teaching of the early church fathers is accurate—that the Romans tried to kill him . . . and couldn't.

In a work called *On Prescription against Heretics*, Tertullian—often called the "father of Latin theology"—made a stunning claim: "The apostle John was first plunged, unhurt, into boiling oil, and then remitted to his island exile!"[73]

Very few scholars question the reliability of the early traditions held about Peter's death on a cross to which Tertullian referred. Likewise, I've never read a commentary that cited reason to question the traditional information that Paul was beheaded like John the Baptist. I certainly don't know if the account regarding John's plunge into boiling oil is reliable, but if you ask me if such an event is possible, I could only answer yes! In Acts 12, God wasn't ready for Peter's work on earth to end, so He loosed his chains and caused him to walk right out of the prison. I can't even count the times the apostle Paul narrowly escaped death. I seem to recall a trio in the Old Testament who experienced fire without even the smell of smoke (see Dan. 3). Beloved, don't let the modern church make you cynical. Ours is a God of wonders, and don't you forget it!

# DAY 340
## Revelation 1:4–11

—⟨∞⟩—

John, your brother and partner in the tribulation, kingdom,
and perseverance in Jesus, was on the island called Patmos
because of God's word and the testimony about Jesus (v. 9).

—⟨∞⟩—

We can be quite sure that John never sketched Patmos on his personal itinerary. I wonder what the old man felt as he was shipped like a criminal from his loved ones in Ephesus to a remote, unfriendly island. He had no idea what awaited him. God's ways are so peculiar at times. Yet the greatest privilege of John's life waited for him in these gravest of circumstances.

The most profound revelation in Revelation is the revealing of Jesus Christ Himself, not only in visions but in authority. The word "revelation" (meaning "unveiling") is translated from the Greek word *apokalupsis*. Thrown onto a boat transferring criminals, John had no idea what God would "unveil" to him upon the island of Patmos.

Imagine John's frail, aging frame as he held on tight while the sea vessel tossed its long way across the Aegean. John probably pushed his gray hair out of his face to look at the few other prisoners sharing his destination. Don't picture a bonding experience. No one would likely carry him through a small group of worshipers while he said, "Dear children, love one another." Exile was intended not only for overwork and overexposure to elements; it was purposed for crazing isolation. Yet the tactic would be wasted on John—just as it can be wasted on us when Satan tries to force us into isolation.

John most likely would have preferred death. His long life may have frustrated him. If forced to remain on earth, exile from ministry and isolation from those he loved was certainly not the way he envisioned spending his senior years. I can't imagine at one point or another in the labors forced upon him that John didn't slip on the jagged, rocky surfaces and rip his thinning skin like paper. He had no bedding for his aching body at the end of a day.

I also can't imagine that he thought, "Finally! A little peace and quiet for writing a new book!" He couldn't have expected to meet Jesus on that island as he did. Beloved one, how many testimonies do we need to hear before we accept that sometimes the places and seasons we expect Jesus least, we find Him most? And oddly, sometimes the places we expect Him most, we find Him least?

Yes, when Christ returns to this groaning soil in His glorious splendor, every eye will see Him. But until then, He sometimes comes with clouds. God's glory is so inconceivably brilliant to the human eye that He often shrouds His presence in a cloud (see Exod. 16:10; 24:15–16; Lev. 16:2; 1 Kings 8:10; Luke 9:34). But one day, as Revelation 1:7 says, the clouds will roll back like a scroll and Christ will stand before us revealed.

He has much to disclose to us in the meantime, and we'll be greatly helped when we accept that clouds are not signs of His absence. Indeed, within them we most often find His presence. In the July 29 entry of his classic devotional *My Utmost for His Highest*, Oswald Chambers wrote figuratively of clouds:

> In the Bible, clouds are always associated with God. Clouds are the sorrows, sufferings, or providential circumstances, within or without our personal lives, which actually seem to contradict the sovereignty of God. Yet it is through these very clouds that the Spirit of God is teaching us how to walk by faith. If there were never any clouds in our lives, we would have no faith. "The clouds are the dust of His feet" (Nahum 1:3). They are a sign that God is there. . . . Through every cloud He brings our way, He wants us to unlearn something. His purpose in using the cloud is to simplify our beliefs until our relationship with Him is exactly like that of a child—a relationship simply between God and our own souls, and where other people are but shadows. . . . Until we can come face-to-face with the deepest, darkest fact of life without damaging our view of God's character, we do not yet know Him.[74]

I've been on Patmos myself when the clouds that settled on the island obscured what might otherwise have been a beautiful view. I wonder if clouds covered the island when Domitian thought he left John to the island's harsh volcanic mercy? I wonder how the old apostle "viewed" his circumstances? I wonder if he ever imagined getting off that island? Or what he'd see while he was there?

John had a critical decision to make while exiled on the unkind island. Would he relax his walk with God at the very least and at most resist? After all, no one from his church or ministry was watching. Would he lie down and die? Goodness knows he was weary. Or would John the Beloved love Christ all the more and seek Him with his whole heart amid the rock and wasteland?

His answer rises like a fresh morning tide baptizing the jagged shore: "I was in the Spirit on the Lord's day" (1:10 HCSB). And there He was: the Alpha and Omega. The first and last Word on every life. Every trial. Every exile.

# DAY 341
## Revelation 1:12–20

⸺∘∞∘⸺

Therefore write what you have seen, what is, and what will take place after this (v. 19).

⸺∘∞∘⸺

Years ago I learned a good rule of thumb that I've tried to keep before me in study: when plain sense makes common sense, seek no other sense. Through the ages various interpreters have sought to make the churches of Revelation 2–3 symbolic, but what we can know for certain is that they were actual believers and real churches at the time of John's exile. The order of scriptural presentation is actually geographic. All seven cities were located in Asia Minor, and their orders in Scripture suggest a very practical route a messenger might take if he began a journey in Ephesus and traveled on to the other six cities.

We will spend much of our time in Revelation on the messages to the seven churches. The fact that God included the communication in Holy Writ tells us they have something to say to us. In fact, Christ Himself pointed out their relevance to others as He drew all seven letters to a close with a broad invitation, first recorded in Revelation 2:7: "Anyone who has an ear should listen to what the Spirit says to the churches" (HCSB).

Now, feel the side of your head. Do you feel an ear? Try either side, for you only need one: "Anyone who has an ear . . ." If you have one, Jesus would like you to hear what the Spirit says to the churches. I have one, too, so I'm in with you. The reason is obvious. We of His church today have much to learn from the successes, failures, victories, and defeats of the early churches. The generations may be far removed, but our basic nature and the truth of Scripture remain consistent.

Actually, Christ had more in mind than talking to people who had at least one physical ear on the sides of their heads. I certainly had ears throughout my young years, but I'm not sure how well I used them to listen to God. For the most part my ears were important hair accessories. Will I put my hair behind both ears today? One ear? Or shall I let my hair hang over both ears? I was so deep. The messages to the seven churches are for people with a little more depth than that. Christ's broad invitation was more like this: What I've said to them will speak volumes to anyone who really wants to hear and respond. So let's each grab an ear and hear!

# DAY 342
## Revelation 2:1–7

———∞∞∞———

You also possess endurance and have tolerated many things because of My name. . . .
But I have this against you: you have abandoned the love you had at first (vv. 3–4).

———∞∞∞———

The letters to the churches in Revelation 2–3 contain several repeated elements that I want you to identify from the very beginning. Although they don't all appear in each of the seven letters, here are the common components:

• *Identification.* Christ identified Himself in a specific way using some element of the first vision in Revelation 1:12–18.

• *Commendation.* While not every letter contains a commendation, all seven include the phrase "I know your . . ." based on His intimate acquaintance with them.

• *Rebuke.* In most cases, He pointed out something that needed correction.

• *Exhortation.* He instructed each church to do something specific.

• *Encouragement.* He always issued an encouragement to overcome. Celebrate the fact that no condition was irreversible!

Using these elements common to each letter to the churches, let's see what Christ had to say to the church at Ephesus.

*Identification.* Note what Christ pinpoints about Himself to the church in Ephesus: "The One who holds the seven stars in His right hand and who walks among the seven gold lampstands" (2:1 HCSB). We would be tragically amiss to think Christ is uninvolved and unmoved by the conditions, activities, and inner workings of His present churches. He walks among us. Nothing is more important to Christ in any generation than the health of His church, since it is the vehicle through which He purposes to reach the lost and minister to the hurting.

*Commendation.* Based on His intimate knowledge of the church of Ephesus, Christ strongly commended them in verses 2 and 3: "I know your works, your labor, and your endurance, and that you cannot tolerate evil. You have tested those who call themselves apostles and are not, and you have found them to be liars. You also possess endurance and have tolerated many things because of My name, and have not grown weary" (HCSB).

*Rebuke.* "But I have this against you: you have abandoned the love you had at first" (2:4 HCSB). Remember, the apostle John was most involved in the church at Ephesus. Knowing what we've learned about him, how do you think he responded internally when he heard this particular rebuke concerning his dear ones in Ephesus? He was the pastor who had sought to teach them to love the Lord Christ. Did he feel a sense of failure or reproof?

*Exhortation.* In verse 5, Christ said, "Remember then how far you have fallen; repent, and do the works you did at first. Otherwise, I will come to you and remove your lampstand from its place—unless you repent" (HCSB). Note a detail about the warning. Christ told the church in Ephesus that if they did not repent and do the things they "did at first," He would come to them and remove their lampstand from its place. The terminology doesn't mean they would lose their place in heaven. We lose our lampstand when we lose a vibrant position of godly influence on earth. In other words, we lose our light in the world.

*Encouragement.* "I will give the victor the right to eat from the tree of life, which is in the paradise of God" (2:7 HCSB). The sins of the church at Ephesus weren't hopeless. Nor are ours! Let's repent, though, so we can overcome!

Somehow in my previous studies of this letter, I have overlooked the original meaning of a critical word in the phrase from Christ's rebuke about abandoning or forsaking their first love. I am astonished to find that the original word for "forsaken" is the same word often translated "forgive" in the New Testament. The word *aphiemi* means "to send forth, send away, let go from oneself."[75] The New Testament uses *aphiemi* in many contexts and simply means giving up or letting go of something, such as in the familiar words of Matthew 6:12 (KJV): "Forgive us our debts, as we forgive our debtors."

I could easily sit right here and sob. The thought occurs to me how often we forsake our first love—our indescribably glorious sacred romance—because we refuse to forsake our grudges and grievances. Please allow me to say this with much compassion as one who has been there: We cannot hang on to our sacred romance with Jesus Christ and also our bitterness. We will release one to hang on to the other.

The room unforgiveness is taking up in your life is cheating you of the very thing you were born (again) to experience. Send it forth! Not into oblivion, but into the hands of the faithful and sovereign Judge of the earth. For unless our lampstands are lit with the torch of sacred love, they are nothing but artificial lights. Fluorescent, maybe. But sooner or later, the bulb burns out.

# DAY 343
## Revelation 2:8–9

⚭

I know your tribulation and poverty, yet you are rich. I know the slander of those
who say they are Jews and are not, but are a synagogue of Satan (v. 9).

⚭

Christ commented about the slander of those who falsely claimed to be
Jews but instead were a synagogue of Satan. This fact may imply that the Jews in
Smyrna identified the Christians to the government and greatly heightened the
persecution against them.

Imagine God's derision for a people who not only looked the other way but
actively enforced poverty and affliction on His children. They had no idea the
King of the earth walked through the perfectly paved streets of their fair city
checking on those who called themselves by His name.

The people of Smyrna took great pride in the beauty of their city. I found the
following quote out of *Biblical Illustrator* quite ironic: "The hills and the sea added
to the picturesque quality of the city. The city itself nestled under the hill Pagos,
which made an ideal acropolis. This beauty was marred, however, by a drainage
problem in the lower city which resulted in the silting up of the harbor and an
accumulation of unpleasant odors."[76]

Try as they might to build the most impressive city in Asia, they just
couldn't do anything about that putrid smell. Don't think for a moment that
their unrelenting persecution of innocent people didn't rise up to the nostrils of
God. Interestingly, the name Smyrna means "myrrh."[77] Yet nothing but stench
ascended to the heavens from the arrogantly pristine, highly educated, and
wealthy of Smyrna. From the hidden slums, however, rose a fragrant incense of
great expense. No perfume is more costly and more aromatic to God than the
faithfulness of believers who are suffering.

I remember serving on a team with a pastor whose son was soon to die of a
malignant brain tumor unless God miraculously intervened. I stood not far from
him during praise and worship. This precious father did not deny his immense pain.
His tears fell unashamedly, but all the while his worship rose just as unashamedly.
I can hardly hold back my own tears as I picture his face. Many of us felt the
favor of God over our interdenominational prayer gathering that night. Somehow,
I believe in the midst of much praise, a fragrance of greater price and exceeding
sweetness ascended to the throne from one grieving servant of God.

# DAY 344
## Revelation 2:10–11

—❦—

Look, the Devil is about to throw some of you into prison to test you,
and you will have tribulation for 10 days. Be faithful until death,
and I will give you the crown of life (v. 10).

—❦—

Smyrna stands out among the churches as one of two that received no rebuke. As Christ walked beside this lampstand, He found no fault in her.

Impressively, she didn't pass her tests because her exams were easy. To the contrary, no other church is characterized by greater depths of suffering. Christ didn't mince words when He described her afflictions and poverty. Christians were despised and terribly mistreated in Smyrna primarily because no other city in Asia Minor held more allegiance to Rome. The obsessive allegiance of the people of Smyrna became deadly for Christians under the rule of emperors like Nero (AD 54–68) and Domitian (AD 81–96). Anything the emperor reviled, the people of Smyrna reviled. For these two emperors and others that followed, Christians were on the top of the hate list.

How are people like the believers in Smyrna able to be faithful through such terrible suffering? As resistant as we are to absorb it, 1 Peter 1:7 indicates one primary reason: ". . . so that the genuineness of your faith—more valuable than gold, which perishes though refined by fire—may result in praise, glory, and honor at the revelation of Jesus Christ" (HCSB).

Those who are faithful in the midst of immense suffering somehow allow their fiery trials to purify them rather than destroy them. If we've never suffered like some of the saints we know or have read about, we tend to indict ourselves with failure before our trials ever come. We must remember that God grants us grace and mercy according to our need. No, I do not have the strength or character to be faithful under such heart-shattering conditions. But when my time comes, the Holy Spirit will impart a power and grace I've never experienced. The challenge is whether or not to accept it.

The tragedy is that in our pride and anger we sometimes refuse the grace of God during our times of suffering. The believers in Smyrna did not refuse the grace. They inhaled it like air because they were desperate. As much as the church in Smyrna had suffered, Christ warned them of more to come. He wanted them to be aware, but He did not want them to be afraid. I believe much of the book of Revelation was written to believers for the same purpose.

Mind you, imprisonment and death awaited some of those among the church of Smyrna. We don't know what Christ meant by the time segment of "10 days" in verse 10. Some scholars believe it was literal. Others think it represented ten years. Still others assume it is a figure of speech for a segment of time known only to God. Whatever the length of trial, Christ called the church of Smyrna to be faithful unto death. His self-identification as the one who died and came to life again reminded them of the absolute assurance of resurrection life. He also promised to reward them with a *stephanos* or victor's crown. They would not be touched by "the second death," a term for the final judgment for all unbelievers.

Sometimes Jesus defines "overcoming" not as living well but dying well. In other words, dying with faith and spiritual dignity. Beloved, dying is the one thing each of us is going to do unless we're the chosen generation to "meet the Lord in the air" without tasting death (1 Thess. 4:17 HCSB).

At least one of the saints in Smyrna to which Christ addressed His letter left us a profound and wonderful example of an overcoming death. His name was Polycarp. He studied directly under the apostle John's tutelage and was alive at the time the Revelation was penned. He became the bishop of the church in Smyrna and served the generation that followed John's heavenly departure. *Foxe's Book of Martyrs* shares the following account of Polycarp's trial and martyrdom.

> He was, however, carried before the proconsul, con-
> demned. . . . The proconsul then urged him, saying,
> 'Swear, and I will release thee;—reproach Christ.'
> Polycarp answered, 'Eighty and six years have I
> served Him, and He has done me no wrong. How
> then can I blaspheme my King who has saved me?'
> At the stake to which he was only tied, not nailed as
> usual, as he assured them he should stand immov-
> able, the flames, on their kindling the fagots, encir-
> cled his body, like an arch, without touching him;
> and the executioner, on seeing this, was ordered to
> pierce him with a sword, when so great a quantity of
> blood flowed out as extinguished the fire.[78]

He had overcome. As long as those moments must have been, noth-
ing could have prepared Polycarp for the sight he beheld when death gave way to life and faith gave way to sight. The only Jesus he had ever seen was in the face and heart of John the Beloved. But that day the old bishop of Smyrna saw the One he loved and had served for eighty and six years. Face to face. With a victor's crown in His hand.

When I get to heaven and meet him, I'm going to try to remember to ask Polycarp if he thought his suffering was worth it. Oh, I already know the answer . . . but I want to see his expression.

# DAY 345
## Revelation 2:12–13

———

The One who has the sharp, two-edged sword says:
I know where you live—where Satan's throne is! (vv. 12–13).

———

We can only imagine what kind and level of warfare the young church in Pergamum experienced. Christ referred to the city as the place "where Satan's throne is." Since Satan is not omnipresent, this claim is hair-raising. We can't be certain what Christ meant, but historical evidence from the first century tells us Pergamum was the uncontested center of pagan worship in Asia Minor.

Keep in mind that Satan's primary goal is to keep people blinded to the truth while providing them with something that momentarily seems to assuage their spiritual hunger. Pergamum delivered. Christ spoke about the church in Pergamum remaining true to His name. Goodness knows, inhabitants had plenty of names to choose from. Within its walls were temples to Dionysus, Athena, Asclepius, and Demeter; three temples to the emperor cult; and a huge altar to Zeus.

Although the philosophy of the city seemed to be "pick a god, any god," two primary religions exceeded all others in Pergamum: the worship of Dionysus, considered god of the royal kings (symbolized by the bull), and the worship of Asclepius, called "the savior god of healing" (symbolized by the snake). Does that second title make your skin crawl like it does mine? I know the Savior God of Healing, and I assure you it isn't the snake. God heals in many ways, but He alone is Jehovah Rapha. I'm reminded of God's words in Hosea 11:3. The prophet said of Israel, "They never knew that I healed them" (HCSB). All healing is meant to reveal the Healer, so Satan will do anything he can to block the connection.

The first psalm I memorized was Psalm 103. I still love it. It urges us to praise the Lord and not to forget His benefits. This is especially important because, given the opportunity, Satan gladly supplies a counterfeit "savior" who claims to provide a dandy benefit package. Any world religion or brand of humanism will do.

But man was created to seek God's benefits. That's why Satan works most effectively if he is able to offer alternatives. For instance, he's sly to suggest other ways for people to unload their guilt. One workable way is to convince them they haven't sinned. He has all sorts of means of providing counterfeit "redemption." Don't fall for them—any of them!

# DAY 346
## Revelation 2:14–17

⊸⊷⊶

I will also give him a white stone, and on the stone a new name is inscribed
that no one knows except the one who receives it (v. 17).

⊸⊷⊶

Not long ago I received a letter from a loved one with whom I shared my testimony about the transforming power of God's Word. He, a practicing Buddhist, wrote me his own testimony about how life had improved since he changed his "karma." My heart broke over the inevitable disillusionment of self-worship. At some point surely a self-worshiper looks in the mirror and says, "If I am as good as God gets, life really stinks." And yet counterfeits continue to be sold and manufactured on every corner.

Christ, for example, rebuked an undesignated number in Pergamum for holding to the teachings of Balaam and the Nicolaitans. The fact that He commanded the repentance of the whole church means the number had to be significant. Although God esteems repentance of the faithful on behalf of the unfaithful, He doesn't require it from people who haven't sinned. Look back at His commendation to the church of Ephesus in Revelation 2:2. I suspect the church in Pergamum may have tolerated "wicked men" and false apostles more than the church of Ephesus.

We can't dogmatically identify the teaching of the Nicolaitans, but they are closely associated with the teachings of Balaam. The account of Balaam and Balak is found in Numbers 22–24. In a nutshell, Balak, the king of Moab, greatly feared the Israelites as they settled in the promised land. He hired Balaam the soothsayer to curse Israel, but Balaam blessed them instead. He did, however, instruct Balak how to defeat the Israelites. He told Balak to seduce them into idolatry through the harlotry of the Moabite women. Based on all I've read, I believe the basic concept of Balaam's teachings is this: If you can't curse them, try to seduce them!

The whole idea makes my blood boil. You see, Satan is waging war on our generation with Balaam's weapon (see 1 Tim. 4:1). Satan can't curse us because we are blessed (Eph. 1:3)—children of God, covered by the blood of the Lamb. If the devil can't curse us, then how can he defeat us? He can try to seduce us! How does seduction differ from temptation? All seduction is temptation, but not all temptation is seduction. Many temptations are just plain obvious and outright. The aim of seduction, on the other hand, is to catch the prey off guard. That's why Satan's best henchmen (or women) are often insiders rather than outsiders. Some in the church of Pergamum were being enticed into sin by others among them, and Christ expected the church to jump to action.

Whether or not the seducers were truly saved is unclear. If the seducers were indeed true believers, they needed to be confronted properly and restored when repentant. Some may wonder how believers could be used by Satan to seduce. Beloved, seduced people seduce people. And if the devil's scheme is not exposed and the chain is not broken, it perpetuates. We must develop discernment and guard our hearts jealously without becoming fearful and suspicious. Authentic godliness rather than religiousness is our best defense against seduction.

Christ's letter to the church in Pergamum must have hit hard, but the tenderness and encouragement of the conclusion spared their hearts.

Christ promised two things to those who overcame: hidden manna and a white stone. The hidden manna contrasts beautifully with the food sacrificed to idols. Jesus Christ was the Bread of Life sacrificed on the altar before the one true God. Now His Spirit falls like manna from heaven to all who hunger. Jewish tradition holds that the ark with the pot of manna in it was hidden by order of King Josiah and will be revealed once again during the earthly reign of the Messiah.

The most probable meaning of the white stone in verse 17 is remarkable. In an ancient courtroom, jurors voting to condemn the accused would cast their vote by tossing a black stone or pebble. In contrast, jurors voting to acquit the condemned would cast their vote by tossing a white stone or pebble. Scripture actually records this ancient practice, but our English translations don't portray it. In the course of sharing his testimony, Paul said he "cast my vote against" the Christians (Acts 26:10). The original wording is *katenegka psephon*. The Greek word *katenegka* means "to deposit or cast." The Greek word *psephon* means "pebble or stone," and is only used in Acts 26:10 and Revelation 2:17.[79] Paul formerly deposited or cast his pebble to vote against the saints.

If we're on target, the terminology Christ used was perfectly fitting for Pergamum, which was the legal center of the district. How I praise God that the Judge of all the earth pitches a white stone to acquit us—not because we're innocent but because Someone has already served our sentence. And the new name on the stone? It could be Christ's, but I also think we each have an overcoming name that's unique and individual to us, not unlike Abram had Abraham, Simon had Peter, and Saul had Paul.

I'll be honest with you. I'll be glad to leave Pergamum and its insider seducers. But the manna and the stone? Those were worth the trip. See you tomorrow in Thyatira!

# DAY 347
## Revelation 2:18–29

---∽∞∽---

*You tolerate the woman Jezebel, who calls herself a prophetess,
and teaches and deceives My slaves to commit sexual immorality
and to eat meat sacrificed to idols (v. 20).*

---∽∞∽---

Scripture associates Thyatira with two different women: Lydia and Jezebel. Acts 16:13–15 tells about Lydia, the businesswoman who became the first named convert in Europe. Lydia was from Thyatira. I love the words of verse 14: "The Lord opened her heart to respond to Paul's message." Then her entire household followed Christ.

Then there's Jezebel. Some scholars interpret Jezebel as a reference to a false doctrine, a type of demonic spirit, or a behavioral concept. Others believe she was a flesh-and-blood woman who played havoc in the church at Thyatira. I am strongly inclined to agree with the latter, but I am also thoroughly convinced she is representative of a kind of woman none of us want to be.

The Revelation 2 Jezebel was a very powerful woman in Thyatira. Likely up to her elbows in secret guilds and society climbs, she did everything she could to infiltrate the church with them. Lydia was also a powerful woman in Thyatira. Together they provide a lesson on abuse versus wise use of authority. Let's perform a character sketch of Jezebel and invite Lydia to hold up a lamp of contrast in her counterpart's insidious darkness.

1. *Jezebel assumed places of authority God did not assign her (v. 20).* Before you jump to the conclusion that her infraction was assuming a role that could belong only to men, note that the New Testament undeniably records the viability of a woman having the God-given gift of prophecy, or what we might generalize as "speaking forth" (Luke 2:36–37; Acts 2:17–18; Acts 21:8–9). Jezebel had no such God-given gift. She wasn't called. She was controlling! She wasn't wisely authoritative. She was bossy! Oh, that none of us—male or female—would confuse the two!

Certainly God calls women into places of leadership, but in the spirit of 1 Corinthians 11:5, I believe our heads must be covered by higher authority. I cannot express how strongly I feel about this issue. As women, we enjoy a wonderful umbrella of protection. The biblical, proverbial buck stops with the men of our households and churches. If God calls a woman to assume a leadership role, I believe with all my heart she is only safe and operating in God's authentic anointing under that umbrella!

Given my past and my lack of credentials, I will never understand the sovereignty of God to appoint *me* to an area of leadership. At the same time, I know what He has called me to do for this season, and I'd be in direct disobedience to

God if I let someone's disapproval dissuade me. I cannot describe, however, the terror that shoots through me over finding myself here. How anyone can have an intimate relationship with God and be arrogant and fearless in a position of authority is beyond me.

James 3:1 warns, "Not many should become teachers, my brothers, knowing that we will receive a stricter judgment" (HCSB). Why would anyone ask for "stricter judgment"? Jezebel was asking for it whether she knew it or not. Please don't miss that Jezebel's most serious infraction was not her sin but her unwillingness to repent! Lydia stands in stark contrast to Jezebel as a woman of success. She was a worshiper of God—not of herself or position. She opened her heart to Paul's message rather than pull rank on him. Both professionally and spiritually, the tone of Scripture suggests she was a servant leader.

*2. Jezebel abused her feminine gift of influence (v. 20).* She misled and deceived. I am convinced that women have a unique God-given gift of influence. I am married to a very strong man. He no doubt wears the cowboy boots in our family. But, if I used my feminine wiles just right (or just wrong), I fear I could talk him into almost anything. I have to be very careful because he loves me and wants to please me. You see, in some ways I am his weakness. Do you understand what I mean?

Many accounts in Scripture attest to the power of a woman's influence. Eve and Sarai represent some biblical blights but, thankfully, we can find many more scriptural examples of positive womanly influence than negative. Lydia is certainly one of them. She influenced her whole household to follow Christ.

*3. Jezebel misused her sexuality (v. 21).* Sisters, I'm not sure our culture has taught us to use anything more powerfully than our sexuality. Don't think for a moment that seducing someone into fornication is the only way a woman can use her sexuality to manipulate. We can be completely clothed and in broad, public daylight and still misuse our sexuality.

I might have a sister in Christ who is horrified right this minute by our discussion of this tawdry topic. True, she may never have dreamed of using her sexuality seductively or manipulatively. Then again, this same woman may wield it like a massive weapon in her marriage.

Sexuality was given by God as a gift. Not a tool. Just because we're married doesn't mean we don't horrifically misuse our sexuality to get what we want. Routine withholding is just one example. God created us to be women complete with all our gifts, contributions, and influences. But let's be women well.

# DAY 348
## Revelation 3:1–6

⊸∞⊶

Be alert and strengthen what remains, which is about to die,
for I have not found your works complete before My God (v. 2).

⊸∞⊶

If we studied the seven churches of Asia Minor and seven hundred more in our cities today, we would quickly discover a disturbing fact. The personalities and moral attitudes of any given city permeate its churches unless the church works to deliberately overcome. For instance, churches in wealthy areas with upper-crust attitudes will have to overcome misguided superiority to keep from portraying the same things. Why? Because the people who comprise churches are also products of their societies. Likewise, churches in cities of deeply ingrained prejudice will carry the same banner unless they deliberately risk being different. A church can be refreshingly dissimilar to its surrounding society only through deliberately renewing their minds.

We might accurately say that the city surrounding the church of Sardis had nearly killed it. Christ had little to say in favor of this ancient church. In fact, I can think of few indictments more serious to a group of believers than these three words: "You are dead" (Rev. 3:1). I believe dead churches are one of the most confounding mysteries to the hosts of heaven. The ministering spirits that invisibly flood the atmosphere must look on the church then back on the radiance of Jesus Christ and wonder how anything that carries His name can be dead. Above all things, Christ is life!

What invaded the church of Sardis with such deadness? The history of this ancient city suggests three permeating contributors:

1. *The people of Sardis were fixated on death rather than life.* Perhaps you'll be as interested as I was to learn that Sardis was best known for a necropolis called the "cemetery of the thousand hills" about seven miles from town. Can you imagine a city known for its cemeteries? But where burial mounds become idols, thoughts of death overtake thoughts of life. I once received a letter from a sister in Christ who was alarmed that I mentioned visiting the graveside of a friend. She was not unkind. She was simply surprised that anyone who believed so strongly in heaven would esteem meaningless remains by visiting a grave. Though I didn't agree with her philosophy, if I were more focused on my believing friend's death than her life, my sister would have a point.

But we don't have to idolize burial mounds like the Sardians to focus on death more than life. Worship in its simplest essence is attentiveness. One way we can focus on death more than life is to possess a life-inhibiting fear of it. I have known people who were so scared of death they could hardly live. You might say they were worshiping burial mounds much like the Sardians—whether or not they realized it. A chronic fear of death can inhibit a believer's entire life and ministry.

2. *The people of Sardis relied on their past achievements.* Sardis was like a leading lady in a Greek tragedy who waltzed around town in riches turned to rags thinking everyone still saw her as she was thirty years ago. In essence, Christ wrote the church of Sardis to hand this self-deceived woman a mirror—just like He's handed one to me a time or ten. Christ does not hand someone a mirror to destroy, however. He hands her the mirror to wake her up!

I was invited a few years ago to attend some special homecoming festivities at my college alma mater. I greatly enjoyed renewing friendships and acquaintances. But I was mystified and somewhat amused as I watched other people "time warp," holding a death grip on the past. If time warping weren't so pitiful, it would be hilarious. Sardis was warped by time. She lived off her past fame, and the results were tragic. Unfortunately, the church within its walls had followed suit.

3. *The people of Sardis likely interpreted rejection as a deathblow.* Though the city of Sardis housed an incomplete temple of Artemis, they lost their bid to build a temple to Caesar in AD 26. Smyrna won the bid instead. Though the church of Sardis had nothing but disdain for pagan practices and temples, my hypothesis is that the people of the church unknowingly wore the same cloak of dejected identity as their surroundings. After all, they too were pagans until the gospel reached their gates—most likely under the preaching of the apostle Paul. I'd like to further hypothesize that the people of Sardis knew they needed a fresh shot of life and vitality when they bid Rome for the new temple. When they were rejected in favor of a rival city, I wonder if they took on an attitude all too common after rejection: Who cares anymore? Unless good reason exists to respond otherwise, rejection can cause people to lose heart faster than almost anything else.

Perhaps the following commentary best sums up the deadness of Sardis at the time of John's vision: "Sardis was a city of peace. Not the peace won through battle, but the peace of a man whose dreams are dead and whose mind is asleep. The peace of lethargy and evasion."[80] I find that statement stunning not because it speaks so perfectly to an ancient city's decay but because it speaks to many of us today.

# DAY 349
## Revelation 3:7–8

—⊶⊷—

Because you have limited strength, have kept My word, and have not denied My name, look, I have placed before you an open door that no one is able to close (v. 8).

—⊶⊷—

Scholars almost unanimously agree that the reference in Revelation 2:8 to the "little" or "limited" strength of the church in Philadelphia was not to spiritual strength, or Christ would not have placed the characteristic in context with such commendation. Christ never commends spiritual weakness. Rather, He views weakness as an opportunity to discover a divine strength beyond our imagination (2 Cor. 12:9–10). Bible commentators believe this referred to their diminutive size and small visible impact, to the fact that lower, less influential classes comprised the church in this city.

In our numbers-oriented society, we can hardly overestimate when we see ourselves as ineffective. I believe outright opposition can often be easier to bear than the thought of futility or incompetence. And don't think for a moment the enemy won't do everything he can to convince you that your efforts in Christ's name are in vain. Nothing is more destructive than feelings of uselessness and worthlessness. That's precisely why the enemy seeks every avenue to fuel and perpetuate them.

Beloved, each of us has a God-given need to matter. You are not self-centered and vain because you have that need; you are human. Sure, the things you and I do with this need can become extremely vain and self-centered, but the need itself is sacred. Fragrant flowers don't need someone to smell them to keep blooming. Lions don't kill their prey for significance—they're simply hungry. Only man yearns to matter.

God acknowledged this need immediately following our creation and before our fall into sin. Notice how He granted purpose to humans in each of these scriptural examples.

- He gave the assignment to be fruitful, fill the earth, and have dominion (Gen. 1:28).
- He gave Adam the charge to care for the garden (Gen. 2:15).
- He commissioned Adam to name the animals (Gen. 2:19).

God could have created the beasts of the field naturally subservient to humans. Instead, He acknowledged our God-given need to matter by telling us to rule over them and subdue them. Furthermore, God could have made the garden of Eden self-maintaining. Instead, He appointed Adam to work it and take care of it. God could have created the animals with names, but He knew Adam could use the challenge and the satisfaction that naming them would bring. In the same way, Eve received a purpose that granted significance. No one else was a suitable helper to Adam.

The Father desires for each of our lives to matter—to bring forth much fruit. The small, seemingly insignificant band of believers in Philadelphia may have been blind to the fruit of their own efforts, but Christ found them beyond rebuke. I think the key word in His commendation is the description He used in verse 10 for how they endured: "patiently." So often we are tempted to give up before the harvest comes.

Ecclesiastes 3:1 tells us, "There is an occasion for everything, and a time for every activity under heaven" (HCSB). God promised, "As long as the earth endures, seedtime and harvest, cold and heat, summer and winter, and day and night will not cease" (Gen. 8:22 HCSB). Though far less predictable than these natural seasons, we experience seasons spiritually as well. The church in Philadelphia had been in the seedtime season without a large harvest probably longer than they wished—yet they continued to endure patiently.

Do you happen to be frustrated by what appears to be a small return on much effort in a ministry opportunity? Keep in mind that God not only allows long seasons of seedtime but also sometimes *appoints* them to enhance the quality of eventual harvest. At times He actively tests our faithfulness in smaller things to see if we can handle bigger things. I hesitate to make this point, because "big" is not the goal; Christ revealed is the goal. However, if a high-volume ministry is one way God chooses to reveal His Son, those to whom He temporarily appoints them by His grace (1 Pet. 4:10) could undoubtedly describe countless appointments to small and frustrating "opportunities" along the way. In retrospect, most now recognize these as crucial tests.

I can remember pouring my heart into preparing several discipleship courses when only two or three people showed up. I sensed God asking me, "What are you going to do now? Cancel the class? Or give them no less than you would give if twenty-five people were here, eager to finish out the semester?" I am certain those were not only precious opportunities; they were tests. I also believe He tested me to see whether I would esteem the opportunity to teach Mother's Day Out or four-year-olds in Sunday school. Both extended the profound opportunity to mark young lives for eternity, yet some would be foolish enough to deem them unimportant.

Thankfully, we obviously don't have to be a genius or particularly gifted to pass God's tests because I certainly would have failed. God is primarily looking for faithfulness to fulfill whatever duty He has placed before us. He formed us to seek lives of purpose and, for those of us who follow His lead, to find them ultimately in Him alone.

# DAY 350
## Revelation 3:9–13

—◆◆◆—

I will make them come and bow down at your feet,
and they will know that I have loved you (v. 9).

—◆◆◆—

One of the meanest tricks Satan ever plays on us is to try convincing us God doesn't love us and that we're exerting all this energy and exercising all this faith for nothing: "Look at all you've done, and He doesn't even care! It's all a big joke!" Detect the smell of devil breath in a statement like that?

Drawn from this passage in Revelation 3, we discover that Satan used the Jews in Philadelphia to demoralize this small church, just as he uses countless puppets in our own lives and times to demoralize us. But Christ promised the church in this city that one day the very people who sneered at them would acknowledge something they would never have confessed on their own. In the end, they would be forced to admit just how much He loves them.

Beloved, you and I are not to be motivated by spite. At the same time, Jesus wants you to know that one day everyone will know how much He loves you. You have been unashamed of Him, and He most assuredly will prove unashamed of you.

What a show of His love, then, that Christ promised to make these over-comers pillars in the temple of God (v. 12). Philadelphia was a city under constant threat of earthquakes. The threat was especially vivid after a devastating earthquake in AD 17. Decades later, some historians say the church had already rebuilt their small sanctuary several times because of tremors. Often the only things left standing in a city lying in ruins are the pillars.

Hebrews 12:26–27 says God will shake both the heavens and the earth so that only that which cannot be shaken will remain. "Therefore, since we are receiving a kingdom that cannot be shaken, let us hold on to grace. By it, we may serve God acceptably, with reverence and awe; for our God is a consuming fire" (Heb. 12:28–29 HCSB).

Christ's promise to the overcomers was that they would be kept from the hour of trial coming upon the whole world, and they would stand like pillars in a kingdom that can never be shaken. Why? Because they were loved and, contrary to popular opinion, they chose to believe it. You, too, are loved, dear one. Let no one take your crown by convincing you otherwise.

# DAY 351
## Revelation 3:14–16

—∞∞∞—

I know your works, that you are neither cold nor hot.
I wish that you were cold or hot. So, because you are lukewarm . . .
I am going to vomit you out of My mouth (vv. 15–16).

—∞∞∞—

We can safely conclude that Christ would not prefer anyone to be spiritually "cold" toward Him rather than lukewarm, which is the way some have interpreted this passage. I believe Christ meant, "For crying out loud, be of one use or the other!" We have much to learn about this distinct city that will shed light on Christ's rebuke and exhortation.

Laodicea lay directly between two other cities, seven miles southeast of Hierapolis and less than ten miles north of Colossae. Hierapolis was famous for therapeutic hot springs. Colossae was known for sparkling cold waters, but ruins reveal a sophisticated six-mile-long aqueduct that drew water from other sources for Laodicea.

In 1961–63 a team of French archaeologists excavated a structure called a *nymphaeum* located practically in the center of the city. The square water basin had stone columns on two sides and two semicircular fountains attached to it.[81] The ornate fountains very likely stood as beautiful centerpieces in the city square. Characteristic of Laodicea, their beauty vastly exceeded their usefulness. You see, by the time the water was piped to the city from miles away, it was neither cold nor hot. You might easily imagine someone cupping her hands under the enticing waters to take a refreshing sip only to spit it out in disgust. Sound familiar? Hot water has therapeutic value, and nothing is like the refreshment of cold water, but lukewarm? If only I knew the Greek word for "yuck!"

Christ's vehement frustration with the church of Laodicea was that she'd be of some use! The last thing I want to tout is a works-centered faith, but we have been called to faith-centered works. Christ intends for us to be useful! Churches are meant to be viable, active forces in their communities.

We talked earlier about how each person's innate need to matter requires us to discover how our gifts and contributions can be useful. In the spirit of Christ's exhortation to Laodicea, anyone can offer a cold glass of water to the thirsty or a hot cup of tea to the hurting. Or how about a frozen casserole? Or a warm pound cake? At times of my life, nothing has ministered to me more than those two things! Christ exhorts His bride, "Be of use to my world!" At times therapeutic. At other times refreshing. Each of us can be hot *and* cold.

# DAY 352
## Revelation 3:17–22

———∞∞———

You say, "I'm rich; I have become wealthy, and need nothing," and you don't know that
you are wretched, pitiful, poor, blind, and naked (v. 17).

———∞∞———

The Laodiceans did what many people in our culture do today. They filled
their gaping need to matter with possessions, then gauged their usefulness by
their wealth. Praise God, neither then nor now can wealth state worth.

Save your breath trying to convince Laodicea, however. When Christ
drafted His letter to John, Laodicea was the capital of financial wizardry in Asia
Minor, a marvel of prosperity. She described herself as rich and in need of nothing (Rev. 3:17).

I discovered some interesting pieces of information that help explain the
audacity and laxity of the Laodicean church. In AD 26 the city placed a bid to the
Roman senate to build a temple to the Emperor Tiberius. They were denied on
the basis of inadequate resources. But their wealth so vastly increased over the
next several decades that by AD 60 after the devastation of an earthquake, they
didn't accept aid from Nero. They had plentiful resources to rebuild themselves.
(Do you hear the hints of independence?) In a nutshell, they thanked Rome but
assured them they didn't need a thing.

Money. The Laodiceans had it. They were in the lap of luxury and didn't
think they had a care in the world. Little did they know, however, that Christ was
walking among their lampstands.

The last portion of Psalm 62:10 speaks a good word to the Laodiceans—as
well as to us. "Though your riches increase, do not set your heart on them." I live
in a city that never expected to be known for the collapse of one of the biggest
financial empires in America. We learned the sobering lesson that billions of
dollars can be lost as instantly as hundreds. We cannot set our hearts securely on
riches no matter how vast.

In Matthew 13:22, Christ addressed another wealth-related issue readily
recognizable in Laodicea. He told of the person who received the Word but then
allowed "the worries of this age and the seduction of wealth" (HCSB) to choke the
fruitfulness out of it. Beloved, wealth by itself is not the issue. We serve a God
of infinite wealth who can distribute the riches of the world any way He sees fit.
Our troubled world certainly needs resources in the hands of wise people. The
problem is the "seduction" or "deceitfulness" of wealth.

Two of my precious friends have not been deceived by wealth. Frankly, I
never knew they were wealthy at all until someone told me. I've served in the
same church with them for several decades and have never met less pretentious,
more generous people. They are constantly involved in inner-city and foreign

missions. I'm convinced their only attitude toward their resources is that of stewards over a trust. While others in their position might have locked themselves behind gates and pretended much of the world wasn't starving to death, they threw themselves right in the middle of it.

The Laodicean church could have used my friends! This wealthy church somehow didn't grasp the principle in Luke 12:48 (KJV): "Unto whomsoever much is given, of him shall be much required." Their worth was so ingrained in their wealth that they honestly saw themselves as utterly independent. We "need nothing." Famous last words.

The older I get and the more my eyes open to the facts of life and ministry, the more my list of needs exceeds my list of wants. For instance, I need to have an active, effervescent daily relationship with Jesus Christ or I'm sunk. I need my husband's blessing. I need my coworkers. I need my church family. I need a friend I can trust. These are just a few necessities of life to me right now.

You see, one reason we readily give is because we, too, need. Taking stock of both our contributions and our needs helps guard us against self-deception. The Laodiceans had needs, too. They just didn't recognize them. But—praise be to God—their self-deceived indifference had not deemed them castaways. Christ had a stunning response and remedy to the Laodicean deception (v. 18).

His first prescription was "gold refined in the fire." Peter gives us a clear idea of what Christ meant. Peter wrote of "your faith—more valuable than gold" (1 Pet. 1:6–7 HCSB).

Christ's second prescription to Laodicea was "white clothes" to wear. The black wool fabric for which Laodicea was famous was the fashion rage all over that part of the world. He suggested they trade their fashions for purity. Ouch.

Jesus' final prescription was "ointment to spread on your eyes." Not only was Laodicea a marketing and financial capital, it also housed a well-known medical center. Ever the marketers, they were best known for Phrygian powder that was used to make salve for eye conditions. All the while, they were blind as bats and poor as beggars. I've been both.

One thing I've learned about God is that He is faithful in every way. He is faithful to forgive, redeem, bless, and provide. He is also faithful to chastise when His child won't readily turn from sin. Yes, the Laodiceans had a prescription, but Christ had no intention of letting them wait a month of Sundays to get it filled without consequences.

# DAY 353
## Revelation 4:1–6a

—⚬⚬⚬—

Also before the throne was something like a sea of glass, similar to crystal (v. 6a).

—⚬⚬⚬—

In reading Revelation's description of the throne room of God, please keep in mind that John related the completely unfamiliar through the familiar. Imagine, for example, escorting an Indian who had never ventured farther than the most primitive part of the Amazon through a tour of the state-of-the-art technology at NASA. When he returned to his fellow tribesmen, how would he describe jets or rockets? He'd probably have to begin his illustration by using birds as an example and try to stretch their imagination from there. Likewise, throughout much of Revelation, John employed known concepts to express images beyond our understanding. The throne of God is simply beyond anything we can imagine.

Yet Hebrews 4:14–16 says that because of Jesus, our great High Priest, we can approach His throne with confidence. No, none of us is without sin (1 John 1:8), but because Christ has become our atoning sacrifice, we need never fear approaching God with our confessions. He wants us to "receive mercy and find grace to help us" in our need (Heb. 4:16).

In the imagery of the throne room, I like to imagine God the Father catching those confessions in the palm of His mighty hand and casting them into the sea. What sea? Perhaps the one most conveniently located right in front of His throne. No matter how many confessions are made, this sea is never muddied by our sins. Rather, as God casts them into the sea, I like to imagine our sins instantly bleached into utter non-existence, swallowed in the depths of crystal-clear waters.

When it comes to dealing with your past sins, are you a deep-sea fisherman? Are you tempted by guilt, condemnation, and unbelief to dredge up old sins and agonize over them? Satan constantly volunteers to be our fishing guide. He even provides a handy lure to cause us to doubt God's forgiveness. How successful has he been with you?

I certainly have done some deep-sea fishing in my lifetime. But what a waste of time and energy—because when we're fishing in the right sea, our line will always come up bare. Anything we think we're seeing on the end of that line is a vain imagination. We won't even catch an old boot. Let's consider giving the enemy one instead.

# DAY 354
### Revelation 4:6b–11

The 24 elders fall down before the One seated on the throne, worship the One who lives forever and ever, [and] cast their crowns before the throne (v. 10).

Much of humanity's trouble stems from our naturally insatiable self-centeredness. We often see ourselves as the center of the universe and tend to describe all other components in reference to us rather than God. The human psyche almost invariably processes incoming information in relationship to its own ego. For example, if the news forecasts an economic slump, the natural hearer automatically processes what it could mean to self, how it affects me, my family, my situation in life.

While this response is natural, in perpetual practice this self-absorption is miserable. In some ways our egocentrism is a secret lust for omnipotence. We want to be our own god and have all power.

Our first reaction upon hearing this bit of truth might be to deny it—that we've never had a desire to be God. But how often do we take immediate responsibility for handling most of the problems in our midst? How often do we try changing the people we know and feeding our control addiction with the drug of manipulation? Simply put, we try to play God, and frankly, it's exhausting.

But thankfully, those of us who are redeemed are also given what 1 Corinthians 2:16 calls the "mind of Christ." Life takes on a far more accurate estimation and perspective when we learn to view it increasingly through the vantage point of the One who spoke it into existence.

Think of some of your greatest challenges. Picture them. Then go back and stamp the words "before the throne" in front of each of these challenges.

The heart of prayer is moving these very kinds of tests and trials from the insecurities and uncertainties of earth to the throne of God. Only then can they be viewed with dependable accuracy and boundless hope. Close your eyes and do your best to picture the glorious seraphim never ceasing to cry, "Holy, holy, holy!" Imagine the lightning emitting from the throne, and hear the rumblings and the thunder. Picture the elders overwhelmed by God's worthiness, casting their crowns before the throne. Approach the throne of grace with confidence, with eyes on Him, not on yourself. Our God is huge! Our God is able!

# DAY 355
## Revelation 5:1–4

—◆◆◆—

*I cried and cried because no one was found worthy
to open the scroll or even to look in it (v. 4).*

—◆◆◆—

We can't be certain what the scroll represents. One possibility is that it is like the one in Ezekiel's vision (Ezek. 2:9–10). That scroll contained words of lament and woe. Certainly the coming chapters announce woes, so the interpretation is plausible for the Revelation 5:1 scroll. But when Christ victoriously claims the scroll, the eruptions of praise cause me to wonder how the scroll can be associated with woes and laments alone. I tend to think the seals themselves involve wrath, but the words within unfold something glorious.

Interpreters pose another possibility—that the scroll represented the will or testament of God concerning the completion of all things on earth and the transition to all things in heaven. The ancient Romans sealed wills or testaments with six seals. A slight variation of this view compares the scene to the Roman law of inheritance. Some scholars believe the scroll is the title deed to earth.

It's all very interesting. And though I'm curious, I am comfortable not knowing the exact identity of the scroll because, whatever it is, it is in the hands of Christ. But I am touched beyond measure by John's response to what happens in verses 2 and 3, when the angel asks if anyone is "worthy to open the scroll and to break its seals" (HCSB). These events may not have happened over a simple matter of seconds. The verb tense of the Greek word for "proclaiming" may suggest the mighty angel could have repeated the question several times, scattering glances to and fro for someone who was worthy. The deafening silence that occurred when no one was able to answer the question only heightened the anxiety of those present. It certainly did for John. He himself admits that he "cried and cried."

His weeping reminds us that the power and presence of the Holy Spirit doesn't make us feel less. The Spirit brings life. Every one of John's senses was surely quickened by what he saw and heard. His response to the sight of the throne must have been indescribable awe. When he heard the angelic proclamation, a tidal wave of grief crashed against that reverent backdrop. Yet John was not too big a man to show both ends of this emotional spectrum. I like that about him.

## DAY 356
### Revelation 5:5–14

——∞∞∞——

Blessing and honor and glory and dominion to the One seated
on the throne, and to the Lamb, forever and ever! (v. 13).

——∞∞∞——

Genesis 1:24–25 tells of the creation of animal life. In the midst of countless creatures, hoofed and not, God created the lamb. I happen to think God is the sentimental type. It shows throughout Scripture, and we as sentimental people were created in His image. I don't think He created the lamb with little notice. He knew the profound significance He would cause this small, helpless creature to have. Adam wasn't created until after the animals. God saved what He considered His best for last. But I think the fact that a lamb was created before a man is quite fitting because throughout the Old Testament, man would require a heap of them.

After sin cost Adam and Eve paradise, "the LORD God made clothing out of skins for Adam and his wife, and He clothed them" (Gen. 3:21 HCSB). This is the first reference to a sacrificial death. Since God dressed them with a skin, we know an animal perished for them to be covered. We have no way of knowing whether the animal was a lamb, but I can hardly picture it any other way.

Genesis 4:4 records the first sacrificial offering. "Abel also presented an offering—some of the firstborn of his flock and their fat portions" (HCSB). Cain brought an offering of fruit, but the Lord looked with favor on Abel's offering.

Not coincidentally, from the moment in Scripture that life appears outside the garden, we see sacrificial offerings. God wasn't partial to Abel. He was partial to Abel's offering. When not distinguished otherwise, a flock almost always refers to sheep in Scripture. From the Old Testament to the New, the Lord looks with favor upon those symbolically covered by the blood of the Lamb. Verse 7 hints that Cain knew the right thing to do and had the same chance to bring a sacrificial offering. The basic tenet of all biblical rebellion is refusing the blood of the lamb.

Genesis 22 contains the account of Abraham's willingness to sacrifice his son Isaac in obedience to God. Far from coincidence, the first time in Scripture the word "lamb" is used is in Genesis 22. Fittingly, the words "sacrifice" and "worship" are introduced in the same chapter, and the word "love" appears for only the second time.

Just before Abraham actually killed his son as an offering to God, the angel of the Lord intervened. God provided a substitute sacrifice in the form of a ram caught in the thicket. I was thrilled when I read the following definition of *ayil*, the word for "ram": "a male sheep generally more aggressive and protective of the flock." Jesus our Lamb is indeed aggressively protective of the flock—even to the spilling of His blood. Galatians calls this drama the gospel preached in advance to Abraham (Gal. 3:8; Rom. 9:7). Glory!

We cannot find a more perfect Old Testament picture of the blood of the sacrificial lamb than the one that's recorded in Exodus 12. The final plague against Egypt came in the form of the death of the first-born. Every Hebrew family found protection through the Passover lamb's blood on the doorpost.

So the concept of substitutionary atonement that unfolded immediately outside the Garden of Eden echoed like a sermon from Isaac's Mt. Moriah, dripped from the doorposts of captive Israel, and remained constant throughout the Old Testament. Innumerable animals were sacrificed throughout the centuries at the altars of the tabernacle and the temple. So many were sacrificed at the dedication of Solomon's temple that they couldn't be counted.

Yet Israel repeatedly fell into idolatry. And after sending the prophets with warnings, Old Testament Scripture comes to an abrupt halt— but not without a promise: "Look, I am going to send you Elijah the prophet before the great and awesome Day of the Lord comes" (Mal. 4:5 HCSB). According to Matthew 11:12–14, John the Baptist fulfilled this prophecy. Look at the first words from John the Baptist's mouth when he saw Jesus: "Here is the Lamb of God, who takes away the sin of the world!" (John 1:29 HCSB).

Luke 22 records the last supper Christ shared with His disciples. Because a Jewish day begins just after sundown and lasts until the next, Christ was actually crucified on the very same "day" they ate their final meal together. According to Luke 22:14 that day was when Jesus' hour had come.

Oh, do you realize we've only seen a glimpse, yet look at the consistency! A lamb, the lamb, the Lamb! So that we wouldn't miss the woolen thread, this book of the Bible that brings all things to completion shouts this title like triumphant bursts from a ram's horn. Not once. Not twice. But twenty-eight times! The Lamb slain from the foundation of the world for the salvation of the world.

Man can shake his arrogant fist all he wants, but he will never shake God. The plan is firm. No plan B exists. All things are going just as He knew they would. We look around us and hang our heads over the miserable estate of this lost, depraved world. And all the while God sits upon His throne saying, "As long as man has breath, I have a Lamb."

# DAY 357
## Revelation 14:1–5

—◈◈◈—

They sang a new song before the throne . . . but no one could learn
the song except the 144,000 who had been redeemed from the earth (v. 3).

—◈◈◈—

I am not a singer, but I dearly love to sing praise songs to my God. My favorite songs are the ones that become "mine" over time as I sing them to God through the filter of my own experience and affection.

Nothing provokes a new song in my heart like a fresh surge of hope in a wilderness season. The song "Shout to the Lord" will forever be special to me because I first heard it at a time of deep personal suffering. The words came to my soul from God as hope that I would survive . . . and even thrive once again. Allow me to use this song as an illustration for Revelation 14:3. First I "heard" the new song, then I "learned" it. My motivation to "learn" it came through its voice to my experience in that difficult but strangely beautiful season with my God.

John "heard" the new song, but "no one could learn the song" except the 144,000 who had been redeemed from the earth. The Greek word for "new" in reference to the new song in Revelation 14:3 implies new in quality as opposed to number. In other words, the song wasn't new like a new release. The song of the 144,000 was "new" because it had an entirely different quality from anything they'd sung before. In other words, it meant something to them no other song had ever meant. Why couldn't anyone else learn it? Because no one else had ever lived it. Out of their unique experience, God gave them a song that only they could learn.

Psalm 40 tells us God gave David a new song when He lifted him out of the slimy pit. I'd like to suggest that each of us who is willing can also receive a new song from God that arises in our souls out of hardship's victories—not necessarily in musical notes but in fresh truths engraved on the heart. These are precious gifts that eventually come to those who keep the faith and wait to see God redeem great difficulty. These songs can be "heard" by others, but they cannot be "learned" secondhand. Songs of the heart are only learned through personal faith experience—through hurts, losses, and failures that have been handed over to Jesus to heal and transform. And once we learn the songs, no one can take them from us.

# DAY 358
## Revelation 15:1–8

—◦◦◦◦—

Then I saw another great and awe-inspiring sign in heaven: seven angels with the seven last plagues, for with them, God's wrath will be completed (v. 1).

—◦◦◦◦—

Perhaps the truest words that ever fall from tainted human lips are these: God is faithful. Indeed He is. What may trouble us is that He is *always* faithful. In other words, God always does what He insists He will whether we like it or not.

The idealist in me wishes the wrath of God didn't even exist and would never be unleashed. Then the realist in me . . .

- reads accounts of unspeakable cruelties and abuses to children;
- reviews a human history blighted by war crimes and bloody crusades;
- hears the name of God mocked, profaned, and publicly derided;
- listens to the arrogant who have convinced themselves they are gods;
- sees the violence bred by hatred, ignorance, and prejudice;
- watches princes of the earth lay bricks on an unseen but very present Tower of Babel.

I look around me and shudder with horror over and over again, asking, "Where is the fear of God?" Then I shake my head and wonder what kind of inconceivable power God must use to restrain Himself.

I don't even have to look as far as the world. At times in my life I've looked no further than my own mirror or my own church and wondered the words of Lamentations 3:22, "Because of the Lord's great love we are not consumed." I have said to Him more times than I can count, "Lord, why You do not rend this earth and swallow up Your own people, not to mention this godless world, is beyond me." Why does God continue to put up with a world that increasingly mocks Him? Why does He wait? For all of time, the most succinct answer to those questions can be found in 2 Peter 3:9: "The Lord does not delay His promise, as some understand delay, but is patient with you, not wanting any to perish, but all to come to repentance" (HCSB).

In some ways the wrath of God will simply finish off what man has started. I am convinced that mankind will do a proficient job of nearly destroying himself and his own planet based on the wars and conflicts prophesied in Scripture. God's Word promises a new heaven and a new earth but not until this one is destroyed. Matthew 24 prophesies increasing wickedness and destruction with a mounting strength and frequency of birth pains. Toward the very end of this age, God will allow the full measure of all permissible wrath to be poured out upon this earth: the wrath of man (never underestimate it), the unholy wrath of Satan, and the holy wrath of God. No wonder this time of great tribulation will be like no other.

The wrath described in the book of Revelation unfolds in a somewhat mysterious sequence: seals, trumpets, and bowls. The seals introduce the trumpets, and the trumpets usher in the bowls. To call this "unsettling" is an understatement. My horror is primarily for those who refuse to believe, of course, because in 1 Thessalonians 1:10, Paul called Jesus the one "who rescues us from the coming wrath."

I am not implying that believers won't go through terrible times. The Word clearly states we will (2 Tim. 3:1), and many Christians already are. My point is that the wrath of God described in the book of Revelation is not toward the redeemed. They will either be delivered *from* it or *through* it.

God will reveal Himself in countless ways toward the end of times, pouring out His Spirit, His wonders, and His mercies. Those mercies, however, are dealt according to demand. In other words, some people respond to *tender* mercies. Others don't respond until God shows *severe* mercies. Others don't respond at all. Never forget that God wants to save people and not destroy them. During the last days, the heavens will show so many signs, and evangelists will preach so powerfully that I am convinced people will practically have to work at refusing Him. Yet many tragically will.

The apostle Paul warned that "because of your hardness and unrepentant heart you are storing up wrath for yourself in the day of wrath, when God's righteous judgment is revealed" (Rom. 2:5 HCSB). People will not refuse Him because God didn't love them or make provision for them. Beloved, please hear my heart. The wrath of God cannot be separated from His character and person. In other words, even in His unleashed wrath, God cannot be less than who He is. God is holy. He is good. He is love. God is righteous, and God is right. The Judge will judge, but His judgments are always based on truth (Rom. 2:2).

Ours is also a God of inconceivable compassion, forgiveness, and mercy. God's heart is neither mean nor unjust. He is holy. And beloved, the holy God will judge this world. The day of the Lord will come, and none will doubt He is God. He will not be mocked. He'd have to be untrue to His own character to do otherwise.

# DAY 359
## Revelation 19:1–10

———⊗⊗⊗———

The marriage of the Lamb has come, and His wife has prepared herself.
She was permitted to wear fine linen, bright and pure (vv. 7–8).

———⊗⊗⊗———

As I was preparing for our twentieth wedding anniversary, for the life of me I could not think of what I wanted to get my husband. He's a very sentimental man. You have to get him something sentimental because if he can afford it, he already owns anything he wants. So I just said, "God, you need to tell me what I can get my man. I need a really great idea." Honestly, I prayed and prayed over this. Then God began suggesting something to my heart.

He started bringing to my mind the early part of our marriage and the pain of my wedding day. I don't know how to explain this to you, but trust me when I say that it was an extremely hard day for me. I didn't really understand why until many, many years later. I was feeling so much shame on my wedding day because it was a day I was supposed to feel beautiful. And I did not feel beautiful.

I had even gone to a lot of trouble to make absolutely sure that I had an off-white dress instead of a white one, because I didn't want to be a lie. Some of you are already hurting because you know what I'm talking about. It's a horrible feeling. Nothing about that day seemed beautiful to me.

When I was a little girl, I had pictured that when I got married I would have a huge wedding portrait, and it would hang over our blazing fireplace. Well, the nearest thing we had to a fireplace was a heater in the bathroom. And I didn't even have money enough for a photographer. I just spent the bare minimum. I didn't even buy my dress; I just rented it. You know, it just was not the kind of day you picture.

So as I contemplated our twentieth anniversary, the Lord began scratching at this a little bit. He said, "You know, Beth," and of course He was speaking to my heart, "you never did get that picture made."

"What picture?"

"That wedding portrait."

"Well, it's a little too late now, isn't it?"

"Who said?"

The Lord put it on my heart that it was time. He said, "My darlin', we have done so much work. I have restored you. And it is time for you to put on a white wedding gown and get your picture taken for your husband."

So I called a friend of mine who's a makeup artist in Houston, a very godly young woman. I knew she would have a fit. She squealed on the phone and jumped up and down. I said, "You can't tell anyone, Shannon. This is our secret." She said, "I'll set up everything. You just show up and I'll have it all ready."

That's exactly what I did. And I'm going to tell you something, she hid me in a room and would not let me see a mirror. She had my dress sparkling white from head to toe. Zipped that thing up nice and tight. Did my makeup. Did my hair. Put on my veil. Then she pulled me out and brought me in front of the mirror. And I nearly died.

I couldn't even recognize myself. The photographer was so tender that his eyes were continually filled with tears. He said, "I've got to be honest with you. I've never taken a picture of a bride this old." Sheepishly catching his *faux pas*, he said, "That's not what I mean—I mean one that's been married for so long." He was right. This was a forty-one-year-old bride who had been married for twenty years.

I had the picture placed in the most ornate gold frame, 20 x 24. Then I had one made for each of my daughters. I wrote the same letter to Keith and the girls, explaining what the portrait meant to me.

The night of our anniversary, I had the girls stay with us, and I presented Keith with this picture, then presented their pictures to them. They all read their letters at the same time. My husband began to weep. He stood up with that picture, and he began walking all over the house, holding it up to places on the wall.

He would stop at one place and shake his head no, then stop at another and shake his head no. Finally he walked right over to a particular part of the wall. The girls and I caught our breath because we knew what he was looking at. He set the picture down. Then gathering his courage, he pulled his trophy deer off the wall.

As I live and breathe, he had tears streaming down his cheeks, and I thought, "He's crying over that deer." But he hung that picture up right there, and it still hangs there today. He stepped back and said, "That is the trophy of my life." A restored bride. And that is what every single one of us can be—fully restored, fully prepared. For our Groom.

# DAY 360
## Revelation 19:11–21

❦

Then I saw heaven opened, and there was a white horse! Its rider is called Faithful and
True, and in righteousness He judges and makes war (v. 11).

❦

When I first wrote this little piece of creative writing several years ago, I
really thought I understood from Revelation 19 that the wedding supper would
precede Jesus' second coming. But now that I look at the text, I'm not sure of that.
It could be that it comes after, but I wrote this with the first understanding. It's
just a fictional writing anyway. I share the final portion of it with you just to get
your mind going.

The horse's coat was white with a luster like pearls. His mane was strands of
gold. His eyes were like wine. His muscles ridged under his coat, displaying his
impeccable condition. The Groom stared at him with approval, then smiled with
familiarity as His hand stroked his mighty neck. Two cherubim brought forth
a wooden chest laden with gold and brilliant jewels. Saints covered their eyes
from the blinding light as they lifted the lid. The dazzling radiance was veiled as
they brought forth a crimson robe from within and placed it upon the Groom's
shoulders. Gold tassels were tied around His neck, and the seraph spread forth
His train. The words were embroidered in deep purple, "King of Kings and Lord
of Lords." His foot went in the stirrup, and the Faithful and True mounted His
horse. The beast dipped his head as if to bow, then lifted it with an inexpressible
assumption of responsibility. The Groom gently tugged the reins to the right and
the animal turned with exemplary obedience.

Suddenly, a sound erupted like rolling thunder. The earth rumbled beneath
their feet. The walls of the banquet hall gave way with a stunning thud. And
encircling them were horses no man could count, winged and ready for flight.
The four creatures—one with a face like a lion, one like an ox, one like a man, and
one like a flying eagle—flew over the heads of the saints and sang the anthem,
"All rise!" Each saint, dressed in white linen, rose from his chair and mounted
his horse. The attentions of every saint were quickened by the Groom. His back
still turned. His horse made ready. Suddenly, a vapor seeped from the ground
and covered the hooves of the horse of Faithful and True. As the vapor rose to
His thighs, the fog became a cloud enveloping the Rider inch by inch. Brilliance
overtook Him, and He became as radiant as the sun. So great was His glory, the
cloud rose to His shoulders and covered His head to shield the eyes of the saints.

The familiar surroundings of heaven were suddenly transformed, and the
sky appeared under His feet. A deafening sound emitted from the middle of
heaven like the slow rending of a heavy veil. The sky beneath their feet rolled by

like a scroll, and the inhabitants of heaven were suspended in the earth's atmosphere. The planet was their destiny. The Groom was their cue. The cloudy pillar that enveloped Him would plot their course.

With swiftness the cloud descended toward the Earth. The horses behind Him kept perfect cadence. The Earth grew larger as they made their final approach, and oceans could be distinguished from the nations. The Earth turned until Jerusalem faced upward. The cloudy pillar circled widely to the right for the Rider's eastward arrival.

The sun interrupted the night as it rose upon the city of Zion and awakened every inhabitant in the land. The rays that poured through their windows were unlike those of any other morning. All who saw it sensed the imposing arrival of the supernatural. The wicked inhabitants of Jerusalem's houses, those who had forced the people of God from their homes, shielded their eyes as they filled the city streets. All of Israel was awakened, and the valleys were filled with people gazing upward as much as their vision would permit to something awesomely beyond terrestrial. Emaciated humans filtered one by one from every cave and crevice—those who had not taken the mark of the beast. Their eyes tried to adjust to such sudden and abnormal gusts of light after hiding in the darkness for so long. Every eye looked upon the amazing cloudy pillar as it made its approach just east of the city of Zion.

The cloud stopped midair.

Suddenly the divine veil began to roll upward inch by inch, exposing first only the hooves of the great white horse then the feet of the Rider. They looked like burning brass in the stirrups. His crimson robe was exposed little by little until it seemed to blanket the sky. His name ascended above all names. The cloud lifted above His shoulder, and the knowledge of God was unveiled in the face of Jesus Christ. His eyes burned like fire into every heart. Those who had taken the mark of the beast ran for their lives, shoving the people of God out of the way as they took cover in the caves. The people of God's covenant and those who had come to their aid remained in the light, entranced by the glorious sight. Moaning filled the air. The Rider on the white horse dismounted His beast, and His feet touched down on the Mount of Olives. The earth quaked with indescribable force. And all who were hiding lost their cover.

The large brown eyes of one small boy remained fixed upon the sight. The whiteness of his teeth contrasted with the filth covering his face as he broke into an inexperienced smile. He reached over and took his mother's bony hands from her face and held them gently. "Look, Mom, no more crying. Surely that is our God. We trusted in Him and He saved us." Even so, Lord Jesus, come quickly.

# DAY 361
## Revelation 20:1–6

---

I saw an angel coming down from heaven with the key to the abyss and a great chain
in his hand. He seized . . . Satan and bound him for 1,000 years (vv. 1–2).

---

What irony that there are references to a "great chain" and being "set free"
right here in passages prophesying the devil's future. Scholars are very divided
over the meaning of the 1,000-year time reference in verse 2. But no matter the
time frame, Satan will be bound. That's all that matters.

And I for one couldn't be happier that the means the Lord uses to bind him
is a great chain. How appropriate! Some may wonder why God will bother chain-
ing him for a time rather than simply casting him immediately into the lake of
fire. Beloved, as far as I'm concerned, the last days will be high time for Satan to
be bound in chains! For all of us who have cried, "How long, O Sovereign Lord,
until You avenge our bondage?" we will be able to enjoy watching him see how
chains feel. In fact, I hope the "great chain" is made from all the ones that have
fallen off our ankles!

I want Satan to experience the same sense of powerlessness with which he
deceived many of us—the same powerlessness we felt when seeing others who
were free yet not knowing for the life of us how to become one of them. Praise
God for truth that sets us free! Satan tried his hardest to keep me bound and to
destroy my life, my family, my testimony, and my ministry, but God defeated
him by the power of His outstretched arm. The future will show Satan not only
defeated but his wickedness toward us avenged. I suspect you feel the same way,
that you share my glee at seeing him get what he has coming to him—and more!

What will the world be like while Satan is in chains? Based on my own
personal study of last things, I tend to think the period of Satan's bondage in the
abyss coincides with the kingdom of Christ on earth, a kingdom characterized
by peace, righteousness, and security. Keep in mind, however, that faithful students of God's Word see a variety of ways to understand the passage. God will
accomplish His will in His own way regardless of opinion. But when all is done,
we will probably all stand with our mouths open in wonder.

And Satan, well—his mouth we won't have to worry about anymore.

# DAY 362
Revelation 20:7–15

∞

Then I saw a great white throne and One seated on it. Earth and heaven
fled from His presence, and no place was found for them (v. 11).

∞

Based on my understanding of Scripture and the final judgments, only the
lost will stand at the great white throne. This seat of judgment seems to differ
from the one described in both 1 Corinthians 3:10–15 and 2 Corinthians 5:1–10.
Those who know Christ will stand before the judgment seat of Christ where
those who have served Him lovingly and obediently will receive rewards. The
judgment seat for the saved will not be a place of condemnation (Rom. 8:1).

Our passages in Revelation, however, describe a very different scene. The
great white throne appears to be a seat upon which only condemnation takes
place. Every person who has refused God will stand before Him on this dreadful
day. Though the earth and sky will try to flee from His awesome presence, those
who have refused God will have no place to run. I am convinced, in fact, that
Revelation 20:13 suggests differing levels of punishment according to the depths
and lengths of the evil accomplished by each person. Why would I have ever
thought otherwise? Is our God not just? Does He not look upon the individual
hearts and deeds of every responsible man and woman? The lake of fire will be
a place of torment for every inhabitant, but I believe Scripture clearly teaches
that punishment will vary according to each person's deeds. The Righteous Judge
knows every thought, and He rightly discerns every motive of our hearts.

Though planet Earth now bulges with billions of people, God still breathes
life into each being, one at a time. We were fashioned for God and designed to
seek Him. He created a universe and an order with the divine purpose of bearing
constant witness to His existence. Heaven unceasingly declares His glory, and all
who truly seek Him find Him.

Not one person's absence from heaven will go unnoticed by God. Not one
will get past God haphazardly. Not one will accidentally get swept away in a sea
of nameless souls. God is not careless. He intimately knows every soul that will
refuse to know Him. Because He created us for fellowship, God's judgments
cannot be rendered with cold, sterile detachment. For God so loved the world
that He sent His Son to seek and to save the lost. Though none can refuse to be
seen, many will incomprehensibly refuse to be "found."

# DAY 363
### Revelation 21:1–8

---

I also saw the Holy City, new Jerusalem, coming down out of heaven from God,
prepared like a bride adorned for her husband (v. 2).

---

I am confident that most of us Gentiles cannot relate to the attachment many Jews through the centuries have felt toward their homeland. Even those whose feet never touched the Holy Land yearned for it like a lost child longs for its mother.

I saw this peculiar bond just weeks ago in the face of my Hebrew friend and ancient lands guide, Arie. He and his family are now residents of Tel Aviv, but his heart never departs Jerusalem. The turmoil erupting within and around Jerusalem doesn't just concern or upset him. It brings him pain. I asked him how he felt about the ongoing crises in the Holy Land. As I witnessed the agony in his face, I sorrowed that I had asked something so obviously intimate. I consider myself very patriotic, yet I had to acknowledge that I knew nothing of his attachment to his own homeland.

If Arie and other Jews through the ages have experienced an indescribable attachment to the Holy City, try to imagine the strength of John's ties. He grew up on the shores of Galilee at the peak of Jerusalem's splendor since the days of Solomon. Herod's temple was one of the greatest wonders of John's world. No Jew could behold her splendor without marveling. Even weeping.

John knew every wall and gate of the Holy City. He walked the lengths and breadths with the Savior Himself. He sat near Him on the Mount of Olives, overlooking its beauty. John was also part of the generation who witnessed the total destruction in AD 70. By the time Jerusalem fell, John probably was already stationed in Ephesus, but the news traveled fast, and the sobs echoed louder with every mile. The grief of the diaspora mixed with the unreasonable guilt of not having died with the city surely shook their homesick souls.

Then how his heart must have leapt upon seeing the new Jerusalem! There it was! Not just restored but created anew with splendor beyond compare. I wonder if John was weeping at the sight. Some people say that we won't be able to cry in the new heavens and earth. Clearly we get at least one last good cry, though, since God will wipe away every tear! I cannot imagine that I will see my Christ, my God, and His heavenly kingdom with dry eyes. Our last tears, however, will no longer be those shed in mourning.

# DAY 364
## Revelation 21:9–21

—∞∞∞—

The city wall had 12 foundations, and on them
were the 12 names of the Lamb's 12 apostles (v. 14).

—∞∞∞—

Throughout our various looks at Revelation over these many days and weeks, we have preoccupied ourselves with what John saw, beginning with the moment a loud voice sounded behind him like a trumpet, saying, "Write on a scroll what you see." Let's now take one last glimpse at a detail in the new Jerusalem that might have had a fairly profound impact on John—the sight of the heavenly city's foundations, upon which were written the names of the twelve apostles.

Beloved, do you realize that among them John saw his own name? In the days he remained on this earth, can you imagine what kinds of thoughts he had as he recaptured that sight in his memory? I have no idea what being one of Jesus' apostles was like, but I don't think they felt superhuman or vaguely worthy of their calling. I'm not even sure those original disciples ever grasped that what they were doing would make a world-changing impact. I can't picture them thinking, "What I'm doing this moment will go down in history and be recorded in the eternal annals of glory." I think they probably got down on themselves just like you and I do. I also think they were terribly overwhelmed at the prospect of reaching their world with the gospel of Christ and seeing only handfuls of converts most of the time.

Days and months later, when John stared at that wall and its foundations again in his memory, can't you imagine he was nearly overcome that God esteemed them? Don't you think he marveled that the plan had worked . . . considering the mortal agents Christ had chosen to use?

Every day I deal with a measure of low self-esteem in ministry. I never feel up to the task. Never smart enough. Never strong enough. Never prayed up enough. Never prepared enough. Do you feel the same way? Then perhaps you also feel the same flood of emotions when this truth washes over you: God loves us. He prepares an inconceivable place for those who receive His love. He highly esteems those who choose to believe His call over the paralyzing screams of their own insecurities. No, our names won't be written on the foundations of the new Jerusalem, but they are engraved in the palms of His hands.

# DAY 365
## Revelation 21:22–27

———

I did not see a sanctuary in it, because the Lord God the Almighty
and the Lamb are its sanctuary (v. 22).

———

Seven blessings are pronounced during a Jewish wedding ceremony, each of which comes from the dignitaries at the wedding, my friend Arie tells me. Usually the rabbi begins it. Then maybe a father-in-law, maybe an uncle, maybe an older brother. But there are seven blessings spoken. And the seventh blessing is always the blessing over Jerusalem. I find this to be very intriguing. The blessing goes something like this: "Bless You, Lord, the Builder of Jerusalem, who will rebuild the temple one day."

Then what do you suppose they do? What is the part you and I probably know the best? Right—they break the glass.

Arie said, "There are some who think that the broken glass just begins the great ceremony, but that is not what it's about. The breaking of the glass is to bring them to a very sober time of thinking that in the midst of great celebration, we must remember"—and I'm quoting his exact words—"that our joy is incomplete."

I said, "Okay, Arie. What makes our joy incomplete?" (Remember all the times that Christ said, "Make My joy complete"?) "What makes our joy incomplete, Arie?"

"Two things," he said. "The first thing is that some of our loved ones are missing from the wedding, those who have already died. The second one is because there is no temple for now in Jerusalem."

But for us as New Testament believers, both of those longings have been satisfied. Regarding our loved ones: those in Christ will be present at the wedding supper of the Lamb. And regarding the temple: well, no, there's not a temple in this new Jerusalem. But that's okay, "because the Lord God Almighty and the Lamb are its temple" (Rev. 21:22). Who needs a place of worship when the object of our worship is right here before us, not seen through representation and symbolism, but here for the enjoying?

Isn't that enormous? No more sadness, reflection, regret, or mourning. No more holes in our happiness—having someone who's not there to share it with, a shoe waiting to drop. No more taking worship to a level that only makes our heart ache for more. Do you understand that our joy gets to be complete, just as John had reported, just as Jesus had said?

## DAY 366
### Revelation 22:1–21

—&infin;—

I, John, am the one who heard and saw these things (v. 8).

—&infin;—

Face-to-face. I can't think of a more fitting focus for our last few moments together. I don't want you to miss the most beautiful statement in the final chapter of Scripture: "They will see His face" (Rev. 22:4 hcsb). For many of us, the very sight of Christ's face will be heaven enough. Everything else is the river overflowing its banks.

Until then we who are redeemed are like spirit-people wrapped in prison walls of flesh. Our view is impaired by the steel bars of mortal vision. We are not unlike Moses, who experienced God's presence but could not see His face. To him and to all confined momentarily by mortality, God has said, "You cannot see My face, for no one can see Me and live" (Exod. 33:20 hcsb).

When all is said and done, we who are alive in Christ will indeed see His face and live. Happily ever after. I can hardly wait!

Yet right this moment I am absorbed by the thought of someone else seeing that face. Someone I've grown to love and appreciate so deeply through the months of study for this book. Several of the early church fathers plant the apostle John back in the soil of Ephesus again after the conclusion of his exile on the Island of Patmos. I wonder what kinds of thoughts swirled through his mind as the boat returned him to the shores of Asia Minor. I've made this trip by sea, and though it is beautiful, it is not brief. As his thinning gray hair blew across his face, he had time to experience a host of emotions. We have gotten to know him well. What kinds of things do you imagine he thought and felt on the ride back to Ephesus?

John lived to be a very old man. We have no idea how many years he lived beyond his exile. The earliest historians indicate, however, that the vitality of his spirit far exceeded the strength of his frame. His passionate heart continued to beat wildly for the Savior he loved so long. John took personally the words God poured through him. They did not simply run through the human quill and spill on the page. John's entire inner man was indelibly stained by *rhema* ink. In closing, read some of the words obviously inscribed on his heart from that last earthly night with Jesus:

> *This is My command: love one another as I have loved you. No one has greater love than this, that someone would lay down his life for his friends. You are My friends if you do what I command you. I do not call you slaves anymore, because a slave doesn't know what his master is doing. I have called you friends, because I have made known*

*to you everything I have heard from My Father. You did not choose Me, but I chose you. I appointed you that you should go out and produce fruit and that your fruit should remain, so that whatever you ask the Father in My name, He will give you. This is what I command you: love one another (John 15:12–17 HCSB).*

John lived the essence of these verses. He ended his life a true "friend" of Christ, for he took on God's interests as surely as Elisha took on the cloak of Elijah. Early church fathers reported that long after John lacked the strength to walk, younger believers carried the beloved disciple in a chair through crowds gathered for worship. His final sermons were short and sweet: "My little children, love one another!" He poured his life into love. Christ's love. The focus of his final days captures the two concepts I've learned above all others in this journey:

• Christ calls His beloved disciples to forsake ambition for affection. John moved from his "pillar" position in the Jerusalem church to relative obscurity. Better to pour out our lives in places unknown than to become dry bones in the places we've always been.

• Only disciples who are convinced they are beloved will in turn love beyond themselves. Actively embracing the lavish love of God is our only means of extending divine love to injured hearts. We simply cannot give what we do not have.

Don't think for a moment the Savior wasn't nearby when the sounds of an old Son of Thunder grew faint and then silent. After all, John was the solitary remaining apostle who could make the claims of his own pen: "That which was from the beginning, which we have heard, which we have seen with our eyes, which we have looked at and our hands have touched—this we proclaim concerning the Word of life" (1 John 1:1). "We" had turned to "I," and soon "I" would turn to "they."

Somehow I picture him in his death much like he had been in his life. To me, the scene that captures the beloved disciple most is recorded in John 13:23. The event occurred at a certain table decades earlier. The Amplified Bible says it best. "One of His disciples, whom Jesus loved [whom He esteemed and delighted in] was reclining [next to Him] on Jesus' bosom" (John 13:23). Yes, I like to think that John died just as he lived. Nestled close. Reclining on the breast of an unseen but very present Savior, John's weary head in His tender arms. The Spirit and the bride said, "Come!" And in the distance could be heard a gentle thunder.

# NOTES

1. Rabbi Solomon Ganzfried, trans. Hyman E. Goldin, *Code of Jewish Law* (New York: Hebrew Publishing Company, 1993), I, 1.

2. Ibid., IV, 43.

3. Ibid., IV, 44.

4. Ibid., II, 62.

5. Ibid., I, 27.

6. Warren Baker, general editor, *The Complete Word Study Old Testament* (Chattanooga, Tenn.: AMG Publishers, 1994), 2372.

7. Trent Butler et al, editors, *Holman Bible Dictionary* (Nashville: Holman Bible Publishers, 1991), 774.

8. Baker, 2363.

9. Baker, 2306

10. Baker, 2318

11. James Strong, *Strong's Exhaustive Concordance* (Grand Rapids, Mich.: Baker Book House, 1982), 95.

12. Butler et al, 21.

13. Baker, 106.

14. Baker, 2300.

15. Butler et all, 946.

16. Baker, 2326.

17. Butler et al, 45.

18. Baker, 86.

19. Baker, 2339.

20. Baker, 2340.

21. Butler et al, 553.

22. Butler et al, 553.

23. Baker, 2344.

24. Baker, 2375.

25. Baker, 2317.

26. Baker, 2306.

27. R. Alan Culpepper, *John, Son of Zebedee* (Minneapolis: First Fortress Press, 2000), 7.

28. Matthew Henry, *Matthew to John: Matthew Henry's Commentary on the Whole Bible*, vol. 5 (Grand Rapids: Fleming H. Revell Company, 1985), 456.

29 Frank Gaebelein and J. D. Douglas, *The Expositor's Bible Commentary*, vol. 8 (Grand Rapids: Zondervan Publishing, 1984), 629.

30. Colin Brown, *The New International Dictionary of the New Testament Theology* (Grand Rapids, Mich.: Zondervan, 1986), 614.

31. Beth Moore, *Things Pondered: From the Heart of a Lesser Woman* (Nashville: B&H Publishing Group, 1997), 7.

32. Robert H. Stein, *Jesus the Messiah: A Survey of the Life of Christ* (Downers Grove, Ill.: InterVarsity Press, 1996), 106.

33 Ronald F. Youngblood and F. F. Bruce, eds. *Nelson's New Illustrated Bible Dictionary* (Nashville: Thomas Nelson, 1999), 473.

34. Dr. Chuck Lynch, *I Should Forgive, But . . .* (Nashville: Word, 1998), 33–34.

35. Matthew Henry, *Matthew Henry's Commentary on the Whole Bible* (New York: Fleming H. Revell), 634.

36. Francis Frangipane, *Exposing the Accuser of the Brethren* (Cedar Rapids, Iowa: Arrow Publications, 1991), 37.

37. Spiros Zodhiates, ed. T*he Hebrew-Greek Key Study Bible* (Chattanooga, Tenn.: AMG Publishers, 1966), 1647.

38. Jim Cymbala, *Fresh Wind, Fresh Fire* (Grand Rapids, Mich.: Zondervan, 1997), 19.

39. Kevin Howard and Marvin Rosenthal, *The Feasts of the Lord* (Orlando, Fla.: Zion's Hope, Inc., 1997), 55.

40. Ibid., 57.

41. Frank E. Gaebelein, ed. *The Expositor's Bible Commentary* (Grand Rapids, Mich.: Zondervan, 1984), 1049.

42. Spiros Zodhiates, *The Complete Word Study Dictionary; New Testament* (Chattanooga, TN: AMG Publishers, 1994), #5485, 1469.

43. Augustine, *Confessions*, trans. R. S. Pine-Coffin (New York: Penguin Books, 1961).

44. Jonathan Edwards, "The End for Which God Created the World," *The Works of Jonathan Edwards* (New York: Yale University Press), 495.

45. C. S. Lewis, *The Weight of His Glory and Other Addresses* (Grand Rapids: Eerdmans, 1965).

46. *The Worldbook Encyclopedia 2001*, vol. 8 (Chicago: World Book Inc., 2001), 8–8a.

47. John Piper, *The Dangerous Duty of Delight* (Sisters, OR: Multnomah Publishers, 2001), 21.

48. Andreas J. Köstenberger, *Encountering John* (Grand Rapids: Baker Books, 1999), 56.

49. Eusebius, quoted in Köstenberger, Encountering John, 35.

50. Augustine, quoted in Köstenberger, Encountering John, 19.

51. Spiros Zodhiates, "Lexical Aids to the Old Testament," #344 in Spiros Zodhiates, Warren Baker, and David Kemp, *Hebrew-Greek Key Study Bible* (Chattanooga, TN: AMG Publishers, 1996), 1503.

52. F. B. Meyer, Paul, *A Servant of Jesus Christ* (Fort Washington, Penn.: Christian Literature Crusade, 1995), 26.

53. Ernle Bradford, *Paul the Traveller* (New York: Barnes & Noble, 1993), 35.

54. Ibid.

55 James Stalker, *The Two St. Johns of the New Testament* (New York: American Tract Society, 1895), 148.

56. Cited in Joan Comay, *Who's Who in the Old Testament* (Crown Publishers, 1980), 322.

57. Patrick Johnstone, *Operation World* (Grand Rapids, Mich.: Zondervan Publishing House, 1993), 643.

58. Butler, et al., 406.

59. Bradford, 196.

60. John F. Walvoord and Roy B. Zuck, eds., *The Bible Knowledge Commentary New Testament* (Wheaton, Ill.: Victor Books, 1983), 421.

61. Ibid., 422.

62. Ibid., 640.

63. Ibid., 735.

64. Robert Graves, *The Twelve Caesars* (New York: Penguin Books, 1957), 222.

65. Ibid., 226.

66. Ibid., 226.

67. John Foxe, *Foxe's Book of Martyrs* (New Kensington, Penn.: Whitaker House, 1981), 12.

68. Zodhiates, "Lexical Aids to the Old Testament," #344 in Zodhiates, Baker, and Kemp, *Hebrew-Greek Key Study Bible*, 1437.

69. Zodhiates, *The Complete Word Study Dictionary; New Testament*, #3674, 1046.

70. Ibid., #3670, 1045.

71. Lynn M. Poland, "The New Criticism, Neoorthodoxy, and the New Testament," quoted in Culpepper, *John, Son of Zebedee*, 139.

72. "John, A Last Word on Love," *Biblical Illustrator*, Summer 1976, 26.

73. Tertullian, On Prescription Against Heretics, as quoted in Culpepper, *John, Son of Zebedee*, 140.

74. Oswald Chambers, *My Utmost for His Highest* (New York: Dodd Mead & Company, 1963), 211.

75. Zodhiates, "Lexical Aids to the New Testament" #918 in Zodhiates, Baker, and Kemp, *Hebrew-Greek Key Study Bible*, 1596.

76. E. Glen Hinson, "Smyrna," *Biblical Illustrator*, Winter 1980, 72, 86.

77. Youngblood and Bruce, *Nelson's New Illustrated Bible Dictionary*, 1187.

78. Taken from *Foxe's Book of Martyrs* by John Foxe, chapter 2, www.biblenet.net/library/foxesMartyrs.

79. A. T. Robertson, *Word Pictures in the New Testament*, vol. 5 (Nashville: Broadman Press, 1960), 307.

80. William Barclay, *Letters to the Seven Churches* (New York: Abingdon, 1957), quoted in Expositor's

81. Henry L. Peterson, "The Church at Laodicea," *Biblical Illustrator*, Spring 1982, 74–75.